'The position of religion in British public life is discussed and contested today more than ever; but the question is not often thought through in relation to wider issues about conscience and the moral accountability of public life. The authors of this highly original and intelligent book examine carefully the way in which legal approaches to religion in the UK help to safeguard the possibility of conscientious diversity and moral debate in British society. A very important book for all who are concerned about preserving ethically literate democracy.'
– *Archbishop Rowan Williams, United Kingdom*

'This timely book is a subtle and in places provocative meditation on the place of religion in the constitutional framework of Great Britain. While the framework prioritises the rule of law, parliamentary sovereignty, checks and balances, and protection for human rights it also, argue the authors, contains a valuable soft presumption in favour of religious practice. This aspect of legal and political culture, they suggest, has produced over time a system that is broadly liberal. It is also tolerant not only of a wide range of religious practices but also, by analogy and extension, of the practices of many other belief systems including atheism.' – *Dawn Oliver, Emeritus Professor of Constitutional Law, UCL, United Kingdom*

Religion, Law and the Constitution

This book examines the existing constitutional and legal system in England, Wales and Scotland, through the prism of its treatment of religion and belief. The study encompasses questions of Church/state relations, but pushes far beyond these. It asks whether the approach to religion which has spread out from establishment to permeate the whole legal framework is a cause of concern or celebration in relation to individual and collective freedoms.

The primary focus of the work is the synergy between the religious dimension of the juridical system and the fundamental pillars of the Constitution (parliamentary sovereignty, the rule of law, separation of powers and human rights). Javier García Oliva and Helen Hall challenge the view that separation between public and religious authorities is the most conducive means of nurturing a free and democratic society in modern Britain.

The authors explore whether, counter-intuitively for some, the religious dynamic to the legal system actually operates to safeguard liberties, and has a role in generating an inclusive and adaptable backdrop for our collective life. They suggest that the present paradigm brings benefits for citizens of all shades of religious belief and opinion (including Atheist and Humanist perspectives), as well as secondary advantages for those with profound beliefs on non-religious matters, such as pacifism and veganism. In support of their contentions, García Oliva and Hall examine how the religious dimension of the legal framework operates to further essential constitutional principles in diverse settings, ranging from criminal to family law.

In a groundbreaking move, the authors also set the legal discussion alongside its social and cultural context. They consider how the theological perspectives of the larger faith traditions might influence members' ideas around the key constitutional precepts, and they include extracts from interviews which give the personal perspective of more than 100 individuals on contemporary issues of law and religious freedom. These voices are drawn from a range of fields and positions on faith. While the authors are at pains to stress that these sections do not support or advance their legal or theological conclusions, they do provide readers with a human backdrop to the discussion, and demonstrate its crucial importance in twenty-first century Britain.

Dr Javier García Oliva, Senior Lecturer in Law, University of Manchester.

Dr Helen Hall, Lecturer in Law, Nottingham Trent University.

Law and Religion

The practice of religion by individuals and groups, the rise of religious diversity and the fear of religious extremism, raise profound questions for the interaction between law and religion in society. The regulatory systems involved, the religion laws of secular government (national and international) and the religious laws of faith communities, are valuable tools for our understanding of the dynamics of mutual accommodation and the analysis and resolution of issues in such areas as: religious freedom; discrimination; the autonomy of religious organisations; doctrine, worship and religious symbols; the property and finances of religion; religion, education and public institutions; and religion, marriage and children. In this series, scholars at the forefront of law and religion contribute to the debates in this area. The books in the series are analytical with a key target audience of scholars and practitioners, including lawyers, religious leaders and others with an interest in this rapidly developing discipline.

Titles in this series include:

Law, Religion and Love
Seeking Ecumenical Justice for the Other
Paul Babie and Vanja-Ivan Savić

Distinguishing between Islam, Islamism and Violent Extremism
A Philosophical-Legal Guide
Matthew Wilkinson

Religion, Law and the Constitution

Balancing Beliefs in Britain

Javier García Oliva and Helen Hall

Routledge
Taylor & Francis Group
LONDON AND NEW YORK

First published 2018
by Routledge

2 Park Square, Milton Park, Abingdon, Oxfordshire OX14 4RN
52 Vanderbilt Avenue, New York, NY 10017

Routledge is an imprint of the Taylor & Francis Group, an informa business

First issued in paperback 2019

British Library Cataloguing in Publication Data
A catalogue record for this book is available from the British Library

Library of Congress Cataloging in Publication Data
Names: García Oliva, Javier, author. | Hall, Helen, (Law teacher), author.
Title: Religion, law and the constitution : balancing beliefs in Britain / Javier García Oliva and Helen Hall.
Description: New York : Routledge, 2017. | Series: Law and religion | Includes bibliographical references and index.
Identifiers: LCCN 2017012353| ISBN 9781138838352 (hbk) | ISBN 9781315734361 (ebk)
Subjects: LCSH: Freedom of religion—Great Britain. | Church and state—Great Britain. | Constitutional law—Great Britain.
Classification: LCC KD4100 .G37 2017 | DDC 342.4108/52—dc23
LC record available at https://lccn.loc.gov/2017012353

ISBN: 978-1-138-83835-2 (hbk)
ISBN: 978-0-367-31312-8 (pbk)

Typeset in Galliard Std
by Swales & Willis Ltd, Exeter, Devon, UK

www.manchester.ac.uk/balancing-beliefs

To our parents, Gloria, Paco, Kit and Richard, for their support and love throughout the years.

To Irene, Manolo, Manuel, Javier and Sidney, for bringing so much joy to our lives, and to the memory of David and Fred.

Contents

Table of statutes

Table of cases

Table of secondary legislation

Anglican ecclesiastical law

International conventions and treaties

Acknowledgements

Writing this book has been a fascinating adventure, and a life-changing journey which could have never been achieved without the assistance of a large number of people. Whatever impact this book may have in academic terms, it has been profoundly important for us as authors.

We have been touched and honoured by the help that we have received from many directions. At the outset we should express our gratitude to both Baroness Elizabeth Butler-Sloss and Dominic Grieve QC MP for their willingness to provide us with an Introduction and Foreword respectively. We are thrilled to have had the support of two such illustrious figures in the legal world.

We are indebted to Norman Doe for his support throughout the last few years and his belief in this project. His comments on the first draft of our book proposal and avenues for research which the questions could open were tantalising, and his inspiration in the initial stages of the project was decisive. We would also like to extend our thanks to a number of colleagues in various British universities, who have provided us with guidance, advice, comments, suggestions, and who have kindly read different drafts of all chapters: Frank Cranmer, David Feldman, Jeff King, Roger Masterman, Ronan McCrea, Dawn Oliver and Adam Tucker. All of them are, of course, extremely busy colleagues; they have gone beyond the call of duty in providing feedback and their insightful comments on the constitutional sections of the book have been crucial.

Furthermore, we were determined to avoid a predominantly English narrative in our book and, as we are undeniably more familiar with the English and Welsh dimension, Janette Wilson's comments on the Scottish sections were invaluable. We are also most grateful to Mihai Popa, who gave us helpful advice in relation to the anthropological aspects of our book, and the Rt Rev'd Dominic Walker, who advised on the theological dimension of our study.

We would like to thank our colleagues and friends at the University of Manchester and Nottingham Trent University as well as the universities of Cardiff and Bangor for their help in relation to this project. We could not possibly name everyone in these institutions who have assisted, but their collective support has been inestimable. Importantly, we appreciate the generosity of our more than 100 interviewees. We have been blessed by so many fascinating accounts and by memorable visits to locations across England, Wales and Scotland. We never imagined that constitutional law would take us to dressing rooms in West End theatres, teashops in Welsh market towns or ferries in driving rain to the Outer Hebrides. The interviews that we conducted in these and so many other locations provided us with a dazzling array of perspectives and countless shades of opinion. It has been a humbling and rewarding journey, and we have found the warmth and enthusiasm of people – many of whom we didn't know before starting this project – most inspirational.

We would also like to thank Sara Acuña, Juan Antonio Alberca, Carmen Asiaín, Tim Bainbridge, Paul Barber, Santiago Cañamares, John Cartwright, Oscar Celador, Ana María Celis, Miguel Cobano, Simon Deakin, Jenny Dix, Rocío Domínguez, John Duddington, Jessica Giles, Diana Ginn, Sion Hughes Carew, Noelia González , Neil Jones, Mark Landon, Enrique López, Fernando Llano, Javier Martínez-Torrón, Claire McCourt, David McIlroy, Roderick Munday, Juan Pablo Murga, Juan Navarro, Roberto Ombres, Sebastian Payne, Paul Russell, Jesús Sáez, John Stanton, Irene Sobrino, Jennifer Welsh and Isabel Zurita, for their assistance in arranging interviews and forming our thoughts on themes in this work.

Needless to say, we could not have completed this task without the tireless patience and professionalism of the members of the Routledge team: Brianna Archer, Lucy Buchan, Alison Kirk, Olivia Manley and Mark Sapwell, as well as their colleagues who have assisted in the production of the book, Elizabeth McElwain and Julian Webb.

We would also like to pay tribute to the countless individuals who have gone out of their way to come to our aid in one capacity or another: busy colleagues and family members of our interviewees who have taken messages and had their days interrupted, kind owners of bed-and-breakfast establishments, taxi drivers and Post Office workers who have pointed us in the right direction when lost in strange towns, and many more. The generosity of all of these, as well as our interviewees, in giving their time and deepest thoughts, and also the help of those who put us in contact with several of them, is a testimony to human kindness.

Foreword

Dominic Grieve QC MP

As the Member of Parliament for Beaconsfield, it is only a few months ago that I was invited, in my official capacity, to go to Oxford for the enthronement of the new bishop of its diocese, which includes my constituency. It was a splendid event, beautifully choreographed and with music from the best Anglican choral tradition.

Looking around the cathedral, I noted with interest the range of other guests present. They included the Lords Lieutenant and High Sheriffs of the three counties covered by the diocese, representatives of the judiciary, the police, fire and ambulance services, and the armed forces, as well as fellow MPs. Then there were the mayors of the towns in the diocese and the chairmen of the County and District Councils and representatives of many charities and national and local voluntary organisations. There were representatives of most Christian denominations and of every major faith. There were also the senior office holders of the University of Oxford and other places of learning, including the Church of England schools that serve the local population. With all of these were the many members of the clergy and laity of the Church of England for whom the bishop had the most direct responsibility. After the ceremony we all gathered together at a reception and made or renewed acquaintance.

I can think of no other event which could bring together in one place, in our country, such a diverse group of those with the principle responsibility of local leadership and governance. Just as tellingly, many other events I attend more regularly as an MP, such as civic services or Remembrance Sunday, are nearly all under the aegis of the Church of England. The same can be said of the prayers which start each day's sitting of the House of Commons and which are led by the Speaker's chaplain. The principal prayer enjoins us 'to never lead the nation wrongly through love of power, desire to please or unworthy ideas but laying aside all private interests and prejudices keep in mind (our) responsibility to seek to improve the condition of all mankind . . .' It was pointed out to me, in a discussion that took place in the House of Commons Standards Committee by a lay member, that in the absence of any job description for MPs, this is the closest we get to any guide as to the ethical standards we should follow.

It is indeed the central feature of the establishment of the Church of England that it is present so widely and is so routinely encountered by those working within the public sphere. It could be said that in the absence of a written constitution, it is the oaths or affirmations of office to the Queen, taken by many of those I have just listed, that forms the framework of their obligation to serve the public and enables the Queen in her turn to discharge her promise to serve her subjects taken in her Coronation Oath. Yet, as the option of affirmation as well as oath-taking attests, this framework places, save for the Queen, no obligation of adherence to Christianity as practised by the Church of England or to any religious belief at all, and both England and the rest of the United Kingdom have long ceased to be confessional states.

So it is a particular pleasure to see the publication of this book by Javier García Oliva and Helen Hall, which explores what some might see as this curious and rather eccentric national phenomenon. The authors have set out to examine how it has developed, its advantages and drawbacks in the present day, and the impact it has on our society. There is no doubt that some in our country dislike it and it is certainly possible to present reasoned criticisms of its continuing existence. Equally, though, many clearly value its presence even when they do not manifest or even share the Christian religious foundations on which it is based. Perhaps unconsciously they sense the important role it seems to play in bringing us together in collective actions based ultimately on Christian principles, which reinforce group identity and bring with it a willingness to co-operate together with others to promote the common good. The present Archbishop of York noted what has previously shaped our history when he reminded us that the Venerable Bede wrote in the midst of the turmoil of the seventh century 'of how not only were the English converted but how the Gospel played a major socialising and civilising role, by uniting the English from a group of warring tribes and conferring nationhood upon them'. As our authors here show, in a society that it is increasingly secular, this part of the work of the Church of England remains key to its relevance and contribution to wider society.

I very much hope that this book will not only be informative but can also serve as a springboard for further discussion of this important aspect of our unwritten Constitution. For, as our country becomes more diverse, so the need to identify and encourage all benign forces that bring us and keep us together becomes more important.

Introduction

Baroness Elizabeth Butler-Sloss

In former times, guides to etiquette used to advise against discussing religion and politics, particularly at the dinner table. However, we have moved into a world in which it is rare for a day to pass in which religion does not feature in one way or another in the news headlines. There is an increasing awareness that whatever our personal perspective on faith, as a society we cannot afford to push it to the margins of our collective consciousness or conversations. Consequently, this work by Javier García Oliva and Helen Hall is set to make a timely, but also an enduring, contribution within the field of law and beyond it.

In general, legal studies of the Constitution have tended to relegate the religious dimension of our system almost to a footnote. They have also traditionally been quite rigidly compartmentalised in terms of the public and private law divide. *Religion, Law and the Constitution: Balancing Beliefs in Britain* breaks the mould. It seeks to address how the responses of both judiciary and legislature have been influenced by the backdrop of establishment, and the authors argue that a religious character has come to suffuse the entire legal framework in fields as diverse as family law, equity, tort and criminal law. They investigate topics as wide ranging as ritual male circumcision, judicial review, violation of sepulchres and defamation.

The work is also somewhat unusual in academic terms, in that it contains a mixture of light and shade. While García Oliva and Hall find aspects of the current law which they suggest are in need of re-examination and reform, they also identify elements which they believe should be celebrated and cultivated. Criticism is, of course, necessary grist to the academic mill and, more importantly, a necessary contribution if we are to improve and maintain our legal machinery. However, discerning positives as well as negatives is essential if we are to move forward in the optimal way. It is refreshing in a climate in which many commentators either problematise religious faith as a phenomenon, or alternatively focus exclusively upon aspects of the legal system which cause difficulties or anxieties for religious individuals or groups, to be reminded of contexts in which there is harmony and an appropriate balancing of interests.

One important window to the book, which undoubtedly lets the light in, is the authors' treatment of religious belief groups. In the course of their substantial study, García Oliva and Hall give space to consider how the teachings and ideas of these groups might influence the thinking of their members in relation to our core constitutional principles, including human rights, and at times reach some surprising conclusions.

In addition, they append interview material at the end of each chapter, which gives voice to a kaleidoscope of perspectives. The authors have spoken to well over a hundred different people, from across the religious spectrum. Their reach includes Anglicanism, Wee Frees, Zoroastrians, followers of Shintoism, Humanists, Quakers, the undecided and many others. They have also cast their net widely in terms of professional background and their interviewees include (inter alia) judges, doctors, actors, scientists, religious ministers, dancers, football and rugby players, students, politicians, waitresses and retired people. García Oliva and Hall are keen to stress that the interview material is not included to support any of the academic arguments which they make, and it is not there to prove any particular point except one. The reason for its inclusion is to remind readers that while citizens might have strongly differing opinions on issues of law and religion, very few people are indifferent. The legal questions which the book addresses have a direct impact upon the lives of all members of society and we all have a vested interest in finding answers which are broadly acceptable to all parties. Appended as they are at the end of each chapter, the interviews also intersperse some humanity and colour with the densely packed legal analysis which forms the meat of the book.

Ultimately, whether or not readers are persuaded by any or all of the authors' conclusions, the work is a fascinating and exuberant one. It holds together an exploration of complex issues of law, which touch every level of our juridical framework, and an acute awareness of human implications of our treatment of these matters. The current climate, both on the national and geopolitical level, is such that we desperately need dialogue on how our societies and legal systems should deal with religion. With this work, García Oliva and Hall are making a significant and unique contribution to our necessary and shared conversation.

Preliminary thoughts

Javier García Oliva and Helen Hall

Viewed from a wider European perspective, the Constitution of the United Kingdom is unique. Even from a global standpoint, it is a rare specimen, ranking alongside Israel and New Zealand as one of the only three uncodified constitutions currently in existence. Not surprisingly, its idiosyncratic nature has always inspired a wealth of doctrinal discussion. For instance, although the codification debate is not at present high on the agenda of the British Government, it is a perennial issue within legal and academic circles. Equally, commentators have found other features of the Constitution to be most enticing subjects for exploration. For example, there has been a plethora of academic papers on the nature and future of the monarchy, not to mention the hotly contested character of parliamentary supremacy. More recently, the Constitution has become increasingly decentralised from a territorial point of view. Since 1998 many of the powers previously in the hands of Westminster have been transferred to the Scottish and Welsh nations, as well as the Northern Irish province. Furthermore, a prominent dialogue is currently taking place about the future of the English nation, and regionalisation within England is still on the radar of the present Conservative Government.

Yet, despite the oceans of ink which have been spilt, public lawyers in Great Britain have been inclined to overlook the religious dimension of the Constitution. It is striking that many of the leading contemporary textbooks on public law neglect to even mention this feature, and one aim of our book is to address this gap in the commentary. Of course, we do not claim to be trekking through steamy intellectual jungle, where academic commentators' feet have never trod. Impressive work on the religious dimension of the Constitution (and indeed the entire legal framework) has been carried out by distinguished public law scholars such as David Feldman and Ian Leigh.

Moreover, in the last few decades British academia has witnessed the development of the study of Law and Religion as a distinct discipline. This subject is now taught in more than thirty universities across the country. A debt of great gratitude is owed to scholars such as Norman Doe, Anthony Bradney, Mark Hill and David Harte, who took the lead in the inception of this academic phenomenon. We have now reached the stage where Law and Religion can claim to be an independent field, with strong links to core legal subjects, such as public law, contract law and family law. The very heterogeneous membership of the Law and Religion Scholars Network, based at Cardiff University, and also the International Consortium for Law and Religion Studies, is a testimony to the number of areas of study which this discipline touches, as well as its widespread appeal.

Nevertheless, in so far as such categories and labels are useful, our book does not sit primarily within the blossoming topic of Law and Religion, and our focus has been quite different from that of scholars concentrating on questions within this subject. We are considering an aspect of the UK Constitution, namely its religious dimension, and see this book as addressing the mainstream audience within the public law world.

We are also very aware that too much of the existing commentary on the Constitution is Anglo-centric in focus and, therefore, ultimately incomplete and distorted in terms of the state as a whole. For this reason, we were concerned to give appropriate attention to the Welsh and the Scottish contexts. In addition, we were eager to deal thoroughly with all three nations within Great Britain, as each of them has its own established or quasi-established Church.[1] Each context is unique and each has distinct revelations about the impact of an establishment model on constitutional arrangements. However, it would be disingenuous to suggest that we have the same level of expertise in Scottish law as we do in the system south of the border. The consequence of this is that the lion's share of examples from the legal framework provided in our book has been drawn from either England or Wales, jurisdictions with which we are undoubtedly more familiar.

In addition, readers will rightly notice the omission of Northern Ireland from our study. This was partly because of the extremely loose nature of its quasi-establishment (as the Church of Ireland was disestablished in 1870). However, our concern primarily was that it would be impossible to meaningfully explore this setting without considering in detail, as well, the history and the contemporary context of the Republic of Ireland. Clearly, undertaking an analysis of another state would have considerably changed the dynamics of our study, and we were also satisfied that, for our particular purposes, an exploration of the UK Constitution as applied in England, Wales and Scotland was methodologically sound.

Undoubtedly, Great Britain is not unique in having a religious constitution. However, it is unusual in an increasingly culturally pluralistic and politically secular Western world. This apparently anomalous situation has given rise to widespread criticisms from some academic and social groupings, and there have been calls for secularising reforms and the conscious uncoupling of Church and state. However, it struck us as curious that these arguments were generally not being made by British scholars within the Law and Religion field, and this

1 We are aware that these terms are controversial for some, and that in Scotland, in particular, many people prefer to speak of a 'national Church'. We are also conscious that whatever terminology we adopt will be contested in some quarters. In the course of this book, we have decided to use 'established/quasi-established' and 'national Church' interchangeably.

made us realise the general disparity between differing academic tribes. This led us to question where the most convincing arguments lay: were they with those advocating change, or those supporting the status quo?

The primary research question of our book is whether the constitutional arrangements and wider legal framework concerning religion enhances or weakens the four constitutional foundations of Great Britain: (i) the rule of law; (ii) parliamentary supremacy; (iii) the separation of powers and checks and balances; and (iv) human rights.

Chapter 1 focuses on the historical development of the legal, political and constitutional framework within the three nations of Great Britain: England, Wales and Scotland, while Chapter 2 discusses both establishment and the wider juridical system concerning religion. We trace the trajectory from exclusion to inclusion, as England (and subsequently Great Britain, and then the United Kingdom) changed from a state in which members of the Anglican religion were uniquely privileged to one in which, first, other Protestant Christians, and later other religions, came to enjoy similar freedoms and benefits. The law had always advanced the interests of the official religions. However, as society became liberalised, both common law and statute widened this favourable treatment to take on board the interests of citizens of other faiths. The religious character of the Constitution and law, flowing from establishment, came to mean that religion as a phenomenon was regarded in positive terms by the legal system.

Furthermore, from the nineteenth century onwards the respect accorded to religious beliefs came to influence the way in which freedom of conscience was understood more widely. Profound beliefs which did not necessarily flow from, or touch upon, religious questions came to be recognised as being of special significance by the law, at least in certain contexts. An analogy with religious beliefs was one important factor in this development, and the protection given to religious beliefs brought benefits to non-religious beliefs as well. This remains the case nowadays, and we discuss in the third chapter (see below) how in Great Britain the legal protection of freedom of conscience extends beyond the requirements of Article 9 of the European Convention on Human Rights. We are not asserting that the religious character of the legal framework has been the only factor in this, but we are arguing that it has played a key role.

In the course of Chapter 2, we also critically analyse the features of establishment in England and Scotland, as well as the quasi-established status of the Church in Wales. Undoubtedly, the UK public authorities still favour the unique position of these three denominations, despite vociferous criticisms from some secular quarters, claiming that this is an unacceptable privilege in a society which takes pride in treasuring values like respect, freedom and equality. However, there remains considerable support for establishment and, as explained above, this is part of a much wider (and usually overlooked) picture: public authorities in Great Britain regard religion as a beneficial social reality, and respect the interests of religious citizens as a result. Not only English and Welsh law, but also Scottish law, provide us with a wide range of examples of this favourable treatment of religion as a phenomenon. In light of this, we are eager to stress that our book pushes beyond the constitutional questions surrounding establishment and seeks to assess the desirability of maintaining this positive legal view of religion. We also note that at times the establishment dimension of the debate has overshadowed questions about religion, belief and the legal framework more generally. In concluding this chapter, we reflect upon how this overall framework provides direct benefits to citizens with a religious belief, regardless of what that faith might be.

We then move on, in the course of Chapter 3, to consider how a juridical system which supports religious belief might have relevance for citizens who adhere to or manifest beliefs in non-religious matters. We explore ways in which a positive approach towards religious belief translates by analogy and association into a positive approach to belief more widely, and assess some of the indirect benefits which the current structure has for individuals and groups motivated to express non-religious beliefs.

Having considered the ways in which the religious character of the public and private law framework generally furthers the interest of those pursuing religious and non-religious beliefs, we turn our attention to its implications for core constitutional principles. In the four succeeding chapters (4 to 7) we discuss whether the British constitutional and legal framework on religion supports each of the four constitutional foundations (such as the rule of law, parliamentary supremacy, and so on). We adopt the same methodology in each chapter. There is an analysis of the relevant constitutional principle, which is followed by the most important section of the chapter: the exploration of the outworkings of the current legal framework in relation to the constitutional pillar in question. We do this by providing a wide range of examples of how the juridical system in connection with religion actively promotes the functioning of this key component of our Constitution. Afterwards, each chapter contains some consideration of the ways in which the worldview of religious groups might influence the thoughts of their members with regard to that particular foundation, and finally we discuss whether this religious legal framework is a catalyst towards developing a more cohesive society. We do not embark on any detailed sociological analysis, but we provide a range of examples of religious denominations that contribute in practical terms towards the operation of the constitutional foundations. It should be emphasised that with this section in Chapters 4 to 7 we do not attempt to stray beyond discussions of the legal framework, this being our primary area of expertise; nor, as stated, have we carried out the kind of empirical work that would be required to substantiate sophisticated sociological conclusions. However, it should be pointed out that we do not aim to test whether 'religion is good' for society. We simply observe some practical ways in which religious bodies are contributing towards social cohesion and this does furnish us with evidence of some practical benefits to the current system. Nevertheless, we do not speculate as to whether the positive contributions being made by religious groups outweigh any negative impact that religious practices may have on our society. It is indisputable that the question of whether religion is a blessing or a curse for humankind belongs firmly in the realm of philosophy and not of law.

Furthermore, we would stress that we are not suggesting that all of the elements within the current paradigm are perfect. In fact, we acknowledge that some aspects are deeply unsatisfactory and, in the course of our discussion, we shall highlight instances where the present arrangements give rise to inequality or potentially problematic outcomes for various groups (either religious or ideological) within society. Nevertheless, we maintain that there is no overarching inequality or detriment imposed by the current framework concerning religion, and suggest that the need to reform component parts of the system does not equate to a need to abandon the system as a whole.

Borrowing an image from the animal world, we argue that the evolving relationship between public authorities and religious bodies can be illustrated by the changing use, but continuing importance, of wings for penguins. In the past, the ancestors of penguins used their wings for flight. Obviously, modern penguins are flightless, but this has not rendered their wings redundant. On the contrary, these limbs are now adapted to enable the bird to swim and move with great efficiency through water. Their nature and function have changed, but they have remained a necessary part of the organism. For the purposes of this metaphor, the penguin represents the state, while the fundamental structure of its wings is provided by the established churches, and other groups which benefit from the systemic support for religion are now integrated within these wings as part of the feathers and cartilage. Therefore, the role of religious groups within the collective life of the state has altered radically, but they remain key social players.

Nevertheless, having acknowledged that the structures generated by establishment provide organisations with the means of becoming institutional participants in the system, we accept that many citizens do not self-identify as members of any such organisations, and we are concerned to explore whether the present system is an acceptable one in relation to such individuals who are not engaged in any form of institutional participation. Needless to say, such an analysis is only feasible to a limited extent without the kind of sociological and anthropological research which lies beyond the scope of our study. Yet, despite this, purely on the basis of considering the law, we suggest that, on balance, citizens in this category are not unduly disadvantaged. In the course of our discussion we advance two primary reasons for this. First, it is inevitably difficult, perhaps impossible, structurally to further the ideological and identity-based needs of such individuals in a collective manner; second, there is no basis for assuming that such individuals regard the institutional participation of other groups of citizens in a negative way, or that they do not benefit from their activities. In tangible terms, for example, a person with no religious identity might welcome a faith group collaborating with their local authority in providing services for homeless people. Equally, a non-practising (but still believing) Catholic might welcome the capacity of Humanists in Scotland to carry out marriage ceremonies for those who desire it.

Without a shadow of a doubt, exploring these questions has been an engaging and thought-provoking exercise, and one which we have thoroughly enjoyed. However, in addition to this doctrinal study, we are eager to show that the topics which are the scope of our analysis are not exclusively theoretical and academic.

They also have a very real impact on the daily lives of all citizens in Great Britain. For this reason, we have conducted more than 100 interviews with a variety of citizens from different sections of our society, including religious and other belief-based organisations, the arts, science, politics, law, commerce and the service industry, sports and education. These interviewees were chosen to give a diversity of perspectives formed by a range of experiences, professional concerns and personal convictions. Most interviews were held from September 2014 to December 2015, although a handful of them were carried out in the course of 2016. We stress that although many are associated with particular organisations, the views and opinions expressed are purely personal and not representative of the views of their organisations.

These interviews are additional material: they are the icing on the cake, rather than the cake itself. It cannot be over-emphasised that they are ***not*** included to prove or support any of our doctrinal conclusions. They are emphatically ***not*** empirical evidence, and must not be treated as such. From that point of view, their value is not 'sociological', as they do not follow any of the recognised methods in the field of sociology and, therefore, such material will be presented at the end of each chapter. Nevertheless, the insights of our interviewees have been illuminating. They have made our work even more rewarding, and have given us perspectives and reflections which we would never otherwise have encountered. We feel privileged to have had these insights and are very keen to share them with our readers.

1 Church/state relations and their historical evolution

Whale knees or penguin wings?

1.1 Introduction

How does the law of Great Britain relate to religion and belief, and is its approach fitting for a liberal democracy in the twenty-first century? One of the main questions at the heart of our study is whether a constitution with a religious dimension can be desirable, or even defensible, in the contemporary world. In searching for a meaningful answer, it is vital to begin with some consideration of how both the overall legal framework and the UK Constitution have developed over the course of history, and also what the evolutionary process has left behind. The present complexity and idiosyncrasy of Great Britain only make sense in light of the events which have shaped it.

It is also helpful to note at the very outset that, unlike many other jurisdictions, there is no 'bright line' between constitutional and general law in the British setting, and that the stories of these strands of legal development are inseparably bound together. Therefore, whilst this book encompasses far more than a purely constitutional discussion, our intention is to use the constitutional structure as scaffolding around which our investigation can be built. For this reason, we shall start our journey with some consideration of the way in which the Constitution has formed over time. It goes without saying that historical context is crucial to understanding *any* complex situation with a political aspect, but it is especially pressing for our purposes because:

1. The journey of legal and political evolution has a particular importance within an uncodified constitutional regime.
2. The existing literature has tended to address *either* Church history or the constitutional framework. Our analysis is different, because it focuses specifically on the religious dimension of the Constitution. Neither the religious nor the constitutional dynamic is squeezed out of the limelight in the course of the study.
3. For the most part, previous academic discussion has tended to concentrate on one component nation within what is now Great Britain. This work attempts to give appropriate weight to all three nations.

The first and third of these factors are closely linked. In order to properly explore the issues around a religious constitution in a British context, it is necessary to examine the very different ways in which various religious threads are interwoven within the unique legal and social fabric of each national setting. What emerges in all three cases is a colourful patchwork quilt, regrettably spattered with a few dubious stains, and the constitutional quilt as a whole makes sense only in light of its component panels and splotches. Furthermore, there are numerous very contemporary challenges which have their roots in centuries-old tensions. On many occasions we have to look back in order to imagine the way forward.

For these reasons, our study begins with some discussion of the process by which the current situation evolved. Moreover, as stressed within point one above, the absence of a codified constitution does give the path of evolutionary development an even greater significance.

Admittedly, it is possible to exaggerate the difference between codified and non-codified regimes in this respect. In reality, codified constitutions do not appear magically overnight, any more than non-codified ones do. The original drafters who framed what have become long-standing codified constitutions, like that of the United States of America,[1] were inevitably very heavily influenced by pre-existing philosophical ideas and political realities. Nor are successful codified constitutions static. If allowed to ossify, they are liable to shatter, rather than bend, when pushed and pulled by a shifting political landscape. Consider, for instance, the response within Japan to attacks by Islamic extremists on citizens abroad in early 2015.[2] This sparked questions in relation to Article 9 of the Japanese Constitution, which prohibits both the use of force to settle international disputes and the maintenance of regular armed forces.[3] Even a constitutional pillar as fundamental for a particular system as pacifism has been for post-war Japan is still open to being revisited, remoulded, and potentially even abolished, in response to a changing world.

Consequently, it would be inaccurate to state that the British Constitution is the product of evolution *because* it is uncodified. However, its uncodified nature does nevertheless add a heightened significance to the evolutionary process. As expressed in a House of Commons briefing note on constitutional reform, the

1 See, e.g., D.W. Howe, 'Why the Scottish Enlightenment was Useful to Framers of the American Constitution', *Comparative Studies in Society and History*, Vol. 31, No. 3 (1989) 572–87; R.A. Ames & H.C. Montgomery, 'The Influence of Rome on the American Constitution', *The Classical Journal*, Vol. 30, No. 1 (1934) 19–27; P.A. Hamburger, 'Natural Rights, Natural Law, and American Constitutions', *The Yale Law Journal*, Vol. 102, No. 4 (1993) 907–60.

2 'Constitutional Change Necessary to Protect Japanese Citizens: Abe', *The Japan Times* (3 Feb 2015), http://www.japantimes.co.jp/news/2015/02/03/national/politics-diplomacy/constitutional-change-necessary-protect-japanese-citizens-abe.

3 Constitution of Japan, Article 9: 'Renunciation of War: Aspiring sincerely to an international peace based on justice and order, the Japanese people forever renounce war as a sovereign right of the nation and the threat or use of force as means of settling international disputes. In order to accomplish the aim of the preceding paragraph, land, sea, and air forces, as well as other war potential, will never be maintained. The right of belligerency of the state will not be recognized', http://japan.kantei.go.jp/constitution_and_government_of_japan/constitution_e.html

absence of a codification means that there is no clear and universal definition of what amounts to constitutional change.[4]

This means that developments have to be viewed in their context, and also that innovation at times takes place in a gradual and even unconscious fashion.[5] There are, of course, on occasion, very deliberate legislative moves, like the Parliament Act 1911,[6] or the Fixed-Term Parliament Act 2011,[7] but equally there are gradual shifts in convention. For instance, during the eighteenth and nineteenth centuries it was clear that Prime Ministers could be appointed from either the House of Commons or the House of Lords, but a modern convention has arguably been established that the Prime Minister must be appointed from the Lower Chamber.[8]

Like the gradual deposition of sedimentary rock, these changes may be scarcely perceptible whilst they are taking place, but ultimately they dramatically reshape the constitutional geography. Therefore, development over time is key to understanding both the current reality and the possible future trajectory of malleable uncodified constitutions. This point returns us to the second of the three factors which we have indicated above: the limited attention given to religion in studies of the UK Constitution.

Whether or not commentators are approving of the religious dynamic of the present constitutional arrangements, the religious dimension is undoubtedly there, as the British Human Association ('BHA')[9] loudly points out when calling for its removal;[10] and it is unquestionably there, precisely because the state has evolved with this characteristic embedded deep within its structures. Entwined religious and secular elements have *always* been a feature of the governing arrangements within this territory, and this in itself does not make the religious dimension either positive or negative.

The British Humanist Association terms it 'anachronistic',[11] but is this term really justified? Deep historical origins do not, in and of themselves, make a phenomenon obsolete, unwieldy or unjust. The appropriateness of a religious constitution for a contemporary Britain must depend upon how it is actually operating for the citizens of the state.

The world of biology provides some enlightening analogies. Whales kept their knees for a long time after they did any walking, crawling or even dragging.

4 K. Parry, 'Constitutional Change: Timeline for 1911: House of Commons Background Paper, Standard Note SN/PC 06256', *Parliament and Constitution Centre* (21 Dec 2012) 2.

5 House of Lords, 'Constitution Committee – Fifteenth Report: The Process of Constitutional Change' (11 Jul 2011) Ch. 1, para 8, http://www.publications.parliament.uk/pa/ld201012/ldselect/ldconst/177/17702.htm.

6 Parliament Act 1911, c. 13.

7 Fixed-Term Parliament Act 2011, c. 14.

8 Cabinet Office, 'The Cabinet Manual: A Guide to the Laws, Conventions and Rules on the Operation of Government', 1st edn (Oct 2011) 21, https://www.ppforum.ca/sites/default/files/uk_cabinet_manual.pdf.

9 Please note that this organisation has now become `Humanists UK'. However, since it was the BHA at the time when the research for this book was carried out, we have used the former appellation in the text.

10 British Humanist Association, 'Campaigns, Constitutional Reform', https://humanism.org.uk/campaigns/constitutional-reform.

11 Ibid.

Ancestors of modern whales, like *Basilosaurus* and *Dorudon*, never set their perfectly formed, but small residual limbs on dry land.[12] For a while, these distinctive, but impractical, appendages may have played some role in helping to manoeuvre partners into a convenient mating position, but around 34 million years ago the basilosaurids began the transition to modern whales, and slowly lost their vestigial legs in the process. Whale knees had outstayed their usefulness and had to go.

In contrast, penguin wings are extremely valuable assets.[13] Just because penguins are not going to be soaring with the albatrosses any time soon, this does not mean that their wings are not vital for them. Penguin wings are crucial for their swimming abilities, and although their function has changed radically, they remain a vital structure for the organism within which they are set.

It is uncontroversial both that religion occupies the place that it does within the public life of Great Britain for historical reasons, and also that the function of religious institutions like the established and quasi-established Churches[14] has continually, and radically, altered over the passage of time. This chapter explores this process and its continuing evolutionary impact. It is a necessary foundation for the subsequent chapters' analysis of whether the religious dimension of the UK Constitution is beneficial, or is a regrettable historical encumbrance which should be removed.

We shall begin with an examination of each national context, before drawing the strands together to set out the current picture across the portion of the United Kingdom covered by England, Wales and Scotland.[15]

1.2 England

1.2.1 England in the Middle Ages

Obviously, both England and Scotland share in the wider narrative of the developments and spread of Christianity within northern and western medieval Europe. In the Scottish context, we consider in detail a number of issues equally relevant for England, with particular focus on the contrasting elements of tension and mutual interdependence between temporal and spiritual powers. In both national paradigms, the same development unfolded from the early Church patronage of warrior kings to a symbiotic relationship between Throne and Altar, and a gradual progression towards theories of the Divine Right of Kings. To avoid repetition, we shall therefore not rehearse all of this discussion here. However,

12 T. Mueller, 'Whale Evolution', *National Geographic* (Aug 2010) 7, http://ngm.nationalgeographic.com/2010/08/whale-evolution/mueller-text.

13 B. Handwerk, 'Why Did Penguins Stop Flying? The Answer is Evolutionary', *National Geographic* (May 2013), http://news.nationalgeographic.com/news/2013/13/131320-penguin-evolution-science-flight-diving-swimming-wings.

14 We are conscious that applying the terminology established to the Church of Scotland and quasi-established to the Church in Wales is, by no means, uncontroversial. We shall detail the reasons for this choice of language in Chapter 2.

15 For a full and necessary explanation of our reasons for omitting an analysis of Northern Ireland from this discussion, please see the Introduction to this book.

it should be noted that, in contrast with Scotland, the territory which became England was successfully incorporated within the Roman Empire.

Christianity first came to the British Isles with the Roman legions. As a consequence, it was almost from the outset both socially prestigious and politically advantageous for ambitious members of the indigenous population to embrace the new faith. Like Latin and literacy, adopting the official religion of the Empire was a facet of the shrewd Romanisation of British social climbers.

Even after the armies departed, many of the elite continued to look towards Christian powers in continental Europe. Forging cultural and other alliances with these forces could help to confer an impression of legitimacy and sophistication on the contending warlords who assumed kingship over chunks of England. As a result, for some members of the elite Christianity remained a socially aspirational religion. Equally, there were others who either reverted to or continued with their pre-Christian practices, whilst Norse and Germanic invaders brought their own Pagan deities and habits with them.

One consequence of this multi-faith and multi-lingual society was that the dominance of Christianity was only established slowly and by a number of different routes. The convergence of two of the main streams of influence in the Christianisation of the British Isles resulted in a clash between Roman Christianity, and what is (not entirely accurately or helpfully) frequently labelled 'Celtic' Christianity.[16] Those in the Roman camp had either maintained their allegiance to the new faith, or been converted by missionaries from the Roman Church hierarchy. However, alongside this Roman mode of Christianity, there was an understanding of the faith planted by the wave of missionaries who came from the north and west, and who brought with them a very different Church culture.

The two groups disagreed on matters which might sound of secondary importance to modern ears, such as the correct dating of Easter. However, as far as the people involved were concerned, these were issues which placed eternal salvation at stake. Clergy of the two factions were instantly identifiable from their differently tonsured hair, and often refused to even eat meals or share accommodation together if they met by chance on the road. The rift was eventually resolved at the Synod of Whitby, an event hosted by the Abbess Hilda, but at which a King (Oswin) acted as arbiter.[17]

At one level, placing the decision in royal hands was simply a matter of pragmatic necessity, since there were two clashing ecclesiastical hierarchies and no appropriate spiritual tribunal. However, it should be noted that royal power ultimately determined the shape of the spiritual landscape. In the later Middle Ages, as we shall see again with Scotland, there were further instances of the Church acting as an arbitrator between clashing temporal powers, both domestically and at an international level, and there were also times when ecclesiastical authority itself clashed directly with the Crown. Nevertheless, the spiritual authority brought by the Church hierarchy was part of the scaffolding of a Western medieval state.

16 P. Cavill, *Anglo-Saxon Christianity* (Fount: London) 1999, Ch. 5
17 B. Yorke, *The Conversion of Britain 600–800* (Pearson: Edinburgh) 2006, 126.

The most dramatic instance of Church and monarch on a collision course in this era was probably the spectacular meltdown between Thomas Beckett and Henry II. It was accepted as an abstract principle that the King had jurisdiction over temporal matters and the Church over spiritual, but difficulties arose in where the dividing lines lay.[18]

Henry II got into a disastrous conflict with his Archbishop of Canterbury over the trial of clergy for serious temporal crimes. Thomas Beckett refused to accept the compromise of having clergy dealt with by the Church courts for trial, deprived of their orders if found guilty and then returned to secular courts for sentencing, on the basis that this would amount to double punishment. A stand-off developed, and the Pope tried unsuccessfully to broker a negotiated settlement. Instead, the saga famously ended with Beckett being hacked to death by some apparently over-enthusiastic knights.

Beckett became a saint; Henry was disgraced on the international stage and the Archbishop enjoyed a posthumous victory. Again, the episode demonstrates the accepted concept of royal authority being limited by both legal norms and the boundaries of secular jurisdiction. Henry was forced to accept not only that there were areas into which his rightful power did not stretch, but also that it was not for him alone to determine where the division lay.

An equally dramatic example of royal limitation took place in the reign of King John, with the crisis which led to the signing of the Magna Carta.[19] John was despotic, greedy, paranoid and vindictive, and understandably not a popular ruler. He got into a dispute with the Papacy, when the Church was formulating more concrete policies on the limitation of secular interference in Church matters (such as ecclesiastical appointments), and John predictably resented what he saw as an encroachment on his rights. At the same time, he also managed to alienate a large section of the nobility, as the barons had lost patience with punitive taxation and other methods which John employed to plunder their resources and deprive them of their property.

The upshot was that the King faced war with the barons, and the Magna Carta (as it later became known) was the document that embodied an attempt to resolve the conflict. It was famously brokered by Archbishop Stephen Langton. It is interesting that, despite being heavily embroiled in the power struggles (in fact, the Church's insistence on Langton as Archbishop over his favoured candidate was one of John's grievances with the Pope), the Church was able to mediate in the conflict. Nederman argues that:

> Magna Carta hints that a precondition of resolving temporal difficulties in the kingdom depends upon the restoration of the proper status of the Church's liberties. Without the prior establishment of good relations between the king and the English Church we may infer it would be impossible to achieve any viable resolution between King John and the discontented nobles.[20]

18 J.H. Baker, *An Introduction to English Legal History* (Butterworths: London) 3rd edn, 1990, 148.
19 R.V. Turner, *King John* (Longman: London & New York) 1994.
20 C.J. Nederman, 'The Liberty of the Church and the Road to Runnymede: John of Salisbury and the Intellectual Foundations of the Magna Carta', *PS: Political Science and Politics*, Vol. 43, No. 3 (2010) 456–61, 460–61.

This is an insightful and helpful observation. It is true that the Magna Carta was not a stunning success as a peace accord, and its fortunes also illustrate both the complexity of Church politics and the potential for tensions between central and regional ecclesiastical authority. Characteristically, after signing the document, John broke his promise at the first opportunity and appealed to the Pope (despite having agreed not to do so). The Pope took John's side over Langton and the barons, effectively overturning the Charter and sparking off more fighting. Yet, even in light of these considerations, Nederman's point has validity.

As was demonstrated in relation to the Beckett crisis, the Church was a source of accepted authority within the state, distinct from royal authority. As such, it could function as a check and balance against abuses of kingly power. If not unduly controlled by the Crown, it could mediate in disputes involving royal actions. It was not an accident that the first clause of the document stated: 'the English Church shall be free, and shall have its rights undiminished, and its liberties unimpaired'.[21]

Furthermore, it should be remembered that the independence of the Church was not only critical at the level of disputes surrounding the exercise of royal power in the government of the realm. It was also vital in relation to marriage and property. Many aspects of family law and inheritance were directly or indirectly within the Church jurisdiction, and it was essential that the Church could be seen to be unmolested in administering these, especially where the Crown might have potential fiscal interests.[22] To import the terminology of a different period, the independence of the Church was required if citizens were to have confidence in 'private' as well as 'public' law matters.

Moreover, the fact that Church authority was embedded within the structure of the medieval state anchored that state to its European context, and necessitated the acknowledgement of an external authority. Even accepting that intra-Church politics could be complex, and that there was often a degree of *Realpolitik* in interactions between popes and temporal monarchs,[23] it still remained the case that monarchs exercised their power within a wider legal framework and were expected to operate within trans-European moral and jurisprudential norms.

This was not only true in a practical sense, and in terms of decisions and appeals the international nature of the medieval Church structure meant that there was also an intellectual dimension to this. For instance, in relation to Magna Carta Helmholz[24] points out, first, that the role of the Church in formulating the document is often underestimated by commentators and,

21 British Library, 'English Translation of the Magna Carta', Clause 1, http://www.bl.uk/magna-carta/articles/magna-carta-english-translation.

22 See, e.g., ibid., Clause (27): 'If a free man dies intestate, his movable goods are to be distributed by his next-of-kin and friends, under the supervision of the Church. The rights of his debtors are to be preserved'.

23 For instance, in the Beckett affair discussed above, the Pope's pragmatic need to have Henry's military support made a negotiated solution seem preferable to issuing demands, at least prior to the Archbishop's assassination. The very possession of temporal interests forced the Church to involve itself in human politics. See Baker, n. 17 above, 148.

24 R.H. Helmholz, 'Magna Carta and the Ius Commune', *University of Chicago Law Review*, Vol. 66, No. 2 (1999) 297–371, 301.

second, that this clerical involvement and impact was shaped by academic developments on the continent, specifically in this case a revival in the study of Roman law.

Therefore, during the medieval period, the Crown and Altar both exercised authority within their respective spheres of jurisdiction. The Church, as an alternative source of authority, could both act as a check on royal abuses at internal state level and, at the same time, legitimate kingly power and its exercise by divine mandate. Furthermore, in having the Church embedded within the state, the state itself was anchored to an international legal framework and a set of moral norms during the medieval period.

1.2.2 European reformations and the Early Modern era in England

The medieval trans-European context described above broke apart dramatically during the era of European Reformations, and perhaps nowhere more forcefully than England. Unlike Scotland, where the impetus for reform came largely from nobles and clerics influenced by Protestant and Humanist ideas from the continent, in England the drive came mainly, if not exclusively, from the personal desires of the king. Furthermore, these desires owed more to dynastic ambition than spiritual conviction. In fact, prior to the Henrician religious revolution, there had been vigorous campaigns to clamp down on the Lollard and Lutheran heresies.[25]

Of course, the fact that such repression was deemed necessary demonstrates that the ideas had gained currency in some quarters, but there is little evidence that there was a groundswell of either elite or popular opinion clamouring for reform, and the religious turmoil of the mid-sixteenth century was very much a top-down phenomenon. Undoubtedly, there were men and women with passionate spiritual convictions on both sides, but for many people it must have been a confusing and frightening period.

For over a generation, liturgies and laws went backwards and forwards in a religious Hokey Cokey.[26] Henry VIII forced through a transition from Roman to English Catholicism: the figure of the King replaced the Pope as head of the Church, services (aside from the Lord's Prayer) remained in Latin and clergy were unable to marry. An English Bible was adopted, however. During the reign of Edward VI (1547–53) the King remained as Head of the Church, but the faith became firmly Protestant. Services took place in English, a new English Prayer Book was introduced and, perhaps even more dramatically, for the first time in many centuries priests were permitted to marry. However, Edward's early death meant that his Roman Catholic sister Mary came to the throne, re-establishing the old order, with force where necessary.

25 E. Duffy, *The Stripping of the Altars: Traditional Religion in England 1400–1580* (Yale University Press: New Haven and London) 2005, 379.

26 For a simple, but helpful overview, see J.F. Aylett, *In Search of History 1485–1715* (Hodder & Stoughton: London) 1984, 21.

Assessments of Mary's reign radically differ even in the hands of contemporary historians. See, for example, the contrasting accounts of Ridley[27] and Duffy.[28] It is undeniable that the execution of more than 280 Protestant men and women by fire, in the space of less than four years, is horrific by any standard.[29] However, Mary's Protestant siblings presided over their share of what we would now regard as atrocities; religious dissent was equated with sedition by the early modern state, and met with the brutal political response of the time.

There is, undoubtedly, an element of historical perceptions being moulded by the victorious tradition. It is interesting, for instance, that the regime of 'Bloody Mary' employed a judicial process in dealing with suspected heretics.[30] In contrast, as will be discussed below, the regime of Charles II sanctioned the immediate, extrajudicial killing of covenanters in Scotland. Yet English history has characterised him as the 'Merry Monarch', and remembered him as a party animal, rather than a tyrant.

Nevertheless, whilst there may be academic disagreement about whether Mary's reign was exceptionally barbaric even by contemporary standards, it was without doubt disruptive. When Elizabeth came to the throne, there was another upheaval, but her long tenure as queen (1558–1603) did eventually bring about some sort of stability. She was an unambiguously Protestant monarch, but hoped to appear to steer a conciliatory course in certain respects, declaring herself 'Governor', rather than Head of the Church. Services, of course, reverted to English, a new Prayer Book was issued and priests were again permitted to marry.

To the general population in the midst of this turmoil, the world must have seemed at times to have gone mad. Eamon Duffy's evocative work *The Voices of Morebath* tells the story of how these times were experienced by one Devonshire village, and gives a window into what must have been the reality for many communities. For instance, there were times when people (at least outwardly) conformed with the requirements of central authority, even when it was against their natural inclination,[31] and at other times rebelled. The often contradictory changes and the zealousness with which they were pursued must have been bewildering. Morebath kept the same priest throughout this time (known by the courtesy title of Sir Christopher), and Duffy records poignantly at his death:

> He asked to be buried in the chancel, above the Communion table. So on the 27th May 1574 they laid him there between the site of the altar where he had sung the Mass and the table where he had celebrated the Supper.[32]

27 J. Ridley, *Bloody Mary's Martyrs* (Constable and Robinson: London) 2001.

28 E. Duffy, *Fires of Faith: Catholic England under Mary Tudor* (Yale University Press: New Haven and London) 2010.

29 Ibid., 7.

30 Ibid., 102.

31 E. Duffy, *The Voices of Morebath* (Yale University Press: New Haven & London) 2003, 103.

32 Ibid., 190.

The story of Morebath and Sir Christopher is a powerful reminder that even in the midst of turbulent and perplexing times, the Church as an institution was at the heart of many communities, and people cared deeply about its life. It continued to provide rites of passage, comfort in times of distress, and hope of a better hereafter.

The stability which Elizabeth's long reign finally brought, combined with Mary's traumatic legacy and the threat of the Spanish Armada, allowed anti-Roman Catholic feelings to ferment, and the old faith to be associated with sinister foreign powers.

This was to be one of the numerous factors in the unravelling of relations between Parliament and the early Stuarts. Neither James nor his son Charles welcomed Parliament's resistance to royal marriages with Roman Catholics (in James' case arranging these for others, his own wife being respectably Protestant). England was now firmly Protestant and nervous about having this jeopardised.

James I and VI may have found the model of religion adopted by the Church of England more in keeping with his understanding of the Divine Right of Kings than that of the Scottish Kirk, but he did not find the English Parliament inclined to conform to his views on his authority or his demands for cash. James, therefore, dismissed Parliament and found alternative means of raising revenue.[33]

His son, Charles I, faced similar conflicts and exacerbated his problems by pursuing a disastrous policy in relation to the Scottish Kirk. Whereas in the Middle Ages the Church had been in a position to mediate in disputes between secular ruling factions, both internally and from Rome, this safety valve had been removed. The Church was no longer part of an international structure, and had the monarch as its Governor.

The causes of the English Civil Wars were complex, but at one level might be boiled down to Charles desiring a greater degree of executive power (including fiscal control) than his subjects were willing to permit him. The dispute famously erupted into armed conflict and the King ultimately suffered decisive military defeat by the summer of 1646.[34] However, at that stage there was a general acceptance of the notion that the King had been within his rights to pursue a war, even amongst his opponents. It was widely assumed that a settlement would be achieved and that Charles as King would play a part in governance afterwards. The picture was complicated, however, by the fact that Parliament, the Scots and the New Model Army were increasingly developing divergent agendas.

Having said that, in starting a second Civil War, Charles effectively engineered his own death. As Kelsey describes:

> He was executed by those amongst his English subjects most alarmed by their King's refusal to bow to the verdict of heaven, coupled with his propensity for collusion with his 'malignant', even his Catholic, subjects in Scotland and Ireland in a bid to revive his ill-fated fortune.[35]

33 Aylett, n. 25 above, 54.

34 S. Kelsey, 'The Trial of Charles I', *The English Historical Review*, Vol. 118, No. 477 (Jun 2003) 583–616.

35 Ibid., 584.

At this stage, political and military events were still understood in the light of an interventionist God. To the devout Puritans ranged against him, Charles was not only causing unnecessary suffering and death, but he was also defying the divine judgment issued on the battlefield. Furthermore, in colluding with a Scottish invasion, Charles was seen to have betrayed the English national interest.

Not only were key players like Cromwell undoubtedly angry at the second 'mischievous' war; so were many of the ordinary soldiers who fought.[36] There was indeed an even greater bitterness about this second conflict than there had been about the first.

From Charles' perspective, he had absolute right on his side and there was no other moral or spiritual choice. At his trial, he refused to acknowledge the authority of the court or to engage with its proceedings, and there are valid, theoretical questions about how the trial of a king could fit within the legal and constitutional framework of the time.[37] However, in pragmatic terms, the distinction between regicide and tyranicide is one of ideological conviction. Given that Charles was not prepared to co-operate in a settlement which would be acceptable to a critical mass of the key military and political players, and for as long as he lived he was going to continue to encourage both foreign and Roman Catholic powers to take up arms against England, it is difficult to see how his death could have been avoided. The nation was appalled at the killing of its king, but both sides were backed into a corner.

The Commonwealth period which followed is often associated with religious and political repression, and certainly England appears not to have been ready for even proto-democratic rule. Cromwell was ultimately nominated 'Lord Protector', and effectively functioned as a military dictator until his death from natural causes. He was briefly followed by his son, Richard, and the very fact of a return to a dynastic pattern is telling.

The comparative speed with which the monarchy was restored afterwards is often taken to be indicative of dissatisfaction with a regime which clamped down on the celebration of festivals, replaced feast days with fast and introduced fines for mild swearing.[38] In fairness to Oliver Cromwell, this had far more to do with pressures from his supporters than his personal, more moderate inclinations.[39] However, the fact remains that the essentially Puritan regime was out of step with the religious and cultural consensus of the majority of the population, as the social context in England was very different from that of the genuinely Presbyterian lowland Scotland.

Yet, balanced against this, there were a minority of religious and political radicals who sprang up during the mid-seventeenth century, and who explored new and sometimes creative ways of thinking and living.[40] There were limits to

36 A. Fraser, *Cromwell, Our Chief of Men* (Mandarin: Reading) 1993, 256–7.

37 Kelsey, n. 33 above.

38 Aylett, n. 25 above, 62–3.

39 Fraser, n. 35 above, 256–7.

40 C. Hill, *The World Turned Upside Down: Radical Ideas During the English Revolution* (Penguin: London) 1991.

how far the governing authorities allowed them to get, but to paint the period as straightforwardly and intellectually repressive is misleading. Some people found the chaos and the shattering of apparent social certainties a stimulus to new patterns of thinking.

The Levellers are probably the best remembered group, and Lilburne, as one of the leading figures, appealed to the principles of Magna Carta.[41] They were not a cohesive group with an easily summarised agenda, but they generally promoted ideas of extended suffrage, equality before the law, religious tolerance and government by consensus of the people. Clearly, they were a long way ahead of their time, and their legacy is complex.

It is true that, as Burgess[42] argues, later radical thinkers and eventually Marxist historians may have constructed a narrative of a connected radical tradition of working-class activism, which does not always bear scrutiny. Nevertheless, the very fact that names and traditions of groups like the Levellers, the Ranters and the Diggers were there to be rediscovered and used by later generations, as a kind of cultural talisman, is important. One further key point which Burgess[43] makes, and which should not be overlooked for our present purposes, is that the religious motivation of the seventeenth century radicals is often pushed aside by later commentators. What, from a later perspective, has been characterised as a struggle for political and social justice was to contemporaries a *religious* endeavour to conform to the will of an omnipotent God.

Ironically, this is a dynamic which the Levellers, Cromwell, Charles I and most of their generation held in common. For them the question was not simply how the state should deal with the Church or religious questions, but how the state could align itself best with the reality and values of God's Kingdom. Furthermore, there was an understanding that failure in this endeavour would lead to divinely inspired repercussions. This was a paradigm which shifted in the eighteenth century, and was never to be re-established.

1.2.3. The eighteenth, nineteenth and twentieth centuries in England

The Restoration of Charles II did not usher in a lengthy period of Stuart rule. The downfall of his successor, James II and VII, will be discussed below in relation to Scotland, but for present purposes the key point is that however much regicide might have been condemned in hindsight, the genie was not going back in the bottle. The de facto position was that kings could now rule only if their policies, religious and otherwise, were kept within parameters broadly acceptable to the nation. Furthermore, the constitutional settlement of 1688 made it clear that royal power was limited by an identifiable legal framework.

41 Fraser, n. 35 above, 214.

42 G. Burgess, 'Introduction', in G. Burgess & M. Festenstein, *English Radicalism 1550–1850* (Cambridge University Press: Cambridge) 2007, 1, 10.

43 G. Burgess, 'Radicalism and the English Revolution', in Burgess & Festenstein, ibid., 62.

The Church of England had a firm place within this constitutional structure, but its role could be seen to have altered dramatically from previous centuries. The mechanism of checks and balances on the exercise of royal power no longer employed the authority of the Church as a counterweight to maintain balance. Rather, it was the function of Parliament to keep executive power within bounds.

The essentially self-contained, internal governance set up by the Tudor state persisted in this regard. The power and position of the monarch had shifted radically from that seen in Elizabethan times, but the Church was in no position to regain temporal authority and, for many, it seemed to have lost its spiritual zeal.

The eighteenth-century Church of England, and particularly its clergy, were lampooned at times for being lazy, self-serving and spiritually lax. It was during this period that the currently known version of the satirical folk-song 'The Vicar of Bray'[44] became popular. The lyrics are sung in the person of a shamelessly pragmatic parson who changes his spiritual and political convictions whenever necessary to ensure that he keeps the only immovable law and principle in his universe:

> And this is the law, I will maintain
> Until my dying day, sir
> That whatsoever king may reign,
> Still I'll be the Vicar of Bray, sir!

However, the line between cynicism and pragmatism is often in the eye of the beholder. The 'latitudinarian' approach, adopted by many clergy of this period, may have seemed a gentler and more socially cohesive attitude than the religious fire of some of their forbears. In fact, Rack[45] describes it as 'a plea for concentration on essentials and toleration on other matters, a taste for the benefits of science and reason, but also for Episcopacy and the beauties of English liturgy'.

Rather than kicking against the values of the Enlightenment, many clerics were happy to embrace them. Furthermore, the Church of England had by this stage developed a discernible culture and identity, which at least some members valued for its own sake. Nevertheless, it was undeniable that belonging to the Church of England was socially and politically shrewd for ambitious families in a nation where entry to Parliament was closed to Catholics and difficult for Dissenters, office holders under the Crown and in corporations were supposed to qualify by a sacramental test, universities were Church of England institutions[46] and the Church itself could provide lucrative career opportunities.

There were, nevertheless, complaints expressed by contemporaries that although the Church of England was present in most aspects of national life,

44 For a version of the lyrics, see Nash Ford Publishing, Royal Berkshire History, 'The Vicar of Bray', http://www.berkshirehistory.com/legends/vicarofbray_bal.html.

45 H.D. Rack, *Reasonable Enthusiast: John Wesley and the Rise of Methodism* (Epworth Press: London) 2002.

46 Ibid., 10.

the nature of its presence was unsatisfactory. There were criticisms about clergy who had multiple livings and were more or less permanently absent from some of their parishes; there were also concerns that the process of industrialisation and urbanisation was leaving the growing city populations with sparse clerical cover.[47] Ecclesiastical boundaries had been established centuries before, and the Church was slow in responding to change.

There were those who wished to reform the Church of England from within, including John Wesley and his brother Charles, believing that the population needed and deserved better spiritual and pastoral care. Nor were they alone, as there were other Anglican Evangelicals and also dissenting groups who sought to bring about a Christian revival.[48] Furthermore, they frequently had considerable success during the course of the eighteenth century.

Evangelicalism continued in its various guises during the succeeding hundred years, and increasingly there was not just the domestic mission field to think about. In fact, Christianity became closely intertwined with the British Empire and the national Church was obviously heavily implicated in this.[49] The task of converting and therefore 'civilising' supposedly primitive peoples gave the process of colonisation a legitimacy and benevolence in the eyes of contemporaries,[50] however misguided this may seem to modern commentators.

Christianity was also perceived as a means of bolstering British citizens for service in the Empire and at home, particularly in the influential incarnation of 'muscular Christianity' from the mid-nineteenth century onwards. This ideology spanned denominational borders and associated Christian values with physical fitness and robust masculinity.[51]

However, the Low Church evangelicals were not the only group fighting to rouse the Church of England from the drowsy comfort of polite social observance and inject a new passion into its life, as the Oxford Movement (also known as the Ritualists and the Tractarians) sought to rediscover the ancient Catholic spirit and identity of the Church.[52] The Anglo-Catholic party in the Church aimed to reintroduce Catholic vestments and patterns of worship,[53] complete with bells

47 J. Munsey Turner, *John Wesley: The Evangelical Revival and the Rise of Methodism in England* (Epworth Press: Peterborough) 2002, 33.

48 Rack, n. 44 above, see in particular 282–305.

49 See A. Johnston, *The British Empire, Colonialism, and Missionary Activity* (Cambridge University Press: Cambridge) 2003.

50 C. Williams, 'British Religion and the Wider World: Mission and Empire 1800–1940', in S. Gilley and W. Sheils (eds), *A History of Religion in Britain: Practice and Beliefs from Pre-Roman Times to the Present* (Blackwell: Oxford) 1994, 381.

51 D.E. Hall, *Muscular Christianity: Embodying the Victorian Age (Cambridge Studies in Nineteenth-Century Literature and Culture)* (Cambridge University Press: Cambridge) 1994.

52 J. Shelton Reed, *Glorious Battle: The Cultural Politics of Victorian Anglo-Catholicism* (Vanderbilt University Press: Nashville) 1996.

53 P.B. Nockles, *The Oxford Movement in Context: Anglican High Churchmanship 1760–1857* (Cambridge University Press: Cambridge) 1994, Ch. 4.

and incense, a focus on the sacraments (including sacramental confession), and to revive the monastic tradition within Anglicanism. They also built numerous 'slum churches' in poor districts of industrial towns. Whilst many people were enchanted with this revival of mystical Christianity, an awful lot were disgusted.

It is difficult, from a twenty-first century perspective, to understand the venom and drama which the Anglo-Catholics aroused. However, the controversy is relevant for our study, given that the opposing forces attempted to use parliamentary legislation to quash the movement by prohibiting many of its practices by statute. The Public Worship Regulation Act 1874 was, as Reed[54] argues, very ill-considered legislation. Attempting to use an Act of Parliament to regulate worship and arranging for it to be supervised by a secular court was found distasteful by many citizens. It also inspired Anglo-Catholics to mobilise their resistance, and raised the status of the handful of clergymen who were imprisoned for contempt of court to that of heroes and martyrs.

Even amongst those who disliked the Tractarians, there were many who disliked this kind of secular coercion even more. It was no longer widely deemed acceptable within English society to have Parliament interfere so fundamentally in the life of the Church, nor to see essentially law-abiding citizens imprisoned for their religious convictions.

Anti-Catholic feeling was still strong, but few people wished to have Popish practices outlawed, and many of the legal disadvantages suffered by Roman Catholics had been removed as long ago as 1829.[55] Furthermore, other aspects of Anglican privilege and monopolies were dismantled in the course of the century (for example, the Universities Tests Act 1871 permitted non-Anglicans to attend Cambridge and Oxford),[56] and against this backdrop, the Public Worship Regulation Act 1874 seemed inappropriate and heavy-handed. Two Commissioners (John Duke Coleridge and Arthur P. Stanley) in a Royal Commission summarised this view well, even before the legislation was passed:

> The Church of England has always contained within it two parties, one caring much for outward observance and ceremonial, the other careless about or even hostile to them; and these two historical parties represent two classes of minds which always have and probably always will exist, and proclaim their existence, in a free country. If, therefore, the Church of England is to remain the National Establishment of a free country, room for both must be found in it, as far as is consistent with general uniformity.[57]

54 Shelton Reed, n. 51 above, 238.

55 Catholic Emancipation Act 1829.

56 R. Sandberg, *Law and Religion* (Cambridge University Press: Cambridge) 2011, 153.

57 Project Canterbury, 'Second Report of the Commissioners Appointed to Inquire into the Rubrics, Orders and Directions for Regulating the Course and Conduct of Public Worship, &c' (1867), http://anglicanhistory.org/pwra.

In 1906, another Royal Commission essentially recommended religious toleration within Anglicanism,[58] and in many ways the ritualist controversy reflected a wider attitude towards religious questions. Issues of faith were still of great importance to many people, but the idea of coercing others into conformity was no longer acceptable. It was now permissible for people to choose not to be members of the established Church, without appearing to be disloyal to the state or infringing social norms, and it was accepted that a national Church with a wide membership *needed* to have room for a diversity of opinion. If the Church of England was to maintain its status and its legitimacy, it had to reflect the respect for liberty, which was understood to be part of the national character.

The next hundred years saw seismic shifts in the place of the Church. At the start of the twentieth century, church membership was important in relation to identity, networking and social opportunities, as well as solace in times of financial or emotional crisis. By the year 2000, society had altered radically, and the majority of the population had found alternative means to define their identity and seek support when required.

Since the Second World War, England has become a far more multicultural and multi-ethnic society, thus making expectations of religious conformity seem even more inappropriate. Furthermore, the association between the Church and British imperialism was now viewed very differently, and much of the missionary work and its association with racial and cultural superiority came to be regarded as an extremely negative aspect of the Empire.

Again, as we shall see in the case of Scotland, the growth of the welfare state and social provision removed a very practical reason for many more economically deprived people to maintain a link with the Church. Bishop Mervyn Stockwood wrote movingly in his autobiography on the change, and expressed a sentiment which many Anglican clergy of his generation might echo:

> The main difference between being a parson in such an area in the 1930s and one in the 1980s is that a parishioner can now tell him to go to hell! Formerly he would not have dared because he knew he might have to creep to him for charity. Hence common sense demanded no unnecessary enemies. Today the welfare state guarantees a minimum standard and society's casualties are no longer dependent upon Lady Bountifuls in clerical collars. Thank God for the change. I prefer to meet my parishioners as equals, without enforced patronage on my side or false subservience on theirs.[59]

1.3 Wales

In contrast with Scotland (which will be discussed below) the Welsh nation was subjected to tight English controls (and in the eyes of some, repression) from a

58 Project Canterbury, '*Legislation related to Liturgy in the Church of England*, Public Worship Regulation Act, *Report of the Royal Commission on Ecclesiastical Discipline*', presented to both Houses of Parliament by Command of His Majesty (1906), http://anglicanhistory.org/pwra.

59 M. Stockwood, *Chanctonbury Ring: The Autobiography of Mervyn Stockwood* (Hodder & Stoughton: London) 1982, 28.

comparatively early period. Therefore, much of the political dynamic of Wales reflects the story of the emergent English state, and we shall avoid repeating the common elements with regard to the Reformation process and Civil Wars, as well as the more contemporary developments. For this reason, this section is somewhat briefer than those for England and Scotland, but we would stress that it is of no less profound significance.

In common with the other territories discussed in our study, early medieval Wales was a patchwork of different (frequently feuding) warlords, although the population shared a language and many cultural practices. The building of Offa's Dyke[60] may also have had an influence in consolidating a sense of shared identity even in the absence of political unity: an imposing territorial boundary carved into the landscape may have fostered an even greater feeling of distance between the peoples to the east and west of it.

Similarly, Wales was subject to comparable Christianising influences as England, both during and after the Roman Empire. In common with much of the west of mainland Britain, it heavily felt the influence of so called 'Celtic' Christianity.[61]

In the years following the Norman conquest of England, large parts of Wales came under Norman control, although Welsh rulers managed to retain their territory in the west for several centuries. Furthermore, the Norman lords who ruled in the borderlands as Lords of March effectively had quasi-autonomous fiefdoms and the power to build castles, wage war and hold courts. Welsh law codes governed civil law matters until Henry VIII introduced legislation effectively bringing Wales fully within English administrative and legal control.[62] This also meant that the Welsh language ceased to be used for most official government purposes, until it was reintroduced in the twentieth century.

In relation to the unfolding story of Church and state, this was critical in light of Henry's break with Rome. Although English accounts tend to focus on the north and the Pilgrimage of Grace, there was considerable opposition and resentment within Wales to the forced religious changes. In addition, as Marshall argues,[63] the resistance was not purely internal, and there were figures capable of agitating on the international stage.

However, as outlined above, the process of religious reform in England rolled on, and the 'Church of England' was imposed on Welsh territory. Initially, the intention was to have the Prayer Book and Bible only in English. Fortunately, a number of enthusiastic Welsh Protestants, influenced by the Humanist movement, fought against this. In 1563 Parliament was persuaded to pass legislation ordering that the Bible and Prayer Book be translated into Welsh by St David's Day (1 March) 1567. Then, as now, academic projects were apt to overrun, but

60 An earthwork dyke along the boundary between the Kingdom of Mercia and Wales, constructed in the eighth century: see Offa's Dyke Association, 'King Offa and the Dyke', http://www.offasdyke.demon.co.uk/dyke.htm.

61 F. Sampson, *Visions and Voyages: The Story of Our Celtic Heritage* (Triangle: London) 1998, 47–50.

62 Laws in Wales Acts 1535 and 1542.

63 P. Marshall, 'The Greatest Man in Wales: James Ap Gruffydd Ap Hywel and the International Opposition to Henry VIII', *The Sixteenth Century Journal*, Vol. 39, No. 3 (2008) 681–704.

a translation of the Prayer Book and New Testament did arrive in 1567 and in 1588 a complete edition of the Bible.[64]

There was (and indeed remains) an enduring link between the Welsh language, culture and religion. The ancient tongue was used by many of the Methodist and other evangelical preachers and hymn-writers in the eighteenth and nineteenth centuries. Even though many accepted as a matter of pragmatism that English was the language of business and government, they argued that Welsh had a nuance and beauty which made it especially suited for preaching.[65]

The evangelical movement was highly successful in Wales and by the end of the nineteenth century there were more people who identified themselves as Non-Conformist than Anglican, although the Church of England remained the biggest single grouping. The issue had been revealed by the 1851 Religious Census, which yielded the following data.[66] Of the 898, 442 sittings available in Welsh places of worship, the percentages of the various denominations were as follows:

- Established Church – 32%
- Calvinistic Methodists – 21%
- Congregationalists – 20%
- Baptists – 13%
- Wesleyans – 12%
- Others – 2%

The Church of England did make some effort to respond, investing in repair to church buildings and developing a network of Anglican Church schools. However, the established Church remained unpopular, particularly with the working-class population. It was quite justly associated both with England and the owners of land, mines, steelworks and factories. In the mid-nineteenth century, there was an understandable resentment about the fact that there had not been a Welsh-speaking bishop appointed since 1702,[67] and it did not help matters that that bishops of Llandaff at times resided not just in England, but as far away as Cambridge. This was a cause of scandal to contemporaries, and trying to win a battle for hearts and minds against this backdrop was a bitter struggle.

Furthermore, xenophobic antipathy towards the influx of Irish immigrants had fuelled anti-Catholic feelings in some quarters, and the Anglo-Catholic movement did nothing to assist the popularity of the Church. To add insult to

64 The National Library of Wales, 'Collections, Welsh Bible 1588', http://www.llgc.org.uk/index.php?id=292.

65 E.W. James, 'The New Birth of a People: Welsh Language and Identity and the Welsh Methodists c1740–1820', in R. Pope (ed.), *Religion and National Identity: Wales and Scotland c1700–2000* (University of Wales Press: Cardiff) 2001, 14, 28.

66 BBC History Home, Wales History, Ch. 16, 'Religion in the Nineteenth and Twentieth Centuries', http://www.bbc.co.uk/wales/history/sites/themes/guide/ch16_religion_19th_and_20th_centuries.shtml.

67 R.L. Brown, 'In Pursuit of a Welsh Episcopate', in Pope, n. 64 above, 84–102.

injury, in some Non-Conformist eyes the Church of England was just popery by the back door.

The campaign for disestablishment in Wales gathered momentum and, driven largely by the Welsh Non-Conformist David Lloyd George, came to fruition with the Welsh Church Act 1914 (although its effects were deferred until after the First World War). It was seen as a victory for the assertion of Welsh national identity, although it was, of course, not welcomed in all quarters. The Conservative politician F.E. Smith (later the first Earl of Birkenhead) championed the opposition, characterising Welsh disestablishment as a move which would shock and distress every Christian community in Europe. The Roman Catholic author G.K. Chesterton penned a somewhat acidic ode in response, ending with the stanza:

> It would greatly, I must own,
> Soothe me, Smith!
> If you left this theme alone,
> Holy Smith!
> For your legal cause or civil
> You fight well and get your fee;
> For your God or dream or devil
> You will answer, not to me.
> Talk about the pews and steeples
> And the Cash that goes therewith!
> But the souls of Christian peoples . . .
> Chuck it, Smith![68]

Whilst not everybody necessarily agreed with Chesterton, both his retort and the disestablishment (and disendowment) of the Welsh Church reflected the change in attitude from previous centuries. Religion was still seen as being an important social issue, and it was openly acknowledged that faith debates often had important financial and property implications. Nevertheless, it was not deemed acceptable for the state to demand conformity (although, as Kent[69] correctly points out, there was never a sustained attempt in the United Kingdom to create a confessional state, in which members of the state were automatically members of the Church and vice versa, requiring all who refused to conform to be expelled. Whilst Roman Catholics and Protestant dissenters may have been persecuted and subjected to a number of serious disadvantages, they were for the most part tolerated, albeit with varying degrees of reluctance. The same, at least from early modern times onwards, could be said of the Jewish community).

68 G.K. Chesterton, 'Antichrist, or the Reunion of Christendom: An Ode', http://www.cse.dmu.ac.uk/~mward/gkc/books/smith.txt.

69 J. Kent, *Wesley and the Wesleyans: Religion in Eighteenth Century Britain* (Cambridge University Press: Cambridge) 2002, 3.

Neither was it considered acceptable (at least for many) to suggest that Christian political opponents were endangering people's eternal salvation in proposing changes to the legal framework connecting Church and state.

The Welsh population, like their contemporaries in England and Scotland, disengaged from active participation in organised religion during the course of the twentieth century. Commentators like Chambers have characterised this change as 'rapid and deep secularisation'.[70] How valid this assertion is depends rather upon what is actually meant by the term 'secularisation', as will be explored in later chapters. However, it is certainly true that attendance at church and chapel drastically declined in this period.

Nevertheless, Robbins[71] argues that even this secularisation has a distinctively Welsh character. He hints that secularisation is defined as the absence of, or at least the departure from, a particular past, and it is not a position reached from a cultural vacuum. He talks of visitors to museums experiencing coal mines and chapels alike as things of the past. However, as things of a specific and shared past, they shape the present.

1.4 Scotland

1.4.1 Scotland in the Middle Ages

As we saw above, unlike the lands that were eventually to become known as England and Wales, not all of the territory which is now Scotland was ever part of the Roman Empire. Indeed, the Romans famously built Hadrian's Wall,[72] and later the Antonine Wall,[73] with the express aim of keeping the thieving, violent and (in their eyes) generally undesirable barbarians on the far side, out of their domain. This meant that the peoples of Northern Britain were not subject to centralised law and control, nor to the influence of Roman Christianity, in the same way as the populations further south.

In contrast, missionaries became seriously active in Scotland in the course of the fifth century and, by the seventh century, Christianity had become the dominant religion, particularly in political terms.[74] As was the case in many other parts of Europe, secular and spiritual authority were enmeshed from the very beginning of the history of both Church and state. The mechanics of government and administration, relating both to lordship and to the embryonic

70 P. Chamber, *Religion, Secularisation and Social Change in Wales: Congregational Studies in Post-Christian Society* (University of Wales Press: Cardiff) 2005, 7.

71 K. Robbins, 'Religion and Community in Scotland and Wales since 1800', in Gilley and Sheils, n. 49 above, 363, 380.

72 'Visit Hadrian's Wall, Why was the Wall Built?', http://www.visithadrianswall.co.uk/hadrians-wall/about-hadrians-wall/why-was-the-wall-built.

73 'The Antonine Wall: Frontiers of the Roman Empire', http://www.antoninewall.org.

74 S. Driscoll, *Alba: The Gaelic Kingdom of Scotland AD 800–1124* (Birlin: Edinburgh) 2002, 40.

parish and diocesan structures, were closely tied together. Not only were they mutually dependent in practical terms, they frequently involved members of the same families, drawn from the local ruling elite.[75] Whilst, in theory, the son of a swineherd might become a bishop or the daughter of a brewer might become an abbess, in practice it did not tend to happen all that often.

An additional dimension in Scotland was the strong link between spiritual authority and linguistic and tribal identity.[76] In the early Middle Ages, the northern part of mainland Britain was a veritable cultural kaleidoscope. A considerable number of different kingdoms occupied distinct regions, and four large ethnic groups could be identified: the Picts, the Gaels, the Britons and the Angles – not to mention, of course, the Vikings,[77] who first raided and then settled in Scottish territory. Saints' cults and the large churches that developed from them were all tied to local identity.[78]

For instance, Cuthbert had a strong following amongst the Angles and the native British population in the south, whilst Columba was called upon by the Gaelic people of the west. It is no coincidence that the names of Cuthbert[79] and Columba[80] are still familiar to us, whilst Pictish saints such as Serf, Ethernan and Drostan have slipped into relative obscurity, melting into the mists along with the mysterious Picts who were loyal to them.[81] As Veitch observes, the transference of St Columba's relics from Iona to Dunkeld in the ninth century was closely related to the rising tide of Gaelic ascendancy and the assimilation of the Pictish people.[82] In the early Middle Ages the power of clerics and cults waxed and waned according to the battlefield prowess and wealth of the kings and nobles who supported them, and equally kingly success or failure in warfare was seen to relate to having retained or lost God's favour.[83]

However, it would be very misguided, therefore, to imply that the Church was a parasitic institution, which simply used the power of the kings and tribal warlords as a vehicle for attaining influence and material possessions. In reality, there was always a symbiotic relationship between Throne and Altar, and the approval of clerics provided evidence of divine mandate, and thereby legitimated kingly rule. For example, in the Chronicle of the Kings of Alba it is stated:

75 R. Fletcher, *The Conversion of Europe: From Paganism to Christianity 371–1386 AD* (Fontana Press: London) 1998, 130.

76 Driscoll, n. 73 above, 9.

77 M. Wood, *In Search of the Dark Ages* (Ariel: London) 1981, 110–12.

78 Driscoll, n. 73 above, 10–11.

79 G. Bonner, D. Rollason and C. Stancliffe, *St Cuthbert, His Cult and His Community to AD 1200* (The Boydell Press: Woodbridge) 1989.

80 P. Sheldrake, *Living Between Worlds: Place and Journey in Celtic Spirituality* (DLT: London) 1995, 8.

81 Driscoll, n. 73 above, 9.

82 K. Veitch, 'The Alliance between Church and State in Early Medieval Alba', *Albion: A Quarterly Journal Concerned with British Studies*, Vol. 30, No. 2 (1998) 193–220, 196.

83 F.H. Russell, *The Just War in the Middle Ages* (Cambridge University Press: Cambridge) 1976, 26.

> Certainly in the following year the Norsemen were beaten in Strathearn, and in his 6th year King Constantine, and Bishop Cellach, vowed that the laws and teachings of the faith, and the rights of the churches and gospels, to be protected equally with the Scots on the hill of Credulity, near to the royal city of Scone.[84]

This is a useful illustration of the Church being, as Driscoll describes, 'fully integrated into the physical and conceptual arrangements of kingship'.[85] A nascent concept of the rule of law could be seen to go hand in hand with maintaining the Christian faith. King and bishop vowed together to assert the legitimacy of rule.

It is also worth emphasising that even in early Christian times, kings were themselves sacred figures, and the Biblical narratives of figures like Saul[86] and David[87] contributed to developing notions of sacral kingship in western Europe. Both royal and episcopal power derived from the same source, and kings possessed a form of spiritual authority. The idea of a division between the religious and political sphere was not only alien to the medieval worldview, but it was effectively incompatible with it.

Thus, as the governance of Scotland gradually coalesced into the Gaelic kingdom of Alba – a territory which stretched from Carlisle to Inverness, and which was the true precursor of the modern Scottish State – the Church developed within it as an intrinsic part of its structure. Yet, having acknowledged all of this, it is important not to adopt a one-dimensional view of the Church as simply another facet of elite control. The story of Church and state is certainly not a narrative confined to the manoeuvres of the ruling classes; nor is it one confined to the world of politics.

First, a seemingly obvious point which may be obscured by a haze of post-Enlightenment cynicism is that there is ample evidence of people across the social spectrum being deeply devoted to their Christian faith. In fact, the Church could only be part of the communal social structure because a critical number of individuals genuinely believed it to be of value. Even in an undemocratic, pre-industrial world, those who wield military or spiritual power can only do so if they can garner sufficient support.

Death rituals provide useful evidence of confidence in the Christian God, and archaeological findings demonstrate a marked transition from Pagan to Christian burial practices.[88] It is highly unlikely that families would wish to take risks with

84 T.H. Weeks (translation), The Pictish Chronicle MS. COLB. BIB. IMP. PARIS, 4126. 'The Chronicle of the Kings of Alba, Constantine II 900-943', http://www.kjhskj75z.talktalk.net/pictish.html#third. The Latin text reads: *In sequenti utique anno occisi sunt in Sraith Herenn Normanni, ac in vi. anno Constantinus rex, et Celachus episcopus, leges disciplinasque fidei, atque jura ecclesiarum ewangeliorumque, pariter cum Scottis in colle credulitatis, prope regali civitati Scoan devoverunt custodiri.*

85 Driscoll, n. 73 above, 37.

86 See 1 Samuel.

87 See 1 Samuel, 2 Samuel, 1 Kings and 1 Chronicles.

88 Yorke, n. 16 above, 216.

their loved ones in the next world, and a change in funeral customs is indicative of a high degree of trust in the God of the Church. Doubtless, on some occasions people practised Christianity whilst retaining pre-Christian beliefs and rituals,[89] but this does not mean that their Christianity was not sincere and important to them. The contemporary academic consensus is that Christianity was embraced as a reality by the majority of people during the Middle Ages, and was not just a necessary veneer to cover Pagan practices from a judgemental ruling class.[90]

The Church in the early Middle Ages provided pastoral care, learning, medicine and services which were of benefit to the whole community. It also taught that all individuals had souls regardless to their status, were children of God and were worthy of compassion and respect.[91] Bede's 'Life of Cuthbert' describes the model Church leader: 'He strictly maintained his old frugality and took delight in preserving the rigours of the monastery amidst the pomp of the world. He fed the hungry, clothed the destitute and had all other marks of the perfect bishop'.[92]

Whether bishops, other than Cuthbert, always attained this ideal may be somewhat questionable, but it is significant that the accepted understanding was that the Church and its clergy were supposed to be both self-sacrificing and benevolent. The intention was that the Church existed to make a social contribution, to be the voice of conscience and a source of practical help.

There is evidence of spiritual authority functioning to check abuses and excesses of secular power in early times. For example, St Aidan is recorded as having rebuked King Oswin for material indulgences and apparently caring more about expensive horses than he cared about people. St Aidan eventually died whilst camping outside the gate of another king who needed shaming for bad behaviour, possibly whilst on a protest hunger strike.[93] Again, it is far from clear that all, or even most churchmen and women, were as outspoken as Aidan. Nevertheless, the ideal is itself significant, even if it was very imperfectly realised.

89 Ibid., 106–09.

90 See R. Hutton, 'How Pagan Were the Medieval English', *Folklore*, Vol. 122, No. 3 (2011) 235–49. Although this article deals specifically with the English context, much of the argument could be generalised to Scotland and indeed Europe more widely. In essence, 'the medieval English Christian religion was of a kind that matched paganism in so many structural respects that it provided an entirely satisfactory substitute for it'. Hutton's case is essentially that the practices and ideas of medieval Christianity, with a multiplicity of saints, assurances and rituals gave people the freedom, security and colour which they desired. There is little evidence of a survival of Pagan practice, at least beyond the eleventh century, and when the picture is considered in its entirety it is unsurprising that this should be so.

91 See, e.g., Bede, *The Age of Bede* (Penguin: London) 1998, 131: 'Eddius Stephanus: Life of Wilfred'. The early medieval author gives an account of a young mason called Bothelm who fell from a building. The virtuous bishop wept when he was taken to the dying man, and his prayers are credited with miraculously restoring him to life. Interestingly, the doctors then provide him with rather more mundane and practical care for his broken bones. However, in the account it is considered normal and appropriate for the bishop to care about a young labourer and the chronicler records his name.

92 Bede, ibid., 79; Bede, ibid., Life of Cuthbert, Ch. 26 'His Way of Life as a Bishop'.

93 Sampson, n. 60 above, 124–5.

The shared understanding was that the Church hierarchy had both the right and the duty to criticise inappropriate royal actions.

This social pattern continued for the later Middle Ages, when the Church was a major force in the collective life of the Scottish people. It was a player on the political and administrative stage from the level of the court to the village, although the nature and terms of its engagement at the courtly level altered during the course of the medieval period. However, it was also a feature of everyday life and experience, and this dynamic must not be squeezed out of our consideration.

The story of the Scottish nation continued to unfold through the turbulent and violent times of the later Middle Ages, inevitably influenced by changes south of the border. Whilst the territory of England was in the hands of a number of different kings, or weak rulers besieged by Viking incursions,[94] it was no serious threat to Scotland. However, once it came under united and effective control, that was a very different ball-game, especially after the Norman Conquest. King Malcolm III unwisely encouraged some aggrieved Northumbrian earls to rebel,[95] and this resulted in an angry William I taking action. Provoking William was highly counterproductive, as the Anglo-Saxon chronicle records:

> A.D. 1072. This year King William led a naval force and a land force to Scotland, and beset that land on the sea-side with ships, whilst he led his land-force in at the Tweed; but he found nothing there of any value. King Malcolm, however, came, and made peace with King William, and gave hostages, and became his man; whereupon the king returned home with all his force.[96]

However, although the Scottish King had in theory done homage to William, the reality was that the Anglo-Norman ruler of England had neither the capacity nor the inclination to bring Scotland within his empire in any meaningful sense, opting instead for constructing frontier castles.[97] As a result, the stage was set for England and Scotland to be less than cordial neighbours for the next few hundred years, with English kings generally seeking to annex Scotland or, failing that, to obtain as much loot as possible in ransoms and fines. Fascinating though the history of this period is, a detailed examination of the bloody tussles between the two kingdoms is beyond the scope of this study. For present purposes, however, the following points are worthy of note.

First, some Scottish Kings, such as David I, very effectively used relations with the English court for their own benefit and in the process brought significant English influences north of the border. Some of these imported ideas had crucial

94 D. Hadley, *The Vikings in England* (Manchester University Press: Manchester) 2006.

95 Driscoll, n. 73 above, 63.

96 *The Anglo-Saxon Chronicle*, Year AD 1072 (the Project Gutenberg ebook of *The Anglo-Saxon Chronicle*), http://www.gutenberg.org/cache/epub/657/pg657.html.

97 Driscoll, n. 73 above, 63.

implications for the evolution of the Scottish state, and David grew up as a prince in the famous court of Henry I.[98] It is easy to exaggerate both the distance and enmity between the ruling classes of the two nations (who were, of course, both every bit as capable of slaughtering their own countrymen and families in civil wars and dynastic squabbles as they were of fighting each other).

David I held extensive estates in England from the Crown, had personal relationships and connections, and in due course imported various Norman concepts of feudalism into Scotland. The adoption of a feudal structure had profound implications for the development of Scottish thinking on royal power and the means and appropriateness of limiting its exercise. It is well established that what was to become known as the Divine Right of Kings had deep medieval roots.[99] However, Oakley has creatively and persuasively argued that feudalism and sacral kingship also contained seeds which were 'destined to germinate in the thirteenth, fourteenth and fifteenth centuries into those institutional arrangements for constitutional restraint upon the abuse of executive power'.[100]

Oakley suggests that feudalism elevated the status of the king, but it also bound him to his lords. In other words, it placed the exercise of royal power within a framework of mutual obligations. This laid the foundations for later debates about the duties and limitations attached to the power of the Crown. If Oakley's contention is accepted, the impact of David I's time in the Anglo-Norman court was to have an influence that rippled down the centuries.

Second, during what became known as the Scottish Wars of Independence, the 'Auld Alliance' was forged.[101] This was the historic name given to the pact of mutual support between Scotland and France in dealing with the English, and this alliance was to have far-reaching implications in the era of the European Reformations. It is also worth noting that from quite ancient times, Scotland was accustomed to looking to the continent and acting as a player in a European context.

Third, the role and nature of the Western Church evolved during the course of this period.[102] Once Christianity became embedded, and as Papal power increased, the fortunes of bishops and others became less straightforwardly tied to the patronage of local secular leaders, and ecclesiological hierarchies had their own

98 C. Warren Hollister, 'Courtly Culture and Courtly Style in the Anglo-Norman World', *Albion: A Quarterly Journal Concerned with British Studies*, Vol. 20, No. 1 (1988) 1–17, 5.

99 G. Burgess, 'The Divine Right of Kings Reconsidered', *The English Historical Review*, Vol. 107, No. 425 (1992) 837–61.

100 F. Oakley, *Empty Bottles of Gentilism: Kingship and the Divine in Late Antiquity and the Early Middle Ages (to 1050)* (Yale University Press: New Haven) 2010, 176.

101 See further N. MacDougall, *An Antidote to the English: The Auld Alliance 1295–1560* (Tuckwell Press: East Lothian) 2001.

102 The topic of Church government in this period is, in and of itself, a vast field of academic endeavour, both then and now. Any detailed assessment is outside of the scope of this book, but see, e.g., C. Zuckerman, 'The Relationship of Theories of Universals to Theories of Church Government in the Middle Ages: A Critique of Previous Views', *Journal of the History of Ideas*, Vol. 36, No. 4 (1975) 579–94.

interests and agendas. In addition, both England and Scotland acknowledged the role of the Papacy as an international arbitrator with power to pronounce on the legitimacy of territorial claims. The English and the Scottish Crowns alike petitioned the Pope for support in the disputes over England's assertion of feudal lordship over Scotland, most famously perhaps with the Declaration of Arbroath from the Scottish side.[103] What began as a letter to the Pope asking England to stop molesting Scotland (and lift the excommunication which Robert the Bruce had suffered for murdering someone in a church[104]) effectively became a proud declaration of Scottish independence.

From the point of view of the present study, however, the critical factor to note is that a spiritual authority, outside of either jurisdiction, was accepted as having power to intervene and pronounce judgement by virtue of divine mandate. As had been the case in earlier centuries, secular power continued to be legitimated and limited by those embodying spiritual status (distinct from the spiritual status embodied within kingship).

Furthermore, secular parties accepted this situation even when it was counter to their interests. The Scottish nobles clearly did not appreciate what the Pope had previously said, but their response was to petition Papal authority, rather than attempt to dismiss it. Obviously, this acceptance of extra-national spiritual jurisdiction residing in the Pope would ultimately change radically with the Reformation. Yet, as will be discussed below, the notion of spiritual power limiting secular power did not die out. Instead, there was a shift in the mechanisms and perceived seats of spiritual power.

Finally, it is key to note that even in this period spiritual power resided in more than one place and the Church had more than one voice. It was Bishop Alexander de Kininmund who took the document to the Papal court in Avignon, and he may in fact even have been the main author of the document.[105] In a world in which spiritual authority could endow leaders with legitimacy, there could potentially be a complicated trade-off between differing sources of such authority. In this case, the Scottish nobles were fortunate to have a local bishop who might well have also had the Pope's ear. However, at other times it may have been necessary to consider whether it was better to have the endorsement of a geographically distant but prestigious Pope or a known, immediate Church presence on the ground.

1.4.2 European reformations and the Early Modern era in Scotland

Tensions between local and centralised Church authority were nothing new; nor were grievances over perceived abuses or differences of theological

103 E.J. Cowan, *For Freedom Alone: The Declaration of Arbroath 1320* (Tuckwell Press: East Lothian) 2003.

104 M.F. Graham, 'Conflict and Sacred Space in Reformation-Era Scotland', *Albion: A Quarterly Journal Concerned with British Studies*, Vol. 33, No. 3 (2001) 371–87, 374.

105 G.W.S. Barrow, *R. Bruce and the Community of the Realm of Scotland* (Edinburgh University Press: Edinburgh) 1988, 305–08.

opinion.[106] However, what had been tensions in the past became irreconcilable differences with the European Reformations and Counter Reformations.

In contrast to England, where the Reformation was driven largely by the personal agenda of the monarch, the Scottish Reformation was powered to a great extent by the ideological convictions of the people. It started with the nobles and clergy, those in an economic or educational position to be exposed to ideas from the continent, but rapidly trickled down to have wider appeal. In Scotland, as elsewhere, the transitional period between Catholicism and Protestantism was fraught, amongst a maelstrom of competing religious passions and political ambitions. King James V had resisted attempts by English diplomats to persuade him to follow the example of his uncle, Henry VIII (James V's mother was Henry's elder sister, Margaret), in closing the monasteries and reforming the Church. In fact, James V had a low tolerance for heresy and Patrick Hamilton, the first martyr of the Scottish Reformation, was famously burnt at the stake during his reign.[107]

However, the execution of Hamilton proved counterproductive, and an associate of the Cardinal responsible warned that the 'smoke of Patrick Hamilton has infected as many as it blew upon'.[108] Considerable numbers of people were drawn towards the new Protestant ideas. James V died suddenly, being succeeded by his infant daughter, Mary.[109] Her tragic life was played out against a background of clashing religious and political factions. It was initially agreed that she would be married to the English heir, Prince Edward (later Edward VI), but voices for the Roman Catholic cause prevailed and she became the bride of the French Dauphin. John Knox, the Calvinist reformer and agitator, never being a man for understatement, opined that she had been sold to the devil.[110]

Whilst she was in France, the reform movement gathered steam and the Scottish Reformation Parliament met and passed the Confession of Faith Ratification Act 1560[111] and the Papal Jurisdiction Act 1560.[112] These outlined the tenets of the faith of the Scottish Church and explicitly repudiated Papal authority in Scotland. Although Mary herself never ratified this legislation, it could be argued that from this point onwards Scotland was de facto a Protestant state.

When her teenage husband sadly died of an ear infection, she returned to Scotland to face a stormy and unpopular reign, being a Roman Catholic Queen in a now zealously Protestant setting. Few fictional heroines could hope to compete with Mary for dramatic events. She had two husbands after the French Prince,

106 See, e.g., J.W. Gray, 'The Problem of Papal Power in the Ecclesiology of St Bernard', *Transactions of the Royal Historical Society*, Vol. 24 (1974) 1–17; M. Chibnall, 'The Empress Matilda and Church Reform', *Transactions of the Royal Historical Society*, Vol. 38 (1988) 107–30.

107 J.E. McGoldrick, 'Patrick Hamilton, Luther's Scottish Disciple', *The Sixteenth Century Journal*, Vol. 18, No. 1 (Spring 1987) 81–8.

108 Ibid., 87.

109 A. Fraser, *Mary Queen of Scots* (World Books: London) 2nd edn, 1971, 26.

110 Ibid., 50.

111 Confession of Faith Ratification Act 1560, c. 1.

112 Papal Jurisdiction Act 1560, c. 2.

and both marriages were to arrogant, ambitious men, who ultimately succeeded in alienating people at all levels of Scottish society, including the Queen herself. Furthermore, her third husband was widely (and possibly not unfairly) believed to have murdered the second. At the time, Mary herself was also implicated in the assassination, although Fraser[113] and the balance of modern historical opinion lean against this conclusion.[114]

Faced with scandal, criminality and armed rebellion by Protestant nobles, Mary was forced to abdicate, and spent the final period of her life as a prisoner in England. When she was accused of involvement in a plot to assassinate her cousin, Elizabeth I, the English Queen had her beheaded, although she managed to squirm out of taking responsibility for the execution.

Mary's baby son, James, succeeded to the throne and it speaks volumes that John Knox preached at his coronation.[115] Within a generation, Scotland had passed not only into Protestant, but Presbyterian and Calvinist control. The national reformed Church in Scotland looked very different from what lay to the south in England. It was governed by elders (the General Assembly) rather than bishops, and it adopted far more austere attitudes towards ritual and a hard-line theology of predestination. It was in this climate that the baby King was raised. As a young man, James VI expressed his views on the Church of England to the General Assembly in 1590:

> As for our neighbour kirk in England, it is an evill said masse in English, wanting nothing but the liftings. I charge you, my good people, ministers, doctors, elders, nobles, gentleman and barons to stand to your puritie, and to exhort the people to do the same.[116]

As Macdonald notes, this speech contrasts dramatically with what he had to say in England to the Star Chamber some 26 years later: '[O]f any Church I know that ever I read or knew of, present or past, [the Church of England] is most pure and nearest the Primitive and Apostolicall Church in Doctrine and Discipline'.[117]

Outstanding changes had taken place in the intervening years. In one of the ironies of history, the Union of the Crowns, which Henry VIII had failed to engineer by marrying Mary Queen of Scots to his son Prince Edward, had come about when his daughter, Elizabeth, died without issue and the throne passed to James. James liked being king of the richer southern nation, and his words to the Star Chamber may simply reflect his pragmatism. However, Macdonald puts forward a very convincing additional reason why he may have revised

113 Fraser, n. 108 above.

114 See also J. Guy, *Queen of Scots: The True Life of Mary Stuart* (HMH: Boston) 2005.

115 American Missionary Fellowship, *The Life of John Knox* (Attic Books: Green Forest, Arizona) 2011, 100.

116 A.R. Macdonald, 'James VI and I: The Church of Scotland and British Ecclesiastical Convergence', *The Historical Journal*, Vol. 48, No. 4 (2005) 855–903, 886.

117 Ibid., 886–7.

his opinion: the English model better suited his notion of how a national Church should treat its monarch.[118]

In Scotland, the position was, as Andrew Melville indicated, less than diplomatically put to James: 'I mon tell yow, thair is twa Kings and twa Kingdomes in Scotland. Thair is Chryst Jesus the King and his Kingdome the Kirk, whase subject King James the Saxt is, and of whose kingdom nocht a king nor a lord nor a heid, bot a member'.[119]

As stated, James found a hierarchical structure with himself at the top to be a more appealing prospect, and Patterson[120] has argued that the King had a genuine intellectual commitment to the idea of reuniting Christendom. This may well have been the case, but the idea of bringing the Church of Scotland into closer line with England would certainly have expanded his personal authority and, indeed, status.

James became deeply committed to the notion that kings ruled by divine right, and famously published a tract setting forth his opinions: 'Kings are called Gods by the prophetical King Dauid, because they sit vpon GOD his Throne in the earth, and haue the count of their administration to giue vnto him'.[121]

It is true that it is possible to oversimplify, and thereby caricature, the political doctrine of the Divine Right of Kings, as it was expressed in the sixteenth and seventeenth centuries. There were differing understandings of what the theory meant and, as Russell[122] has argued, it is misguided to equate espousing the Divine Right of Kings with asserting that the monarch was in no way constrained by the law. Nevertheless, it is reasonable to assert both that James adopted an extremely high view of the doctrine, and also that there were some essential features which both Parliament and society in Scotland would struggle with.

The notion of an anointed king as an intermediary between the nation and God was instinctively repugnant to Calvinist sensibilities. As Chapman suggests, part of the appeal of Protestantism for many was 'its promotion of practical, non-mystical contact with the Deity'.[123] Therefore, sacral kingship itself was problematic, and the notion of a king as Head of the Church still more so. Having rejected bishops and a sacramental priesthood, what logic could there be in a human, kingly intercessor?

With the union of the Crowns, Scotland lost a resident monarch who felt the heartbeat of the Scottish nation. Even before the death of Elizabeth, James had shown a marked interest in her kingdom.[124] However, James' abandonment of

118 Ibid., 887.

119 A. Nicholson: *Power and Glory: Jacobean England and the Making of the King James Bible* (Harper Perennial: London) 2003, 6.

120 W.B. Patterson, *James VI and I and the Reunion of Christendom* (Cambridge University Press: Cambridge) 2000.

121 Constitution Society, King James, *The Trew Law of Free Monarchies*, http://www.constitution.org/primarysources/stuart.html.

122 C. Russell, *Causes of the English Civil War* (Oxford University Press: Oxford) 1990, 150.

123 H.W. Chapman, *Lady Jane Grey* (Pan Books: Bucks) 1962, 18.

124 Nicholson: n. 118 above, Ch. 1 'A poore man now arrived at the Land of Promise'.

the faith of his homeland was to have profound implications for the reign of his son, Charles I. Charles' intense belief in the Divine Right of Kings set him on a trajectory of almost inevitable confrontation with the Kirk and opened up bitter divisions within the Scottish nation. It also sparked off armed conflict throughout the British Isles. As Fissel argued: 'Charles I's obsession with redefining orthodoxy and imposing uniformity within the churches of his kingdoms led to a grave political miscalculation'.[125]

Charles attempted to impose both bishops and what was essentially an Anglican Prayer Book on the Scottish Church. This resulted in rioting and also the National Covenant of 1638. The latter was a document signed by individuals at all levels of society, which in the words of the Scottish Covenanter Memorial Association was intended to 'confirm their opposition to the interference by the Stuart kings in the affairs of the Presbyterian Church of Scotland'.[126]

The Covenanters raised an army and defeated Charles in the 'Bishops' Wars'.[127] The crisis was one of the sparks that lit the blue touch-paper for the Wars of the Three Kingdoms (which included the English Civil War, the Scottish Civil War and the Irish Confederate Wars).[128] The mayhem and carnage which raged throughout the seventeenth century is too complex to recount in detail here. In a nutshell, the Covenanters fought and won a war in Scotland against Charles I. However, they then got into conflict with the English Parliament and supported the claims of Charles II to the thrones of England and Scotland (hoping and believing that he and his involvement in the kirk could be controlled). Ultimately, Cromwell and his New Model Army invaded and occupied Scotland, and an Act of Union was passed by Parliament in 1657.[129]

It is important to note, however, that a significant number of Scots remained staunchly Royalist. The Roman Catholic and Episcopalian population had no desire to champion Presbyterianism, and although the Puritan faith was strong in the Lowlands, the north and the Highlands inclined more to these religious persuasions. In addition, there was the distinct culture of the Highlands to be factored into the equation.[130] The Gaelic language still persisted there, as did the clan system and its customs, including that of 'human rent' in the form of providing fighting men to the lord when required.[131] Of course, political and religious

125 M.C. Fissel, *The Bishops' Wars: Charles I's Campaigns against Scotland, 1638–1640* (Cambridge University Press: Cambridge) 1994, 1.

126 Scottish Covenanters Memorial Association, 'Who were the Covenanters', http://www.covenanter.org.uk/whowere.html.

127 See further Fissel, n. 124 above.

128 See further M. Bennett, *The Civil Wars in Britain and Ireland: 1638–1651* (Wiley: Chichester) 1997.

129 Fraser, n. 35 above, 364.

130 A.D. Kennedy, 'Reducing that Barbarous Country: Center, Periphery, and Highland Policy in Restoration Britain', *Journal of British Studies*, Vol. 52, No. 3 (2013) 597–614.

131 For an evocative, artistic depiction of Highland culture, only slightly later in time, see the classic documentary drama *Culloden* (1964), written and directed by Peter Watkins.

loyalties could not be neatly decided along geographical lines, and there were royalists in Edinburgh and Protestant clans in the Highlands. Nevertheless, there were definite regional trends and cracks along ancient fault lines.

Neither the Act of Union 1707 nor the Commonwealth were destined for longevity, and at the Restoration of Charles II the Covenanters faced severe persecution in what became known as 'The Killing Time'. Parishes were given into the charge of Episcopalian curates, and those who refused to conform faced fines, torture and execution. Not surprisingly, this generated civil unrest and violence.

Both academic and popular opinion remain divided as to whether the Covenanter rebels were martyrs for freedom of conscience or violent, religious fundamentalists.[132] The assassination of the Scottish Primate, Archbishop Sharpe, in Fife in May 1679,[133] followed by the battles of Drumclog and Bothwell Brig, raised the stakes still further. The Government responded with the extrajudicial execution of anyone caught in arms, or who refused to swear loyalty to the King and take the 'Oath of Abjuration' renouncing the Covenant. It exacerbated intra-Scottish tensions that many of the Government troops sent into the Lowlands to crush and root out rebels were Highlanders.[134] The memories of these bitter events were still fresh during the following century when it came the turn of many (although by no means all) Highlanders to be opposed to the Government in Jacobite risings.

The period of bloodshed has left a deep imprint on Scottish psyche and culture, and there are memorials to the Covenanters throughout the nation.[135] Sir George Mackenzie, the man responsible for some of the greatest excesses in the repression, became a folk-monster after his death and remains at the centre of one of Edinburgh's most notorious ghost stories.[136] Inevitably, the understandable place of horror which these times held in Presbyterian popular culture has fed into enduring sectarian divisions.

132 E.H. Hyman, 'A Church Militant: Scotland, 1661–1690', *The Sixteenth Century Journal*, Vol. 26, No. 1 (1995) 49–74.

133 Ibid., 68.

134 Scottish Covenanters Memorial Association, n. 125 above.

135 Scottish Covenanters Memorial Association, http://www.covenanter.org.uk: Airds Moss, Battle of 1680 Auchengilloch, Bothwell, Battle of 1679, Brechin & Fenwick – Rev William Guthrie Campsie – William Boick, Carluke – Rev Peter Kid, Carsgailoch Hill Covenanters Cumnock – Dun & Paterson, Dalry (Galloway) Stewart & Grierson, Dalry (Galloway) – Covenanter Sculpture, Dolphinton – Major Joseph Learmont, Douglas Covenanter Connections, Drumclog, Battle of Dumfries – Rev William Veitch, Durisdeer –Daniel MacMichael, East Kilbride Covenanters, Earlstoun Castle and the Gordons, Edinburgh – Greyfriars Kirkyard-Covenanters' Prison, Greyfriars, Hamilton – Earnock Graves, Inveraray – Executions—1685, Kippen–James Ure of Shirgarton, Lanark Covenanters Lanark – William Hervi (Harvey) Lesmahagow – Rev Thomas Linning Linn's Tomb (Wigtownshire), Muirkirk – John Brown of Priesthill—1685 Muirkirk Heritage Layby, etc, New Cumnock – Corson & Hair New Cumnock – Martyrs' Moss, Pentland Rising—1666 Sorn – George Wood—1688 Stonehouse – James Thomson, Strathaven Covenanters, Tynron – William Smith.

136 City of the Dead, Haunted Graveyard, 'The World Famous Edinburgh Ghost and Graveyard Tours', http://www.cityofthedeadtours.com/tours/city-of-the-dead-haunted-graveyard-tour.

1.4.3 The eighteenth, nineteenth and twentieth centuries in Scotland

Although driven by forces in the Hague and London, rather than Edinburgh,[137] the Glorious Revolution of 1688 turned political and religious fortunes in Scotland upside down. James VII and II – the ill-fated Roman Catholic successor to his brother, Charles II – was ousted from the throne in favour of his daughter, Mary, and son-in-law, William of Orange. Not only did this bring the persecution of the Covenanters to an end, but it was a crushing blow for the Divine Right of Kings as a political force. A monarch who had proved unacceptable to the wider ruling classes had effectively been sacked and replaced by a more appropriate candidate. In 1688[138] the Bill of Rights[139] set aside the exercise of royal power within a legal framework and asserted the rights of Parliament.[140]

In Scotland, a Convention of the Scottish Estates sat and voted that James had forfeited the Crown by acting contrary to Scottish constitutional law. They set out the basis for this with stark clarity in the Claim of Right Act 1689, namely:

> Wheras King James VII being a profest papist did assume regall power and acted as King without ever takeing the oath required by law wherby the King at his access to government is obliged to swear to maintain the Protestant religion and to rule the people according to the laudable laws And Did By the advice of evill and wicked Counsellers Invade the fundamentall Constitution of this Kingdome and altered it from a legall limted monarchy to Ane arbitrary despotick power.[141]

In accordance with this understanding, royal power is limited by the law and the Constitution. The monarch does have a spiritual role, but it is to use the power vested in him or her by the Constitution to uphold the Protestant faith. Of course, not everybody agreed, and those loyal to the Stuart line, and frequently also the Divine Right of Kings (known as Jacobites from the Latin 'Jacobus' for James), were both a perceived and actual threat to the Government for the first half of the succeeding century.

The other less immediate, but equally direct, consequence of the 1688 settlement was the Parliamentary Union of 1707.[142] Queen Anne succeeded her sister, and her Government decided that uniting the two Parliaments was essential if the

137 R.P. Barnes, 'Scotland and the Glorious Revolution of 1688', *Albion: A Quarterly Journal Concerned with British Studies*, Vol. 3, No. 3 (1971) 116–27, 117.

138 For an explanation of the conventions of dating statutes from this period, see that given by the UK Government at http://www.legislation.gov.uk/aep/WillandMarSess2/1/2/introduction.

139 Bill of Rights 1688, c. 2, 1 Will and Mar Sess 2.

140 E.g., see ibid, 'Dispensing Power: That the pretended Power of Suspending of Laws or the Execution of Laws by Regall Authority without Consent of Parlyament is illegall. Late dispensing Power: That the pretended Power of Dispensing with Laws or the Execution of Laws by Regall Authoritie as it hath beene assumed and exercised of late is illegall'.

141 Claim of Right Act 1689, Preamble.

142 Act of Union 1707.

arrangements of 1688 were to achieve enduring stability.[143] Previous attempts at parliamentary union (aside from the brief Commonwealth experience) had foundered because neither side was especially keen. The Scots feared losing their autonomy, particularly in religious matters, and the English did not like the idea of the Scottish involvement in the free trade with the American colonies.

However, Anne's lack of an heir and Edinburgh's failure to follow Westminster in settling the succession on Hanover made England twitchy, particularly with the French King Louis XIV egging on the Jacobites;[144] consequently, they placed considerable economic pressure on Scotland to consent. Initially the Scottish Kirk was bitterly opposed to the proposals, which was unsurprising given the struggles of the previous century, but legislation guaranteeing the historic freedoms of the Church and a Presbyterian system of government won enough of the churchmen round to make moving forward possible. The preservation of Scots law was also a fundamental aspect of the deal. These two factors together helped to shift opinion in enough crucial quarters. Even so, Devine argues that the union was in reality a marriage of convenience between the governing classes in Edinburgh and London, and that many ordinary Scots were left feeling resentful and betrayed.[145]

However, as Harris suggests, it would be unjust to attribute the union to nothing more than self-seeking elite Scots who recognised an opportunity for personal gain.[146] His case is that in reality many of those considering the proposals from a Scottish perspective could consent, if not exactly cheerfully, then at least with a clear conscience, on the basis that it genuinely appeared to be in the national interest, particularly in economic terms.

An additional consideration is that there were ideological as well as financial incentives. Harris quotes with approval[147] the persuasive case made by Stephen[148] that many pro-unionist Scots saw in parliamentary unity a safeguard against the return of the Stuart dynasty, Roman Catholicism and French influences. Given that the horrors of the Killing Time were still very fresh, it is easy to imagine that this may well have been a strong incentive to draw closer to the Protestant powers south of the border.

On the other side of the coin, of course, there were those who devoutly believed that rejecting an anointed monarch was a crime against God, and a transgression which would bring down divine retribution if not rectified. There were also others who, after the death of Anne and the accession of George I, preferred

143 T.M. Devine, *The Scottish Nation 1700–2000* (Penguin: London) 1999, 3.

144 Ibid., 6–7.

145 Ibid., 17.

146 B. Harris, 'The Anglo-Scottish Treaty of Union, 1707 in 2007: Defending the Revolution, Defeating the Jacobites', *The Journal of British Studies*, Vol. 49, Special Issue 01 (2010) 28–46, 35.

147 Ibid., 46.

148 J. Stephen, *Presbyterians and the Act of Union 1707* (Edinburgh University Press: Edinburgh) 2007, 31.

the idea of a Scottish Stuart to a German Hanover. The relationship between religion and national, regional, familial and personal identity in this period was extremely complex and, as McLynn demonstrates, the motivating factors driving Jacobitism were by no means straightforward.[149]

Having said that, one key consideration united all sides at the start of the eighteenth century: religion was a political matter which concerned the state and was not something to be relegated to the private sphere. As the century progressed, the union became increasingly firmly established and, despite various armed uprisings, Jacobitism ceased to be a viable military or political force after the defeat of Culloden in April 1746.[150] Furthermore, Scotland began to see some economic benefits, as free trade and the expanding Empire started to provide a host of career and money-making opportunities for ambitious Scots.[151] Indeed, so many Scots benefited from the opportunities offered by England and its colonies that there was a rise in 'Scottophobia' in the mid-eighteenth century.[152] The anxiety about those from less wealthy regions arriving *en masse* to snaffle jobs and resources from the domestic population has parallels with some of the contemporary debate about relations with the European Union. Samuel Johnson famously opined that '[t]he noblest prospect which a Scotchman ever sees, is the high road that leads him to England!'[153]

However, as might be expected, this fear and anxiety about Scotland was more nuanced than it might first appear. It relates closely to religion in public life because anti-Scottish feeling in England was targeted and received differently in relation to differing cultural and faith identities. Of all Scottish groups, the Highlanders undoubtedly came in for the most brutal and dehumanising portrayal in popular culture.

The monstrous figure of Sawney Bean provides an interesting example. He was a huge hit in the chapbooks of the eighteenth century, although many academics now believe him to have been entirely the invention of English propaganda.[154] Even if the tale did not originate in England, it certainly fuelled the fires of prejudice. The stories about Sawney Bean were presented as true, the eponymous anti-hero being the head of a clan of cannibals who enthusiastically practised incest and lived in a Scottish cave. The Highlanders were effectively presented as the 'other': savage, menacing and a threat which needed to be neutralised, and these were lapped up by the English population.

Although not all clans within the Highlands were Roman Catholic, anti-Catholic and anti-Irish feeling served only to pour paraffin on the flames. Gaelic

149 F. McLynn, 'Issues and Motives in the Jacobite Rising 1745', *The Eighteenth Century*, Vol 23 (2) 1982, 97.

150 Devine, n. 142 above, 24 5.

151 Ibid.

152 Ibid., 27.

153 J. Boswell, *The Life of Johnson* (Westminster, A, Constable & Co: Philadelphia) 1901, 493.

154 'Sawney Bean the Cannibal: All the Product of English Propaganda', *The Scotsman* (30 Jan 2008), http://www.scotsman.com/news/sawney-bean-the-cannibal-all-a-product-of-english-propaganda-1-1076320.

culture was presented as barbaric and something to be eradicated, and this was an idea which had appeal in Lowland Scotland as well as in England. Sir John Clark, the contemporary Scottish historian, even claimed that the early Scots in fact spoke Saxon![155] Roman Catholicism in general was associated with disloyalty to the state, and it was regarded as incompatible with the developing concept of 'Britishness'.

Whilst Highlanders were given a starring role in that smear campaign, it was ordinary and vulnerable men, women and children who were left feeling the effects of burning, pillage and the start of the High Clearances.

It is true that, as modern commentators like Mackillop[156] correctly point out, Highlands politics did not disappear after Culloden, and that elites in the region continued to engage with state power emanating from Westminster. Furthermore, many of the changes which took place in the Highlands over the eighteenth and nineteenth centuries flowed from the political and economic interests of the land-owning lairds, and it is not a simple narrative of external oppression by either the English or the Lowland Scots. However, this cannot have been of any great comfort to the powerless and vulnerable in their hunger and misery when they lost homes, loved ones and a way of life. Religion and nationality were just two of the dynamics in a cultural and political struggle which, quite simply, saw many individuals and families in the wrong place at the wrong time.

Furthermore, Lowland Scots may have been less susceptible to dehumanising tendencies in cheap literature, but at times the middle classes preferred a degree of assimilation to retaining their identity. Even the philosopher David Hume was not too sophisticated to fret about his accent,[157] and he was by no means alone in this insecurity. Many aspects of identity, including those of a religious nature, came in for reassessment. Notably, Scottish intellectuals on both sides of the border became increasingly embarrassed by the behaviour of the Covenanters, dismissing them as religious fanatics. Nevertheless, for many at all levels of society, these figures remained heroes, and the ancient fissures along religious lines did not disappear overnight.

It is indisputable that the place and perception of religion in Scottish public life altered radically in these two centuries, but a straightforward narrative of decline and marginalisation would give a very misleading picture. As the Scottish people redefined their identity within a united British context, they were also grappling with the forces of the Enlightenment and Industrialisation, both of which had a profound impact on religious practice.

At the start of the eighteenth century,[158] Church courts were still policing the morality of the population, at least in the Lowlands, hearing cases on fornication, adultery, drunkenness and profaning the Sabbath, as well as on occasions more

155 Devine, n. 142 above, 29.

156 A. Mackillop, 'The Political Culture of the Scottish Highlands from Culloden to Waterloo', *The Historical Journal*, Vol. 46, No. 3 (2003) 511–32.

157 Devine, n. 142 above, 29.

158 Ibid., Ch. 5.

'secular' crimes such as assault (particularly in a domestic context) and theft. Although the state ceased to assist the Kirk in enforcing sanctions in the first half of the eighteenth century, it was another hundred years before the framework of Kirk discipline completely crumbled.

This community-level supervision of spiritual correctness was a different aspect from the imposition of national religious orthodoxy, and distinct from struggles over whether church governance should lie in the hands of the monarch or the General Assembly, but it was one which probably touched more directly upon the lives of individuals, at least in times of peace.

In addition, the Kirk had a key role in the provision of education. Although by no means perfect, the availability of elementary education to the population was more comprehensive and egalitarian than it was in England, and the Kirk was a major player in this.

However, both of these phenomena were rocked by the intellectual, social and technological upheavals of this period. Brown,[159] in his landmark book on religion in Scotland, argues that the process of industrialisation and the social conflicts which this bred were responsible for the national Church losing its grip on the life of the nation. In his thesis, as patterns of occupation and employment changed, social classes became increasingly segregated in terms of residential area. Groups could foster a sense of self-worth and identity by taking on a unique and cohesive religious identity. This, for Brown, explains why some Presbyterian sects dramatically broke away from the national Church and also in part why Roman Catholicism in Scotland enjoyed a resurgence in the nineteenth century. The national Church was grievously wounded by divisions in the course of this era, but at that stage Christian participation itself was not so beleaguered. It is an interesting thesis, and academic debate on the reality and causes of the secularisation phenomenon is something to which we shall refer in the next chapter. In terms of the shaping of the Scottish nation as far as religion is concerned, the salient point is that the dominant position of the national Kirk was now no longer unassailed and, crucially, by the Victorian era this was not the source of anxiety it would once have been. Violent unrest was far more likely to bubble to the surface over political injustices, such as campaigns for suffrage and economic discontent, than over religious divisions.

It is also key to note that perceptions about the sources and functions of executive power in relation to religion had shifted. Enlightenment ideas, and the nineteenth-century political philosophy which built upon them, increasingly came to see freedom of religion and conscience as a right, rather than a threat. It was not the role of the government to impose religious conformity, either by divine mandate or because it was deemed necessary to protect the common peace.

However, this shift does not equate to an accepted assumption that religion had no place in the collective life of the Scottish nation. As Devine[160] acknowledges,

159 C.G. Brown, *The Social History of Religion in Scotland since 1730* (Methuen: New York) 1987.
160 Devine, n. 142 above, 364.

even a superficial examination of Victorian Scotland reveals that religious observance remained a significant social force; and not because it was imposed by force of law, as much of the rigid Sabbath observance, including the closing of shops and businesses, was not required by secular legislation. It happened because of a social consensus. Without this ever having been articulated in a conscious way, religion went from being *required* by the legal framework to being *supported* by it. The constitutional structure which had once imposed Christianity now gave it a legal basis to remain at the heart of national life.

Furthermore, as Cheyne[161] argues, the Kirk was not immune to the spirit of progress and reform which permeated Victorian society, and experienced changes in its collective attitudes towards the Bible, worship and social issues. It would be inaccurate to present it as an institution trapped in ossified and unyielding modes of Puritan thought from a bygone era. It did not remain untouched by the debates which individuals like Darwin unleashed on society, nor the new social problems raised by an increasingly urban and industrialised world.

Nevertheless, according to Brown's[162] thesis, the twentieth century saw an irreversible erosion of the place of Christianity within the life of the Scottish nation, primarily because the factors which had driven participation in the previous hundred years gradually lost relevance. As the welfare state developed and social inclusion increased, individuals had less to gain materially and socially from active membership of churches.

Yet, balanced against this, is the more general analysis of Britain in the interwar years, given by David Hempton,[163] and aptly applied to the Scottish context by Devine:[164]

> [E]ven non-churchgoers sent their children to Sunday School, dressed up on Sundays, used religious affiliations to obtain jobs and welfare relief, sang hymns as a means of cementing common solidarity, respected 'practical Christian virtues', relied heavily on Christian sexual ethics (at least as a point of departure), derived comfort from religion at times of suffering or disaster, accepted that church or chapel or Catholic or Protestant were fundamental social divisions and used the church's social facilities without any need for more overtly 'religious' activities.

Religion had less direct relevance to periodic debates about devolution and independence for Scotland. Ironically, on one occasion they were more relevant for discussion about the establishment of the Church of England, when Non-Conformist Scottish MPs famously voted down changes to the Book of

161 A. Cheyne, *The Transforming of the Kirk: Victorian Scotland's Religious Revolution* (St Andrews Press: Edinburgh) 1983.

162 Brown, n. 158 above.

163 D. Hempton, *Religion and Political Culture in Britain and Ireland* (Cambridge University Press: Cambridge) 1996.

164 Devine, n. 142 above, 387.

Common Prayer, which were approved by the majority of English members whose constituents would actually be affected by it.[165]

The contemporary place of the Church of Scotland will be set out more fully in the next chapter, but it is worth noting at this point that the continued decline in active attendance from the 1950s onwards does not automatically equate to a lack of social relevance. A flaw in Brown's thesis is the emphasis placed on religious observance as the litmus test for importance. In his view, religion in Scotland has now 'been relegated to the margins of social significance'.[166]

This is not an inevitable conclusion from a drastic reduction in active participation on a regular basis. The nature of its social significance may have changed, but this should not unquestioningly be characterised as a marginalisation. Robbins[167] makes the intriguing argument that there are 'Presbyterian atheists' who are attached to the idea of the Church of Scotland remaining part of the landscape, because its disappearance would remove a still major aspect of Scottish identity. Both secularists and religious believers might find reasons to dispute this analysis, but Robbins' case does at least remind us that a lack of inclination to attend worship (and even to comply with religious norms of behaviour in relation to sexual or economic ethics) does not equate to repudiation of the Church as an institution. The dynamics of individual and community interaction with organised religious structures are nuanced and complex.

1.5 Great Britain in the twenty-first century: whale knees or penguin wings?

All of the foregoing poses two crucial questions: (i) what are we left with in terms of religion and legal framework; and (ii) are the existing arrangements an anachronism in need of reform, or have they been adapted to perform still useful, if different, functions? In all three national settings, the social and political place of the Church – and religion in general – has radically altered, but how should its *legal* place be described?

According to the classical ecclesiastical law analysis of Church/state relations, there are three models which may be employed to assess these arrangements: national Church, separatist, and hybrid/cooperationist.[168] Although these models are open to criticism[169] and, like any analytical tool, are subject to limitations, they provide a useful starting point.

165 C. Garbett (Archbishop of York), *The Claims of the Church of England* (Hodder & Stoughton: London) 1947.

166 Brown, n. 158 above, 256.

167 Robbins, n. 70 above, 373.

168 J. García Oliva, 'The Denominational Teaching of Religion in Spanish State Schools', in M. Hunter-Henin (ed.), *Law, Religious Freedoms and Education in Europe* (Ashgate: Surrey) 2011, 183–206, 185.

169 N. Doe & R. Sandberg, 'Church-State Relations in Europe', *Religion Compass*, Vol. 1, No. 5 (2007) 561–78.

Scotland and England have national Church models, whereas the Welsh nation is arguably cooperationist. However, given that some key features of establishment were retained by the Welsh Church Act (for example, the Church in Wales is still established for the purposes of marriage law) it might be more accurate to describe it as quasi-established[170] rather than disestablished. Therefore, Great Britain as a whole retains a religious dimension to its constitutional arrangements, both at state and national level in each context.

Furthermore, as we shall explore in the next chapter, this religious character has diffused out beyond the constitutional level, colouring the juridical system as a whole. The legal framework in general adopts a positive, rather than a neutral attitude towards religious practice. In a variety of ways, religion as a phenomenon is actively promoted and facilitated.

Are the current patterns of Church/state relations, and the deeper systemic treatment of religion as a phenomenon, justified on the basis of anything other than an historical accident?

170 N. Doe, *The Law of the Church in Wales* (Cardiff University Press: Cardiff) 2002, 11.

2 Religion in the current paradigm

The flight of the penguin?

2.1. Introduction

The final sections of the preceding chapter traced the gradual decline in participation in organised religion in the course of the nineteenth and twentieth centuries. Inevitably, this decline has had a profound impact upon all three of the national Churches in Great Britain.

One possible interpretation of this downward trend might be that establishment is going the way of whale legs, and that national Churches are fast becoming small and embarrassing appendages, dragged along by the body politic. If this analysis is accepted, then the only remaining question is whether these unused limbs are essentially harmless and can be allowed to gradually evolve away with the passage of time, or whether they are an encumbrance which should be removed with a legislative scalpel.

However, there are alternative ways of viewing the current picture, and these generate very different questions. A contrasting interpretation would be that instead of having receded, the role of national Churches (and alongside them, other faith groups) within British society has in fact *transformed*, and that *the whole legal framework has shifted* (and continues to shift) to reflect and enable this. Rather than doing what they have always done, only with less support and less significance, these bodies are in fact doing something different. This reconfigured role does not require any creedal consensus, and has the capacity to benefit *all* citizens regardless of their religious outlook or lack of it. Instead of being whale knees, the national Churches are in fact penguin wings, and have found a new and vital function within the organism.

Our thesis is that establishment in its contemporary form, signifying the unique legal and social position of the three national Churches,[1] cannot be adequately understood in isolation. It has to be seen in terms of its place within a suite of characteristics which make both the current Constitution and the remaining legal system religious, rather than separatist, in nature.

While these other characteristics have grown out of the historical context of establishment, they now have a life and identity of their own. In fact, these

1 In relation to the Church in Wales, please see the discussion below for an explanation of our decision to categorise it as having 'quasi-established' status, and to describe it as a 'national Church'.

secondary religious characteristics have attained greater significance in the contemporary setting than establishment itself, and they would persist even if the formal legal ties between the state and its national denominations were severed. For example, the law actively facilitates religious practice in a variety of ways: faith-based activities enjoy exemptions from the general criminal law on assault[2] and equality legislation.[3]

This chapter explores the suite of characteristics which define the modern Constitution *and* the wider legal framework as religious. We set out our conception of the juridical system in relation to religion, presenting a new analytical model – 'the Russian Doll' paradigm – and we discuss how this operates in practice within the three nations under consideration, with particular emphasis on the positive treatment by the legal system as a whole of 'religion' as a phenomenon. We also consider the limitations of this positivity, and how faith-based rights and interests are balanced against other societal needs and objectives, as well as setting out some of the most prominent criticisms of the current framework.

2.2 A suite of religious characteristics: the Russian doll model

The religious nature of the legal framework in the twenty-first century is not manifested solely, or even primarily, in terms of the establishment link between national denominations and the state. It is reflected in a suite of three, related but separate, characteristics which are all a product of the way in which the juridical and political system has developed since the seventeenth century. The structure can be linked to a nesting *Matryoshka*, or Russian doll.

The biggest doll, containing all of the others, is the overarching positive stance which the state still takes towards religion as a phenomenon. The legal system has moved, gradually and incrementally, from supporting the practice of established religion, to supporting Christianity more widely, to finally supporting religion in general. This has not been the consequence of any orchestrated policy, but is the result of shifting perceptions of the judiciary, the Government and Parliament.

As we shall explore, there are now a significant number of instances where different areas of the legal framework (for instance, family law, education law, criminal law, property law, employment law, equality law, contract and tort) operate to facilitate the practice of religion. Effectively, there is a soft-presumption in favour of permitting and endorsing religious practices where possible. It is soft in the sense however, that it is easily rebutted, if there are other factors weighing against it. These positively enabling features often either have origins pre-dating modern human rights legislation, or go beyond what would be required in order to comply with the obligations placed upon the state under Article 9 of the European Convention on Human Rights (ECHR).

They reflect a legal system which initially regarded support for the established Churches to be axiomatic, and privileged the practice of official religion.

2 *R v Brown* [1994] 1 AC 212.
3 E.g., Equality Act 2010.

Over time the disadvantage to which this subjected citizens of other faiths came to be seen as increasingly unacceptable. Rivers is correct in noting that a recognition of individual religious liberty is a 'remarkable social achievement'.[4] Achievements of this kind are gradual, and progress was incremental. Furthermore, the response to inequality was frequently not to deprive Anglicans of the benefits which they enjoyed, but to extend these to other faith groups – for example, the capacity to carry out legally binding marriages.

As we consider the examples of this, it should always be borne in mind that they are, for the most part, discreet. There was never a moment when a root-and-branch overhaul of establishment privilege took place. Rather, it was a question of a court having to decide whether to allow a particular religious organisation or cause charitable status, or a given Parliament legislating on anomalies in marriage law. Consequently, the developments were in many cases haphazard, and the generally positive stance towards religion which has emerged was never fully debated or consciously engineered.

This raises the legitimate question of whether the current position is defensible, or even desirable. We shall argue in the course of this book that it is both. The general umbrella of support for religion need not, in and of itself, be seen as harming those who do not have a faith or inclination to practice.

Religion is not the *only* phenomenon to be treated positively or in a unique manner by the legal framework. It would be rather absurd to assert that the state should *only* support practices which directly involve all citizens. For instance, individuals who decide to become parents are supported in this choice in a variety of ways by the law. There are legal provisions about maternity and parental leave, a variety of fiscal concessions and state benefits when required, free primary and secondary education, etc. While there may be voices arguing that the childless population bears an unjust burden as a result,[5] and there is clearly scope for debate about the structure of the current arrangements, there is also widespread acceptance of the underlying principle that the choice to become a parent and raise children is one which the state should facilitate.

Therefore, enabling an individual choice in one area of life is not intrinsically problematic. In tangible terms, the ability to set up a religious charity granted to persons of faith does not interfere with the freedom of an Atheist to set up an animal welfare charity or a football charity, for example. Neither does the ability of parents to consent to ritual male circumcision disadvantage other parents who would not choose this for themselves or their sons.[6]

In the course of our analysis we shall explore the most relevant examples of the legal system supporting faith groups and, crucially, the organised practice

4 J. Rivers, *The Law of Organised Religions: Between Establishment and Secularism* (Oxford: Oxford University Press) 2010, x.

5 P. Dunbar, 'Why Should Childless Women Like Us Do Longer Hours to Cover for Working Mothers?', *The Daily Mail* (28 Jul 2013), http://www.dailymail.co.uk/femail/article-2380473/Why-SHOULD-childless-women-like-longer-hours-cover-working-mothers.html.

6 We should stress that there is a debate as to whether the positive aspects of accommodating this practice justify an exception to the general approach towards protecting the corporeal integrity of minors. We shall discuss this issue in detail below.

of non-faith-based religious beliefs (such as Humanist societies, as will be explained). We argue that, taken in the round, the current system is not detrimental either to citizens who consciously have no faith, or to those who are indifferent to religious matters (however, in assessing the possible criticisms of the existing arrangements, we acknowledge that there are some areas which may be in need of reform). Then, looking ahead to Chapter 3, we shall at that stage suggest that there are a number of ways in which the religious character of the legal framework is also *indirectly* beneficial to citizens in respect of their non-religious beliefs. Having made this detour to address beliefs which do not concern religious matters, we shall then return to the primary focus of our study in Chapters 4 to 7, addressing how the religious character of the Constitution relates to its foundational pillars.

Opening this outer doll, there is a second inside, which represents a supportive stance towards the Christian religion in general. There is the recognition within the legal framework that the cultural heritage of Britain is in the Christian tradition and that the majority of citizens still self-identify in this way. As a result, there are some aspects of the law (for example, relating to the dates of many public holidays) that reflect this.

Again, this second doll in the set need not be automatically labelled as problematic, provided always that those who are not Christian are not disadvantaged by the recognition given to the Christian context. Undoubtedly, there is legitimate scope for debate in some areas, such as whether the right to opt out of predominantly Christian collective worship in state schools is enough to spare non-Christian school pupils from stigma. However, overall, this aspect of the legal framework does not seem to be an obstacle to inclusion and social cohesion by its very nature.

Then, opening up this second doll, the littlest figure inside is the establishment doll. She does need to be peered at carefully. But again, when considered as a whole, the way in which establishment operates at the current time does not seem to be oppressive either to Anglicans, Presbyterians or other citizens. The controls which the Crown and other branches of the state exercise over the national Churches are now very loose, and many of the special roles of the Churches need not affect citizens who do not wish to participate. For instance, if a couple do not wish to avail themselves of the right to marry in a parish church in England or Wales, there are religious and secular alternatives open to them.[7] In the following section we shall explore the ways in which these three legal and constitutional layers operate in each of the national contexts being considered.

2.3 England[8]

2.3.1 England – the social context

In his Easter message of 2015, the then Prime Minister David Cameron described Britain as a 'Christian country'. It is interesting that he saw fit to do this in the lead

7 It must be highlighted that there are some interest groups, such as the British Humanist Association, campaigning for an expansion of the secular options to encompass Humanist ceremonies.

8 See J. García Oliva, 'The Favourable Legal View of Religion in England in the XXI Century', *Derecho y Religión*, Vol. X (2015) 163–82.

up to what was at that time expected to be a closely fought general election, with the balance of power teetering on a knife-edge.[9] Furthermore, he asserted that this statement went beyond an acknowledgement of the nation's historical and cultural heritage, and reflected the tangible impact which this faith continues to have:

> Across Britain, Christians don't just talk about 'loving thy neighbour', they live it out ... in faith schools, in prisons, in community groups.
>
> And it's for all these reasons that we should feel proud to say, 'This is a Christian country'. The Church is not just a collection of beautiful old buildings. It is a living, active force doing great works across our country.[10]

This statement was controversial and responses were predictably mixed, ranging from the warm to the sharply critical.[11] However, the Prime Minister's address undeniably generated a lively debate, and it is interesting to ask how his claim relates to the available objective evidence about the religious make-up of Britain. It must, however, be acknowledged that everything turns on what the label 'Christian country' is in fact intended to mean, and crunching numbers cannot hope to resolve such a question.

The 2011 census data revealed that Christianity remains the biggest religious or ideological group in England and Wales:[12] in total 59% of the population opted to self-identify within this category,[13] and the second most favoured option was 'no religion', accounting for 25% of the respondents. Of the religious choices, Islam came second to Christianity, being the stated religious identity of 4.8% of those who answered. The other listed faith groups were represented as follows: Hindu 1.5 %, Sikh 0.8%, Jewish 0.5% and Buddhist 0.4%.

Of course, great caution needs to be exercised in interpreting statistics and what they might actually mean. Any attempt at sophisticated sociological analysis

9 See, e.g., reports of a YouGov pole from April 2015, predicting a hung parliament: M. Wilkinson, 'Election 2015 Latest Poles and Odds: Labour Take Two-Point Lead but Punters Prefer Tories', *The Telegraph* (8 Apr 2015), http://www.telegraph.co.uk/news/general-election-2015/11519632/Election-2015-latest-polls-and-odds-Labour-take-two-point-lead-but-punters-prefer-Tories.html.

10 R. Prince, 'David Cameron Declares Britain is Still a Christian Country', *The Telegraph* (5 Apr 2015), http://www.telegraph.co.uk/news/general-election-2015/11516804/David-Cameron-declares-Britain-is-still-a-Christian-country.html.

11 See, e.g., P. Vale, 'David Cameron Uses Easter Message to Praise Britain as a "Christian Country"', *Huffington Post UK* (5 Apr 2015), http://www.huffingtonpost.co.uk/2015/04/05/cameron-uses-easter-message-to-praise-church-as-living-active-force-doing-great-works_n_7007134.html; and National Secular Society, 'As Cameron Says UK Still a Christian Country, 62% tell YouGov They are not Religious' (8 Apr 2015), http://www.secularism.org.uk/news/2015/04/as-cameron-says-uk-still-a-christian-country-62-percent-tell-yougov-they-are-not-religious

12 The census data relates to both England and Wales. However, as discussed earlier, since the Welsh Church Act 1914 came into force in 1920, the Church of England has not had jurisdiction within Wales. The Welsh Church was partially disestablished and the Anglican province in that nation is completely autonomous and self- governing.

13 Office for National Statistics, 'Religion in England and Wales 2011', Key Points (11 Dec 2012), 1–2, http://www.ons.gov.uk/ons/dcp171776_290510.pdf.

is beyond the scope of this book. Nevertheless, it may be useful to note a few points about the published numbers. First, the faith question was voluntary and 7.2% of people declined to give any answer.[14] This means that considerably more citizens failed to respond at all than identified as members of *any* of the minority faiths. It is clear, therefore, that there are a considerable number of pieces missing from this jigsaw.

Second, the census form is inevitably quite a blunt instrument. It cannot express the possibility of an individual having multiple religious identities, not simply in the course of their lifetime, but at the *same* point in time. As well as the people who convert from one religious tradition into another, there are those who embrace more than one religious identity at the same time.

There is convincing academic evidence to suggest that this is a reality for many people in Western societies.[15] An individual might have one identity in one context and for one set of purposes, and another in a different sphere (even if this may be repugnant to the official doctrines of one of their religious identities). People might conceivably see themselves as Muslims *and* Agnostics, or Christians *and* Pagans.[16] Third parties may regard this as defying logic, but neither religious belief nor human self-perception are necessarily rooted in logic.

In addition, the available categories on the form each cover a range of possible beliefs and levels of practice. The British Humanist Association (BHA) is, perhaps understandably, keen to point out that despite the statistics in the census, in a 2014 survey only 13.1% of the population reported that they attended a religious service once a week[17] and, as a result, the BHA asserts that the religious character of the nation portrayed by the census data is misleading.

Furthermore, even the statistics produced by the Church of England itself are striking when read alongside the census data: its figures for 2013 claim that only 785,000 people attended church on a usual Sunday.[18] Of course, the 59% of the population who identified as Christian included members of all Christian denominations, so it would be unreasonable to expect the entirety of them to be worshipping in Anglican services. Nevertheless, given that there are

14 Office for National Statistics, ibid.

15 L. Beaman, *Religion and Canadian Society: Context Identities and Strategies* (Canadian Scholars Press: Toronto) 2005, 5.

16 This could be possible in the sense of having personally concluded that the two identities are compatible – see, e.g., Christian or Trinitarian Wicca, 'Christian Wicca: The Kingdom is Within You and All Around You', http://christianwicca.org – or, conversely, in adopting different identities and practices in different contexts. Opting to go to church while visiting family; having a church wedding and children baptised, etc, while at the same time celebrating Pagan festivals and reading Pagan literature; this might come about through a mixed marriage or relationship, or simply through personal choice.

17 British Humanist Association, 'Campaigns, Religion and Belief: Some Surveys and Statistics', https://humanism.org.uk/campaigns/religion-and-belief-some-surveys-and-statistics.

18 The Church of England Research and Statics Department, Archbishops' Council, 'Statistics of Mission 2013', 6, https://www.churchofengland.org/media/2112070/2013statisticsfor mission.pdf.

approximately 52.6 million people living in England,[19] 785,000 is a very small number for attendees of the established Church.

However, this does not mean that the census data can or should be lightly dismissed as lacking significance, despite the suggestions of the BHA. As their secular critics have pointed out, there are compelling reasons why non-practising and even non-believing citizens might elect to have a religious identity, and this personal choice should be taken seriously.[20] Officially recorded and recordable evidence of religious practice in no way invalidates the way in which people choose to define themselves in spiritual or ideological terms. In choosing to mark the Christian box, every individual who did so was electing to own that label in preference to all of the others on offer, and also rejecting the possibility of opting out of making any decision. It is, therefore, inaccurate to suggest that their choice in many cases had no meaning. In fact, having been immersed in the cultural and ethical values of a religion, a person continues to feel that influence, whether he or she regards this as positive or negative, and ingrained habits or patterns of thought may remain, even though conscious belief might have ebbed away years beforehand. Many citizens understandably claim to remain Jewish or Sikh in terms of their morals or culture, even if they no longer hold the core beliefs of the faith.

Furthermore, not only does dismissing the statistics from the census data on the basis of church attendance raise logical problems, it is also doubtful from an ethical standpoint. Is it really appropriate for third parties to demand reasonableness and logic from individuals in this context, and dismiss their choices if they do not meet an externally imposed standard? The way in which a person chooses to self-identify should not be a matter for debate, and requiring a certain level of observance before an individual's asserted faith identity can be accepted is hard to justify in terms of respecting individual autonomy and dignity. How observant is observant enough to count, and who could possibly judge? How could this kind of approach relate to religions or belief systems which do not demand outward, structured acts of observance? Should Anglicans be subjected to tests not applied to Hedge Witches before their religious self-understanding can be taken seriously?

Plus, of course, in terms of the census data, what is sauce for the goose is sauce for the gander: it might well be the case that some people opting to identify as 'no religion' offer private prayers to a deity or even join in public worship. Interestingly, this point was not highlighted by the BHA. Statistics and their attendant flaws are a double-edged sword. Therefore, we would emphasise that the census data should be handled appropriately, and not used as the foundation for conclusions which it cannot support. However, the following general propositions may legitimately be drawn out.

19 Office for National Statistics, 'Population Estimates for UK, England and Wales, Scotland and Northern Ireland, mid 2001–mid 2010 Revised' (17 Dec 2013), http://www.ons.gov.uk/ons/rel/pop-estimate/population-estimates-for-uk--england-and-wales--scotland-and-northern-ireland/mid-2001-to-mid-2010-revised/index.html.

20 Bagehot, 'There is a Difference between Lacking Faith and Having No Religion', *The Economist* (10 Mar 2011), http://www.economist.com/blogs/bagehot/2011/03/british_2011_census

First, it is apparent that England and Wales are now diverse societies in relation to religion.

Second, it is evident that Christianity continues to be the majority religious identity. Even though there has been a sharp decline since 2001 (when 71.7% ticked the Christian box on the form[21]), it remains significant that almost six out of ten people still chose to define themselves in this way. How this relates to practice and/or active participation is a moot and complex point, but self-identification is in itself significant.

However, this is not to assert that numerical dominance in terms of self-identification justifies an establishment relationship, nor that its absence would necessitate dismantling the arrangement were the picture to move in that direction. It is merely to note the current social context in so far as it is available.

2.3.2 England – the legal context

In this section, we shall explore some of the discrete instances in which the legal framework treats religion as a positive phenomenon, in so far as it actively enables or facilitates its practice. Some of the areas – for instance, the law relating to education and marriage – also provide examples of the Christian religion in particular continuing to receive special treatment. For ease of analysis, we have therefore considered both of the two inner layers of the suite of religious characteristics together.

It should also be noted that another important manifestation of this second religious characteristic, not dealt with in detail below, is the relevance of Christian festivals to the public calendar in Britain. Bank Holidays, as well as the academic and parliamentary timetable, are all related to the Christian year and, consequently, practising Christians do not have to arrange time off work or full-time study in order to celebrate these Holy Days. We have not focused on this in depth, as it is straying beyond the realms of law and into social policy. Nevertheless, we would observe in passing that it would be somewhat impractical for the religious festivals of every faith to be given the status of public holidays. Furthermore, the two most religiously significant occasions for Christians, Easter and Christmas, are times when many people who would not identify as Christian enjoy cultural traditions and family celebrations. Also, previous parliamentary attempts to ban Christmas and other festivals have proved somewhat unpopular.[22]

2.3.2.1 General provisions within the legal framework (the Outer Doll)

2.3.2.1.1 EQUALITY AND DISCRIMINATION LAW

Religion and belief constitute one of the protected characteristics in current equality legislation,[23] so citizens may not be subjected to discrimination on the

21 Office for National Statistics, 'Religion in England and Wales 2011', n. 13 above.

22 C. Durston, 'The Puritan War on Christmas', *History Today*, Vol. 35 (12 Dec 1985).

23 Equality Act 2010, s. 4.

grounds of their faith or lack of it. In this respect, religious citizens are in the same position as those with strong non-religious beliefs, who also enjoy legal protection.[24] However, as well as providing this layer of protection, discrimination law also furnishes religious believers with a number of exceptions and dispensations from the general framework. In certain defined circumstances, what would otherwise amount to unlawful discrimination is permitted because of the faith context surrounding it.

One of the most significant arenas in which this operates is that of employment law. The Equality Act 2010[25] expressly permits discrimination on grounds such as sex, marriage and sexual orientation, if this is done in order to avoid conflicts with religious doctrine in the context of organised religion. Therefore, faith groups are free to demand that persons occupying certain roles must be male and celibate or female and married, if these criteria are in accordance with doctrine. They are also permitted to discriminate on the grounds of religion or belief where this relates to a genuine occupational requirement.[26]

In addition, as will be discussed further below in the context of education, discrimination on grounds of faith is permitted in connection with schools with a religious character, in ways which concern both staff employment and pupil selection.[27] As far as staff are concerned, religious employers in this context enjoy even greater freedom than that accorded by the general exceptions in the Equality Act.[28] Although different provisions apply to different types of school, a common theme is the lack of any requirement for the religious criteria being imposed to be proportionate, and Vickers argues that this is incompatible with the requirements of the EU Employment Equality Directive.[29] In other words, schools are free to discriminate in this regard if they wish to do so, and need not demonstrate that alternative, less discriminatory measures could not have achieved their stated and legitimate objectives. This latitude reduces the potential for monitoring and accountability in the system, and increases the possible negative impact on the careers and freedom of individual teachers.

Clearly, these points cannot be disentangled from the wider political debate about schools with a religious ethos, popularly known as faith schools. We shall use both terms interchangeably for the purposes of our analysis. The counter argument to Vickers' point would be that the religious requirements are necessary in terms of maintaining the religious ethos of the school, and that it would be problematic to uphold this if the genuine occupational requirement test were applied to every appointment. For instance, an individual teaching Maths or

24 We shall return to this theme in detail in the course of Chapter 3.

25 Equality Act 2010, Sch. 9.

26 Ibid.

27 UK Government, Schools Admissions, 'Admission Criteria', https://www.gov.uk/schools-admissions/admissions-criteria.

28 School Standards and Frameworks Act 1998, ss 58 and 60.

29 L. Vickers, 'Religious Discrimination Against Teachers in Faith Schools', *Public Spirit* (22 Oct 2013), http://www.publicspirit.org.uk/religious-discrimination-against-teachers-in-faith-schools/#_edn1.

Chemistry might well be able to do his or her job to a high standard despite not identifying with the faith of the school. Nevertheless, the impact of a high percentage of staff from outside the faith group might alter the ethos and character of the community considerably.

How persuasive this argument appears is contingent upon the view which is taken of the purpose and desirability of faith schools. This is a highly complex and politicised question, and not one which we are currently seeking to address. The point for present purposes is that, in this respect, the legal framework in relation to discrimination appears to go beyond the minimum requirements imposed by the state's international obligations (in Vickers' view it even arguably crosses the line in the other direction and infringes them).

Yet commentators also suggest that other aspects of discrimination law are insufficiently open to the needs of religious citizens. Gibson[30] asserts that the protection in place for employees wishing to manifest their faith at work is effectively weighted too far against the individual. He argues that the resolution which UK courts tend to reach, in relation to disputes concerning religion in the workplace, ordinarily necessitate a dilution of religious liberty for the individual involved, especially when questions of disadvantage or proportionality are involved. He addresses whether adopting a North American-style duty of 'reasonable accommodation' would be desirable.

Interestingly, in this context, Vickers[31] also wonders whether religious liberty might be being undervalued by the legal framework. This commentator asks whether a 'hierarchy of rights' might be developing, with religious liberty being treated as less than other protected grounds, and suggests that this could leave citizens with views which are not in line with what is considered 'respectable' in a democratic society effectively enjoying a lower level of protection.[32]

It is true that many of the high-profile cases which have been litigated in both the United Kingdom and Strasbourg have gone against individuals asserting their religious freedoms in the workplace. For example, three of the four applicants in the *Eweida* litigation were unsuccessful.[33] We would argue, though, that this does not in itself prove that individual religious liberties have been watered down, nor that there is a hierarchy of rights. It could equally well show that religious liberties are generally well respected by employers, that appropriate requests are ordinarily met positively, and that it has tended to be weaker claims that have been litigated.

Furthermore, cases which involve a balance of conflicting rights must, by their very nature, be fact specific. Just because in a particular decision the balance came down against religious liberty, it cannot be claimed that religious freedom was seen

30 M. Gibson, 'The God "Dilution" of Religion, Discrimination and the Case for Reasonable Accommodation', *Cambridge Law Journal*, Vol. 72, No. 3 (2013) 578–616.

31 L. Vickers, 'Religious Discrimination in the Workplace: An Emerging Hierarchy', *Ecclesiastical Law Journal*, Vol. 12, No. 3 (2010) 280–303.

32 Ibid., 303.

33 *Eweida and Others v United Kingdom*, 15 January 2013, [2013] ECHR 37 (ECtHR).

by the court as a lesser right. All the decision shows is that in those circumstances the religious claims were less weighty than other factors.

The complexity here also demonstrates the other way in which discrimination law flexes to allow conduct which would otherwise be prohibited when religious factors are involved. The recognition of religious freedom and the status of religion and belief as a protected characteristic enable individuals at times to act in ways which employers might otherwise frown upon, or even be under a positive duty to prohibit.

So, for example, if a male engineer refused to shake hands with female clients and colleagues because he regarded them as inferior and out of place in the industry concerned, his employers would be highly likely to fall foul of the Equality Act were they to allow this to continue. However, if another male engineer tried to avoid physical contact with women because of his orthodox Jewish or Muslim faith, but was still respectful and courteous to everyone regardless of gender, then his employer would be both obliged and entitled to respond very differently.

Consequently, discrimination law functions to both protect religious individuals and groups from adverse treatment, but also in certain circumstances insulates faith-based discrimination from liability, which would otherwise apply.

2.3.2.1.2 CHARITY LAW

Charitable status brings a number of attendant legal and tax benefits for organisations that are able to attain it.[34] In order to qualify as being set up for charitable purposes, a trust must be able to demonstrate that (i) it is of public benefit, and (ii) it falls within one of the statutory descriptions of charitable purposes.[35] The advancement of religion is listed among the possible categories of charitable purposes.[36]

The current legislative position has developed from the regime previously existing at common law. Religion was always accepted to be a positive force in society, but originally it was understood very much in terms of doctrines of the official faith.[37] For instance, 'superstitious uses'[38] were considered void, which made it difficult for Roman Catholics to make charitable bequests for what they would have deemed religious purposes, even where there was discernible public benefit:

> As if a man gives land of the value of £20 and that the feoffees of the profits of the land shall pay to a priest £10 and the residue for books, bread, wine etc for the celebration of Mass, etc, or to one or divers to visit, and see that the service

34 National Anti-Vivisection Society v IRC [1948] AC 31.

35 Charities Act 2011, s. 2(1).

36 Ibid., s. 3(1)(c).

37 C.E.F. Rickett, 'An Anti-Roman Catholic Bias in the Law of Charity', *Conveyancer and Property Lawyer* (1990) 34–44.

38 The word 'use' in this context is a noun, rather than a verb, and refers to the legal entity from which the modern trust evolved.

> be done, or that the reparation of the chappel in which the service is to be done, or to the reparation of the tenements, or to poor people to be present at it, or some such like intents or purposes which depend upon the superstitious use, or for an ornament or continuance of it, there all is given to the King.[39]

Nevertheless, as the law developed, the courts acknowledged that the religious purposes of other Christian denominations, including Roman Catholicism, could come within the charitable fold. Furthermore, by the nineteenth century it was clear that other non-Christian faiths could also, in principle, be included, although like all trusts they would have to demonstrate public benefit.[40]

This is not to suggest that the current situation is perfect or uncomplicated. There still, to a degree, remains debate about the proper definition of 'religion'.[41] Inevitably, judges define and understand concepts from their own cultural perspective, and this runs the risk of religions from minority cultural paradigms being inadvertently excluded. However, as commentators such as Sandberg acknowledge, there has been a marked and welcome judicial shift away from a theistic conception of faith, which inevitably favoured Christianity, Islam and Judaism over Eastern belief systems, and a move towards a more expansive assessment.[42] Writing in an academic capacity, the Deputy President of the Supreme Court of the United Kingdom, Baroness Hale, has also endorsed the current broad and inclusive approach to the understanding of religion.[43]

There are few, if any, commentators pressing for a return to a more restrictive model. Consequently, the benefits flowing from charitable status, once confined to the Church of England, are now available to almost all individuals and groups who wish to advance the purposes of their faith.

It might be asked whether this situation is, nevertheless, still unsatisfactory on the basis that it appears to favour citizens who have some form of religion over their Agnostic and Atheist counterparts. It is legitimate to consider whether the modern law, which has grown from the root of bolstering the practice of the established faith to branching into recognising and privileging *all* faiths in this regard, has in the process marginalised individuals without religion in their lives. Yet a careful assessment of the overall picture reveals that the charge of disadvantage cannot be sustained in the field of charity law.

39 *The Reports of Sir Edward Coke in English, compleat in thirteen parts, with references to all the antient and modern books of the law. Exactly translated and compared with the first and last edition in French, and printed page for page with the same. To which are now added the pleadings to the cases,* Part IV, Adams and Lambert Case, 112, https://play.google.com/books/reader?id=O9YsAAAAYAAJ&printsec=frontcover&output=reader&hl=en_GB.

40 *Yeap Cheah Neo and Others (Appellants) v Ong Cheng Neo (Respondents) (on appeal from the Supreme Court of the Straits Settlement, in its division of Penang)* (1875) LR 6 PC 381.

41 See, e.g., *R (on the application of Hodkin) v Registrar General of Births, Deaths and Marriages* [2013] UKSC 77.

42 R. Sandberg, 'Defining the Divine', *Ecclesiastical Law Journal*, Vol. 16, No. 3 (2014) 198–204.

43 Baroness Hale, 'Secular Judges and Christian Law', *Ecclesiastical Law Journal*, Vol. 17, No. 2 (2015) 170–181, 172.

Indeed, there are other charitable purposes which some groups of citizens regard as immoral and harmful to society, and recognising *any* given purpose as charitable obviously benefits those who wish to pursue that purpose, but it does not automatically disadvantage citizens who are indifferent, or even hostile. For example, legislation recognises the advancement of the promotion of the efficiency of the armed forces of the Crown as a charitable purpose.[44] Is this incompatible with the fundamental rights of those, such as the Peace Pledge Union,[45] who oppose the maintenance of armed forces on pacifist or other ideological grounds? Unless the answer is in the affirmative, it is difficult to assert that the rights of non-religious citizens are automatically infringed by permitting religious causes the benefits of charity law in this regard. Not *all* charitable purposes will be considered as good or desirable by all of the population.

2.3.2.1.3 EDUCATION[46]

Education is another forum within which religion receives special treatment by the legal framework. We confess at the outset that this topic in itself has given rise to libraries full of learned books, and we can only hope to provide a general overview in this chapter. We stress that our current concern is to indicate ways in which the legal framework accommodates believers, not to provide a comprehensive assessment of religion, education and the legal system.

Religious education (RE) is a subject which all state-funded schools are required to provide,[47] and it comprises one of the basic elements of the essential curriculum in all schools.[48] However, although the importance of religious education is recognised, it is acknowledged to be an area in which parental freedoms are particularly at stake, and there is a statutory right for parents to withdraw their children should they so wish, as well as provision (subject to certain conditions) for them to opt to take their children out of school in order for them to receive alternative religious instruction.[49] The Government declined to grant children themselves an independent right to decide whether to participate, arguing that the guarantee of free parental choice was sufficient to protect the liberty of citizens.[50]

As Harris and García Oliva[51] and also Lundy[52] argue, this stance is highly unsatisfactory from the point of view of respecting the human rights of minor

44 Charities Act 2011.

45 Peace Pledge Union, http://www.ppu.org.uk.

46 Education Law and Religion is a legal discipline in and of itself, and we are therefore able only to give a general overview of the position here.

47 Education Act 2002, s. 80.

48 Schools Standards and Framework Act (SSFA) 1998, s. 60(1).

49 SSFA 1998, s. 71(1) and (2)(a) (as substituted/amended by the 2006 Act) s. 55(3) and (4)

50 Jim Knight, Schools Minister, *House of Commons Debates*, Vol. 451, col. 502 (2 Nov 2006).

51 N. Harris and J. García Oliva, 'Adapting to Religious Diversity: Legal Protection of Religious Preference in State Funded Schools in England', in C. Russo (ed.), *International Perspectives on Education, Religion and Law* (Routledge: Abingdon) 2014, 134–54.

52 L. Lundy, '"Voice" is Not Enough: Conceptualising Article 12 of the United Nations Convention on the Rights of the Child', *British Educational Research Journal*, Vol. 33 (2007) 927–42.

citizens, in accordance with the UN Convention on the Rights of the Child[53] (UNCRC). Presumably, the fear was that given the chance, too many pupils would use the right as an opportunity to skip a lesson without repercussions, or decide that they needed time out of school for religious education in an unconventional denomination.

Whether or not this paternalistic approach is defensible or reconcilable with the dignity of young citizens is a moot point, but the value which the state places upon religious education as a force for social cohesion is evident. Successive Governments have maintained its place as a legally required element within state education.

Furthermore, in addition to religious education – which is academic and non-denominational (although predominantly Christian),[54] rather than devotional – there also remains a statutory duty imposed on state schools with no religious ethos to hold a daily act of worship,[55] which is 'wholly or mainly of a broadly Christian character'.[56]

Therefore, the current framework treats spiritual activity as being beneficial enough to justify imposing a requirement on otherwise secular schools to offer it to their pupils. The provision is weighed in favour of Christianity as the dominant religion within the culture, although not in specifically Anglican terms. The national Church and other denominations benefit alongside one another.

The requirement is sufficiently flexible to include some worship specifically drawn from other religions and also to construct worship which would be acceptable to believers in other faiths. Expressing thanks to God as Creator, for example, or a spiritual message about compassion and kindness, would be of a broadly Christian character, but also in keeping with many other faith-based belief systems. Nevertheless, parents who wish may still choose to withdraw their children[57] and students themselves have an individual right to opt out.[58]

There are groups, however, such as the National Secular Society (NSS),[59] which argue that the right of withdrawal is insufficient as a means of rendering the legal framework inclusive for people of all faiths and none. In their view, exercising the right to withdraw means separating students from their peers, which may lead to stigmatisation or exclusion. In response to this point, it could be argued that there are more appropriate ways of addressing concerns about marginalisation than seeking to deny differences between pupils. If young people were subjected to bullying and peer pressure on the basis of a withdrawal from collective worship, it would indicate serious failings in relation to building a culture of respect and inclusivity, as in a healthy educational environment students

53 Arts 12 and 14(2).
54 Education Act 1996, s. 375.
55 SSFA 1998, s. 70.
56 Ibid., Sch. 20.
57 Ibid., s. 71(1).
58 Ibid., s. 71(1B).
59 National Secular Society, 'Collective Worship', http://www.secularism.org.uk/collective-worship.html.

should be helped to understand different beliefs and cultural backgrounds among their peers and see this diversity in a positive light.

However, in raising the point about social marginalisation, the NSS does not address the detriment to which its preferred solution of eradicating all religious content from collective school gatherings would subject a different group of pupils. In fact, were that path to be followed, members of the school community who value the spiritual dimension of collective worship would be permanently deprived of it.

In addition to these provisions, the legal framework also demonstrates its support for religion in an educational context in relation to schools with a religious ethos, which are wholly or partly funded by the state.[60] As has already been noted above in relation to discrimination law, we recognise that this is a highly controversial situation. Petchey perceptively argues that while it may be possible to rebut legal challenges to state-supported faith schools, attacks grounded in human rights law are to be expected while such public funding remains contested.[61] Faith schools are an emotional and divisive issue for many people. It would be neither practical nor appropriate to attempt to rehearse all aspects of the social and political debate within our present work, which is primarily legal in nature. For current purposes, we shall simply note the different ways in which schools with a religious ethos can operate within the public sector.

There are various types of governance and financing arrangements for public sector schools, and faith schools can operate on the basis of available structures. They may be inter alia voluntarily aided schools, free schools or academies.[62]

As already discussed, faith schools are exempt from certain provisions of the Equality Act 2010,[63] and are therefore allowed to apply faith-based selection criteria where they are oversubscribed[64] (we note that at the time of writing there are proposals to further extend the scope for such selection, but it is not yet clear what legislative changes, if any, will come to fruition).[65] What constitutes oversubscription is in itself potentially controversial, as it requires some determination of what it means for an individual to be a member of a given faith community. However, as Barber[66] observes, the courts are in general reluctant to interfere

60 See further, UK Government, 'Schools Admissions and Transport to School', https://www.gov.uk/types-of-school/faith-schools.

61 P. Petchey, 'Legal Issues for Faith Schools in England and Wales', *Ecclesiastical Law Journal*, Vol. 10, No. 2 (2008) 174–90.

62 UK Government, 'Faith Schools', https://www.gov.uk/types-of-school/faith-schools.

63 R. Long and P. Bolton, 'Faith Schools: Frequently Asked Questions', House of Commons Library Briefing Paper (14 Oct 2015).

64 UK Government, 'Statutory Guidance: Schools Admissions Code Department for Education' (19 Dec 2014, updated 17 Sept 2015), https://www.gov.uk/government/publications/school-admissions-code--2.

65 C. Cook, 'New Grammars and More Selection by Faith Proposed, *BBC News* (8 Sept 2016), http://www.bbc.co.uk/news/uk-politics-37312625.

66 P. Barber, 'State Schools and Religious Authority – Where to Draw the Line?', *Ecclesiastical Law Journal*, Vol. 12, No. 2 (2010) 224–8.

with the determination of religious authorities on this point. Rosenberg and Desai[67] also highlight problems with the ways in which faith-based discrimination criteria are sometimes applied, and point to the potential for both undue rigidity and unjustifiable discrimination. Furthermore, as discussed above, faith schools are able to select staff as well as students on the basis of religious related criteria. Some of the same issues would apply in this context. How is membership of a faith group determined? How practising must an individual be in order to be deemed 'acceptable'? Who should determine this and how open is it to adjudication on the basis of objective criteria which third parties can apply?

Different arrangements apply to the teaching of religious education in this setting from that of state schools without a religious character. Government guidance summarises the provision of religious education as follows:

> RE in a school with a religious character must be provided in accordance with the school's trust deed or, where provision is not made by a trust deed, in accordance with the beliefs of the religion or denomination specified in the order that designates the school as having a religious character. RE in a foundation or voluntary controlled school with a religious character must be provided in accordance with the locally agreed syllabus for the area. However, where parents request it, provision may be made in accordance with the school's trust deed or, where provision is not made by trust deed, in accordance with the beliefs of the religion or denomination specified in the order.[68]

So, in essence, faith schools have the freedom to provide religious education which is in keeping with their particular ethos, although in some cases if they have not opted out, their provision will be in line with what has been agreed locally for all public sector schools in the area.

It is not merely the provision of religious education which marks them out as different, however. A controversial issue has been the teaching of 'creationism' in faith schools. The current position is that it may not be taught in science lessons, but it may be referred to in religious education lessons 'provided that it does not undermine the teaching of established scientific theory'.[69]

Clearly, this is a governmental attempt to tread unstained through a moral and political quagmire. On the one hand, it is difficult to see how teaching creationism in RE, while acknowledging it to be a mainstream part of the faith being promoted by the school, could not at some level undermine the teaching of established scientific theory delivered in biology lessons. On the other, the guidance effectively bans creationism being presented as an alternative theory to evolution within the context of science teaching.

67 D. Rosenberg and R. Desai, 'The Admissions Arrangements of Faith Schools and the Equality Act 2010', *Education Law Journal* (2013) 93.

68 Long and Bolton, n. 63 above, 7.

69 Long and Bolton, ibid., 10.

It should perhaps be acknowledged that it is possible to overstate the issue of the teaching of creationism, given that the majority of faith schools have either an Anglican or a Roman Catholic ethos, and neither denomination encourages or expects believers to renounce Darwinian theory. However, this issue is by no means purely hypothetical, as acknowledged by respected scientific figures like Professor Martin Rees, who has expressed concern about promising students being lost to science if these issues are mishandled.[70]

This point also raises another key issue concerning religion and education law. In addition to questions about whether the state should support religious schools in financial and other respects, there are issues concerning the responsibilities which the state owes to *all* children. Independent schools[71] must comply with independent school standards, and are subject to inspection by OFSTED or an alternative inspectorate, and this imposes some monitoring and quality control in respect of the content and delivery of curriculum.[72] Consequently, even parents who are able and willing to entirely fund their children's schooling cannot buy the right to exercise unfettered discretion over the education which they receive. Although education law is extremely generous in accommodating parental religious choices in many respects, there are necessarily limits to this liberty.

These issues do not just, of course, apply to conventional, school-based education. The United Kingdom has an extremely permissive legal regime in respect of home-schooling, and while this educational route is chosen for a wide variety of reasons, religion is the primary motivating factor for many families.[73] Parents have a legal duty to ensure that children of compulsory school age receive a full-time education, but this need not be in a school environment.[74] Consequently, religious parents have a great deal of freedom to educate their children in a setting over which they have complete control, should they so desire.

As Monk argues, this is a potentially problematic position, especially in the current political climate regarding radicalisation,[75] but it should be stressed that contemporary concerns about terrorist indoctrination are by no means the only reason for dissatisfaction with the present framework on education outside conventional schools. For instance, it has recently come to light that some sections of the Jewish Charedi community are failing to provide appropriate and adequate education, especially for boys.[76]

70 I. Sample, 'Martin Rees – I've Got No Religious Beliefs at All', *The Guardian* (6 Apr 2011), https://www.theguardian.com/science/2011/apr/06/astronomer-royal-martin-rees-interview.

71 UK Government, 'Regulating Independent Schools' (Jan 2016), www.gov.uk/.../file/492994/Regulating_independent_schools.pdf.

72 Long and Bolton, n. 63 above, 10.

73 See, e.g., Home Education UK, 'Why Home Educate?', http://www.home-ed.co.uk/whyhomeed.html.

74 Education Act 1996, s. 7.

75 D. Monk, 'Out of School Education and Radicalisation: Home Education Revisited', *Education Law Journal*, Vol. 1 (2016) 17–31.

76 'Concern Over 1000 Boys in 'Illegal' Schools Over Narrow Curriculum', *The Telegraph* (1 Apr 2016), http://www.telegraph.co.uk/education/2016/04/01/concern-for-1000-boys-in-illegal-schools-over-narrow-curriculum.

There have also been a number of tragic cases in which children being home-schooled have died through abuse or neglect.[77] In practice, the arrangements for monitoring these children in general terms, not simply in relation to curriculum, should be considerably more robust.

Once again, the values and dangers of home-schooling (and 'out of school' education more generally) are the subject of fierce social debate, and we do not presume to offer an opinion on the topic more widely in this book. For present purposes, we simply acknowledge that the legal framework gives religious parents the freedom to determine the methods, environment and place of their children's education, in practice with little interference if the threshold for state intervention on the grounds of neglect or abuse is not being met.[78] The local authority does have the right to check that a child is receiving an adequate education,[79] but cannot block a parent's decision to withdraw a child from the school system if the child in question is being educated. However, the requirements in relation to the nature of the education provided are sparse. Parents or others who undertake home education are not bound to have any qualifications, for example, nor to conform with any set curriculum or pattern.

It should also not be forgotten that there are issues relating to tertiary education and religion. Obviously, the context here is very different, as the participants are ordinarily legally adults, and the education is entirely voluntary. Nevertheless, students may at times object on religious grounds to the content of their chosen course and, interestingly, there remains a statutory guarantee of their right to do so. This is a surviving provision of the Universities Tests Act 1871, s. 7: 'No person shall be required to attend any colleague or university lecture to which he, if he be of full age, or, if he be not of full age, his parent or guardian, shall object upon religious grounds'.

2.3.2.1.4 CRIMINAL LAW

Another striking example of the positive light within which the current system views religion can be seen in the area of criminal law. Not only are religious believers protected from being targeted and harmed by others on the basis of their faith identity;[80] in some circumstances they are effectively shielded from liability for what would otherwise amount to criminal conduct, as long as they are acting with a religious motivation.

In terms of protection, the Religious and Racial Hatred Act 2006 is an important, although controversial, piece of legislation. As Jeremy[81] observes, rather than taking the approach of making religious hatred an aggravating factor in the

77 I. Pollock, 'Boy's Scurvy Death Prompts Home-Schooling Register Call', *BBC News* (8 July 2016), http://www.bbc.co.uk/news/uk-wales-36746094.

78 Children Act 1989, Part IV.

79 UK Government, 'Home Education', https://www.gov.uk/home-education.

80 E.g., Racial and Religious Hatred Act 2006.

81 A. Jeremy, 'Practical Implications of the Enactment of the Racial and Religious Hatred Act 2007, *Ecclesiastical Law Journal* (2007) 187–201.

commission of existing crimes (which would effectively increase the tariff upon sentencing), this legislation created a wholly new offence. Since the passage of the Act, it is a criminal offence to intentionally stir up religious hatred. The *mens rea* required means that in practice it is difficult to bring successful charges under the legislation, as intentionality is difficult to prove. However, as Jeremy argues, the introduction of this crime may have symbolic value, and its very presence on the statute book sends a message to minority faith groups who may feel beleaguered, and also to would-be abusers, that this is not behaviour which our society is willing to tolerate.

In addition to this, an element of religious hatred will be an aggravating factor in the commission of other criminal offences,[82] and this confers an additional layer of security on believers.

As well as these provisions – which are geared towards safeguarding citizens from suffering harm or intimidation on the basis of their faith – there are elements of criminal law which actively enable the practice of religion. It is not possible within the law of England and Wales to consent to an assault if the relevant contact amounts to actual bodily harm[83] or more serious injury, unless the conduct comes within one of the categories of recognised exemptions.[84] Although this approach has received widespread criticism from academic commentators like Tolmie,[85] Giles,[86] Streets[87] and Bix,[88] primarily on the basis that it amounts to an unjustifiable restriction of individual autonomy, this position has remained unchanged since it was brought to light by a high-profile case in the mid-1990s.[89]

Nevertheless, 'religious mortification' is acknowledged as one of the excepted categories of activity,[90] as is ritual male circumcision.[91] Others relate to medical treatment and contact sports, for instance.

While at first sight a defence to criminal assault on the basis of religious mortification might sound more an issue for legal textbooks than the real world, it has undeniable practical application. In 2006, the New Zealand courts were faced

82 See, in particular, the provisions of the Crime and Disorder Act 1998 and Criminal Justice Act 2003.

83 Actual bodily harm has been defined by the courts to mean harm which is more than transient or trifling, but need not be permanent: R v Donovan [1934] 2 KB 498, 25 Cr App Rep 1 (CCA); *R v Miller* [1954] 2 QB 282; *R v Chan Fook* [1994] 2 All ER 552. Psychological harm is included, but only where identifiable psychiatric injury can be demonstrated: *R v Dhaliwal* [2006] EWCA Crim 1139.

84 *R v Brown* [1994] 1 AC 212.

85 J. Tolmie, 'Consent to Harmful Assaults: The Case for Moving Away from Category Based Decision Making', *Criminal Law Review* (2012) 656–71.

86 M. Giles, 'R v Brown: Consensual Harm and the Public Interest', *The Modern Law Review*, Vol. 57, No. 1 (1994) 101–11.

87 S. Streets, 'S&M in the House of Lords', *Alternative Law Journal*, Vol. 18, No. 5 (1993) 233–6.

88 B.H. Bix, 'Assault, Sado-Masochism and Consent, *Law Quarterly Review*, Vol. 109 (1993) 540–4.

89 *R v Brown* [1994] 1 AC 212.

90 Ibid., per Lord Mustill, 267.

91 *Re S (Specific Issue Order: Religion: Circumcision)* [2004] EWHC 1282 (Fam); *Re J (Specific Issue Orders: Child's Religious Upbringing and Circumcision)* 1 FLR 571 (CA).

with considering capacity to consent in a religious context following the death of a woman during an exorcism ritual,[92] and similar deaths have been considered by the criminal justice system in the United Kingdom.[93]

Equally, family courts have made it clear that the capacity to consent to male circumcision is at the very outer limits of what can or will be permitted, particularly where minors are involved.[94] Unlike most decisions, which can be made unilaterally by any person with parental responsibility,[95] circumcision of boys requires consensus among all of the holders of parental responsibility or a court order. In practice, in cases of dispute, the courts have consistently refused to grant such an order, given the serious and irreversible nature of the intervention, and the attendant risks.

Therefore, the gravity of matters potentially covered by the exceptions to criminal law should not be underestimated. Religious freedoms are accorded a genuine privilege in this regard, and the otherwise rigid criminal law is prepared to bend to accommodate them.

2.3.2.1.5 FAMILY LAW

In addition to the special role of the established Church in relation to marriage,[96] there are a variety of ways in which family law demonstrates a commitment to the promotion and safeguarding of religion in general.

First, there are mechanisms in place to enable other religious denominations to carry out wedding ceremonies in accordance with their own rites and customs.[97] All marriages which are solemnised other than according to the rites of the Church of England or the Church in Wales are conducted on the authority of a superintendent registrar's certificate or the Registrar General's licence. Although this is not expressly provided for in the Marriage Act 1949, as Lowe and Douglas argue, this is the obvious intention and necessary effect of the statute.[98] A marriage on the authority of a superintendent registrar's certificate may be solemnised in a registered building, according to the usages of the Society of Friends, the Jews or in any place where a housebound or detained person is situated.[99]

92 *R v Lee* [2006] 5 LRC 716. See H. Hall, 'Exorcism, Religious Freedom and Consent: The Devil in the Detail', *Journal of Criminal Law*, Vol. 80, No. 4 (2016) 241–53.

93 *R. v Rabiya Patel and Others* [1995] 16 Cr App R (S) 827.

94 *Re B (Children) (Care Proceedings) (also known as Leeds City Council v M)* [2015] EWFC 3; *Re S (Specific Issue Order: Religion: Circumcision)* [2004] EWHC 1282 (Fam); *Re J (Specific Issue Orders: Child's Religious Upbringing and Circumcision)* 1 FLR 571 (CA).

95 Children Act 1989, s. 2.

96 See the section below ('Establishment') on low establishment of the Church of England.

97 See N. Lowe and G. Douglas, *Bromley's Family Law* (Oxford University Press: Oxford) 10th edn, 2007.

98 Ibid., 57, fn 116.

99 Marriage Act 1949, s. 26(1) (as amended by the Marriage Act 1983, Sch. 1 and the Marriage Act 1994, s. 1(1)).

Any building which is registered as a place of worship under the Places of Worship Registration Act 1855 may be registered by the Registrar General for the solemnisation of marriages.[100] A marriage in a registered building may take place only in the presence of a registrar or an authorised person,[101] and authorised persons will ordinarily be ministers of the relevant faith or denomination. This is significant because only *religious* buildings may be registered for *religious* marriage. A wholly different regime and legislative provisions apply to registering non-religious premises.[102] The venue must not have any continuing connection with religion. So, for example, a chapel in a stately home or mock Celtic wooden circle would be prohibited.

The marriage rites for non-established religious marriages may take any form, provided that they contain a declaration similar to that required when the marriage is in a register office, and the parties contract the union *per verba de praesenti* (present vows: an exchange of promises in the present tense with present intention, not a declaration about what may happen in the future).[103] In contrast, secular marriages must not contain any religious elements. In fact, readings from sacred texts and religious music are banned, as is anything which might be construed as religious worship or ritual.[104]

These unusually strict provisions demonstrate how the legal framework treats religious marriage as a distinct institution worthy of special protection and respect. Religious groups are permitted to carry out wedding ceremonies (provided that they are able to comply with the necessary formalities), but those offering civil wedding venues for commercial profit may not incorporate religious elements to make their product more marketable. Couples in contemporary England may not

100 Marriage Act 1949, ss 41 and 42 (as amended by the Marriage Acts Amendment Act 1958, s. 1(1) and the Marriage (Registration of Buildings) Act 1990, s. 1(1)).

101 Marriage Act 1949, s. 2.

102 Ibid., s. 26(1).

103 Ibid., s. 44.

104 UK Government, 'The Registrar General's Guidance for the Approval of Venues for Civil Marriages and Civil Partnerships', 5th edn (revised May 2014), https://www.gov.uk/government/publications/guidance-on-registering-a-venue-for-civil-marriage-and-civil-partnership, Annex C:

> 11.—(1) Any proceedings conducted on approved premises shall not be religious in nature.
> (2) In particular, the proceedings shall not—
> (a) include extracts from an authorised religious marriage service or from sacred religious texts;
> (b) be led by a minister of religion or other religious leader;
> (c) involve a religious ritual or series of rituals;
> (d) include hymns or other religious chants; or,
> (e) include any form of worship.
> (3) But the proceedings may include readings, songs, or music that contain an incidental reference to a god or deity in an essentially non-religious context.
> (4) For this purpose any material used by way of introduction to, in any interval between parts of, or by way of conclusion to the proceedings shall be treated as forming part of the proceedings.

choose a faith-lite wedding, and a sharp and impenetrable divide is maintained between secular and religious ceremonies.

There is scope for debate about the appropriateness of this arrangement, but as it currently stands religion is given special and jealously guarded treatment where marriage ceremonies are concerned.

It should also be noted that in England and Wales (unlike Scotland) there is no framework which allows Humanist celebrants to conduct legally binding marriages. Only religious ministers (or others appointed by a religious group as an authorised person) or civil registrars have the capacity to preside at weddings with effect in state law.

2.3.2.1.6 GLOBAL PICTURE – A LEGAL FRAMEWORK WITH A RELIGIOUS CHARACTER

Taken together, the aspects of equality, charity, education, criminal and family law set out above all demonstrate that religion in general is treated as a positive phenomenon and something which the state ought properly to foster and protect. Although some of the specific doctrinal examples we have produced may be novel, that contention in itself is not. For example, Doe and Sandberg have maintained that in western Europe functional co-operationism is the normal pattern within juridical systems.[105]

In broad terms, as charity law illustrates well, this has come about because the state historically treated Anglicanism as deserving respect and promotion, and gradually came to acknowledge that other faith traditions required comparable assistance and recognition.

Furthermore, the general pattern is one of helping citizens who wish to engage in religious activities to do so, and of supporting activities in which some citizens freely elect to take part. Although there are those who would vociferously criticise this overall legal structure,[106] it is one which has grown up in a responsive manner, and is not intended to be exclusive. It has long since moved from defending the established Church for political reasons to recognising the wider benefits of religious practice, and supporting the spectrum of faiths active in the modern nation.

However, because the cultural and historical context has been predominantly Christian and Anglican in nature, and this tradition remains the numerically dominant one, the Church of England is inevitably a highly significant beneficiary of this overarching treatment of religion, and inevitably it is against this backdrop that establishment[107] must be considered.

105 R. Sandberg, 'Church-State Relations in Europe: From Legal Models to an Interdisciplinary Approach', *Journal of Religion in Europe*, Vol. 1 (2008) 329–52.

106 National Secular Society, 'Challenging Religious Privilege', http://www.secularism.org.uk; British Humanist Society 'Campaigns', https://humanism.org.uk/campaigns.

107 For a more in-depth analysis of the English model of establishment, see J. García Oliva, 'Church, State and Establishment in the United Kingdom in the 21st Century: Anachronism or Idiosyncrasy?', *Public Law* (July 2010) 482–504.

2.3.2.2 Establishment

Commentators like Carr[108] draw a useful distinction between the features of high and low establishment. In his analysis, high establishment covers the very visible, constitutional aspects of the current Church/state relationship – for example, Church of England bishops in the House of Lords and the position of the monarch as Supreme Governor of the Church. The counterpoint to this is the phenomenon of low or 'earthed' establishment, which covers the practical ways in which the Church of England has an impact on the lives of citizens through parishes, hospitals, prisons and schools.

As McClean[109] has argued, high establishment has traditionally tended to steal the limelight in academic commentary on establishment. This is regrettable, as low establishment in many respects has a greater practical effect on contemporary society. However, both features are important for the purposes of the present analysis, and we shall consider each in turn, starting with high establishment.

2.3.2.2.1 HIGH ESTABLISHMENT

A. The Monarch The compromise title of 'Supreme Governor' adopted by Elizabeth I has survived and been retained.[110] Whether this situation should continue is the subject of debate, and commentators such as Morris[111] suggest that the title of Supreme Governor should be removed, while the role of Defender of the Faith ought to be re-imagined and reinterpreted. Yet, for the moment it remains, and the personal link between the Monarch and the Church is evident.

The Act of Settlement 1701 still means that the Monarch cannot be Roman Catholic, although the prohibition on marriage to a person of that faith has now been lifted.[112] When the law was in the process of reform, the Church of England wrote to express its support for the change removing the bar to succession which was operative in the case of such marriages.[113] However, there were voices of dissent from within the Church, and a former Archbishop of Canterbury (Lord Carey) publically expressed concern that such a move could 'upset the delicate constitutional balance'.[114]

108 W. Carr, 'A Developing Establishment', *Theology* (Jan 1999) 2–10.

109 D. McClean, 'The Changing Legal Framework of Establishment', *Ecclesiastical Law Journal*, Vol. 7, No. 34 (2004) 292–303.

110 Church of England, Canon A7, of the Royal Supremacy: 'We acknowledge that the Queen's excellent Majesty, according to the laws of the realm, is the highest power under God in this kingdom, and the supreme authority over all persons in all causes, as well ecclesiastical as civil'.

111 R.M. Morris, 'Towards a New Balance', in R. Morris (ed.), *Church and State in 21st Century Britain: The Future of Church Establishment* (Palgrave McMillan: London) 2009, 226–41, 238–9.

112 Succession to the Crown Act 2013, s. 2.

113 R. Mason, 'Nick Clegg Urges "Equal Rights" for Royal Girls as MPs Prepare to Debate Rules of Succession', *The Telegraph* (22 Jan 2013), http://www.telegraph.co.uk/news/uknews/theroyalfamily/9816620/Nick-Clegg-urges-equal-rights-for-royal-girls-as-MPs-prepare-to-debate-rules-of-succession.html.

114 Ibid.

Despite this anxiety, the passage of the legislation so far has not caused protest or disquiet within the United Kingdom, although, as Twomey argued, it did present some legal and constitutional challenges for some Commonwealth countries.[115] Given that this step has been taken without disaster, an obvious question to ask is whether the prohibition on Roman Catholic monarchs might also be lifted.

Interestingly, Leigh[116] had argued against this, asserting that the House of Windsor only now occupies the throne by virtue of the guarantee of Protestant succession. Without this provision, there is no logical reason why Prince Charles should succeed his mother, as his claim is not based just on hereditary principles, but hereditary principles with this added gloss. He also maintains that severing the link between the Church and Monarch as Supreme Governor, would be a secularising move and therefore contrary to the interests of social cohesion. In Leigh's view, developments towards secularisation are more apt to threaten than reassure followers of minority faiths, as they are interpreted as an attack on *all* religions.

This is an important point to be considered, and certainly demonstrates that the continued role of the Monarch in relation to the Church could potentially have a tangible social influence. However, it is key to highlight that removing the Monarch as Supreme Governor would not necessarily be a step towards disestablishment or even a secular state, as this would depend upon the reasons for the change and the circumstances within which it took place.

As Scotland demonstrates, it is perfectly possible to have a national, established Church, with a system of governance independent of the Monarch. As will be discussed below, the Queen sends a representative (the Lord High Commissioner) to meetings of the General Assembly of the Kirk, but he or she is not permitted to speak, much less exercise authority.[117]

Furthermore, as García Oliva notes,[118] there are the institutions of Royal Peculiars and Chapels Royal, which operate in a manner distinct from the usual Anglican ecclesiastical structures and retain a particularly intimate relationship with the Crown.

B. Appointment of bishops Sixteenth century legislation[119] means that in strict legal terms the Sovereign appoints bishops, archbishops and suffragan bishops in England. However, there is a constitutional convention that the Monarch appoints on the advice of her or his ministers.[120] Until the 1970s, the Prime

115 A. Twomey, 'Changing the Rules of Succession to the Throne', *Public Law* (2011) 378–401.
116 I. Leigh, 'By Law Established? The Church of England and Constitutional Reform', *Public Law* (2004) 266–73, 269.
117 The Church of Scotland, 'General Assembly', http://www.churchofscotland.org.uk/about_us/general_assembly.
118 García Oliva, n. 107 above, 489.
119 Bishops Act 1534; Suffragan Bishops Act 1534.
120 J. García Oliva, n. 107 above, 489.

Minister unilaterally decided on the appointment of bishops. James Callaghan agreed to reform, but rejected proposals to end prime ministerial involvement altogether, opting instead for a 'halfway house' in which the Prime Minister selected from names put forward by the Church.[121] Since that time the level of ministerial involvement has gradually decreased into the modern era. On 3 July 2007, the Government announced that 'the Prime Minister should not play an active role in the selection of individual candidates. He should not use the royal prerogative to exercise choice in recommending appointments of senior ecclesiastical posts to the Queen'.[122]

The procedure now is for the Crown Nominations Commission[123] to send only one name to the Prime Minister, who transmits it to the Queen, thereby making him no more than an official postman in the process. It may even be that the passive prime ministerial stance will in time ossify into a constitutional convention in its own right, comparable with the non-interventionist role of the Monarch in the modern system.

C. Legislation and the Church of England The Church of England Assembly (Powers) Act 1919 means that the Church of England is empowered to enact measures – legislation which forms part of the corpus of state law. On the one hand, this gives the Church of England a uniquely privileged position, as it has both autonomy and a power which other religious groups lack. However, there is a sting in the tail. Draft measures must be submitted to the Ecclesiastical Committee of both Houses of Parliament,[124] and each House must pass a resolution that the measure be laid before Parliament and submitted to the Monarch for Royal Assent.[125] Until the measure receives Royal Assent, it does not become operative. As a sign of the Church's autonomy, it may withdraw but not amend a measure that it has presented.[126]

Canons – which are the internal rules of the Church, binding only upon the clergy and certain lay office-holders (but not the general population or even all communicant members of the Church) – do not need to go through Parliament. However, the Submission of the Clergy Act 1533 provides that the convocations of the clergy may not 'make, promulge and execute' canons without having received 'the King's most royal assent and licence',[127] and prohibits the making

121 J. Wynne Jones, 'Bishops Fear Position of Church under Threat', *The Telegraph* (17 Feb 2008), http://www.telegraph.co.uk/news/uknews/1578893/Bishops-fear-position-of-Church-under-threat.html.

122 The Secretary of State for Justice and the Lord Chancellor, *The Governance of Britain*, CM 7170 (The Stationery Office: London) July 2007, https://www.gov.uk/government/uploads/system/uploads/attachment_data/file/228834/7170.pdf.

123 The Church of England, 'Crown Nominations Commissions', https://www.churchofengland.org/clergy-office-holders/asa/senappt/dbnom/cnc.aspx.

124 Church of England Assembly (Powers) Act 1919, s. 3(1)

125 Ibid., s. 4.

126 Ibid., s. 3(5).

127 Submission of the Clergy Act 1533, s. 1.

of canons that are 'contrary or repugnant to the King's prerogative royal or the customs, laws or statutes of this realm'.[128] Moreover, Royal Assent and Licence are required for the making of new canons and this is not granted until the Ministry of Justice has scrutinised the draft legislation to ensure that it complies with the Submission of the Clergy Act 1533.[129]

Therefore, it can be seen that, although not a branch of the state, the Church of England has a special, cosy relationship with it. This brings powers which are not available to other faith groups, but also constraints to which other denominations are not subjected.

D. Lords Spiritual A number of Church of England bishops continue to sit in the House of Lords.[130] There are many critics of this arrangement, such as Morris,[131] who does not consider it appropriate or defensible in the twenty-first century. A Royal Commission, commonly referred to as the 'Wakeham Commission', was set up to consider the future of the Upper Chamber and attempted to address some of the concerns in this area, recommending that leaders of other denominations be appointed to join the bishops.[132] This suggestion was not taken up by the Government.

It is probable that in pragmatic terms the future of the bishops will be determined by wider reform of the House of Lords, although this is unlikely to be a political priority under the current Government. Despite the fact that it is not on the immediate political horizon, the appropriateness of an entirely unelected second Chamber of the legislature is one which may well be revisited by the United Kingdom in the course of the twenty-first century. However, at present, the Church of England has a guaranteed opportunity to have its senior representatives playing a role in debates in the House of Lords, which is a perk not enjoyed by other denominations. While the former Chief Rabbi, Jonathan Sacks, was granted a place, and there are other peers who are distinguished representatives from other faith groups, none of them have their place as of right.

It is perhaps important to note that, while in theory the general pattern of widening benefits would be the obvious way to remedy the present inequality between faith groups, this would be by no means straightforward in practice. How would representatives from other religious communities be chosen? Not all groups have formal structures and hierarchies which would make the selection of a figurehead easy to achieve. How could a Lord Spiritual for the Buddhist or Pagan community be selected, for instance? Furthermore, there is room for considerable (perhaps endless) wrangling as to where the line should lie between faith groups.

128 Ibid., s. 3.

129 García Oliva, n. 107 above.

130 P. Edge, 'Religious Remnants in the Composition of the United Kingdom Parliament', in R. O'Dair and A. Lewis (eds), *Law and Religion: Current Legal Issues*, Vol. IV (Oxford University Press: Oxford) 2001, 443–55.

131 Morris, n. 111 above, 239.

132 Royal Commission on the Reform of the House of Lords, *A House for the Future*, Cm 4534 (The Stationery Office) 2000, https://www.gov.uk/government/uploads/system/uploads/attachment_data/file/266061/prelims.pdf.

Is it equitable to have the Chief Rabbi representing Judaism, for instance, when Reformed Jews would be likely to disagree with his stance on many issues (same-sex marriages, for example)? Even if the Jewish/Muslim/Hindu population were entitled to vote for a representative or number of representatives, how could the authorities determine which citizens were entitled to vote?

If anyone who self-identified as a particular faith group could vote on the basis of his or her own assertion, there would be the potential for people to cynically self-identify on an official form in order to influence the election of a representative. This does not mean that the difficulties are insurmountable, but some careful and creative thought would need to go into tackling them to achieve a fair and workable system.

If this aspect of establishment privilege cannot be opened up and shared, should it be dismantled in the interests of promoting equality and social cohesion? A number of academic commentators argue that removing bishops from the House of Lords would, in fact, have the opposite effect. For instance, Baldry endorses the description that Archbishop Justin Welby gave of the Church of England as 'glue' holding society together, and goes on to argue that it should remain a cohesive factor in the fabric of parliamentary life.[133]

It is also important to observe that commentators from non-Christian faiths, such as Tariq Modood[134] and Nasar Meer,[135] have strongly defended establishment on the basis of its benefits for religious people in general. Many citizens of faith welcome religious voices, even if they come from a different tradition. Therefore, it is by no means clear that removing the bishops would help to foster a sense of justice or inclusion.

Harlow, Cranmer and Doe[136] have noted a number of serious concerns with the functioning of the Lords Spiritual in practical terms (such as the unregulated nature of their participation), but also observed that a lot of good will towards their presence in the Upper House remains. This is undoubtedly a supportable conclusion, but it must be acknowledged that there is also considerable hostility in certain quarters, particularly from secularist campaign groups.[137]

In summary, we find little evidence that having bishops in the House of Lords is causing any sort of detriment to individuals not of the Anglican faith, and voices from a number of quarters suggest that there may be social value in retaining them.

133 T. Baldry, 'Parliament and the Church', *Ecclesiastical Law Journal*, Vol. 17, No. 2 (2015) 202–14, 211.

134 T. Modood, 'Establishment, Multiculturalism and British Citizenship', *The Political Quarterly*, Vol. 65, No. 1 (1994) 53–73.

135 N. Meer and T. Modood, 'A Jeffersonian Wall or an Anglican Establishment: The US and UK's Contrasting Approaches to Incorporating Muslims', LSE US Centre, http://blogs.lse.ac.uk/usappblog/2016/04/25/a-jeffersonian-wall-or-an-anglican-establishment-the-us-and-uks-contrasting-approaches-to-incorporating-muslims/#Author.

136 A. Harlow, F. Cranmer and N. Doe, 'Bishops in the House of Lords: A Critical Analysis', *Public Law* (2008) 490–509.

137 National Secular Society, 'Religion and State', http://www.secularism.org.uk/religion-and-state.html.

For these reasons, we suggest that removing them from the Second Chamber, as it is currently composed, would not be a beneficial move for society unless further compelling evidence is provided. However, were the Upper Chamber to be reformed more widely, it would of course be appropriate to assess the position of the Lords Spiritual.

E. The Church Commissioners For the sake of completeness, the Church Commissioners should be alluded to in the context of high establishment. They are a statutory body, created in 1949 to manage the land and property owned by the Church of England, and in order to replace both the Governors of the Bounty of Queen Anne for the Augmentation of the Poor Clergy and the Ecclesiastical Commissioners.[138]

The Church Commissioners include, inter alia:

- the First Lord of the Treasury;[139]
- the Home Secretary;
- the Speaker of the House of Commons;
- the Speaker of the House of Lords;
- the Secretary of State for the Department of Culture, Media and Sport;
- the three Church Estates Commissioners (crucially the Second Church Estate Commissioner is a member of the House of Commons, taking the government whip);
- three persons nominated by Her Majesty, as well as three persons nominated by the Archbishops of Canterbury and York acting jointly after consultation with the Lord Mayors of the Cities of London and York;
- the Vice-Chancellors of the Universities of Oxford and Cambridge; and
- such other persons as appear to the Archbishops to be appropriate.[140]

On one level, the link between control of the Church's property and those running the state is, therefore, extremely tight. However, the day-to-day functioning of the institution is more detached, as the routine business is dealt with by the much smaller Board of Governors.[141] Despite this trade-off, the element of state control remains. It is clear that secular authority in England, having looted the Church and made off with its assets once in the Reformation era, is still keen to ensure that nobody else should have an opportunity to do so.

2.3.2.2.2 LOW ESTABLISHMENT

A. Education As discussed above, religious education is something which non-denominational state schools are required by the legal system to provide.

138 M. Hill, *Ecclesiastical Law* (Oxford University Press: Oxford) 2007, 50.
139 i.e. the Prime Minister.
140 Church Commissioners Measure 1947, Sch. 1, s. 1(2) para. 1.
141 Ibid., Sch.1, s. 1(2) para. 1(b).

The Education Act 1996 demands that the content of religious education must be decided by a Standing Advisory Committee on Religious Education (SACRE), appointed by the local education authority. The Church of England has a special place on the committee in so far as the committee must be composed of the following members: the Church of England representative; representatives of other faiths (Christian or otherwise) which are located in the area; teachers' associations and the local education authority.[142]

Low establishment is also often reflected in informal arrangements in respect of schools. In many communities there is a pattern of inviting the local vicar into schools to conduct assemblies or to become a governor, even in the case of non-denominational schools. Where there is a sizeable community of another faith, a representative of that community may also step into this model and play a similar role, either instead of or alongside the Anglican cleric.

Again, this is a model of widening participating from the basis of establishment. Rather than dismantling Anglican privilege, other groups are invited to share in it. The system has the merit of flexibility, allowing for discretion to be used on the ground in order to accommodate the very different faith landscape in different communities, and also to allow for changes over time with shifting populations.

Nevertheless, there are those who would question why the Church, or indeed religious groups more widely, should have any privileged position.[143]

B. Prisons It is a requirement that prisons in England have a chaplain,[144] and that this chaplain be Anglican, although he or she has a duty to extend help to all inmates regardless of faith, particularly in an emergency situation in which a representative from their own community is not readily available.[145] Entrusting the Church with the responsibility to care for vulnerable individuals in the custody of the state should not be underestimated in terms of significance. Furthermore, the fact that the legislature saw fit to extend the provisions to the Church in Wales in 1952, three decades after its statutory disestablishment, is indicative of how much the Government apparently valued the service in practical terms.

Moreover, there are good objective reasons to believe that a spiritual and pastoral service offered to all regardless to belief may be especially welcomed in this context. As Beckford and Gilliat-Ray[146] rightly point out, the religious needs of prisoners may be a low priority for faith communities once they have been convicted and sentenced, and Edge[147] observes that fear of social stigma for the

142 Education Act 1996, s. 390.

143 National Secular Society, 'Challenging Religious Privilege', n. 106 above; British Humanist Society, 'Campaigns', n. 106 above.

144 Prison Act 1952, s. 7(1).

145 Prison Rules 1999, r. 14.

146 J.A. Beckford and S. Gilliat-Ray, *Religion and Prison: Equal Rites in a Multi-Faith Society* (Cambridge University Press: Cambridge) 1998.

147 C. Bakalis and P. Edge, 'Sentencing the Religious Defendant: The Constraints of the European Convention on Human Rights', *European Human Rights Law Review*, Vol. 5 (2009) 659–69.

group as a whole may discourage religious people from championing the spiritual requirements of their co-religionists in prison.

Given the vulnerability of the prison population (one tragic illustration of which is that 82 prisoners in England and Wales took their own lives in 2014, of whom 14 were aged between 18 and 24[148]), the provision of chaplaincy services should be a key concern for society as a whole, especially when for a variety of reasons minority faith groups may find it challenging to advocate the needs of community members behind bars.

C. Sacraments and religious duties Church of England clergy have a duty to baptise any infant from within their parish if such a service is requested.[149] They may not refuse on the grounds that the parents themselves are neither baptised nor believing.[150]

Furthermore, as García Oliva argues, there is a generally accepted – although not an academically unquestioned[151] – right,[152] vested in all citizens to be married in their parish church or a church with which they have a qualifying connection.[153] Clergy undoubtedly have a number of canonical duties[154] towards couples in respect of pastoral care and legal formalities surrounding marriage: they must explain to the couple the nature of the obligations which they are undertaking, for example,[155] and enquire about any impediments to the marriage.[156]

As with baptism, this right is not contingent upon belief or practice. Church of England clerics are not required to be *impressed* about marrying Atheists who want picturesque churches on their wedding photos, but they are obliged

148 'Prison Suicide Rate at Highest since 2007 Figures Show', *The Guardian* (22 Jan 2015), http://www.theguardian.com/society/2015/jan/22/prison-suicide-rate-82-deaths.

149 Church of England, Canon B 22(4).

150 There may be complications where there are disputes between those who exercise parental responsibility for the child (Children Act 1989, s. 2). The Clergy Terms of Service require respect for secular law, so the provisions of the Children Act 1989 should be heeded. Canon law dates from a time when it was understood that, in the case of married parents, the father had complete authority, and similarly that an unmarried mother was free to act as she saw fit. However, modern family law now places the emphasis on children's rights rather than adult rights, and parental responsibility is given by statute to further the child's best interests. Clergy should check that adults bringing children for baptism have the legal authority to make decisions on their behalf. If a cleric has reason to doubt this, or is aware of a dispute between those with parental responsibility, then he or she may be justified or even required to withhold the sacrament. This is not about policing the beliefs or conduct of the adults involved, but about upholding what secular law has laid down to protect vulnerable minors.

151 N. Doe, *The Legal Framework of the Church of England* (Oxford University Press: Oxford) 1996, 358–62.

152 Subject to the exceptions discussed below. In strict terms, it is a right to marry someone of the opposite gender to your birth gender provided that neither party has been previously married. In any other circumstance, the position is more complex.

153 García Oliva, n. 107 above, 496; see also Marriage Measure 2008.

154 Church of England, Canon B 30-B36.

155 Church of England, Canon B 30.

156 Church of England, Canon B 33.

to do the task. Again, it can be seen that establishment is a burden, as well as a benefit. It is hard to imagine that the majority of other faith groups would welcome the powers which the Church of England has in relation to marriage, in exchange for an obligation to conduct ceremonies for all comers of whatever faith or outlook. Indeed, such an arrangement would be repugnant to the doctrines of many groups.

It is also controversial that the *right* to marry in an Anglican church is not extended to divorced persons, those who have changed their gender or same-sex couples. In the case of the former two categories, individuals may marry *if* the clergyperson responsible is willing to assist, which is clearly a very different position. Same-sex couples are at present entirely excluded until such time as the Church of England sees fit to alter its policy. So, it cannot be claimed that all citizens have a right to marry in all circumstances according to the rites of the Church of England.

The canonical provisions relating to carrying out funeral services are more inclusive. Essentially, there is a duty upon clergy to bury the corpse or ashes of any deceased person within his or her cure, or on the relevant electoral roll.[157] There are some historical exceptions, allowing for variation in the wording of a service where the deceased was unbaptised, committed suicide while of sound mind, was excommunicated for some notorious crime without evidence of repentance, or a variation is requested by the next of kin or legal representative of the deceased.

In their modern application, the exceptions should be interpreted as enhancing pastoral care, rather than applying stigma. The canon effectively acknowledges that there might be reasons why an Anglican burial might be desired, but with some elements omitted at the request of the deceased's loved ones, and in so far as doctrinally possible this may be accommodated with appropriate permissions. The wording also recognises that suicide is frequently tied up with mental illness, or such extreme emotional anguish as to impair judgment and, even where this is not the case, the bereaved may have particular feelings and needs which should be taken into account.

The provisions relating to a notorious criminal are very rarely used, but it is possible to imagine circumstances in which the Church of England would not deny a human being made in the image of God a funeral service, while omitting some of usual wording might be appropriate in light of the feelings of victims or their families. Consider, for example, the position had the crimes of Jimmy Savile come to light prior to his funeral and had he been an Anglican.

2.3.2.2.3 OVERVIEW OF ESTABLISHMENT IN ENGLAND

All things considered, we are not suggesting that the way in which the legal system deals with religion in an English context is completely perfect or free

157 Church of England, Canon B 38.

from controversy. There are clearly voices within society that would question the appropriateness of bishops in the House of Lords, or the favouring of Christianity within the provision for collective worship within state schools, for example. Nevertheless, in our view, on the whole, the system is not demonstrably oppressive or exclusive towards non-Anglicans.

The existence of establishment *per se* is not problematic from the point of view of human rights in a European context. In fact, it has been clarified that as far as the European Union is concerned, it is certainly permissible to have a national Church, as is evidenced by the treaties of Amsterdam and Lisbon.[158] Of course, after Brexit our dependence on these sources remains to be seen, but they will still be applicable for the time being. Academic commentators such as Ahdar and Leigh[159] have defended a soft model of establishment as convention-compliant in relation to the European Convention on Human Rights, and the Strasbourg Court itself came to the same conclusion that the Swedish national Church (prior to disestablishment) was acceptable.[160] It is also the case that other signatory states (such as Denmark) retain national Churches. Furthermore, the Danish Church plays a far greater role in the affairs of the state.[161]

2.4 Wales

2.4.1 Wales – the social context

As set out earlier, the general census data laid out above for England encompasses both England and Wales. However, broken down there are some key distinctions which should be noted.[162] Fifty eight per cent (1.8 million) of residents of Wales described themselves as Christian in 2011, which was a 14 percentage point drop from the previous count in 2001. This was a larger decrease than was recorded for any of the regions within the neighbouring England. Furthermore, nearly one third (32% – 983,000) of the population in Wales stated they had no religion in 2011, which again exceeded the figure for any area in England.

The representation of minority religions was also considerably less,[163] although Islam again came in as the second largest faith, accounting for 1.5% of those who responded. Tantalisingly, the next biggest religious identity came out as 'Other'.

158 Declaration of November 10, 1997 on the Status of Churches and Non-Confessional Organisations [1997] OJ C340/133 (appended to the Treaty of Amsterdam). See also the Lisbon Treaty 2007.

159 R. Ahdar and I. Leigh, *Religious Freedom in the Liberal State* (Oxford University Press: Oxford) 2005, 127. There is now a more recent edition of this book.

160 *Darby v Sweden* (A/187) (1991) 13 EHRR 774, [45] (ECtHR).

161 In fact, the Church of Denmark is directly controlled by the state through the Ministry of Ecclesiastical Affairs, and its indirect influence is arguably more relevant.

162 Office for National Statistics, '2011 Census: Key Statistics for Wales, March 2011', http://www.ons.gov.uk/ons/rel/census/2011-census/key-statistics-for-unitary-authorities-in-wales/stb-2011-census-key-statistics-for-wales.html.

163 Ibid., Table 2 'Religion', http://www.ons.gov.uk/ons/rel/census/2011-census/key-statistics-for-unitary-authorities-in-wales/stb-2011-census-key-statistics-for-wales.html#tab--.

It is tempting to consider some of what this 'Other' basket may have contained. There may well be representatives of smaller Dharmic faiths such as Jainism, as well as other ancient religions or spiritual systems,[164] such as Zoroastrianism or Shinto. There is also ample evidence of more modern religious movements being active in Wales, such as Mormonism[165] and Neo-Pagan groups.[166]

Furthermore, it is equally possible that some of those ticking this box were doing so as a form of creative protest. The 'Church of the Flying Spaghetti Monster' movement has reached the United Kingdom. It claims to be a genuine religion rather than a joke,[167] although outsiders often assert it to be a deliberate parody of religion. Certainly, it seeks to protest about what its members perceive to be harmful practices carried out on the basis of faith, such as giving creationism space within the school teaching curriculum. In 2015 a Mr Ian Harris attempted to assert his right to have his official driving licence photo taken wearing a colander.[168] Although Harris was based in Brighton, the movement is active in Wales.[169]

Therefore, it may well be the case that the 'Other' category contains a wide variety of very different positions on faith and accompanying social attitudes. Equally, as was the case in England, a significant section of the population simply declined to answer (7.6%). Once again, it is impossible to know the religious views of those within this category. Therefore, taken together, almost 8% of the Welsh population are without an ascertainable religious identity, but rejected the option of selecting 'no religion'.

Of the other minority faiths, Hindus and Buddhists each accounted for 0.3%, and Sikhism and Judaism were also both recorded as representing 0.1% of the Welsh population. So, overall, it can be seen that Wales is a diverse society in terms of religious belief, but that minority faiths account for a smaller slice of the pie than across the English border.

It is also critical to note that many complex subdivisions lie behind the majority 'Christian' label. As we have seen in the previous chapter, in the nineteenth century the Anglican Church was deeply unpopular and lost vast swathes of ground to the various Non-Conformist denominations.[170] However, the Anglican

164 Describing Shinto as a 'belief system' is problematic, in light of the absence of doctrine: see S. Ono, *The Kami Way* (Tuttle Publishing: Singapore) 1962.

165 The Church of Jesus Christ and the Latter Day Saints, United Kingdom and Ireland, 'Locations', http://lds.org.uk/locations.

166 The Pagan Federation, Mid-West and Wales, http://www.paganfed.org/index.php/pagan-federation-districts/midwest-wales-pf.

167 Church of the Flying Spaghetti Monster, http://www.venganza.org/about.

168 'Meet the Spaghetti Worshipper Battling the DVLA to Wear a Colander on his Head on his Driving Licence', *Wales Online* (7 Apr 2015), http://www.walesonline.co.uk/news/wales-news/meet-pastafarian-member-church-flying-8997070.

169 Facebook, The Church of the Flying Spaghetti Monster Wales, https://www.facebook.com/pages/The-church-of-the-Flying-Spaghetti-Monster-Wales/1486947134916477.

170 G.E. Jones, *Modern Wales: A Concise History* (Cambridge University Press: Cambridge) 1994, 274.

Church remained the biggest single denomination and, rather than disappearing on disestablishment, declined at a slower rate than its dissenting counterparts, leaving it still as the largest Christian group within the Welsh nation.

2.4.2 Wales – the legal context: when is an established Church not an established Church?

In terms of the general legal framework, most provisions apply to both England and Wales.[171] We shall, therefore, not repeat the discussion set out above, as all of the examples given of the law treating religion as a positive phenomenon are as relevant in the Welsh context as they are in on the other side of the border.

As has already been recorded, the Church of England within Wales was disestablished by legislation in the twentieth century.[172] Therefore, the features of high establishment disappeared in relation to Wales. However, many of the crucial features of low establishment were retained, to the point that it seems justifiable to refer to the Church as 'quasi-established'.

There are, undoubtedly, some legal differences. For example, in Wales there is no requirement for a Church in Wales representative on the SACRE in an educational context,[173] although given the frequency with which Church in Wales representatives in fact sit on such Committees this may be an exception which proves the rule. Nevertheless, as has been noted above, marriage law and education law operate for Wales on essentially the same basis as they do in England. The arrangements for prison chaplains which were introduced in 1952 treated Wales as a national Church long after the disestablishing Act.[174]

Also, many of the informal features of establishment apply in Wales as much as they do across Offa's Dyke. So when there is a cause for either mourning or celebration, the Anglican Church will often be the focal point and Church in Wales clergy will frequently be required to take a leading role. For example, when a young girl tragically disappeared in the small town of Machynlleth, the local church held a candlelit vigil, and other churches, including Bangor Cathedral, opened prayer books.[175]

The Church provided the community with a physical and spiritual space in which to express its hope and fear, and enabled people to come together in a time of crisis. In theory, any other building or institution could have been the vehicle for this, but in practice it was the Church which fulfilled this function.

Disestablishment in Wales has addressed what for contemporaries were understood to be real injustices, but what has been the practical impact of severing the ties, especially given the quasi-establishment relationship that has continued?

171 For a detailed discussion of the background and explanation for this, see T.G. Watkin, *A Legal History of Wales* (University of Wales: Cardiff) 2007.

172 Welsh Church Act 1914.

173 Education Act 1996, s. 390.

174 Prisons Act 1952.

175 'Candlelit Vigil for April Jones in Machynlleth', *Wales Online* (3 Oct 2012), http://www.walesonline.co.uk/news/local-news/candlelit-vigil-april-jones-machynlleth-2019746.

Clearly, the Anglican Church within Wales is not subject to any control from secular authority; it may govern itself as it pleases without needing Parliament to endorse or ratify its decisions. The downside of this, of course, is that it lacks the capacity to enact provisions that take effect directly in secular law.

This lack of capacity can cause problems when the Church in Wales finds itself falling between the two stools, having the duties of an established Church but lacking its legislative powers. For example, the Marriage Measure 2008 drastically widened the eligibility criteria for marriage in a particular parish, and it became possible for couples to get married in a church by virtue of a 'qualifying connection',[176] which was defined more broadly than residence or status as a regular worshipper. In effect, it became easier for people to get married in what they regarded as their 'family church', even though they were not resident within the parish boundaries or in the habit of attending on a Sunday.

The snag, however, was that the Church of England could not and did not legislate for Wales, which left Wales stuck with the previous regime. The problem was eventually resolved by an Act of Parliament, introduced in the House of Lords as a private members' bill by Lord Rowe Beddoe.[177] However, in the interim, the Church in Wales as a faith organisation was left in a sticky situation: clergy were faced with explaining to aggrieved brides and grooms that the arrangements that applied to their friend or cousin in Bristol or Shrewsbury were not available to them, and, of course, the population of Wales as a whole was disadvantaged by being deprived of the more relaxed regime enjoyed by their English neighbours. It was not a situation which affected only practising Anglicans in the Welsh nation.

However, the flipside of the coin is that it would have been problematic on a number of levels for Parliament to interfere with the system in Wales without a request from the Welsh Church. It would defeat the point of the disestablishing Act itself if the legislature acting of its own accord simply changed the rules by which the Church in Wales was required to operate, and it is conceivable that the Church might not have wished to widen the number of weddings it was likely to perform for couples with no professed commitment to its practice or doctrines.

176 Marriage Measure 2008, s. 1(3). A qualifying connection with a parish exists if: '(a) that person was baptised in that parish (unless the baptism took place in a combined rite which included baptism and confirmation) or is a person whose confirmation has been entered in the register book of confirmation for any church or chapel in that parish; (b) that person has at any time had his or her usual place of residence in that parish for a period of not less than six months;(c) that person has at any time habitually attended public worship in that parish for a period of not less than six months, (d) a parent of that person has during the lifetime of that person had his or her usual place of residence in that parish for a period of not less than six months or habitually attended public worship in that parish for that period; or (e) a parent or grandparent of that person has been married in that parish'.

177 C. Fairbairn, Parliamentary Briefing Paper, Marriage (Wales) Bill [HL] Standard Note SN/HA/05347 (3 Mar 2010), http://researchbriefings.files.parliament.uk/documents/RP13-8/RP13-8.pdf.

The problem could have been averted by better consultation in advance. Indeed, the stage at which Parliament considered the Church of England Measure would have been the obvious opportunity to ascertain the views and wishes of the Church in Wales. That would have been a more reliable resolution than the pragmatic, sticking-plaster solution of the Church finding a friendly peer to introduce appropriate legislation.

Arguably, therefore, the real problem was not with the system as such, but the manner in which it was operated. One justification for Parliament supervising the legislative capacity of the Church of England is to monitor the impact of changes on the legal system as a whole. A more satisfactory process was applied in relation to the passage of the Same-Sex Marriage Act. In that instance the unique position of the Church in Wales was considered before the bill became law,[178] and the legislation built in provision for Wales to have the same freedom as England to decide whether and when to marry same-sex couples, without the need for a further Act of Parliament.[179]

Another anomaly left behind by legislative disestablishment, and which applies equally (although for different historical and ecclesiological reasons) to the Scottish nation, is the absence of spiritual representatives for Wales in the House of Lords. As will be discussed further in Chapter 5, one of the arguments in favour of retaining Church of England bishops in the Upper Chamber is that they provide a voice for a specific geographical region, whereas other peers do not.

Clearly, whether any or all of these points is sufficient to outweigh the considerations *against* having bishops in the House of Lords is a debate to which we shall return. However, for the present moment, it is simply worth noting that there are some discernible benefits for the community beyond the Anglican Church in having bishops in Parliament, and in the modern system these benefits are conferred only upon the English nation.

Taking the Welsh context as a whole, it might be argued that it both benefits and suffers from being neither fish nor fowl.[180] Many of the features of low establishment are in place, and the Church is available to provide services to those who wish to receive them (in the form of, for example, wedding ceremonies, funerals and associated pastoral care), but at the same time the Church is free from constraints in terms of its internal governance, and its role in civic or governmental occasions is exercised by mutual consent, rather than right.

In general terms, this fluidity is positive, but it is complicated by the retention of certain establishment obligations, which persist in the absence of accompanying

178 UK Government, 'Marriage (Same-Sex Couples) Act – A Factsheet', https://www.gov.uk/government/publications/equal-marriage-documents-explaining-our-policy; D. Cornock, 'Church in Wales Exempt from Same-Sex Marriage Law', *BBC News* (11 Dec 2012), http://www.bbc.co.uk/news/uk-wales-politics-20682574.

179 Marriage (Same Sex Couples) Act 2013, s. 8.

180 For a full discussion of vestiges of establishment in canon law context, see T.G. Watkin, 'Vestiges of Establishment: The Ecclesiastical and Canon Law of the Church in Wales', *Ecclesiastical Law Journal* Vol. 2, No. 7 (1990) 110–15.

legal powers. The practical difficulties caused by this can generally be worked around if both Church and state remain alert to possible issues, as was the case with the passage of the Marriage (Same-Sex Couples) Bill. However, if both sides fumble or drop the ball, as happened with the Marriage Measure 2008, practical problems arise and there are no streamlined legal mechanisms in place to deal with them (for instance, a procedure whereby the Church in Wales could request Parliament to legislate to harmonise its position with new arrangements arising from a Church of England measure).

The complexity of this situation is illuminating in terms of Church/state relations more widely. There is a real risk of focusing too much on labels and too little on substance. Whether or not a system is termed 'established' or a Church is acknowledged and labelled as a 'national' Church can be a debate which develops talismanic status, but at the same time obscures the reality of what is happening.

When examined closely, as previously stated, the majority of European regimes are 'co-operationist' in the sense that governmental authorities collaborate at a legal and practical level with what has been historically the dominant religious denomination within the jurisdiction. Whether or not the arrangements are characterised as 'establishment' is a secondary question to the issue of how the state's legal structures function in practice for citizens of all faiths and none.

It is also an inescapable truth that no legislature has magical powers and fairy dust, and the historical and cultural slate can never be wiped clean. Consider, for example, the conspicuous failure of the Soviet regime in Eastern Europe to eradicate the influence of both Orthodox and Roman Catholic Christianity.[181] Even brutal and oppressive measures could not achieve this, much less legal developments which would be compliant with the European Convention on Human Rights.

The quasi-established nature of the Church in Wales is a powerful reminder that the legal and political debate around the place of religion within constitutional structures needs to be nuanced if it is to relate to the real world. Rather than placing different states in separate categories, it might be more helpful to see them in terms of being at different points on a continuum. To imply that there is an ontological difference between a separatist and a national Church regime, at least when both are embedded within liberal democracies, is to over-egg the philosophical pudding. When all of the regimes provide mechanisms in order to facilitate and accommodate joint working in some spheres between state authorities and religious bodies, the distinction is one of degree, rather than kind. Wales illustrates that legal disestablishment of the Church of England would not necessarily give rise to immediate social disestablishment.

181 J. Anderson, *Religion, State and Politics in the Soviet Union and Successor States* (Cambridge University Press: Cambridge) 1994.

2.5 Scotland

2.5.1 Scotland – the social context

The 2011 census data for Scotland[182] revealed a picture that was significantly different from that of England and Wales. Once again, there were some frustrating and tantalising gaps, even allowing for the limitations of a broad-brush approach. Nevertheless, it is clear that some useful insights can be gleaned.

Overall, 56.3% of the population identified themselves with some form of religion, whereas 36.7% opted for 'no religion'. Again, a significant number of people chose not to answer the question. The final figure for non-respondents was 7%, which is striking given that the largest non-Christian minority religion (Islam) accounted for only 1.4% of Scots. It is impossible, of course, to know what the chosen religious identity of those non-respondents would have been, but if a large percentage of them were from one particular faith group, their inclusion would have changed the data dramatically.

Similarly, the statistics for the other non-Christian religious groups were as follows:

- Buddhist – 0.2%
- Hindu – 0.3%
- Jewish – 0.1%
- Sikh – 0.2%
- Another religion – 0.3%

Once again, had a large number of the 'Another religion' group identified with a specific choice had it been available to them (such as Neo-Paganism or Zoroastrianism), this would have produced a significant change in the appearance of the figures. However, while speculating about these matters might be intriguing, in the absence of alternative evidence it is not very fruitful.

In relation to Christianity, 32.4% identified as Church of Scotland, 15.9% Roman Catholic and 5.5% Other Christian. Therefore, at first glance, it appears that Scotland is a more secular society than that of England and Wales. However, it is important to appreciate the diversity within Scotland. There are undoubtedly a significant number of Scottish people who live in communities where the religious demographic makes a dramatic contrast with the national average.

For example, on Barra and Vatersay[183] 68% of the population identified as Roman Catholic, 13.2% as Church of Scotland and only 11.2% as having no religion. Nevertheless, on the nearby Isle of Lewis only 3.2% of the population

182 Scottish Government, 'Summary: Religious Group Demographics', http://www.gov.scot/Topics/People/Equality/Equalities/DataGrid/Religion/RelPopMig.

183 Comhairle nan Eilean Siar, '2011 Census Barra and Vatersay Key Statistics', available via http://www.cne-siar.gov.uk/index.asp?tabindex=1.

identifies as Roman Catholic.[184] Therefore, the experience which a person living in Scotland will have of his or her religious context will be entirely dependent upon their geographical location. While, as we have seen, there has been a dramatic move towards secularisation across the Scottish nation as a whole, there are places where the picture is radically different. The same point is true in relation to whether individuals will be in a religious minority or majority in terms of their immediate surroundings. Arguably, all generalisations are dangerous, but generalisations concerning religion and Scotland are especially so.

2.5.2 Scotland – the legal context

2.5.2.1 General provisions within the legal framework (the Outer Doll)

As is the case in England, the established national Church in Scotland is only a very small part of the way in which religion is dealt with by the state legal framework. There are many provisions which, although distinct, largely parallel the position in England.

2.5.2.1.1 CRIMINAL LAW

For example, the law relating to assault also generally precludes consent as a defence for anything other than a 'minor injury'.[185] Despite this, ritual male circumcision is permitted as it is south of the border, for both adults and children.

There are also some distinct attributes of the Scottish legal system – for example, the crime of 'violation of sepulchres',[186] which forbids the disinterment of human remains after burial. Although not explicitly religious, the existence and survival of this offence has strong religious connotations. As Ferguson and McDiarmid argue,[187] it cannot be justified on the basis of proscribing behaviour which causes or threatens harm to a living person. Its roots lie in the affront to sensibilities, not just of the loved ones of the deceased, but of the wider community.

We do not, after all, routinely criminalise actions which might cause distress to the bereaved. There are no effective criminal or civil provisions in Scotland (or indeed England and Wales) which protect the reputation of the dead; in fact, newspapers, social media and other fora are routinely vehicles for sharing gossip, insults and lurid speculation about the recently departed. Yet the act of interfering with a corpse evidently has a cultural and spiritual dimension to it, which places it in a different category of conduct.

Although the offence of violating sepulchres evolved largely to deal with the problem of body-snatchers, who plied their trade to supply medical professionals

184 Comhairle nan Eilean Siar, '2011 Census Lewis Key Statistics', available via http://www.cne.siar.gov.uk index.asp?tabindex=1.

185 P. Ferguson and C. McDiarmid, *Scots Criminal Law: A Critical Analysis* (Edinburgh University Press: Edinburgh) 2nd edn, 2014, 305.

186 Ibid., 439.

187 Ibid.

and their students with specimens, it nevertheless still has application and approval in the modern era. In 2004 two teenagers broke into the tomb of Sir George McKenzie in Greyfriars Kirkyard, hacked the head off a corpse and played with their trophy, using it like a glove puppet and to simulate a sex act.[188] When they were tried and sentenced to probation, their conviction received widespread approval and some voices, including the Scots Tory leader at the time (David McLetchie MSP), questioned whether they should have received a harsher sentence.[189] There is consequently still support for legal provisions which criminalise violation of the sacred in Scots law.

2.5.2.1.2 CHARITY LAW

Again, the position here parallels that of England. Scottish charities are subject to different legislation[190] and have their own regulator[191] (the Scottish Charity Regulator as opposed to the Charity Commission),[192] but it is still the case that the advancement of religion is a charitable purpose, and that the regulator adopts a generous approach to assessing public benefit.[193]

2.5.2.1.3 EDUCATION LAW

The legal and social backdrop in Scotland is, in some respects, very different from that of England, although still supportive of religion. It is important to note at the outset that the context is very different from that south of the border. Government statistics in December 2013 showed that out of 370 state-funded faith schools, there were 366 Roman Catholic, three Episcopalian and one Jewish.[194] It is also interesting to note that this was against the background of 2,569 schools in Scotland. In contrast to England, where the majority of faith schools are Church of England, the overwhelming majority north of the border have a denominational character which was in historical terms at odds with the national Church.

However, it must be remembered that the Church of Scotland has a special position in relation to education, and has done so since 1872. Church of Scotland representatives are still present on local authority education committees; the

188 'Corpse Ghouls Walk Free', *The Scotsman* (23 Apr 2004), http://www.scotsman.com/news/corpse-ghouls-walk-free-1-1009541; K. Scott, 'Boys Avoid Jail for 'Violating' Tomb and Beheading Corpse', *The Guardian* (24 Apr 2004), http://www.theguardian.com/uk/2004/apr/24/ukcrime.scotland.

189 'Corpse Ghouls Walk Free', ibid.

190 Charities and Trustee Investment (Scotland) Act 2005; Charities Accounts (Scotland) Regulations 2006.

191 See pages 60–62.

192 OSCR Scottish Charity Regulator, 'About OSCR', https://www.oscr.org.uk/about/about-oscr.

193 OSCR Scottish Charity Regulator, 'Meeting the Charity Test, Guidance: the Advancement of Religion', https://www.oscr.org.uk/charities/guidance/meeting-the-charity-test-guidance/c-the-advancement-of-religion

194 Scottish Government, 'Schools, Frequently Asked Questions', http://www.gov.scot/Topics/Education/Schools/FAQs.

Church takes this role very seriously, and issues detailed guidance on how it should be carried out.[195] The Roman Catholic Church also has a representative on these committees, along with a 'third representative', who reflects the interests of other Churches and denominations in the area.[196] Therefore, religious, and specifically Christian, voices do have a privileged opportunity to contribute to policy-making and debate.

In non-denominational schools, pupils receive 'religious and moral education', rather than 'religious education', although pupils attending Roman Catholic schools do receive 'religious education'. However, in both contexts, there is emphasis on respect, embracing diversity and social cohesion.[197] Having had a past scarred by sectarianism, government policy aims to help in fostering an inclusive and positive society for the present and future Scottish nation.

However, it would be misleading to present a picture of complete harmony and contentment. For example, guidance for teaching the 'Health and Wellbeing' element of the curriculum relating to Relationships, Sexual Health and Parenthood Education[198] permits faith schools to deliver their own material in place of government-produced resources, and allows individual teachers to opt out. On the one hand, this is a powerful indication of the respect which Government shows for religious freedom in the implementation of 'soft law', but on the other it has drawn criticism and hostility from both the Humanist Society Scotland and LGBT campaign groups.[199]

Permitting state-funded faith schools inevitably causes difficulties when the doctrines of the faith groups running them are at odds with the values of the state. This is, if anything, thrown into even sharper focus when one denomination in particular dominates the educational landscape.

Another controversial area of religious accommodation relates to home education. Although different legislation applies, the practical position is essentially the same as that in England and Wales: Scottish parents have a duty to ensure that children of compulsory school age receive full time education, but not necessarily in a school setting.[200] The same dilemmas and questions arise in this context as have already been rehearsed above in respect of England. For present purposes,

195 The Church of Scotland, 'The Church of Scotland and Education: A Guide to Good Practice for Church of Scotland Representatives on Local Authority Education Committees', http://www.churchofscotland.org.uk/speak_out/education/articles/the_church_of_scotland_and_education.

196 The position of these three religious representatives comes from the Local Government (Scotland) Act 1973, s. 124, and the Local Government (Scotland) Act 1994, s. 31.

197 Education Scotland, 'Religious and Moral Education', https://education.gov.scot/parentzone/learning-in-scotland/curriculum-areas/Religious%20and%20moral%20education.

198 Scottish Government, 'Conduct of Relationships, Sexual Health and Parenthood Education in Schools' (11 Dec 2014), http://www.gov.scot/Publications/2014/12/8526/downloads.

199 N. Duffy, 'Scotland: Faith Groups can Opt Out of New Guidance Teaching Gay Relationships', *Pink News* (13 Dec 2014), http://www.pinknews.co.uk/2014/12/13/scotland-faith-schools-can-opt-out-of-new-guidance-on-teaching-gay-relationships.

200 Education (Scotland) Act 1980, ss. 28, 30 and 35.

the key point is that parents enjoy considerable latitude in providing education for their children in a faith-environment of their choosing.

2.5.2.1.4 FAMILY LAW

Given its troubled religious history, Scotland has suffered from sectarian conflicts, particularly as between Roman Catholics and Protestants, for longer than most communities in England. It speaks volumes that one of the 'frequently asked questions' in relation to church weddings is whether one party being a Roman Catholic will be a barrier to a church wedding.[201] Even though the Presbyterian Church gives an assurance that it will not, and that official structures on both sides of the denominational divide are striving to heal the wounds of the past, the very fact that the issue must still be specifically referenced and addressed is telling.

As recently as 2012, legislation was passed to try to deal with anti-social sectarian behaviour at football matches.[202] Falsone asks whether the ambit of this offence has been adequately considered, either by the legislature or Church bodies, and whether it could effectively function as a kind of renewed blasphemy law.[203] In our view, the key point for present purposes is not whether the legislation is well or badly conceived, but the function which it is intended to fulfil. As would be expected, it criminalises equally offensive and inflammatory behaviour regardless of the direction in which the traffic of abuse is flowing. In other words, Presbyterians insulting or intimidating Roman Catholics would be equally caught.

The move can be seen as an attempt not only to foster social cohesion, but also to vindicate the right of individuals to live in safety and comfort with their faith identity. Religion itself is being defended, rather than attacked, by the provision. Once again, faith is seen to be accepted by the legal framework as a positive asset, and one which can be legitimately promoted for the common good.

2.5.2.2 Establishment (The Inner Doll)

The Church of Scotland Act 1921 contained a schedule of 'Articles Declaratory of the Constitution of the Church of Scotland'.[204] The status and effect of these articles is set out in s. 1 of the statute,[205] providing for a clear division

201 The Church of Scotland, 'Frequently Asked Questions, Marriage', http://www.churchofscotland.org.uk/__data/assets/pdf_file/0019/2449/guide_marriage.pdf.

202 Offensive Behaviour at Football and Threatening Communications (Scotland) Act 2012.

203 A. Falsone, 'Redundant Crimes of Blasphemy in Scotland', *Ecclesiastical Law Journal*, Vol. 16, No. 2 (2014) 190–7.

204 The Church of Scotland, 'Church Constitution', http://www.churchofscotland.org.uk/about_us/church_law/church_constitution.

205 'The Declaratory Articles are lawful articles, and the constitution of the Church of Scotland in matters spiritual is as therein set forth, and no limitation of the liberty, rights and powers in matters spiritual therein set forth shall be derived from any statute or law affecting the Church of Scotland in matters spiritual at present in force, it being hereby declared that in all questions

of authority. The Church of Scotland is to be free from temporal powers interfering in spiritual matters.

The complete autonomy of the Kirk and freedom from state interference in all matters spiritual is expressly set out, in particular, in Articles IV, V and VI.[206] Article III makes it clear that the state is not *granting* this independence to the Church, but acknowledging the independence which has existed since the Scottish Reformation:

> This Church is in historical continuity with the Church of Scotland which was reformed in 1560, whose liberties were ratified in 1592, and for whose security provision was made in the Treaty of Union of 1707. The continuity and identity of the Church of Scotland are not prejudiced by the adoption of these Articles.[207]

of construction the Declaratory Articles shall prevail, and that all such statutes and laws shall be construed in conformity therewith and in subordination thereto, and all such statutes and laws in so far as they are inconsistent with the Declaratory Articles are hereby repealed and declared to be of no effect.'

206 Church of Scotland Act 1921, Schedule, Articles IV, V and VI:

'IV This Church, as part of the Universal Church wherein the Lord Jesus Christ has appointed a government in the hands of Church office-bearers, receives from Him, its Divine King and Head, and from Him alone, the right and power subject to no civil authority to legislate, and to adjudicate finally, in all matters of doctrine, worship, government, and discipline in the Church, including the right to determine all questions concerning membership and office in the Church, the constitution and membership of its Courts, and the mode of election of its office-bearers, and to define the boundaries of the spheres of labour of its ministers and other office-bearers. Recognition by civil authority of the separate and independent government and jurisdiction of this Church in matters spiritual, in whatever manner such recognition be expressed, does not in any way affect the character of this government and jurisdiction as derived from the Divine Head of the Church alone, or give to the civil authority any right of interference with the proceedings or judgments of the Church within the sphere of its spiritual government and jurisdiction.'

'V This Church has the inherent right, free from interference by civil authority, but under the safeguards for deliberate action and legislation provided by the Church itself, to frame or adopt its subordinate standards, to declare the sense in which it understands its Confession of Faith, to modify the forms of expression therein, or to formulate other doctrinal statements, and to define the relation thereto of its office-bearers and members, but always in agreement with the Word of God and the fundamental doctrines of the Christian Faith contained in the said Confession, of which agreement the Church shall be sole judge, and with due regard to liberty of opinion in points which do not enter into the substance of the Faith.'

'VI This Church acknowledges the divine appointment and authority of the civil magistrate within his own sphere, and maintains its historic testimony to the duty of the nation acting in its corporate capacity to render homage to God, to acknowledge the Lord Jesus Christ to be King over the nations, to obey His laws, to reverence His ordinances, to honour His Church, and to promote in all appropriate ways the Kingdom of God. The Church and the State owe mutual duties to each other, and acting within their respective spheres may signally promote each other's welfare. The Church and the State have the right to determine each for itself all questions concerning the extent and the continuance of their mutual relations in the discharge of these duties and the obligations arising therefrom.'

207 Church of Scotland Act 1921, Art. III.

The Articles are phrased in the present tense, making it clear that they are descriptive, rather than proscriptive of change. They use the language of rights in relation to the Church and its governance, and Article IV expressly states that the Church receives its 'right and power, subject to no civil authority' to govern itself in spiritual matters from Christ, its Head. In other words, its rights come from God, not from the grant of any human monarch or legislature. Therefore, the separation between Church and state is key to the Church of Scotland.

It is legitimate to question whether a Church so expressly free from all forms of state control is indeed established in the conventional sense of the term. It is a question which Cranmer[208] has addressed and, as his piece acknowledges, much turns on what is meant by establishment in a Scottish context. Again, there is the danger, referred to above, of allowing the ship of discourse to drift onto unproductive sandbanks, and get stranded on an essentially circular debate about labels and terminology. Cranmer is wise to be alert to this peril. It is clearly possible to mould the definition of establishment to include or exclude almost any given context, but this does not move the dialogue forward.

One important feature of Scottish establishment was noted by Lyall,[209] – namely, that civil authorities look to Church authorities for involvement with suitable ceremonial occasions. As Cranmer observes, Lyall is at the end of the spectrum of opinion which questions the appropriateness of applying the term 'establishment' to the Scottish context, a point of view which is shared by McClean.[210]

However, McClean's basis for rejecting the establishment principle in the modern Scottish context is that it does not resemble the civil provision of religion in terms which Calvin would have recognised and, therefore, does not amount to an established Church within the reformed theological understanding. Having said that, there is a huge leap from stating that the Presbyterian Church has a reformed theology of sacraments to concluding that the political understanding of a sixteenth-century pastor should be the determinative factor in characterising the contemporary Church of Scotland. Whether or not the Church of Scotland is established in the terms of the UK legal framework is a different matter from whether it matches up to Calvin's ideas about state religion.

Nevertheless, it is striking that the feature of establishment which Lyall cites could equally well be ascribed to the Anglican Church in Wales.[211] Despite having been disestablished by statute, it often functions as the established Church on civic

208 F. Cranmer, 'Scottish Independence and the Establishment Principle', *Law and Religion UK* (19 May 2014), http://www.lawandreligionuk.com/2014/05/19/scottish-independence-and-the-establishment-principle.

209 F. Lyall, 'Church and State (Legal Questions)', in Dictionary of Scottish Church History and Theology (T&T Clark : Edinburgh) 1993, 180.

210 M.A. MacLean, 'The Church of Scotland as a National Church', *Law & Justice*, Vol. 149 (2002) 12.

211 On civic occasions the Church in Wales is still often the denomination invited by secular authorities to lead ceremonial activities. See, for example, J. Flynn, 'Welsh Medics who Received Gallantry Medals in WW1 to be Honoured in Ceremony', Wales Online (15 Apr 2015), http://www.walesonline.co.uk/news/local-news/welsh-medics-who-received-gallantry-9048653. In this instance, the Anglican Archbishop led the service, which was attended by the Duke of Gloucester.

occasions, moments of national or local tragedy or celebration. Therefore, this characteristic alone cannot evidence a fully fledged, established Church within the UK legal framework.

However, Munro[212] makes a persuasive case for interpreting the Church of Scotland as both established and free, arguing cogently that it is difficult to construe the 1921 Act as a disestablishing measure, either in the understanding of the time or with the benefit of historical perspective. Bearing in mind that the ratification of the Church by the Scottish Parliament in 1592 effectively established it as a national Church, and the Treaty of Union of 1707 guaranteed security of its status, it is difficult to claim convincingly that it could be disestablished without an express and clear legislative statement to that effect.

We concur that the mere fact that establishment in Scotland takes a very different form from that in England does not signify that it is not 'true' establishment, as all relationships between religious authorities and states are the unique product of a particular series of legal and cultural developments.

It may be enlightening at this point to consider some of the features of establishment within Scotland. For the purposes of analysis, the division between high establishment features (those elements of establishment which played out on the national, political stage) and low establishment features (those which touch upon the everyday lives of citizens) may be useful.[213]

However, it should be stressed that, as with so many features of Church/state relations, the boundary between these is blurred. For example, are high-profile services attended by political figures, business and community leaders, which the Church is expected to host and preside over, instances of high or low establishment? Consider the memorial service held on the 25th anniversary of the Pipa Alpha disaster, for instance. This took place in St Nicholas Kirk[214] in Aberdeen and was attended by figures such as Alex Salmond, representatives of the oil and gas industry, and, of course, the victims' families and friends.[215] Was that a sign of high or low establishment?

2.5.2.2.1 HIGH ESTABLISHMENT

The Queen appoints her Lord High Commissioner to act as her representative at the General Assembly of the Church of Scotland.[216] However, it is crucial to note that the Royal Representative is present as an observer, and not as a participant in the proceedings. The symbolism is doubled-edged. On the one hand, there

212 C. Munro, 'Does Scotland Have an Established Church', *Ecclesiastical Law Journal*, Vol. 4, No. 20 (1997) 639–45.

213 See the analysis in Carr, n. 108 above.

214 This church actually has membership of the United Reformed Church, as well as the Church of Scotland, an arrangement expressly permitted and indeed encouraged by Art. VII of the Articles Declaratory, n. 204 above.

215 'Piper Alpha Memorial Service Takes Place', *STV News* (8 July 2008), http://news.stv.tv/scotland/30409-piper-alpha-memorial-services-take-place.

216 The Church of Scotland, 'General Assembly', n. 117 above.

is a public demonstration of the link with the monarchy and the Church, but the silence of this figure is also a visible reminder that the authority which he or she represents does not have the right to an active involvement within the spiritual business of the Kirk. Although presented in courteous terms by the modern Church, the Lord High Commissioner arguably has a role which in some ways is akin to Black Rod at the State Opening of the Westminster Parliament,[217] who summons the House of Commons to hear the Queen's Speech, and symbolically has the door slammed in his face. There is an element of the performance which suggests that royal authority may extend so far, but no further.

In addition to the Lord High Commissioner's role, sometimes the General Assembly will invite a distinguished visitor to give an address, which may be used as a symbolic platform for communicating with the Scottish nation. For instance, in 1999 the then Chancellor, Gordon Brown, used it as an opportunity to set out his philosophy for international debt reduction.[218] Margaret Thatcher gave what was to become known as 'The Sermon on the Mound', and Archbishop Desmond Tutu has also been invited to speak. Although less formal than the Lord High Commissioner, the potential for an address before the General Assembly to reach a wide audience and to be interpreted as an opportunity to speak to Scotland as a whole might be construed as a feature of high establishment.

However, because the division between spiritual and temporal power is crucial to the self-understanding, and indeed the statutory basis of the Church of Scotland, there is no feature of high establishment akin to the representation of bishops in the UK Parliament, or the legislative links between Church and state (for instance, the procedure for approval of measures by Parliament before they can pass into law).[219] Neither Westminster nor the Scottish Parliament have a say in the approval of legislation of the Church of Scotland.

It should also be noted for completeness that the Church courts have been acknowledged by the Court of Session to be courts of the land.[220] However, because of the Church's autonomy in spiritual matters, the civil courts have no appellate or supervisory role in relation to them.[221]

2.5.2.2.2 LOW ESTABLISHMENT

Like the Church of England, the Church of Scotland has a parish structure, and is understood to have both an obligation and a right to minister in every community within the nation.[222] Church of Scotland clergy are treated differently from

217 UK Parliament, 'Black Rod', http://www.parliament.uk/about/mps-and-lords/principal/black-rod.

218 The Church of Scotland, 'General Assembly', n. 117 above.

219 Church of England Assembly (Powers) Act 1919.

220 *Presbytery of Lewis v Fraser* (1874) IR 888.

221 For a detailed discussion of these issues see F. Cranmer, 'Judicial Review and Church Courts in the Law of Scotland', *Denning Law Journal*, Vol. 13, No. 1 (1998) 49–66.

222 The Church of Scotland, 'How We Are Organised', http://www.churchofscotland.org.uk/about_us/how_we_are_organised.

other ministers in relation to marriage law, being entitled to solemnise marriages as of right, whereas other clergy require an approval procedure.[223]

However, it is interesting to note that the Church of Scotland is in a very different position from that of the Church of England in relation to marriage. Although respected commentators like Doe[224] have questioned this, the general social and academic consensus, as expressed by García Oliva[225] and others, is that all citizens in England have the *right* to be married in the parish in which they are resident or with which they have a 'qualifying connection' as defined by statute.

In stark contrast, the Church of Scotland undertakes that parish clergy will enter into a discussion with anyone living in their parish boundary to discern whether a church ceremony is appropriate in their circumstances.[226] In other words, citizens have a right to request a wedding ceremony, but not to demand one.

A similar pattern applies where baptism is concerned, and again this is in contrast to England where Anglican clergy must baptise any child within their parish presented to them. The Church of Scotland (at least in theory) restricts this sacrament for infants to circumstances where at least one parent or other close family member is a church member or willing to become one.[227] As a compromise position, the possibility of a service of thanksgiving and blessing is offered to all children, regardless of the confessional status of the adult family members.[228]

However, in relation to funerals the Church takes a radically different view, and adopts a compassionate 'open-door' policy in response to the needs of all citizens:

> Through its parish system and territorial ministry the Church of Scotland seeks to serve all the people of Scotland and not just the membership of the Church. Nobody in the situation of bereavement should hesitate to seek the services of the parish minister, either directly or through the undertaker.[229]

The Church of Scotland also has a special role in relation to education. Since the state assumed the responsibility for education in 1872, the Church has been granted the statutory privilege of having representatives on local authority

223 Marriage (Scotland) Act 1924, s. 18.
224 Doe, n. 151 above, 358–62.
225 García Oliva, n. 107 above, 496. See also Marriage Measure 2008.
226 The Church of Scotland, 'Frequently Asked Questions, Marriage', n. 200 above: 'The Church of Scotland is "national", in that every district has its parish church. The parish minister is willing to discuss conducting marriage for any member of the parish. If you are not a church member, the minister will want to discuss with you whether a religious ceremony is what you are looking for, whether it will have meaning for you, and whether he or she agrees it is appropriate in your situation'.
227 For the church law on this, see General Assembly 2000 Act 5, Sacraments Consolidating Act.
228 The Church of Scotland, 'Life Events', http://www.churchofscotland.org.uk/connect/life_events.
229 Ibid.

committees dealing with education,[230] which was in recognition of the role that the Church has historically assumed in relation to education. Although the guidance which the Church publishes deals with the need to provide some Christian input into the discussion and decision-making process, and a special interest in religious and moral education, it also demonstrates an ongoing commitment to furthering the provision of high quality education across the board (such as tackling barriers to literacy). Again, this is an example of the Church embracing a pastoral duty towards the nation as a whole, and an endeavour to assist in promoting the collective interest, rather than just the welfare of its members.

A more problematic arena, however, is undoubtedly in relation to equality legislation. It is here that there is perhaps the greatest potential for conflict between Church and state, and a perception that the terms of the 1921 Act may be threatened even in the twenty-first century. In order to understand this, it is necessary at this point to consider the Percy case – a seismic legal event which sent shock waves beyond employment law. We consider it in this context primarily for its relevance to state involvement in the governance of the Church.[231] A female minister was accused of having an affair, and complained that she was treated differently and more harshly by the Church than male ministers who had found themselves in a similarly sticky situation. She brought an action in the secular courts. Although the House of Lords rejected the argument that she was an employee in the sense of having a civil employment contract, they nevertheless concluded that the terms of the Sex Discrimination Act 1974 were applicable.

However, the fact that the Court determined that it had jurisdiction to hear the case at all was controversial. There were two stumbling blocks: (i) the ongoing and vexed question as to whether religious ministers can be employees in legal terms, and (ii) the Church of Scotland Act 1921.

Lord Nicholls affirmed that the Church had exclusive jurisdiction over spiritual matters, but declared that a sex discrimination claim was not a spiritual matter:[232]

> A sex discrimination claim would not be regarded as a spiritual matter even though it is based on the way the Church authorities are alleged to have exercised their disciplinary jurisdiction. The reason why a sex discrimination claim would not be so regarded is that the foundation of the claim is a contract which, viewed objectively, the parties intended should create a legally binding relationship. The rights and obligations created by such a contract are, of their nature, not spiritual matters. They are matters of a civil nature as envisaged by section 3 . In respect of such matters the jurisdiction of the civil courts remains untouched.

230 The Church of Scotland, 'The Church of Scotland and Education: A Guide to Good Practice for Church of Scotland Representatives on Local Authority Education Committees', http://www.churchofscotland.org.uk/speak_out/education/articles/the_church_of_scotland_and_education.

231 *Percy (AP) v Church of Scotland Board of National Mission* [2005] UKHL 73.

232 Ibid., per Lord Nicholls, para. 40.

Lord Hope came to essentially the same conclusion,[233] as did Lord Scott.[234] Baroness Hale expressly doubted that it was likely that Parliament had intended to grant the Church of Scotland special immunity denied to other religious groups when it passed the 1975 Act outlawing discrimination on grounds of sex.[235] In our view, this must logically be the correct conclusion, as the purpose of the 1921 Act was to protect the Church of Scotland from interference in matters of spirituality and doctrine, not to grant it special immunity from litigation denied to other religious bodies.

McClean and Peterson[236] interpret this decision as an erosion of the protection offered by the 1921 Act, before going on to discuss the *Rennie* controversy as a further example of the dangers posed. In this instance, a dispute arose over the appointment to a parish of a minister who was in a committed homosexual relationship. In the end, the matter was resolved in favour of the appointment by a vote of the General Assembly, but McClean and Peterson maintain that, had the minister lost, there would have been potential for him to appeal to the secular courts. If they had accepted jurisdiction, the autonomy of the Church in spiritual matters would have been attacked.[237]

In our view, this concern is misplaced, partly for reasons which McClean and Peterson draw out of their own analysis of the situation. They are looking at the question of entrenchment within the UK Constitution, and arguing that an abandonment of a Diceyan view in favour of an understanding of UK parliamentary democracy, which permitted a legislature to bind its successors, would be valuable. The merits of this specific argument are not within the scope of this study, although, as Cranmer argues,[238] conflicts about the placement of homosexual ministers within the Church of Scotland raise legal and constitutional issues beyond the clash of individual rights being assessed. McClean and Peterson present the following argument:

> Up to this point we have identified three types of conflicts. First are the *Ladele* and *Begum* cases, where individuals' religious interests conflict with an employer or a school; second, the instances of Greenshields and Scottish Episcopalians Act, in which non members of a religion or denomination are protected (free exercise). Third is government intervention in a religious denomination, as happened in the Church Patronage (Scotland) Act, 1712, the Prayer Book Crisis of 1927–28, and the Percy and, potentially, Rennie cases (the parameters of establishment).[239]

233 Ibid., per Lord Hope, para. 133.
234 Ibid., per Lord Scott, para. 138.
235 Ibid., per Baroness Hale, para. 152.
236 I. McClean and S. Peterson, 'Entrenching the Establishment and Free Exercise of Religion in the Written U.K. Constitution', *International Journal of Constitutional Law*, Vol. 9, No. 1 (2011) 230–50, 244.
237 Ibid., 245.
238 F. Cranmer, 'Human Sexuality and the Church of Scotland: Aitken et al v Presbytery of Aberdeen', *Ecclesiastical Law Journal*, Vol. 11, No. 3, (2009) 335–9.
239 McClean and Peterson, n. 236 above, 246.

They go on to assert that the first category may appropriately be dealt with by the secular courts on the basis of the provisions of the Human Rights Act 1998 and a case by case approach to proportionality. They contrast this with the second two categories, which are best dealt with on the basis of entrenched legislation and are less susceptible to changing political tides or powerful interests of the moment.

Irrespective of the merits of the entrenchment argument, the existence of the first category (and to a certain extent the second and third categories as well) demonstrates that there *are* spheres in which secular courts should quite properly involve themselves in spiritual matters. Furthermore, in our view, it would be desirable in a Scottish context, and indeed in most others, if the establishment status played no part in determining whether or not a matter came within the ambit of secular jurisdiction.

2.5.2.2.3 OVERVIEW OF ESTABLISHMENT IN SCOTLAND: REFLECTIONS ON THE 1921 ACT – A SIEVE, NOT A BASIN

The historical development of the Church of Scotland discussed above led up to the 1921 Act and the Articles Declaratory because there had been, throughout the last few centuries, persistent and justified grievances about the executive and legislative power of the secular state interfering with the governance of the Church. A succession of (primarily Westminster-based) regimes attempted to control patronage and worship within the national Church of Scotland and members of the Kirk resisted this, even to the point of self-sacrifice and martyrdom.

However, it is neither reasonable nor acceptable to suggest that the 1921 legislation should shield the Church from *all* state intervention and, presumably, few commentators would advocate this. Were the Church of Scotland to decide that because of a shift in doctrine, all female ministers should be dismissed and deprived of any financial compensation, it is unlikely that many voices would deny that the state had a right and a duty to intervene.

The reality is that the 1921 Act should function as a sieve, and shift out any attempted interventions which are being made *because the Church has a special relationship with the state*, but it is not a basin which should catch *all* proposed interventions of the secular courts. It would not be in keeping with the light and flexible understanding of contemporary Scottish establishment. Furthermore, for the Kirk to enjoy special immunity from state intervention in its life would not be easily defensible in terms of respecting the religious diversity within Scottish society and the liberties of individual citizens. The Church of Scotland should not be accorded any privilege in this way not extended to other faith groups.

There is an ongoing debate about when the state should properly involve itself in the conduct of religious groups. Commentators like Rivers argue that the United Kingdom is moving in an increasingly secular direction, and is in danger of allowing collective religious freedoms to be eclipsed by too great a focus on individual rights,[240] while voices like Vickers suggest that society and secular

240 J. Rivers, 'The Secularisation of the British Constitution', *Ecclesiastical Law Journal*, Vol. 14, No. 3 (2012) 371–99.

courts are required to give due weight to all interests at stake where clashes of rights occur, and that collective religious concerns must not be given more than their fair share of consideration.[241]

> Rivers does not fully explore the metaphorical weight of other interests with which religion is competing, such as equality, and so his model would seem to leave equality interests somewhat under-protected.

We would argue that however these disputes are resolved, national Churches should be in the same position as other religious denominations. Clearly, because of their unique relationship with the state and place in national life, these Churches are special and different, but difference should not amount to privilege. For instance, the same principles that determine whether Methodist or Sikh clergy can bring a claim for unfair dismissal should apply to the Church of Scotland. There are legitimate questions with no easy answers as to how far faith groups should be exempt from equality legislation, or indeed have the perk of side-stepping ordinary employment law for what would otherwise be contractual breaches unrelated to spiritual matters (such as the failure to provide a safe working environment, freedom from harassment, and so on). How these questions are answered cannot and should not turn on whether the faith group has a 'special status' as a national Church.

The beliefs of the group may matter – for instance, in terms of parties' intention to enter into a contract binding in secular law,[242] – and these beliefs may be found in part in documents such as the Declaratory Articles. In these kind of cases, however, they should be treated no differently from a document such as the Roman Catholic Code of Canon Law. Any other approach would be to give the Church of Scotland a statutory 'Get Out of Jail Free' card not available to other faith groups, and also to prejudice its ministers and members by potentially denying them the jurisdiction of the secular courts.

2.5.2.2.4 CONCLUSIONS ON THE SCOTTISH MODEL OF ESTABLISHMENT

As noted above, Munro described the Church of Scotland as established but free, and this assessment has some merit[243] because the bonds between Church and state are looser than those in other establishment regimes. Despite interesting academic attempts to suggest that *any* national Church is problematic and even contrary to international law,[244] the unquestionable truth is that the Court of Strasbourg has confirmed the legitimacy of such legal arrangements, and the point

241 L. Vickers, 'Twin Approaches to Secularism: Organized Religion and Society', *Oxford Journal of Legal Studies*, Vol. 32, No. 1 (2012) 197–210.

242 *JGE v Trustees of the Portsmouth Roman Catholic Diocese Diocesan Trust* [2012] EWCA Civ 938.

243 Munro, n. 212 above.

244 J. Temperman, 'Are State Churches Contrary to International Law?', *Oxford Journal of Law and Religion*, Vol. 2, No. 1 (2013) 119–49.

is not really moot.[245] The question is really whether the specific arrangements in Scotland are desirable and beneficial for Scottish society.

It can be argued convincingly that a flexible and light touch establishment, which does not disadvantage those of other faiths and none, is benign, rather than destructive.[246] The role of the Church provides some tangible advantages to society as a whole (for instance, in relation to its work in education and the platform available to address the General Assembly).

Ironically, the only area of concern lies in relation to the freedom from oppression which it fought so bravely and tenaciously to maintain. It is important that this should continue to function to shield the Church from state interference, but not to give it an added layer of protection from litigation not available to other faith groups. To do so would indeed unjustifiably disadvantage those outside the Church and, in some cases, those within it as well. Subject to this proviso, however, the current arrangements appear in our view to function positively in many respects.

2.6 Assessment of the current position in Britain as a whole

As the discussion above shows, each of the three component nations within our study has a unique pattern of Church/state relations, the imprint left by its own particular shared cultural journey. However, all three are embraced within the Russian doll paradigm that we have set out. The constitutional and legal system of Britain as a whole treats religion as a positive phenomenon, acknowledges the special cultural place of the Christian faith in particular and maintains a unique position for the three established/quasi-established denominations.

However, before moving on with our study and testing the desirability of the favourable view of religion in Great Britain, by analysing the compatibility of the legal framework with its constitutional foundations (such as the rule of law and parliamentary supremacy), it is important to consider the scope of the religious dimension to the juridical system, and also some of its criticisms.

2.7 The protective limitations of the religious dimension to the legal framework and Constitution

Having characterised the Constitution and the legal system in Great Britain as religious, it is important to state clearly what this characterisation is, and is not intended to mean. It is vital to be precise about both: (i) the scope of our academic claim, and (ii) the scope of the third layer of this suite of religious characteristics. How far does the positive treatment extend?

245 Darby v Sweden, n. 160 above, [45].

246 For a positive assessment of public religion in general, see R. Trigg, *Religion in Public Life: Must Religion be Privatised?* (Oxford University Press: Oxford) 2007.

2.7.1 The scope of our academic claim

Our thesis is that, as a matter of observation, the Constitution and legal framework treat religion as a positive phenomenon in the sense of promoting and enabling its practice. There is effectively a soft presumption in favour of facilitating religious activity unless contraindicated by other factors. As already discussed, we do not assert that this is the result of any deliberate political policy; rather, it is the product of the way in which the system has evolved.

Even more crucially, however, we do not set out in the course of this book to argue that in abstract, philosophical terms, religion *is* a positive phenomenon for humankind or the planet we inhabit. Whether or not the practice of religion does more good than harm is a question for academics in disciplines other than law. We both have a religious faith, but the value or danger of religion for our species is not the issue which we are seeking to explore. Instead, we are describing the religious juridical system which is at present operative in Britain, and address the question of whether it is functioning in a way that safeguards fundamental freedoms and fosters social cohesion. Is a framework that treats religion positively (rather than adopting a neutral or even negative stance) enhancing the foundations of our Constitution in the twenty-first century? Is this more conducive towards a cohesive society?

2.7.2 The scope of the third layer – what are the limits of positivity?

It is important not to lose sight of the reality that treating religion as a positive phenomenon, and actively enabling faith-based practices, does not equate to allowing religious considerations to trump all others. It is clearly the case that there are some circumstances in which competing societal needs and rights will outweigh religious claims. Furthermore, there are undoubtedly some manifestations of some beliefs which the legal system rightly categorises as harmful and unacceptable.

The legal framework is sufficiently sophisticated to treat religion as a positive phenomenon in general, while acknowledging that there are certain manifestations of it that must be limited or even forbidden. In this sense, religious practice is no different from other rights that are safeguarded and promoted. For example, freedom of expression is an important value which the Constitution respects, and which Article 10 of the European Convention on Human Rights now explicitly defends. There are nevertheless occasions when the legal system limits freedom of expression: for instance, many types of hate speech are banned expressly,[247] whereas others might be dealt with by way of public order offences.[248] Equally, civil law provides defamation[249] as a means for citizens to seek redress for harmful and false assertions. Consequently, although the legal system is supportive of freedom of expression, this support is not unconditional.

Similarly with religion, not all expressions of religious belief are deemed appropriate or acceptable by the legal system, and some must be restrained, as the following examples illustrate.

247 See, e.g., Racial and Religious Hatred Act 2006.

248 Criminal Justice and Public Order Act 1994.

249 Defamation Act 2013.

Expressions which interfere with the rights of others

Some religious practices and manifestations of belief are restrained because they are inimical to the rights of third parties. Those who wish to engage in commercial activity cannot, generally speaking, discriminate against customers on the basis of their sexual orientation, even if they have a religious motivation in doing so.[250] Similarly, schools may not use faith-based doctrine as a justification for racial discrimination.[251] Furthermore, employers are entitled to limit the religious freedoms of their employees at work, if this is a proportionate means of safeguarding the rights of their fellow workers or clients.[252]

When the prevent duty applies

Specified authorities in England and Wales[253] and Scotland[254] are required by the Counter-Terrorism and Security Act 2015 to have due regard for the need to prevent people from being drawn into terrorism, and government guidance has been issued on carrying this out. This guidance explicitly acknowledges that some extremist religious groups are potentially agents for drawing citizens into terror;[255] therefore, the destructive potential of religion in this context is explicitly highlighted. At the same time, however, it is also recognised that non-religious extremist groups pose a similar threat.[256] Arguably, therefore, the issue is not one of religious ideologies but malign, extremist ideologies, although we do not seek to minimise the danger and destruction caused by some groups in the name of religion.

When the objective best interests of vulnerable people are threatened or compromised

An example is the situation where parents object on religious grounds to 'non-Gillick' competent[257] children receiving medical treatment, which is determined by a court to be in their best interests. Here the legal system will promote the welfare of the child in preference to parental freedoms.[258] Once again, however,

250 *Bull and Another v Hall and Another* [2013] UKSC 73; *Lee v Asher Bakery Co Ltd* [2015] NI Cty 2 (transcription).

251 *R (E) v Governing Body of JFS* [2009] UKSC 15.

252 *Eweida and Others v United Kingdom* [2013] ECHR 37 (ECtHR).

253 HM Government, 'Revised Prevent Duty Guidance: for England and Wales', originally issued on 12 March 2015 and revised on 16 July 2015.

254 HM Government, 'Revised Prevent Duty Guidance: for Scotland', originally issued on 12 March 2015 and revised on 16 July 2015.

255 HM Government, 'Revised Prevent Duty Guidance: for England and Wales', n. 253 above, para. 10; HM Government, 'Revised Prevent Duty Guidance: for Scotland', n. 254 above, para. 7.

256 HM Government, 'Revised Prevent Duty Guidance: for England and Wales', n. 253 above, para. 11; HM Government, 'Revised Prevent Duty Guidance: for Scotland', n. 254 above. para. 10.

257 *Gillick v West Norfolk & Wisbech Area Health Authority* [1986] AC 112. Children who are deemed 'Gillick competent' in relation to a particular decision have the capacity to make that decision, and their parents have no responsibility or right in relation to the issue in question.

258 *An NHS Trust v Child B and Others* [2014] EWHC 3486 (Fam).

it should be noted that the same issues arise where parents object to necessary clinical interventions for ideological reasons which are not faith-based.[259] Although these are instances when manifestations of religious beliefs are quite rightly restrained, it is a question of harm rather than faith which necessitates state action. Both religious and secular beliefs can and do produce identical problems in this regard.

Expressions which conflict with the wider societal interest

As has already been discussed, there are various provisions that criminalise hate speech and aggressive or intimidating behaviour with a specifically religious element.[260] These laws address potential problems of sectarian or interfaith conflict, but they also deal with attacks made by secularists or other non-religious individuals on believers.[261] As a result, religious expressions which fall foul of these laws will be criminalised, but so will equally problematic behaviour with a non-religious motivation.

Similarly, public bodies are under no obligation to collaborate with, or enable, the activities of religious bodies if these conflict with legitimate policies which have been adopted to pursue communal interests. For example, Transport for London was entitled to decline to allow a fundamentalist Christian group to buy advertising space, which would have resulted in offensive, anti-gay messages appearing on the side of London buses.[262] In this instance, support for religious freedom and practice, along with freedom of expression, gave way to concerns about protecting vulnerable groups from intimidation and abuse, and the need to promote equality, diversity and mutual respect within society.

Thus, it can be seen that treating religion as a positive phenomenon and supporting it in general terms does not preclude the legal system from acknowledging that there are some manifestations of religious faith which are extremely negative, and dealing with these robustly. Nevertheless, there are still some commentators, academic and otherwise, who assert that having a legal framework with a religious character is inherently problematic, or who strongly take issue with some key elements of the existing suite of religious characteristics. Before beginning our own analysis of the framework in relation to the constitutional principles or foundations, it is crucial to give some attention to these voices of dissent.

259 See, e.g., *Re JM (A Child)* [2015] EWHC 2832 (Fam); *F v F (Welfare of Children: Immunisation)* [2013] EWHC 2683 (Fam).

260 E.g., see the Racial and Religious Hatred Act 2006 or Offensive Behaviour at Football and Threatening Communications (Scotland) Act 2012.

261 'Atheist Guilty over Cartoons left at Liverpool Airport', BBC News (4 Mar 2010), http://news.bbc.co.uk/1/hi/england/merseyside/8549613.stm; M. Moore, 'Philosophy Tutor in Court for leaving Anti-Religious Cartoons in John Lennon Airport', *The Telegraph* (3 Mar 2010), http://www.telegraph.co.uk/news/religion/7353643/Philosophy-tutor-in-court-for-leaving-anti-religious-cartoons-in-John-Lennon-airport.html.

262 *R (on the application of Core Issues Trust) v Transport for London* [2014] EWHC 2628 (Admin).

2.8 Criticisms of the current framework

In spite of the limitations and safeguards described above, there remain those who legitimately argue that the present legal and constitutional framework does not enjoy a healthy relationship with religion. We shall now consider these notes of caution, dividing them into three categories: (i) academic criticisms at a systemic level; (ii) academic criticisms of specific aspects of the current legal framework – in this section we will include the findings of a recent report by the Woolf Institute[263] – and (iii) criticisms from secularist and Humanist campaign groups.[264]

For the first of these categories we will engage in detailed analysis in this chapter. The nature of these holistic arguments about the overall legal framework means that it is appropriate to deal with them here. In relation to criticisms of specific aspects of the current system, however, we have adopted a different approach. Many of these are considered in subsequent chapters and, where this is the case, we will simply state them and move on in order to avoid repetition. We will only assess the merits of these specific criticisms in detail in the instances where they do not arise elsewhere in the book.

Nevertheless, we considered that it was appropriate to include all of the specific criticisms at this point, if only in the form of a brief mention, as they demonstrate that the debate in which we are engaging is a live one. There are voices at present arguing strongly that our society needs to renegotiate its legal and political treatment of religion. These voices raise principled concerns, which deserve academic attention, including our own.

2.8.1 Academic criticisms at a systemic level

There are commentators at one end of the spectrum who argue that a legal framework which incorporates a state Church (or by implication, state Churches) is not simply a suboptimal arrangement, but in breach of international law. Temperman,[265] in a fascinating and detailed article, advocates a separatist state, claiming that there is an inevitable correlation between establishment and 'governmental favouritism', and that this inherent bias necessarily brings increased restrictions on religious and other liberties. Accordingly, he categorises the concept of 'benign establishment' as a myth.

263 The Woolf Institute, http://www.woolf.cam.ac.uk.

264 In this chapter we have grouped secularist and Humanist organisations together, as both are campaigning in a non-party political sense for reform of the place of religion in public life. However, we should stress that from Chapter 3 onwards, we will place them in separate categories for the purposes of analysis. This is because humanism can be understood as an identity and position in relation to personal religious beliefs. In contrast, secularism is a position in relation to the political structure of the state. An individual could plausibly be a secularist, and desire a secular legal and political system, while personally being a member of a particular religion. We discuss in greater detail in Chapter 3 why we are treating humanism as a form of religious identity/conviction, and what this means for the purposes of our study.

265 Temperman, n. 244 above.

Although strongly argued, there are a number of flaws in Temperman's thesis, the most serious being that his central contention is not tenable: the European Court of Human Rights has definitively pronounced that establishment arrangements are not incompatible with the ECHR.[266] Furthermore, it is difficult to see how it would be viable for international law to truly progress to a point where states were not free to recognise and embrace ties with particular religious groups or traditions. At present there are a number of states with special links to a given faith or faiths, and a very significant proportion of these would have to radically change their position for a new international norm to be imposed.

Furthermore, stating that 'benign establishment is a myth' is not robust enough to stand testing. For it to survive, a clear and uncontroversial definition of establishment would need to be reached. As has already been discussed in relation to Wales, and as will be detailed further below, the terminology here is both key and slippery. Furthermore, as the work of Vazquez Alonso[267] demonstrates, there is a great deal of complexity and variety across different paradigms of separatism.

Nieuwenhuis[268] cogently argues that there are many layers to Church/state relations, and that the traditional models for describing them are too rigid and simplistic to be serviceable.

The borders between establishment, co-operationism and separatism are in reality fluid. Formal disestablishment in Wales has made little difference in many legal contexts. Therefore, an academic case attacking establishment risks is nothing more than an assault on a label, and a poorly defined and understood label at that. While Temperman in fairness does acknowledge a degree of complexity in the application of the traditional models, if the boundaries between them are understood to be fluid and perhaps even illusory, it is hard to locate the foundation for his objections.

Even if this issue is set aside, Temperman struggles to substantiate the claim that establishment *necessitates* favouritism. Some incarnations of establishment are pluralist and inclusive by nature. For example, Alsace-Moselle is a pocket of the French state insulated from the general principle of *laïcité*.[269] As it was annexed by the German Empire when the law of separation between Church and state was adopted in 1905, it survived as a relic of the Napoleonic Concordat of 1801. The Concordat recognised four religious traditions – Judaism, Roman Catholicism, Lutheranism and Reformed Protestantism – and the arrangements in that context never sought to promote a single cultural and religious paradigm as the norm for citizens. Given the difficulty in defining, and indeed reshaping, ties between states and religious bodies and also the multiplicity of forms which

266 *Darby v Sweden*, n. 160 above, [45].

267 V. Vazquez Alonso, *Laicidad y Constitución* (Centro de Estudios Políticos y Constitucionales: Madrid) 2012.

268 A. J. Nieuwenhuis 'State and Religion, a Multidimensional Relationship: Some Comparative Law Remarks', *International Journal of Constitutional Law*, Vol. 10, No. 1 (2012) 153–74.

269 Vie Publique: Au coeur du débat public, 'Les exceptions au droit de cultes issu de la loi de 1905', 24 May 2015, http://www.vie-publique.fr/politiques-publiques/etat-cultes-laicite/droit-local-cultes.

these ties take, it is not really sustainable to condemn establishment as a concept. It is more useful to consider whether establishment relationships in particular contexts are functioning in an acceptable and even beneficial manner for citizens of the jurisdiction in question.

There are similar problems with generality and rigidity of categories in the case put forward by Laborde.[270] This author argues that the notion of a separatist state was based upon a structural template provided by religion, and that the Euro-Atlantic concept of a separatist state is based upon the double protection of the state from religion and religion from the state. Effectively, this thesis presents the mirror image problem to that of the definition of establishment. What is a 'separatist' state, and are the ways in which particular separatist legal systems interact with religious groups, including those with cultural dominance, markedly different from other co-operationist or establishment regimes?

Of course, we do not suggest that these labels are meaningless and, in fact, we have spent a considerable amount of time explaining our understanding of Great Britain as a religious and established legal framework. However, we would question their utility in the abstract, because in reality all secular states are the products of their own unique and complex historical journey, and to apply a universal narrative would be counterproductive. In our current study, we are not presuming to assert that secularism is harmful and that establishment is benign. We are interested in examining the concrete question of whether or not the current religious characteristics of the British state are a help or a hindrance to our constitutional foundations and social cohesion.

Domingo[271] presents a nuanced case. He does not argue that establishment is necessarily and invariably problematic in legal or philosophical terms, but he makes it clear that his preference would be for a disestablished model. For Domingo the priority is to create a dualist structure, in which both the political and religious communities keep to their proper sphere. He acknowledges that this is possible within an establishment regime, such as Britain, but considers a separation between Church and state to be preferable.

His argument is rooted in the unique nature of religious belief and interests. Domingo asserts that religion is supra-rational, and therefore beyond the extrinsic limit of secular law in the same way in which land is beyond the extrinsic limit of the sea: 'By granting the religious exception, the secular legal order acknowledges the existence of another dimension of the human being and the priority of human dignity over political sovereignty'.[272] On this basis, his case is that secular legal systems should protect the right to religion and recognise that it is something distinct from other constitutional liberties.[273]

270 C. Laborde, 'Equal Liberty, Non-Establishment and Religious Freedom', *Legal Theory*, Vol. 20, No. 1 (2014) 52–77.

271 R. Domingo, 'The Constitutional Justification of Religion', *Ecclesiastical Law Journal*, Vol. 18, No. 1 (2016) 14–35.

272 Ibid., 35.

273 R. Domingo, 'Religion for Hedgehogs? An Argument against the Dworkinian Approach to Religious Freedom', *Oxford Journal of Law and Religion*, Vol. 2, No. 2 (2013) 371–92.

Interestingly, Domingo does acknowledge that religion has a part to play in the political arena, which he sees as broader than the legal sphere. Furthermore, he is critical of the French model of *laïcité*, seeing it as failing to protect the religious rights of citizens, and, as noted above, Domingo is open to the possibility that an establishment framework such as that found in Britain might be capable of delivering the kind of dualist protection which he desires. Having a special link between the secular authorities and a particular religious group does not, in his eyes, automatically preclude achieving an appropriate dualism.

Domingo is by no means unique in questioning establishment, but also rejecting secularism. In fact, Bhandar is explicitly critical of the British paradigm, but regards the French model as being no better.[274] In Bhandar's view, the British concept of multiculturalism is functionally biased towards a Christian world view, because it emerged from an intellectual and cultural context which was shaped by Christianity. However, she also regards French *laïcité* as having the same philosophical roots, and claims that this has a negative impact on Muslim women and girls who wish to veil themselves. Bhandar's case is original and creative, but its foundations are questionable. First, she fails to substantiate the assertion that British multiculturalism and French secularism were forged in the same *Christian* intellectual crucible. It is an academically arguable contention for two reasons.

To begin with, Christian philosophical sources were not the only intellectual fuel for the Enlightenment fire and the cultural developments which followed it (which include both French secularism and British multiculturalism). Classical writers were a powerful influence for almost all Enlightenment figures,[275] as Latin and Greek were a required feature of education at the time. Furthermore, some significant contributors to the Enlightenment were from non-Christian religious backgrounds: for example, Spinoza[276] and Ricardo[277] were both Jewish.

Moreover, simply because two streams of intellectual thought shared some of the same origins, this does not mean that they are not capable of having diverged and become dramatically distinct. To make a convincing case, Bhandar would need to set out reasons why modern French secularism still bears the 'taint' of Christian thought. In what identifiable ways can its present conception of citizenship be traced to Christian ideas? Bhandar must implicitly acknowledge the significance of divergence from a point of common origin if her own overall thesis is to be applicable, given that Christianity and Islam have a lot of shared heritage.

Yet, even in so far as multiculturalism and secularism have been influenced by Christian thought patterns, Bhandar does not demonstrate why this has been problematic or what should be done about it. Her thesis appears to be

274 B. Bhandar, 'The Ties That Bind: Multiculturalism and Secularism Reconsidered', *Journal of Law and Society*, Vol. 36, No. 3 (2009) 301–26.

275 Consider, e.g., Voltaire (see A. Alridge, *Voltaire and the Century of Light* (Princeton University Press: Princeton) 1975), or Locke (see W. von Leyden (ed.), *Essays on the Law of Nature and Associated Writings* (Clarendon Press: Oxford) 2002).

276 S. Nadler, *Spinoza: A Life* (Cambridge University Press: Cambridge) 1999.

277 D. Weatherall, *D. Ricardo: A Biography* (Martinus Nijhoff: The Hague) 1976.

heavily influenced by her dissatisfaction with the outcome of some disputes concerning veiling, but disappointment for some individuals in some circumstances does not in itself demonstrate that a different system would produce a better outcome for the majority of female Muslims, nor for society as a whole. As would be expected, there is a wide spectrum of opinion among Muslim women, and women of Muslim origin, in relation to human rights, multiculturalism and religious dress codes.[278] Neither all voices from this sector, nor society as a whole, would share Bhandar's perspective, and she produces limited external support for her assertions.

A very different type of systemic criticism comes from Bonney,[279] who argues that prior to devolution the Church of England was in the de facto position of state Church of the United Kingdom as a whole. Given that the devolved Assembly in Wales and the Scotland Parliament have declined to adopt a pattern of parliamentary religion in line with Westminster, this can and should be seen as an implicit criticism of that *modus operandi*. The Welsh and Scottish Assembly/ Parliament declined to adopt the Westminster template because it was unsuited to the twenty-first century, and Westminster should take this as a cue for reform.

Again, it is a colourful and creative thesis, but is based upon too many assertions which are weakly supported. For instance, Bonney argues that the Anglican Church remains allied with the Conservative Party, without providing sufficient evidence to justify this. In addition, the central claim that the Church of England was in the position of being the de facto state Church is open to dispute. Arguably, this issue goes to the heart of what establishment truly means and, more deeply, what it really signifies to have a legal framework with a religious character.

It is true that bishops from the Church of England (in preference to bishops from Wales or ministers from Scotland) preside on state occasions such as coronations and royal weddings. However, do these unusual celebrations truly mean that citizens living in the Outer Hebrides on the Isle of Lewis or Barra, heavily involved with their Free Church or Roman Catholic community, would perceive the Church of England as *their* national Church?

Similarly, Bonney cites the funeral of Princess Diana as an example of the Church of England acting as the 'official' Church for the state as a whole. Yet, this was essentially because the deceased and her family were English and Anglicans. In contrast, at the reburial of King Richard III, which had all of the pomp of a state funeral, representatives from other denominations were included.[280] It is by no means the case that the Church of England takes an exclusive lead on all collective state occasions.

278 See, e.g., H. Elver, *The Headscarf Controversy: Secularism and Freedom of Religion* (Oxford University Press: Oxford) 2012, and A. Hirsi Ali, *Heretic: Why Islam Needs a Reformation Now* (Harper Collins: Glasgow) 2015.

279 N. Bonney, 'Established Religion, Parliamentary Devolution and New State Religion in the UK', *Parliamentary Affairs*, Vol. 66, No. 2 (2013) 425–42.

280 Channel 4, 'Richard III: The Reburial', http://www.channel4.com/programmes/richard-iii-the-reburial.

However, it would be disingenuous to deny the social and cultural weight of the Church of England. Cobb[281] argues for disestablishment on the basis of the damage done to LGBT citizens when a denomination with political privilege and state sanction is predominantly hostile towards the interests of these vulnerable minority groups, particularly in relation to marriage. We must acknowledge that Cobb's essential contentions are solid and difficult to dispute. The Church of England does indeed have a unique degree of cultural influence, and has at an official level adopted an oppositional stance towards inclusive developments such as same-sex marriage.[282] Yet it is significant that Cobb himself recognises that the formal disestablishment of the Church would not in reality be sufficient to neutralise the harmful impact of its public stance in this regard, and his proposal is that in addition to disestablishment, the law of marriage should be replaced by a voluntary adult partnership scheme.

Whether or not this contention about family law is accepted, it is insightful to appreciate that establishment does not exist in a vacuum, but as part of a wider legal and social framework.

It is striking, too, that other commentators have argued that severing the ties of establishment would be liberating not just for the state, but also for the Church. Smith[283] makes this case, as does Engelke,[284] and in the mid-1990s the then Bishop of Woolwich, Colin Buchanan, published a book on this basis.[285] Buchanan was especially concerned with the control which Parliament exercises over the Church and (perhaps a touch ironically) the process of appointment of bishops.

However, it could not be said that this is the majority view, nor that disestablishment is at present being pursued by the Church of England, which on its official website acknowledges and embraces its established position.[286]

2.8.2 Academic criticisms of specific aspects of the current legal framework

Having considered the academic criticisms of the current structure at a systemic level, it is necessary now to turn to objections to specific elements of the present arrangements. Some of the issues raised have already been considered in detail above or will be dealt with in subsequent chapters, so they will not be scrutinised

281 N. Cobb 'The Church of England's Hold Over Marriage: The Queer Case for Disestablishment', in A. Carling (ed.), *The Social Equality of Religion or Belief: A New View of Religion's Place in Society* (Palgrave Macmillan: Basingstoke) 2016, 200–15.

282 J. García Oliva and H. Hall, 'Same Sex Marriage: An Inevitable Challenge to Religious Liberty and Establishment?', *Oxford Journal of Law and Religion*, Vol. 3, No. 1 (2014) 25–56.

283 R. Smith, 'Caesar's Palace, not Lambeth's', *New Law Journal*, Vol. 158 (2008) 229.

284 M. Engelke, *God's Agents: Biblical Publicity in Contemporary England* (University of California Press: California) 2013, Ch. 3 'Kingdom and Christendom'.

285 C. Buchanan, *Cut the Connection: Disestablishment and the Church of England* (DLT: London) 1994.

286 The Church of England, 'A Detailed History', https://www.churchofengland.org/about-us/history/detailed-history.aspx.

in depth in this section. Whereas in the foregoing passage we assessed the validity of the arguments being put forward on the framework as a whole, here we are more concerned to acknowledge and set out the questions about particular provisions and practices.

Furthermore, we are mindful that criticism aimed at a particular problem does not necessarily amount to an expression of doubt about the framework as a whole. Therefore, the views of the following authors should not automatically be interpreted as pressing for the reform of the wider juridical system in relation to religion.

2.8.2.1 Education

In considering issues with the decentralisation of education policy, Harris[287] discusses the teaching/promotion of creationism in free schools and academies as one of the potential areas of controversy. Similarly, in an earlier article he raised the question of religion in schools in relation to issues such as sex education, casting doubt on whether the present system does sufficient to ensure that all of the competing interests are adequately balanced.[288] Both of these matters concern whether the state is seen to be going too far in enabling the religious choices of some parents within the provision of public education, to the detriment of other families and possibly even their own children.

Closely related points are raised by Lundy,[289] who argues that the way in which Britain currently deals with clashes between educational policy and parental/familial beliefs is not compatible with international human rights obligations. Lundy also suggests that the present systemic support for Christianity 'paves the way' for conflict with more fundamental forms of Christianity, non-Christian religion and secular values. Similarly, Evans[290] suggests that plural religious education is the optimal method of complying with human rights in a liberal democracy. Implicit within this perspective is a criticism of current practices in some state-funded schools in the United Kingdom.

Monk takes a slightly different angle, highlighting the past and continuing influences of the Church of England and Roman Catholic Churches in relation to homophobic bullying, their stance on human sexuality being more likely to exacerbate than ameliorate such problems.[291]

287 N. Harris, 'Local Authorities and the Accountability Gap in a Fragmenting Schools System', *The Modern Law Review*, Vol. 75, No. 4 (2012) 511–46.

288 N. Harris, 'Playing Catch-Up in the Schoolyard? Children and Young People's "Voice" and Education Rights in the UK', *International Journal of Law, Policy and the Family*, Vol. 23, No. 3 (2009) 331–66.

289 L. Lundy, 'Family Values in the Classroom? Reconciling Parental Wishes and Children's Rights in State Schools', *International Journal of Law, Policy and the Family*, Vol. 19, No. 3 (2005) 346–72.

290 C. Evans, 'Religious Education in Public Schools: An International Human Rights Perspective', *Human Rights Law Review*, Vol. 8, No. 3 (2008) 449–73.

291 D. Monk, 'Challenging Homophobic Bullying in Schools: the Politics of Progress', *International Journal of Law in Context*, Vol. 7, No. 2 (2011) 181–207.

All of these commentators raise valid and real concerns, but they are all ultimately issues which turn on government social and educational policy. At present, the democratically expressed will of the legislature and executive is to support faith schools and enable parents to make choices about whether their children should have access to some elements of the curriculum in relation to religion and sex education. It should be noted that there is no legal opportunity for parents to veto their child's involvement with these topics in *all* areas of study. If explanations or discussions of these matters are required for a lesson in science or English literature, then there is no right to withdraw.

2.8.2.2 Family law

Interestingly, but perhaps unsurprisingly, in this arena academic commentators adopt radically different views on the approach which the state should take to accommodating and enabling religious practice.

In relation to the parental choices in the upbringing of children, Shelley[292] and Taylor[293] both acknowledge that the state has a legitimate interest in the welfare of children and the right to intervene in family life where this is compromised or threatened. However, they both caution that this should be used sparingly, especially where cultural and religious minorities are concerned. If anything, they characterise the state as too restrictive, rather than too permissive, in relation to religion freedoms.

It is striking that this is in sharp contrast to the perspective of some of the non-academic commentators we shall consider below, who argue that the legality of ritual male circumcision for minors (at least in relation to minors lacking the capacity to consent) is unacceptable.

Similarly, Cohen[294] and Cumper[295] advocate in different ways for a more sensitive form of 'transformative accommodation' – in effect a greater willingness for secular law to make concessions and allow for religious communities to resolve at least some disputes in accordance with their own laws and norms. In common with the authors on parental rights, the suggestion is that, if anything, the current framework is insufficiently open to furthering religious needs. Again, this is at odds with some of the perspectives from non-academic commentators who question the capacity of faith groups to adequately safeguard the interests of women and children.

292 C. Shelley, 'Beating Children Is Wrong, Isn't It? Resolving Conflicts in the Encounter between Religious Worldviews and Child Protection', *Ecclesiastical Law Journal*, Vol. 15, No. 2 (2013) 130–43.

293 R. Taylor, 'Responsibility for the Soul of the Child: The Role of the State and Parents in Determining Religious Upbringing and Education', *International Journal of Law, Policy and the Family*, Vol. 29 No. 1 (2015) 15–35.

294 J. Cohen, 'The Politics and Risks of the New Legal Pluralism in the Domain of Intimacy', *International Journal of Constitutional Law*, Vol. 10, No. 2 (2012) 380–97.

295 P. Cumper, 'Multiculturalism, Human Rights and the Accommodation of Sharia Law', *Human Rights Law Review*, Vol. 14, No. 1 (2014) 31–57.

2.8.3 The Woolf Institute Report[296]

This thought-provoking report was produced by a think-tank dedicated to the academic study of relations between Christians, Muslims and Jews. It organised a commission chaired by Baroness Butler-Sloss, which generated a number of criticisms about the current legal, social and political framework in relation to religion and belief, as well as some suggestions for moving forward. The topics covered were wide ranging, and many of the suggestions are discrete, in the sense that it would be rational to accept one without being convinced by the merits of another. Given that this report attempted a global assessment of religion and belief, we concluded that its findings, most appropriately, belong within the systemic criticisms of the current framework. Nevertheless, as previously noted, the report does make specific, as well as general, recommendations.

All of these issues will be dealt with elsewhere in the course of this book, so for present purposes it is appropriate simply to provide a summary of the most significant proposals. In this section and others we have attempted to set them out succinctly and clearly for ease of reference.

1. Constitutional/legal

(a) The plural character of modern UK society should be reflected in national civil events and ceremonies. The report expressly acknowledges that the Church of England has a role in facilitating this.
(b) Where a religious organisation is best placed to deliver a social good, it should not be disadvantaged (including in relation to law/public funding). Once again, it should be noted that some of the non-academic commentators take a strongly opposing stance in relation to the provision of services by faith groups.
(c) The Ministry of Justice should issue guidance on compliance with UK standards of gender equality and justice by religious courts and tribunals. The report does not indicate whether there should be any sanctions in the event that such tribunals fail to engage with this guidance.
(d) The Ministry of Justice should instruct the Law Commission to review the anomalies in the ways in which the legal definitions of race, ethnicity and religion interact in practice.
(e) In framing counter-terrorism legislation, the Government should promote, rather than limit, freedom of enquiry, speech and expression.

2. Social

(a) A national conversation should be launched on shared understanding and fundamental values, across religious and ethical traditions.
(b) Greater religious and belief literacy is needed and steps should be taken by the Government to promote this.

296 The Woolf Institute, *Report of the Commission on Religion and Belief in British Public Life: Living with Difference – Community, Diversity and the Common Good* (7 Dec 2015), http://www.woolf.cam.ac.uk/uploads/Living%20with%20Difference.pdf.

(c) The BBC Charter should mandate the Corporation to reflect the range of religion and belief in the modern United Kingdom.
(d) A panel of experts on religion and belief should be established to advise the Independent Press Standards Organisation.
(e) Public bodies and voluntary organisations should promote opportunities for interreligious/inter-worldview encounters.

3. Educational

(a) All pupils in state-funded schools should have a statutory entitlement to a curriculum that includes religion, philosophy and ethics. This leaves open the question of the situation of children who are home-educated and in private schools. Is it legitimate for parents to effectively buy the freedom to deny their children what would otherwise be a statutory right? It is also unclear how this statutory entitlement would be reconciled with parental rights and choices about family life.
(b) Bodies responsible for admission and employment in faith schools should take measures to reduce selection of pupils and staff on religious grounds. Again, as with the religious tribunals, there is no indication of what consequence, if any, should be imposed in the event that certain faith schools choose not to comply. Given that their policies will have been determined after some consideration and will be tailored to the wishes of the community they presently serve, there is a high risk in some instances that these suggestions would not be taken up.

2.8.4 Criticisms from lobbying organisations

We will now turn to the points raised by the three largest groups in contemporary Britain, with the express purpose of furthering a secularist or Humanist agenda. In common with the Woolf Institute, each of these groups raise a variety of mutually independent concerns about the current legal and political systems. We shall consider every one of these issues as they arise elsewhere. For the moment, therefore, we will content ourselves simply with acknowledging and summarising the concerns, flagging up some points of divergence and contrast with other voices.

Because each of these groups has its own distinct lists of concerns and points of emphasis, we will set them out in turn. As might be expected, there is some overlap, but there is no universal consensus or viewpoint.

2.8.4.1 British Humanist Association

Disestablishment and secularism[297]

(a) Disestablishment is necessary for a secular state. The British Humanist Association (BHA) explicitly claims that state secularism guarantees the maximum freedom for all members of society.

297 British Humanist Association, 'Campaigns, Secularism', https://humanism.org.uk/campaigns/secularism.

(b) Establishment in England gives rise to and allows many of the inequalities outlined in the BHA's education and human rights campaigns.
(c) The Head of State should not also be Head of the Church.
(d) Bishops in the House of Lords are an example of discrimination, religious privilege and undemocratic politics.

Specific issues within the legal framework

1. Education[298]

The BHA is campaigning to:

(a) end religious discrimination in school admissions;
(b) end religious discrimination in the employment of school staff;
(c) end the expansion of faith schools;
(d) reform the law on assemblies and collective worship;
(e) reform the existing school curriculum, in relation to religion, science (especially in connection with creation and evolution), personal, social, health and economic education (including sex and relationships);
(f) reform existing faith schools so that they can be inclusive schools for the whole community (NB Obviously this is the terminology adopted by the BHA and not that of the authors; in fact, many faith schools would argue that they are already doing exactly this).

2. Human rights[299]

(a) The BHA is campaigning to preserve the Equality Act 2010 in its current form, in terms of resisting any proposal to 'accommodate' currently unlawful behaviour on grounds of conscience.
(b) It has concerns about the use of legal provisions against harassment and incitement on grounds of religion or belief in equality legislation leading to unwarranted free speech restrictions by the back door.
(c) It is campaigning to change UK libel laws to prevent victimisation of scientists, journalists and human rights campaigners.
(d) It will work with others to make legislation less restrictive of valid expressions of free speech, such as liberalising the Public Order Act 1986 in relation to 'insulting' behaviour.
(e) It is campaigning for reform of the regulations and practices which lead bodies such as the Advertising Standards Authority and advisory bodies such as the Committee on Advertising Practice to 'chill' free speech in the name of preventing 'offence' and cause commercial interests to do the same.

298 British Humanist Association, 'Campaigns Schools and Education', https://humanism.org.uk/campaigns/schools-and-education.
299 British Humanist Association, 'Campaigns, Human Rights and Equality', https://humanism.org.uk/campaigns/human-rights-and-equality.

3. Marriage law[300]

The BHA is campaigning for Humanist celebrants to be able to conduct marriage ceremonies in England and Wales in the same way as they currently do in Scotland. They object to the present legal position in which religious people can choose between a religious or civil ceremony, whereas Humanists have a civil service or nothing.

4. Service delivery by faith groups/'Big Society'[301]

(a) The BHA argues that the legal/political framework is developing in ways which exclude Humanists, because of the increased emphasis on working with 'faith groups' as opposed to working with the whole community in the development and provisions of services. This is effectively presented as systemic prejudice against Humanists.
(b) The BHA would like the Human Rights Act to be amended so that religious bodies delivering services on behalf of public sector are treated as public authorities, and for the exemptions in the Equality Act to be suspended when religious bodies are working in this context.

5. Public ethical issues[302]

(a) The BHA campaigns for *assisted dying*, arguing that the current law does not meet the needs of patients or show due regard for individual autonomy. It would like to see assisted suicide to be available for all, and not just the terminally ill. It notes that some religious people believe that the time and manner of death are matters for the deity to decide, and states its rejection of this position. Interestingly, the BHA does not address the complicated arguments against this legal change which have nothing whatsoever to do with religious faith. It is a striking choice to present this as a faith versus Humanism issue, when in reality individuals from within both groups hold opposing, but carefully thought out, positions.
(b) *Abortion*: The BHA campaigns to liberalise abortion law in Northern Ireland.
(c) *Human tissues* (including *stem cells and embryos*): The BHA is not campaigning for any changes to the current law, but sets out its commitment to ensuring that the law is made and developed on rational/scientific lines, and criticises the way in which religious voices tried to have the Human Fertilisation and Embryology Bill amended, accusing them of spreading misinformation.

300 British Humanist Association, 'Marriage Law', https://humanism.org.uk/campaigns/human-rights-and-equality/marriage-laws.
301 British Humanist Association, 'Public Service Delivery', https://humanism.org.uk/campaigns/secularism/public-service-reform.
302 British Humanist Association, 'Public Ethical Issues', https://humanism.org.uk/campaigns/public-ethical-issues.

(d) *Organ donation*: The BHA is campaigning for an opt-out as opposed to an opt-in scheme.
(e) The BHA is campaigning for the NHS to stop funding *homeopathy*, as the evidence is clear that it has merely a placebo effect. It should be noted that the BHA opposed 'irrational' and non-evidenced based beliefs being given publicly funded support, even where such beliefs are not religious or spiritual in nature.
(f) *Animal welfare/ritual slaughter*: The BHA wants to end the religious exemptions allowing kosher and halal slaughter to take place without pre-stunning the animal.
(g) The BHA campaigns on what it characterises as the *genital mutilation of children*. It wishes to outlaw any non-medically necessary procedures for boys and girls. The BHA does not use the words 'ritual male circumcision', but it is clear that this is the only way in which its policy can be interpreted. As noted above, there is a striking contrast between this and the views of many of the academic commentators in the field of family law, who were keen to safeguard the space for parental decision-making, especially in so far as it related to minority groups.

2.8.4.2 Humanist Society Scotland

Disestablishment and secularism

Interestingly, the Humanist Society Scotland (HSS) does not mention this as an issue. This is a situation which must surely reflect the very different shape of establishment north of the Tweed.

Specific issues in the legal framework

1. Education[303]

(a) The HSS campaigns to end religious selection policies for state-funded schools.
(b) It campaigns to end religious appointment policies/exemptions for state-funded schools.
(c) Religious observance (equivalent of collective worship) is no longer predominantly Christian and in 2014 the HSS issued a joint statement with the Church of Scotland calling for religious observance to be replaced by a more inclusive 'time for reflection'.

2. Restricting the right to protest outside abortion clinics[304]

The HSS campaigns to establish 'protest-free zones' around abortion clinics. This is an interesting contrast to the robust view which the BHA adopts in relation to freedom of speech, even where its exercise may affect the vulnerable.

303 Humanist Society Scotland, 'Humanists and Education', https://www.humanism.scot/what-we-do/education.
304 Humanist Society Scotland, 'Female and Reproductive Rights', https://www.humanism.scot/what-we-do/policy-campaigns/female-and-reproductive-rights.

3. Family law[305]

The HSS campaigns to make civil partnerships available to mixed-sex couples.

4. Assisted suicide[306]

The HSS campaigns for law reform allowing assisted suicide.

2.8.4.3 The National Secular Society

Disestablishment and secularism[307]

(a) The National Secular Society (NSS) campaigns for disestablishment for both England *and* Scotland. It sees this as a primary, long-term aim for society. The NSS also supports a 'written'[308] Constitution to help in guaranteeing its secular nature.
(b) The NSS is campaigning for the removal of the *Lords Spiritual*.
(c) *Religious influence in Parliament*: The NSS argues that there is a growing religious influence in Parliament and that a secular government is the only way to ensure equality for all citizens:

> We campaign against the growing influence of religion on Government and the increasing desire of the current Government to involve religious bodies and individuals in the decisions of state, often in the name of multiculturalism or the 'Big Society'. We believe this puts the large minority (maybe even a majority) of the population who are not religious at a disadvantage.[309]

This hostility towards the involvement of faith groups in the provision of services is shared with the BHA.

Specific issues within the legal framework

1. Education[310]

(a) *Faith schools*: The NSS campaigns for an inclusive secular education system in which religious organisations play no formal role, and therefore for the abolition of publicly funded faith schools.

305 Humanist Society Scotland, 'LGBTI Campaigns and Policy', https://www.humanism.scot/what-we-do/policy-campaigns/lgbti-equality.
306 Humanist Society Scotland, 'Assisted Dying Policy and Campaigns', https://www.humanism.scot/what-we-do/policy-campaigns/assisted-dying.
307 National Secular Society, 'Religion and State', http://www.secularism.org.uk/religion-and-state.html.
308 This terminology is adopted by the NSS rather than by us.
309 National Secular Society, 'Religious Influence in Parliament', http://www.secularism.org.uk/religious-influence-in-parliamen.html.
310 National Secular Society, 'Religion and Schools', http://www.secularism.org.uk/religion-in-schools.html.

(b) *Religious education*: It campaigns for reform of the curriculum and the way in which this subject is taught in publicly funded schools (whether or not they are 'faith schools'). Teaching should be neutral and no religious groups should have a privileged position in terms of content or delivery.
(c) *Creationism*: The Society campaigns to eradicate the teaching of creationism in schools, even as an alternative theory to evolution.
(d) *Collective worship*: It campaigns for the requirement for schools to hold acts of worship to be removed.
(e) *Evangelism in schools*: The NSS is concerned about external groups visiting schools with an evangelical agenda, doing pastoral work, setting up clubs, and the like. It argues that the current legal framework, including the obligation to hold collective worship, gives such groups a foot in the door. It campaigns for non-statutory guidance to be issued, making it clear to head teachers that evangelising groups should not be invited into schools.
(f) *Religious selection*: The NSS campaigns for an end to laws which allow publicly funded schools to apply religious criteria in deciding which pupils to admit.

2. Freedom of expression[311]

The NSS actively opposes any changes to national or international law which would have a detrimental effect on freedom of speech, in particular by protecting the sensibilities of religious believers.

3. Human rights and equality[312]

(a) The NSS accepts the general position that Article 9 ECHR is a qualified right and stresses that the right to religious freedom should never be used to justify limiting the human rights of third parties, such as the right of freedom from discrimination.
(b) *Burka/niqab*: The NSS opposes a general ban on wearing these garments and defends the autonomy of the wearer to choose how she dresses. However, it endorses the right of the state to require these garments to be removed when there are legitimate reasons, such as at airports and in courtrooms. The NSS would also support a ban on the wearing of such clothing in schools.
(c) *Caste-based discrimination*: The NSS campaigns for equality law to be widened to cover this form of discrimination.
(d) *Sharia law*: This is the NSS statement on Sharia law (we would stress that it is the view of the NSS rather than our own perspective, but we have included it as it provides a valuable insight into the perspective of this group):[313]

311 National Secular Society, 'Freedom of Expression', http://www.secularism.org.uk/freedom-of-expression.html.

312 National Secular Society, 'Human Rights and Equality', http://www.secularism.org.uk/law-equality-and-human-rights.html.

313 National Secular Society, 'Sharia Law', http://www.secularism.org.uk/sharia-law.html.

Sharia law fundamentally undermines the rule of law in this country and represents a division of rights among racial and religious lines. Muslim women and the children of Muslim parents are particularly vulnerable under this system and our society has a responsibility to protect them.

a. In sharia law, a woman's word is worth half of that of a man. Child custody is awarded to fathers regardless of the circumstances of the case. A man can obtain a divorce by repudiation whereas it is extremely difficult for women to show grounds for divorce, even if abuse or violence has been proved.
b. The European Court of Human Rights in Strasbourg has stated: 'The Court concurs in the Chamber's view that sharia is incompatible with the fundamental principles of democracy, as set forth in the Convention'.
c. We regard it a national scandal that the UK government tolerates, respects, or in any way accommodates a legal system which discriminates so openly against women and children, and we believe it to be a threat to community cohesion and the legal and political equality of all women. As recent legal rulings have shown, religious freedom does not – and should not – include the freedom to overrule the fundamental human rights of others.

(e) *Anti-Muslim bigotry*: The NSS states clearly that it opposes anti-Muslim bigotry, and emphasises that it treats Islam in the same way as all other faiths. However, it believes that a liberal society protects individuals and not ideas, and opposes criticism of damaging ideas rooted in Islam being labelled Islamophobia. For instance, objecting to homophobic views does not equate to Islamophobia.

4. Roman Catholic Church and sexual abuse[314]

The NSS argues that the scale of abuse in Ireland was possible because until recently it was one of the 'least secular' states in Europe, and that secularism could have prevented much of the abuse and suffering.

5. Healthcare[315]

(a) *Hospital chaplains*: The NSS argues that hospital chaplains are a waste of public money, of no clinical benefit and no value of any sort to the majority of patients. If churches, mosques and the like want someone to minister to the needs of their own community, they should pay for it.

314 National Secular Society, 'Clerical Child Abuse', http://www.secularism.org.uk/child-abuse-and-the-catholic-chu1.html.

315 National Secular Society, 'Healthcare', http://www.secularism.org.uk/health.html.

(b) *Female genital mutilation*: The NSS expresses concern that there have been very few prosecutions and no successful ones, and queries why the legal/political system is not doing more to eradicate this practice.
(c) *Male circumcision*: The NSS argues that this should be banned for non-therapeutic reasons.

6. Chancel repair liability[316]

The NSS campaigns for its abolition.

7. Non-stun slaughter[317]

(a) The NSS campaigns for the abolition of exemptions allowing religious groups to slaughter animals without stunning them first.
(b) It also campaigns for proper labelling for as long as non-stun slaughter remains lawful, so that consumers can make an informed choice.

2.9 Interim conclusions and questions for the remainder of our study

As we have seen, the current legal framework has a suite of religious characteristics which justify its classification as religious, and establishment and quasi-establishment represent just one factor in this. The present system has many benefits, but there are those who object both as a matter of principle to a religious legal framework, and to specific manifestations of these religious characteristics. So where does this leave us?

At present it must be acknowledged that there is not a groundswell of popular opinion for disestablishment in England or Scotland, or full disestablishment in Wales, and the subject is not even high on the agenda for debate. In the 2015 and 2017 general election campaigns, none of the major parties highlighted the issue, and it was not a featured, much less a hot, topic of discussion in the media and television debates.

It is true that the subject was at least referred to by the then Liberal Democrat leader, Nick Clegg, in interviews, some time before the 2015 election campaign got under way.[318] Clegg self-identifies as an Atheist and stated that he favoured a 'secular state' which protected all religions, but privileged none. However, this was neither party policy nor a major campaign point, and in any event the Liberal

316 National Secular Society, 'Chancel Repair Liability', https://www.secularism.org.uk/chancel-repair-liability.html.
317 National Secular Society, 'Non-Stun Slaughter', https://www.secularism.org.uk/chancel-repair-liability.html.
318 G. Eaton, 'Clegg Calls for the Disestablishment of the Church of England – and He's Right', *The New Statesman* (24 Apr 2014), http://www.newstatesman.com/politics/2014/04/clegg-calls-disestablishment-church-england-and-hes-right.

Democrat party did not succeed in that particular election. While we are not suggesting that there was any causal connection between this and Mr Clegg's comments, it would be hard to construe a strong popular mandate for anything which the former Deputy Prime Minister put forward during that period.

Even in relation to social and political controversies around religion which have been high profile – for example the so-called 'Trojan Horse' affair (involving allegations of an extreme Islamic agenda being pushed in Birmingham schools[319]) – calls for disestablishment and a secular state have simply not featured strongly in the debate.

Equally, in the contemporary academic world, the primary focus is not on achieving the (un)holy grail of total disestablishment, much less on seeking to pick out all of the many religious elements embedded within the legal framework. Inevitably, there are some issues which are perceived to be unsatisfactory by some commentators, and we would agree that there are without doubt some areas in urgent need of reform. However, our initial contention is that the triune religious nature of the legal framework and Constitution is positive, rather than problematic. Consequently, we would wish to make the following points.

2.9.1 There can be no clean slate: we have to address the reality of our current paradigm

The Constitution is not an Etch-A-Sketch. Unlike with the classic toy, there is no possibility of shaking the Constitution clean and beginning with a wholly new picture on a blank screen. In all three nations, there is an embedded legal, historical and cultural structure which cannot be simply or cleanly removed. Even if it were deemed desirable, in practice it is not possible to clear away all features of the pre-existing Church/state relations by Act of Parliament.

2.9.2 The terminology trap

As the Welsh context demonstrates, in practice establishment or disestablishment is not really a straightforward binary choice. It is possible to get into a lengthy debate about what establishment means and what qualifies as establishment, and it is also equally easy to discuss at length what a separatist constitution looks like, as well as what this would in theory mean for our society. These questions are legitimate, and indeed interesting from an academic point of view but, as we have seen, relabelling will not change the flavour of the jam in the jar. In some sense, all states are in reality co-operationist in nature, and the key issue has to do with the character of co-operation which is embedded within the legal and political system. The real question is whether the kind of co-operationism made manifest by our threefold Russian

319 'Trojan Horse Reaction to Council and Government Reports', *BBC News* (18 July 2014), http://www.bbc.co.uk/news/uk-england-birmingham-28374058.

doll model functions in a way that is positive or negative for our constitutional foundations and social cohesion.

This is not to imply that it is unimportant whether a state collectively chooses to place itself on the establishment or the separatist end of the Church/state relations spectrum. However, it should not be forgotten that there is a spectrum, rather than a series of either/or choices. In practice, there will be features of co-operation between the state and both the historically dominant religious tradition and other faith- and belief-centred groups. The nature of the mechanisms which enable this and the context within which it takes place are more critical than the terminology adopted.

As we shall explore in Chapters 4 to 7, there are many ways in which the legal framework concerning religion and belief,[320] as well as the social contribution of religious and non-religious organisations, have a beneficial effect upon the constitutional foundations of Great Britain. There is no reason to assert that adopting a 'secular' framework would improve the overall situation, confer greater freedoms on citizens, or more effectively foster social cohesion.

As we have already stressed, this is certainly not to imply that the current system is entirely perfect, or that there are not aspects which require reform. There are undoubtedly features of the present framework in urgent need of radical reworking, as will be discussed, and others which merit further assessment and consideration. However, our thesis is that the appropriate changes can and should take part within the current paradigm of a religious Constitution and legal system, and are the latest chapter in a long story of evolution. The role of faith groups and the established Churches has changed, but it remains an important and beneficial role. Rather than operating in an exclusionary manner, the establishment settlement can actually be the basis for a collaborative and inclusive society, in which citizens of all faiths and none can feel equally affirmed and equally well placed to contribute to the common good.

2.9.3 A flashing light: the liminal place of established religion

It is true that one way of viewing the national Churches in England and Scotland is as vestigial arrangements from a long-gone era. As we have seen, there was a time when the formal religious tradition of the state was welded to temporal power and the two acted in concert. Following the Enlightenment, religious belief became an increasingly private matter and, by popular consensus, it gradually receded from the public sphere. Furthermore, the twentieth century saw a steep decline in participation in organised Christian religion and self-identification with the same, a trend which continues into contemporary times. On this basis, the established Churches might be seen as a once bright light which is now

320 Our focus up to this point has been on religious beliefs [understood widely enough to include beliefs on religious matters such as Atheism or Humanism]. However, the legal framework with its favourable treatment of religion has implications for other serious and profound beliefs, as we shall explore in Chapter 3.

dying away into darkness. However, an alternative narrative is that the role and the place of the national Churches has changed. Just as the wings of the now grounded penguin have come to be finely honed tools for underwater flight, so the place of the established Churches within society has shifted to new territory.

This change partly explains the trends identified by commentators like Rivers,[321] who argue that establishment is weakening as a legal reality. The validity of this statement is effectively a question of perspective and what is meant by establishment. It is true that the old order is passing away. However, we would suggest that it is not being replaced by secularism, but a new form of religious legal reality.

The light is not fading, but it is flashing. The established Churches have come to occupy a liminal place within the legal structures of the life of the state, and this liminality enables them both to make a tangible difference and to have a real impact on the lives of citizens, while at the same time, by its very nature, it keeps their influence within what are essentially consensual bounds.

Liminality is a feature which can be identified within the very different models of Church/state relations operational within England, Scotland and Wales, and although any detailed examination of other jurisdictions is beyond the scope of this book, it is suggested that it may be found in many other European regimes. Anthropologists use the term 'liminal' to refer to people, places, or situations which exist on the boundary between categories or states of being: to be liminal is to be both and neither. Often liminality is associated with fluidity and the capacity for change. It may be feared or prized, depending on the context. It may provide possibility for experiment, exploration or discussion, because where liminality is a feature, normal rules and expectations are inapplicable, suspended or softened.[322]

The established (and quasi-established) Churches now occupy a liminal space within the contemporary society; their clergy are often in the position of liminal figures. They are associated to some extent with the official structures of authority and government, and yet are recognised, both in law and in practice, as being distinct. They are often given a voice within public dialogue, but wield influence rather than decision-making power. This may happen through rigid legal structures, such as the place of the bishops in the House of Lords, or more informal and permissive routes. For example, it is not uncommon for Anglican clergy in England and Wales to be invited to serve as 'community governors' on state schools without a religious ethos.

321 J. Rivers, n. 4 above.

322 See, e.g., M. Rudwick, 'Geological Travel and Theoretical Innovation: The Role of "Liminal" Experience', *Social Studies of Science*, Vol. 26, No. 1 (1996)143–59; G. Dowling, 'The Liminal Boundary: An Analysis of the Sacral Potency of the Ditch at Ráith na Ríg, Tara., Co. Meath', *The Journal of Irish Archaeology*, Vol. 15 (2006) 15–37; B.W. Derr, 'Implications of Menstruation as a Liminal State', *American Anthropologist New Series*, Vol. 84, No. 3 (1982) 644–5; and M.C. Hwangpo, ' El Compadre: Un tipo porteño liminal y espacial', *Revista de Crítica Literaria Latinoamericana*, Año 35, No. 70 (2009) 257–72.

The liminal nature of these roles means that they are inherently flexible, and that their significance can ebb and flow naturally with changing dynamics within communities.

2.9.4 Establishment: providing a structure and a pattern

The inherent flexibility of the establishment model within Britain provides a structure and a blueprint for social engagement by other faith and ideological groups. Establishment furnishes the bone structure of the penguin wings, but the individual feathers now include a variety of faith traditions and their make-up can depend upon the context at a local level. For instance, in the example given above, there is a pattern which allows for a representative from a different faith community being invited onto a school governing body, alongside or in place of the local vicar, if this reflects the demographic of the area more appropriately. Admittedly, there can be issues in finding an appropriate representative. It should not be assumed that religious ministers are isomorphic, and that the priest at a Hindu temple will do the same tasks within his community as an Anglican priest; but again, finding appropriate ways of working can be done at a local level where there is good communication. The structure given by the establishment framework provides a basis from which other faith groups can engage with community life.

Because the liminal nature of establishment confers Anglican clergy with a quasi-official role, others alongside or in place of such clergy may either share or take over that mantle. Again, because this role and status is liminal, no group can exercise it as of right: there must be a weight of social consensus in order for it to be operative.

2.9.5 A religious legal framework

In summary, our contention is that the religious legal framework with which we are working in twenty-first century Britain is not merely functional, but positive for society and in harmony with the fundamental pillars of our modern Constitution. This is the thesis which we are going to test in the following chapters. The established Churches have, like the wings of the penguin, found a new and dynamic role within the present organism. This role is creative and valuable, but it is only one element in the suite of religious characteristics which we now observe. As we move forward, we will test the application of all three in relation to our core constitutional principles from Chapters 4 to 7.

The study is not concerned exclusively, or even primarily, with the question of establishment. We are interested in moving beyond this, to look at the many ways in which a positivity towards religion permeates the whole legal framework. We explore aspects of this which have frequently been overlooked, delving into fields such as family and criminal law. We consider how the individual component parts are functioning, and assess whether there is any need for reform or replacement. What are the competing claims for change and the driving forces behind them?

Having said that, we also keep our attention focused on the system as a whole. Is it helping to promote a cohesive, positive and mutually respectful society? Is there any evidence that a legal system which were to adopt a more neutral stance towards the practice of faith would be a more equitable and inclusive regime? In addition, a question all too frequently overlooked by academics, in the constant push to find material to criticise and proposals to make: What do we currently have which is positive and valuable? What are the elements within our religious legal system, and indeed characteristics as a whole, which we should seek to preserve, whatever befalls us on our journey forwards as a nation and juridical system?

However, before we turn to the core part of our book (Chapters 4 to 7), it is important to illustrate how our religious Constitution is also indirectly beneficial to beliefs unrelated to religion (such as veganism) and this will be the scope of Chapter 3.

3 Non-religious beliefs in the current paradigm

3.1 Introduction: the meaning of religious and non-religious beliefs

As we set out at the beginning, the primary focus of our study is on the religious character of the Constitution. For this reason, we have concentrated our attention in the preceding two chapters upon the ways in which the legal system has evolved in relation to beliefs on religious matters. For the avoidance of doubt, it should be stressed that beliefs on religious matters encompass worldviews which explicitly reject religion (at least, as it is conventionally understood), such as Atheism and Humanism, as declaring oneself an Atheist is to assume an identity and stance in the context of faith. As freedom of religion has advanced, citizens whose self-definition is consciously non-religious have benefited alongside all other non-Anglican and non-Christian faith groups and positions.[1]

Moreover, Atheists, Humanists and others who join coordinated bodies with operations that mirror organised religion can and do slot into the same structures that establishment provides for faith groups. So, for example, they may provide representatives for civic occasions,[2] visit schools[3] to gives talks and assemblies, and take part in lobbying and consultation exercises.[4] Not only do societies like the British Humanist Association (BHA) afford many of the internal dimensions of organised religion for their members (such as offering rituals to mark major life events), but they also operate as a form of organised religion in terms of their external dealings with society beyond their membership.

1 E.g., the Universities Tests Act, s. 3, was passed to allow individuals from religious minorities to take up fellowships at Oxford, Cambridge and Durham. The final impetus came from the high-profile case of Numa Edward Hartog who, despite having being Senior Wrangler, was effectively barred from a Cambridge fellowship on the grounds of his Jewish faith. The abolition of a religious test for such appointments clearly benefited Atheists and Agnostics as much as it did Jews, Non-Conformists, Roman Catholics and other minority faiths.

2 Humanist Society Scotland, 'Humanists Join Tributes at National Remembrance Day Ceremony' (Nov 2016), https://www.humanism.scot/what-we-do/news/humanists-join-tributes-at-national-remembrance-day-ceremony.

3 British Humanist Association, 'Education for Teachers', https://humanism.org.uk/education/teachers.

4 Humanist Society Scotland, 'Assisted Suicide Consultation Closes Soon', http://www.humanism.scot/what-we-do/news/assisted_suicide_consultation_closes_soon/.

We should stress that we do not question their self-definition as non-religious, as that is uncontroversial and wholly accepted. Nonetheless, we do assert that the values of Humanism in the lives of members occupy the space of religion for many persons of faith, and furthermore that the manner in which these organisations engage with the world parallels that of faith groups. Therefore, is it appropriate for our specific purposes to refer to all beliefs on religious matters as 'religious beliefs' and, furthermore, it is logical and necessary for us to recognise organised manifestations of religious beliefs as forms of organised religion (even when for other purposes this categorisation might appear counterintuitive, Humanism being for some the antithesis of religious belief). In reality, bodies such as the BHA and the Humanist Society Scotland (HSS) are *functioning* as organised religion for many purposes.

Of course, there are times when such groups express dissatisfaction about their level and manner of inclusion, and argue for a larger slice of the pie (or sometimes even to be permitted a bite). For example, the BHA has long been campaigning to participate in *Thought for the Day* on Radio 4.[5] It must be stressed that such activism proves, rather than disproves, the point about their participation within the establishment structure. A degree of wrangling over who gets on what platform and when is an inevitable facet of something as loose and flexible as 'low establishment'. Its very fluidity means that there are not always hard-and-fast rules as to what must be done, when, and by whom. Faith groups (including the established Churches) also sometimes actively seek a different manner or level of participation in a given situation, with varying degrees of success; in this sense, Humanist groups operating as forms of organised religion are in no different a position from that of their faith-based counterparts. For instance, both the Church of England[6] and the Church in Wales[7] argued that they were not sufficiently consulted in relation to the legal arrangements surrounding same-sex marriage, and some Pagan commentators feel that their faith does not receive adequate treatment and recognition in British schools.[8]

Precisely because the patterns given by establishment are flexible, a continual process of renewal and adjustment in particular contexts is part of its fundamental nature. Inevitably, all parties will at times experience the frustration of failing to convince the majority of other stakeholders about the merits of some claim which

5 British Humanist Association, 'Human Rights and Equality Broadcasting', https://humanism.org.uk/campaigns/human-rights-and-equality/broadcasting.

6 D. Wilcock, 'No Consultation: The Church of England attacks Government over Gay Marriage Plans', *The Independent* (14 Dec 2012), http://www.independent.co.uk/news/uk/home-news/no-consultation-church-of-england-attacks-government-over-gay-marriage-plans-8414180.html.

7 S. Jones, 'Church of England and Church in Wales Protest at Gay Marriage Ban', *The Guardian* (13 Dec 2012), https://www.theguardian.com/society/2012/dec/13/anglican-church-protests-gay-marriage-ban.

8 Simple Magick, 'Pagans Want to be Included Too', 24 April 2007, http://www.simplemagick.com/2007/04/pagans-want-to-be-included-too.html.

they wish to assert. In fact, any group or individual engaging in a collaborative endeavour must, on occasion, accept that their point of view has not prevailed in a specific situation.

Moreover, the very fact that Humanist groups functioning as forms of organised religion actively assert their claims for greater inclusion within the structures supported by an establishment framework demonstrates that these groups enjoy considerable de facto benefits from the system. There would be no logic in demanding more of something which was perceived as being of no value.

In short, as was outlined in Chapter 2, the religious character of the Constitution and legal machinery confer advantages on those who wish to practise religion or manifest their religious beliefs, especially in the form of organised religion. Therefore, bodies which operate as a form of organised religion – regardless of their beliefs about divinity, the supernatural or rationality – *directly* benefit.

We are aware that it may be counterintuitive to suggest that groups which consciously see themselves as non-religious, and are even bound together by a shared rejection of religion, should benefit from a religious legal system. Nevertheless, our contention is that this is in fact the case. In providing an alternative religious identity for the consciously non-religious, with a collective ethical voice and rituals to mark life events, groups like the BHA might appropriately, if controversially, be understood to be fulfilling the functions of organised religion for their members.

For this reason, for the remainder of the book, we shall include the BHA and HSS within our understanding of religious belief groups, in the sense of being organisations formed around shared convictions on religious matters and participating in the social and political arena as such.[9] Even though these organisations may be highly critical of the establishment framework and religious legal system, they nevertheless enjoy some direct benefits and in certain respects actively seek greater involvement.

Yet, we would argue that the beneficial impact of the religious legal system, in its tripartite, Russian doll form, extends even further. In our view, there are *indirect* benefits for beliefs which do not in any way relate to religious matters.

Our contention is that the development of religious liberty was instrumental to the development of freedom of conscience. A respect for religious belief led, naturally and incrementally, to a respect for other profound and serious beliefs. We do not assert that having a religious Constitution was the only factor in the development of freedom of conscience, nor certainly that it is a *sine qua non* for the same. Nevertheless, we do suggest that, in the particular context of Great Britain, the religious legal environment has been, and remains, conducive to the development of freedom of conscience, and we suggest that this can be seen in three primary ways:

9 As we noted in Chapter 2, they are distinct from organisations which exist to promote secularism, and are gathered around a common desire to end legal links between Church and state. Secularist groups do not seek to replace organised religion in members' lives, and might indeed draw members with a wide variety of personal faith convictions.

(a) the treatment of beliefs which have been protected by association with religious beliefs;
(b) the treatment of beliefs which have been protected by analogy with religious beliefs; and
(c) a presumption in favour of supporting and respecting beliefs within the legal framework has the potential to provide claimants who cannot meet the requirements of Article 9 of the European Convention on Human Rights (ECHR) with an alternative gateway to recognition and protection.

3.2 Non-religious beliefs protected by association with religious beliefs

We would argue that there are a variety of instances in which non-religious beliefs have been protected by association with religious beliefs. Where religious groups have secured a concession on the ground of their beliefs, it is difficult for public authorities to justify refusing to make a parallel concession to those who demand it in respect of non-religious beliefs.

In other words, on a number of occasions, religious groups have mounted a successful campaign to be permitted to either do or not do something which would otherwise have been legally problematic. Their calls for distinct treatment were accepted by state authorities in part because of the special perception of faith by the juridical and political system, and, as a result, a smaller number of citizens who wished to obtain the same distinct treatment on the basis of deeply held convictions, not religious in nature, were also successful in gaining an exception.

This was partly on the basis of fairness and rationality – if one person's beliefs merited respect, then logically so should those of other citizens – and partly on the pragmatic ground that the clamour made by the religious bodies enabled the voices of all parties requesting the same concessions to be heard. We will now move on to consider some examples of protection by association.

3.2.1 Conscientious objection to military service

Principled objections to engagement in military activity were recognised in law in 1757 when Quakers[10] were exempt from the provisions of the Militia Ballot Act 1757. This legislation was passed with the intention of providing a national military reserve in England and Wales. Men were to be chosen by ballot, but permitted to pay substitutes to take their place, and it was accepted that Quakers should not be required to compromise their pacifist beliefs by participating in this system.

There is less clarity with regard to the position in relation to the dreaded press-gangs, which were used particularly by the Georgian navy to man warships. Getting drunk, or even simply being in the wrong place at the wrong time in a coastal town, could result in an unwary young man being forcibly taken to serve

10 G. Russell-Jones, *Conchie: What My Father Didn't Do in the War* (Lion Hudson: Oxford) 2016, 167.

in the navy. Both law and society in general held contradictory views towards the practice of impressments,[11] and individuals effectively had their freedom taken away in order to defend freedom. It was impossible to square the moral circle, but equally it was impossible to operate the navy without the press-gang, and consequently it was tolerated and even romanticised. In some respects, allowing people to object to what basically amounted to kidnapping made little sense. By definition, everyone who resisted the press-gang and, as a result was roughed up and forcibly dragged on board ship, had had their liberty dramatically removed. However, it was possible for victims of the press-gang to petition the Admiralty for their release and, as Brunsman notes, being Quaker was one basis upon which a man might successfully secure his escape.[12]

Thus, from at least the eighteenth century onwards, there was an understanding that objections to military service based on religious beliefs ought to be respected by law, even when the state was using exceptionally coercive measures in the interests of national security. Crucially for our purposes, this acceptance that a man's religious beliefs necessitated excusing him from a burden imposed upon other citizens opened the door to allowing other beliefs to operate in the same way.

Only a very weighty consideration could justify excusing one individual from a serious detriment which others were expected to bear for the common good, and the conceptual door which had been opened by the early legal accommodation of Quaker conscientious objection helped to shape the systemic response towards other forms of belief-based opposition to military service when conscription was introduced during the First World War. Military service for men aged between 18 and 41 (who did not fall within one the statutory exemptions) became compulsory in 1916,[13] but the expectation, based on earlier frameworks, was that there would be some space to allow for those whose beliefs were incompatible with military service.

The truth is that by the early twentieth century, it was no longer tenable to treat one set of beliefs differently from another when it came to the fundamental freedoms of citizens. The legislation recognised both implicitly and explicitly that religious beliefs for many individuals would be a driving force behind a principled objection to fighting, and affirmed that these should be respected. For example, religious ministers were among those explicitly excluded from mandatory service. However, at the same time, it was recognised that there were others with equally strong personal convictions against military service which were *not* religious in nature. These non-religious beliefs were also matters of conscience and, therefore, accorded special protection and respect, even in a time of national crisis, and the term 'conscientious objector' unambiguously

11 D. Ennis, *Enter the Press-Gang: Naval Impressment in Eighteenth Century British Literature* (Associated University Presses: London) 2002, 19.

12 D. Brunsman, *The Evil Necessity: British Naval Impressment in the Eighteenth Century Atlantic World* (University of Virginia Press: Virginia) 2013, 192.

13 Military Service Act 1916.

encompassed ideological perspectives which were non-religious in nature. The stance of the Quakers had long since carved out an exception to military service rooted in a conflict of belief, and this exemption could no longer be confined to one particular form or style of belief.

Non-religious conscientious objectors fell into a number of categories:[14] (i) those with left-wing political views who perceived the conflict as an Imperialist War, in which oppressed workers were being forced to fight one another by the respective ruling elites in their nations; (ii) those with a non-religious objection to killing – for example, one man explained that he had worked as a butcher and knowing what it was to end the life of a pig, he could not contemplate doing the same to a human being;[15] and (iii) anti-interventionists who objected to governmental interference and control, and regarded the fighting in continental Europe as having no relevance to their individual lives and concerns.

Regrettably, it has to be stressed that the manner in which the legislation was applied frequently led to arbitrary and oppressive decisions. Local tribunals decided whether a particular conscientious objector was sincere or not, and their wide discretionary powers were sometimes abused. Moreover, society in general viewed conscientious objectors negatively, and the stigma and hostility which they faced meant that in practice men often received a less than sympathetic hearing.[16]

Although there was an appeal procedure, this too was imperfect, and exemption could be absolute or conditional. Some men were required to serve in the army in a non-combatant role, while others were exempt from military service on the condition that they performed an alternative service. Consequently, there were conscientious objectors who either had their claims for exemptions entirely rejected, or who were presented with a conditional exemption which they felt unable to accept, because it involved too active a role in assisting in the war. In either case, the men faced prison in harsh conditions and, in a few tragic cases, ultimately death (because they were deemed to have joined the army and were brought before a court-martial for refusing to obey orders).

Yet, while it must be acknowledged that the functioning of the system left a lot to be desired, the basic principle that individuals with a conscientious objection to participating in armed conflict should not be compelled to do so was present and applied. The practical treatment of conscientious objectors during the First World War unfortunately makes uncomfortable reading, but religious and non-religious objectors were protected by the same law, and both groups suffered equally in cases where it was poorly implemented.

Furthermore, had it not been for the pre-existing religious precedent, it is unclear whether the concept of conscientious objection would even have been

14 M. Brooks, 'Conscientious Objectors in Their Own Words', *Imperial War Museums*, http://www.iwm.org.uk/history/conscientious-objectors-in-their-own-words.

15 Ibid.

16 A. Kramer, *Conscientious Objectors of the First World War: A Determined Resistance* (Pen & Sword: Barnsley) 2002, 2.

recognised at that stage, given the widespread anger directed at men who refused to take up arms. It is also important to try to understand where this aggression and bitterness came from. For some people, seeing some of their contemporaries escape the trenches, when they had lost family members and friends, would have been very difficult to bear. In addition, the heroism of many of the conscientious objectors, who received conditional exemptions and performed services like rescuing and caring for the wounded, may have only fuelled the resentment against those who refused to play any part at all. Tragically, there were all too many parents, wives and children who would probably far rather have seen their loved one imprisoned in Britain than dead or maimed fighting abroad. Accommodating the beliefs of some citizens in the context of war and conscription, while others not saved by the shibboleth of conscience are compelled to suffer, inevitably raises emotive issues, and we should not be surprised that the system was less than perfect.

A similar but better regulated regime for managing conscientious objection was adopted in the Second World War.[17] Conscientious Objection Tribunals were chaired by judges rather than untrained volunteers (who were frequently members of the local squirearchy and accustomed to be being obeyed). Consequently, the underlying legal principle of respecting conscientious objection was maintained, and strengthened with a more just and coherent application; even after compulsory military service ceased, the principle was maintained in British law by virtue of the international law commitments of the state. For example, Article 18 of the International Covenant on Civil and Political Rights provides for freedom of religion and conscience, and in 2006 the majority of the Human Rights Committee of the United Nations expressed the view that this encompasses the right to conscientious objection to military service.[18] Furthermore, the European Court of Human Rights has also confirmed that Article 9 requires states to respect the right of individuals to object to military service on conscientious grounds.[19]

Although the applications were driven principally by religion – given that it is uncontroversial that the scope of Article 9 extends to non-religious beliefs[20] – it is clear that all forms of sincere conscientious objection are equally protected. Moskos and Chambers even went so far as to argue in the 1990s that modern objections to military service were more likely to be secular than religious.[21] Their perspective was heavily influenced by the North American paradigm, and the geopolitical situation has changed considerably in the last twenty years. We do not have sufficient data to assess whether the assertion of Moskos and Chambers would hold good in contemporary Britain, but it is certainly the case that equally

17 National Service (Armed Forces) Act 1939.

18 *Yoon and Choi v Republic of Korea* (Communications nos 1321/2004 and 1322/2004).

19 *Bayatyan v Armenia*, App no. 23459/03, Judgment, 7 July 2011 (ECtHR).

20 *R (on the application of Williamson) v Secretary of State for Education and Employment* [2005] UKHL 15; [2005] 2 AC 246.

21 C. Moskos and J. Chambers, *The New Conscientious Objection: From Sacred to Secular Resistance* (Oxford University Press: Oxford) 1993.

strong principled objections to military service come from both religious and secular standpoints. The genesis of the conscientious objection is not material to the protection which the modern legal framework accords it.

To conclude, we do not claim that the positive treatment of religion as a phenomenon has been the *only* factor in the legal framework coming to recognise the right to conscientious objection to military service as an essential facet of the right to freedom of religion and belief. However, it is indisputable that it was a driving force in the establishment of the principle that personal convictions should, at times, insulate individuals from burdens imposed on society as a whole, and it helped the principle to survive even in times of hostility and crisis.

3.2.2 Veganism

The Oxford English Dictionary defines 'vegan' in the following terms: 'A person who abstains from all food of animal origin and avoids the use of animal products in other forms'.[22] Thus, veganism itself is not technically a belief, but a lifestyle choice. Nevertheless, for many people who adopt it, veganism is a choice which flows from very deeply held convictions, and it was accepted by the (then) European Commission for Human Rights that beliefs relating to veganism can amount to a matter of conscience or belief for the purposes of Article 9 (see, for example, *W v United Kingdom*[23]). It should be noted, though, that the UK government did not dispute this particular point in the case, and we would be cautious about assuming that all persons who self-identify as vegan would clear the belief-related hurdles in order to show that Article 9 was engaged. Many vegans are motivated by a desire not to cause pain or suffering to non-human animals,[24] while others may be driven by environmental concerns.[25]

However, some religious traditions either encourage or demand a vegan or vegetarian lifestyle,[26] or require believers to abstain from eating or contact with certain types of animal life – for example, the familiar prohibitions on pork and shellfish in the Jewish dietary laws.[27]

In both cases, the religious beliefs in question may require abstention from animal products in circumstances where vegans might also wish to avoid contact. We would argue that the legal and social necessity to recognise, and where possible meet, these religious needs strengthens the potential protection available to non-religiously motivated vegans. Consider, for example, the recent and ongoing

22 *Oxford English Dictionary* (2016), http://www.oed.com/view/Entry/221868?rskey=3l3EwX&result=1#eid.

23 *W v United Kingdom*, App no. 18187/91, 10 February 1993 (ECtHR).

24 R. Roth, *That's Why We Don't Eat Animals* (North Atlantic Books: Berkley) 2009.

25 Vegan Outreach, 'Environmental Destruction', http://www.veganoutreach.org/whyvegan/environment.html.

26 E.g., some Buddhist traditions: N. Phelps, *The Great Compassion: Buddhism and Animal Rights* (Lantern Books: New York) 2004, 129.

27 L. Stern, *How to Keep Kosher: A Comprehensive Guide to Understanding Jewish Dietary Laws* (Harper Collins: London) 2009.

controversy over the use of animal fat in the new polymer £5 notes. The inventor, Professor David Solomon, was reported in the press as having labelled vegetarian protestors as 'stupid'.[28] Vegan and vegetarian calls for a reappraisal of the introduction of polymer money are clearly being met with resistance, but it is striking that there have also been high-profile objections from religious groups,[29] and the seriousness with which religious concerns are treated by the legal and political framework can only boost the chances of the equally important and legitimate non-religious vegan voices being heard.

Similarly, some of the concessions won by religious individuals working in the public sector contexts would be of benefit to non-religious vegans. For instance, a Sikh guardsman was granted permission not to wear the bearskin busby ordinarily required for his regiment, and paraded instead in a black turban.[30] This appears to have been more on the grounds of the busby being incompatible with a turban than any objection to its controversial construction from bear skin. However, given that the army has now accepted that the busby may be replaced with alternative headgear on the grounds of personal belief, it would be difficult to see how it could justify treating a vegan or vegetarian soldier differently and demanding that the busby be worn.

3.2.3 Other examples

Clearly, conscientious objection to military service and veganism are just two examples of non-religious beliefs that potentially require similar concessions to those rooted in religious beliefs, but there are, undoubtedly, other paradigms that we could have chosen to explore if space permitted. For instance, a similar pattern might be traced in relation to parental conscience provisions with regard to state education.[31] In the nineteenth and twentieth centuries, much of the pressure for flexibility and choice in this regard came from religious groups, who had concerns about the content of religious education, sex education or participation in religious worship. However, the statutory provisions safeguarding parental decision making in this context provide equal protection for those who wish to withdraw their children on the basis of non-religious beliefs. For instance, some parents might object to the delivery of sex education in schools on the basis that the topic was addressed in what they perceived as too strongly heteronormative terms, a manner which failed to give sufficient weight to feminist concerns and

28 Australian Associated Press, '£5 Animal Fat Bank Note: British Vegetarians being "Stupid" says Inventor', *The Guardian* (2 Dec 2016), https://www.theguardian.com/business/2016/dec/02/5-animal-fat-bank-note-british-vegetarians-being-stupid-says-inventor.

29 'Animal Fat in New Five Pound Note Offensive, says Sikh Activist', *BBC News* (30 Nov 2016), http://www.bbc.co.uk/news/uk-38160291.

30 'Sikh Soldier First Guardsman to Parade Outside of Buckingham Palace Wearing a Turban', *The Telegraph* (11 Dec 2012), http://www.telegraph.co.uk/news/religion/9737480/Sikh-soldier-first-guardsman-to-parade-outside-Buckingham-palace-wearing-turban.html.

31 See Chapter 2 above, for a detailed discussion of the same.

theories, or quite simply because they had a strong belief that such matters should be taught and discussed primarily in the home.

All of these non-religious beliefs are accommodated in the global right to withdraw, and the same can be stated in a healthcare context where legislation sets out provisions on conscientious objections in connection with the termination of pregnancy[32] and the treatment of human embryos.[33] In all of these spheres, non-religious beliefs are protected by association with religious beliefs. Significantly, the legislation does not require an individual to justify the grounds for the conscientious objection. This is important, because it respects the privacy and dignity of all citizens exercising these rights, but it does mean that it is difficult to know the proportion of people withdrawing or abstaining on religious and non-religious grounds. Moreover, given that all beliefs are protected equally, we would not expect to see a significant amount of litigation from individuals asserting that their particular motivation for objection is catered for, as it clearly holds all viewpoints within its ambit.

3.3 Protection by analogy: refusal of medical treatment

Important though protection by association is in practice, there is another distinct form of assistance that religious beliefs may confer upon deeply held non-religious beliefs: protection by analogy. This applies when beliefs receive recognition and protection, not because *their outward manifestation* is similar to recognised manifestations of religious beliefs, but because the *inner depth and seriousness* is recognised as being *qualitatively akin* to a religious belief.

We have chosen to focus on the field of refusal of medical treatment. It is settled and well established law that an adult with full capacity may refuse medical treatment regardless of 'whether the reasons are rational, irrational, unknown or non-existent, and even if the result of the refusal is the certainty of death'.[34]

However, complicated questions arise in relation to capacity. In those situations where a person may lack capacity and a third party has assumed a duty of care, that third party may be liable if he or she failed to seek or provide appropriate medical and practical care.[35] In examining how the courts have dealt with these cases, it is possible to discern how their treatment of religious beliefs in this context has been one factor in influencing judicial treatment of non-religious beliefs.

The case of *R (on the application of Jenkins) v HM Coroner for Portsmouth and South East Hampshire*[36] concerned the judicial review of a coroner's decision, and turned on whether the only rational verdict on the facts was one of

32 Abortion Act 1967, s. 4.

33 Human Fertilisation and Embryology Act 1990, s. 38.

34 *HE v A Hospital NHS Trust* (*by her Litigation Friend, the Official Solicitor*) [2003] EWHC 1017 (Fam), per Munby J., para. 20.

35 *Re Land (Dec'd)* [2007] 1 WLR 1009.

36 *R (on the application of Jenkins) v HM Coroner for Portsmouth and South East Hampshire* [2008] EWHC 3229 (Admin).

unlawful killing. The deceased, Jenkins, was a diabetic who stepped on the the plug of an electrical appliance in his home and, despite being aware of the dangers of not attending properly to foot injuries for sufferers of diabetes, he resolutely refused all conventional medical treatment. As a result, the wound did not heal and became infected, which ultimately caused gangrene and death from septicaemia. The deceased's partner, Ms Cameron, was a registered nurse; her account was that she shared the deceased's beliefs and respected his wishes not to have recourse to conventional medicine. It was accepted both that she was well aware of the course that his illness would inevitably take once a serious infection had set in, and also that she had lied to his family about his condition (had they known, it was clear that they would have sought medical help whether the deceased wished it or not). The question arose as to whether Ms Cameron had any duty to summon an ambulance once Jenkins lost capacity to make decisions for himself. The court found that on the facts she did not.

Pitchford J considered and distinguished a number of cases in which defendants were found to be liable for not having summoned help for a person, even though the deceased had been resistant to this,[37] and one common thread which he identified in all of them was that 'the deceased had become incapable of taking care of and making decision for themselves'.[38]

As stated above, an individual with capacity can refuse medical treatment on *any* basis that they choose, and they need not be motivated by a principled belief which they are able to articulate. In pragmatic terms, it is frequently the case that if a person with capacity and no desire to die is refusing medical treatment, he or she is doing so on the strength of some principled belief. Nevertheless, this is not invariably so. Patients might refuse, for example, because they suffered from an extreme form of trypanophobia; in such an instance, provided that their mental state was not such that they had lost capacity, their choices would be respected and protected by the legal framework. The point at issue in *Jenkins*, however, was not whether the deceased was free to decline treatment, but whether his partner had assumed a duty of care and was, consequently, criminally culpable for not obtaining medical help when he lost capacity.

In this context, we would suggest that the beliefs held by the deceased were a key consideration before the court. The judgment refers specifically to the testimony of one witness who had compared the strength of Jenkins' belief in his alternative therapies and rejection of conventional medicine to a religious conviction: 'The Coroner asked Mr Cooter whether he might have advised Mr Jenkins to see a doctor had he known the condition of his foot. Mr Cooter replied "In my mind, it would have been in the same league as trying to convince a Jehovah's Witness to have a blood transfusion"'.[39]

37 *Stone v Dobinson* [1977] 1 QB 354; *Re Hood* [2004] 1 Cr App R (S) 73; *Re Land (Dec'd)*, n. 35 above.

38 *R (on the application of Jenkins) v HM Coroner for Portsmouth and South East Hampshire*, n. 36 above, per Pitchford J, para. 38.

39 Ibid., para. 16.

This was a highly persuasive factor in the judge's analysis and conclusion: 'Mr Russell Jones had his own strongly held, if idiosyncratic views about self-care . . . the evidence before the Coroner was that Mr Jenkins was resolute in his determination not to accept conventional medical help'.

Therefore, the court appreciated the parallel between the deceased's beliefs in his form of alternative medicine and the beliefs of a religious person. By analogy, it was important that his beliefs be respected. We suggest that this element of a clearly expressed belief, on the part of the deceased, tipped the balance and led the court to distinguish these facts from those of earlier cases where a duty to provide care or to seek medical help had been found. In *Stone v Dobinson*[40] the deceased had neglected herself while she was still able to have some agency in her own life, but there was no identifiable belief driving her actions. She had a fear of being forcibly institutionalised, but there was no suggestion that she had a belief that was incompatible with any of the help which might have been on offer, had the brother with whom she lived sought or given it. Indeed, the fact that the brother had made some fleeting and rudimentary efforts to assist demonstrated that she was prepared to accept aid.

> This was not a situation of a drowning stranger. They did make efforts to care ... The jury were entitled to find that the duty had been assumed. They were entitled to conclude that once Fanny had become helplessly infirm, as she had by July 19, the appellants were, in the circumstances obliged to summon help or else care for Fanny themselves.[41]

In *Re Hood*[42] the deceased was apparently reluctant about going to hospital, but did not refuse this when the defendant finally and belatedly summoned assistance. There was nothing to suggest that she had had any principled objection to any help or treatment that might be offered. Equally, in *Re Land*,[43] the deceased had disliked and distrusted officialdom, but there was no suggestion that any intervention would have violated her personal beliefs.

A key factor in *Jenkins* appears to have been the clear and specific beliefs which the deceased held, and which were treated as having a gravity and relevance akin to religious beliefs. This analogous treatment radically altered the way in which the court interpreted the duties of the defendants once the deceased had lost capacity to make decisions. Consistent and deeply held beliefs were given far more weight than apparent preferences, which might be subject to change.

Similarly, although the analogy with religious beliefs was not made as explicit, in *F v F*[44] the resistance of two minor sisters to receiving vaccinations was given considerable weight, on the basis that it stemmed in part from the veganism

40 *Stone v Dobinson*, n. 37 above.
41 Ibid., per Geoffrey Lane, 361.
42 *Re Hood*, n. 37 above.
43 *Re Land (Dec'd)*, n. 35 above.
44 *F v F* [2013] EWHC 2683 (Fam).

of one child and the discomfort which she felt with the idea of having animal products in her body. The parents of the two sisters could not agree on whether they should be vaccinated, and it therefore fell to the court to make a 'best interests' determination. Of course, s. 1(3)(a) of the Children Act 1989 always requires that the ascertainable wishes and feelings of the child be taken into account by the court when exercising its powers in this regard, but the fact that the child's wishes were rooted in matter of conscience gave an added dimension to the case, and the point was emphasised in both the judgment and the CAFCASS report.

In the event, the court ordered that the children be vaccinated. This was partly because their objections were based on misinformation (such as thinking that measles involved merely getting a rash) and also their objective physical best interests in terms of avoiding the risk of infections and serious complications of the disease. However, it was highly relevant too that there was a real question about the extent to which the girls' protests were really based upon their own deeply held beliefs, and how far they were seeking to support their anxious mother (who vehemently opposed the vaccine) and save her from distress. Nevertheless, the potential issue of conscience for the girls was by no means swept under the carpet: it was given serious and careful judicial treatment.

We suggest that a legal system which demonstrates respect for religious beliefs is, in practice, inclined to show comparable respect for other forms of strong, subjective beliefs. An additional recent example comes from the tragic case of *Re JS (Disposal of Body)*.[45] A terminally ill fourteen-year-old wished to have her body cryogenically frozen upon her death, in the hope that she could one day be revived and cured. Her mother supported this preference, whereas her father opposed it.

The court stressed that its role was not to determine the merits or rationality of JS's wishes or beliefs, and that she had every right to form her own beliefs in relation to life and death.[46] It was also clear that the decision to order that the arrangements for the disposition of JS's body after her death should lie with her mother (thereby ensuring that JS could feel confident that her wishes would be followed, and allowing her some measure of peace in her final days) was not an affirmation of her beliefs per se. Mr Justice Peter Jackson reiterated that in English law a person cannot dictate the treatment of his or her body after death, regardless of testamentary capacity or religion.[47] Ultimately, it was (quite properly) a decision aimed at advancing her welfare as effectively as possible, but the importance that JS's beliefs had for her demanded that the court treat them with weight and respect in evaluating her best interests.

Effectively, the approach to the question about dealing with her body was the same as it would have been had JS had a strong religious belief, which one parent shared and the other rejected. The assurance that her belief about a profound matter would be respected was important, as was the idea that the 'correct' treatment of her body would ensure her chances of survival beyond her death.

45 *JS v M and F; Re JS (Disposal of Body)* [2016] EWHC 2859 (Fam).

46 Ibid., para. 31.

47 Ibid., 48.

Effectively, the basis of JS's concern was the same as that of the applicant in the celebrated *Ghai* case,[48] in which the applicant was concerned that if he could not secure cremation in the appropriate, outdoor form, his soul might suffer irreparable damage, and the process of rebirth could be adversely affected. Although not religious, the foundation of JS's belief and concern was the same: she was equally worried about having her body dealt with in a way that would promote her ongoing existence. In neither instance was the belief the sole determinative factor, but in both cases it was treated with the utmost seriousness and respect by the courts. In *JS* the court found that supporting her belief was in the best interests of the minor, and in *Ghai* the Court of Appeal found a way of interpreting the relevant legislation which allowed for the applicant's desires to be honoured.

Thus, taken in the round, we argue that a legal system which directly benefits religious believers also indirectly benefits, by analogy, those who hold non-religious beliefs. A support for religious belief incrementally and naturally translates into a supportive stance towards other profound and sincere beliefs. Furthermore, the scope of this benefit extends beyond that which is provided by Article 9 ECHR, and we turn to this in the last section of this chapter.

3.4 An alternative gateway to protection: beyond the boundaries of Article 9

We shall explore in detail in Chapter 7 how the current legal framework deals with human rights. However, for present purposes we would observe that human rights developed within the domestic legal system long before the Human Rights Act 1998 was passed, and indeed before the United Kingdom ratified the European Convention on Human Rights in 1951. We do not, in any way, wish to downplay the significance of these groundbreaking legal instruments, but would like to emphasise that they exist to further rights, rather than to limit them. The truth is that human rights continue to develop within domestic law outside the parameters of the statutory regime.

As we set out in Chapter 2, our thesis is essentially that the legal framework adopts a positive stance with regard to religious belief, and goes further towards recognising and supporting it than what is required by the framework of the Human Rights Act. In this chapter, as stated, we have taken a step further, and have suggested that the positive stance towards religious belief has also led to a positive stance towards 'belief', more broadly understood.

There is a soft presumption that religious beliefs should be respected and facilitated where possible, and we would argue that this has led to a secondary soft presumption: that *any* belief which is of deep importance to the holder will be recognised by the courts as being worthy of respect.

Where matters of conscience are concerned, the practical need for protection is now met in many instances by Article 9 ECHR, but we would suggest that there

48 *R (on the application of Ghai) v Newcastle City Council (Ramgharia Gudwara, Hitchin and Another intervening)* [2010] EWCA Civ 59.

are two instances in which Article 9 may not assist individuals in asserting their right to express a belief. First, there are situations in which the belief will not pass the *Williamson* test,[49] and therefore no Article 9 rights will be engaged; second, there are occasions where the application of Article 9 invites the courts to conduct a balancing exercise which would otherwise have been unnecessary. Following Cumper and Lewis,[50] we would suggest that there are some instances when courts relying on the Human Rights Act may reach an unfavourable conclusion for a party trying to manifest a belief, but might find a different answer if the questions were approached through the alternative prism of the common law. Consequently, non-religious beliefs are favoured because of the nature of our Constitution, which is inherently religious and therefore, supportive of belief in general.

3.4.1 The scope of Article 9

As a preliminary step in answering this question, we need to assess the scope of Article 9 itself. If the manifestation of a belief is to be protected by Article 9(2) it must satisfy the test laid out by the House of Lords in *Williamson*: 'The belief must relate to matters more than merely trivial. It must possess an adequate degree of seriousness and importance. As has been said, it must be a belief on a fundamental problem'.[51]

It is not clear whether some of the beliefs discussed above – for example, the faith which the deceased in the *Jenkins* case placed in his brand of alternative therapy – would qualify.[52] Moreover, it is even less certain whether some of the other examples of beliefs dealt with elsewhere in this book would pass through the filter. For instance, in Chapter 6 (on the separation of powers) we address how state authorities have accommodated folk beliefs in fairies and nature spirits.[53] Nevertheless, the juridical system demonstrates its support for both types of belief.

In the course of this section, we would like to illustrate how the traditional common law model, which is a facet of the religious character of the UK Constitution, has worked favourably towards the protection of non-religious beliefs. Its scope is to highlight the possible shortcomings which an exclusive reliance on Article 9 would have.

We are certainly not the first commentators who have identified the weaknesses of the Article 9 framework. It must also be acknowledged that there are voices that strongly assert that going beyond Article 9 is necessary if the values

49 *R (Williamson and Others) v Secretary of State for Education and Employment*, n. 20 above.

50 P. Cumper and T. Lewis, 'Last Rites and Human Rights: Funeral Pyres and Religious Freedom in the United Kingdom', *Ecclesiastical Law Journal*, Vol. 12, No. 2 (2010) 131–51, 151.

51 *R (Williamson and Others) v Secretary of State for Education and Employment*, n. 20 above, per Lord Nicholls, para 23.

52 *R v (on the application of Jenkins) v HM Coroner for Portsmouth and South East Hampshire*, n. 36 above.

53 Whether a belief in fairies should properly be deemed religious or non-religious is, of course, a moot point, but then, of course, fairies themselves are apt to resist easy categorisation.

and freedoms of citizens are to be adequately respected, and the scope (or at least judicial interpretation of the scope) of Article 9 has received considerable academic criticism.

Some of this relates directly to non-religious as well as religious beliefs. For instance, Ouald Chaib[54] argues that the Strasbourg Court all too often fails to examine Article 9 claims when they are pleaded alongside other issues, suggesting that this is problematic on two grounds. First, it raises questions about procedural fairness; second, it risks undermining the legitimacy of the judicial process by denying litigants the sense that their claims have been fully heard and considered. We are persuaded that Ouald Chaib's logic is sound in both of these respects.

In addition to this general challenge, there appear at times to be higher hurdles in the Strasbourg jurisprudence for non-religious beliefs than for the religious beliefs. While it is true that some non-religious beliefs (such as pacifism) have been recognised as coming within the ambit of Article 9,[55] applicants who assert non-religious beliefs have tended to struggle to satisfy the courts that their Article 9 rights have been engaged at all. For example, in *Pretty v United Kingdom*[56] the European Court of Human Rights (ECtHR) refused to accept that the practice of assisted suicide would come within the umbrella of Article 9(2):

> Her claims do not involve a form of manifestation of a belief through worship, teaching, practice or observance as described by the first paragraph. As found by the Commission the term 'practice' as employed in Article 9 s. 1 does not cover each act which is motivated or influenced by religion or belief.[57]

Similarly, in *Jones v United Kingdom*[58] the ECtHR refused to accept that the placement of a memorial photo in a burial ground could amount to a manifestation of belief for the purposes of Article 9.

We would suggest that one reason why the Court has frequently found non-religious beliefs to be a stumbling block relates to a perceptive criticism which Su[59] made of the jurisprudence of both North American and European courts when faced with assessing the sincerity of religious beliefs for the purposes of discrimination and accommodation claims. The point which she made in relation to religious beliefs is amplified considerably if we translate it to the context of non-religious beliefs. Su argues that, although courts assert that they avoid involving themselves in questions of religious doctrine and focus on the sincerity of the believer as opposed to the orthodoxy of the belief, the reality is far more

54 S. Ouald Chaib 'Procedural Fairness as a Vehicle for Inclusion in the Freedom of Religion Jurisprudence of the Strasbourg Court, *Human Rights Law Review*, Vol. 16, No. 3 (2016) 483–510, 509.

55 *Arrowsmith v United Kingdom* (1978) 3 EHRR 218.

56 *Pretty v United Kingdom*, App. no. 2346/02, Judgment, 29 July 2002 (ECtHR).

57 Ibid., para. 82.

58 *Jones v United Kingdom*, App. no. 42639/04, Judgment, 13 Sept 2005 (ECtHR).

59 A. Su, 'Judging Religious Sincerity', *Oxford Journal of Law and Religion*, Vol. 5, No. 1 (2016) 28–48, 43.

complex than this. In fact, a 'hands off' approach to doctrine is impossible to sustain and, at times, courts even resort to expert testimony on the normative content of religions.

We would concur with this assessment, and suggest that it raises a double complexity in the case of non-religious beliefs. First, a non-religious belief may not be tied to a group or tradition with any identifiable norms or parameters – for example, there are vegan groups and support groups, but no schools or denomination of veganism in the same way in which there are identifiable religious groupings and subgroupings. Second, since the courts are reluctant to admit their concern with the normative status of beliefs, it is difficult for them to articulate this problem, and it is therefore more straightforward for judges to dismiss or sideline any Article 9 issues raised in litigation surrounding non-religious beliefs.

This issue alone would raise sufficient barriers in many cases, but we further suggest that another challenge has been identified in the religious context, which has even greater implications for a negative bearing upon non-religious Article 9 claims. Peroni[60] asserts that by framing religion primarily in terms of freedom of conscience or belief, the Court is implicitly characterising religion *as* belief or conscience and, in practical terms, it is privileging a Western, Protestant understanding of religion.

Here the criticism is being levelled as much at the drafting of Article 9 as at its judicial interpretation. The Convention itself casts freedom of religion in the mould of a manifestation of a belief. We have criticised this in previous work, on the basis that it fails adequately to deal with the religious freedom of children[61] and adults who lack full mental capacity, either on a temporary or a permanent basis.

McIvor[62] also points out the problematic dynamic of this dimension of Article 9. She argues that the 'inbuilt privileging of the *forum internum* over manifestation' has made it difficult to protect objects used for religious purposes. In McIvor's analysis, this emphasis on a belief-based approach to the total exclusion of alternative or complementary forms of embodied engagement is deeply unsatisfactory – or, in other words, the practice of religion is more than the acting out of an intellectual belief. If protecting religion in law is reduced to safeguarding the freedom to act out an intellectual belief, then we are left with a legal framework which protects only one dimension of religious practice. Even worse, minority faith groups within the western European context are those most likely to fall through the holes in the safety net of the Convention, as they are generally further from the Protestant/intellectual religious paradigm.

We would endorse this criticism, but crucially would also extend it to non-religious beliefs. In some senses, applicants seeking to assert a non-religious belief

60 L. Peroni, 'On Religious and Cultural Equality in European Human Rights Convention Law', *Netherlands Quarterly of Human Rights*, Vol. 32, No. 3 (2014) 231–4, 231.

61 J. García Oliva and H. Hall, 'Religious Decision-Making and the Capacity of Children in the United Kingdom', *Laicidad y Libertades: Escritos Jurídicos*, Vol. 1 (2013) 137–70.

62 M. McIvor, 'Carnal Exhibitions: Material Religion and the ECHR', *Ecclesiastical Law Journal*, Vol. 17, No. 1 (2015) 3–14, 13.

are in an even weaker position by virtue of the point which we made in relation to Su's analysis. If, despite their protests to the contrary, courts are inclined to look for normative criteria when assessing the sincerity of their beliefs, applicants who are not coming from a tradition of religious belief, with a set of established norms, are in a weaker position to demonstrate the sincerity and seriousness of the belief or practice for which protection is sought.

Essentially, the alternative gateway of the Common Law presumption also allows for non-religious beliefs which may not be matters of rational, intellectual conscience, but are nonetheless deeply significant for the people who hold them. A juridical framework which can embrace religious beliefs – which, as Domingo argues, by their very nature are apt to be suprarational[63] rather than rational – can logically also take cognisance of non-religious beliefs which are profound but not necessarily rooted in logic. In this sense, a religious legal system is arguably better placed than one which lies closer to the secular end of spectrum of Church/state relations to meet the needs of citizens with some types of non-religious belief; conversely, a consciously secular juridical system is more likely to adopt an intellectual, rationalist model of belief. Worryingly, citizens with non-religious beliefs which neither fall within the category of religion, nor appeal to the world of abstract ideas, are likely to find themselves unprotected in such a paradigm.

3.4.2 Non-religious folk beliefs and customs

In contrast, the religious juridical system in Great Britain at times bends for non-religious beliefs that are not related to matters of conscience. We would suggest that this is important in any society, but especially perhaps in one in which many citizens are disengaged from organised religion.

Brown argues that many people act upon the basis of beliefs[64] that do not take the form of religion as the Anglo-American imagination is inclined to categorise it. This is a view borne out by anthropological study. Take, for example, spontaneous 'shrines', which are apt to spring up when a person dies a sudden and usually violent death. Flowers, cards, cuddly toys and other tokens are placed at the sight of the tragedy, or other significant location such as the home, school or workplace of the deceased. Santino argues that spontaneous shrines create a link between mourners and the departed: they 'insert and insist upon the presence of absent people'.[65] Yet many of those who create them would deny that they are inspired by any 'religious' impulse; neither could they, nor would they claim that

63 R. Domingo, *God and the Secular Legal System* (Cambridge University Press: Cambridge) 2016, 96.

64 A. Brown, 'Paganism is Alive and Well – but you won't find it at a Goddess Temple', *The Spectator* (14 Feb 2015), https://www.spectator.co.uk/2015/02/paganism-is-alive-and-well-but-you-wont-find-it-at-a-goddess-temple.

65 J. Santino, 'Performative Commemoratives: Spontaneous Shrines and the Public Memorialization of Death', in J. Santino (ed.), *Spontaneous Shrines and the Public Memorialization of Death* (Palgrave Macmillan: Basingstoke) 2006, 5–16, 13.

they were acting on the kind of belief which would satisfy the criteria laid down in *Williamson*. If a local authority wished to ban or remove such tributes from a particular location, those wishing to leave them in place could not have recourse to Article 9. Yet, presumably people do these things out of a belief that it will bring them comfort, demonstrate solidarity with other mourners or make some symbolic or literal connection with the departed.

Similarly, as the outcome of *Jones v United Kingdom* demonstrates, non-religious wishes in respect of funerals and memorials will often not come under the protective umbrella of Article 9. Yet, as far as the significance for the deceased is concerned, is there really a difference in terms of the need to act out a ritual, which brings comfort and has meaning for their inner life? A Roman Catholic parent who tragically loses a child may find solace from leaving a lighted candle burning in front of a statue of the Virgin Mary, asking the Mother of God to pray for their loved one. Equally, a non-religious parent might go and place a toy windmill on the child's grave, finding some small sense of peace and connection. Surely, both actions are equally meaningful and significant for the individuals involved. Yet the former would qualify as a manifestation of a religious belief, and secure protection via Article 9, while the latter comparable action probably would not.

A similar point may be made in respect of more everyday or joyful expressions of belief and custom, and it can be seen that the law in practice often accommodates them. For example, it is well established law that ear piercing is one of the common law exceptions to the general principle that individuals may not consent to actual bodily harm or more serious harm.[66] However, at first sight it is less clear why the ear piercing of non-competent minors is permissible, because generally the law does not allow parents to modify their children's bodies for non-medical reasons outside the now controversial realm of ritual male circumcision.[67] Yet, ear piercing is relatively common and not subject to legal challenge, even in respect of babies and toddlers who can have no meaningful agency in the decision.

We would suggest that it is no coincidence that ear piecing is a mainstream part of many cultures.[68] While some critics of the practice regard it is unnecessary mutilation, even describing it as 'child cruelty' inflicted for the vanity of the parents,[69] the parents who choose it are frequently following some cultural practice in which they believe. It is often not tied to a religion, and many would probably struggle to articulate a self-consistent coherent underlying rationale which would travel through the hoops of Article 9. In reality, however, parents

66 *R v Brown* [1994] 1 AC 212.

67 Consider, e.g., the Tattooing of Minors Act 1969.

68 See, e.g., A. Gottlieb and J. Deloache, *A World of Babies: Imagined Childcare Guides for Eight Societies* (Cambridge University Press: Cambridge) 2016, 179.

69 R. Sanghani, 'Thousands Call for Ear-Piercing to be Banned for Children in the UK', *The Telegraph* (11 June 2015), http://www.telegraph.co.uk/women/life/thousands-call-for-ear-piercing-to-be-banned-for-babies-in-the-uk.

often make this choice because they hold a belief that it is part of the process of the girl-child taking on her gender identity.[70] For people who are part of a culture in which women have both ears pierced, and men have one or neither ears pierced, modifying a female infant's body in this manner is one way in which she takes her place within her community.

Of course, there are those who strongly disagree for a myriad of reasons. If actual bodily harm is not permitted in relation to corporal punishment, why should it be allowed on *any* other non-medical basis? If the practice is carried out by some cultural groups as part of the process of acquiring a gender identity, is it not harmful for individuals whose gender identity turns out not to match their biological sex? While arguments like this are powerful, we suggest that the practice is ultimately admitted on the strength of cultural beliefs. These would not satisfy the rigours of Article 9, but they do pass through the filters of a legal framework which has a soft presumption in favour of supporting the beliefs of individuals, unless there is a good reason to displace this.

A similar pattern can be found in the arena of folk customs. A number of societies and communities believe in following ancient customs and traditions, some of which would fall foul of modern legislative demands if the law did not flex to accommodate folk beliefs. Practices which may not be the manifestation of beliefs that would satisfy the *Williamson* test may nevertheless be an expression of values and bonds which run very deep for those involved.

The culture of Morris dancing provides an interesting example. As Mac-Sithigh[71] observes, Morris dancers have been granted a number of concessions in both primary and secondary legislation.[72] In essence, they are permitted to perform without seeking an entertainment licence from the local authority, when this would now ordinarily be required for the performance of live music. In addition, the drafting of the Equality Act 2010 is broad enough to permit Morris organisations that wish to maintain male-only dancing to do so.[73]

There are other folk groups with cultural beliefs and practices which are accommodated by the legal framework – cheese rolling in Gloucestershire is one such example.[74] Participants in the event chase a wheel of cheese down an extremely steep slope, often falling and sustaining injury in the process, but the event is permitted and even facilitated by public authorities; the only disruption to have occurred in recent times arising from the level of risk came in 2010,

70 C. Mitchell and J. Reid-Walsh, *Girl Culture: An Encyclopaedia* (Greenwood Press: London) 2007, 195.

71 D. Mac Sithigh, 'Flags, Priests and Morris Dancers: a Case for Medium Law', *SLS Paperbank* (2016).

72 Licensing Act 2003, Live Music Act 2012, and Legislative Reform (Entertainment Licensing) Order 2014.

73 J. Copping, 'Morris Men Must Allow in Morris Women, but not to Dance', *The Telegraph* (24 Apr 2011), http://www.telegraph.co.uk/news/newstopics/howaboutthat/8469817/Morris-men-must-allow-in-morris-women-but-not-to-dance.html.

74 See the official website for the Cooper's Hill event: 'Cheese Rolling in Gloucestershire', http://www.cheese-rolling.co.uk/index1.htm.

when the event was cancelled because of fears about the safety of the spectators.[75] There have been no attempts to stop it on the basis that it is dangerous for those actually taking part. The event was cancelled again the following year, but this was because of a dispute over charging a £20 entry fee and the indignant response from the local community.[76] Feelings ran high with verbal abuse and threats of serious violence. Clearly, to those involved, the cheese rolling was anything but trivial.

Just as religious groups have rituals which express their values and cement their ties, so do citizens brought together by non-religious beliefs and customs. A belief in maintaining tradition and community ties can be of immense importance, and the legal support for customs like Morris dancing and cheese rolling demonstrate this.

3.4.3 Non-religious beliefs and lifestyle choices

A third category of non-religious beliefs are those which cannot comfortably be categorised as matters of conscience, in the sense that an individual feels compelled to act in a particular way by his or her personal ethics, but nor are they related to folk beliefs. They might be categorised as conscious lifestyle choices. Those who manifest such beliefs would not claim a sense of ethical duty, but nevertheless have a strong preference for a particular lifestyle choice which flows from the belief in question.

One example of such a choice would be naturism. Undeniably, some naturists behave in a way which appears to be closely akin to those acting out of an imperative ethical duty, but many do not. Some see it as an activity which they enjoy and can pursue when circumstances permit, whereas others are driven to take a principled stand. In *Gough v DPP*[77] the so-called 'naked rambler' sought to challenge the sentence he had received for insisting on appearing in public, hiking naked apart from walking boots, socks and a hat. Recourse to human rights arguments did not help him and, in fact, took the same trajectory identified by Cumper and Lewis.[78] He sought to apply Article 10 ECHR, rather than Article 9, but the outcome was no different. It was found that while his Article 10 right was engaged, it did not entitle him to 'trample roughshod'[79] over the rights of the majority to 'enjoy a shared public space without being caused distress and upset'.[80]

75 'Gloucestershire Cheese-Rolling Off due to Safety Fears', *BBC News* (12 Mar 2010), http://news.bbc.co.uk/1/hi/england/gloucestershire/8563692.stm.

76 'Spitting, Threats and … Arson? Gloucestershire Cheese-Rolling Festival Cancelled for the Second Year Running after Organisers Receive Abuse over £20 Entry Fee', *The Daily Mail* (25 Mar 2011), http://www.dailymail.co.uk/news/article-1369824/Thoroughly-cheesed-Gloucestershire-cheese-rolling-festival-cancelled-second-year-running-organisers-receive-abuse-20-entry-fee.html.

77 *Gough v Director of Public Prosecutions* [2013] EWHC 3267 (Admin).

78 Cumper and Lewis, n. 50 above.

79 *Gough v Director of Public Prosecutions*, n. 77 above, para. 12.

80 Ibid.

Papworth[81] has characterised this as an endorsement of human rights, but the human rights of citizens who wanted to go about their business without being confronted with the applicant's nudity. Yet another element of the judgment is striking: the court did explicitly accept that Gough's perspective was a minority view which had to be respected and, although there was no recourse to Article 9, the significance of a conscientious position was duly noted and affirmed by the court.

It should also be observed that being naked in public is not, in and of itself, a criminal offence, and the Crown Prosecution Service has issued guidelines on what may be construed as criminal conduct.[82] Generally speaking, if there is an offence it will fall under the Public Order Act 1986; other possibilities include exposure contrary to s. 66 of the Sexual Offences Act 2003 (which criminalises the exposure of genitals with the intent that another person will see them and suffer alarm or distress), and the common law offence of outraging public decency.

Although at first sight the variety of possible criminal offences might suggest that the legal framework is hostile towards naturism, closer examination reveals a far more nuanced picture. It is clear that it is a minority practice, and one which generally stems from abstract beliefs about what is natural and healthy. If put into practice in some contexts, this belief will have what is currently judged to be a negative impact upon other citizens. However, if undertaken in appropriate locations, such as recognised nudist beaches, no criminal sanctions will be triggered. Furthermore, the state has issued guidance on what is deemed problematic, partly to help citizens who wish to engage in this minority practice.

Therefore, the legal system provides some space and support for a manifestation of naturist beliefs, without direct recourse to human rights law.

3.4.4 An alternative approach to Article 9

It is interesting that in the case of naturism, the legal system has flexed to accommodate a non-religious belief without recourse to human rights law. In fact, Article 9 may not always be the only means of securing protection, or even the most effective means of doing so. There are, in fact, some circumstances in which commentators have suggested that it may hinder rather than help.

Cumper and Lewis[83] make a persuasive, but in some ways disturbing case that there are occasions when invoking arguments based on human rights has the effect of weakening, rather than strengthening, protection for religious practices. They argue that the Administrative Court in the *Ghai* litigation[84] applied the criteria contained in Article 9 and found that the applicant's deep

81 N. Papworth, 'A Right to be Naked in a Public Place', *Criminal Law and Justice Weekly*, 177 JPN (2013) 843.

82 Crown Prosecution Service, 'Nudity in Public – Guidance on Handling Cases of Naturism', cps.gov.uk/legal/I_to_o/nudity_in_public.

83 Cumper and Lewis, n. 50 above, 151.

84 *R (on the application of Ghai) v Newcastle City Council*, n. 48 above.

need to practise his faith and secure the future of his soul could be overridden on the basis that the state was pursuing a legitimate aim in seeking to protect others from being offended by an open-air cremation, despite the fact that they would not actually see it. In other words, the mechanism of Article 9 allowed for a form of cultural relativism to take over, and the assumed offence to the majority justified curtailing religious practice by the minority.

Given the challenges inherent in the drafting of Article 9, it may be helpful for litigants in some contexts to focus on the seriousness and integrity of their non-religious belief, and the importance which it has for them. In other words, instead of going through the gateway of Article 9, it may be preferable to access protection and recognition via other routes.

Instances like the partial accommodation of naturism and the folk beliefs described above strengthen the argument made by Cumper and Lewis'[85] that there should be room for compassion in the courts' treatment of freedom of belief, and we would assert that this should apply as much to non-rational, non-religious beliefs as to religious beliefs. We would argue that compassion is not merely desirable, as it is already in place. In fact, it is shown in the soft presumption that favours the accommodation of non-religious beliefs where this is possible.

3.5 Final reflections and the specific contribution of a sample of non-religious belief groups

3.5.1 Final reflections

Just as in Chapter 2 we identified that there were direct benefits flowing from the religious legal framework for citizens with religious beliefs, we have demonstrated that there are *indirect* benefits to citizens who wish to express non-religious beliefs, worldviews or lifestyles.

As set out above, these indirect benefits take three forms:

(a) protection of beliefs by association;
(b) protection of non-religious beliefs by analogy; and
(c) recognition of beliefs and expressions of belief which would not meet the *Williamson* criteria, but nevertheless have deep significance for those who hold them.

We have argued that a religious legal system is actually better equipped than a secular system to give space to these non-religious needs, because in embracing religion it necessarily encompasses a conception of belief and manifestations of belief which goes beyond adherence to an abstract intellectual position. In our view, this support for belief beyond religious belief is highly positive, as many

85 Cumper and Lewis, n. 50 above.

non-religious beliefs enrich the lives of individuals who hold them and contribute to our collective cultural and legal life.

For the remainder of this book, we shall return to our primary focus of religion and the legal framework, exploring in the following chapters how the religious character of the juridical system relates to the foundational pillars of the Constitution, and the contributions that faith communities might make towards this. In each chapter, we shall include reflections about the ways in which religious-based groups influence the thinking of their members in relation to the constitutional principles. However, bearing in mind that our assertion is that non-religious groups are also supported by the current system, we will pause, in the next and final sub-section of this chapter, to consider the ways in which the ideas and aims of some groups bound together by non-religious beliefs might influence the thoughts of their members in relation to the pillars of the Constitution.

3.5.2 The specific contribution of a sample of non-religious belief groups

If the current framework benefits 'belief' more widely than religious belief, do the manifestations of these non-religious beliefs feed back positive ideas into the system? Obviously, all we can do in the space available is to give a sample, and we freely acknowledge the point that among non-religious and religious groups there will be both constructive and destructive traits. Nevertheless, if we later include some instances of supportive themes (to the constitutional pillars) among religious-based communities, it appears only just and appropriate to include some comparable intellectual contributions from non-religious belief groups. It should also be recognised that the pillars of the Constitution will be thoroughly explained in Chapters 4 to 7, and we invite our readers to bear in mind our analysis of those constitutional foundations for the present purposes.

3.5.2.1 The Badger Trust and the rule of law

The Badger Trust is an organisation allied to beliefs about animal welfare and the need to safeguard badgers in particular. While not all of its members and supporters could necessarily be said to hold beliefs of the kind that would pass the *Williamson* test, nevertheless there is undoubtedly a shared vision.

The mission of the Badger Trust is described as follows: '. . . to use all lawful means to campaign for the improved welfare, protection, and conservation of badgers, their setts and habitats'.[86]

As an organisation, it can be seen to have strong support for the rule of law in two respects: first, the Trust co-operates with statutory authorities and other organisations in the voluntary sector in an effort to further the prevention and prosecution of illegal actions by third parties; second, it encourages individuals with a concern for badgers to use only lawful methods to pursue their cause.

86 The Badger Trust, 'What We Do', http://badger.org.uk/about/what-we-do.aspx.

In terms of addressing unlawful action, the Trust undertakes the following:

> Our members remain active and vigilant and often appear for the prosecution as expert witnesses when lawbreakers appear before the courts. Badger groups work constantly with developers and planning authorities to minimise the wilful illegal destruction of badger setts.[87]

Thus, the Trust aids the detection and reporting of unlawful activity, as well as the appropriate juridical process in respect of the same. Its role is equally important in terms of persuading those who feel passionately about badgers to use only legitimate methods to protest about government policy or to tackle abuses by third parties. Given the strength of feeling generated by the current debate around the culling of badgers, this is a valuable and much needed contribution to the collective dialogue on the matter.[88] The Badger Trust urges its members, and others willing to listen to its views, to bear in mind that it is both possible and necessary to save the badger population from the cull without resorting to illegal methods or intimidation. Consequently, a non-religious organisation with a focus on a particular area of wildlife protection can be seen to be working actively to promote the rule of law.

3.5.2.2 Stonewall and parliamentary sovereignty

Stonewall is an organisation with clearly stated ideological values. It supports lesbian, gay, bisexual and transgender people in particular, indicating that its work will be complete 'when everyone feels free to be who they are, wherever they are'.[89] It would be unjust to suggest that its primary focus indicates an indifference to other concerns – for example, some of their educational material on the theme 'Different Families: Same Love'[90] promotes the idea that families with same-sex parents are equally loving and nurturing as those with heterosexual couples in parenting roles. The same artwork also includes positive depictions of other families which depart from some societal expectations, such as families with grandparents in parenting roles. These are also promoted and affirmed. Consequently, although Stonewall has a clear agenda, it is not exclusivist or narrow in focus. Its values are aligned towards fostering a positive and cohesive society.

As an organisation, Stonewall is by no means negative towards religious people or practice and, in fact, campaigns for an end to discrimination in relation to faith communities and worship. In its priorities, for example, it includes the following comment in relation to 'empowering individuals': 'We will empower people of all ages and backgrounds to be role models and allies wherever they live, work,

87 Ibid.

88 The Badger Trust, 'Stop the Cull', http://badger.org.uk/campaigns/stop-the-cull.aspx.

89 Stonewall, 'Our Mission', http://www.stonewall.org.uk/about-us/our-mission.

90 Stonewall, Education, 'Different Families: Same Love', http://www.stonewall.org.uk/get-involved/education/different-families-same-love.

shop, socialise and pray. We will support them, and the people they reach, to be themselves and achieve their full potential'.[91]

In the context of transforming institutions Stonewall 'will work with all organisations, including workplaces, schools, healthcare providers, sports clubs and religious institutions, here and abroad, to ensure they offer inclusive, equal and inspiring environments for lesbian, gay, bi and trans people'. It also includes in its literature a booklet of Christian role models, with stories from individuals who have reconciled their faith and sexuality.

Stonewall is extremely supportive of and actively engaged in the democratic process, lobbying Parliament and MPs in relation to its various campaigns. It also seeks to contribute to the collective dialogue, both as an institution and through helping and empowering individuals. Stonewall sees legal reform through legislative change as being an important tool for reshaping society along more inclusive lines. Its message of respect and inclusion, and *modus operandi* of dialogue and education are by nature fundamentally in harmony with the democratic principles which are at the heart of parliamentary sovereignty. When we address the activities of faith groups in Chapter 5 (relating to this constitutional pillar), it will be seen that many groups driven by religious beliefs make a comparable contribution.

3.5.2.3 Woodcraft Folk movement and checks and balances/separation of powers

Once again, this is a good illustration of how the contribution of non-religious belief groups can very much parallel the kind of support for constitutional structure that religious belief groups also offer. As an organisation, the Woodcraft Folk is held together by shared values which are clear and identifiable, but which might be too loose to satisfy the *Williamson* criteria.

It developed in the early twentieth century, and grew out of individuals who were drawn to some aspects of scouting, but found other areas difficult.[92] It has continued to provide some of the outdoor and collaborative experiences available through Scouting and Guides, but without elements which some people found personally problematic (such as a perceived militaristic ethos, religious dimension, gender division, perceived age discrimination and support for the monarchy). It has had strong links with the Co-operative movement[93] from its early days, and these have been maintained. Woodcraft Folk is still represented on the Co-op's values and principles committee, which ensures the Co-op fulfils its ethical principles and uses some of its profits to strengthen local communities.

91 Stonewall, 'Our Priorities', http://www.stonewall.org.uk/about-us/stonewalls-key-priorities.

92 Woodcraft Folk, 'History', http://woodcraft.org.uk/history.

93 See further, The Co-operative Groups, 'Values and Principles', http://www.co-operative.coop/corporate/aboutus/The-Co-operative-Group-Values-and-Principles.

It would be fair to say that Woodcraft Folk has a pronounced left-wing ethos, although there is no requirement for any political affiliation in order to join. It is also religiously open, but requires that members must not practise their faith in a way that contravenes the aims of the movement:

> The Woodcraft Folk welcomes all children, young people and adults, who wish to become members of the movement, and it asserts the right of all its members to practice the faith of their choice providing it does not contravene the aims and principles of the movement.[94]

In practical terms, some faith groups and/or traditions within faith groups would find active participation in activities harder than others. Clearly, any group that requires rigid gender segregation would not find the way in which Woodcraft Folk operates to be an appropriate environment, but equally many religious people would find the ideals of the movement and its manner of operating to be very much in harmony with their values and lifestyle.

Importantly, for present purposes, the five common themes which are shared by the religious traditions that will be explained later in this book are all equally relevant in so far as the Woodcraft Folk movement is concerned. Its values and beliefs are set out in a range of policy documents, including their 'Educational Aims and Principles'.[95] The second of these aims and principles is explicitly:

> We seek to develop in our members a critical awareness of the world. We will work to develop the knowledge, attitudes, values and skills necessary for them to act to secure their equal participation in the democratic process that will enable them to bring about the changes that they feel are necessary to create a more equal and caring world. As an educational movement, we believe that equal opportunities should extend to all aspects of activity and participation in the Woodcraft Folk. We will combat oppression or discrimination in our movement, whether on grounds of age, class, gender, race, sexual orientation or for reasons of disability. We will educate our members so that they may take these issues into the wider community.

As with most of the religious groups, the express *aim* is not to keep a check on the way in which authority structures in society use their powers. Nevertheless, in order to pursue this goal, it is a practical necessity to engage with authority figures and structures, and there is express mention of participation in the democratic process with a view towards shaping a more 'equal and caring world'. Clearly, monitoring and challenging injustices and improper use of power is one obvious element of furthering this endeavour.

94 Woodcraft Folk, 'Woodcraft Aims, Principles and Programme', https://woodcraft.org.uk/aims-and-principles.

95 Ibid.

Furthermore, the movement places great emphasis on respect for others, peace and collaboration. Like the religious groups, dialogue and a collaborative approach to problem solving would be the first and preferred recourse where issues arise.

3.5.2.4 The National Secular Society and human rights

As might be expected from its name, the National Secular Society (NSS) states its purpose in the following terms:

> The National Secular Society works towards a society in which all citizens, regardless of religious belief, or lack of religious belief, can live together fairly and cohesively. We campaign for a secular democracy with a separation of religion and state, where everyone's Human Rights are respected equally.[96]

Clearly, while in many people's minds secularism might be associated with Atheism, the agenda set out above is one to which religious believers could and do subscribe. The NSS defines secularism as the separation of religion from the state and the principle that different religions and beliefs should be equal before the law.[97] Moreover, the NSS asserts that this protects both religious and non-religious citizens.

It must be acknowledged that the chosen strap line of the society 'Challenging religious privilege'[98] could be seen as antagonistic towards religion, and there are those who would suggest that the NSS in reality has had a negative and confrontational attitude towards faith from its early days.[99] Nevertheless, it should be stressed that this is a matter of external perception, rather than its stated agenda.

What is clear is that the NSS does set out an express commitment to human rights. Obviously, as we will see in Chapter 7 (on human rights), there is a necessary and ongoing social dialogue about which rights should be included in the legally recognised canon of fundamental rights, how these should be interpreted and what should be done to resolve clashes appropriately between competing rights. Religious belief groups contribute to this wider dialogue, and the NSS is an example of a non-religious belief-based group also participating. Voices from a variety of perspectives (which will be mutually complementary on some issues and mutually antagonistic on others) are beneficial if the political and legal framework is to reflect the ideological centre of gravity when it comes to human rights.

96 National Secular Society, 'About the National Secular Society', http://www.secularism.org.uk/about.html

97 National Secular Society, 'What is Secularism?', http://www.secularism.org.uk/what-is-secularism.html.

98 National Secular Society, 'Homepage', http://www.secularism.org.uk.

99 H. Carey, 'Secularism v Christianity in Australian History', in C. Hartley (ed.), *Secularism: New Historical Perspectives* (Cambridge Scholars Publishing: Newcastle) 2014, Ch. 2, 8–33, 19.

In campaigning from its particular standpoint, therefore, the NSS is adding value to this national dialogue on human rights. Moreover, it enhances the operation of the current human rights framework by highlighting apparent instances where the present system is not being implemented, and human rights are therefore being undermined. For example, it published concerns over faith schools which were operating outside the law, to the potential detriment of the rights of children to receive an appropriate and adequate education.[100]

Taken in the round, when the activities of this non-religious belief-based group are considered together, it can be seen that it does help in promoting the functioning of key pillars of the British Constitution.

100 NSS, 'News', http://www.secularism.org.uk/news.html.

4 The rule of law and the religious character of the Constitution and the wider legal framework

4.1 Introduction – penguins and catching fish

In the preceding chapters, our journey through history and the contemporary legal world has revealed how dramatically the role of religion within the juridical system has changed over time, and the question remaining is whether the model which has emerged from the evolutionary process is fit for purpose. Is the current treatment of religion positive and beneficial for citizens and the state, a cumbersome and anachronistic irrelevance, or even an actively damaging force?

In the concluding part of Chapter 2, we suggested that there are good reasons to assert that this current structure, like the wings of a penguin, has altered but remains a valuable asset. Furthermore, although the *form and role* of penguin wings are very different for a swimming bird than a bird that flies, some of the underlying *purposes* of the wings have remained constant. In the days when penguins flew and swooped like guillemots, they spent a great amount of their time and energy catching fish. Modern penguins still require nutrition, but they now have a very different technique for capturing their prey.

Similarly, is it possible that some continuity might be discerned in the deep collective needs of the state? It could be suggested, for example, that the problem of keeping an appropriate check on the exercise of executive power is a recurring theme in the history of Great Britain. Are there some repeated patterns to be found in the wrangling over the Divine Right of Kings in the Stuart era, and modern judicial review actions brought against government ministers? Arguably the core issue of keeping executive action accountable and within identifiable boundaries remains. It is true that the parallels are not entirely unproblematic. For instance, how far is the basis and nature of accountability within an early modern state truly comparable with that in a twenty-first century representative democracy? We will return to the specific issue of judicial review later in our study. Nevertheless, the overarching question of continuity at a deep level certainly merits exploration.

Essentially, in this and the following chapters, we shall be taking one of the founding pillars of the British Constitution and asking how it relates to the religious character of the legal framework – the religious character in this sense being understood to reflect the tripartite structure set out in the preceding chapter, and to distinguish it from secular frameworks such as those of France or the United States of America. In the first section we shall explore the operation of the principle in the contemporary context. We shall then move on to analyse whether the principles enshrined within that pillar are strengthened or weakened by the British legal framework concerning religion, and this will be followed by a discussion of how the teachings and perspective of the various religious groups (including Humanist organisations, as described at the beginning of Chapter 3) influence their members' perceptions of the rule of law. The final section will explore some of the practical ways in which the activities of faith groups facilitate or promote the practical outworking of this constitutional principle. As set out in the Introduction, this is not intended to be a sociological exercise, and certainly not to balance the benefits and detriments of faith-based activities. It is simply an observation of some tangible ways in which such groups currently enrich these constitutional foundations.

In concrete terms, this chapter will adopt the following structure (and Chapters 4 to 6 will be essentially isomorphic):

1. What does the rule of law mean in the context of the UK Constitution?
2. Does the religious character of the legal and constitutional system enhance or weaken the rule of law?
3. How do the teachings and perspective of the various religious groups influence their members' perceptions of the rule of law?
4. From a more practical point of view, do faith communities in Great Britain make a tangible contribution to the operation of the rule of law?
5. Conclusions.

4.2. What does the rule of law mean in the context of the UK constitution?

Before assessing the impact that religious bodies have upon the functioning of the rule of law, it is obviously necessary to establish what the term 'rule of law' actually means. This is a challenging task, because as Elliott and Thomas rightly observe,[1] of all of the main constitutional principles, the rule of law is probably the most elusive.

Commentators have produced varying schools of thought on the concept, and although we shall consider each of them in detail below, our aim is not to carry out a thorough analysis of the doctrinal understandings of every principle in every chapter, as this has been successfully done elsewhere.[2] However, it is crucial not

1 M. Elliott and R. Thomas, *Public Law* (Oxford University Press: Oxford) 2nd edn, 2014, 62.

2 T. Bingham, *The Rule of Law* (Penguin: London) 2011; B. Tamanaha, *On the Rule of Law: History, Politics, Theory* (Cambridge University Press: Cambridge) 2004; T. Etherton, 'Religion, the Rule of Law and Discrimination', *Ecclesiastical Law Journal*, Vol, 16, No. 3 (2014) 265–82 ; A. Staiculescu and M. Bala, 'The Rule of Law: Challenges and Opportunities', *Contemporary Readings in Social Justice*, Vol. 5, No. 2 (2013) 837.

to allow the rule of law (or, indeed, any of the other constitutional foundations) to disappear into the mist of political philosophy by virtue of its contested nature, like the Loch Ness monster of doctrines. Just because the rule of law is a much debated principle, it does not follow that it is vague or without substance. It has long been firmly established as one of the pillars of the UK legal framework.[3]

In some senses, the content of the rule of law resembles the formula for creating the perfect pancake. Pancakes are different according to varying national and cultural contexts (spongey, cakey American breakfast pancakes are very distinct from their refined French cousin, crêpes); similarly, the way in which the rule of law is understood to operate in Great Britain, particularly in terms of notions such as legal certainty, is quite distinct from that of jurisdictions such as Japan.[4] However, even when the national context is established, there is scope for endless dispute about the best recipe and method of serving.

There are, undoubtedly, many variations on the traditional British Shrove Tuesday pancake. Should it be served with sugar and lemon juice, or butter and golden syrup? Is the European innovation of Nutella now an accepted component? Nevertheless, there are some core elements (flour, milk, eggs, butter and salt) which are universally agreed to be non-negotiable ingredients. Furthermore, it is possible to put forward a reasoned justification as to why the other possible additions are either beneficial and/or essential (for example, to avoid blandness, or to use up sugar before Lenten austerity commences).

In a similar way, it is also feasible to identify certain key components widely understood to be included in the UK conception of the rule of law, and further to examine the merits of the arguments for incorporating other factors within its formulation. On this basis, having a focused discussion about the rule of law and to arrive at a rationally defensible definition of the doctrine is an achievable aim, even though no one definition would ever be accepted by all commentators in the British context.

4.2.1 The principle of legality (plain pancake)

In his insightful book on the rule of law, Tamanaha observes that a common strand in all understandings of the principle is the contrast between the rule of law and the rule of man. This commentator states as follows:

> To live under the Rule of Law is not to be subject to the unpredictable vagaries of other individuals, whether monarchs, judges, government officials or fellow citizens. It is to be shielded from the familiar human weaknesses of bias, passion, prejudice, error, ignorance, cupidity of whim.[5]

3 J.H. Baker, *An Introduction to English Legal History* (Butterworths: London) 3rd edn, 1990, 165.
4 See, e.g., M. Dean, *Japanese Legal System* (Cavendish Publishing: London) 2002.
5 Tamanaha, n. 2 above, 122

The principle of legality requires that society operates in accordance with rules, and that the rules are introduced in the prescribed and approved manner. Anyone who has ever had the experience of playing board games with younger children (and, indeed, certain adults) knows how frustrating it is when a small arbitrary tyrant purports to make up and change the rules from minute to minute to suit his or her purposes. Arbitrary powers are the antithesis of the rule of law. In order to satisfy the principle of legality, rules must be properly enacted in accordance with the requirements of the relevant legal system.[6] Therefore, in the case of an Act of Parliament in the United Kingdom, the provisions must be approved by both Houses of Parliament.[7] Although this might at first sound rather obvious and somewhat theoretical, the principle of legality does have practical application and is called upon by the courts. The classic example is the celebrated case of *Entick v Carrington*:[8] a government minister purported to issue a warrant authorising his agents to burgle Mr Entick's house in search of seditious papers. The court found that the minister had no legal power to issue such a warrant, and held that his agents had committed trespass in violating the plaintiff's home and damaging his property.

However, it would be wrong to think that the need to call upon the principle of legality disappeared when powdered wigs fell out of fashion. In the far more recent case of *Witham*[9] a government minister attempted to make rules which were beyond the scope of the power delegated to him. Here again the court cited the principle of legality in striking the rules down.

Similarly, in *Beghal v DPP*[10] the courts highlighted the importance of the principle of legality in relation to protecting fundamental freedoms. In this case, the appellant was questioned at an airport on the basis of Schedule 7 of the Terrorism Act 2000. She was not formally detained, but the questioning process lasted for around an hour and three quarters. During this time, she refused to answer any questions and was subsequently convicted of wilfully refusing to answer questions contrary to Schedule 7, paragraph 18 of the 2000 Act.

The Supreme Court considered, among other factors, whether the legislation relied upon was compatible with the principle of legality. The decision stressed that in order to comply with this principle, the law must contain sufficient safeguards to prevent powers from being arbitrarily exercised and fundamental rights being potentially interfered with in an unjustified manner. Although in this instance the Court found that sufficient safeguards were in place to satisfy this requirement, it remains important that the issue was the subject of judicial scrutiny, and it was emphasised that government action had to be taken on the basis of identifiable legal rules.

6 Elliott and Thomas, n.1 above, 64.

7 Unless the provisions of the Parliament Acts 1911 and 1949 apply, in which case approval by the House of Lords may be dispensed with.

8 *Entick v Carrington* (1765) 19 St Tr 1030.

9 *R v Lord Chancellor, ex parte Witham* [1998] QB 575.

10 *Beghal v Director of Public Prosecutions* [2015] UKSC 49.

4.2.2 Formal conception of the rule of law (pancake topped with butter and sugar)

However, while the principle of legality is a *necessary* component of the rule of law, most commentators would deny that it is *sufficient*. The legal pancake needs topping to be palatable for society. The formal conception of the rule of law, famously asserted by commentators like Joseph Raz,[11] defines the doctrine as a set of principles which enable the law to perform its function effectively. In Raz's view, the function of law is to enable citizens to make choices and order their behaviour in accordance with known rules. He sees this as essential if human dignity is to be respected and individual autonomy is to be maintained.

In practical terms, the rule of law, therefore, has to include formal rules. These must be clear, ascertainable and non-retrospective. They must also be binding on all citizens. On this basis, individuals can suffer adverse consequences only for failing to comply with rules which they knew, or at least could have chosen to know about, before falling foul of them.

A notorious example in the English and Welsh context was the judicial treatment of marital rape. Until the late twentieth century, it was legally impossible for a man to rape his wife within this jurisdiction, as she was deemed to have given her irrevocable consent to intercourse.[12] In *R v R*[13] the House of Lords declared that such implied consent was a common law fiction which had never been a true rule of English law, and defendants could no longer rely on it to avoid a rape conviction. The decision was highly controversial and Strasbourg considered the judicial removal of the UK marital rape exemption in relation to another case with similar facts.[14] The Court found that the trajectory of the law towards abandoning the immunity was obvious at the time when the offences were committed.[15] Consequently, the appellant, on the facts, was not being subjected to sanctions as a result of retrospective lawmaking; nor was the position unclear.

Furthermore, the leading speech in *R v R*, given by Lord Keith in the House of Lords, had stressed that the Court was *not* creating a new criminal offence to impose liability on unacceptable conduct, but removing a legal fiction which had historically allowed a certain category of offenders to escape liability.[16]

It was apparent from the judgments of both the domestic courts and Strasbourg that the repugnance of the behaviour at issue would not itself have

11 J. Raz, 'The Rule of Law and its Virtue', *Law Quarterly Review*, Vol. 93 (1977) 195–211, 201.

12 *R v Miller* [1954] 2 QB 282; *R v Kowalski* (1988) 86 Cr App R 339; *R v Sharples* [1990] Crim LR 198.

13 *R v R* [1992] 1 AC 599

14 *SW v United Kingdom*, App. no. 20166/92, Judgment, 22 November 1995 (ECtHR).

15 Ibid., para. 43: 'Moreover, there was an evident evolution, which was consistent with the very essence of the offence, of the criminal law through judicial interpretation towards treating such conduct generally as within the scope of the offence of rape. This evolution had reached a stage where judicial recognition of the absence of immunity had become a reasonably foreseeable development of the law'.

16 *R v R*, n. 13 above, per Lord Keith, 611: 'This is not the creation of a new offence, it is the removal of a common law fiction which has become anachronistic and offensive and we consider that it is our duty having reached that conclusion to act upon it'.

been a justification for suspending the rule of law and imposing a retrospective sanction. Ultimately, the case did not turn on whether the defendant had wilfully committed a heinous act (that much was uncontroversial), but whether the formal requirements of the legal process could be satisfied.

This is in keeping with the view often understood to be espoused by commentators like Raz, that the rule of law as a concept is a morally neutral tool.[17] The reasoning behind this is that the function of the rule of law is to enable the law to fulfil its purpose efficiently, and there is a moral dimension to this only in so far as morality is *instrumental* in furthering this purpose. A favoured analogy employed by Raz is that of sharpness being of instrumental value to knives, because (butter knives aside) this quality is a requirement for fulfilling their purpose as cutting tools. Thus, moral considerations are relevant for Raz, at least in relation to the rule of law, *only* where they advance its core purpose.

However, it must be acknowledged that the argument is more nuanced than this. Although, as Hamara argues,[18] it is difficult to read Raz in the round as advocating anything other than a morally neutral conception of the rule of law, he nevertheless 'tries to make room for understandings which link "The Rule of Law" to some desirable state of affairs'.[19]

While not a moral value in his terms, the rule of law is nevertheless a value which society sustains. Therefore, although on this basis the rule of law cannot be characterised as *good* or linked to the pursuit of moral good, it is nevertheless cast as a necessary tool for the common pursuit of good, or at least the collective interest, as may be determined on the basis of identifiable goals with a moral dimension to them (such as respect for human dignity and autonomy). These last considerations make the formal conception of the rule of law likely to be subject to robust criticism.

4.2.3 Substantive conception of the rule of law (pancake topped with butter and sugar with golden syrup inside)

Nevertheless, a significant number of commentators still regard this formal conception of the rule of law as deeply problematic. Sharp knives may be used in a street fight or for peeling apples, rendering the use to which they are put crucial to their desirability in any given context. If the rule of law is to be a *universally* desirable principle, then the argument goes that it must have an inbuilt moral compass which governs the uses to which it may be turned.

The substantive conception of the rule of law rejects the notion that the principle could be applied in the service of totalitarian regimes which trampled human rights. Proponents of this school of thought, such as Allan,[20] point out

17 J. Waldron, 'Why Law? Efficacy, Freedom and Infidelity, *Law and Philosophy*, Vol. 13 (1994) 259–84.

18 C.T. Hamara, 'The Concept of the Rule of Law', in I. Flores and K. Himma (eds), *Law, Liberty and the Rule of Law* (Springer: Heidelberg, London, New York) 2013, 11–26.

19 Ibid., 16.

20 T.R.S. Allan, *Law, Liberty and Justice: The Legal Foundations of UK Constitutionalism* (Clarendon Press: Oxford) 1993.

that formal understandings of the rule of law, put forward by Raz and others, are themselves based upon substantive, moral foundations.[21] Why should the purpose of the law be to enable individuals to enjoy autonomy and dignity? Surely the answer can only be that these things have been deemed to be morally good.

Furthermore, Allan observes that the courts have to apply principles, rather than simple formulaic rules, and make determinations based on abstract notions of justice and fairness; this process would not be possible without an ethical dimension being present.[22] The judicial task is not akin to following directions for building flat-pack furniture: it is one of adjudication, rather than the straightforward application of rules. He notes also that this reality is demonstrable in the way in which common law courts in the United Kingdom operate in practice.[23]

Other commentators are similarly persuaded. Laws,[24] for example, adopts a rights-based approach to the rule of law and, indeed, the legal system and Constitution more generally. It must be acknowledged, of course, that the influence of the acclaimed twentieth century philosopher Dworkin can be felt strongly in the writing of both Laws and Allan. Dworkin[25] rejected the formal understanding of the rule of law, and built a case instead upon the idea that citizens owe one another moral rights and duties, and have political rights vested in them against the state. In this understanding, the legal system embodies these rights in positive law, knitted together by liberal principles.

Dworkin rested much of his discourse on a particular understanding of the role of judges within the rule of law.[26] He sought to draw a distinction between law and moral principles, and cast the judiciary in the role of guardians of unchanging moral obligations, which might be threatened by the democratic tyranny of the majority should the elected legislature see fit to enact morally repugnant law. As Dyzenhaus argues:

> Dworkin relied explicitly and with wholehearted approval on Hart's account in 'The Concept of Law' of the relationship between moral and legal obligation, specifically on the section where Hart maintained that certain important differences between law and morality arise from the fact that morality, unlike law, is immune from deliberate change.[27]

Inconveniently for both Hart and Dworkin, this fundamental assertion is by no means irrefutable. In fact, an inconvenient puff of analysis threatens to bring

21 Ibid., 28–39.
22 Ibid., 39.
23 Ibid., 28–43.
24 J. Laws, 'The Constitution, Morals and Rights', *Public Law* (1995) 622; and 'Law and Democracy', *Public Law* (1995) 72.
25 R. Dworkin, *A Matter of Principle* (Oxford University Press: Oxford) 1985.
26 Ibid.; R. Dworkin, 'Political Judges and the Rule of Law', British Academy, *Proceedings of the British Academy*, Vol. 23, No. 3 (1980).
27 D. Dyzenhaus, 'The Rule of Law as the Rule of Liberal Principle', in A. Ripstein (ed.), *Ronald Dworkin* (Cambridge University Press: Cambridge) 2007, 56–79, 73.

down the whole house of cards. In practice, moral principles are subject to dramatic and sometimes rapid social changes. Furthermore, legal development may be a catalyst for, rather than a consequence of, evolving moral principles.

Various contemporary examples throw this into sharp focus. Within living memory in the United Kingdom, homosexuals could face criminal sanction for loving and consensual sexual activity between adults,[28] while owners of boarding houses could freely display signs proclaiming 'No blacks, No Irish',[29] and parents could beat their children, using rubber slippers or belts, without risking legal or social censure.

In recent decades there has been a paradigm shift in both the legal *and* the moral centre of gravity with regard to all of these issues. However, it would be a gross oversimplification to state that the legal framework has simply *responded* to shifting moral principles. For instance, in outlawing racial discrimination, legislation may well have played a role in actively reshaping perceptions about acceptable and desirable behaviour. The law was one of the many social forces that encouraged a change in both culture and morality.

It would, therefore, be wrong to present a substantive conception of the rule of law as being without philosophical challenges of its own, or the end point of our collective dialogue on the question. If law can be deemed legitimate only if it is within the territory laid out in a moral map, how and by whom is the map to be drawn?

4.2.4 Choosing a pancake recipe

As Craig[30] notes, it is no coincidence that Raz, one of the principal advocates of the formal conception of the rule of law, is also a card-carrying legal positivist. Bennett perceptively and helpfully observes that academic dialogue about the rule of law often becomes obscured by the wider positivist versus anti-positivist debate.[31]

Defining legal positivism is a complex endeavour in itself,[32] and it is certainly beyond the scope of our analysis. However, in essence, legal positivism is the intellectual tradition which asserts that the validity of legal norms and rules depends

28 The Sexual Offences Act 1967 decriminalised consensual acts in private between two men where both parties were aged 21 or above. However, it applied only to England and Wales, it excluded the army and merchant navy and imposed a higher age of consent than that applicable to heterosexual activity.

29 'Signs of the Times of Racism in England that was All Too Familiar', *The Guardian* (22 Oct 2015), http://www.theguardian.com/world/2015/oct/22/sign-of-the-times-of-racism-in-england-that-was-all-too-familiar.

30 P.P. Craig, 'Formal and Substantive Conceptions of the Rule of Law: an Analytical Framework', *Public Law* Vol. 21 (1997) 467–87, 477.

31 M.J. Bennett, 'Hart and Raz on the Non-Instrumental Moral Value of the Rule of Law: A Reconsideration', *Law and Philosophy*, Vol. 30, No. 5 (2011) 603–35.

32 D. Plunkett, 'Legal Positivism and the Moral Aim Thesis', *Oxford Journal of Legal Studies*, Vol. 33, No. 3 (2013) 563–605.

upon the legitimacy of the source, rather than their intrinsic moral merits. In other words, law is law because the legal system says it is. It is the positive assertion which makes law (hence the name). In contrast 'anti-positivists' maintain that a link between the law and moral argument is necessary.[33] Unsurprisingly, as we have seen, philosophers like Dworkin, whose work bolsters the substantive model of the rule of law, tend to be anti-positivists. Consequently, clashes between the formal and substantive concepts of the rule of law are played out in the shadow of this larger debate about the very nature of law itself. This fascinating discussion is extremely complex and exploring this further would detract from the purpose of our analysis.

At this point, worryingly, it might well feel that despite earlier promises, the tangible doctrine of the rule of law is starting to slope off, Nessie-like, into the mist of philosophical wrangling. However, it is possible to coax the beast back into the sunlight.

4.2.4.1 The function of academic theories of the rule of law: an explanation rather than a blueprint

First, it should be remembered that while these underlying theories are important in understanding the deep background to what is going on within the legal framework, they ***explain, rather than dictate*** what actually happens in the courts of Great Britain. On most occasions, judges in applying principles contained within the rule of law do not need to decide whether they are subscribing to a substantive or a formal understanding of the same. In the *Pierson*[34] case, for instance, the Court found that it was unlawful for the Home Secretary to retrospectively increase a sentence for a criminal conviction when it had been lawfully passed. Whether the rule of law is driven by formal rules that demand openness and clarity and forbid retrospective change, or is driven by a set of ethical values which encompass fundamental human rights, the destination is the same: actions with retrospective legal effect are incompatible with the rule of law.

It should also be remembered, and indeed stressed, that the academic identification of many of the core principles of the rule of law, in particular by the influential commentator, A.V. Dicey,[35] took place prior to the philosophical debates within the twentieth and twenty-first century jurisprudence. Furthermore, there is judicial awareness that many of the precepts of the rule of law are of ancient pedigree and unquestioned application. In *Re M*[36] the House of Lords roundly rejected the Home Secretary's contention that government ministers should not be liable, in the same way as other citizens, to fine or imprisonment for the flagrant breach of a court order (in this instance directing

33 S. Taekema, *The Concept of Ideals in Legal Theory* (Kluwer Law International: The Hague) 2003, 206.

34 *R v Secretary of State for the Home Department, ex parte Pierson* [1998] AC 539.

35 A.V. Dicey and J.W.F. Allison (eds), *The Law of the Constitution* (Oxford University Press: Oxford) 2013.

36 *Re M* [1994] 1 AC 377.

the deportation of an asylum seeker). Lord Templeman stated that if the Home Secretary's reasoning were followed, 'the executive would obey the law as a matter of grace and not as a matter of necessity, a proposition which would reverse the result of the Civil War'.[37]

We are not suggesting, therefore, that it does not matter whether a formal or a substantive conception of the rule of law is adopted, rather that both schools of thought are attempts to explain the same constitutional principle. In other words, the system is older and deeper than either conception in its modern form.

4.2.4.2 Points of convergence

It must certainly be acknowledged that many followers of both schools of thought would be unimpressed by the pancake analogy, on the basis that it at first *appears* to treat the substantive conception as nothing more than the formal understanding with an added dimension. However, this would be an inaccurate understanding of our proposal, as the picture being painted is rather more nuanced than this.

It is, of course, uncontroversial that at one level the two systems are distinct, each having an entirely separate basis. The formal conception is essentially positivist and rule-based, whereas the substantive conception is anti-positivist and held together by moral precepts. Notwithstanding, when the situation is looked at on another level, there are many harmonious elements and the intrinsic differences are no longer observable. The level at which the question is approached is key. Borrowing an image from science, it is uncontroversial that the concept of temperature does not exist at the level of individual particles,[38] but this does not mean that temperature is not a highly real and relevant consideration when deciding whether oven gloves are necessary to lift a lasagne. Whether substantive and formal conceptions of the rule of law are *functionally* distinct depends upon the level at which they are analysed. Not only are the practical effects of both systems frequently identical, there are points of theoretical convergence as well.

Bennett argues persuasively that many commentators are misguided in assuming that advocates of the formal conception, such as Raz and Hart, dismiss the idea that the rule of law is entirely without non-instrumental moral value (in other words, moral value that does not directly further its purpose).[39] In Bennett's analysis, their writing reveals instrumental moral value and non-instrumental moral value side by side. Even within what is ultimately a positivist paradigm, there is a necessary place for ethical principles. This echoes an important element of Allan's[40] critique of their position – namely that their conception of the purpose of the rule of law is itself constructed upon substantive moral values. The imperative to promote human autonomy and dignity itself originates from ethical considerations.

37 Ibid., 395.
38 L.M. Brown and F. Rohrlich, 'Chapter 17 Comments', in T.Y. Cao (ed.), *Conceptual Foundations of Quantum Field Theory* (Cambridge University Press: Cambridge) 1999, 261.
39 Bennett, n. 31 above, 612.
40 Allan, n. 20 above.

The flip side of the coin, however, is the acknowledgement by advocates of the substantive conception, such as Bingham, that attaining consensus on moral principles, and therefore 'good' law, is deeply problematic.[41] Even among liberal Western democracies there is scope for near endless debate over which values and rights are so fundamental as to form part of the rule of law. How is 'good law' to be determined?

In reality if either position is pushed to the extreme, it becomes difficult to sustain. Few voices for the formal conception would wish to endorse an understanding of the rule of law which could support a regime like that of ancient Sparta, where clear law, legitimately enacted, demanded the exposure of sickly and disabled infants.[42] On the other hand, those who favour a substantive understanding of the concept are faced with an insurmountable challenge in identifying and achieving consensus on the substantive moral principles which they claim suffuse the doctrine.

Some illumination can be found in the terminology adopted by commentators like Bingham,[43] who refer to 'thin' (formal) and 'thick' (substantive) understandings of the doctrine. This language implies a spectrum of understanding, rather than rigid binary division, and in our view, at least for present purposes, this is a far more productive approach. Hence, a return to the image of the pancake, with a non-negotiable base of ingredients, but scope for debate about additions to the recipe.

In relation to the UK Constitution, the rule of law encompasses the principle of legality and the recognised rules within the formal conception. In essence, the law must be clear, ascertainable and non-retrospective, and it must apply equally to all persons regardless of status or role. Furthermore, the rule of law pancake is currently folded to contain a layer of golden syrup (or possibly continental Nutella), which is the recognition of human rights as set out in the European Convention on Human Rights (ECHR). While respect for human rights is now arguably a separate constitutional principle (and, indeed, has its own chapter in this book), it is also a component element of the rule of law. This dimension provides an identifiably substantive layer to the principle, as it now functions.

Nevertheless, it would be wrong to suggest that the substantive element is an entirely modern innovation, transplanted Nutella-like from the wider European context. The practical problems of identifying the moral principles underpinning the law must be acknowledged, as ethics are complex, subjective and constantly shifting sands. Despite this difficulty, it remains the case that down the centuries a procession of distinguished jurists have accepted, both implicitly and explicitly, that such ethical foundations are present within the common law and the UK Constitution.

In *Somerset*[44] Lord Mansfield CJ was required to decide whether chattel slavery was recognised by English law. On his decision rested the fate of James Somerset,

41 Bingham, n. 2 above, 68.

42 H. Michell, *Sparta* (Cambridge University Press: Cambridge) 1964, 165.

43 Bingham, n. 2 above, 162.

44 *Somerset v Stewart* (1772) 98 ER 499; 1 Lofft 1 (KB).

who was imprisoned on a slave ship by his purported owner, facing a future of suffering and degradation on a plantation in Jamaica. His abolitionist friends and supporters made an application for habeas corpus. In an often quoted passage from his judgement Mansfield CJ held:

> The state of slavery is of such a nature, that it is incapable of being introduced on any reasons, moral or political; but only positive law, which preserves its force long after the reasons, occasion, and time itself from whence it was created, is erased from memory: it is so odious, that nothing can be suffered to support it, but positive law. Whatever inconveniences, therefore, may follow from a decision, I cannot say this case is allowed or approved by the law of England.[45]

In other words, because of the immoral nature of slavery, the common law could not and would not recognise it. Such an institution could only enter the corpus of the law of Great Britain by virtue of 'positive law' or statute. As this was not the case, there was no legal justification for treating a human being as property. Thus, the developments which have flowed from the Human Rights Act have been an additional layer, rather than a change of direction, in relation to the substantive component of the rule of law.

Judges in Great Britain, like Mansfield, have always been alive to the risk of cutting themselves adrift from the legal principles which they are required to apply, and substituting their individual moral assessment of the case. He was very clear that his decision could not rest simply on his sense of compassion for James Somerset. However, judges have been equally aware that an application of legal principles to a given factual context cannot be correct if the outcome would be a gross violation of overarching moral precepts, which are the foundation of the law.

The courts' treatment of *R v R*[46] and *SW*[47] provides a helpful illustration of this dichotomy in the modern context, and an essentially harmonious approach from domestic and international tribunals when it came to reconciling the clash. In deciding what could be deemed an *acceptable* interpretation of *existing legal provisions*,[48] human rights and human dignity were key considerations. As noted above, the morally repugnant nature of the crime and its impact upon the rights and dignity of the victim would not have justified setting aside the rule of law. However, the human rights implications of interpreting the law in a way which

45 Ibid., para. 19.

46 *R v R*, n. 13 above.

47 *SW v United Kingdom*, n. 14 above.

48 Ibid., para. 43: 'There was no doubt under the law as it stood on 18 September 1990 that a husband who forcibly had sexual intercourse with his wife could, in various circumstances, be found guilty of rape. Moreover, there was an evident evolution, which was consistent with the very essence of the offence, of the criminal law through judicial interpretation towards treating such conduct generally as within the scope of the offence of rape. This evolution had reached a stage where judicial recognition of the absence of immunity had become a reasonably foreseeable development of the law'.

would have effectively shielded a sub-category of rapists from prosecution, was highlighted by the European Court of Human Rights in support of the stance taken by the House of Lords:

> The essentially debasing character of rape is so manifest that the result of the decisions of the Court of Appeal and the House of Lords – that the applicant could be convicted of attempted rape, irrespective of his relationship with the victim – cannot be said to be at variance with the object and purpose of Article 7 (art. 7) of the Convention, namely to ensure that no one should be subjected to arbitrary prosecution, conviction or punishment (see paragraph 34 above). What is more, the abandonment of the unacceptable idea of a husband being immune against prosecution for rape of his wife was in conformity not only with a civilised concept of marriage but also, and above all, with the fundamental objectives of the Convention, the very essence of which is respect for human dignity and human freedom.[49]

Neither the domestic courts nor Strasbourg were prepared to allow legal rules to be interpreted in a manner which was fundamentally incompatible with human rights and dignity. The case was undeniably controversial, and the decision close to the margins of what the European Court of Human Rights could be expected to permit in relation to retrospective change.[50] However, it is precisely for this reason that it is so instructive. On the one hand, it demonstrates that there clearly is a substantive dimension to the way in which the rule of law is applied in a UK context. The principles at its core are undoubtedly now consciously viewed through the prism of human rights. Yet, on the other hand, it reveals how malleable and uncertain this substantive ethical aspect is in practice. Both the right of citizens not to be subjected to retrospective criminal sanction, and the right of citizens to enjoy corporeal integrity and freedom from inhumane and degrading treatment, are non-negotiable in a civilised society which upholds *any* understanding of the rule of law. A head-on collision between the two was always going to be difficult to resolve. As with other constitutional principles, the reality of the rule of law in its practical application is one of balance and compromise between opposing needs and demands.

4.3 Does the tripartite religious character of the legal and constitutional system enhance or weaken the rule of law?

4.3.1 Establishment and quasi-establishment: preliminary observations about possible challenges to the rule of law in the field of marriage

As we have discussed at length, the British Constitution and its religious character are the results of haphazard historical evolution. Within the United Kingdom

49 Ibid., para. 44.
50 R. Beddard, 'Retrospective Crime', *New Law Journal*, Vol. 145 (1995) 663.

no founding fathers set out to draft a coherent Constitution and craft its terms carefully around any guiding principles. Just because the constitutional system embraces both establishment relationships and a robust doctrine of the rule of law, it does not automatically follow that the two are mutually compatible. There are potential challenges and they should not be underestimated. One clear point of possible tension lies in the exercise of clerical discretion in relation to the remarriage of divorcees within the Church of England[51] and the Church in Wales.[52] We have identified this as an area which is capable of presenting challenges for the rule of law and it would be disingenuous to pretend that it does not exist.

One facet of establishment which has survived in both England and Wales is the implicit right vested in all citizens, regardless of personal dogma, to marry in their parish church (or indeed any church with which they have a qualifying connection).[53] However, if one or both parties has/have been divorced, this right becomes contingent upon the willingness of the cleric involved to conduct the ceremony.

Because this arrangement is in place to safeguard freedom of conscience for clergy in this matter, the exercise of discretion cannot be subject to challenge on grounds that it is arbitrary or irrational. On one level, this appears to be unsatisfactory, because a ruling which could be construed as having quasi-judicial effect is not open to review. Furthermore, an individual cannot know in advance what conduct will render him or her unable to marry in a particular church. For example, some ministers might marry a person who had committed adultery in a previous marriage some years ago, provided that the person expressed regret and a sincere intention to remain faithful to his or her current fiancé(e), whereas others might consider adultery a permanent bar. Therefore, while it seems fairly unlikely that anybody would pause before undressing a clandestine lover in order to check the canon law implications of their actions, the fact remains that were they to do so, they would not find a clear answer as to the consequences.

Nevertheless, despite being problematic in some respects and without underestimating the possible challenges to the rule of law, in our view this state of affairs does not render the legal framework fundamentally incompatible with this constitutional foundation, and it simply demonstrates the limits of the territory into which the legal framework should extend. An established Church is still a faith group, and as such its members are entitled to their collective and individual Article 9 right to freedom of conscience and belief. The legal system in the United Kingdom allows all faith groups the flexibility to decide whom they wish to marry according to their rites (whether or not in the particular circumstances of the case those rites have consequences in secular law), and there is no reason to restrict this in the case of the Church of England and the Church in Wales. Moreover, a couple who may not marry in an Anglican church can still contract a valid marriage in the eyes of secular law.

51 The Church of England, 'Marriage after Divorce', http://www.yourchurchwedding.org/youre-welcome/marriage-after-divorce.aspx.

52 The Church in Wales, 'Marriage – Frequently Asked Questions', http://www.churchinwales.org.uk/life/marriage/faq.

53 Marriage Measure 2008.

It should also be noted that in conceptual terms, the Church of England and the Church in Wales could remove the potential for arbitrary decision making by simply refusing to marry *any* person with a former spouse still living. Although this might make for a system more smoothly compliant with an abstract understanding of the rule of law, it would also deprive many more citizens of the church wedding which they might otherwise be offered. It would seem on balance that the practical cost would outweigh the theoretical benefits. Aside from this one example, it is difficult to find facets of establishment relationships in Great Britain which might be deemed incompatible with the rule of law.

However, compatibility does not equate to desirability. Is the current model in any way positively beneficial for the functioning of the rule of law? Or are we dealing with vestigial whale legs, a harmless but unhelpful relic from the past that should be allowed to fade? We would argue that if the legal landscape is properly surveyed, there are some elements of its functioning in relation to religion which do positively enhance the rule of law. Examples of this can be discerned not only in relation to establishment, but also much more widely.

Taking establishment first, despite the fact that there are some controversial areas of the marriage law framework, there are also some other dimensions within this field and beyond that can be seen, on balance, as being advantageous to the rule of law.

While it is not conceived of as a branch of the state, the Church of England has retained a unique function in relation to marriage law.[54] As already observed, this element of establishment was not dismantled by the Welsh Church Act 1914, and the position in Wales remains essentially the same. An undeniable question which arises from this relates to whether the unique treatment of the established/quasi-established Churches in this regard is in harmony with the rule of law principle of equality before the law. Are members of these Churches either favoured, or perhaps even disadvantaged, by being subject to specific legal arrangements?[55]

In England[56] and Wales[57] Anglican clergy have a *duty* to solemnise marriages of individuals resident in their parish if requested to do so. There is an exemption, as discussed, where one or both parties is divorced and has a surviving spouse.[58]

54 The Church of England, 'A Response to the Government Equalities Office Consultation: Equal Civil Marriage', Annex, 'Marriage Law: the Position of the Church of England', para. 6.

55 In the political debate that preceded the introduction of same-sex marriage, the Church of England highlighted its special situation and argued that this could potentially be disadvantageous for the religious freedom of its members if the proposed changes were introduced: see, e.g., The Church of England, Marriage (Same Sex Couples) Commons Second Reading Briefing, 'The Unique Position of the Established Church', p. 2.

56 Faculty Office of the Archbishop of Canterbury, 'A Guide to the Law for Clergy' (1999); see also *Davis v Black* (1841) 1 QB 900.

57 Welsh Church Act 1914.

58 Matrimonial Causes Act 1965, s. 8(2): 'No clergyman of the Church of England or the Church in Wales shall be compelled – (a) to solemnise the marriage of any person whose former marriage has been dissolved and whose former spouse is still living; or (b) to permit the marriage of such a person to be solemnised in the church or chapel of which he is the minister'.

In that case Anglican clergy have a discretion, rather than an obligation, to carry out the marriage. Special provision is also made where one party has undergone gender reassignment. The Gender Recognition Act 2004 amended the Marriage Act 1949[59] to the effect that '[a] clergyman is not obliged to solemnise the marriage of a person if the clergyman reasonably believes that the person's gender has become the acquired gender under the Gender Recognition Act 2004'.[60]

Furthermore, unless and until the Anglican Churches of England and Wales decide that they wish to conduct same-sex marriages, these provisions will be of no benefit to same-sex couples.[61]

The above regime leaves us with several distinct but related questions: (a) Are these provisions imposing an undue burden on the established and quasi-established Churches? (b) Are these provisions placing other faith groups who lack these powers and duties at an unfair disadvantage? (c) Are these provisions leaving some groups of citizens in a less favourable position than others?

Questions (a) and (b) can helpfully be taken together. First, it should be observed that marriage law in England in Wales has been assembled bit by bit. There are several ways in which religious marriage may be carried out.[62]

Basically, all marriages which are solemnised other than according to the rites of the Church of England or the Church in Wales are conducted on the authority of a Superintendent Registrar's certificate or the Registrar General's licence. Although this is not expressly provided for in the Marriage Act 1949, as Lowe and Douglas argue, this is the obvious intention and the necessary effect of the statute.[63]

A marriage on the authority of a Superintendent Registrar's certificate may be solemnised in a registered building, according to the usages of the Society of Friends and the Jews, or in any place where a housebound or detained person is situated.[64] Any building that is registered as a place of worship under the Places of Worship Registration Act 1855 may be registered by the Registrar General for the solemnisation of marriages.[65]

A marriage in a registered building may take place only in the presence of a registrar or an authorised person;[66] 'authorised persons' will ordinarily be ministers of the relevant faith or denomination. The marriage rites in this instance

59 Ibid., Sch. 4.

60 This provision has now been replaced by the Equality Act 2010, Sch, 3, Pt 6, s. 24(4): 'A person does not contravene section 29, so far as relating to gender reassignment discrimination, by refusing to solemnise, in accordance with a form, rite or ceremony as described in sub-paragraph (3), the marriage of a person (B) if A reasonably believes that B's gender has become the acquired gender under the Gender Recognition Act 2004'.

61 Marriage (Same-Sex Couples) Act 2013.

62 See further N. Lowe and G. Douglas, *Bromley's Family Law* (Oxford University Press: Oxford) 10th edn, 2007, Ch. 2 'Formation and Recognition of Adult Partnerships'.

63 Ibid., 57.

64 Marriage Act 1949, s. 26(1) (as amended by the Marriage Act 1983, Sch. 1, and the Marriage Act 1994, s. 1(1)).

65 Marriage Act 1949 ss. 41–42 (as amended by the Marriage Acts Amendment Act 1958 s. 1(1) and the Marriage (Registration of Buildings) Act 1990 s. 1(1)).

66 Marriage Act 1949, s. 2.

may take any form, provided that they contain a declaration similar to that required when the marriage is in a registry office,[67] and the parties contract the union *per verba de praesenti* (present vows – that is, an exchange of promises in the present tense with a present intention, rather than a declaration about what may happen in the future).

Unpacking all of the above, Jewish and Quaker couples who wish to marry are subject to special rules, because historically they were granted exemptions from the general regime of Anglican marriage. Other religious groups may choose to have marriages on their premises if they have a registered building, and may do so either by arranging a secular registrar or by having one of their ministers approved as a registered person. The other option, of course, is for religious groups to advise their prospective spouses to arrange a civil law marriage with the registrar, and to separately conduct a religious marriage with no legal force, whenever and however they choose.

Therefore, the precise legal provisions that will apply to any given religious couple will depend upon their particular context. It would be deeply misleading to present a picture of a dual regime for religious marriage, with a choice between established and quasi-established Churches on one side, and other faiths groups on the other.

Arguments might be made for harmonising and simplifying what has become a rather cluttered legal space, with a plethora of applicable provisions scattered in different statutes and case law. However, this (essentially administrative) issue does not, in and of itself, demonstrate that there is a lack of equality before the law. The truth is that differing situations require different treatment and it is far from clear that a one-size-fits-all regime would dramatically advance religious liberty. At the risk of stating the obvious, an acceptance of the duty to marry all-comers (aside from statutory exemptions prompted by the state changing its definition of marriage) is part of Anglican theology and self-understanding (at least within a UK context). It is what these Churches do and have always done and, in our view, dismantling this would strip them of a part of their self-identity and disable them from putting some of their beliefs into practice.[68]

However, to state the even more obvious, expanding the scope of this legal duty and imposing an obligation on all faith groups to marry anyone who asked within a defined geographical area would not be a popular or a practical move. In fact, it would undeniably be the subject of a successful challenge founded on Article 9 of the European Convention. Imagine the feelings of a priest from a conservative Christian denomination on learning that he had an obligation to marry two Atheists who had once attended a christening in his church and just adored the pretty statues and the lingering smell of incense.

Neither would the third option of constructing a middle ground necessarily resolve the issue. Even if all religious groups were given the theoretical power

67 Marriage Act 1949, s. 44.

68 The Church of England actively promotes the church weddings that it offers: The Church of England, 'Thinking of a Church Wedding', https://www.churchofengland.org/weddings-baptisms-funerals/weddings.aspx.

to elect to marry couples within their buildings on the same legal basis, this would still not create a level playing field. There would be the obvious problem of administration and accountability, and the law would have to require appropriate procedures and registration of documentation. This would be difficult for some faith traditions which do not adopt a formalised, central structure with trained and monitored ministers. Furthermore, not all groups choose to have buildings or records. So, how could they fit within such a framework? In fact, not all religious pathways even involve groups: there are, for example, solitary Pagans.

To sum up, we do not suggest that the marriage law framework in the United Kingdom is perfect at present, or that reform of some areas would not be beneficial. However, arguably, the gradual evolution of the legal system in this regard, with establishment holding it all together like the bone structure of a penguin wing, has enabled the needs and circumstances of various groups to be met as society has changed and new challenges have arisen. The principle of equality and, indeed, the rule of law in general are not offended, as citizens effectively have a variety of legal pathways towards marriage, all of which are known and identifiable. They are in a position to choose an appropriate route depending on their personal belief system. Thus points (a) and (b) do not reveal this aspect of the establishment to be problematic for the rule of law. In fact, they demonstrate how a soft and pliable establishment model has helped to develop a framework which bends to accommodate evolving needs.

A far more compelling issue, however, is raised by question (c). Given that the established and quasi-established Churches have a basic duty to marry all citizens who request this service, why should divorcees, those wishing to marry someone of the same sex and individuals who have had their gender reassigned be excluded? This aspect has already been discussed at length in this chapter. It seems especially harsh that individuals from vulnerable minority groups, and those who have experienced the trauma of divorce, should be placed at a comparative disadvantage. The answer ultimately lies in the need to balance individual and collective rights. The acknowledged reality is that it is the state, rather than the Churches, that moved the goal posts in relation to the eligibility criteria for marriage, and the beliefs of conservative Anglicans were accommodated in the legal reforms. Carving out exemptions was deemed preferable to either attempting to forcibly drag the Church along with the state, or to slow secular legal reform to the pace of continental drift/Anglican doctrinal debate. This flexibility is a feature of the soft and collaborative model of establishment that is in operation in Great Britain.

Marriage within the established and quasi-established Churches is expressly acknowledged to be a religious matter and the executive and legislature continue to demonstrate concern for the collective rights of the Anglican provinces in England and Wales.[69] From this perspective, it would be as inappropriate to force these denominations to carry out marriages for all divorcees as it would

69 See, e.g., the ministerial response to consultation prior to the introduction of Same Sex Marriage in England and Wales: M. Miller, 'Ministerial Foreword', *Equal Marriage: The Government's Response* (Dec 2012).

be to attempt to compel an Orthodox Synagogue to facilitate the wedding of a same-sex couple. Individual religious freedom cannot extinguish collective religious freedom.

4.3.2 Prison chaplains

Prisons are contexts in which the courts have acknowledged that citizens are especially vulnerable and disempowered, and in which particular vigilance towards their legal rights and due process is required.[70] Legislation[71] provides that every prison in England and Wales must have an Anglican chaplain.[72] This does not operate to the exclusion of other religious and secular traditions. In fact, there are arrangements for the spiritual and emotional care of all prisoners, and religious prisoners who are not Anglican have the right to receive spiritual care from a minister of their own faith should they wish to access this.[73]

However, the mandatory presence of a representative of the established or quasi-established Church in every facility helps to ensure that the rule of law is applied to even the most vulnerable members of society. The availability of an Anglican chaplain provides an unofficial form of internal oversight, and thereby functions as an additional safeguard against prisons becoming an enclave where the rule of law might be entirely suspended. Not all faith groups require clergy to undergo formal training and not all faith groups would see prison visiting (or sick visiting for that matter) as part and parcel of the role of their priests or ministers. If the guaranteed Anglican presence in prisons were to be removed, some facets of prison chaplains could be lost. The mandatory appointment of an Anglican chaplain means that in every prison there is at least one chaplain who has the training and support of a large national organisation, as well as a framework for comparison in terms of other prisons. The link means that Anglican chaplains should always be in a position to seek guidance about normal and acceptable practice and standards if they are in any doubt. They also should have support from wider Anglican authorities should they ever need to be in the position of whistle-blower. If there was no requirement for at least one Anglican representative, arguably there would be no guarantee that any of the active chaplains had access to a way of benchmarking standards of prisoner treatment, nor of assured backing in the event of those standards being breached. They might or might not have this, depending upon the faith group or secular tradition to which they were attached.

70 See, e.g., *Shahid v Scottish Ministers (Scotland)* [2015] UKSC 58.

71 Prison Act 1952.

72 J. Beckford and S. Gilliat-Ray, *Religion in Prison: Equal Rights in a Multi-Faith Society* (Cambridge University Press: Cambridge) 1998.

73 P. Phillips, 'The Statutory Presence of the Church of England in Prisons Should Give It a Voice on Issues of Imprisonment, but it Remains Largely Silent', London School of Economics and Political Science, http://blogs.lse.ac.uk/religionpublicsphere/2016/09/the-statutory-presence-of-the-church-of-england-in-prisons-should-give-it-a-voice-on-issues-of-imprisonment-but-it-remains-largely-silent.

In addition, the liminal position of the Anglican prison chaplain allows him or her to function as an intermediary between inmates and officials. There can be a balance between a figure perceived as official and powerful enough to receive grievances or even fears and make a tangible difference, yet sufficiently detached from the source of the actual or perceived problem to appear safe and approachable. Authors like Scott have specifically argued for the potential of the chaplaincy role to bring about challenge in the prison context.[74]

Once again, we are not suggesting that the current system is the *only* way of achieving the ends described above. There are other mechanisms which could be conceived of which might function and have merit: for example, it could become mandatory that every prison has an official 'Lead Counsellor' who is trained to counsel prisoners and is backed up by a specially established independent organisation or network. This might achieve success in terms of winning prisoner trust, and providing a system for internal oversight and a conduit for communication. Such a system, however, would have to be set up from scratch and does not exist in Great Britain at the present time. The statutory regime of Anglican prison chaplains, on the contrary, does. We would like to emphasise that we are not asserting that the current establishment framework is the *only* method of achieving these benefits; rather we are observing the system as it has evolved and the benefits that it currently confers. The present discussion is grounded in how things are, rather than how they might be.

4.3.3 *The chameleon character of clergy employment*

Turning now to the legal framework beyond establishment, the way in which UK employment law deals with ministers of religion is another complicated and ongoing story.[75] However, for present purposes, the salient point is that British courts have essentially moved away from a position where there was at least a strong presumption that ministers of religion were bound by spiritual rather than temporal ties;[76] as such, their working arrangements were not subject to the jurisdiction of secular courts. The courts will now examine the circumstances on a case-by-case basis, and decide whether there was an intention to create legal relations as far as state contract law was concerned. The courts have been and remain crystal clear that they will not impose a contract where this would be a legal fiction, and would fly in the face of the parties' understanding and beliefs.[77]

In respect of contract law, this is a relatively orthodox conclusion. In fact, an intention to create legal relations is a necessary element of any contract. However,

74 D. Scott, *Heavenly Confinement: The Role and Perception of Christian Prison Chaplains in North East England's Prisons* (LAP Lambert: Saarbrucken) 2011.

75 See, e.g., *Sharpe v Worcester Diocesan Board of Finance Ltd* [2015] EWCA Civ 399; Moore v President of the Methodist Conference [2013] UKSC 29; *Percy v Church of Scotland Board of National Mission* [2005] UKHL 73.

76 *Re National Insurance Act 1911* [1912] 2 Ch 563.

77 *Macdonald v Free Presbyterian Church of Scotland* [2010] All ER (D) 265 (Mar).

the legal framework has been flexible enough to recognise that the status and role of religious ministers is unique. Instead of categorising clergy as employees or self-employed persons, the courts have been prepared to adopt different definitions for various contexts. Chameleon-like, ministers are effectively able to be employees for some purposes, but not others. Perhaps the most striking and significant context where this plays out relates to vicarious liability. In the case of *Maga*[78] a Roman Catholic priest was treated as an employee solely for the purposes of a claim in tort with the agreement of all parties to the litigation.

Vicarious liability attaches to an employer where an employee commits a tort which is related to his or her employment.[79] However, the matter is always particularly complicated where the tortious conduct is contrary to the express commands and desires of the employer: see, for example, the recent litigation involving Morrisons supermarkets, in which the Supreme Court disagreed with the Court of Appeal as to where the boundary lay.[80] The Supreme Court found an employer vicariously liable for a vicious and unprovoked assault which an employee inflicted on a customer entering a petrol station kiosk. In such cases the courts are required to determine if there is a sufficient nexus between the tort and the employee's role to fasten the employer with liability for the conduct. It is not relevant whether the employer was at fault or in any position to prevent the harm. Vicarious liability is a form of strict liability. The Court of Appeal determined that there was an insufficient link between the assault and the employment relationship to justify the imposition of liability, but the decision was finely balanced and, as we have seen, the Supreme Court took the opposite view.

In *Maga* the Court of Appeal had to consider how these principles might apply where a Roman Catholic priest had groomed and assaulted a boy who was not part of the church congregation and with whom he did not have a spiritual relationship, but whose trust was nevertheless gained in part by the priest's standing in the local community. The court found that there was a sufficiently strong connection between the tortious assault and the role to which the priest was appointed in order to justify the imposition of liability on the diocese. In reaching this conclusion, the judges applied essentially the same legal principles as they would for a secular employee in an unusual working context.

In *JGE*,[81] the Court of Appeal went even further, and was prepared to expressly find that the priest was in a position 'akin' to employment, *for the purposes of vicarious liability*. Thus, the legal framework has adopted a creative and flexible approach to the employment status of religious ministers. It is possible for an individual to be treated as an employee for some purposes, but not for others. The Roman Catholic diocese in the *JGE* case did not succeed in using its theological position to justify avoiding vicarious liability, but the court engineered its finding to achieve this outcome without altering the status of Roman Catholic priests in

78 *Maga v Roman Catholic Archdiocese of Birmingham* [2010] EWCA Civ 256.

79 *Lister and Others v Hesley Hall* [2001] UKHL 22.

80 *Mohamud v W.M. Morrison Supermarkets plc* [2014] EWCA Civ 116; [2016] UKSC 11.

81 *JGE v Trustees of the Portsmouth Roman Catholic Diocesan Trust* [2012] EWCA Civ 938.

contract law.[82] In allowing clerics to adopt this chameleon legal existence, judges have strengthened the rule of law in a number of important respects.

First, they have maintained the basic principle of freedom of contract, and have refrained from imposing what must necessarily remain voluntary obligations where this was clearly never the intention of the parties (and the motivation for avoiding it was spiritual, rather than economic). Thus, they have avoided any allegation of having retrospectively altered the fundamental rules of contract law, or driving a coach and horses through the Article 9 rights of the parties involved.

Second, they have prevented a situation where religious beliefs could be a mechanism for ousting the jurisdiction of the courts and depriving vulnerable victims of deliberate wrong-doing (tragically often of a heinous nature) of an action in tort. It would be incompatible with concepts of natural justice and fairness to simply state that because the Roman Catholic Church (or any other faith organisation) had a doctrinal objection to treating its clergy as employees, it could enjoy complete immunity in terms of vicarious liability. Put another way, the chameleon solution avoids a victim of sexual assault being informed by a court that he or she has no claim, because to allow a cause of action would be incompatible with the spiritual beliefs of the perpetrator and/or the organisation for which he or she worked.

Consequently, treating ministers of religion as a special case and dealing with them as such proves to be beneficial for all parties to the litigation, and to the legal system as a whole. Ironically, in later cases, which are arguably less satisfactory, unfortunate decisions have been made on the basis of inadequate attention being paid to the beliefs of the parties. At present, where vicarious liability is concerned, it could be argued that, if anything, too little (rather than too great) emphasis is placed on the unique dimension which a religious context may give to cases.

In *Various Claimants*,[83] the Supreme Court found that lay brothers in a religious order could be vicariously liable for the actions of one another. The decision was heavily influenced by *JGE* and relied heavily on the principle of a relationship akin to employment. However, unlike the connection between a priest and his bishop, monks or nuns have a relationship ordered upon family, rather than working or quasi-employment lines. The British legal system does not impose vicarious liability upon married people for the torts of their spouse, so it is not self-evidently appropriate to impose vicarious liability upon individuals who choose to 'marry' their religious order. Arguably, the Court was comparing apples and oranges in this case, and ought not to have applied the principles in *JGE*. Just as those who form their long-term adult relationships on the basis of marriage or civil partnership are not responsible for the torts of their spouse or civil partner, arguably those who enter into alternative family relationships should not be liable for the torts of their elected spiritual family. Religious brotherhoods and sisterhoods are understood by their members

82 Ibid.

83 *Catholic Child Welfare Society and Others v Various Claimants (FC) and Others* [2012] UKSC 56.

(at least in a traditional Christian context)[84] as being based on familiar rather than employment structures. Significantly, had the Court adopted a more nuanced understanding, it would not have left the victim without a solvent defendant to sue, given that the perpetrator had an employer who was also found to be liable. Importantly, the case also confirms the proposition that more than one party may be vicariously liable for the same tort.

Thus, in general terms, from the perspective of tort, treating religious contexts differently from other settings is beneficial for the administration of justice and the rule of law. If anything, it would be preferable for judges to pay more attention to the factors which genuinely make religious contexts unique and address these in the application of legal rules.

4.3.4 Oaths

The Oaths Act 1978 acknowledges that the legal system in England and Wales provides for an oath to be taken on Holy Scripture.[85]

The Act specifically provides that the oath shall be valid and binding, even if it is later revealed that the person taking it had no religious belief at the time it was sworn.[86] This provision would need to be applied only in the case of a person who, either through cynicism or mistake, had opted to swear an oath, despite not having any underlying faith conviction. The Act also explicitly provides for individuals to take a solemn oath if this is more appropriate to their wishes and beliefs.[87]

The continuing appropriateness of oaths in criminal proceedings was debated by the Magistrates' Association in 2013, and the majority of members opted to retain it.[88] The practice is not uncontroversial and faced some criticism after a trial in 2015 was halted when a Muslim witness swore on the Bible, rather than the Quran.[89] The judge decided that his evidence could not be accepted in that form, and ordered that a new trial be commenced.[90]

However, it was accepted by all parties, including the unfortunate judge, that this decision had been a mistake. The witness asserted that he had been happy

84 See, e.g., the Rule of St Benedict: Order of St Benedict, 'Rule of St Benedict', http://www.osb.org/rb/text/toc.html; also the Rule of the De La Salle brothers themselves: De La Salle, 'The Rule of the Brothers of the Christian Schools', Rome (2008), http://www.lasalle.org/wp-content/uploads/pdf/institucionales/fsc_rule.pdf.

85 Oaths Act 1978, s. 1(1).

86 Ibid., s. 4(2).

87 Ibid., s. 5.

88 R. Pigott, 'Motion of End Bible Oaths in Court Defeated', *BBC News* (19 Oct 2013), http://www.bbc.co.uk/news/uk-24588854.

89 C. Howse, 'The Trouble with Swearing an Oath on a Holy Book', *The Telegraph* (7 Mar 2015), http://www.telegraph.co.uk/comment/11455853/The-trouble-with-swearing-an-oath-on-a-holy-book.html.

90 H. Saul, 'Judge Stops Robbery Trial when Muslim Witness Swears on Bible instead of Koran', *The Independent* (28 Feb 2015), http://www.independent.co.uk/news/uk/crime/judge-stops-robbery-trial-when-muslim-witness-swears-on-bible-instead-of-koran-10075745.html

to take an oath on the Holy Book of the country in which he lived and, as noted above, the Oaths Act 1978 is explicit that oaths remain valid and binding even if they are for some reason made without the support of an appropriate underlying belief. The person giving evidence was satisfied with the proceedings, and statute prevented third parties from attacking his evidence on religious grounds.

The problem arose not really from the law, but the manner in which it had been understood and applied. Until such time as scientists working on artificial intelligence develop judicial droids, we shall be reliant on fallible human beings who will make mistakes whatever legal rules are in place. It is not difficult to conceive of circumstances in which a judge might call into question a solemn affirmation on the basis of some practical or administrative error.

In any case, the present legal framework is flexible and inclusive. It allows individuals giving evidence or making a commitment in public life to swear a religious oath, and one that is in keeping with their individual beliefs. For instance, Hindus sometimes opt to swear by the Gita and Sikhs by Guru Nanak.[91] Equally, those with no religious belief are free to solemnly affirm, and the law is explicit that their word in this context is to be given equal weight to that under oath. Everyone may express themselves in the way in which they feel is most appropriate for them when making a profound, personal commitment to act with honour and integrity. Yet, there are some citizens who wish to remove this freedom and impose a blanket secular affirmation in all cases.[92]

It is hard to see how this could be defended as a move in the direction of advancing individual or collective liberty. Ian Abrahams, the magistrate who proposed the motion to remove religious oaths, argued that the spiritual dimension made people no more likely to tell the truth, and maintained that the point to be emphasised to individuals was that if they lied in court they could face a prison sentence.[93] However, Nick Freeman, a solicitor arguing for the retention of religious oaths, asserted that for some people the religious character of an oath has meaning, and that '[t]he way you stamp out lying under oath is to punish people who do so, not to get rid of the religious oath. By changing it you are depriving people with a religious faith of the chance to reinforce their evidence by swearing on their religious text'.[94]

Both points have merit. First, it is not clear that the religious or secular character of a promise to tell the truth relates to an understanding on the part of those making it that they will be punished by the legal system if they break their word. Second, in removing the choice to swear a religious oath, some people of faith would feel a sense of genuine deprivation. Why should they suffer this detriment?

Prior to the introduction of same-sex marriage, there were some religious voices who argued that the proposed changes would damage faith communities and others opposed to same-sex unions, as it would deprive them of an exclusively

91 Howse, n. 89 above.
92 Ibid.
93 Pigott, n. 88 above.
94 Ibid.

heterosexual legal institution.[95] The persuasive response from many within the LGBTQ community can be summed up with the slogan 'If you don't like gay marriage, don't get gay married'.[96] Introducing same-sex marriage for those who wanted it in no way prevented other citizens, whose beliefs were incompatible with such unions, from contracting a heterosexual partnership with the legal status of marriage, and ordering their relationships in accordance with their beliefs. In a similar way, citizens who wish to continue to have the capacity to make religious oaths could equally assert 'If you don't like religious oaths, don't make one'. Allowing all citizens to make the choice which feels most appropriate for them, in expressing their commitment to the truth and the judicial process, would appear to be a more positive way forward than forcing some citizens to conform with the worldview of others.

The current legal framework uses the serious nature of religious oaths to reinforce the strength of the commitment that individuals are making to the words which they speak. Arguably, some secular individuals might even feel an added sense of solemnity, conferred by the understanding that their personal promise is *as important* as an oath which a religious person would make before their conception of the divine. Therefore, religious oaths might be seen to enhance the rule of law by supporting the collective belief in the importance of legal proceedings, the powers of the courts and evidence given before them. In recent debates, magistrates have considered them sufficiently valuable and powerful to retain, and they are not simply a vestige of former times, which have survived because they have been overlooked and ignored.

As a secondary point, the present system is respectful and inclusive of all beliefs and none. Making a solemn promise and tying this commitment to your sense of integrity and identity is a grave and deeply personal matter. It is not a coincidence that the verb 'to perjure' has retained its reflexive character in the transition from French to English. For some individuals, both religious and Atheist, a personal commitment to the truth is greater and more fundamental than the fear of prison or other state-imposed punishment. Consider, for example, Camus' lyrical and heartbreaking account in *L'Étranger*[97] of a man whose sense of self is so linked to a commitment to truth and his lived reality that he ultimately faces execution for his refusal to abandon this.

For many people, telling the truth in a courtroom or other solemn situation is about something more profound than the avoidance of prison, and this conviction is by no means confined to religious people (indeed, it would be insulting, as well as inaccurate, to suggest that it was).

95 See our analysis of this argument in J. García Oliva and H. Hall, 'An Inevitable Challenge to Religious Liberty and Establishment', *Oxford Journal of Law and Religion*, Vol. 3, No. 1 (2014) 25–56.

96 M. Moore, 'If You Are Against Gay Marriage Don't Get Gay Married', *Pink News* (25 Oct 2016), http://www.pinknews.co.uk/2016/10/25/michael-moore-if-you-are-against-gay-marriage-dont-get-gay-married.

97 A. Camus, *L'Étranger* (Gallimar: Paris) 1972.

In light of this, moving from a legal framework where all individuals are free to make this kind of public commitment in a manner which reflects their personal worldview, to one in which everybody would have to make a secular affirmation, would curtail, rather than promote, liberty and diversity. Given that individuals of faith would mostly be well aware that the format had been changed and that the option of making a religious oath had been removed, this could indeed be perceived as a 'deprivation', as rightly argued by Freeman.[98] Some witnesses, and indeed others, could feel alienated by a process which they perceived as having dismissed their worldview as an option, and enforced a secular one. This would not be conducive to the effective functioning or legitimacy of the justice system. Consequently, the current framework, which respects and accommodates all spiritual and secular outlooks, is better equipped to bolster the rule of law than one stripped of its religious dimension.

4.3.5 Violation of sepulchres

Violation of sepulchres is a common law offence which appears to have its origins in responding to the problem of 'body-snatching'.[99] It is a crime without a direct human victim, although clearly the relatives of the recently bereaved may suffer if a corpse is disturbed, or even if this is known to be a threat. However, the offence has been used in recent years, in relation to ancient tombs, where no close family members of the deceased were in a position to be distressed.

In 2004 some teenagers, who broke into an ancient grave in Greyfriars Kirkyard in Edinburgh,[100] hacked the head off a corpse and used it as a puppet,[101] were convicted of this offence. Judge Lord Wheatley[102] observed during the case '[w]hat lies behind this offence, and always has done, is the notion that in any civilised society there should be respect for the dead. The essence is the dead should be treated with a proper degree of reverence'.

Therefore, while it might be debatable whether this offence is religious in nature, there is undoubtedly a recognition that it exists because there is an accepted societal understanding that human remains should be treated with dignity. This is a shared cultural belief, which for many people has an ethical or spiritual dimension. As the maximum penalty for the offence is life imprisonment, desecrating a sepulchre is manifestly treated differently from other acts of criminal damage or vandalism, which do not have the potential to attract such a lengthy sentence. The relevant conduct is specifically criminalised precisely

98 Pigott, n. 88 above.

99 P. Ferguson and C. McDiarmid, *Scots Criminal Law: A Critical Analysis* (Edinburgh University Press: Edinburgh) 2014, 440.

100 'Corpse Ghouls Walk Free', *The Scotsman* (23 Apr 2004), http://www.scotsman.com/news/corpse-ghouls-walk-free-1-1009541.

101 'Teenagers Deny Violating Corpse', *BBC News* (25 Mar 2004), http://news.bbc.co.uk/1/hi/scotland/3568075.stm.

102 'Corpse Ghouls Walk Free', n. 100 above.

because of the 'belief' held by citizens that the dead should be 'treated with a proper degree of reverence'.

The social response to this kind of behaviour is demonstrated by press reports which suggest that the crime haunted the offenders in later years.[103] The conviction appears to have been one factor in one of the defendants losing his job as a traffic warden in later life. While we do not condone the persecution of offenders after they have served their lawfully imposed sentences, this story does suggest that irreverent behaviour in relation to graves is still a cause of shock and outrage. Although the offence is rarely used, it appears that there is support within Scottish society for maltreatment of graves to be treated as a serious and special offence under criminal law.

The surprising survival and acceptance of what at first sight appears to be a somewhat archaic crime demonstrates a subjective, moral dimension to the rule of law, especially where beliefs are concerned. Many legal rules are observed, and their enforcement is supported, not simply because they have been lawfully enacted, but because they are in harmony with widely held values. Although 'body-snatching' is no longer a widespread problem in Scotland, there remains a general consensus that disturbing human burials in a disrespectful manner is culpable behaviour worthy of criminal sanction. Thus the respect which the juridical system accords to beliefs about the dignity of the dead and the feelings of their loved ones helps to strengthen the rule of law, as it can be seen that this offence safeguards values and social norms which remain important to many citizens.

4.4 How do the perspective and teaching of different religious belief groups influence perceptions of the rule of law?

Undoubtedly, this is a question which needs to be approached with caution. It is important to bear in mind the radically different nature, hierarchical structure and self-understanding of the various religious belief groups that are represented in contemporary Britain. It would be easy for commentators coming from a Western Christian paradigm to fall into the trap of asking what does a particular denomination teach about the rule of law. For many Christian denominations, this would be a viable investigation, at least on one level. Many Churches have a clear hierarchical structure, with a body and process for declaring official policy and doctrine. They also frequently have their own body of canon law or comparable regulations, and a long tradition of engaging with the secular state in which they are set. They may well have an official position in relation to the rule of law. It might, however, be legitimate to question how far this official position of the Church reflects the beliefs and opinions of its membership. For example, some polls suggest that the attitude of Anglicans at grassroots level towards

103 'Former Grave Robber Loses Job after Colleagues Discover Past', *Daily Record* (31 Jul 2009), http://www.dailyrecord.co.uk/news/scottish-news/former-grave-robber-loses-job-1032478.

same-sex marriage is radically at odds with the institutional stance of the Church of England, as asserted by its Archbishops.[104]

So even though such a line of enquiry would be possible and meaningful in many Christian contexts, at least, generally speaking, the value and scope of its conclusions would be open to debate. However, when this kind of enquiry is transposed into different faith settings, it can become even more problematic in a number of respects.

For many religious belief groups, there is no single figure or assembly able to give a definitive or universal interpretation of doctrine. Within Judaism[105] and Islam,[106] individuals frequently seek advice from local scholars and experts when faced with moot points. Furthermore, not all such groups accept even the abstract idea of a single truth, and do not regard a set of shared abstract beliefs as the tie which binds them together as a community. For example, many of those who self-define as Neo-Pagan would not regard this as requiring them to subscribe to a single, common theological understanding of the universe.[107]

Moreover, not all religious beliefs embrace the idea of exclusivity, membership or identity. Many branches of Buddhism, for example, not only operate without the need or desire to foster conformity in terms of belief,[108] but can be embraced alongside other faith traditions. Even among faith traditions which invest members with a sense of identity and shared doctrinal beliefs, these beliefs are not concerned with earthly politics: Zoroastrianism is arguably a good example of a religious path in this category.[109]

Furthermore, as we discussed in Chapter 3, for many of our very specific purposes, some Humanist and Atheist organisations can be properly termed 'religious belief groups'. They are held together by shared beliefs on religious matters and function along lines which are parallel to organised religion as it is conventionally understood. The selection of religious belief groups which we deal with in each chapter will be slightly different, to give a variety of perspectives and, in some instances, to avoid repetition,[110] and in Chapter 7 we include the British

104 H. Sherwood, 'The Church of England Backs Same-Sex Marriage', *The Guardian* (29 Jan 2016), https://www.theguardian.com/world/2016/jan/29/church-of-england-members-back-same-sex-marriage-poll.

105 J. Baskin and K. Seeskin (eds), *The Cambridge Guide to Jewish History, Religion and Culture* (Cambridge University Press: Cambridge) 2010.

106 J. Esposito, *The Future of Islam* (Oxford University Press: Oxford) 2010.

107 S. Hawkings, *Goddess Worship, Witchcraft and Neo-Paganism* (Zondervan/Harper Collins: Michigan) 1998, 35.

108 M. Spiro, *Buddhism and Society* (George All & Unwin: London) 1971.

109 M. Boyce, *Zoroastrians: Their Religious Beliefs and Practices* (Routledge and Kegan Paul: London) 1987.

110 In particular, because different Christian denominations in Britain have had differing experiences of the operation of the legal system and continue to have different links with the state, it is logical to consider them separately when discussing matters such as the rule of law and parliamentary sovereignty. However, in doctrinal terms they are likely to occupy broadly the same theological territory in relation to concepts such as human rights. Similarly, among the Dharmic religions, there are instances of convergence and divergence, and we have tried to tailor our analysis to reflect this, attempting to strike a balance between avoiding repetition on the one hand and doing justice to each unique tradition on the other.

Humanist Association. As with some of the faith traditions we have discussed, it is not in the nature of Humanism to demand subscription to any identifiable creed when an encouragement of free thought is one of its core values.[111]

Taking all of these factors into account, it would not be fruitful to ask simply 'How do the various religious belief groups represented in contemporary Britain regard the rule of law'?' Put starkly, it is not helpful to explore what members of X tradition believe about the rule of law (or, indeed, the other constitutional pillars discussed in later chapters). In fact, it is not the primary function of most religions to provide a blueprint for the political structure of society, and even religions which have firm doctrine and mechanisms to interpret and maintain this do not generally deal in detail with how to arrange the Constitution of a nation state. In some ways, it could be argued that Christianity is an excellent paradigm example of this. The religious wars and political turmoil of the seventeenth century, discussed in Chapter 1, were possible precisely because there was no clear answer as to what model of government would be desirable and pleasing to the Christian God.

Yet, at the same time, as we noted earlier, ideas from Christian Scripture and tradition fuelled and inspired the debate. All sides believed that their perspective was at least compatible with Christian values and ideas, and religious faith and identity have enormous influence in shaping the thoughts and actions of individuals. It does not necessarily give the answer to political questions, but it may provide intellectual building blocks from which to construct an answer.

Given the diversity of human character and creativity, it is not surprising that there will be huge variation in the sculpture constructed from the available blocks. This is why it is only to be expected that not all Methodists, Orthodox Jews or Hindus will come to the same conclusion about the rule of law or human rights in a particular context. Equally, however, the building blocks do provide some common possibilities and constraints.

To take a dramatic example to illustrate this point, the sanctity of human life is a core principle within all branches of Judaism. The rabbinic principle *pikuach nefesh*[112] means that almost any of the commandments may be suspended in order to preserve an endangered human life. The willingness to dispense with other fundamental requirements indicates just how profound and far-reaching this imperative is. For example, if an individual is faced with starvation or eating non-kosher food, he has a duty to eat non-kosher food. Equally, taking a sick person to the hospital both justifies and necessitates driving on the Sabbath. In light of this, it would be extremely difficult to construct any governmental or legal system which requires the destruction of human life, and claims that this is compatible with a Judaic understanding of the world. Because the ideas and values imparted by religious traditions are important to those who subscribe to them, it is useful to consider how these might relate to abstract concepts such as the rule of law,

111 British Humanist Association, 'Humanist Thinking', https://humanism.org.uk/humanism/humanism-today/humanists-thinking.

112 R. Eisenberg, *The JPS Guide to Jewish Traditions* (The Jewish Publication Society: Philadelphia) 2004, 548.

not in an effort to assert what members of the different groups might think in concrete terms, but to understand some of the factors which mould their thinking on these topics. Bearing all this in mind, we now turn to consider what building blocks might be imparted by the perspectives of religious groups in Great Britain.

4.4.1 The Church of England

The established denominations in Great Britain are all Christian, and these relationships are important for members of these Churches in terms of their understanding of temporal authority. Furthermore, until the twentieth century, Judaism was the only non-Christian faith group with a strongly entrenched presence in England, Scotland and Wales. Therefore, religious minorities were seen mainly in terms of Christians from outside the establishment settlement. The other Christian groups also inevitably understood their identity and place within society in the shadow of establishment, and were well aware that they were not worshippers within the 'state religion'. Essentially, establishment moulded the perceptions of all Christian groups in one way or another.

For this reason, in this chapter (and also in the following discussion of parliamentary supremacy in Chapter 5) we will consider the teachings of these and other Christian denominations separately, whereas we will not always divide other faiths into distinct subgroups. This clearly should not be taken to imply that the non-Christian faith groups are of any lesser significance, but simply to deal with the nuance of the particular cultural paradigm in which we are working, shaped by its history.

For good or ill, the Church of England is part of the constitutional framework of the state.[113] The unique position of Anglicanism means that the beliefs which it fosters must, in general terms, be supportive of the legitimacy of the state and its Constitution. Its own canon law exists within the corpus of national law and has the power to enact legislation.[114] Some of its bishops sit in the House of Lords and take part in the debates of that chamber. Given that the Church forms part of the constitutional structure, exercises its own legislative powers, and actively assists in the general legislative process via its participation in the House of Lords, its doctrines generally approve accepted constitutional principles and the legal system more widely. In fact, it could not reject the system of governance to which it owes its form and powers, if not its existence.

Indeed, in the recent debates before the introduction of same-sex marriage in England and Wales,[115] there were voices from within the Church asserting that a legal change (even in relation to family rather than constitutional law), which left the secular rules at odds with Anglican doctrine, would be an innovation that would lead to the breakdown of establishment.[116]

113 The Church of England, 'Detailed History', https://www.churchofengland.org/about-us/history/detailed-history.aspx.

114 The Church of England, 'Measures', https://www.churchofengland.org/about-us/structure/churchlawlegis/legislation/measures.aspx.

115 Marriage (Same Sex Couples) Act 2013.

116 García Oliva and Hall, n. 95 above.

As we argued in a journal article,[117] this extreme position was difficult to defend, not least because the state introduced divorce long before the Church accepted the possibility of dissolving a valid marriage (as opposed, of course, to setting aside an invalid one). Even today there continues to be a gulf (in fact, in some instances a yawning chasm) between what the state permits in connection with remarriage and what the Church will allow. Secular law would have no difficulty in validating the fifth marriage of an individual divorced for adultery four times and demonstrating not a shred of remorse for the pain this behaviour had caused to others. The Church, however, would take a very different line. The establishment relationship managed to flex, rather than snap, when faced with legal divergence in the past. Nevertheless, the very fact that the argument could be made sufficiently credibly, and could also require consideration and rebuttal, demonstrates the undeniably close bond that continues to exist between state and canon law.

Yet equally, secular law on divorce, and now same-sex marriage, prove that a close bond does not equate to state and canon law being coterminous on all matters. Therefore, it is helpful to find support for the rule of law elsewhere within Anglican formularies. Article 37 of the Thirty Nine Articles deals with 'the Civil Magistrates', and affirms the legitimacy of the power of the Crown and the right to govern and uphold the laws of the realm.[118]

> Of course, the individual clauses of the Thirty-Nine Articles are now somewhat antiquated. The official position of the Church of England is that Anglican clergy and officers are required to affirm them as part of the historic development of the Church, while acknowledging that the Gospel must be proclaimed afresh in every generation.[119] In other words, they are not accepted wholesale as a modern statement of belief. A useful test case is Article 37 itself, and its explicit endorsement of capital punishment.[120] The Church of England debated capital punishment in the General Synod (its governing body) in 1983, and passed the following motion: 'That this Synod would deplore the reintroduction of capital punishment into the United Kingdom sentencing policy.'[121]

117 Ibid.

118 Book of Common Prayer, Articles of Religion, Article XXXVII.

119 See further, The Church of England, 'Being An Anglican', https://www.churchofengland.org/our-faith/being-an-anglican.aspx, and in particular the oath required of clergy, readers and some lay officers: 'I, [name], do so affirm, and accordingly declare my belief in the faith which is revealed in the Holy Scriptures and set forth in the catholic creeds and to which the historic formularies of the Church of England bear witness; and in public prayer and administration of the sacraments, I will use only the forms of service which are authorized or allowed by Canon'.

120 Book of Common Prayer, Articles of Religion, Article XXXVII: 'The Laws of the Realm may punish Christian men with death, for heinous and grievous offences'.

121 The Church of England, 'Justice Issues and Prisons', https://www.churchofengland.org/our-views/home-and-community-affairs/home-affairs-policy/justice-issues-prisons/capital-punishment.aspx.

Therefore, despite the content of Article 37, the Church is supportive of the state having rejected capital punishment, and by extension arguably the developments from the European Court of Human Rights which now require the state to protect even non-citizens from exposure to capital punishment abroad in some circumstances.[122]

Taken in the round, the Church of England can be seen as a national Church which is part of the constitutional framework, and therefore is, in broad terms, supportive of the Constitution and its principles. However, the Church as an institution is not required to approve of every aspect of secular law. On the contrary, it promotes the idea that people of faith should engage in constructive criticism of political and social decisions, both individually and collectively, if they conflict with core Christian values, such as compassion for the suffering and oppressed. Also, in many of its policy statements,[123] the Church demonstrates an ethical concern for the weak and those at risk. Furthermore, it is important to remember that engaging in dialogue within the democratic framework is in itself supportive of the rule of law, and a commitment to bringing about change from within the existing system.

It is also useful to note that the Church itself has a conception of the rule of law in relation to its internal framework. This was one of the identified principles of canon law common to the whole Anglican Communion.[124] The definition and understanding adopted is narrower in scope than that which sits within the UK Constitution, but it is undoubtedly compatible with it:

1 The Law binds the bishops, clergy and lay officers.
2 The law may bind lay people who do not hold office.
3 No-one shall be above the law. All institutions and persons in positions of authority or office, ordained and lay, shall act in accordance with law.
4 Rights, laws and duties are enforceable within a church by its own ecclesiastical authorities by executive action or judicial process.
5 Any person or body injured by a violation of law should be able to obtain a remedy before a competent ecclesiastical authority in accordance with the law.
6 A voluntary declaration, or other form of assent prescribed by law, to comply with ecclesiastical jurisdiction, binds the person who makes that declaration.[125]

122 European Court of Human Rights, Press Unit, 'Factsheet, Death Penalty Abolition' (Feb 2015), http://www.echr.coe.int/Documents/FS_Death_penalty_ENG.pdf.

123 See, e.g., its statement on immigration and asylum: Church of England, 'Immigration and Asylum', https://www.churchofengland.org/our-views/home-and-community-affairs/asylum-and-immigration.aspx; and on social care: Church of England, 'Social Care', https://www.churchofengland.org/our-views/medical-ethics-health-social-care-policy/socialcare.aspx.

124 Anglican Consultative Council, *Principles of Canon Law Common to the Anglican Communion* (Anglican Communion Office: London) 2008.

125 Ibid., Pt 1, Principle 5.

This understanding is, of course, shared by the Church in Wales and the Scottish Episcopal Church in Great Britain, also being provinces within the Anglican Communion. A crucial caveat must be added, however. The Church of England does not give unconditional support for the rule of law in all circumstances, and its understanding of the concept must undoubtedly be of a substantive nature, with an inbuilt ethical compass. Within its Holy Days, it commemorates as saints and exemplars men and women who resisted the lawful but immoral exercise of power. For instance, Dietrich Bonhoeffer is remembered on 9 April and Oscar Romero on 24 March.[126]

4.4.2 The Church in Wales

As explained in the previous chapter, until it was forcibly disestablished by Act of Parliament, the Church in Wales formed part of the Church of England. It therefore shares the same theological tradition set out above and, as already outlined, its members were not actively seeking to break away from it. Indeed, pre-establishment ecclesiastical law remains part of the law of the Church in Wales unless and until the Church elects to alter it.[127] (As Doe observes, however, *in general*,[128] it no longer applies as it does in England as part of the law of the land. Instead, it takes effect by virtue of the statutory contract.)[129]

Consequently, as a matter of overarching principle, the Church in Wales shares with its sister province the stance of being broadly supportive of the state legal framework, including the rule of law. Having existed within the Church of England from the sixteenth to the twentieth centuries and has only reluctantly departed, very similar doctrinal considerations apply to those set out above in relation to England.

4.4.3 The Church of Scotland

As our historical discussions above have revealed, the Church of Scotland has always had a very different relationship and bond with temporal authority from that of the Church of England. Nevertheless, its teachings have always recognised and upheld the right of secular authority to operate in the secular sphere. Obedience to lawful and just commands of the earthly state is one facet of the lifestyle it promotes. This is reflected by section 3 of the Church of Scotland Act:[130]

126 The Church of England, 'Common Worship Daily Prayer', https://www.churchofengland.org/prayer-worship/worship/texts/daily2.aspx.

127 Welsh Church Act 1914, s. 3.

128 There are exceptions, e.g., in relation to marriage and burial. This is one reason why, as discussed in Chapter 2, the Church in Wales is more appropriately described as 'quasi-established' than it is as 'disestablished'.

129 See further, N. Doe, *The Law of the Church in Wales* (University of Wales Press: Cardiff) 2002, 15–18.

130 Church of Scotland Act 1921, s. 3.

> Jurisdiction of civil courts.
>
> Subject to the recognition of the matters dealt with in the Declaratory Articles as matters spiritual, nothing in this Act contained shall affect or prejudice the jurisdiction of the civil courts in relation to any matter of a civil nature.

Furthermore, as can be seen from its Standing Orders,[131] the life and governance of the Church is arranged in accordance with identifiable rules and principles. These incorporate provisions which guard against conduct that would amount to an arbitrary exercise of authority or offend the concept of natural justice: for example, decisions in contentious cases must be made by impartial judges who have heard the relevant evidence:

> 74. Announcement. Before parties are heard in any contentious case the Clerk shall read the following announcement, viz – 'The Commissioners are reminded that justice requires that all the pleadings at the bar should be heard by all those who vote in this case, and that their judgement should be made solely on the basis of the pleadings.' Immediately before a vote is taken in such a case, the Clerk shall read the following further announcement, viz – 'The Commissioners are reminded that only those who have heard all the pleadings at the bar are entitled to vote in this case.'

Thus, as we observed with the Church of England, the Church of Scotland runs its own internal affairs in way which affirms the concepts underpinning the rule of law. Therefore, in adopting this template, it encourages its membership to value and support the principle.

4.4.4 The Roman Catholic Church

The Roman Catholic Church has a long tradition of co-operating with temporal authority, and a respect for secular law continues to be enshrined in its canon law.[132] Yet, as with the Church of England, it is clear that obedience to secular laws is not an absolute mandate. Moreover, the mere fact that conduct is permitted by secular law will not, in and of itself, be sufficient to render it licit in the eyes of the Church. There is also an acknowledgement that secular law may not be in compliance with the beliefs and values of the Church. For example, Can 1259 states: 'The Church can acquire *by every just means* of natural or positive law permitted to others'.[133]

131 The Church of Scotland, General Assembly, 'Standing Orders', http://www.churchofscotland.org.uk/__data/assets/pdf_file/0012/705/standing_orders.pdf.

132 See, e.g., CCI Canon 231, s. 2, which deals with the payment of laymen fulfilling certain offices, and specifically demands that the prescripts of civil law be observed; and Canon 1259, which stipulates that the Church may acquire temporal goods in any way which, by natural or positive law, it is lawful for others to do. It therefore expressly accepts that it may properly make use of secular law.

133 CCI Canon 1259 (emphasis added).

In other words, the Church is permitted to make use of secular law in this regard only in so far as it is just in the Church's understanding, and the same logic applies to the Roman Catholic faithful. Furthermore, it is clear that the Church will not defer to or recognise civil law that it deems to be in conflict with its teaching: 'Civil laws to which the law of the Church yields are to be observed in canon law with the same effects, insofar as they are not contrary to divine law and unless canon law provides otherwise'.[134]

In contrast to the canon law of the two Anglican provinces described above, the canon law of the Roman Catholic Church has to be drafted to fit an international framework. There are, of course, provisions which allow for specific regulations to apply to designated locations and people,[135] but the general norms of the Church have to be of worldwide application. An unqualified affirmation of civil law would be difficult to justify, as there are many Roman Catholics living within oppressive, totalitarian regimes with little or no regard for human rights.

In addition to this, as noted above, there are national and cultural differences when it comes to defining the juridical concept of the rule of law. An international Church cannot engage with only one understanding of a secular legal term when multiple understandings of it exist among the temporal systems that affect its members, and its explicit doctrines cannot shape the views of all members in relation to a concept which is not universally shared. However, the core aspects of the particular understanding of the rule of law, which forms a pillar of the UK Constitution, are compatible with, and indeed supported by, the theology of the Roman Catholic Church. Squeezed into a nutshell, Roman Catholic teaching supports secular law where it is for the common good and is compatible with natural law and justice.[136]

For instance, Aquinas in the *Summa Theologica* deals with the need for law to be promulgated for it to be valid:

> In order that a law obtain the binding force which is proper to a law, it must needs be applied to the men who have to be ruled by it. Such application is made by its being notified to them by promulgation. Wherefore promulgation is necessary for the law to obtain its force.[137]

This relates directly to the ideas discussed above: that in the United Kingdom laws must be known, clear and identifiable. It can be seen, therefore, that in this regard the principle of Roman Catholic teaching and the constitutional understanding of the rule of law are coterminous. Nevertheless, as we have seen, it should not be forgotten that there is a dark side to state law in relation to the Roman Catholic

134 CCI Canon 22.

135 See, in particular, CCI Part 2, 'Hierarchical Constitution of the Church, Section 2, Particular Churches and their Groupings.

136 T. Aquinas (trans. Fathers of the English Dominican Province), *The Summa Theologica of St Thomas Aquinas*, 2nd and revised edn, 1920, Questions 90–108.

137 Ibid., Question 90, Art. 4.

Church in Great Britain. We should not underestimate the degree to which the state, historically, used its powers of lawmaking and enforcement in ways that were deeply oppressive, both for the Roman Catholic Church as an institution and for its individual members. As a result, many worshipping communities and families chose to break the law in preference to abandoning their faith, and were forced to risk torture and death in doing so.[138] This is now part of our history, as these forms of abuse, alongside legislation excluding Roman Catholics (or any other religious group) from Parliament and universities, would not be compatible with the rule of law as it operates in contemporary Britain. The plain pancake of legality has now been enhanced with the treacle and butter of human rights and substantive ethical considerations.

Thus, in functional terms, the Roman Catholic Church is in a similar position to that of the Churches discussed previously. It is essentially supportive of the rule of law as it is embedded within the Constitution, because its structure fits well with its own ethical stance. However, like other Christian denominations, it teaches its followers that there may be extreme circumstances in which deference to secular law must be sacrificed to higher spiritual and moral principles.

4.4.5 The Methodist Church

Methodism grew out of the Anglican tradition, and it was the intention of its founder, John Wesley, to revitalise, rather than escape from, the Church of England.[139] It, therefore, had embedded within its ideological DNA a respect for the rule of law and those who administered it, and Wesley was anxious that his followers should be respectable and law-abiding citizens. Even in the nineteenth century, as Methodism went its own way and also splintered into numerous factions, this trait continued within the predominant groups. It has even been argued by academics that Methodism was a force in holding back the tide of revolution.[140] Despite a passion for social justice, the consensus of opinion within the movement was that it was preferable to work towards reform from within the political and social system, rather than seeking to overturn it. Munsey Turner quotes the response of the local preachers in Burnley, when asked about individuals using sermons as a vehicle to further radical politics:

138 J. Childs, *God's Traitors: Terror and Faith in Elizabethan England* (Oxford University Press: Oxford) 2014.

139 Despite the controversy sparked by the very elderly John Wesley's laying hands on individuals for the purposes of ordination, in response to the refusal by the Church of England to assist the rebel side in the American War of Independence, he died as he had lived, a member of the established Church: see further H.D. Rack, *Reasonable Enthusiast: John Wesley and the Rise of Methodism* (Epworth Press: London) 3rd edn, 2002, Ch. XIV 'I Live and Die in the Church of England: Methodism in the 1780s'.

140 J. Munsey Turner, *John Wesley: The Evangelical Revival and the Rise of Methodism in England* (Epworth: Peterborough) 2002, Ch. 7 'Did Methodism Prevent Revolution?'.

> We are unanimous in our opinion that as preachers of righteousness and followers of Christ whose Kingdom is not of this world, we ought to respect every ordinance of man for the Lord's sake, whether of the King as Supreme Governor of the Realm or of the magistrates acting under authority.[141]

However, this respect for the legal system and its principles again should not be equated with blind and unquestioning acceptance of everything done with appropriate legal sanction. The same pattern of respect for the rule of law as applied by the state, but with vigilance as to how this might be worked out in practice, can be found in Methodism as in other Christian denominations.

The explicit statement of 'Vision and Values' made by the contemporary Methodist Church in England and Wales draws out the importance of justice for this faith group: 'The Church exists to be a good neighbour to people in need and to challenge injustice'[142] and 'we share with one another our concerns about things which do not seem right, or cause trouble in our community, or appear unjust'.[143]

Therefore, the principles of justice and fairness rooted in the rule of law, as well as the impact their operation may have on the poor and vulnerable, are serious concerns for modern Methodists.

4.4.6 Judaism

Sadly, Judaism too has known its share of persecution, oppression and marginalisation. Throughout much of its history, the faithful have had to live as members of a religious and ethnic minority group. Unlike Christianity and Islam, Judaism has not been closely tied to regimes that exercise temporal power for much of the last two thousand years. Consequently, it is no surprise that the interface between religious law (Torah) and secular law is dealt with in the Talmud.[144]

As a general rule, observant Jews are expected to abide by the laws of the country in which they reside.[145] The guiding principle which has emerged is *dina d'malchuta dina*:[146] in other words, the law of the land is the law. In essence, where there is no conflict between religious and secular law, and the state has a legitimate interest, the observant Jew should obey the law. So, for instance, it is clear that a good Jew should pay taxes and avoid speeding; neither of these injunctions conflict with the Torah, and it is appropriate for secular authorities to be using tax money to fund hospitals and legislative power to minimise road

141 Ibid., 141.

142 The Methodist Church, 'Vision and Values', http://www.methodist.org.uk/who-we-are/vision-values.

143 Ibid.

144 Collective authoritative rabbinical teachings.

145 J. Rosen, *Understanding Judaism* (Dunedin Academic Press: Edinburg) 2003, 111.

146 S. Atlas, 'Dina D'Malchuta Delimited', *Hebrew Union College Annual*, Vol. 46 (1975) 269–88.

accidents. Clearly, as the experience of the Jewish community in historic times demonstrates, the position is more complex where there is a conflict.[147]

As might be expected, Rabbinic opinion is divided over exactly when the principle of ***dina d'malchuta dina*** is engaged. The entirety of Jewish law is predicated on the opinion of an expert.[148] It is generally accepted that the principle applies between individuals and government; it is also generally accepted that it does *not* apply to ritual matters, while everything in between is up for grabs. A detailed assessment of when it should be called upon is beyond the scope of this book (and our expertise), but for present purposes the point is that Judaism, broadly understood (encompassing Reform, Conservative, Orthodox and Ultra-Orthodox groups), acknowledges the legitimacy of the law of the land in 'public law' matters. In a state such as the United Kingdom, which guarantees the right to both hold and manifest religious beliefs,[149] this should equate to a general support for the rule of secular law within its proper remit.

Furthermore, respect for justice and the rights of the individual, combined with a need to contribute to communal life, is another theme which is common to Jewish groups across the religious spectrum. For instance, the UK-based Movement for Reform Judaism defines its core values as being:

> Creating inclusive, egalitarian communities, valuing difference
>
> Bringing Holiness into the world by seeking meaning in our lives and a just society for all
>
> Treasuring the autonomy of the individual, Jewish tradition and the insights of the wider World.[150]

Speaking recently from an Orthodox perspective, Rabbi Jonathan Sacks made the following comments on the current political debate surrounding immigration to Britain:

> They [his parents and their contemporaries] were doing what Jews have been doing since the days of the prophet Jeremiah, twenty six centuries ago, when he wrote to the Jews who'd been taken as captives to Babylon. Don't weep, he said. Seek the welfare of the city where you have been taken, and pray to God on its behalf, for in its peace you will find peace. In other words, keep your identity but contribute to society. That's what my parents taught us to do. They had a Hebrew phrase for Britain. They called it a ***malkhut shel chessed***, a 'kingdom of kindness'.[151]

147 M. Motis Dolander, 'Estructura interna y ordenamiento juridico de las aljames judias del Valle del Ebro', *Segunda Semana de Estudios Medievales* (1993) 111–52.

148 Rosen, n. 145 above, 111.

149 Art. 9 ECHR.

150 The Movement for Reform Judaism, 'Our Core Values', http://www.reformjudaism.org.uk/about.

151 J. Sacks, 'Living in a "Malkhut Shel Chessed", a "Kingdom of Kindness"', The Office of Rabbi Sacks (28 Oct 2014), http://www.rabbisacks.org/living-malkhut-shel-chessed-kingdom-kindness.

In summary, observant Jews of all shades of opinion acknowledge the importance of respecting state law, but also of contributing towards a cohesive and mutually respectful society. This, therefore, suggests a similar desire to that observed in a Christian context: to collaborate with the rule of law in so far as it furthers justice and enables the state to carry out its proper duties, while at the same time questioning any abuses which are problematic. Again, we have an example of a faith group supporting the rule of law, provided that it has an acceptable moral guiding compass.

4.4.7 Islam

As we have observed within Judaism and Christianity, Islam encompasses a wide spectrum of opinion on most topics. In addition to the divergence between Sunni and Shia, there are of course many shades of thought within these two groups. Furthermore, in common with all other religions, Islam cannot exist in a cultural vacuum. It is not always easy, either for insiders or external observers, to disentangle what is an Islamic belief or practice from what is in reality a Pakistani or Turkish cultural belief or practice. In fact, as Lewis observes, young British Muslims are increasingly using Islam to critique their parental culture.[152]

In contrast with Roman Catholicism, for example, there is no structure with accepted spiritual authority to determine what a demand of the faith is, and what a matter of cultural habit or preference is instead. So, for instance, the Congregation for the Doctrine of the Faith pronounced in 1976 that it was no longer mandatory for women to cover their hair in church,[153] and this position was affirmed when the 1983 Code of Canon Law did not reissue previous canons about veiling.[154] However, within Islam there are several perspectives on the religious obligations of women in terms of dress and veiling, and no single hierarchical structure to arbitrate.[155] This leaves young British Muslim women able to argue that the habits adopted by their mothers, grandmothers and aunts are either greater or lesser than the demands of their faith, properly understood. Of course, the flip side of the coin is that since there is no universality, some anthropological commentators, such as Green, prefer to talk of 'Islams', rather than Islam.[156] (Although Green's study is historical, the recognition of a lack of homogeny, and even more crucially the ***equal validity*** of differing strands within a faith tradition, is a valuable insight into the contemporary context).

152 P. Lewis *Young, British and Muslim* (Continuum: London) 2011, 150.

153 The Vatican, Sacred Congregation for the Doctrine of the Faith, Declaration *Inter Signiores* on the Question of Admission of Women to the Ministerial Priesthood, http://www.vatican.va/roman_curia/congregations/cfaith/documents/rc_con_cfaith_doc_19761015_inter-insigniores_en.html.

154 The Vatican, Code of Canon Law 1983.

155 R. Aluffi Beck-Peccoz, 'Burqa and Islam', in A. Ferrari and S. Pastorelli (eds), *The Burqa Affair Across Europe: Between Public and Private Space* (Ashgate: Farnham) 2013, 15.

156 N. Green, *Bombay Islam: The Religious Economy of the West Indian Ocean 1840–1915* (Cambridge University Press: Cambridge) 2011.

In other words, if an individual or group understands a particular practice as being a requirement of Islam, then it is indeed a requirement of *their* Islamic faith. This conception is, of course, reflected in the approach of the ECtHR in interpreting Article 9, as it is now well established that a belief or practice need not be doctrinally orthodox or accredited in order to be protected.[157] In the *Eweida* and *Chaplin*[158] cases, for instance, the fact that mainstream Christian denominations do not teach that their members are required to wear a visible cross was no barrier to the applicants arguing that the display of such a symbol was a manifestation of their beliefs for the purposes of Article 9.

However, it would be disingenuous, and in pragmatic terms futile, to pretend that the current geopolitical situation does not complicate the dialogue in respect of understandings of Islam. When terrorist atrocities and acts of war are being committed by individuals and groups asserting that they are motivated by the teachings of Islam,[159] to treat all incarnations of the faith as having parity in terms of authenticity becomes deeply problematic. Put another way, are the elements of the ideology espoused by ISIS and similar movements, which drive acts of hatred, in fact present within the various understandings of Islam adopted by the majority of people living in Britain who self-identify as Muslim? If the answer is no, then to simply give both the label 'Islam' is troubling. Such terminology potentially exposes people following an ideology devoid of such deeply destructive elements to misunderstanding and stigma. Tragically, at the time of writing, Islamophobic incidents are dramatically on the rise in Great Britain, and Muslim citizens are increasingly subject to abuse for their spiritual identity and choices.[160]

So we are caught on the horns of a dilemma. On the one hand, our general default position is to accept that people have a right to self-identify as *they* choose, and that it is neither appropriate nor rational for third parties to deny this personal election. We were critical of organisations like the British Human Association for attacking the validity of citizens' self-identification on census forms, and we have also acknowledged that it is difficult to defend the proposition that there is one, authentic and objectively discernible form of Islamic doctrine and practice, against which beliefs and praxis can be judged. However, equally, we do not wish to ascribe the same terminology to differing worldviews, when some contain highly destructive elements and others do not.

One possible response is to adopt a similar approach to that taken by Hirsi Ali,[161] and impose an additional layer of labelling on different groups within Islam, from the perspective of an external observer. However, taking on this model, we do not assert that we wholeheartedly endorse all of her contentions

157 *Eweida and Others v United Kingdom*, App. no. 48420/10, [2013] ECHR 37 (ECtHR).

158 *Chaplin v Royal Devon & Exeter Hospital NHS Foundation Trust* [2010] ET 1702886/2009.

159 A. Hirsi Ali, *Heretic: Why Islam Needs a Reformation Now* (Harper: London) 2015.

160 T. Jeory, 'UK Entering Uncharted Territory of Islamophobia after Brexit Vote', *The Independent* (27 Jun 2016), http://www.independent.co.uk/news/uk/home-news/brexit-muslim-racism-hate-crime-islamophobia-eu-referendum-leave-latest-a7106326.html.

161 Hirsi Ali, n. 159 above, 13–19.

and, partly for this reason, we do not adopt the same labels which she ascribes to differing groups. In her controversial work, *Heretic*, Hirsi Ali assumes a role in relation to the Islamic community, which is somewhere between critical friend and dissenting member. She argues that there are aspects of Islamic doctrine itself which do in reality run counter to liberal values such as tolerance, individual autonomy and respect for the dignity and freedoms of others, regardless of their beliefs or status. Furthermore, she divides the global Muslim community into three groups: (i) Medina Muslims; (ii) Mecca Muslims; and (iii) Modifying Muslims. In Hirsi Ali's terminology, Medina[162] Muslims are fundamentalists who believe in forcible conversion and the imposition of Sharia law by violent means if necessary. In contrast, Mecca Muslims are 'loyal to the core creed and worship devoutly but are not inclined to practice violence'.[163] Hirsi Ali states that the vast majority of the world's Muslim population belong to this group. In her analysis, there is an inevitable cognitive dissonance between their faith and their experience of living with rationalism, modernity and science, but Mecca Muslims learn to cope with this disconnect. In her view, one strategy for achieving this is 'cocooning', or opting to live within self-contained and frequently self-governing enclaves. However, her third and final category is that of Modifying Muslims, who are attempting to generate reform and dialogue, and find ways of living out their faith without a cognitive dissonance.

We are not in a position to analyse in detail the strengths and weaknesses of Hirsi Ali's analysis, nor do we adopt her categories. However, we suggest that a similar categorisation exercise might be helpful in resolving the dilemma set out above. Instead of three groups, we will divide understandings of Islam into two categories for our purposes: Exclusivist and Pluralist Muslims. Exclusivist Muslims are those who regard an Islamic regime governed by Sharia as the only acceptable context for the faithful to make a home, and clearly this group would include Hirsi Ali's Medina Muslims, but would also encompass individuals from the more conservative end of the Mecca Muslims, who would never contemplate using violence to further this religious end. They might be present in Britain upon what they regard as a temporary basis, with a plan to return 'home' to another jurisdiction when economic conditions allow;[164] or they may be saving money in order to move for the first time to what they regard as a better religious environment.

Pluralist Muslims, our second category, would of course include the more open Mecca Muslims, as well as the Modifying Muslims. Pluralist Muslims have an understanding of Islam which accepts that living in a non-Islamic regime is entirely compatible with a devout lifestyle, provided that individuals enjoy sufficient freedom to live in accordance with their faith and have the required inclination and self-discipline to do so. In choosing to live in Great Britain, either

162 Hirsi Ali adopts the term 'Medina' because this group aims to emulate the warlike approach and enforced conversion tactics adopted by the Prophet Muhammad after his move to Medina: Hirsi Ali, n. 159 above, 15.

163 Ibid., 16.

164 G. Marranci, *The Anthropology of Islam* (Berg: Oxford) 2008, 55.

by rejecting the option of emigration if they were born here, or having elected to come and remain if they were born elsewhere, the vast majority of British Muslims are by definition Pluralist.

Having said that, it cannot be denied that there is a complexity for Muslims living outside Muslim majority countries where the rule of law is concerned, because initially Islam developed in a context where both temporal and spiritual power were wielded by the Prophet Muhammad.[165] Furthermore, the strong links between temporal and spiritual authority, and a fusion of religious and secular law, continued in many succeeding Islamic regimes.

Contemporary opinion is divided about whether, in an ideal context, there should be a boundary between sacred and secular authority. Some surveys have suggested that a significant number of Muslims in the West regard the introduction or maintenance of Islamic principles within political and legal life as being optimal,[166] and we do not deny the existence of Exclusivist Muslims in Britain, as elsewhere. However, it is essential for us to highlight that many others argue that observance of Islamic law should be voluntary to be of any true spiritual value, and assert that Islam has tragically lost touch with its proud heritage of multiculturalism and tolerance.[167]

Yaran notes that Muslim countries were among the founding states of the United Nations.[168] This demonstrates willingness by the states concerned to be an active and collaborative part of a legal framework, which is shared with non-Muslims and not constructed along specifically Islamic lines. Of course, this is not uncontroversial, and at the present time there is an ongoing conversation within the Muslim world about the degree of accommodation that is desirable and acceptable, both in relation to Muslims living in non-Muslim majority contexts and vice versa.[169] Although we have referred to Exclusivist and Pluralist Muslims, we do not claim that the issues are black and white, with no shades of grey in between. Against this backdrop, however, it is significant that in a speech on British and Islamic Values given by the Secretary General of the Muslim Council for Britain,[170] Dr Shuja Shafi, the rule of law was cited as a gateway to inclusion and justice for Muslims in this society: 'Nevertheless, it is the Magna Carta and the rule of law that I point to when I talk to young people and encourage them that they do have a stake in this society'.[171]

165 Z. Sardar and Z. Abbas Malik, *Introducing Islam* (Icon Books: Royston) 2004.

166 M. Lutz, 'Muslim World: Poll shows Majority want Islam in Politics; Feelings Mixed on Hamas, Hezbollah', *Los Angeles Times* (5 Dec 2010), http://latimesblogs.latimes.com/babylonbeyond/2010/12/hamas-hezbollah-islam-sharia-public-opinion-muslim-countries.html.

167 Sardar and Abbas Malik, n. 165 above, 125.

168 C. Yaran, *Understanding Islam* (Dunedin Press: Edinburgh) 2007, 89.

169 Ibid.

170 The Muslim Council of Britain is a national representative Muslim umbrella body with over 500 affiliated national, regional and local organisations, mosques, charities and schools, http://www.mcb.org.uk.

171 The Muslim Council of Britain, 'Speech by Dr Shuja Shafi on British and Islamic Values' (29 Jan 2015), http://www.mcb.org.uk/shuja-shafi-speech-british-values-290115.

Although there is a genuine debate in both global and domestic Muslim circles about the compromises which can and should be made when living in a non-majority Muslim context, there is widespread recognition that all countries, Muslim or otherwise, are distinct. Clearly, living in a country that permits the Islamic faith to be practised openly and with respect is essential to Muslims. Followers of this faith in Britain in general find this compatible with their conscience because it is possible to live freely and practise their faith (the same statement could, of course, be made about Christian and Jews), and given that these rights and liberties are supported by secular law, there are strong pragmatic reasons to endorse the British constitutional model.

Furthermore, Muslims also have a duty to keep promises and covenants, and to act honourably in their dealings with others,[172] and there is a strong imperative to promote justice for all. It is very difficult to see how these key spiritual obligations could be fulfilled by anyone not respecting the rule of law. Therefore, for the majority of British Muslims, who should properly be thought of as Pluralist, the teachings of their faith encourage individuals to support and engage with the values underlying the rule of law.

4.4.8 Hinduism

We now turn our attention to the Dharmic faiths, and must therefore change our approach in some respects. First, it is advisable to be cautious in terms of what we infer from the Western term 'religion' in this context. Is this even an appropriate label to apply to what are arguably ways of life, which bind together spirituality, philosophy and ethics?[173] Certainly, it is acceptable only if we understand the term to mean something beyond a belief system which is isomorphic to the Abrahamic faiths, as these Eastern faith groups do not assert a monopoly on spiritual truth and sit more naturally within a pluralistic context. Although they have holy writings, they do not have a corpus of 'law' laid out in codes in the same sense as the Abrahamic faiths.[174]

This is not to suggest that these spiritual traditions have not shaped highly sophisticated legal systems where they have been an integral part of an intellectual and cultural paradigm.[175] Although Hinduism does not seek to answer questions akin to the debates about 'Church and state', which have moulded Anglican history and self-understanding, it undoubtedly does provide its followers with ideas and perceptions which shape their approach to the underlying questions and principles at issue.

172 S. Al-Oadah, 'Obeying the Law in Non-Muslim Countries', *Islam Today*, http://en.islamtoday.net/node/604.

173 A. Bahnot (General Secretary, Hindu Council UK), 'The Advancement of Dharma: A Discussion Paper for Faith Leaders', Hindu Council UK (20 Nov 2011), http://www.hinducounciluk.org/images/stories/report/the_advancement_of_dharma.pdf.

174 W. Menski, *Hindu Law: Beyond Tradition and Modernity* (Oxford University Press: New Delhi) 2012, 545.

175 See, e.g., Menski, ibid.; M.A. Nathan, *Buddhism and the Law: An Introduction* (Cambridge University Press: Cambridge) 2014.

Hinduism is an ancient faith, encompassing many strands of belief and a rich diversity of traditions, customs and practices. However, there are some themes common to all branches, one being the central endeavour to live a virtuous life. What this means in terms of individual duties and concerns varies both according to the characteristics of an individual and the stage of life which that individual has reached. The priorities and duties of a 10-year-old girl at school are not seen to be the same as a woman of 40 with a family and profession or an elderly great-grandmother of 95. Equally a priest will not have the same obligations as a warrior.

This proposition flows from the concept of Dharma, revealed in the Holy Scriptures (Vedas). Dharma is the spiritual power which drives all natural forces and also which gives human beings the potential to live a virtuous life (and ultimately to escape the cycle of rebirth and unite with the Divine). Dharma is a universal force, but its practical requirements will depend upon the precise circumstances. Perhaps one parallel for those from a Judeo-Christian background might be drawn from the words of Ecclesiastes 3:1-8:

> For everything there is a season, and a time for every matter under heaven:
> a time to be born, and a time to die;
> a time to plant, and a time to pluck up what is planted;
> a time to kill, and a time to heal;
> a time to break down, and a time to build up;
> a time to weep, and a time to laugh;
> time to mourn, and a time to dance;
> a time to throw away stones, and a time to gather stones together;
> a time to embrace, and a time to refrain from embracing;
> a time to seek, and a time to lose;
> a time to keep, and a time to throw away;
> a time to tear, and a time to sew;
> a time to keep silence, and a time to speak;
> a time to love, and a time to hate;
> a time for war, and a time for peace.

The demands of Dharma and a virtuous life will depend upon the circumstances and the characteristics of the individual. This is the focus of Hinduism, so at one level drawing out a perspective on the rule of law is problematic. However, at another level, it is possible to see that the core values of the faith are very much in harmony with the principle. For all Hindus a virtuous life requires a commitment to serve both divinity and humanity, and serving humanity necessarily encompasses an interest in charity, compassion and justice. In helping to maintain a peaceful society, in which individuals can work, study and prosper while suffering can be minimised, the rule of law is in harmony with the goals and desires of those striving to live in accordance with Hinduism. Therefore, while the teaching may not be direct, the effect may be profound. Those who follow this pathway should be drawn towards supporting the application of just and transparent rules, and the resolution of disputes without corruption or oppression.

4.4.9 Sikhism

Similarly, Sikhism promotes the values of community, justice and mutually respectful relationships:

> At the same time, we have to knock down the false barriers of belief and exclusivity between religions. When we do so, we will see our different religions as they really are: overlapping circles of belief, in which the area of overlap is much greater than the smaller area of difference. In that area of overlap, we find common values of tolerance, compassion and concern for social justice: values that can take us from the troubled times of today, to a fairer and more peaceful world.[176]

Furthermore, Juss[177]argues that Sikhism, on its collective journey to date, has been a moderate 'middle of the road' religion, which is essentially in harmony with the values of a liberal, secular state. Principles such as equality, universal brotherhood and hard work mean that Sikhs are often motivated by their faith to strive towards a cohesive and mutually respectful society. Disregarding laws imposed by a democratically elected administration, disturbing the peace or depriving others of their rights would be incompatible with Sikhism in the eyes of many of its followers.

It is also interesting to note that in many cases the Sikh community has been successful in advocating a relaxation of legal rules which are problematic for them in terms of observance. For instance, before laws on religious equality were introduced, Sikhs gained an exemption from the general obligation to wear motorcycle crash helmets.[178] Again, the interest in pursuing and gaining legal concessions demonstrates a desire to work within the legal framework, rather than seeing it as an oppressive or negative force.

4.4.10 Buddhism

In common with Hinduism, Buddhism is not concerned primarily with temporal politics. In fact, for many branches of Buddhism, the primary spiritual focus is on promoting a detachment from all earthly concerns and distractions. Notwithstanding, it is important to remember the rich diversity of traditions, beliefs and practices within Buddhism, and some Buddhist groups present in contemporary Britain very actively promote social and political engagement as part of their worldview – for example, Soka Gakkai.[179]

176 I. Singh, 'Religion and Society: A Sikh Perspective', Network of Sikh Organisations (20 Oct 2013), http://nsouk.co.uk/religion-and-society/#more-105.

177 S. Juss, 'The Secular Tradition in Sikhism', *Rutgers Journal of Law and Religion*, Vol. 11 (Spring 2010) Pt 2, 271, 275.

178 Motorcycle Crash Helmets (Religious Exemption) Act 1976.

179 Soka Gakkai International UK, http://www.sgi-uk.org.

It is also the case that Buddhism has a long heritage of engaging both directly and indirectly with secular legal systems. The Buddha is believed to have given rules to his followers in order to assist them on their spiritual journey.[180] It is, therefore, not unreasonable to assert that Buddhism does have an internal concept of law, but equally it is important to exercise a degree of caution in doing so. As Voyce[181] argues, the concept of law within a Buddhist paradigm is not in reality isomorphic to the concept of law within either the Abrahamic traditions or within Western secularism.

First, the rules given by the Buddha are not spiritual goods in themselves, akin to the Jewish understanding of Torah, but effectively mere tools. In other words, the rules are a means rather than an end. So, unlike the Abrahamic faiths, there is no acceptance of a need to abide by rules for their own sake and a support for the rule of law in that sense. However, there is an understanding that observing the rules will advance progress towards spiritual liberation, whereas breaking them will not.[182]

Moreover, a person acting in accordance with the Buddha's teachings will not engage in the kind of activities that would be prohibited by the secular legal system in Great Britain, such as assault, murder, theft or fraud. The idea is that if such a person is free from greed, hatred and delusion, he or she will inevitably not be drawn into such forms of behaviour, any more than water will flow uphill. Therefore, in practical terms, pursuing Buddhism will encourage citizens to live in a way that supports the rule of law.

In addition, there is also some strong indirect support. The Vinaya is part of the canon of Buddhist sacred texts, although multiple versions of it have been transmitted by different schools of Buddhism.[183] It is believed to be the word of the Buddha himself, and is effectively a Buddhist monastic legal code. Many of the principles within it have influenced secular law in Buddhist societies[184] and much of the substance resonates with the rule of law, as it exists in contemporary Britain.

For instance, the principle of *nullum crimen, nulla poena sine lege* (no crime or penalty unless there is a law to justify it) effectively prohibits retrospective and arbitrary sanctions. Furthermore, there must be no punishment without culpability, so those lacking mental capacity must not suffer detriment for actions beyond their control – an idea that chimes with the concept of natural justice. Therefore, taken in the round, Buddhist teachings encourage followers of this pathway to act in a manner which is supportive of the rule of law.

180 R. Gethin 'Keeping the Buddha's Rules: The View from the Sūtra Pitaka', in R. French and M. Nathan (eds), *Buddhism and the Law* (Cambridge University Press: Cambridge) 2015, 63–77, 76.

181 M. Voyce, 'Ideas of Transgression and Buddhist Monks', *Law Critique*, Vol. 21, No. 2 (2010) 183–98.

182 Gethin, n. 180 above, 76.

183 P. Kieffer-Pulz, 'What the Vinayas Can Tell Us about Law', in R. French and M. Nathan (eds) *Buddhism and the Law* (Cambridge University Press: Cambridge) 2015, 46–62, 46.

184 Ibid., 53.

4.4.11 Paganism

Very similar considerations apply to Paganism. Once again, despite not being prescriptive, the label 'Paganism' embraces a variety of worldviews[185] which, in general, value community in the widest sense and respect the rights of individuals. Consider, for instance, from the Wiccan branch of Paganism, the three-fold law:

> Mind the Threefold Law you should,
> Three times bad and three times good.

and the close of the Wiccan Rede:

> Eight words the Wiccan Rede fulfill:
> An' it harm none,
> Do what ye will.

In essence, these statements champion freedom of individual choice, but with the accompanying notion of individual responsibility for choices. Actions should not have a negative impact upon others, and both good and evil deeds will rebound on the doer with triple impact.

While the imposition of external rules do not at first appear to sit comfortably with this, recalling the philosophical basis of the rule of law (at least in the formal sense outlined by Raz) has, at its heart, a respect for personal autonomy and a need to safeguard the vulnerable from the consequences of anarchy. Couched in those terms, it can be observed that although Paganism does not sit within a structure which imposes juridical notions that support an express doctrine of the rule of law, it does foster an understanding which would lead its followers towards supporting the concept in general terms, while being alert for potential abuses and transgressions in relation to individual freedoms.

4.4.12 Zoroastrianism

Interestingly, much the same point might be made of Zoroastrianism, an ancient faith which straddles the border between Eastern and Western thought patterns. It is a monotheistic faith with surviving scriptures, which tend not to unpack its tenets in great detail. Nevertheless, one of its core maxims is '*Humata, Hukhta, Huvarshta*'', which translates as 'Good Thoughts, Good Words, Good Deeds'.[186]

It would be disingenuous to assert that there is an articulated Zoroastrian response to the rule of law. Despite this, it is a religion which encourages a sense of active social responsibility and engagement, and it is interesting to note that the first three Asian MPs in Westminster were all Zoroastrians (and they each stood for a different political party).[187] In upholding the importance

185 The Pagan Federation UK, 'Homepage', https://paganfed.org/index.php

186 Zarathustra, http://www.zarathushtra.com/z/article/overview.htm.

187 P. Allen, 'Zoroastrian Faith Joins Queen's Coronation Celebrations', *The Telegraph* (4 Jun 2013), http://www.telegraph.co.uk/news/uknews/10097326/Zoroastrian-faith-joins-Queens-Coronation-celebrations.html.

of justice and positive collective action, the Zoroastrian faith can be seen to be supporting the rule of law, at least in a functional sense. An acceptance of the need for agreed norms which govern a communal life, taken together with a concern for individual needs, flow from the kind of social engagement which Zoroastrianism promotes.

4.5 Do faith communities make a practical contribution towards the functioning of the rule of law?

Religious groups, including the established and quasi-established Churches, have a role not merely in responding to the rule of law, but also in playing an active part in its administration. It would not be possible to assess all current examples of formal and informal co-operation in this regard, but it is nevertheless helpful to focus on a few instances which illustrate this in practice.

4.5.1 The efforts of religious communities in tackling the problem of spiritual marriage without legal force

An important example of how the social contribution of faith groups may enhance the rule of law is demonstrated by the efforts of some religious communities in tackling the problem of spiritual marriages without legal force.

In fact, the established Churches are not the only religious bodies to collaborate with the state in relation to the rule of law where marriage is concerned. At present, there remains the problem in Great Britain of some religious couples marrying according to the rites of their faith without ensuring that the accompanying civil law requirements are fulfilled. This leaves the parties with no greater claims than any other cohabiting partners in the event that the relationship breaks down, which has serious implications for the economically weaker member of the partnership.

For illustrative purposes we will consider this in the Muslim context, but we are in no way suggesting that the difficulty is confined to Islam.[188] In fact, the issue is not even an exclusively religious one. Many people who have never been through *any* form of marriage ceremony, sacred or secular, still harbour the erroneous belief that they are protected by a mythical institution unhelpfully dubbed 'common law marriage'.[189]

However, a religious setting can increase the chance of misunderstanding arising, as it is easy to see how couples who have experienced a religious marriage ceremony of some sort might wrongly assume that it had legal force, especially if accompanied by 'formal' papers. The risk is even greater where one party originates from a jurisdiction with a very different legal framework, for whom English is a second language, and for whom accessing independent information can be challenging as a result of linguistic barriers.

188 D. Talwar, 'Wedding Trouble as UK Muslim Marriages Not Recognised', *BBC News* (3 Feb 2010), http://news.bbc.co.uk/1/hi/uk/8493660.stm.

189 C. Fairbairn, '"Common Law Marriage" and Cohabitation', House of Commons Library, Briefing Paper 03372 (9 Mar 2017), http://www.parliament.uk/business/publications/research/briefing-papers/SN03372/common-law-marriage-and-cohabitation.

At present there remains the acknowledged problem that a large number of Islamic marriages are unregistered in Great Britain. However, the Muslim community is working positively with the Government to try to improve the position. In January 2012, a Round Table meeting was held at the Foreign Office,[190] and a number of influential members of the Muslim community attended, including Baroness Warsi. The meeting was addressed by Lord Tariq Ahmad with the aim of launching the Muslim Marriage project, which seeks to tackle the issue of unregistered marriages.

It is significant to note that even though a legislative requirement for the registration of Muslim marriage was not ruled out, and was in fact flagged as a probable way forward, it was also made clear that it was crucial to put resources into raising awareness and moving towards a consensual change of culture. Aina Khan, a solicitor involved in the initiative, drew up a number of resources to assist, which significantly included the following:

> A 2-page simple Islamic narrative is being drafted, to be downloaded and given out at Mosques and other places frequented by Muslims. This has been given the support of key Islamic scholars; emphasizing that 'Islam was the first religion to introduce the concept of marriage as a contract, with clear terms to protect the interests of both parties and the children – secret marriages or those that exploit or hurt one party are not acceptable in Islam'.

Remarkably, proper engagement with secular law in order to protect the interests of those involved was effectively presented as a religious obligation for good Muslims, and a failure to register a marriage with the civil authorities, taking advantage of the other party's legal vulnerability, could be said to amount to non-Islamic behaviour. A similarly strong message was given by the Muslim Parliament of Great Britain:[191]

> For the marriage to be properly valid in the UK, it must be registered according to UK law. No Muslim should seek to contract a marriage without the full protection of the law of the land. If the marriage is not registered in a civil ceremony it is not recognised legally, and although the couple may feel married before Allah, they are in effect committing zina (adultery) so far as UK law is concerned. The husband, wife and children would therefore have

190 Duncan Lewis Solicitors, 'Aina Khan and Baroness Warsi Kickstart Muslim Marriage Project' (14 Jan 2014), http://www.duncanlewis.co.uk/news/Aina_Khan_and_Baroness_Warsi_kickstart_Muslim_Marriage_Project_%2814_January_2014%29.html#sthash.u3HEQ64F.dpbs.

191 The Muslim Parliament of Great Britain is 'a forum whose purpose is to debate, campaign and lobby on issues concerning the Muslim community in Britain. It is a non-governmental organisation dedicated to promoting community interests. It operates through a number of committees, each with its own remit. These committees work along with related campaign groups in the country': Muslim Parliament of Great Britain, 'About the Muslim Parliament', http://www.muslimparliament.org.uk/about.htm.

> no rights in law as regards pensions, benefits etc, and the children would be regarded as illegitimate.[192]

On the one hand, it must be acknowledged that the very existence of these statements and campaigns evidences that there is a problem with large sections of this religious community failing to properly engage with the secular legal framework, to the particular detriment of vulnerable women and children. We do not seek to minimise the seriousness of this point. Yet, crucially, influential members of these communities are seeking to engage their fellow believers in bringing about a paradigm shift, and are appealing to the principles of their faith in order to do so.

In some sense, the campaign is aimed at bringing the principle of the rule of law into practice as far as marriage is concerned, and it is trying to ensure that individuals are aware of their rights and obligations, are treated equally and have access to a judicial hearing if wronged. Where parties fail to engage with voluntary aspects of secular law in relation to personal obligations, they are in practice denied the protection of its rule. This situation leaves vulnerable individuals exposed to harm and exploitation. Co-operation between the state and religious authorities, therefore, strengthens the reach and effect of the rule of law.

In this context it is perhaps appropriate to note, in passing, the anxiety sometimes expressed in the popular press over Muslim Sharia law encroaching on British soil.[193] The implication is almost that the rule of law might be undermined by citizens preferring to live in accordance with, or even being coerced into 'opting in' to an alternative religious legal system which would be incompatible with the secular understanding of the rule of law. For instance, Sharia law treats men and women differently for a large number of purposes, in a way that many commentators would view as irreconcilable with a substantive concept of the rule of law which embraces European notions of human rights.

In many ways this debate is primarily sociological, rather than legal, and therefore beyond the scope of this book. The reason for this contention is that the legal framework itself, including the rule of law, has shifted little in this regard, and the questions are more about the use that citizens choose to make of it.

For these purposes, there are two types of legal regulation: that which is universal and involuntary, and that which citizens may opt into by action or express agreement. Clearly, the former binds all citizens, regardless of their religious affiliation. So, if a marriage breaks down, it does not matter what documentation the parties have signed: they cannot oust the jurisdiction of the court to determine the best interests of any children involved if those with parental responsibility cannot agree a way forward. To do so would run counter to the welfare principle at the heart of s. 1 of the Children Act 1989.

192 Muslim Parliament of Great Britain, 'Getting Married – Some Guidelines: Validation of Marriage', http://www.muslimparliament.org.uk/marriage_guidelines.htm.

193 See, e.g., J. Bingham, 'Sharia Law Guidelines Abandoned as Law Society Apologises', *The Telegraph* (24 Nov 2014), http://www.telegraph.co.uk/news/religion/11250643/Sharia-law-guidelines-abandoned-as-Law-Society-apologises.html.

In contrast, with regard to voluntary legal regulation and private matters with no legal effect, Muslims and other citizens have always been free to order their affairs as they see fit. Contractual agreements and wills may be drawn up along Sharia lines if this is the basis upon which the parties choose to operate. There is nothing new or revolutionary about Muslim or Jewish citizens electing to order their affairs in accordance with their religious laws and, at times, making use of the secular courts to enforce agreements. The extent to which religious laws are in harmony with, or contrary to, human rights and other aspects of the constitutional rule of law is, of course, a matter for intense and complex academic debate, although in one sense it is irrelevant given that non-religious citizens frequently enter into contracts or make wills about which the same criticism could be levelled.

There is nothing to stop an Atheist testator in the United Kingdom deciding to leave his entire estate to his son, rather than his daughter. It makes no legal difference whether he did this because (a) he believed that men should inherit and women should be cared for financially by their husbands, (b) he and the daughter had agreed that he would pay out her 'share' early during his lifetime because she needed it when her business became insolvent, or (c) she insulted his pet cat. Provided that he is of sound mind and the formalities are complied with it is equally valid in each case: it does not matter whether his motives are unjust, irrational or even offensive.

Religious and non-religious citizens alike are equally free to order their affairs as they desire within the parameters allowed by the law. If more Muslim citizens are opting to arrange their lives in accordance with the demands of Sharia, it may be interesting and important for academics to explore the reasons behind this. However, it is not something which need directly undermine the rule of law, provided always, of course, that those involved are making conscious and free choices, which is why the problem of unregistered marriages is critical. Having said that, as outlined above, Muslim authorities in Great Britain are commendably seeking to address this issue and strengthen the application of secular law and the reach of its protection.

4.5.2 Religious bodies and individuals, litigants and campaigners in relation to the rule of law

Religious groups also arguably have a role in supporting the rule of law from their position as litigants and campaigners. As outlined above, they are placed to challenge what they perceive as abuse of executive or legislative power and a threat to the rule of law. At times, they do this through judicial means and in their own perceived interest. For example, in *Core Issues v London Transport*,[194] a conservative Christian group protested against a decision by Transport for London not to allow them to run an advertising campaign on the side of London buses proclaiming 'Not gay! Ex-gay, post-gay and proud. Get over it!' It was done in direct response to the Stonewall campaign 'Some people are gay. Get over it!'

194 *R (on the application of Core Issues Trust) v Transport for London* [2014] All ER (D) 285 (Jul).

The Christian group was evidently pleased with its slogan and aggrieved when Transport for London declined to plaster homophobic slogans across its iconic vehicles. The applicant sought judicial review on the grounds of improper purposes, claiming that Transport for London had been unduly influenced by the London Mayor who was concerned about the possible impact of the 'bigot-buses' on his chances of re-election. The court found that the decision had not been made for the improper purpose of advancing a political campaign, and that it was legitimate for the Mayor to express his views on the issue. The decision had ultimately been made by Transport for London on the grounds that the slogan contravened its advertising policy.

Perhaps unsurprisingly, the Christian group involved was not impressed with the decision, describing it as 'contrived and punitive'.[195] However, despite the lack of success, the claim itself arguably had a beneficial influence upon the functioning of the rule of law. Periodic judicial review actions provide citizens with some reassurance that those exercising executive power will be held accountable for their behaviour. They also serve as a disincentive to politicians, officers and civil servants who may be tempted to abuse their discretion. Obviously, faith groups are by no means the only sections of society with a role to play in this process, but they are certainly among the players who contribute by making judicial review applications.

Therefore, in common with other parties who bring such actions to challenge executive decision making, the Christian group in this case was participating in the system of constitutional checks and balances which keep the exercise of power within appropriate bounds. However, it is hardly the raison d'être of faith groups to bring judicial review actions, and this procedure is in any case available exclusively to parties who have *locus standi*. The law allows only those who are directly affected to intervene in this way: the doors of the administrative courts are not open to any party with an inclination to go in and stir the pot.

Similar considerations could be said to apply to individuals who bring private claims in respect of discrimination, family law disputes or other issues which may relate to religion. Faith groups may support members of the faithful in this position, and may on occasions even join as intervening parties,[196] but litigation is by no means their primary purpose or focus. Consequently, while faith groups can and do actively respond when they or their members are subjected to the rule of law, this is not their greatest contribution to the functioning of this principle.

4.5.3 Religious bodies: a voice in the collective dialogue from a liminal place

As outlined above, religious bodies have a significant part to play both in collaborating with the state in relation to the application of the rule of law, and in helping to challenge it from the position of subjects. In addition to these contributions, they have a third and critical crucial role. It is one which owes much to the way in which the establishment framework has reshaped itself to

195 J. Miller, 'Bus Ad Ban Was Lawful', *New Law Journal*, Vol. 164, No. 7618 (2014).
196 See, e.g., *Eweida and Others v United Kingdom*, n. 157 above.

encompass the contributions of other belief communities, and we referred to it in the latter part of Chapter 2.

The penguin wings of the state are no longer used for flying, and their function in swimming relies on the help of more than simply the established Christian communities. The third vital role of all faith communities in relation to the Rule of Law is to be a voice in the arena of public debate, highlighting injustices and campaigning for change. The commitment to social concern and compassion, which is deeply rooted in almost all of the religious traditions, encourages and enables this. Not coming generally from a professional or economic perspective, faith communities are equipped to advocate on behalf of many groups of vulnerable people and to challenge a range of abuses of power, not just through the highly formal channels of litigation but also in more fluid ways at varying levels of our collective life. When the substantive moral dimension to the rule of law appears to be lost in its practical application, faith groups are in a position to point this out. They can and do make a noise when the pancake needs more treacle to be poured on.

The establishment framework has provided a structure and platform from which this can take place, but there is now an expectation that the established Churches will share this platform with other faith groups, where appropriate. The tradition of having religious representatives taking part in public life, at every stratum from the House of Lords to the village fête, has given an opportunity and legitimacy to faith groups in seeking to point out flaws and injustices. Yet, at the same time, it has always been a liminal voice, both connected and disconnected from official power structures. At its best the religious voice can raise concerns and influence the behaviour of secular decision makers, without being tainted with direct responsibility, or political and financial motives.

This can operate in many ways when the rule of law appears to lose its moral way or proper application. Responses and opportunities range widely: comments in the press, local clergy liaising with councillors and sitting on school governing bodies, and chaplains making the needs of the communities that they serve heard in practice. For instance, a number of senior faith leaders in Great Britain (including Archbishop Barry Morgan, primate of the Church in Wales; Rabbi Laura Janner-Klausner, Head of the Jewish Reform Movement; and Shaykh Ibrahim Mogra, Assistant Secretary General of the Muslim Council of Great Britain) spoke in protest at the failure of the United Kingdom to do more to provide a safe haven for Syrian refugees in line with promises which the Government had made. It is striking that the highly influential secular pressure group, Amnesty International, regarded this as a sufficiently important and valuable contribution to highlight it in a press release.[197] While this kind of response may not at first seem to relate directly to the rule of law, it in fact demonstrates

197 Amnesty International, 'Great Britain Has a "Moral Responsibility" to Refugees from Syria Say Faith Leaders' (28 Jan 2015), https://www.amnesty.org.uk/press-releases/great-britain-has-moral-responsibility-refugees-syria-say-faith-leaders.

a sense of responsibility to monitor and comment upon the manner in which legal and executive power is exercised. It enhances the ethical dimension identified in the substantive understanding of the rule of law. It also reveals the role of religious bodies within the modern legal framework, echoing the part played by the medieval Church in questioning excesses and injustices perpetrated by secular authority. In some sense, the penguin is indeed still catching fish, albeit in a radically different manner with very different wings.

4.6 Conclusion

To sum up, on balance our analysis demonstrates that the functioning of the religious dimension to the legal framework operates to enhance the rule of law, as the concept is understood in a British context. There are some problematic elements within the current legal landscape (such as marriage law), but taken in its entirety the vista is a positive one. Moreover, the ideological building blocks supplied by the faith traditions considered also in general terms would encourage adherence to those traditions to respect and support the rule of law (within a liberal democratic society). Finally, we observe that there are a number of practical ways in which faith communities are among the forces in society that support the day-to-day outworking of the rule of law.

Chapter 4 appended interview material

Bharti Tailor

Is it important for you always to act within secular law?

Sadly the Prison Service does not provide culturally acceptable food and therefore, Hindus who are in prison really struggle. . . particularly if they don't eat meat; the vegetarian diet is dire.

There is only one thing which has hurt the Hindu Community in Britain. Other than that, we all act in a democratic way; a few of us vote (not many); we always accept the laws passed by Parliament, except the law on caste which we feel casts a cloud over us and our progeny and it discriminates against us.

David Pollock

Is it important for you always to act within the law?

I certainly wouldn't rule out civil disobedience on principle. Yes, I would be prepared to contemplate that as a possibility in extreme circumstances. As a matter of fact I have never come near to civil disobedience in my whole life, but that is the consequence of living in a country which is well run and where the laws are tolerable, even if you disagree with them.

Andrew Copson

Is it important for you always to act within state law?

I do not find it problematic to live within the bounds of the law, although I have broken the law many times and I think that in every case I have been justified in doing so, because the law was immoral. I broke the law when I was young, when I first had sex, because the law of consent was very unequal. I probably wasn't thinking of civil disobedience at the time.

Constance Jackson

Is it important for you always to act within state law? Are there circumstances which justify or necessitate breaking the law?

As a member of society, it is important to respect the law. However, the whole US civil rights movement was based on civil disobedience to protest unjust laws; an unjust law is an unjust law. When the Iraq war protest broke out, they estimated we had half a million to one million people in London on that Saturday. I remember that it was an unseasonably hot day in spring. It was such a long march that you could go into a bar, have a drink and rejoin it. I called my sister in Los Angeles as things were wrapping up; she was watching the New York protest on TV. None of the London protest was reported on the news, no pictures. The US media 'cropped' the protest to fit the frame. It was as if to say we are going to do this war and everybody is going along with it, except for these few rabble-rousers. If we had had Twitter then, it would have been a lot harder for them to crop the protest and tell everyone that most people were going along with the decision to go to war. That is what democracy is all about. Sometimes, the majority makes a stupid decision and the minority needs to agitate to say that you guys need to reconsider this.

Lord Richard Harries of Pentregarth

Is it important for you always to act within secular law?

I do believe there is a moral obligation to keep secular law. In terms of disobeying it should only be in extreme circumstances where there is very good reason for it. I am happy to go along with St Thomas Aquinas, where he said if a person is starving they might be justified in stealing food.

Mona Bayoumi

Is it important to act within state law?

To be completely honest, and I was having this discussion recently in a different context, it is actually a very important part of being a Muslim; it is respecting the laws of the land that you choose to live in. There are no exceptions to that really. If it gets to the point in which you feel that the laws of the land are in conflict with your beliefs, then you need to make a choice about where you live.

Patricia Travis

Is it important for you to act within state law? Could you envisage circumstances in which you would feel morally compelled to break the law?

I would never ever break the law.

I cannot think of a hypothetical situation breaking the law. I could never do that. I would never ever break the law. I wouldn't because I haven't been brought up that way. I have never ever been in trouble and I don't want to be.

The Rev'd Professor Martin Henig

Is it important for you always to act within secular law? Are there circumstances which might justify or necessitate breaking human law?

Yes, I think that there can be. When I was young I marched against the bomb and I can see myself doing things like that again, perhaps with the badger cull. I think that there are a lot of situations in which high-minded people might be on the edge of breaking the law, but not in ways that would be morally wrong. It would be true to say that there were a few grey areas.

The Rt Rev'd Tim Thornton

Is it always important for you to act under the law of the land? Are there any circumstances under which you would feel compelled to break the law?

The short answer is 'Yes'. I feel bound to respect the law of the land. It is important for our system, because of the checks and balances model. However, I could feel I need to break the law if I felt that the law is based on wrong principles or brought about for wrong principles. I have thought a lot about what I would do in some situations. In my last job I had to travel a fair bit, and I had to go to South Sudan . . . talking with my colleagues there about their lives, and particularly in North Sudan, where there was persecution against Christians by Muslims. I am sorry to say, it is happening . . . I think therefore that there would be circumstances under which I would feel compelled to break the law, but I can't think that would happen in this country at this stage.

Aled Griffiths

Is it important for you always to act within secular law?

I can envisage situations in which I would feel compelled to break the law on moral and religious grounds [. . .] Jo and I have different views about assisted dying, but if Jo were ill I would have to help her. I know that is her very deep conviction and, although I don't share it, I have to respect her views on such an important matter. I cannot really think of a clearer example, particularly bearing in mind the current legal framework.

The Most Reverend Professor Rowan Williams

Is it important for you personally always to act within secular law? What circumstances, if any, justify breaking human law?

[. . .] once I was arrested for saying public prayers on an airfield as part of an anti-nuclear protest. I was never brought to court because I don't think anyone was quite sure of what precise illegality I had committed [. . .]

It is rooted in the (often misunderstood) Anglican doctrine of 'passive obedience'. Active obedience means cooperating freely with what the Government does. Passive obedience is saying 'Well, I'll do what I am told to a point, but if I can't, ok, I'll go to jail'.

Janette Wilson

Is it important for you personally always to act within secular law?

[. . .] I think that there would be occasions when people have not entirely gone along with immigration law, because of feelings about immigrants who are going to be removed. There have been discussions about giving sanctuary in churches, so there are some cases where people would nail their colours to the mast.

Frank Williams

Is it important to act within secular law?

I don't know the answer to your question. I think I am by and large law abiding and I do uphold secular law, and I can't think of an occasion where I would deliberately want to break secular law, because it has moved forward in the last 30 or 40 years, beginning to understand that people have different viewpoints in various things. When I look back at my younger age, we still had capital punishment. I remember as a young man speaking against it, because I thought it was totally unacceptable. Therefore, I don't know . . . I have often thought if I were on a jury and someone were accused of murder in the days we had capital punishment . . . would I have actually been able to exercise my jury thing or would I have said I don't care if he or she is guilty or not . . . I will say he/she is not guilty, because what is going to happen to him/her is so immoral . . . By and large, I would uphold secular law nowadays, because it seems to me it is much more moral and understanding anyway.

Chikwan Nam

Are there any circumstances or countries in which breaking the law might be justified or necessary?

Yes, I suppose for me it's mainly because of China. Their laws are quite restrictive for things that we take for granted here. So, I think that it is morally justified to break those laws, not that I think I would have the guts to do it myself. And they do, there are lots of people out there who do and are punished for it.

Sir Mark Hedley DL

Are there conflicts between your faith and secular law? How would you resolve them?

[. . .] I have undoubtedly authorised same-sex families, surrogacies; I have authorised things that in my personal life I would not want to be associated with. I have given my reasons in public for doing it and they stand or fall on their own merits, but that I think it would be the nearest I have come to it. In my personal life, I am not aware of having come anywhere near to having to make a decision like that.

Dr Hilary Firestone

Are you aware of any legal rules which might have an adverse impact on you personally?

Yes, the rules of ritual slaughter of animals. It would create enormous problems for those of us who only eat kosher meat if laws were passed which prevented this.

Are you aware of any more local problems?

Oh, you mean the Eruv going around? The Eruv in Whitefield, in North Manchester is up. I live in South Manchester and there is talk of getting one up. It doesn't bother me if it is there or not. I am not going to see it, it's just a bit of wire. The thing about Jews is we are quite difficult people. Have you listened to Jackie Maso? We are caricatures of ourselves, so we can be difficult. I think that at the back of some people's minds is this ghetto feeling, but we already live in a ghetto.

Alison Steadman

Are there any particular laws which you would like to see changed?

I think that the whole situation with the way we manufacture plastic now, I can only see a future where there is something catastrophic and I really think that we have to start to say that we cannot allow our world to fill up with plastic the way it is. When I first started becoming aware of this, the plastic in the Pacific, because of the current it all bunches together and has made this island, it used to be the size of Wales, now it's the size of Germany.

Fr Iain Paton

Are there any legal rules which you find restrictive?

I would have been marrying same-sex couples for years.

Anne Duddington

Are there any legal rules which you currently find restrictive?

I can't think of any particular examples of laws which are restrictive of my freedom as a Roman Catholic. I can only think of the laws on education. If you cannot have your child in a Catholic school then you have to abide by a syllabus which I would regard as restrictive, but that has to do with education law.

The Most Reverend Dr Barry Morgan

Do you believe that you have a duty to speak out about injustices that affect third parties?

Absolutely. If the leader of a Church does not speak out on issues which cause grave injustice to others, he or she is abrogating their duty. Minorities expect you to do that. The Church should always stand up for the voiceless and marginalised. People quite frequently ask me to sign letters to ministers to get laws changed. I have done so over the issue of asylum seekers.

Bharti Tailor

Do you feel that you have a responsibility to speak for the vulnerable?

Absolutely . . . we need to speak on behalf of the vulnerable and the weakest. To put up with unfairness is an atrocity in itself, so we must speak against atrocities which effect the weak and the vulnerable first.....The world is one family.

The Rt Rev'd Christine Hardman

Do your beliefs require you to speak out for third parties, especially the weak and the vulnerable?

Yes. It's an absolute requirement. That is part of what I would see as being at the heart of what I am called to be and to do. A bishop has a tremendous opportunity to be heard, and I consciously try to use my voice on behalf of those whose voices are not heard.

Baroness Haleh Afshar

Do your beliefs require you to speak out against injustices, especially those affecting the vulnerable?

Yes! Absolutely, that is very much part of Shi'ism; it brings a strong commitment to justice as a central tenet of the faith. It is required of us to be just, to expect justice and to demand it, so I am duty bound to speak out against injustice and I would have no hesitation about doing that.

Baroness Elizabeth Butler-Sloss

Do you believe that you have a duty to speak out for third parties, especially the vulnerable?

[. . .] This is an area on which I speak of injustices in the rule of law, particularly in the provision of legal aid, where there are people who are denied access to justice.

Of course it is ironic that we are celebrating the success of Magna Carta at the same time that access to justice is being curtailed. It makes me mad that Britain, and its former Lord Chancellor, is going around the world advocating Magna Carta, when he has been responsible for a great deal of deprivation of access to justice.

Professor Dame Nancy Rothwell

Do your beliefs require you to speak out for the vulnerable?

I don't think religion has complete ownership of moral positions. I think most people, religious or not, have strong moral views.

I have spoken about persecution of scientists and of an organisation called CARO, which brings refugee scientists in, which I support, but I have kept it to science, rather than more widely.

Sam Dick

Do your beliefs require you to speak out on behalf of third parties, especially the vulnerable?

[. . .] Now that we have achieved legal equality, we've been able to talk about and deal with the many complexities within the LGB community. You need to secure peoples' basic fundamental rights first before you can adequately address their complex needs. When you are focused on trying secure basic human rights, you need to advocate clearly and succinctly. However, it is absolutely clear that you can be treated less equally not only because of your sexual orientation, but because of your economic status, religion, etc., and they are not separate issues. So, for example, a lesbian with a poor education and a difficult economic background has different experiences from somebody else. You can't address the sexual orientation discrimination aspect without looking at all other aspects: their gender, economic status, education and so on. So, now we have secured LGB peoples' basic rights we need to look at the whole range of social injustices LGB people experience more and more now.

Dr Adrian Crisp MD

Do your personal beliefs require you to speak out against injustices affecting third parties?

Yes, they do; and in medical practice the GMC in its code of principles enjoins us if we see bad practice to identify it and do something about it. That has been an improvement in my time in medicine. In the past it was important to keep your mouth shut and that was very wrong.

Professor Steven Jones

Do you think that it is important to speak for the vulnerable?

Yes, of course I do. One of the strongest and most powerful arguments you could make is to say that I am vulnerable because that makes you invulnerable. That is what religious minorities often do, saying that we are vulnerable, you are bullying us, disregarding the fact that they often bully other people far more.

Professor Linda Woodhead

Is the rule of law applied equally? Do some groups receive preferential or prejudicial treatment?

[. . .] It is clear that people who are convicted of crimes are not representative of the general population, of course, but there is such complexity about what is cause and what is effect that the answer is not straightforward. In the USA it seems they have a real problem in the way black people are treated by the police and by the law. I don't think we have anything on that scale any more. I would be more worried about things like Rotherham, the way in which young girls, working-class girls have been treated. There is something really worrying there. Sex abuse, children rights . . . why haven't they been protected? I would be more worried about that sort of area in this country, because we have a different history.

Jim Sutcliffe

Would you say that the rule of law is applied equally?

No. Again, possibly this might not be politically correct, but I don't trust a single policeman that walks this earth; and, yes, they're there the same as the rest of the justice system for the greater good and a lot of the time it probably works all right. But I think that there is a lot of bentness inside it, and some people get away with a lot of things which they shouldn't, whereas other people don't. But I think it probably goes back to the question about people in power: once you give out that power it gets abused anyway. It's human nature. But I don't think it's dealt out fairly by any stretch.

Sam Dick

Is the rule of law applied equally? Do some people experience either prejudicial or preferential treatment?

Yes, theoretically we are all equal before the law. In law do I think some people are treated preferentially? There is the argument particularly coming from some religious communities that LGBT people are preferred by the law than those people with religious faith. I disagree with that. Some believers would say that gay people have been afforded a right to do something and they have been denied their rights as a result. I don't think it is true. The law is quite clear. No matter who you are, you have the right to be respected and be treated equally.

Lucy Powell MP

Do you think that the rule of law is applied equally to everyone in British society? Do some groups experience preferential or prejudicial treatment from public bodies (e.g. schools, the criminal justice system)?

Yes, they do; not knowingly, but it happens. I think people of different backgrounds . . . often there are assumptions about people. For example, former criminals, you know . . . when they serve their time, people treat them very badly in terms of employment and future prospects, how they get treated even if they have become completely different people. Those convictions seem to follow them their whole lives. They would be discriminated against . . . Or for faith reasons, I think there is still a lot of antisemitism or islamophobia . . . it is hard to accept it, but those situations happen in society more generally.

Eamonn O'Brien

Do you think that the rule of law is applied equally to all citizens in Great Britain?

In theory it largely does, but in practice there are lots of examples where people aren't treated equally; stop and search powers are interesting. Who gets stopped has changed; now it is perhaps Muslim people who get searched, 40 years ago it was Irish people. My dad used to be constantly stopped in airports.

Dominic Dyer

Do you think that the rule of law is applied equally?

[. . .] When it comes to animal welfare, that is a problem. With badger baiting it is illegal to put dogs down setts and kill them, people can go to prison for six months and face £5,000 fines for that, and we are involved in bringing people to court for that. But I don't see fox hunting any differently. Fox hunting is illegal under the law, but fox hunts go around the country every weekend killing foxes, but these might be MPs, members of the House of Lords, close to David Cameron, hence he would like to repeal the Hunting With Dogs Act, so that is a class issue.

Samantha Chandler

Do you think that the rule of law is applied equally to everybody in UK society? Do some groups experience preferential or prejudicial treatment from the police or the justice system? How do you think that Great Britain compares with other countries in this regard?

I've had some experience with a good friend of mine who was going through a particularly acrimonious divorce. She was married to a barrister, who obviously had a vastly superior knowledge of the law and useful contacts to assist him. She had very little money of her own and did not know how the system worked. As a result, she had a very difficult time and there seemed to be very little in the legal system to protect her interests.

The Rev'd Professor Thomas Watkin

Do you think that the rule of law is applied equally?

Difficult question, because I don't think we know the extent to which there are certain interest groups in British society promoting or protecting one another. That has become clear in relation to child abuse enquires, certain aspects of policing, Hillsborough. I think that in theory the rule of law applies, but in practice I am less sure.

Faisal Khan

Is the rule of law applied equally? How does it compare with other countries?

Unfortunately, at the moment the Asian community is regarded as terrorist . . . not always, but many times . . . by the police. When I go to the airport,

I always get questions such as 'Where am I going?', 'Who am I going with?', and it is just . . . not very nice, especially when you go to places like Spain or Paris. Even when I went to Canada . . . 'Why are you going to Canada?', 'Who are you going to see?'. . . It is not very nice. They don't ask anybody else. When I went to Amsterdam . . . they were checking passports and it was only me, a black guy and a Jewish guy who were stopped . . . and we were waiting there . . . It is not very nice . . .

People like politicians, on the contrary, receive preferential treatment. They get away with all this fraud, taxes, all these loopholes . . . They are not held accountable, but they hold you and me accountable . . . we get fined . . . They don't treat people the same and the rich are treated completely differently.

Michael Kennedy QC

Would you say that the rule of law is applied equally to everyone, or do some groups experience either prejudicial or preferential treatment?

Preferential treatment I have never given, but I don't know how other people would perceive it, or whether the sights of those perceiving are correctly zeroed in. It's all perceptions. Two reports from Lewes prison: one was that they were terrified of me and the other that I was Father Christmas. I don't believe either.

What about access to justice?

When I was with the CAB I tried to organise some of our volunteers to come down to court to help people, especially women who were victims of what is called domestic violence, to help them fill in forms and hold their hands. The volunteers were scared and felt that they couldn't undertake it. There are other examples: dyslexia – I nearly locked a builder up in a civil dispute for failing to bring his documents and get them in order. He explained that his accountant was on holiday. In the end I understood that he couldn't read the documents. If I hadn't been married to a teacher who knew about all these things I mightn't have sensed it. If you know that somebody has got a problem, an incapacity you deal with it, you take a practical step. A mother came in one early morning for an emergency application, a Spanish woman who didn't speak English. Her son was with her, aged about nine, and I asked him to help. I had him sworn as a juvenile interpreter; he was the best interpreter I have ever had, direct, nothing added. My clerk brought me some headed note paper and several court stamps and I gave him a document telling him he was the best interpreter. That was a practical solution.

Dr Myriam Hunter-Henin

Do you think that the rule of law is applied equally to everyone in British society? Or do you think some groups experience preferential or prejudicial treatment from public bodies (e.g. schools, the criminal justice system)?

[. . .] I am struck as well by social divides and there is a bit of perversion when religion becomes a way to surpass social divides. Faith schools are criticised as a safe haven for the middle class . . . the middle class who cannot afford to pay, and a very well-known saying is that you pay or your pray in England, and I think that is offensive for those who attend faith schools because they believe in the ethos of that school, and it is also unfair on faith schools. If there is a dilemma between paying and praying, we should look at resources, rather than attacking faith schools. I find that social divides are very sharp and where I live in the south-east, at secondary level, there is an enormous gap between the independent and the state sector.

Carole Emmerson

Do you believe that the rule of law is applied equally? Do some groups receive preferential or prejudicial treatment?

I don't think we are all on an equal footing before the law. There is definitely racism. For example, I imagine young black men are more likely to be stopped and searched if they look in the least suspicious, and I am sure they have a harder time. Not all police would do that. I think there will be some though. In more deprived areas I am sure they have a harder time with the police, and also I think there is a different approach to people who break the law depending on their social class. Sometimes when people are more articulate they can be treated better. The system can be unjust at times.

Rev John Chalmers QHC

Do you think that the rule of law is applied equally? Do some groups receive preferential or prejudicial treatment?

[. . .] there are migrant groups that are at the very bottom of the pile. The mix in a place like Govan Hill in Glasgow, densely populated, the most multi-ethnic part of Scotland, where I think that there are 3,000 Romany people living there (out of 5,000 in Scotland). Some of them living 15 to a room, exploited by all of the other ethnic groups; they are the ones who will work for £1.95 an hour at the car washes. They are the lowest of the low and not even on the ladder, and the protection of the law just doesn't belong to them. Some of the streets in these places are run by gang masters, not the police.

Naveed Choudhry

Do you think the rule of law applies equally to everyone in British society or are there some groups which experience either preferential or prejudicial treatment, in terms of the criminal justice system, schools, etc?

No, unfortunately not. Islamophobia exists. I feel there is a witch-hunt against Muslims in the media. It is easy to help people to form a negative opinion. It is easy to fuel that. It is easy to blame a group for all the problems in the world.

Baroness Ros Altmann

Do you think that the rule of law is applied equally to everyone in society?

If I am honest, and seeing what I have seen, I would say sadly not. There is an element of power that does play a role and favoured groups who get treated better and less favoured groups who get treated worse. I think, though, that is an extreme case, and that normally there are great attempts, especially in the courts, for justice to be done. But, then again, justice isn't an absolute either, and what one person thinks of as justice another disagrees. There have certainly sadly been examples where powerful vested interests have been treated better and have had better legal and financial outcomes than the person in the street.

Danny Batth

Do you think that the rule of law is applied equally? Do some groups experience prejudicial or preferential treatment?

I don't think some races will be picked up more easily than others . . . I think the police are really good in England.

On the whole the police do pretty well. At times they could act stronger in some circumstances, not being worried about what it might look like, how it would be portrayed by the media . . . I think the media, the TV, dictate quite a lot to the police what they should or shouldn't be doing.

I think the media is very negative in the UK. I am a positive person, so I don't like seeing the news much because it is all bad news, and they never show anything positive.

Generally speaking, citizens are on an equal footing in Britain.

Sir Gareth Edwards CBE

Would you say that the rule of law is applied equally and fairly?

We were brought up where the policeman in your village would know you: the threat that he would tell your parents was enough. If you really deserved it, a little nudge here and there did you a bit of good rather than taking you to court. Justice was dished out in a different way. The thought that your parents would find out about something naughty was more than enough. We seem to have lost that. You do something wrong, you are dragged before court, everyone wants to sue you. I am a little bit more dubious and less sure about whether justice is done.

Dr Hema Radhakrishnan

How do you feel about the general trend towards an increase in police powers and state surveillance?

[. . .] I think that they could be using those resources more efficiently and public money could be spent in better ways than showing everyone we are on alert.

That probably just makes the terrorists proud that they have made us do this, and that they are getting attention.

Lucy Skilbeck

How do you feel about the general trend towards an increase in police powers in recent years?

[. . .] If the police have a legitimate concern they should be able to investigate it, but the widespread surveillance culture and paranoia is really detrimental to social cohesion and mental health. If you spend the whole time thinking that the person next to you is plotting against you, it doesn't do much for society or for your own peace of mind.

Lillie Flynn

How do you feel about the increase in police powers over the last 15 years or so?

It is hard to say . . . of course, you don't want people to do terrible things. So, you want to stop them, but banging into someone's home, when he or she is innocent . . . Police coming to your house . . . Shooting an innocent man just because of his skin colour . . . We live in a world in which if you see the police you feel paranoid and not protected. That is not the way it should be, but I think most people feel that way nowadays even if you are the most innocent person in the world. If you see a policeman, you feel threatened, and that is so backwards . . . But then, sadly, there are so many extremists at the moment so, I think a balance must be reached.

Dr Tobias Lock

How do you feel about the general increase in police powers and state surveillance in this country over the past 15 years or so?

In this country people don't seem to have a big problem with data collection. The continental experience is different . . . in Germany, for example. You cannot see all these CCTV cameras . . . some people would love it, but it doesn't happen.

The Rev'd Dr Jason Bray

How do you feel about the extension of police powers over the past ten years or so?

I am exceedingly concerned. There's another series of Bills going through Parliament to give police even more powers. The Snoopers' Charter got thrown out, mainly because one of the government partners jumped up and down about it; otherwise anyone could have access to more or less any data. You do wonder whether Britain has become much more of a police state since Tony Blair came into power. So it's not just the Conservatives or the Coalition, it was actually Tony Blair's government that introduced so many additional legal measures which closed down a lot of loopholes and gave the police enormous powers, which they do abuse. They have always abused such powers as they've had, but now that they've got even more. When the police ask for more powers the response should be 'Why', rather than 'When do you want them?'

Fr Roddy Johnston

How do you feel about the general trend towards an increase in police powers?

I don't know what it is like in Wales or England, but in Scotland the police have been pulled up because of an overuse of stop and search. It was felt that the pendulum had swung too far in the direction of stopping anyone for the flimsiest of reasons, so that has now been brought back. The press have been very instrumental in bringing that to attention, so the police have declared that that is no longer their way of working. The stop and search practice has had some benefit, as there was very much a knife culture . . . everyone carried a knife and said that it was because everyone else carried a knife. The authorities wanted the police to act on this, but there has not been a withdrawal. There are now more stringent procedures around stop and search and the recording of it.

Sarah Miles

How do you feel about the general trend which we have seen in the last 15 years or so towards an increase in police powers and state surveillance? Has that been an inevitable evil in a changing world, or has it been an overreaction which is a threat to our society?

Personally, I think we are over-watched, to an extent that takes away our freedoms.

Nico McNenzie-Juetten

How do you feel about the way in which state powers have generally increased in the past 15 years or so?

There has been a huge focus on police powers ever since the 1970s in a 'law and order' frame of reference; people end up in the criminal justice system who really shouldn't be there. I think that in Scotland we are retreating from that gradually, and even some important figures in the police are beginning to see that it is essentially about social justice. I read this extraordinary statistic suggesting that only around 22% of police call outs in England relate to criminal behaviour, and I think that police are facing difficult issues in handling those other situations, involving safety, emergencies with children and mental health.

Rev David Robertson

Should the same rules which apply to private citizens, apply equally to public authorities, including the police? Should they be allowed to suspend certain rules under specific circumstances?

[. . .] A useful illustration is my daughter, when she was younger . . . she is now 17 . . . there was one way I could actually guarantee that she wouldn't get beaten up, raped or become pregnant, and that would be to lock her up in her room. You could say I was caring for her . . . actually I would destroy her . . . at the age of 12 or 13 I let her go to town, catch the bus . . . and to get her own independence. I think in a civilised culture you will have to allow freedoms which may be abused [. . .] A Conservative MP recently said that the anti-terrorist legislation could be used against evangelical Christians who oppose same-sex marriage. There we have reached the level of insane, but that is to me the logical way where we are going. I think we'll fight that tooth and nail.

For example, I don't agree with Islam, but I will defend the right of an Islamic preacher to preach in this country, provided that they don't break the law [. . .] Freedom is far too important to sacrifice freedom for people's safety. I would wonder what freedom would be for.

Jon Nott

How do you feel about the general increase in the powers of the police over the last 15 years or so?

[. . .] I mentioned earlier things like the Prevent legislation. Also, as an employer I now have obligations to police part of the immigration system, which I am not qualified to do, and that puts me in a position where I have to behave towards people in a way that I wouldn't choose to do, or risk breaking the law. I think that kind of privatisation of the criminal justice system – giving powers to employers, teachers and landlords – is incredibly problematic.

Thomas Nichols

How do you feel about the general increase in police powers and state surveillance? What institutions do you trust more?

[. . .] I trust the judiciary, less the politicians . . . and certainly at the very bottom, the police.

5 Parliamentary supremacy and the religious character of the Constitution and the wider legal framework

5.1 Introduction

Having examined the rule of law, we now move on to another key facet of the Constitution, namely the concept of parliamentary sovereignty. Unlike the rule of law, which is arguably an abstract idea applied by various organs and representatives of the state, parliamentary sovereignty is tied to a specific institution with a collective voice. Strikingly, the United Kingdom Parliament[1] itself makes the following declaration about this principle, via its explanatory website:

> Parliamentary sovereignty is a principle of the UK constitution. It makes Parliament the supreme legal authority in the UK, which can create or end any law. Generally, the courts cannot overrule its legislation and no Parliament can pass laws that future Parliaments cannot change. Parliamentary sovereignty is the most important part of the UK constitution.[2]

As we have already established in our discussion of the rule of law, the closing sentence is by no means uncontroversial. If parliamentary sovereignty really were the unquestioned king of the jungle in relation to constitutional principles, then Parliament would be entirely free to repeal any inconvenient legislation guaranteeing human rights and other safeguards, withdraw from international frameworks such as the Council of Europe, and rampage about gobbling up whatever rights and freedoms of citizens it desired.

Nevertheless, even though its asserted dominance over all other principles should be treated with caution, parliamentary sovereignty is undoubtedly one of the essential pillars of the UK Constitution. At one level, it can be seen as a manifestation of the idea that the destiny of the state should be determined by the collective will of the people, as expressed through the democratic process, and once again we are left with the question of whether the current balance of Church/state relations and the wider approach of the legal system towards religion enhance

1 Given that the focus of our constitutional discussion is Great Britain, rather than national level, our consideration of parliamentary sovereignty relates to the United Kingdom Parliament, and we do not deal with how variant understandings of the concept might function in the context of devolved administrations.

2 UK Parliament, 'Parliamentary Sovereignty', http://www.parliament.uk/about/how/sovereignty.

the functioning of this principle. The following discussion is structured along the same lines as the previous chapter. First, we consider in detail what the label of parliamentary sovereignty truly encapsulates before going on to assess whether the current legal arrangements in respect of religion are conducive towards advancing this ideal. This will be followed by a consideration, similar to that undertaken in respect of the rule of law, about the doctrines of faith groups considered and the manner in which they might influence thought in relation to this constitutional foundation. We close the chapter with some discussion of the contribution of religious bodies, in practical terms, to the principle of parliamentary supremacy.

5.2 What does parliamentary supremacy mean within the context of the UK Constitution?

5.2.1 Academic theories related to the Diceyan understanding of parliamentary supremacy

The Oxford jurist A.V. Dicey[3] occupies a place in the pantheon of British constitutional theorists, which is arguably akin to that of Sir Isaac Newton in physics. While later commentators have sought to analyse his contribution critically on the basis of subsequent developments as well as doubts about its original correctness, his work nevertheless remains the point of departure for most constitutional investigation. It is also helpful to recall that just because, for example, we no longer generally favour a corpuscular picture of light,[4] it does not mean that the theories of Newton have disappeared from physics textbooks. It may be the case that some of Dicey's ideas fit more easily than others within a twenty-first century paradigm, but accepting or dismissing a commentator wholesale is generally not a productive approach to academic discourse. Therefore, 'What can we take from Dicey?' is probably a more helpful question than 'Was Dicey right or wrong'? He famously formulated an understanding of parliamentary sovereignty with two core components:

1 Parliament has the right to make or unmake any law that it chooses.
2 No person or body has the right to set aside legislation passed by Parliament.[5]

The crispness and clarity of these assertions lend them a certain elegance, but not an impenetrability. Even before the current debates relating to the European Union or the Human Rights Act emerged, commentators took issue with the Diceyan line. As Tomkins[6] noted, Sir Ivor Jennings, a leading constitutionalist of the 1930s,

3 Lord Plant of Highfield, 'Foreward', in P. Raina (ed.), *A.V. Dicey: General Characteristics of English Constitutionalism – Six Unpublished Lectures* (Peter Lang: Oxford and New York) 2009, 9.

4 Nuffield Foundation, Practical Physics, 'Light: Wave or Particles?', http://practicalphysics.org/light-%e2%80%93-waves-or-particles.html.

5 A.V. Dicey, *An Introduction to the Study of the Law of the Constitution* (ed. E.C.S.Wade, Macmillan: London) 10th edn, 1959, 40.

6 A. Tomkins, 'Talking in Fictions: Jennings on Parliament', The *Modern Law Review*, Vol. 67, No. 5 (Sept 2004) 772–86, 776.

successfully burst the bubble of an all-powerful Parliament in terms of political reality. He saw the role of Parliament as being to question and debate government policy, and asserted that in a pragmatic sense real power lay with the executive. Furthermore, Jennings argued that neither Parliament nor the Government could act in a way which outrages public opinion. In other words, even though the UK democratic model is one of representative democracy, the elected representatives cannot ignore the collective consensus of those outside Parliament. For Jennings, the ultimate reality is *vox populi vox dei*, and both Parliament and the executive must remain conscious of this.

Jennings also challenged Dicey's conception of Parliament as a body which should be thought of in purely, or even primarily, legislative terms, this being an idea which has been embraced by some more contemporary commentators, including Tomkins.[7] Indeed, Jennings saw the capacity of Parliament as a body to create law being constrained and controlled by the political reality of the House of Commons, in which a majority government had effective control. However, Jennings could conceive of no circumstance in which a government in the United Kingdom could harness the legislative power of Parliament to enable some morally heinous policy, such as the 'killing of all blue-eyed babies',[8] but again he saw this not as a product of 'any legal limitations in the power of Parliament, but to the fact that both Parliament and the House of Commons derive their authority from the people'.

It is chilling to read this with the benefit of historical hindsight and an awareness which Jennings could not then have possessed about the full horrors of Nazi Germany. Authors like Rawlings highlight the difficulty of having Parliament restrained only by the 'sweet reason' of MPs and the constituents.[9] It is a tragic irony that he wrote these words in an era when babies, and indeed others, in western Europe were being killed and persecuted on grounds every bit as arbitrary as eye colour. There is perhaps scope for debate about the full extent of popular knowledge of the Final Solution, but events like *Kristallnacht* did not happen in secret, and should serve as a permanent reminder that public opinion will not always protect the innocent and the vulnerable.

This is a key consideration, because both the European Union and the human rights movement developed in response to the atrocities of the mid-twentieth century and the Second World War. Dicey formulated his constitutional theory, and indeed Jennings fashioned his critique of the same, at a time when it must have seemed highly theoretical to imagine in a British paradigm the hijacking of legislative and governmental authority for what we would now term 'crimes against humanity'. Western Europe cannot and should not regain that naivety.

This must be borne in mind in addressing the present debate, and as to whether Diceyan constitutional orthodoxy has survived developments relating to the

7 A. Tomkins, 'What is Parliament For?', in N. Bamforth and P. Leyland (eds), *Public Law in a Multi-Layered Constitution* (Hart: Oxford) 2003, Ch. 3.

8 I. Jennings, *Parliament* (Cambridge University Press: Cambridge) 1939, 9. Also cited ibid., 776.

9 R. Rawlings, 'Introduction: Sovereignty in Question', in R. Rawlings, P. Leyland and A. Young (eds), *Sovereignty and the Law: Domestic, European and International Perspectives* (Oxford University Press: Oxford) 2013, 1.

European Union and the Human Rights Act. We do not deal with devolution as a potential challenge to parliamentary supremacy, because the complications in this regard are more concerned with the political than the legal arena. See further our discussion below in relation to the Supreme Court and the Miller case, and the robustness with which the sovereignty of Westminster was affirmed in this context.

5.2.2 *The challenges to parliamentary supremacy: EU membership, the Human Rights Act and unintended constraints (Jackson)*

5.2.2.1 *EU membership: questions concerning Britain's planned exit from the EU and issues relating to our obligations for as long as we remain*

It should also be acknowledged that the formulation of legal theories does not take place in a sterile intellectual environment, and that academic commentators are inevitably heavily influenced by the political backdrop within which they are working. At the time of writing, the United Kingdom is in the midst of a maelstrom of uncertainty over the constitutional ramifications of the referendum on EU membership, held on 23 June 2016.

Going back a step in order to understand this, the potential for a collision between Diceyan parliamentary sovereignty and the European Community legal framework was present since the passage of the European Communities Act 1972, in light of the following provision:

> All such rights, powers, liabilities, obligations and restrictions from time to time created or arising by or under the Treaties, . . . as in accordance with the Treaties are without further enactment to be given legal effect or used in the United Kingdom shall be recognised and available in law, and be enforced, allowed and followed.[10]

However, a crunch point did not come until many years later, in the early 1990s, with the notorious *Factortame*[11] litigation. The series of cases originated in a game of cat-and-mouse over fishing quotas, in which the UK Government passed legislation requiring that UK fishing vessels be 75% UK-owned.[12] This was obviously very inconvenient for a group of enterprising Spanish fishing companies, which had been buying UK-registered vessels in order to have their catch included within the UK quota (a practice known as 'quota hopping' and much disapproved of by the British authorities). The European Court of Justice ruled that the statute in question was incompatible with European Community law, and

10 European Communities Act 1972, s. 2.

11 Factortame v Secretary of State for Transport (No. 1) [1989] 2 WLR 997 (HL); *R v Secretary of State for Transport, ex parte Factortame (No. 2)* [1990] ECR I-2433; *Brasserie du Pêcheur SA Bundesrepublik Deutschland, R v Secretary of State for Transport, ex parte Factortame and Others (No. 3), Joined cases* C-46/93, 48/93 [1996] ECR I-01029, ECLI:EU:C:1996:79; *R v Secretary of State for Transport, ex parte Factortame (No. 4),* Case C-48/93 [1996] All ER (EC) 301; and *R v Secretary of State for Transport, ex parte Factortame (No. 5)* [1999] 4 All ER 906).

12 Merchant Shipping Act 1988.

that domestic tribunals should not apply such legislation. In referring the case, the House of Lords accepted the supremacy of Community law over national law in the areas where the United Kingdom had accepted this law in acceding to international treaties. This was in sharp contrast to the ordinary doctrine of 'implied repeal', which – as Ahmed and Perry observe – generally compels courts to construe later statutes to have impliedly repealed any parts of earlier legislation in conflict with their provisions.[13]

Academic responses in the aftermath of these judicial pronouncements could essentially be divided into two camps. First, there were those who argued that the fishing battle had confirmed that parliamentary sovereignty had undergone a sea-change, in the full Shakespearian sense. As the mysterious Ariel sprite sang into the tempest:

> But doth suffer a sea-change,
> into something rich and strange,
> Sea-nymphs hourly ring his knell,
> Ding-dong.[14]

For commentators in this camp, the impact of the 1972 Act and these judicial decisions meant that parliamentary sovereignty was either dead or radically transformed. A leading proponent of this position was Wade[15] who, despite being an orthodox Diceyan scholar, argued that the most credible understanding of the speech given by Lord Bridge in the House of Lords in *Factortame* was that the relevant legislation relating to merchant shipping[16] was disapplied precisely because the Parliament of 1972 had succeeded in binding its successors: 'It is for the judges, and not for Parliament, to say what is an effective Act of Parliament. If the judges recognise that there must be a change, as by allowing future Parliaments to be fettered, this is a technical revolution'.[17]

However, there were equally distinguished voices within the world of constitutional law putting forward alternative analyses. Craig preferred what he described as a 'construction view',[18] and Sir John Laws,[19] writing extra-judicially,

13 F. Ahmed and A. Perry, 'The Quasi-Entrenchment of Constitutional Statutes', *Cambridge Law Journal*, Vol. 73, No. 3 (2014), 514–35.

14 W. Shakespeare, *The Tempest*, Act I, Scene II, 'Ariel's Song'.

15 H.W.R. Wade, 'Sovereignty: Evolution or Revolution', *Law Quarterly Review*, Vol. 112 (1996) 568–75.

16 Merchant Shipping Act 1988.

17 Wade, n. 15 above, 574.

18 P. Craig, 'Sovereignty of the United Kingdom Parliament after Factortame', *Yearbook of European Law*, Vol. 11, No. 1 (1991) 221–55: '. . . a rule of interpretation to the effect that Parliament is presumed not to intend statutes to override EEC law. On this view inconsistencies between United Kingdom statutes and EEC law would be resolved in favour of the latter unless "Parliament clearly and expressly states in a future Act that it is to override Community law" . . . The longer that we remain in the EEC the more likely it is that the courts will adopt this rule of construction which serves to preserve the formal veneer of Diceyan orthodoxy while undermining its substance'.

19 J. Laws, 'Law and Democracy', *Public Law* (1995) 72–104, 89: 'Although Factortame and EOC undoubtedly demonstrate what may be described as a devolution of legislative power to Europe, it

also saw the outcome of the *Factortame* litigation as a development which could and should be incorporated within the Diceyan constitutional framework. In other words, the organs of (what was then) the European Economic Community (EEC) were exercising functions at the behest of the UK Parliament. Given that Parliament was free (at least in legal terms) to withdraw from this arrangement at any time, it remained sovereign. It had delegated power, but retained the ability to take it back on demand.

Allan viewed the situation from a different angle again, drawing a distinction between national and parliamentary sovereignty, and arguing that there was a pressing need to understand how the developments could be related to the pre-existing legal framework from which they must necessarily have arisen.[20] In our view, Allan's insight in this respect is a useful one. All constitutional developments which are compatible with the rule of law – in the sense that they are the result of legally mandated processes, rather than violence, civil disobedience or other direct action – *must* necessarily make sense in terms of the preceding constitutional arrangements from which they emerged.

There is an interesting analogy with the current Spanish context, and the recent attempts by the Catalan regional authorities to orchestrate referenda in defiance of the national Constitution and courts. As García Oliva[21] has argued, this is a perilous and illogical direction of travel, because the Catalan authorities are driving a coach and horses through the very Constitution, which is the basis of the democratic mandate for the proper exercise of their powers.

It is not being suggested by any of the academic legal commentators that the 1972 legislation was a similar act of conscious constitutional vandalism. Laws[22] and Craig[23] are also correct in asserting that the understanding of the House of Lords in *Factortame* was clearly that the judges were seeking to interpret the legislation passed by Parliament in 1972. They were attempting to apply the will of a sovereign Parliament expressed through legislation, and not to instigate any judicial innovation.

Boiling an extremely complex debate down to a simple level – as it is not the scope of this chapter to discuss in detail the complexities of the doctrine of parliamentary supremacy – an interpretation based on Laws'[24] understanding is logically

is no true devolution of sovereignty. In legal (though certainly not political) terms, the organs of European legislation may in truth be described, for so long as the Act of 1972 remains on the statute book, as Parliament's delegates; the law of Europe is not a higher-order law, because the limits which for the time being it sets to the power of Parliament are at the grace of Parliament itself'.

20 T. Allan, 'Parliamentary Sovereignty: Law, Politics, and Revolution', Law Quarterly Review, Vol. 113, No. 2 (1997) 443–52.

21 J. García Oliva, 'Catalonia in Spain? The Future Ahead', *UK Constitutional Law Association* (10 Nov 2014), https://ukconstitutionallaw.org/2014/11/10/javier-garcia-oliva-catalonia-in-spain-the-future-ahead; and J. García Oliva, 'Catalonia in Spain: The Significance of the 25th September 2015 Elections', *UK Constitutional Law Association* (25 Jul 2015), https://ukconstitutionallaw.org/2015/07/24/javier-garcia-oliva-catalonia-in-spain-the-significance-of-the-25th-september-2015-elections.

22 Laws, n. 19 above, 89.

23 Craig, n. 18 above, 221.

24 Laws, n. 19 above, 89.

defensible. In other words, a sovereign Parliament in 1972 effectively delegated some of its authority to organs of the then European Economic Community, and this delegation is to subsist until such time as Parliament chooses to revoke it. It is also currently more important than ever not to lose sight of Allan's[25] instructive distinction between national and parliamentary sovereignty.

In terms of purely abstract theory, following traditional, Diceyan principles, the UK Parliament would simply have to pass an Act in order to depart from the European Union. However, our current reality is far more complex. In the real political world, the United Kingdom is now faced with a period of domestic and international horse-trading, while the state negotiates the process of extricating itself from the European Union and what this will mean for all parties. We should pause to acknowledge that at the time of writing there are still internal voices arguing that the exit process can, and must, be halted. However, in our view, the repercussions of the referendum are in themselves an unexpected illustration of Jennings' thesis in action. As early as 9 July 2016,[26] Phillip Kolvin QC and 1,053 other lawyers sent an open letter to the Prime Minister arguing that the referendum was advisory only and that the Article 50[27] mechanism could be triggered only by primary legislation which Parliament should not pass.

This was followed by the *Miller* case,[28] which saw a challenge to the governmental position that the making and unmaking of international agreements was a matter within the remit of the ministerial prerogative,[29] and that no Act of Parliament was needed.[30] The majority of the Supreme Court robustly affirmed the sovereignty of Parliament in relation to the exercise of prerogative powers. Lord Neuberger gave the leading judgment (with which Lady Hale and Lords Mance, Kerr, Clarke, Wilson, Sumption and Hodge concurred) and asserted that, specific exceptions aside,[31] ministers may not exercise the prerogative in ways that alter the law or legal rights of citizens.

Ordinarily, ministers would be acting on prerogatives when entering into, changing or withdrawing from international treaties and agreements. In most circumstances, this does not conflict with the rule against using it to alter the law, because the United Kingdom is a dualist state. In other words, international treaties

25 Allan, n. 20 above, 443.

26 'In Full: The Letter from 1,000 Lawyers to David Cameron over EU Referendum', *The Independent* (10 Jul 2016), http://www.independent.co.uk/news/uk/politics/in-full-the-letter-from-1000-lawyers-to-david-cameron-over-eu-referendum-brexit-legality-a7130226.html (Kolvin letter).

27 The provision which deals with a Member State that wishes to withdraw from the European Union: Art. 50, Lisbon Treaty, http://www.lisbon-treaty.org/wcm/the-lisbon-treaty/treaty-on-European-union-and-comments/title-6-final-provisions/137-article-50.html.

28 *R (on the application of Miller and Another) v Secretary of State for Exiting the European Union* [2017] UKSC 5 (*Miller*).

29 The residual power of the executive to act on behalf of the Crown: see further R. Brazier, *Ministers of the Crown* (Clarendon Press: Oxford) 1997, Ch. 12.

30 See further the blog post by J. García Oliva, 'Expert Comment: The Supreme Court's Decision – Article 50 and Parliament', *The University of Manchester* (24 Jan 2017), http://www.manchester.ac.uk/discover/news/article-50-parliament.

31 *Miller*, n. 28 above, per Lord Neuberger, paras 52–53.

have no legal consequences at the domestic level unless and until Parliament passes legislation to bring them within British law. However, departing from the European Union would mean that EU law would no longer be part of domestic law and, in the view of the Supreme Court, this would conflict with the principle against using the prerogative to make internal legal changes. Therefore, primary legislation must be enacted to achieve this change.

It was argued for the Government that the referendum on EU membership had been authorised by an Act of Parliament in 2015, and that this rendered further legislation unnecessary. Nevertheless, the majority of the court were not convinced, and found that the effect of any particular referendum would depend upon the statute which instigated it.[32] For instance, some statutes, such as the Scotland Act 1978 and the Parliamentary Voting System and Constituencies Act 2011, had provided for very specific consequences.

However, the majority of the Supreme Court noted the contrast between these enactments and the legislation relating to the two referenda on membership of the EU (and its predecessor European Economic Community) in 2015 and 1975 respectively, and, as a result, in the absence of clear advance provision, the judges considered that an Act of Parliament would be required to give effect to a referendum in a way that alters domestic law.

Although the dissenting judges interpreted the situation differently, while essentially agreeing on the two key principles to be applied (namely that ministers are entitled, and are frequently required, to use prerogative powers to make international agreements, and that prerogative powers may not generally be used to alter the law), it is interesting to note for our purposes that, in the opinion of the whole Court, both the right and the freedom to make and repeal laws ultimately rests with Parliament. In the understanding of Lords Reed, Carnwarth and Hughes, the European Communities Act 1972 simply provided that such law would apply while the relevant treaties were enforced in the United Kingdom. The 1972 Act came into force on 17 October of that year, but had no practical legal consequences until the Treaty of Accession was ratified and came into force. Thus, in the view of the dissenting judges, any legal rights were contingent on the treaties according to the conventional rules of statutory interpretation.

It is also important to appreciate that both the majority and dissenting judges dismissed all arguments put forward in *Miller* that the approval of the devolved assemblies in Scotland, Wales or Northern Ireland was needed in order to invoke Article 50. The ruling made it clear that constitutional power to leave the European Union lies exclusively with the UK Parliament. The logical corollary of this, of course, is that Parliament has also retained its freedom to remain.

At the purely legal level this is a convincing argument. There is no real basis in constitutional law or theory for asserting that provision for a referendum amounts to the UK Parliament irrevocably ceding its discretion on the matter in question.

32 Ibid., para 118.

However, in political terms, rejecting the result of the referendum would be extremely damaging to the credibility of both the Government and Parliament, and it would be difficult to claim a democratic mandate while ignoring the expressed will of the majority of those who participated in the referendum.

Kolvin effectively acknowledged this issue, arguing in his letter[33] that many of the citizens had voted to leave the EU because they had been acting upon misinformation. In other words, had people known the truth, they would have voted differently, and in consequence the result does not in reality reflect their collective will. As a result, even those who advocate that Parliament should refuse to abide by the outcome of the referendum accept that, in political terms, this would require robust and convincing justification.

Therefore, Parliament is sovereign in a legal sense, but in pragmatic political terms it cannot afford to disregard the consensus of opinion in the nation as a whole, and this is effectively the same reality that Jennings observed almost a century ago. Despite voices of protest like Kolvin, at present the United Kingdom has triggered Article 50 and looks set to leave the European Union, a situation that reveals the continuing reality of parliamentary sovereignty, but also its practical limitations. The UK Parliament clearly *is* free to remove or retain the constraints which it has placed upon itself, but only insofar as this is compatible with the demands of *realpolitik*. However, it is also the case that, at the time of writing, the United Kingdom is still a Member State of the European Union, and will continue to be so until 'Brexit' transitions from a stated intention to an accomplished reality. For the time being, it is subject to the benefits and burdens that member status confers, so it remains appropriate to consider the nature and extent of the self-imposed restraints on Parliament which are part of this.

The European Union Act 2011, and in particular the 'sovereignty clause', was passed with the express intention of explaining the meaning and scope of Parliament's self-imposed restraint:

> Directly applicable or directly effective EU law (that is, the rights, powers, liabilities, obligations, restrictions, remedies and procedures referred to in section 2(1) of the European Communities Act 1972) falls to be recognised and available in law in the United Kingdom *only* by virtue of that Act or where it is required to be recognised and available in law *by virtue of any other Act*'.[34]

In other words, the statute reiterates the principle that European institutions exercise decision-making and legislative power in a UK context because, and to the extent that, Westminster has given authority for this to happen. Many of the factors which led to the passage of the Act are discussed in the Tenth Report of

33 Kolvin letter, n. 26 above.

34 European Union Act 2011, s. 18 (emphasis added).

the European Scrutiny Committee;[35] one crucial issue was the *Thoburn* case,[36] otherwise known as the 'Metric Martyrs case'. As a result, we feel it would be helpful to explain the background concerning this landmark decision.

The interface between national and European law had been tested against the backdrop of whether greengrocers and other owners of small businesses should be legally obliged to operate primarily in metric measurements. At no point was it ever suggested that there would have been a problem in telling a customer who asked how much a pound of strawberries would cost. Nevertheless, in the eyes of the litigants involved, it was a battle about democracy, freedom and identity, rather than a dispute about managing pumpkins and bananas.[37]

The impact of the *Thoburn* judgment was helpfully summarised by Professor Bradley[38] in evidence to the European Scrutiny Committee. In essence, Bradley's contribution is an acknowledgement that the powers vested in EU institutions subsist by virtue of decisions made by organs of the state in the United Kingdom, in accordance with the requirements of its own legal system and Constitution. Laws LJ, in the *Thoburn* case, had confirmed, although *obiter dicta*, that the European Communities Act 1972 was a constitutional statute and was therefore not subject to implied repeal.

In consequence, as far as the European Union is concerned, the UK Parliament remains sovereign, but has delegated some of its authority until such time as it should expressly decide to take it back. Following the referendum, it appears that this time is now upon us.

5.2.2.2 The Human Rights Act 1998

What is the position with regard to other legislative developments and constitutional statutes, such as the Human Rights Act 1998? What implications do

35 European Scrutiny Committee, Tenth Report, 'The EU Bill and Parliamentary Sovereignty' (6 Dec 2010), http://www.publications.parliament.uk/pa/cm201011/cmselect/cmeuleg/633/63302.htm.

36 *Thoburn v Sunderland City Council* [2002] EWHC 195 (Admin).

37 '"Metric Martyrs" Loose Court Battle', *BBC News* (18 Feb 2002), http://news.bbc.co.uk/1/hi/england/1826503.stm.

38 European Scrutiny Committee, Tenth Report, n. 35 above, para. 20:

> (1) All the specific rights which EU law creates are by the 1972 Act incorporated into our domestic law and rank supreme: that is, anything in our substantive law inconsistent with any of these rights and obligations is abrogated or must be modified to avoid the inconsistency. This is true even where the inconsistent municipal provision is contained in primary legislation.
> (2) The 1972 Act is a constitutional statute: that is, it cannot be impliedly repealed.
> (3) The truth of (2) is derived, not from EU law, but purely from the law of England: the common law recognises a category of constitutional statutes.
> (4) The fundamental legal basis of the UK's relationship with the EU rests with the domestic, not the European, legal powers. In the event, which no doubt would never happen in the real world, that a European measure was seen to be repugnant to a fundamental or constitutional right guaranteed by the law of England, a question would arise whether the general words of the 1972 Act were sufficient to incorporate the measure and give it overriding effect in domestic law. But that is very far from this case.

they have for the Diceyan understanding of parliamentary sovereignty? The Human Rights Act 1998 brought most provisions of the European Convention on Human Rights into the domestic legal framework of the United Kingdom, but the way in which this operates is not always accurately understood. Certain sections of the popular press in Britain gleefully present the domestic and international human rights framework as undermining, or perhaps even usurping, the democratic will of the nation expressed through Parliament. For example, in 2013, *The Daily Mail* reported that 'Judge Spielmann told BBC Radio Four that all decisions reached by his court must be respected – including prisoner votes. This is despite the fact that the democratically elected Westminster parliament has voted overwhelmingly to keep the ban in place'.[39]

Nevertheless, the reality of the interplay between the various bodies involved is far more complex and nuanced than this colourful journalism might suggest. As Lady Hale observed in the *Jackson* case (discussed further below), Parliament has limited its own powers by virtue of the European Communities Act and the Human Rights Act, but in extremely different ways.[40] The nature and form of the constraints imposed by the Human Rights Act 1998 are not at all the same as those concerning the European Union.

The Human Rights Act requires that, in so far as possible, primary and secondary legislation must be read in a way that is compatible with Convention rights.[41] The courts have acknowledged that this legislation can allow for considerable judicial wiggle-room and that the wording of provisions can certainly be stretched in interpretation. In the course of a careful assessment of section 3, Lord Steyn stressed that there was a strong rebuttable presumption in favour of finding an interpretation of a statute which was compliant with the Human Rights Act, and that a section 4 declaration of incompatibility should only be a last resort mechanism.[42]

However, although drafting may be treated as being flexible, it is not infinitely plastic. Judges are required to stop before it reaches snapping point and they are, as a result, effectively amending or creating, rather than interpreting, legislative provisions.[43] If a compatible reading would be to go against the fundamental thrust of the statute, section 3 may not be called upon and a section 4 declaration is the only possible response.

A section 4 declaration of incompatibility does basically what it says on the tin, and it should be stressed that it does not translate to 'striking down' a statute. In fact, section 4(6) explicitly states that a declaration will not affect the validity, operation or enforcement of the law. Non-compliant legislation remains alive and

39 J. Slack and S. Doughty, 'Britain Must Obey Strasbourg Judges or Quit the EU, Warns New Chief of the European Court of Human Rights', *The Daily Mail* (5 Jun 2013), http://www.dailymail.co.uk/news/article-2336021/Britain-obey-Strasbourg-judges-quit-EU-warns-new-chief-European-Court-Human-Rights.html#ixzz3eMMneYaD.

40 *Jackson v Attorney General* [2005] UKHL 56; [2006] 1 AC 262, para. 159.

41 Human Rights Act 1998, s. 3.

42 *Ghaidan (Appellant) v Godin-Mendoza (FC) (Respondent)* [2004] UKHL 30, per Lord Steyn, para. 50.

43 *Re S (Minors) (Care Order: Implementation of Care Plan)* [2002] UKHL 10.

kicking on the statute book, and it is for Parliament to decide whether to amend it. In this respect, the legislature has given the judiciary a monitoring, rather than a supervisory, role and has thus retained its sovereignty.

Similarly, in terms of parliamentary procedure, the legislature is monitored, rather than controlled, by the provisions flowing from the Act. Before the second reading of a bill, a statement must be laid in both Houses of Parliament by the minister in charge, declaring that in the minister's view, the bill is either compatible with Convention rights or it is incompatible, but that the Government nevertheless wishes to proceed with it.[44] There is also a Joint Parliamentary Committee on Human Rights, tasked with scrutinising draft legislation in this regard. These arrangements require both politicians and civil servants to at least think about human rights during the planning and drafting of legislation, as well as encouraging both vigilance and debate in Parliament. They do not, however, actually prevent an Act of Parliament being intentionally passed, even though it is not thought to be Human Rights Act-compliant by either the legislature or the executive.

It should also be noted that section 6 of the Human Rights Act (which provides that it is unlawful for public authorities to act in contravention of the statute) contains a specific exemption to cover a situation in which the authority was required by primary legislation to so act.[45] Once again, the use of Parliament's legislative power is not ultimately curtailed.

As Klug and Wildbore argue,[46] an amendment requiring the UK courts to treat Strasbourg case law as binding was expressly rejected in parliamentary debates leading to the passage of the Human Rights Act, and the statute was deliberately crafted in order to preserve the constitutional principle of parliamentary sovereignty. This is an important consideration when addressing some of the arguments which have been put forward by academic commentators on the nature and continuing existence of absolute parliamentary sovereignty.

Tucker[47] mounts a scholarly attack on the doctrine, but the heavy guns in his artillery are supplied by jurisprudence, rather than legal doctrine. Like many commentators before him, Tucker employs the work of Hart to support his case, but in contrast to Wade[48] and others he relies on Hart to dismantle, rather than prop up, parliamentary sovereignty. Tucker's core argument is that Hart[49] is correct in

44 Human Rights Act 1998, s. 19.

45 Ibid., s. 6(2).

46 F. Klug and H. Wildbore, letter published in *The Times* on the Human Rights Act, the relationship between domestic courts and the European Court of Human Rights and parliamentary sovereignty (24 Oct 2011), available via London School of Economics: Human Rights: http://www.lse.ac.uk/humanRights/documents/2011/KlugTimes24Oct.pdf, and http://www.lse.ac.uk/humanRights/whosWho/helenWildbore.aspx.

47 A. Tucker, 'Uncertainty in the Rule of Recognition and the Doctrine of Parliamentary Sovereignty', *Oxford Journal of Legal Studies*, Vol. 31, No. 1 (2011) 61–88.

48 H.W.R. Wade, 'The Basis of Legal Sovereignty', *Cambridge Law Journal*, Vol. 13, No. 2 (1955) 172–97.

49 H. Hart, *The Concept of Law* (Oxford University Press: Oxford) 1994.

claiming that legal validity ultimately depends upon 'the requirements of a social rule, the ultimate rule of recognition, which binds the officials of a legal system to enforce rules which conform to certain criteria'.[50]

On this basis, Tucker goes on to reason:

> The orthodox Diceyan position, that there are no limits on the law making power of Parliament, is wrong. Our rule of recognition is an indeterminate rule of recognition and this means that we simply cannot say there are no limits on parliamentary power. Rather, the imposition (or not) of such limits will depend on the judiciary's understanding of the point of allocating law-making power to Parliament and their stance on whether this point requires that power to be limited or not.[51]

In other words, social rules are indeterminate; the rule of recognition is therefore indeterminate, and it cannot be said, as a result, that there are no limits to parliamentary power. However, Tucker then immediately goes on to acknowledge that in real terms the constraints or lack of constraints to which parliamentary power is subject will be determined by judicial understanding. Consequently, while the understanding of the judiciary embraces classical parliamentary sovereignty, the doctrine will survive.

Irrespective of whether or not the rule of recognition is determinate in abstract philosophical terms, if people within the group or society where a social rule operates see or understand it as determinate, then it will function as determinate unless or until that understanding changes. Outside the realms of thought experiment, for as long as those charged with interpreting the Constitution believe in parliamentary sovereignty, it will be a constitutional reality.

5.2.2.3 Unintended constraints on Parliament: the Jackson litigation

It is also true that the operation of parliamentary sovereignty has faced challenges in the twenty-first century from quarters other than European Communities and the Human Rights Acts. Interestingly, as explained below, it was discussed *obiter dicta* whether Parliament's powers could face judicial rejection under extreme circumstances. In *Jackson v Attorney General*[52] the courts were asked to consider the validity of the Hunting Act 2004, and the argument mounted was that the Parliament Act 1911 could not be used to pass the Parliament Act 1949, as it effected constitutional change. Therefore, the 1949 Act and any legislation relying on its procedures were invalid.

A key preliminary issue was whether the courts even had jurisdiction in this matter, as in *Pickin v British Railways Board*[53] it was made clear that

50 Tucker, n. 47 above, 62.

51 Ibid., 87.

52 *Jackson v Attorney General*, n. 40 above.

53 *Pickin v British Railways Board* [1974] AC 765.

it was not open for a judge to examine the procedure by which legislation was enacted.

Despite this, the House of Lords concluded, in this particular instance, that it was able to hear the case as the question was essentially one of statutory interpretation. It was, indeed, effectively being asked to determine the scope of the 1911 Act, rather than go delving into the murky world of parliamentary procedure, and statutory interpretation is part of the bread and butter of judicial work. The substantial decision was that there were limitations in the 1911 Parliament Act which were material to the validity of the 1949 Parliament Act, but of greater interest for present purposes are the *obiter* remarks which the Law Lords made about parliamentary supremacy. Some of them gingerly poked at the extremely hypothetical scenario of parliamentary sovereignty being limited by the courts. Lord Steyn ventured:

> The classic account given by Dicey of the doctrine of the supremacy of Parliament, pure and absolute as it was, can now be seen to be out of place in the modern United Kingdom. Nevertheless, the supremacy of Parliament is still the general principle of our constitution. It is a construct of the common law. The judges created this principle. If that is so, it is not unthinkable that circumstances could arise where the courts may have to qualify a principle established on a different hypothesis of constitutionalism. In exceptional circumstances involving an attempt to abolish judicial review or the ordinary role of the courts, the Appellate Committee of the House of Lords or a new Supreme Court may have to consider whether this is a constitutional fundamental which even a sovereign Parliament acting at the behest of a complaisant House of Commons cannot abolish.[54]

Lord Hope adopted a rather more definite stance:

> But Parliamentary sovereignty is no longer, if it ever was, absolute.[55] [. . .] The rule of law enforced by the courts is the ultimate controlling factor on which our constitution is based. The fact that your Lordships have been willing to hear this appeal and to give judgment upon it is another indication that the courts have a part to play in defining the limits of Parliament's legislative sovereignty.[56]

Jowell has suggested that Lord Hope's more emphatic position might be related to the influence of the Scottish context, where the doctrine of parliamentary sovereignty was never accepted in the same manner as it was south of the border.[57]

54 *Jackson v Attorney General*, n. 40 above, per Lord Steyn, para. 102.

55 Ibid., per Lord Hope, para. 104.

56 Ibid., per Lord Hope, para. 107.

57 J. Jowell, 'Parliamentary Sovereignty under the New Constitutional Hypothesis', *Public Law* (2006) 562–80.

Certainly, the remaining Law Lords were all considerably more circumspect. Baroness Hale did not join Lord Hope in attempting to topple the tower of Diceyan parliamentary sovereignty, nor even test its foundations as hard as Lord Steyn: 'The concept of Parliamentary sovereignty which has been fundamental to the constitution of England and Wales since the 17th century (I appreciate that Scotland may have taken a different view) means that Parliament can do anything'.[58]

Hale did go on to observe that the courts would not find that Parliament had interfered with fundamental rights unless its intentions were 'crystal clear',[59] and even tentatively suggested that the courts would look on with suspicion and ***might*** even reject any attempt to 'subvert the rule of law by removing governmental action affecting the rights of the individual from all judicial scrutiny'.[60] She also noted the various voluntary limitations which Parliament had accepted in relation to the European Communities Act and the Human Rights Act, but her ultimate conclusion was: 'In general, however, the constraints upon what Parliament can do are political and diplomatic rather than constitutional'.[61]

Taking her analysis as a whole, it seems that Baroness Hale was willing *at most* to very cautiously dip a toe into the ocean of a general constitutional right of the courts to limit parliamentary sovereignty (as opposed to specific rights conferred by Parliament via constitutional statutes). Lord Steyn was prepared to risk a paddle and Lord Hope was happy to jump in and swim. However, Lords Bingham and Carswell were staying firmly on the sand.

In fact, as Lord Bingham firmly stated:

> The bedrock of the British constitution is, and in 1911 was, the supremacy of the Crown in Parliament . . . *Then, as now*, the Crown in Parliament was unconstrained by any entrenched or codified constitution. It could make or unmake any law it wished. Statutes, formally enacted as Acts of Parliament, properly interpreted, enjoyed the highest legal authority.[62]

And Lord Carswell took a very similar stance:

> As a judge I am very conscious of the proper reluctance of the courts to intervene in issues of the validity of Acts of Parliament. I should be most unwilling to decide this or any other case in a way which would endanger that tradition of mutual respect. I do not, and I have no doubt your Lordships do not, have any wish to expand the role of the judiciary at the expense of any other organ of the state or to seek to frustrate the properly expressed wish of Parliament as contained in legislation. The attribution in

58 *Jackson v Attorney General*, n. 40 above, per Baroness Hale, para. 159.
59 Ibid.
60 Ibid.
61 Ibid.
62 Ibid., per Lord Bingham, para. 9 (emphasis added).

> certain quarters of such a wish to the judiciary is misconceived and appears to be the product of lack of understanding of the judicial function and the sources of law which the courts are bound to apply.[63]

Again, it should be stressed that all of this was in the context of *obiter dicta* speculation. On the one hand, the willingness of the courts to hear the case at all was striking, but on the other, even when speaking entirely in the abstract the most senior judges in the United Kingdom were extremely deferential towards the principle of parliamentary sovereignty. It is tempting to fasten upon the most daring passages in *Jackson*, and hail them as indicative of a rebalancing of the relationship between the courts and Parliament. However, reading the judicial statements in their entirety, it is difficult to support this conclusion.

As Knight and Cross[64] observe, the speeches of the House of Lords in the *AXA* case[65] also raised the theoretical possibility of the courts at some point intervening if Parliament attempted to pass primary legislation which was contrary to the rule of law. However, unless and until the point is actually tested, it is impossible to tell how far the courts would go in this direction. How adventurous individual judges are in this regard varies considerably, but at present it appears that a direct challenge to the concept of parliamentary sovereignty is territory into which the judiciary are reluctant to even consider venturing.

Nevertheless, all of this is based upon the idea that Dicey accurately described the functioning of the British Constitution in the early twentieth century, and that developments since have taken place within an essentially Diceyan paradigm. What if this is not the case?

5.2.3 The case of the empty house

In one of the most notorious and beloved Sherlock Holmes' stories, 'The Case of the Empty House', the hero comes back from the dead, understandably causing the traumatised Dr Watson to collapse in shock. Having duly applied brandy, Holmes reveals how he 'came alive out of that dreadful chasm . . . I had no serious difficulty in getting out of it, for the very simple reason that I never was in it'.[66]

Similarly, is the paradox of the capacity or incapacity of a sovereign Parliament to limit the sovereignty of its successors actually a red herring? What if the UK Parliament never has been sovereign, and we were not in this theoretical chasm in the first place?

63 Ibid., per Lord Carswell, para. 168.

64 C. Knight & T. Cross, 'Public Law in the Supreme Court 2011–12', *Judicial Review*, Vol. 17, No. 4 (2012) 330–55.

65 *AXA General Insurance Ltd and Others v The Lord Advocate and Others* [2011] UKSC 46, [2012] 1 AC 868.

66 A. Conan Doyle, 'The Empty House', in *Sherlock Holmes: The Complete Illustrated Short Stories* (Chancellor Press: London) 1989, 443.

This is a theory which has been cogently put forward in various guises by a number of respected commentators. Joseph[67] argues that the concept of parliamentary sovereignty is in fact a myth, and that in reality the British Constitution operates by virtue of a collaborative exercise between Parliament and the courts. Similarly, Lakin[68] maintains that the scaffolding upholding the Constitution is the common principle of legality, and that the final authority for enforcing this lies in judicial, rather than in parliamentary hands. Building on related ideas, Eldin[69] acknowledges that parliamentary sovereignty has a predominant position in contemporary British legal thought, but proposes that this is a recent and misguided development. His thesis is that courts have lost sight of their previously acknowledged role of acting as a constitutional safeguard against unjust law, and that this now dormant common law tradition should be rediscovered.

Goldsworthy[70] suggests that it is strange that Eldin did not cite the comments by Hope and Steyn in *Jackson*, describing them as 'unprecedented', and asserting that they would have bolstered Eldin's argument.

However, we consider that Eldin was wise to leave his case as it was in this regard. In the first place, he is acknowledging that this aspect of common law, constitutionalism, largely remains on ice as far as contemporary jurisprudence is concerned, and that at present it is still waiting to be warmed up and reanimated. Second, as we saw above, only Lord Hope was prepared to fully embrace the idea. The response of his fellow Law Lords ranged from an ambivalent acknowledgement of the theoretical possibility to a robust defence of parliamentary sovereignty, which was fundamentally at odds with Eldin's approach. Had Eldin followed Goldsworthy's advice, he would not just have been faced with making bricks without straw: he would have been stuck with no straw *and* a pitifully small supply of mud. Not only did the House of Lords in *Jackson* provide little usable material, what did exist was *obiter dicta*.

However, in fairness to Goldsworthy, he is more interested in seeking to dismantle, rather than support, Eldin's analysis. The thread running through his impressively scholarly book is that parliamentary sovereignty is a very real phenomenon, which has survived centuries of constitutional change, and which has the capacity to survive many more.[71] He carefully deconstructs some of the philosophical criticism of the doctrine, arguing that it is an error to seek to discredit it on the basis that it is founded upon a view of sovereignty derived from Hobbes and Austin.[72] Goldsworthy, not unreasonably, summarises these schools

67 P. Joseph, 'Parliament, the Courts and the Collaborative Enterprise', *King's College Law Journal*, Vol. 15 (2004) 321–34.

68 S. Lakin, 'Debunking the Idea of Parliamentary Sovereignty: the Controlling Factor of Legality in the British Constitution', *Oxford Journal of Legal Studies*, Vol. 28, No. 4 (2008) 709–34.

69 D. Eldin, *Judges and Unjust Laws, Common Law, Constitutionalism and the Foundations of Judicial Review* (University of Michigan Press: Ann Arbour) 2008, 173–5.

70 J. Goldsworthy, *Parliamentary Sovereignty: Contemporary Debates* (Cambridge University Press: Cambridge) 2010, 268.

71 Ibid., 280.

72 Ibid., 272–4.

of thought as portraying law as a body of command backed by threats, and issued by a sovereign authority with sufficient power to enforce obedience if necessary.

Nobody could describe Hobbes as an optimist, and much of his outlook is distilled into the iconic phrase so often quoted from *Leviathan* on the natural condition of humankind in time of war: 'and, which is worst of all, continual fear and danger of violent death, and the life of man solitary, poor, nasty, brutish, and short'.[73] In a nutshell, his view was that human beings were naturally vile and savage, and the only way to keep a lid on things was to submit absolutely to a sovereign authority. The alternative was war and chaos, which invariably made a very bad situation worse. In mitigation, his view undeniably was shaped by the horror and carnage of the civil wars of the mid-seventeenth century.

However, Goldsworthy suggests that the doctrine of parliamentary sovereignty came to be widely accepted with the rising of the Whig star and the events of 1688.[74] The Whig outlook recognised that tyrannical behaviour might justify rebellion, although it shied away from defining tyranny. It was recognised that there were *moral* limits to parliamentary authority, but these were deemed too vague to be defined in a legally serviceable way; the jurist Blackstone was writing against this backdrop in the eighteenth century.

Goldsworthy[75] seeks to defend Dicey, arguing that his concept of parliamentary sovereignty was not in fact derived from Austin's legal positivist philosophy, which understood law as the body of rules laid down by a sovereign 'uncommanded commander'[76] and backed by sanctions, echoing Hobbes (although it did not endorse absolute obedience in all circumstances with Hobbes' pessimistic zeal for doom). If the classic principle of parliamentary sovereignty was so closely linked with a purely formal understanding of the rule of law, it would be unpalatable to many contemporary commentators (who want more sauce on their pancake, as we saw in Chapter 4).

However, in Goldsworthy's perception it is not. He maintains that Dicey's doctrine grew from the primordial soup of English[77] legal understanding, and it had its origins in the constitutional settlement of 1688, as well as the outworkings of this in subsequent juridical thought. Not only does he defend the classic principle of parliamentary sovereignty on philosophical grounds, Goldsworthy also champions it on the basis of the practical operation of the law. He attacks the collaborative account of the constitution given by Joseph, questioning whether it is plausible to assert that statutes mean whatever the courts decide that they mean.[78] For Goldsworthy, statutes are not essentially empty vessels until they are filled by the courts, and he asserts that this is the logical implication of Joseph's argument.

73 T. Hobbes, *Leviathan* (Harvard Classics) 1909–14, Ch. XIII 'Of the Natural Condition of Mankind as Concerning Their Felicity and Misery', http://www.bartleby.com/34/5/13.html.

74 Goldsworthy, n. 70 above, 274.

75 Ibid.

76 C. Saunders & K. Le Roy, *The Rule of Law* (The Federation Press: Annandale) 2004, 27.

77 The term 'English' is used here because, as has been noted, the concept of parliamentary sovereignty is regarded differently north of the border.

78 Goldsworthy, n. 70 above, 278.

It is undeniable that Goldsworthy's defence of both Dicey and the doctrine of parliamentary sovereignty is admirable. It is also true that even if parliamentary sovereignty is a myth in the mind of some academics, it is a story in which the judiciary continue to have a strong belief, as the speeches in *Jackson* make clear. However, this does not necessarily mean that some of the insights of Joseph and other commentators are not also of great value.

Even if parliamentary sovereignty is not ready to disappear up the mythical mountain with the yeti, there is still value in a narrative of collaboration. While it is going too far to suggest that the legislature is signing a blank cheque to the courts when statutes are promulgated, it is true that their meaning and application is clarified and shaped by judges and, for that matter, other constitutional actors. For instance, when statutory duties are imposed upon public bodies, they must necessarily be understood and interpreted by those bodies. It is true that there is scope for judicial review, but in the absence of this the way in which the words of an Act of Parliament are given force in the real world depends upon decisions made by, and the understanding of, people on the ground. Parliament might be sovereign in terms of its legislative capacity, but if that legislative power is to be translated into practical effect, it requires the assistance of other parties within the state.

5.2.4 Legislative sovereignty versus practical sovereignty

As explained above, the dominant understanding of parliamentary sovereignty in British courts is that of the Diceyan account, subject to the debated impact of the Human Rights Act and membership of the European Union. Commentators and judges disagree about the scope and trajectory of this influence, but the centre of gravity is around an essentially Diceyan model. Nevertheless, there are valuable insights to be gained from those who put forward a more collaborative understanding of the mechanics of the UK Constitution.

In terms of orthodox legal theory, Parliament is sovereign in enacting legislation, and legislation is the top of the legal food chain. An Act of Parliament can be modified or disapplied only by virtue of another Act of Parliament. Although there are those, like Eldin, who believe in residual common law power vested in the judiciary to police the legal framework, this is not widely accepted or recognised by the majority of Britain's senior judges. Yet, this is not the only relevant question in assessing the real power of Parliament. It should not be forgotten that the bare power to legislate is of little use, and the mere capacity to issue an order is of limited value.

In some senses, the essence of the modern doctrine of parliamentary sovereignty lies in collective responsibility. First, there is the concept of putting into practice the democratic will of the people, and one of the most robust and thorough defences of parliamentary sovereignty in the modern era is provided by Michael Gordon.[79] As he observes:

79 M. Gordon, *Parliamentary Sovereignty in the UK Constitution: Process, Politics and Democracy* (Hart: Oxford) 2015, 55.

> The importance of the doctrine from a functional perspective – as a central organising principle and constitutional focal point – and the virtue of the doctrine from a normative perspective in ensuring the primacy of democracy, mean that a significant challenge is posed to those who would seek to eliminate Parliamentary Sovereignty from the UK's constitutional architecture.

Similarly, although she embarks upon a detailed and nuanced analysis of what the concept of 'sovereignty' truly encapsulates, Young also makes a forceful case for retaining the principle of a Parliament which is unfettered by its predecessors and not unduly constrained by an unelected judiciary. Her reasons for this analysis are again firmly rooted in democratic ideals:

> From a normative perspective, I find it difficult to justify the role of the court in establishing fundamental principles of the common law and the rule of law. However, I acknowledge that this is due to my theory of human rights; regarding human rights as contestable I find it difficult to conclude that the court can, always, determine rights with such certainty that it is justifiable for them to impose rights to limit democratic law-making institutions. This is not to argue that the legislature alone should have a say in the determination of rights, rather that I believe there is a role for both the legislature and the judiciary.[80]

It is interesting to hear what almost sound like echoes of Jennings in her concluding remarks. Specifically in relation to the Scottish and the UK Parliaments Young observes:

> In addition, the threat of a potential constitutional crisis means that both institutions need to pay attention to the wishes of the electorate. A constitutional crisis will, ultimately, be determined by the wishes of the people. As such, neither institution will be tempted to enforce full sovereignty over the other unless there is at least some assurance that this will be supported by the people, should their actions give rise to a constitutional crisis.[81]

Undeniably Young is talking about a radically different constitutional context and adopting a different understanding of sovereignty. Of course, here she is dealing with a particular clash of institutions which Jennings could not, and did not, have in mind. Nevertheless, the common thread which runs through both authors is the notion that parliamentary authority is derived from, and constrained by, the collective opinion of UK society.

Even though the electoral system is open to criticism and the UK model of representative democracy is by no means perfect, legislation is the result of a vote

80 A. Young, 'Parliamentary Sovereignty – Redefined', in R. Rawlings, P. Leyland and A. Young (eds), *Sovereignty and the Law: Domestic, European and International Perspectives* (Oxford University Press: Oxford) 2013, 87.

81 Ibid., 88.

of democratically elected representatives, and it is no accident that the Parliament Acts 1911 and 1949 give the elected Lower Chamber capacity to override the unelected Upper Chamber.

It should be noted also that the current legislative process impliedly takes into account an understanding of collective responsibility which operates at level more complex than the out-working of representative democracy. The very continued existence of the House of Lords provides for voices from different sectors of society to have an input into the decision-making process, and the presence of the Lords Spiritual is a classic example of this dynamic.

However, for parliamentary sovereignty to be meaningful in a real as well as a legislative sense, the dynamic of collective responsibility must be taken seriously; this does not just apply to the need for Parliament to use its legislative powers within the bounds that wider society will deem acceptable, as Jennings and Young in their own ways have argued. Collective responsibility encompasses, but goes beyond, this self-regulation. The population do not simply function passively as a brake on what might be deemed by popular consensus to be unacceptable actions. Indeed, citizens and groups must also actively contribute to the operation of our system of representative democracy, engaging with the electoral process and with politicians between elections, and there must also be a willingness to assist in the understanding and application of legislation. We shall return to this theme later in this chapter. Let us now turn to the key part of our analysis in Chapters 4 to 7 – namely whether the legal framework concerning religion in Great Britain enhances our constitutional foundations, in this case parliamentary supremacy.

5.3 Does the tripartite religious character of the legal and constitutional system enhance or weaken parliamentary sovereignty?

5.3.1 Preliminary considerations

At the structural and constitutional level, the current establishment and quasi-establishment relationships between Church and state have all been created and/or endorsed by primary legislation from Westminster. In particular, we need to highlight the Act of Supremacy 1534, the Welsh Church Act 1914 and the Church of Scotland Act 1921. There appears to be no serious doubt that Parliament has the power to alter these arrangements as and when it may see fit to do so, as the forcible disestablishment of the Church of England in Wales demonstrates.

During the debates prior to the passage of the Marriage (Same-Sex Couples) Act 2013 there were voices suggesting that the anticipated rift between canon law and secular law would precipitate the end of the establishment relationship.[82] As we argued at the time, this was an untenable proposition, given that there was

82 J. García Oliva and H. Hall, 'Same-Sex Marriage: An Inevitable Challenge to Religious Liberty and Establishment?', *Oxford Journal of Law and Religion*, Vol. 3, No. 1 (2014) 25–56.

already a yawning gulf between canon law and secular law in terms of remarriage after divorce, and if a discrepancy between the two regimes was so deeply problematic, establishment would have crumbled to dust long before 2013.

Setting that issue aside, no commentators had seriously suggested that the bonds between Church and state could potentially invalidate primary legislation. Even at a moment when the conservative voices within the realm of ecclesiastical law were anxious to be heard as forcefully as possible, nobody was suggesting that Parliament, acting with a democratic mandate, lacked the capacity to make laws contrary to the will of the Church, or to consciously or unconsciously severe the bonds between Church and state if it so wished.

All things considered, therefore, it would be difficult to argue that the current legal arrangements are in any way incompatible with parliamentary sovereignty. Having said that, is it possible to go beyond this, and find ways in which they are a positive asset for this principle?

We would argue that rather than simply being no threat to the application of parliamentary sovereignty and the democratic ideals which underlie it, there are several ways in which the current legal framework on religion positively assists. We will provide, first, an example of how the model of establishment in England enhances the principle of parliamentary supremacy (as well as the rule of law); this will be followed by other examples drawn from the wider legal framework.

5.3.2 Supervision of the legislative powers of the Church of England

Church of England Measures are legislative instruments passed by the Church, which become part of the general corpus of state law. The legislation receives final approval from the General Synod, but does not become part of state law until there has been a resolution passed by both Houses of Parliament to present it for Royal Assent, and this has indeed been granted.[83]

There is therefore an inbuilt safeguard which preserves the principle of parliamentary supremacy. For example, the Clergy Discipline Measure 2003[84] was passed in response to the discussion document by the then Department of Trade and Industry on labour law rights for atypical workers,[85] but even if the Government had provided much of the impetus for the change, it is hard to imagine that Parliament would have resolved to present a document to the Queen if it had offended the principles of natural justice or otherwise been demonstrably incompatible with the rule of law.

83 The Church of England, 'Church of England Measures', https://www.churchofengland.org/about-us/structure/churchlawlegis/legislation/measures.aspx.

84 The Church of England, 'The Clergy Discipline Measure', https://www.churchofengland.org/about-us/structure/churchlawlegis/clergydiscipline.aspx.

85 The Church of England, *Review of Clergy Terms of Service: Report on the First Phase of the Work* (Church House Publishing: London) 2004.

This is well illustrated by the way in which the representative of the Church Commissioners (Mr Stuart Bell) explained the proposed Measure to the House of Commons:[86]

> I think that you will agree, Mr Deputy Speaker, that the Measure bends over backwards to be as fair as is humanly possible to a cleric who is the subject of a complaint, and I will allude to that later when I touch upon Article 6 of the European convention on human rights.[87]

The Church was at pains to demonstrate compliance both with domestic and international law, but also accepted ideas of fairness and justice which are embedded within the common law, and that the scrutiny of Parliament was genuine, rather than a polite charade. Consequently, it can be argued that establishment has evolved in a way that ensures that the legislative capacity of the Church of England is monitored and compliant with both parliamentary supremacy and the rule of law.

5.3.3 Amber zone offences

There are certain contexts in which the law allows religious motivation for an assault to function as a shield against criminal liability. It is well established, if controversial, law that a person may not consent to an assault occasioning actual bodily harm or more serious injury.[88] However, there are certain recognised exceptions to this general principle, and acts carried out in the name of 'religious mortification' fall within this category, as does ritual male circumcision.[89] It is hard to think of a more serious legal concession than the suspension of criminal liability. However, in two respects, the way in which the legal framework deals with these offences can be seen to support the principle of parliamentary sovereignty.

First, there is the reality that were some of these practices to be invented or popularised now, the law might well not be willing to tolerate them. For example, ritual male circumcision involves subjecting what in many cases is a child who is too young to give consent to an irreversible surgical procedure which carries some physical and emotional risk. Nevertheless, one reason for the courts continuing to accept the legality of such practices must be that Parliament has reformed criminal law on many occasions, and has not chosen to intervene in this matter. There is therefore the recognition that it is not for the courts to disregard this and attempt to alter the accepted position.

86 *Hansard*, HC Deb, 22 May 2003, Vol. 405 cc1174–85, http://hansard.millbanksystems.com/commons/2003/may/22/clergy-discipline-measure.
87 Ibid., c1175.
88 *R v Brown* [1994] 1 AC 212.
89 *Re S (Specific Issue Order: Religion: Circumcision)* [2004] EWHC 1282 (Fam).

Second, however, there is the placing of these offences in the amber zone. Rather than couching their judgment in terms of rights, the courts have focused on capacity to consent. A shield against criminal liability, where it would otherwise strike, serves as a reminder that these situations are at the outer edge of what the law will permit without legislative mandate. This approach encourages judges to adopt a cautious stance in the application of this principle, and be inclined to flag up issues for parliamentary intervention rather than applying judicially created solutions. Thus, overall this area confirms that where freedom of action in the private or family sphere is concerned, fundamental changes are to be introduced by the democratically elected legislature, rather than judge-made law.

5.3.4 The Marriage (Same Sex Couples) Act 2013

Prior to the passage of this legislation, the Church of England challenged the proposals on the grounds that there would be a clash between secular and canon law, and also that despite the guarantees which the UK Parliament would build into the statute, it would remain vulnerable to challenges in the European Court of Human Rights.

The Government acknowledged the concerns raised by the Church of England's response to its consultation exercise in respect of an obvious conflict between state and canon law, were the state to permit same-sex marriage while the Church did not.[90] This is an important issue, because by statute no canon may be made which is contrary to the royal prerogative, customs, laws or statutes of the realm.[91] However, the executive expressly responded that Parliament is sovereign and capable of legislating to avoid a conflict.[92] Section 1(3) of the Act duly provided that '[n]o canon of the Church of England is contrary to section 3 of the Submission of the Clergy Act 1533 . . . by virtue of its making provision about marriage being the union of one man with one woman'.

This enactment and the successful resolution of the potential clash between sacred and secular law bolsters the case for Parliament having retained its sovereign legislative capacity. In some senses, the legislature is sovereign precisely because its members and the judges who interpret its enactments believe it to be so. Therefore, assurances of this kind help to maintain the principle. Furthermore, the ministerial response to consultation in the form of a statement that Parliament remains sovereign, combined with careful drafting to avoid potential pitfalls, demonstrates a willingness on the part of the executive to use legislation in a way that respects, but is not constrained by, the self-imposed limitations adopted by Parliament.

90 *Equal Marriage: The Government's Response* (Dec 2012), paras 1.4 and 1.5; see also Church of England, Canon B30, which sets out the Church's definition of marriage.

91 See Submission of the Clergy Act 1533, s. 3, as applied by the Synodical Government Measure 1969, s. 1(3).

92 *Equal Marriage: The Government's Response*, n. 90 above, paras 1.4 and 1.5.

Similarly, despite the angst from the Church, to date Parliament appears to have attained its aim of designing legislation on this issue which would resist all successful challenges on human rights grounds. Again, this helps to shore up the perception and, therefore, the functioning of the principle. In choosing to submit to judicial supervision in the manner prescribed by the Human Rights Act, Parliament need not be perceived as having hobbled its capacity to move the legal framework in new and creative directions. Rather, it has elected to travel in line with certain guiding principles.

5.3.5 The Children Act 1989: the welfare principle in religious cases

Section 1(1) of the Children Act[93] provides:

> When a court determines any question with respect to –
>
> (a) the upbringing of a child; or
> (b) the administration of a child's property or the application of any income arising from it,
>
> the child's welfare shall be the court's paramount consideration.

According to this section, the welfare of the child who is the subject of the proceedings is the paramount consideration, and this statutory principle triumphs over any agreement which the adult parties to the litigation may have reached.

Commentators such as Herring[94] have questioned whether this provision is compatible with the Human Rights Act 1998, as it appears to subjugate the Article 8[95] rights of parents (and, indeed, other family members) to the best interests of their children; the same logic could, of course, apply equally to the Article 9 rights of adults.[96] It must be acknowledged that the future and the appropriateness of the welfare principle generally is the subject of complex debate, and there are those who would prefer the legal system to focus on children's rights[97] in any event; obviously this debate is beyond the scope of the present work. For current purposes, the important point is that the collective democratic consensus, as expressed in the Children Act 1989, continues to be applied and upheld by the courts. Various judicial decisions have considered the Article 9 rights of adults in relation to disputes about the religious upbringing of children,[98] and although the independent rights of adults to manifest their religious beliefs have been accepted, judges have had no difficulty in finding that this right may be appropriately limited in order to promote the welfare of a minor.

93 Children Act 1989, s. 1(1).
94 J. Herring, 'The Human Rights Act and the Welfare Principle in Family Law – Conflicting or Complementary?', *Child and Family Law Quarterly Review*, Vol. 11 (1999) 223–35.
95 The right to private and family life, home and correspondence.
96 The right to freedom of thought, conscience and religion.
97 See, e,g., A. Bainham and S. Gilmore, *Children: The Modern Law* (Jordans: Bristol) 2013, Ch. 7.
98 See, e.g., *Re G (Children) (Education: Religious Upbringing)* [2012] All ER (D) 50 (Oct).

This is an area of law where the will of Parliament has been clearly expressed, and courts are consistent in following this, even where it may necessitate limiting the exercise of religious freedoms by adults involved in the case. The legal framework has a positive and accommodating approach towards religious belief and practice, but not to the point of circumventing the will of Parliament in terms of its ordering of priorities. Statutory law, at present, decrees that disputes about religious upbringing are resolved by recourse to the welfare principle rather than a balancing of rights, and this is the clear approach which is adopted.

5.3.6 Bestiality

Engaging in sexual relations with a non-human animal is an offence in Scotland, as it is south of the border. Ferguson and McDiarmid argue that this exists purely because such conduct violated Judeo-Christian sexual norms.[99] They assert that it is not based upon animal welfare and that, to the extent that such conduct causes pain or harm to the animal involved, it could and should be dealt with in the same way as any other act of animal cruelty.

This position can be supported by the opinion of Sir George Mackenzie[100] in his work on Scottish criminal law.[101] Mackenzie both makes it clear that the origin of this offence is the prohibition in the *Book of Leviticus*, and also that the animal involved would ordinarily be put to death by fire or drowning. It is hard to claim that an offence which originally demanded such cruel and barbaric treatment of innocent animals could have its roots in animal welfare. Furthermore, the way in which the offence was linked in historical times with other sexual practices that were categorised as deviant or sinful further demonstrates that it was targeted at enforcing moral norms in relation to sexual behaviour.[102]

In our view, the offence of bestiality has survived because the cultural belief that sexual intercourse with animals is inherently wrong and undesirable has not disappeared. Historically, a number of sexual behaviours which are now accepted and embraced within mainstream society were once criminalised. As the perceptions of society have changed, legislation has stepped in to remove prohibitions against conduct which is no longer regarded as either necessitating or justifying state-imposed punishment. For example, private homosexual acts were rendered lawful by the Criminal Justice (Scotland) Act 1980,[103] and the legal framework has gradually moved from condemning to actively supporting same-sex unions, culminating in the introduction of same-sex marriage in 2014.[104]

99 P. Ferguson and C. McDiarmid, *Scots Criminal Law: A Critical Analysis* (Edinburgh University Press: Edinburgh) 2014, 441.

100 Ironically, the same Sir George Mackenzie whose tomb was broken into and desecrated by intruders in 2004, as discussed in relation to 'Violation of a Sepulchre' (see Ch. 2).

101 G. Mackenzie, *The Laws and Customs of Scotland: In Matters Criminal* (Thomas Brown: Edinburgh) MDCLXXVIII (1678), 162.

102 J. Meek, *Queer Voices in Post-War Scotland: Homosexuality, Religion and Society* (Palgrave/MacMillian: Basingstoke) 2015, 16.

103 Criminal Justice (Scotland) Act 1980, s. 80.

104 Marriage and Civil Partnerships (Scotland) Act 2014.

The legal changes in respect of homosexual relations came about through social campaigning and debate in Scotland, as elsewhere.[105] The criminal dimension had made homosexual activity distinct from other forms of consensual sexual activity engaged in by adults, and about which social attitudes transformed in post-war Britain. This was in stark contrast with heterosexual activities. Although any sexual activity outside marriage was socially stigmatised, especially for women, this sort of sexual practice was not unlawful. It would be wrong to underestimate the suffering and prejudice experienced, for example, by many single women who became mothers,[106] but their circumstances did not, in and of themselves, attract criminal sanction. There were, of course, debates about abortion, provision of family planning and the appropriate status of prostitution.[107] Nevertheless, a single woman was not risking imprisonment by having sexual intercourse with a man. In contrast, legal reform and decriminalisation was an absolute requirement if the rights of sexual minorities were to be advanced.

Consequently, democratically elected legislative bodies reworked the law, dismantling prohibitions based on historic interpretations of Judeo-Christian ethics.[108] However, significantly for our present purposes, there was no similar social and political pressure in respect of the decriminalisation of sexual behaviour such as bestiality. The continuing existence of this as a criminal offence demonstrates respect for democratic principles as made concrete through parliamentary action. The religiously based sexual offences, which were increasingly felt to be an affront to a liberal, open and just society, were gradually swept away whereas the crime of bestiality remains in existence. This is not to say that commentators such as Ferguson and McDiarmid[109] do not make interesting arguments for reforming the law in this regard. There is good reason to assert that cruelty to animals should be dealt with consistently and pursuant to legislation constructed to advance animal welfare, and that otherwise the sexual freedoms of adults should not be unduly curtailed. Nevertheless, the fact that the offence has survived to date reflects the concerns and priorities of society. This element of religious morality enshrined in the legal system has not been perceived as deeply problematic by a critical mass of people in order to trigger a movement for reform, and it has remained as part of the legal landscape as a result.

We shall now proceed to discuss the ways in which the teachings and outlooks of religious groups might mould perceptions of parliamentary sovereignty and the democratic principle which underlies it.

105 G. Mucciaroni, *Same Sex Different Politics: Successes and Failure in the Struggles over Gay Rights* (University of Chicago Press: Chicago and London) 2008.

106 K. Kiernan, H. Land & J. Lewis, *Lone Motherhood in Twentieth Century Britain: From Footnote to Front Page* (Clarendon Press: Oxford) 1998.

107 R. Davidson and G. Davis, *The Sexual State: Sexuality and Scottish Governance 1980–1950* (Edinburgh University Press: Edinburgh) 2012.

108 We would stress that not all contemporary Christians or Jews would interpret their faith as condemning loving and consensual sexual relations between persons of the same sex, and we ourselves therefore would not endorse an unqualified and universal term like 'Judeo-Christian ethics' in this context.

109 Ferguson and McDiarmid, n. 99 above.

5.4 How do the perspectives and teachings of different religious belief groups influence perceptions of parliamentary supremacy and the democratic process?

Whichever of the various nuanced understandings of parliamentary sovereignty we choose to adopt, the same concept lies at the heart of the doctrine: namely, that the content of enacted, positive law should ultimately be determined by collective consensus, as mediated through the democratic process. Furthermore, for legislation to be accepted and given force on the ground (as opposed to simply in the statute book), there must be a willingness on the part of the population to recognise its force and co-operate in its implementation. We now consider how the teachings and viewpoints of various faith communities might shape the thoughts of their followers in relation to this concept.

5.4.1 Christianity

Whereas in the chapter on the rule of law (Chapter 4) we assessed the teachings of different Christian Churches separately, in relation the question of democracy there is little identifiable difference between the doctrinal positions of the various denominations. The issue of how these groups interact with secular law and the state on a broader level has already been explored extensively in Chapters 2 and 4, and there is little to be gained by revising the same material here. For this reason, we shall assess instead how Christianity, in general, relates to these ideas.

In common with many of the other faith traditions, Christianity emerged into a society which was not democratic. The figures who shaped its early development did not move in a democratic paradigm and did not perceive or analyse the world in democratic terms.

As Foster[110] argues, in reality Christianity contributed to the development of democracy really only in so far as it contributed to the development of Western civilisation as a whole. Nevertheless, given the magnitude of the influence that Christianity has had on European intellectual ideas, the importance of this contextual contribution should not be lightly set aside.

Furthermore, it is necessary to acknowledge, as Foster does, that there have been times when the institutional voice of Christianity has struggled against, rather than for, democratic government. The two examples he cites are the French[111] and American[112] Revolutions, but Foster also observes that the theological principles of changing the world by persuasion rather than coercion, and engaging in argument and discussion, propel Christians towards democracy as a desirable system of government.

Moreover, there is early and firm evidence of this trend in codes such as the Order of St Benedict. Although not a blueprint for a modern democratic

110 J. Foster, 'Christianity and Democracy', *The Expository Times*, Vol. 63, No. 11 (1952) 350–2.
111 See C. Hibbert, *The French Revolution* (Penguin: London) 2001.
112 See C. Bonwick, *The American Revolution* (University of Virginia Press: Charlottesville) 1991.

community, there is a strong emphasis throughout on processes for collective decision making. While the abbot is invested with wide-ranging powers, he should not exercise these despotically, and must listen to the views of members of the monastery in Chapter meetings, even the youngest and newest members.[113] This is in keeping with Christian ideas that those in positions of leadership should see themselves as servants,[114] and that individuals have a duty to care for the people and society of which they are a part.[115]

This is reflected in practical ways in Great Britain by the support that Churches show for the democratic process. Anglican leaders, for example, actively encourage their members to take part in elections and endorse the contribution that politicians make to society. In the lead up to the general election of 2015, the Church of England bishops issued a Pastoral Letter, entitled 'Who is My Neighbour?'[116] It did not seek to support the agenda of any particular political party, but did attempt to tackle head-on the cynicism with the political process that had developed in Britain. It defended the work and motivation of politicians, and urged Christians (and, indeed, other citizens) to re-engage with the system and consider what kind of society we wish to build together. By way of example:

> As bishops of the Church of England, we are in touch with all kinds of communities across the country through our local churches. And we maintain close links with the elected politicians for the constituencies in our dioceses. In our experience, the great majority of politicians and candidates enter politics with a passion to improve the lives of their fellow men and women. They will disagree wildly about how to achieve this, but with few exceptions, politicians are not driven merely by cynicism or self-interest.[117]

113 The Order of St Benedict, 'The Rule of St Benedict', http://www.osb.org/rb/text/toc.html.

114 See, for instance, Luke 22:24–27: '[24] A dispute also arose among them as to which one of them was to be regarded as the greatest.[25] But he said to them, "The kings of the Gentiles lord it over them; and those in authority over them are called benefactors.[26] But not so with you; rather the greatest among you must become like the youngest, and the leader like one who serves.[27] For who is greater, the one who is at the table or the one who serves? Is it not the one at the table? But I am among you as one who serves.'

115 See, for instance, Luke 10:29–37: '[29] But wanting to justify himself, he asked Jesus, "And who is my neighbour?" [30]Jesus replied, "A man was going down from Jerusalem to Jericho, and fell into the hands of robbers, who stripped him, beat him, and went away, leaving him half dead.[31] Now by chance a priest was going down that road; and when he saw him, he passed by on the other side.[32] So likewise a Levite, when he came to the place and saw him, passed by on the other side.[33] But a Samaritan while travelling came near him; and when he saw him, he was moved with pity.[34] He went to him and bandaged his wounds, having poured oil and wine on them. Then he put him on his own animal, brought him to an inn, and took care of him.[35] The next day he took out two denarii, gave them to the innkeeper, and said, 'Take care of him; and when I come back, I will repay you whatever more you spend'.[36] Which of these three, do you think, was a neighbour to the man who fell into the hands of the robbers?[37] He said, "The one who showed him mercy." Jesus said to him, "Go and do likewise".'

116 Church of England, House of Bishops, 'Pastoral Letter', https://www.churchofengland.org/media/2170230/whoismyneighbour-pages.pdf.

117 Ibid., para. 22.

It also advocated robustly for religion that operates in the public as well as the private sphere, and characterised the perception of faith as a phenomenon exclusively for the private arena as an aberration of modern European society.[118] Therefore, this very public statement bolstered the democratic process, and thereby the legitimacy and effectiveness of parliamentary sovereignty. If Parliament is seen as expressing the collective will of British society, the standing of its enactments must necessarily be held in high regard by all who support democratic decision making and collective responsibility. This does not equate to endorsing a straightforwardly majoritarian understanding of democracy, or implying that the will of the majority must necessarily prevail in all circumstances. It does, however, demand that the expressed will of the legislature is to be treated seriously. Furthermore, in claiming that religion and religious people have a place in the public sphere, and indeed have a responsibility to participate in decisions which affect our collective life, the Church of England supported the place of other faith groups within this arena.

The Anglican tradition is not alone in expressing active support for the democratic process. The Methodist Church makes the following statement:

> We cannot ignore the challenges facing society today, and we need to engage fully with democratic processes and decision-making. By participating in elections, Christians can make their feelings known, and can impact positively on the political landscape.'[119]

Moreover, all of the larger Christian Churches take an interest in secular politics and the decisions made which affect all of society. For example, the Free Churches (the Methodist Church, the United Reformed Church, the Baptist Union of Great Britain, the Salvation Army and the Quakers) send a delegation each year to the three major party political conferences,[120] and the Roman Catholic Church also stresses the importance of political engagement for the faithful.[121]

However, we must also acknowledge that there are some far smaller groupings which adopt a different theological stance that precludes voting or taking any active part in secular government. Among the Plymouth Brethren, for example, Exclusive Brethren do not vote,[122] but they stress that they pray for whichever government is in power, and will lobby politicians about matters of policy if in their view they are issues involving the compatibility of legislation and

118 Ibid., in particular paras 6–9.

119 The Methodist Church, 'Elections', http://www.methodist.org.uk/mission/public-issues/politics-and-elections/elections.

120 Baptists Together, 'Politics and Christian Faith', http://www.baptist.org.uk/Groups/220649/Politics_and_Christian.aspx.

121 The Catholic Church in England and Wales, 'The General Election 2015 – Bishops' Letter to All Catholics in England and Wales' (24 Feb 2015), http://www.catholicnews.org.uk/Home/Featured/Features-2015/General-Election-2015/Election-Letter.

122 Plymouth Brethren Christian Church, 'Plymouth Brethren and Politics', http://www.plymouthbrethrenchristianchurch.org/beliefs/doctrine.

their interpretation of scripture. Furthermore, they explicitly recognise this as a right which they enjoy by virtue of the democratic system: 'On these occasions we actively lobby our representatives, exercising our individual democratic rights as citizens living in a free society'.[123]

On balance, Christianity as an outlook is one which encourages a supportive stance towards democratic government and the principle of parliamentary sovereignty.

5.4.2 Judaism

As will be considered in more detail below, Jewish groups, like the Christian Churches, have produced voting guides and encouraged participation in the democratic process. Again, this evidences their support for parliamentary sovereignty at an intellectual level, as well as a willingness to translate this ideological support into practical action. This is unsurprising in light of the emphasis that Judaism places on communal responsibilities, respecting others in the community and being mindful of public opinion.[124] A failure to engage with wider society in an effort to further the common good would be a spiritual failing for the majority of groups within Judaism, so it is not surprising that involvement in temporal politics (in both a party and non-party political sense) is deemed a positive course of action.

As Fradkin[125] argues, although it is true that (like Christianity) Judaism is not inevitably democratic in the sense that it predates any modern understanding of the concept and has been practised successfully under other forms of government, nevertheless the principles of liberty and equality,[126] which are fundamental to the democratic project, have their origin in the Hebrew Bible. This commentator also acknowledges that Judaism is inclined to critique, constructively and not with hostility, the practical functioning of democracies, on the basis that all human political traditions are inevitably flawed. For Fradkin, Judaism's view of democracy cannot be divorced from the historical experience of the Jewish people, which in the twentieth century demonstrated how damaging the alternatives to democracy can be.

This is not to suggest that there are no challenges. For example, Arkush[127] examines how a number of Jewish thinkers have attempted to deal with the apparent discrepancy between what he characterises as the inherently theocratic principles of Judaism and modern liberal ideas with which they wish to harmonise their faith. However, although the various commentators considered by Arkush

123 Ibid.

124 J. Rosen, *Understanding Judaism* (Dunedin Academic Press: Edinburgh) 2003, 111.

125 H. Fradkin, 'Judaism and Political Life', *Journal of Democracy*, Vol. 15, No. 3 (2004) 122–36.

126 See, e.g., Genesis 1:2: 'So God created humankind in his image, in the image of God he created them; male and female he created them'. All human beings are seen as bearing the Divine image and must, consequently, be treated with dignity and respect.

127 A. Arkush, 'Theocracy, Liberalism and Modern Judaism', *The Review of Politics*, Vol. 71, No. 4 (2009) 637–58.

(namely, Moses Mendlessohn, David Novak and Isaiah Leibowitz) address this challenge in differing ways, the very nature of the project in which they are all engaged is testimony to the commitment which mainstream Jewish thought has to democratic principles.

Interestingly, even the groups within Judaism most inclined to practise separation (not merely from non-Jews, but also in many cases from Jews who interpret the Torah differently) there is still an expectation of engagement with the democratic process, and the intense speculation over voting patterns amongst Haredi communities in the United States in the run-up to the 2016 presidential election is illustrative of this.[128]

Although Judaism has not always existed in a context where democracy has been the norm, it has always been a religion which emphasises the importance of the present world and reality, and has not encouraged too great a preoccupation with life after death (although it certainly does engage with the topic).[129] It does not focus on detaching from the temporal, and in addition taking a full part in the life of the community is regarded as key. For groups now living within democratic countries, participating in the political process is, therefore, an obvious and natural mechanism for achieving this.

5.4.3 Islam

Once again, in common with the other Abrahamic faiths, Islam developed centuries before our contemporary understanding of liberal democracy; consequently its teachings are not geared towards this particular paradigm, as the Prophet and his successors did not arrange the life of Muslim society along what we would regard as democratic lines. The same is true of early figures within non-Abrahamic religions: for example, the Buddha moved in a world ruled by kings and princes and Buddhist scriptures reflect this, but few people would assert that Buddhism is intrinsically anti-democratic.

In Chapter 4, we discussed at length the various approaches in modern Islam towards practising the faith within a non-Islamic context and non-Islamic legal systems. We must also acknowledge here that there is a diversity of opinion about democracy within twenty-first century Islam, certainly in the Western sense,[130] and clearly the group which we termed ‘Exclusivist Muslims’ would not be supportive of democratic principles. However, in Great Britain, as we have previously suggested, the majority of the population come within the group to which we have ascribed the labelled ‘Pluralist Muslims’, and for these individuals, there are many elements of the Islamic faith which encourage support for democracy.

128 B. Sales, ‘The Haredim Look to Trump as a Pro-Israel, Traditionalist Tough Guy, Emphasis on ‘Guy’, *The Times of Israel* (7 Sept 2016), http://www.timesofisrael.com/haredim-look-to-trump-as-a-pro-israel-traditionalist-tough-guy-emphasis-on-guy.

129 J. Ellens, *Heaven, Hell and Afterlife: Eternity in Judaism, Christianity and Islam* (Praeger: Oxford) 2013.

130 C. Yaran, *Understanding Islam* (Dunedin Academic Press: Edinburgh) 2007, 91.

As Moaddel[131] argues, there are several important concepts within Islam which would point to an affinity between Islamic doctrine and democracy. For example, the notion of a *shura* or consultative body, which – coupled with the general Islamic requirement to live in accordance with justice – means that although Islam does not demand a democratic form of government, to many Muslims such a system might appear a reasonable and appropriate system for ordering society, particularly in a pluralistic context. Lewis[132] observes that young Muslims, in particular, want to find ways of retaining their faith identity and embracing a supportive and positive approach to life in a diverse and democratic setting, and there are examples from history where respect and harmony for different creeds was fostered in Islamic contexts.

Commentators like Menocal[133] have held up Islamic Spain as a model of positive religious co-existence within a vibrant and flourishing society, but her work has been criticised as over-idealised by a number of academic commentators.[134] Nevertheless, whatever the historical reality, the fact that this time and place is *seen* as a model of harmony in diversity is, in and of itself, important. It has a talismanic status and the potential to build bridges between intellectual worlds. These visions of societies, within which peoples of different creeds can live with mutual co-operation and even affection, encourage Muslims and non-Muslims alike to embrace democracy as a system of government which accords respect and a voice to all.

Furthermore, as with Christianity and Judaism, there are verses within Islamic Scripture which support the underlying values of the democratic project, such as equality between human beings, regardless of race or culture.[135] Thus, for Pluralist Muslims, there are many streams of Islamic thought and tradition which foster a positive and participatory approach towards democracy.

5.4.4 Hinduism

Much of the discussion around Hinduism and democracy has been generated within the very specific social and political context of India and, needless to say, many issues and considerations apply in this setting, which are not of direct relevance to Great Britain. Nevertheless, it is striking that even against the complicated, and in some ways controversial backdrop of the Hindu Nationalist BJP

131 M. Moaddel, 'The Study of Islamic Culture and Politics: An Overview and Assessment', *Annual Review of Sociology*, Vol. 28 (2002) 359–86.

132 P. Lewis, *Young, British, Muslim* (Continum: London) 2011, 151.

133 M. Menocal, *The Ornament of the World: How Muslims, Jews and Christians Created a Culture of Tolerance in Medieval Spain* (Little Brown: New York) 2002.

134 See, e.g., A. Akasoy, 'Convivencia and its Discontents: Interfaith Life in Al-Andalus', *International Journal of Middle East Studies*, Vol 43, No. 3 (2010) 489–99.

135 'O people, we created all of you from the same male and female, and we made you into nations and tribes to recognize each other. The best among you is the most righteous. God is omniscient cognizant': The Quran [49:13].

party, a Hindu worldview can be seen to co-exist with democratic ideals and 'universalists discourses on rights and entitlements'.[136]

It must be acknowledged that the BJP has been accused by its critics of a discriminatory and negative attitude towards Muslims and other minority groups within Indian society, and clearly an adequate discussion of the justice or otherwise of these claims is well beyond the scope of this book. Suffice it to say that we do not assert that the BJP (or any other political party in any jurisdiction) has impeccable credentials in relation to either democracy or human rights. It is, nevertheless, significant for our purposes that an avowedly Hindu political party adopts a pro-democratic stance. Similarly, in historical terms, Hindu intellectuals were an integral part of the democratic struggle within the movement for Indian independence. As Arvind argues, '[t]he entire independence movement was predicated on the substitution of British raj by a democratically elected raj'.[137]

Therefore, although (as discussed in Chapter 4) Hinduism does not have prescribed and identifiable creeds in the same way as do the Abrahamic religions, it can nevertheless be seen to be a worldview which, in many contexts, is conducive towards acceptance and support for democratic principles. In light of this, it is reasonable to assert that a Hindu perspective tends to be positive towards democracy and, flowing from this, the principle of parliamentary sovereignty, resting as it does upon democratic foundations.

5.4.5 Buddhism

Once again, as we explored in relation to the rule of law, Buddhism as a spiritual pathway does not provide teaching on how to organise a modern society, or even direct guidance on how individuals should relate to their wider community. Buddhist scriptures do contain commentary on the proper conduct of princes and monks, although the manner in which these directly relate to a lay population requires interpretation and cultural translation. In one sense, it would be slightly misguided to state that Buddhism was *pro-democracy*. It simply is not in the nature of Buddhism to be supportive of one particular system of political organisation over another, as these matters are essentially not addressed by Buddhist philosophy. Yet, there are those who would say that a Buddhist view of politics can be extrapolated from Buddhist ethics, with the essential goal of reducing suffering:

> The question of whether Buddhism can or should have any interest in politics, or whether this runs counter to its true and original nature, is a subject of ever recurring debate amongst Western scholars. I believe this to be more or less an artificial problem. Buddhism has always been interested in politics

136 T.B. Hanson, *Saffron Wave: Democracy and Hindu Nationalism in Modern India* (Princeton University Press: Princeton) 1999, 4.

137 S. Arvind, *Modern Hindu Thought* (Oxford University Press: Oxford) 2005, 8.

> for the same reason and to the same extent it is interested in ethics. Morally good behaviour, whether in the private or the social realm, is beneficial to one's own spiritual welfare and the welfare of one's fellow beings. And behaviour is morally good, if in line with the Dharma, it contributes to the reduction or containment of suffering.[138]

However, an added layer of complexity, for present purposes, is that Buddhism does not necessarily tie morally good behaviour in the public arena with the furtherance of democratic principles, and classical Buddhism was formulated with an understanding of a society ruled by a king. Nevertheless, as Schmidt-Leukel goes on to argue:

> The classical Buddhist ideal of monarchy under the Dharma does not tend to be compatible with democracy nor with the concept of a secular state in which no religion is prioritised. Yet it is also true that classical Buddhism does not understand the monarchy as a divine institution . . . In principle then, there is no reason why the task of upholding law and order could not be fulfilled by a democratically elected body instead of a king. And presumably some Buddhists could accept the idea that laws by which such a government rules must not be based exclusively on the Buddhist Dharma but could also rest upon social consensus as long as certain indispensable ethical standards are guaranteed.[139]

In other words, democracy itself is not a concept which can necessarily be drawn easily from Buddhist teaching, but it is reasonable to infer that Buddhists in a democratic country might regard the political system as a means of furthering certain collective ethical outcomes (such as fostering greater social harmony and the reduction of suffering).

A clear example of this is provided by the Komeito[140] in Japan, a political party with close ties to the Buddhist lay organisation, Soka Gakkai. Its policies are moulded by Nichiren Buddhism, centred around humanitarianism, and it is deeply committed to religious freedom and the democratic basis of the Japanese Constitution. Obviously, this is just one example of a particular group within a particular branch of Buddhism, but it illustrates that there is certainly nothing intrinsically anti-democratic about Buddhism, and that for Buddhists living in a liberal, democratic state, working in concert with the democratic system is likely to be an expedient and desirable means to acting ethically and for the common good. Therefore, although indirect, there are solid grounds for suggesting that Buddhist thought within Great Britain is likely to be broadly supportive of the principle that the elected legislature has the final say in making and changing law.

138 P. Schmidt-Leukel, *Understanding Buddhism* (Dunedin Press: Edinburgh) 2006, 86–7.
139 Ibid.
140 Komeito, 'On Politics and Religion', https://www.komei.or.jp/en/about/view.html.

5.4.6 Zoroastrianism

As previously discussed, the ancient teachings of Zoroastrianism do not relate directly to the modern political context. Nevertheless, the emphasis which the faith places on doing good and respecting fellow human beings, as well as animal life, means that it fits well with an understanding of ordering common life on the basis of democracy and justice. As indicated, the first three British Asian Members of Parliament were all Zoroastrian.[141] Building from this, it seems reasonable to assert that Zoroastrianism is a worldview which is compatible with, and broadly supportive of, the parliamentary democracy present in the United Kingdom's Constitution.

5.4.7 Paganism

Paganism encompasses many different spiritual philosophies and most Neo-Pagan movements would reject encouraging (much less demanding) creedal orthodoxy. However, a general reluctance to prescribe or impose ethical norms on the basis of doctrine, and an emphasis on respect, dialogue and acting in harmony with others, where possible, would tend towards supporting a system in which legal rules are ultimately within the control of an elected assembly. Given that living in anarchy would allow for the mistreatment of the weak, it is reasonable to accept that there must be enforceable rules of some sort, and the least oppressive way of discerning these rules might reasonably be deemed to be in some form of collective decision-making.

It is true that some groups within Paganism may be more drawn to alternative forms of political engagement and protest than participation in the formal system. Consider, for example, direct action in the context of eco-Paganism around the construction of roads,[142] and it must also be admitted that a religious label which does not relate to any set of normative doctrines is, by its very nature, impossible to tie to any specific political or philosophical stance. Nevertheless, it is still reasonable to assert that in very broad terms, a Pagan worldview is likely to encourage democratic decision-making, and therefore, be compatible with at least the underlying rationale of parliamentary sovereignty.

5.5 Do faith communities make a practical contribution towards the functioning of parliamentary supremacy and the democratic process?

As stated earlier in this chapter, for the principle of parliamentary sovereignty to function properly, citizens must certainly be engaged with the democratic and

141 P. Allen, 'Zoroastrian Faith Joins Queen's Coronation Celebrations', *The Telegraph* (4 Jun 2013), http://www.telegraph.co.uk/news/uknews/10097326/Zoroastrian-faith-joins-Queens-Coronation-celebrations.html.

142 A. Letcher, 'The Scouring of the Shire: Fairies, Trolls and Pixies in Eco-Protest Culture', *Folklore*, Vol. 112 (2001) 147–61.

legislative process. However, the collective contribution needs to go beyond this, and it must also involve the putting into practice of duly enacted legislation. The remainder of this chapter considers how the established Churches and other faith groups contribute to this.

Legislative sovereignty can have a practical effect only if citizens are prepared to engage in the process of making and implementing the policies which are expressed through legislation. The effectiveness of the system is dependent upon collaboration.

Once again, lessons may be drawn from the penguin world. Emperor penguins survive in astonishingly low temperatures, and distinctively do so by huddling together. Their entire life cycle and survival strategy is dependent upon co-operation. After laying their eggs, female penguins transfer them to their partners and go off for two months to find food. During this time, the penguin fathers huddle together to keep themselves and their eggs as warm as possible, and clearly a single penguin would have no chance of survival. Furthermore, the system works only because the huddle slowly and carefully moves in order to allow the penguins to circulate, and take turns shivering on the edge and being toasty warm in the middle. Without this inbuilt collaborative dimension, the whole strategy would collapse. If the penguins on the edge were stuck there and died of cold, the group would get smaller and smaller and *everyone* would be frozen long before the females could return from the sea. Similarly, parliamentary sovereignty can operate in a meaningful and effective way only if the system is built upon co-operation.

Having established that faith groups in general have a positive approach towards the democratic process and collective decision-making, and in broad terms the principle of parliamentary sovereignty, we are left with the question of how this might translate into practical action to support its functioning. How also do religious citizens assist in making parliamentary sovereignty real by contributing to the understanding and application of enacted legislation?

5.5.1 Faith groups and the encouragement of participation in the democratic process

Of course, we are not suggesting that all faith groups regard involvement in the democratic process as permissible, or even beneficial. Some religious organisations, such as Jehovah's Witnesses,[143] expressly forbid or reject political action. However, as we have already seen in the Christian context discussed above, many faiths do have a commitment to social responsibility and see participation in temporal politics as one important means of furthering this.

For example, the Movement for Reform Judaism produced a guide for voting in the 2015 general election, stressing that Jews had a religious duty to vote. Furthermore, it stated that '[i]t should be stressed that whilst viable economic policies are essential, they are not the only criteria by which parties should be judged,

143 Watch Tower Ministries, http://www.towerwatch.com/Witnesses/Beliefs/their_beliefs.htm.

with the moral and social health of the country being equally important'.[144] The document[145] went on to highlight some of the social issues which Reform Jews should consider in deciding how to use their votes.

This is an excellent example of a transfer of spiritual heat in the social penguin huddle. The Reform Movement can be seen to actively encourage its members to take their share of the collective responsibility for British society, and to consider issues which will affect all people, and not just members of their own group. The substance of the message and the nature of the concerns raised very much echo those contained in the pastoral letter of the House of Bishops.[146] Both documents acknowledge the current cynicism towards the political process, but urge their members not to use this as a reason or excuse to decline to exercise their influence and work for positive change. They both also encourage a sense of collective responsibility and care for the vulnerable.

Taking the above into account, faith groups can be seen to be encouraging participation in two ways: (i) by directly endorsing the involvement in the current democratic system, and (ii) by giving members ideas and guidance about factors to consider in making their democratic choices. Inevitably, these factors are influenced by the values and beliefs of the faith in question, but in many cases there will be an emphasis on collective care for the weak and social justice.

Other groups in society,[147] of course, may wish to put forward other factors for citizens to consider, for example, in relation to economic and business considerations, but this is not at odds with the role played by faith groups; it is simply another form of heat to contribute to the social huddle. We would like to emphasise that we are not suggesting that religious groups are the only groups that encourage participation and provide information, or that the information flowing from faith groups is always both objective and benign. However, it is the case that many religious groups do actively encourage their members to take a responsible part in the political process and that this supports parliamentary sovereignty by bolstering perceptions of the democratic system and its intrinsic value. Furthermore, the special and liminal position of the national Churches means that they are uniquely placed to take a leading role in this contribution.

144 The Movement for Reform Judaism, 'News, A Jewish Guide to Voting' (2 Apr 2015), http://www.reformjudaism.org.uk/rabbi-dr-jonathan-romain-of-maidenhead-synagogue.

145 Ibid: 'Benefits – what changes to the benefits system should be made to ensure those truly in need receive adequate provision? Carers – how should those caring at home for the sick, disabled or elderly be assisted? Disability – what support should be given to the needs of disabled people? Homelessness – what policies will remedy the on-going problem of homelessness? Personal Debt – what controls should be introduced to prevent people from falling into serious personal debt?' Poverty – what is the best way of alleviating the plight of those living in poverty? Racism – what measures can eradicate the various types of prejudice and discrimination in society?'

146 The Church of England, House of Bishops, 'Pastoral Letter', n. 116 above.

147 For instance, at the end of 2014 the Confederation of British Industry (CBI) released a statement looking ahead to the new year, focusing on issues in the upcoming election: CBI, 'Looking Ahead to 2015' (19 Dec 2014), http://www.cbi.org.uk/news/looking-ahead-to-2015.

If these bodies were closely tied to executive and legislative power as was the case in former times, their encouragement and endorsement would carry less weight. It would be the equivalent of a company director assuring the public that its products are safe and of high quality. However, if the Churches had no official place in public life, they would be simply other voices crying in the wilderness. They would have less of a platform, and there would be less perception that the bishops were speaking from an informed and authoritative position. Being both, within and without the system, gives national Churches a particular ability to speak.

5.5.2 Faith groups and the implementation of legislation

The UK Parliament could in theory pass a statute declaring that Canada is part of United Kingdom. This would not alone make that a political or practical reality. It is true that any statute can be made more than words on a page only if there is a willingness on the part of those on the ground to co-operate in its implementation.

As we saw in Chapter 4, both the national Churches and other major faith groups work towards upholding the rule of law as a matter of principle. For this reason alone, they are willing to assist in the application of legislation which affects them and their membership, but their wider commitment towards social engagement means that they frequently and naturally play a role in co-operating with public authorities in the outworking of law and policy. For example, it is possible for Parliament to pass legislation aimed at protecting vulnerable people, such as the Children Act 1989 and the Protection from Harassment Act 1997, but this kind of legislation cannot function effectively without co-operation from society as a whole. Statutory authorities alone can neither make all individuals aware of their rights, nor detect those who might be too vulnerable or incapacitated to seek help.

In fact, organisations like faith groups can play a vital role in maximising the effectiveness of legislation, and allowing parliamentary sovereignty to transcend purely theoretical legislative supremacy. For example, the Church of England has adopted guidelines on dealing appropriately with the signs and disclosure of domestic abuse.[148] Equally, organisations like the Muslim Women's Network UK have adopted or participated in campaigns relating to domestic violence, and offer help and advice.[149]

At first sight, these initiatives might seem very laudable, but are not obviously related to parliamentary sovereignty. However, there is a very real relationship, because without work like this on the ground the legislation which Parliament has passed to try to deter and punish the perpetrators of abuse and to assist their victims would remain largely aspirational. There is a limit to what police, social

148 The Church of England, *Responding to Domestic Abuse: Guidelines for Those with Pastoral Responsibility* (Church House Publishing: London) 2006.

149 Muslim Women's Network UK, 'Campaigns', http://www.mwnuk.co.uk/campaigns.php.

workers and other public servants can achieve, and the laws on domestic violence, in common with the remaining legal framework, can function effectively only through collective participation.

Once again, we are not claiming that faith groups are the only organisations engaged in this kind of work. Nevertheless, it is unquestionable that parliamentary sovereignty, or the expressed collective will of the people, can be made real only through social co-operation. The commitment which faith groups in general have towards the rule of law, as well as social engagement, work together in helping to make parliamentary sovereignty a substantive, rather than a purely legislative concept. It is valuable heat in the shared penguin huddle.

5.6 Conclusions

The following points may be drawn from the foregoing discussion:

1 Parliamentary sovereignty as a principle remains a key facet of the United Kingdom Constitution, although there is an ongoing debate as to the meaning and boundaries of the concept in a twenty-first-century context. Nevertheless, at the heart of all of the posited understandings is the idea that the democratically elected legislature should be the primary agent in the creation and acceptance of legal rules.

2 Furthermore, the power exercised by Parliament can be made real only through the collective collaboration of society as a whole. Without this co-operative endeavour, this constitutional principle would remain an empty shell. Just as penguins can survive only by huddling and sharing heat, and there is a mutual dependency between the individual bird and the group, so parliamentary sovereignty can truly function only through widespread societal acceptance and participation.

3 The liminal position of the established (and quasi-established) Churches places them in a unique position to facilitate this participation, and their capacity to do this provides a template for other faith groups to engage in a similar role.

4 Crucially, the legal framework provides us with a range of interesting examples of how both establishment and the favourable legal treatment of religion enhance the principle of parliamentary supremacy.

Chapter 5 appended interview material

Dr David Perfect

Is living in a Parliamentary democracy a good thing in terms of your faith? Is there another system which you would prefer?

I think that legacy is important in the sense that there is this climate of tolerance, linked to the fact that we have a Parliamentary system, but also linked to the fact that religious tolerance has evolved over time, I think that's significant as well . . . The historical element, of that . . . Of course, as a historian I would say that!

Mona Bayoumi

Is living in a democracy positive? Does it make it easier for you to live in accordance with your faith?

Living in a democracy makes it 100% easier for me to live in accordance with my Muslim faith.

Patricia Travis

Is living in a democracy a positive thing?

I don't follow politics. I don't listen to the Government. They are all the same.

Baroness Elizabeth Butler-Sloss

Do your beliefs mean that you feel that you have a duty to vote?

I feel very strongly about voting. I wouldn't go as far as Australia, but I believe the House of Bishops has written a very interesting letter, 'Who is my Neighbour?', and I have read it today because I have been asked to speak on a debate about this and they are strongly of the opinion that people have a personal responsibility to vote and they are making a point, in that pastoral letter, that very depressing figures of people who don't vote can be identified in many elections. And we have that right.

Jim Sutcliffe

Do you feel that you have a personal duty to vote?

Yes, and it makes me bloody angry when people don't vote. A lot of people have worked hard and people have lost lives for me to have my vote.

Professor Grace Davie

Do you feel that you have a duty to vote?

Yes, I feel I have a personal responsibility to vote, because I have a commitment to the society in which I live. I often think of the suffragettes and what women went through to get the vote, which is one reason why I feel strongly about it.

Grace Hatley

Do you feel that you have a duty to vote?

I have never ever voted, because I have always felt I didn't have much to contribute, but I have come to realise it should be a much bigger deal in schools. I have never been hugely interested in politics, but I realise this is a very naïve thing to say, as it affects your whole life. So, I am becoming aware of the voting system and we need to do more research. Some of my friends have gone to the polling station, spoiling the vote, just to make a point . . . Have they really contributed? I don't know!

Dr Myriam Hunter-Henin

Given that we live in a democracy, does your Catholicism mean that you feel that you have a personal responsibility to vote?

I clearly feel I have a personal responsibility to vote. Whether it is because I am a Catholic or not, I am not sure . . . all the influences I have had in my childhood have pushed me to feel responsible for voting. Some of those influences were not Catholic. Again, I am a Catholic, but I don't want to explain every action of my life in light of my faith. So, I think for me it is broader than being a Catholic, and I hope many non-Catholics would also want to vote.

Dr Elizabeth Healey

Do you feel that you have a duty to vote?

Yes, I do have a duty and personal responsibility to vote, but that is not as a result of being a Catholic, but because I am a citizen. Some people feel this duty very strongly. Let me give you an example. Earlier this year my brother-in-law and sister both had terminal cancer and were expected to die long before the general election. However they didn't die and, despite being very ill and confined to bed, my brother-in-law suddenly decided on election day that he was going to vote. So he got out of bed, put on a suit, roused my sister (who was less enthusiastic) and together they walked to the polling station and cast their votes. He died shortly after. It seems that he must have had a very strong duty to decide to vote despite being so ill. When my sister told me I found it quite moving, but at the same time somewhat crazy!

Professor Ronald Hutton

Does Paganism impose a personal responsibility to vote?

I think that the voting behaviour of Pagans reflects that of the electorate as a whole; some are more politicised than others. One should not forget that democracies can be persecuting societies and within my lifetime, homosexuals and people of a different colour were subjected to quite serious persecution. I am glad that public opinion has changed. But since that public opinion governs a democracy, it is entirely dependent on how liberal that opinion may be.

The Rev'd Dr Will Adam

Do your personal beliefs mean that you feel that you have a duty to vote? If so, why?

I do believe that I have a duty to vote; I'm not particularly sure whether that stems from a religious perspective. It would have to be two steps away. The Christian imperative to look after the vulnerable would mean that voting is an opportunity to influence society in a way which does that. So voting is a way of exercising one's Christian duty of care for society and the environment etc.

Frank Cranmer

Do your beliefs mean that you feel that you have a duty to vote?

It is a difficult one, because I think I am going to write 'none of the above' on the ballot paper [. . .] Out of the three main parties, I despair of all of them; and UKIP is full of mad people.

Fr William Pearsall

Does your Catholicism mean that you feel that you have a duty to vote?

Yes, I do. I am careful not to use my position in the church to influence the vote, but if you don't vote in a democracy then you are voting for some other form of government.

Ruth Jenkins

Do you believe that you have a duty to vote?

[. . .] I think people have the moral obligation to vote . . . so, why shouldn't it also be a legal duty? It is not acceptable that when we have an election and it rains, fewer people vote . . . Is that fair? What would the people who didn't vote have said had they voted?

Stephen Castle

Should Parliament have the final say in making and changing law? Would you like to see a judiciary empowered to strike down legislation?

I wouldn't like to see an empowerment of the judiciary in the UK in that sense. The British system works well in this respect. Essentially the balance is right. Parliament legislates and courts decide case by case. Without a codified Constitution, I don't see how the judiciary should be given those powers and it would only become an issue with a written Constitution.

Sir Mark Hedley DL

Should Parliament have the final say in making and changing law? Would you like to see an empowerment of the judiciary in striking down legislation?

The judiciary unanimously embraces parliamentary supremacy in principle, but they have put down at least three markers as to whether they could challenge it. The first was over the refusal to make decisions about the right to assisted dying . . . that is a matter for Parliament, but they added that if Parliament didn't address it, the judges might . . . I think the second one was when Parliament was threatening to withdraw the right to judicial review . . . the third, of course, is section 3 of the HRA, where there is no doubt that although lip service is paid to parliamentary supremacy, section 3 has been used from time to time to interpret statutes manifestly at variance with what Parliament probably intended . . . I got involved in one where we dealt with reverse standards of proof in terrorist proceedings, and it was obvious to us as a Court of Appeal that Parliament had intended to reverse burdens of proof, and the House of Lords in effect said 'Well, grammatically we understand that, but we are not having that', and they used section 3 in a remarkable way. Therefore, there are those three challenges around, but within that I don't detect amongst judges any 'hunger' to be able to strike down legislation.

Kimberley Long

Should Parliament have the final say in making or changing law, would you like to see the judiciary having greater power?

I think I would have a hesitation; the judiciary is like 95% private school boys, and they seem to be from the same pool of people as the cabinet.

The Most Reverend Professor Rowan Williams

Do you think that an understanding of democracy as the will of the majority of the people is problematic for minority groups? Do you think that parliamentary democracy is inclusive of all groups and citizens in society, or is it more difficult for some people to participate?

There are barriers to participation that are social and educational, and there are attitudes of both apathy and suspicion. Turnouts at elections continue to drop. People don't have much confidence in the process. They feel the parliamentary process is very remote from them, and they increasingly don't want to get involved. This is something which you hear in public, not just in the bar, in the pub. You hear it everywhere. Russell Brand is a well-known public example. So I am a bit concerned that there is a deficit in the sense of ownership of the parliamentary process; and the party system seems at the moment rather stuck. I don't think it is working very well. So this is not the healthiest of times for our system.

Ruth Jenkins

Is a majoritarian understanding of democracy a problem for minorities? Are there barriers for some groups in participating in our democracy?

[. . .] We have so many migrants now . . . I don't think there is anything wrong with that. If we are human beings we have to help disadvantaged people, who were persecuted in their country. How could we live with the thought that we didn't really help those people, that we didn't allow them to come in? However, I don't think that many people realise that or think like that . . .

Thomas Haines

Is majoritarian democracy a problem for minorities? Are there some groups in society who find it easier than others to participate?

[. . .] There are lots of people like that. The language which is used in the legal system is intimidating and it is designed to attract only a very limited number of people, whilst people like me, who don't come from an affluent background . . . the legal terminology is intimidating and off-putting. Costs are also daunting. The system is certainly designed for the elite.

Sam Dick

Is a majoritarian understanding of democracy problematic for minority groups? Are there barriers to participation for some people?

A notion of democracy as the will of the majority of the people is problematic. Twenty-five years ago the Government introduced section 28, which outlawed the promotion of homosexuality by local authorities. It affected a large minority, but a minority at the end of the day.

Una Mary Parker

Is a majoritarian understanding of democracy a problem for minorities? Are there barriers to participation for some groups in our society?

[. . .] I think everyone can participate in the political system if they have the talent and if they have ideas of what the majority wants.

Baroness Kathleen Richardson

Does the understanding of democracy as the will of the majority create problems for minorities? Are there barriers to participation?

There is apathy in this society because people feel they are a long way from it. What disturbs me as much is that people don't even get involved in decisions which affect themselves.

Ioannis Stylianou

Do you think that some groups find it harder than others to participate in our democracy?

I think in British society everyone is on an equal footing.

Shaina Huleatt

Do you think an understanding of democracy as the will of the majority of the people is a problem for minority groups? Do you think that Parliamentary democracy is inclusive of all groups and citizens in society, or is it difficult for some people to participate? If so, what are the barriers?

[. . .] Minority groups which, for any reason (including financial and cultural), cannot muster significant political power face misunderstanding by majority groups that is difficult to overcome and ultimately affects political decision making. A recent example is the 'Trojan Horse' fuss about faith schools, which was misreported by the media and poorly handled by politicians.

Ian Scott

Is Parliamentary democracy sufficiently inclusive of all groups here in Scotland?

I think that in terms of the people who have ended up being representatives, in the most recent SNP intake of MPs, seven or eight of the 56 are LGBT, which makes it the gayest Parliament in the world. Certainly, I'd imagine that people who are not straight, white men would find it easier to notice when things are not in balance, usually in their particular direction. I think that at the moment things are improving in terms of accessibility and inclusivity generally.

Professor Sheila McLean

Is a majoritarian democracy a problem for minorities? Are there barriers to participation for some groups in our society?

I am not a majoritarian. I don't think that just because the majority of the population think that something is a good idea, that you must necessarily do it. If you ask British people whether they would like to have death penalty back, that is the classical example, in which you cannot simply be led by the wishes of the majority. In fact, the majority can be very ill-informed or be very prejudiced.

Imam Irfan Chishti MBE

Would you say that an understanding of democracy as the will of the majority is problematic for minority groups? Is it more difficult for some people to participate?

Ten years ago, with all the scandals of MPs' expenses and other issues, as a nation we started to mistrust our politicians. So, if we say that as Muslims we need more representatives, the whole system has not given confidence to the electorate to come forward and do more. I have spoken with passionate Muslims about this. We need to do more; what can we do about some more important social issues? Some of the responses which young people hear online . . . Syria is an important example at the moment. Young people hear about atrocities; they then just want to jump on a plane, join the battle and physically do 'their bit'. But what they don't realise is that the reality of life out there is very, very different. Death is a real proposition . . . So, what have they then achieved? Nothing, other than their understanding of martyrdom, which from a true Islamic theological perspective, if that war has not been legislated and properly constituted, it is a wasteful death. We try to encourage people to engage and work with the system. That has been my attitude throughout my life. We have to try to encourage people to change things. My father came in the '70s, as I said . . . my sister in law and my own wife . . . they all come from very remote parts of Pakistan, and they know, if I may use the expression, what proper corrupt politicians are like and people can't really make any sort of impact, whereas here we see some solid examples where people have stood up, raised their voices and changes have taken place.

Zerbanoo Gifford

Does your understanding of democracy as the will of the majority present problems for minority groups in society? And do you think our democracy is inclusive of all groups and citizens, or is it in practice here difficult for some people in our society to participate?

And I used to say, I used to get very upset when I was campaigning to be told that I wasn't from the area, even though my children were born in the area, I lived my life in the area . . . . because I was not born in England I found it very unpleasant and there was nothing you could do.

But then, you know foreigners are foreigners forever. There was a letter in the local press in Harrow about how I should go home and fight elections in my own country. And I just thought that that was hitting below the belt, that wasn't proper. I went and saw the editor. I told the editor that the racist letter he printed was objectionable. Firstly I reasoned with him and said it wasn't right. I was a Harrow councillor and I had been elected with a landslide and he'd seen the work that I did. He said that he admired what I did, but there was a feeling among the public that people like me should not be standing for Parliament and that we were foreigners. I told him that it is irresponsible to print letters from people who don't exist, a Mr Smith of some street in Harrow that didn't exist. He just wouldn't listen to me, so I said fine, the next time you print a letter like this, I shall make sure that every newsagent, they were all Guajarati Asians, nobody would sell his newspaper. I told him in no uncertain terms, you leave that to me. I said the newsagents make 5p profit per newspaper they sell, I will make sure they stop selling your paper. Never again did the editor print another racist article because he knew I was serious. So, I was able to use the power of a minority because I knew they controlled sales. I reasoned with the editor, but he wouldn't listen to my reasoning. He was a man that should have understood that all communities should take part in political life. He knew the importance of the work that I was doing, and the need to involve more people who were marginalised in those days.

Fr Paul Stonham

What is your view of establishment?

I'm not bothered by it at all. I do wish, as it is the established Church that the state would provide for the maintenance of the important historic buildings that the C of E has to care for. If you think of any European country, this happens.

Rev John Chalmers QHC

If the Church of Scotland is established, would you like to see it represented in Parliament in the same way as the other established church?

Again, in my Liberal Democratic way of seeing the world, I'd say and what about the rest? And you know ideally I'd like to see some sort of second chamber that was representative of different areas of expertise and different groups across the country. Not just a place where you recycled old politicians . . . that know the ropes.

Rev David Robertson

I am interested in the last point you made . . . could you expand on your views on establishment?

I think what we have in Scotland now is a relic from the past, if you like. It is a bit like an old suit that is hanging in a wardrobe, but in terms of day-to-day use is not used. I think we have the relics of a civic religion in Scotland. We don't even have prayers in the Scottish Parliament. We have time for reflection, which includes different people. You have a certain civil recognition, but that is more associated with Westminster in London than with Scotland.

The Church of Scotland is a Church by law established, but I think it is so weak that it is almost irrelevant.

Given all the challenges posed by secularism which you have identified, would a stronger form of establishment be the solution?

Not now. It is too late for that. You could argue, and I would be prepared to argue, from an ideological point of view in an ideal Scotland, that there should be a recognition of the Christian religion as the religion of the country. I would be happy with that. I would love to see that indeed. But I think that at the moment that would be largely farcical because most people don't have a clue what Christianity is. So, I would like to see a renewal of the Church before anything like that happens. My concern at the moment is that a secular state without a Christian ethos would be belligerent against us. I have no objection to a secular state as long as it has a Christian ethos.

The Most Reverend Professor Rowan Williams

Do you think that the presence of bishops in the House of Lords is defensible?

[. . .] I think there is real truth in the idea that the Church of England can sometimes be at the service of voicing the concerns both of other religions and of the voiceless of our society. Certainly, when I was Archbishop, other religious communities would treat me and my colleagues as people who could speak on their behalf. We would be lobbying together on many occasions. There is also a factor that I pointed out in discussion a while ago: some parts of the country would be underrepresented in the Lords if the bishops were not there. You wouldn't have many peers coming from Cambria or Cornwall. Quite often, it happens that the bishop of Truro or Carlisle would be the one speaking on behalf of the people of their regions. In one instance, I remember vividly a parliamentary debate affecting the city of Manchester (a regulatory proposal about super-casinos), and at that point a number of bishops got up to speak for the communities they knew in the city of Manchester and successfully resisted a proposal that they thought would be damaging for those communities. So it can happen.

Professor Sir John Sulston

How do you feel about Church of England bishops in the House of Lords?

I think that they should not be there as of right. I think that faith should not be a criterion for membership. I think that there should be people of all faiths and no faith in the House of Lords, but faith should not be a criterion for selecting them.

Rabbi Lord Jonathan Sacks

What do you think about the presence of Church of England bishops in the House of Lords?

[. . .] I testified there suggesting that other religious traditions should have a voice but not a vote, that representatives should be chosen *ad hominem* not *ex officio* [. . .] but the existence of 26 Lords Spiritual reflected an historical legacy which has ongoing significance. For instance, an event like a memorial service for the victims of 9/11 or the tsunami, these things are usually in St Paul's or Westminster Abbey. They are Church of England services, but representatives from other Christian denominations take part and representatives from other faiths are seated in a place of honour at those services. That seems to be an admirable British way of doing things. Every country works its own way of doing things. There isn't one way, every country finds its way through the topography. The fact that you will have a service at St Paul' s, presided over by the Archbishop of Canterbury, at which all of the major faiths are there in a place of honour, that seems to be an admirable way of doing things. I do not think there is any way to end the presence of the Lords Spiritual, who are involved in very good and important work.

Lord Richard Harries

What is your opinion of the Lords Spiritual?

[. . .] There are prayers every day in the House of Lords taken by bishops. They are not here to represent the interests of the Church of England. They are here in some sense to represent the concerns of the diocese where they are, not just church-going members, but the diocese as a whole. Sometimes the bishop might have been the only person from a particular part of the country in the House of Lords and he will bring into the debates concerns which might arise over agriculture, or might take some concerns from some of the Muslims in the diocese. The bishop can be the eyes and ears of the diocese and convey what is happening, so in that wider sense they represent an area in the Church of England.

The Rt Rev'd Tim Thornton

In your own experience, are you there to speak on behalf of citizens other than Anglicans?

Yes, I am there to speak out. Full stop. I speak about general matters concerning Cornwall, which is one of the most deprived areas of the country, unknown to many people. I have a huge responsibility to speak out for Cornwall, but I have spoken out on a wide range of issues; that is what I should be doing.

Professor Imre Leader

What do you think of Church of England bishops being given a place as of right in the House of Lords?

It works. If I had the impression that the evil bishops spent their time trying to influence government policy and block things which they shouldn't be blocking, then I wouldn't like it, but that hasn't happened. So, it's fine.

Joaquín Acedo

What do you think of the presence of Church of England bishops in the British Parliament?

Religion should not be within the political sphere; its place is outside. Religion should be in one arena and politics in another. As I have said to you before, you can have diverse ideas about religion within one political party. Politicians should focus on other questions. I believe that religion is something very personal and should never be taken into Parliament.

Baroness Elizabeth Butler-Sloss

How do you feel about bishops in the House of Lords?

I very strongly support the bishops in the Upper House for two reasons: (1) As long as we have an established Church, Lords Spiritual must be there. You would have to make a very important constitutional change to get rid of them; (2) They represent all groups in their dioceses. The bishop of Leicester, for instance, has a very diverse population in his dioceses and he told the House years ago that he is actually approached by Muslim groups who would ask him if he would speak for them in the Lords. And let's bear in mind what the Queen stated in Lambeth Palace in 2012 when the nine main religions met in Lambeth Palace, and the Queen said that the role of the Church of England was not just to serve the CofE, but be the umbrella for all other religions in the UK. That is very well shown in the work that the bishops do, and increasingly bishops are being encouraged to sit in select committees.

Dominic Grieve QC MP

What is your view of the Lords Spiritual and representatives from other faith groups?

I think that my answer to this is 'if it ain't broke, don't fix it'. I think that the 26 bishops in the House of Lords play a very important role in the House of Lords in representing wider faith viewpoints in the national conversation which takes place in Parliament. I've yet to come across a Muslim who is unhappy about there being bishops in the House of Lords. There have been efforts to appoint representatives from other groups . . . ex-chief rabbis, the Roman Catholics don't want to do it as a matter of policy, I respect that. There are ex-senior Methodists. There are an increasing number of Muslims with a faith interest. I'm very keen on that; I think we should continue with it. But do I want to get rid of the bishops? No, I see no need to for it at all.

Carole Emmerson

How do you feel about bishops in the House of Lords?

I do think we are a traditional Christian country. So, although we are multi-faith, Christianity is part of our heritage and I don't have a problem with the bishops in the House of Lords, but I assume there are members of the Lords who do have other faiths, although they may not be there in their faith capacity . . . maybe it would be good to appoint representatives of other religious bodies, but the question would be how to choose them.

Rabbi Reuven Silverman

What do you think about the presence of bishops in the House of Lords?

I don't think the CofE represent all Christians, however much they want to. I think you would get the same question from other Christians. I am interested in the statement that has been made that they may represent the voiceless of our society because the bishops I know really do, and that includes Rowan Williams and the Bishop of Manchester and others. They are very sensitive people and that is a positive thing, but then you don't need bishops to represent the voiceless, as you have former members of the House of Commons who were active in their own constituencies and actually they are now much freer [. . .] It is now common for members of the House of Lords to stand up and speak from Jewish ethical principles. There is the former Chief Rabbi, Lord Jonathan Sacks, and my own colleague, Reform Rabbi, Baroness Julia Neuberger. Our voice is very much represented in the House of Lords.

Professor Dame Jocelyn Bell Burnell

How do you feel about the presence of bishops in the House of Lords as of right?

[. . .] I think bishops of the CofE can speak on behalf of all people of faith, but because they wear their Anglican robes, maybe that breadth is not so visible.

Sam Dick

How do you feel about bishops in the House of Lords as of right?

I don't have a particular strong view about bishops in the House of Lords. I always mistrust anyone in Parliament who claims to speak on behalf of a faith, or cite the views of a faith because a religious leader has said something, because there is such a plurality of views within each denomination [. . .]

I don't have strong views about the bishops. It is the current situation and it should be understood in the wider context of an unelected second chamber. The fact that we have religious leaders of a particular faith in a wholly unelected chamber is just one more strange aspect of a strange institution.

Professor Norman Doe

How do you feel about the presence of bishops in the House of Lords?

My feelings are that it is odd, but I understand it historically. The question is whether the bishops adequately discharge their functions as members of a second chamber. So, we must look at the evidence. What do they do? Do they contribute? How? Do they have a critical attitude themselves about what their position is? I think the gathering of all that evidence and a solid debate about it is needed, and I can't see that has happened, but it should.

Professor John Healey

How do you feel about the presence of bishops in the House of Lords? Can they speak on behalf of other religious communities?

[. . .] essentially I am happy for them to speak for all Christians. I think it is awkward that they put themselves forward to some extent to speak also for Jews and Muslims, who are not represented in the same way. They can't really plausibly do that. They can probably talk vaguely in favour of faith communities, but they cannot really defend particular concerns of the Muslim and Jewish communities.

The Rt Rev'd James Jones

Do bishops speak on behalf of all people of faith?

Yes, we are not there just to speak on behalf of the CofE. We are pastors for all communities. This comes back to the idea of the kingdom of God. If this is the world, and not just the Church . . . well, let me give you an example. If someone calls the vicarage, the vicar will never ask the person whether he/she comes to the church . . . the vicar will ask where the person lives, and if the person lives in the parish, he will be there to help you.

The Most Reverend Peter Smith

What do you think of the Lords Spiritual? The claim by Church of England bishops that they speak on behalf of all people of faith?

The Church of England claims to be an all-enveloping church, whether you want it or not we speak for you; I've never agreed with that. The Church of England is by law the established church; personally I wouldn't want an established Church and you have to separate Church and state. It works in the US.

Dr Catharine Morgan

How do you feel about bishops in the House of Lords?

I don't feel necessarily comfortable with religious voices in Parliament . . . I feel it is probably appropriate to have some religious representatives there, but I don't think they should be there just because they are bishops . . . that doesn't make any sense to me.

The Rev'd Professor Thomas Watkin

What do you think about the presence of Lords Spiritual in the House of Lords?

[. . .] The bishops have as much right to be there as anyone else. The bishops are appointed after a process governed by ecclesiastical measure. The other members of the Lords are not so appointed. The bishops are chosen more carefully than politically appointed life peers, so I wouldn't want to look at their role apart from the wider picture.

Joanna Griffiths

How do you feel about bishops in the House of Lords?

I think bishops of the CofE should remain in the Upper House, because they are there on merit. I think their contribution is very valuable indeed. I think they speak for the voiceless of our society and they must remain in Parliament, but we should also have voices from other religions.

Keith Porteous Wood

What is your view of the Lords Spiritual?

I don't think that bishops should be banned from the revising Chamber as such. The revising Chamber should be taking people on their merits and on some occasions that might include bishops. So the bishops should earn their seats because of any particular expertise they have (other than theological) that will be useful in the lawmaking process. They should not be in it simply because they are bishops, regardless of their suitability. The Westminster Parliament is the only one in the world to have bishops sitting as of right. There are 26 of them – middle class, largely male and largely white, only from English dioceses of a Church that only 2–3% of the population attends on a normal Sunday. The 'right' for them to sit originated in the Church's massive land holdings and is no longer relevant.

It is alarming that those bishops have immense power from their position. Being in the Lords gives bishops access to ministers on a day-by-day basis; they are able to hold ministers to account in a way no one outside Parliament can. It is telling that in the Chamber itself, even now, if a bishop stands up, anyone speaking sits down and allows the bishop to speak. No one else enjoys such primacy.

Kimberley Long

What do you think of the Lords Spiritual? Do they speak on behalf of all faiths?

You can't speak on behalf of all Christians, never mind other faiths. The ways in which different Christians come up with their own decisions are sacred for them; you have to respect that and their processes. Christians have wildly different views on things, for example Quakers and the Free Church of Scotland! To claim to speak for everyone is ludicrous!

Janette Wilson

How do you feel about the presence of Church of England bishops in Westminster?

[. . .] I think I would rather the bishops should be there than that there should be no religious representation. However, I think that it does now in the twenty-first century seem extremely unbalanced that you do have all these Lords Spiritual and they're all from the Church of England. I think they do speak on behalf of all people of faith . . . and I think that's why I say I'd rather them be there.

Joe Ahearne

Do you think that it is appropriate to have Church of England bishops in the House of Lords?

It is fantastically inappropriate.

Jessica Morden MP

Do you consider it problematic that we have an unelected House of Lords?

[. . .] I think they are an anomaly, but they do good work.

Frank Cranmer

Does it concern you that the House of Lords is unelected?

I worked 36 years as a Clerk of the Commons. So, I am bound to have prejudices. You won't find a Clerk of the Commons who is impartial about the Upper House! It is not in our nature. I think that having an unelected second Chamber, with about 800 members is ridiculous. I would abolish it and would start again.

Keith Porteous Wood

Do you think it is problematic that members of the House of Lords are not elected?

The intuitive answer is that it is a problem, but the practical answer is the opposite. I have spent a lot of time in the House of Lords and I think our lawmaking is better because of the Lords. Most of the members are very experienced and have more time to improve the laws made by the House of Commons, which is a very valid and important role in quality assurance. I also worry that there is an unwillingness of elected parliamentarians to deal with sensitive issues. For example, there is a growing unofficial use of Sharia law in this country. The House of Commons will not deal with this because Members are concerned about losing their seats, especially in constituencies with large percentages of Muslims who may be uncomfortable about looking at these issues in a critical, analytical way.

And, finally, I find that the House of Lords regards itself with some justification as being the guardian of people's human rights and the protector of the disadvantaged. For example, they're bringing in an assisted dying bill which 80% of the population want, but the elected Chamber has never decided to take on. The democratic Chamber isn't touching issues like that, and counter-intuitively the House of Lords says that 'the people's will is not being listened to, let's start the bill here'.

Professor David Feldman

Do you find it problematic that members of the House of Lords have some role in the lawmaking process, even though they are not elected?

No, I don't find that problematic. There are different forms of what is sometimes called legitimacy. The House of Commons has elected members, and their legitimacy basically comes from the way in which they get there. It doesn't really depend on what they do while they're there, or what they produce, although there may be political implications later. The House of Lords has a representative role in a different way. It reflects a wide range of interests and fields of activity, and they by and large work extremely well. And I think that their legitimacy comes from the quality of the work which they do, the reports and outcomes which they produce. So it's a different sort of legitimacy, and I think that it is good that we have a Chamber where people are actually pretty good at what they do.

Lucy Gorman

Does it concern you that the House of Lords is unelected?

The House of Lords is probably an old boys' club. I think if the House of Lords were elected, it would probably look very different.

Baroness Haleh Afshar

Does it concern you that members of the House of Lords are not elected?

I think that it is fortunate for many of us – minorities, people who don't conform to the wider norms of society, however defined – who would be highly unlikely to stand and less likely to be elected.

Dr Martin Clarke

Is it a problem that members of the House of Lords are not elected?

Yes, I think it probably is. I don't have a solution. But it does trouble me that there are vast numbers of members of the House of Lords, some of whom don't make a great contribution. How to solve it I don't know; you wouldn't want a system where there was potential for conflict between the Commons and the Lords because both were elected.

Philip Bird

Would you say that public authorities try to respect the will of Parliament as expressed in legislation?

In principle, yes, but it's not very joined-up sometimes, and policies are nowadays invented and then discarded at such speed that it is very difficult to implement them. Government is a slow process. My LA was happy to give the go-ahead to a supermarket in the village which would involve lots of lorry journeys through the narrow High Street and an awful lot of food miles. The supermarket has put small independent shop-owners out of business; and yet someone else from some other bit of government will say that they like small businesses. Where is the plan?

Alison Steadman

What is your perception of public authorities, do they try to respect the voice of Parliament?

I can't think of them ignoring Parliament. Again, nothing is perfect, all of these things as human beings and a nation we have to keep checking. We can't just assume because it is a public authority or the police that it is all fine; we have to listen to people and their grievances. Look at the whole Hillsborough thing that has taken far too long to address and put right. Hopefully that will be an example to everyone. The whole thing of the NHS and whistle-blowers – people should be without fear of losing their jobs in saying that things aren't right.

6 Checks and balances, separation of powers and the religious character of the Constitution and the wider legal framework

6.1 Introduction: the octopus and the coconut shell: same goal, but different tactics

Octopuses are part of a family known, somewhat unflatteringly, as cephalopods. The term comes from the Greek meaning 'head foot', and although somewhat blunt, it does accurately describe the way in which most of their organs are kept within the central sack of their body. Long ago, their ancestors had shells to keep their soft and delicate bodies safe, but around 65 million years ago, they lost this protective armour.[1]

This did not mean, however, that they were doomed to have a future as easy pickings for hungry penguins and other predators. Losing their heavy shell was an evolutionary perk in terms of manoeuvrability, and they found other ways to keep their vulnerable parts secure. Modern octopuses often live in dens, and have even been observed scuttling onto the shore to harvest coconut shells to wear.[2]

They also have an array of other defence techniques: they can change shape, colour and even texture; they have limbs which can be sacrificed, move independently and even grow back; they are venomous, and they squirt ink. Added to which, they are highly intelligent, having been known to escape from domestic aquaria on many occasions. In the wild, they have been reported to break into fishermen's crab traps, gobble all of the crabs in there and scoot off without leaving so much as a thank you note.[3] The octopus is in no way missing its shell. Yet, octopuses are still very much focused on the *goal* behind the shell: the imperative to protect their soft bodies remains. The need is unchanged; it is just that the animal has adapted to find a very different method of meeting it.

Similarly, as we saw in the first chapter, an important role of the Church in historic times was to act as a break on royal power. It helped to ensure that the

1 J. Mather, R. Anderson and J. Wood, *Octopus: The Ocean's Most Intelligent Invertebrate, A Natural History* (Timber Press: London) 2010, 67.

2 Octopuses can survive for short periods out of water, and can 'walk' between rock pools using their tentacles as legs. For some amazing footage of an octopus walking underwater in a similar manner, see the following post by Museums Victoria, 'Coconut-Carrying Octopus', *YouTube*, https://www.youtube.com/watch?v=1DoWdHOtlrk.

3 Mather, Anderson and Wood, n. 1 above, 1.

Crown was not an unchallenged or tyrannical source of authority, and assisted in keeping the action of monarchs within their proper bounds. However, with the Reformations, this facility was lost. The break with Rome meant that there was no longer the connection with a higher appellate authority outside the jurisdiction, and the remit of the Church within the state was clearly limited. In Scotland, the separate spheres of the spiritual and the temporal were emphasised, while in England the Church was effectively subjugated to the power of the Crown.

Having lost the Church as a brake on secular power, were the states on both sides of the English/Scottish border left naked and helpless in the face of its abuse? The answer to this is clearly in the negative: like the octopus, the organism of the state still has to address the same basic need, and has found a variety of alternative means of achieving this end. Furthermore, just because the Churches no longer play the part which they formerly did in achieving this end, it does not mean that they have no contribution to make. As we shall see, the current legal framework and Constitution enable the Churches, alongside other religions, to further this collective objective.

6.2 What do checks and balances and separation of powers mean in the context of the UK Constitution and the wider legal framework?

A common tactic which many modern national constitutions deploy against the misuse of power is the concept of the separation of powers. In simple terms, the various powers of the state (executive, legislative and judicial) are parcelled out so that they are exercised by different bodies and individuals, thus preventing an unhealthy concentration of power in any one place.[4] All holders of power have limited capacity to act without the co-operation of the others.

However, the degree of separation and limitation varies between different state models. Just as there is no universally accepted understanding of the rule of law, there exists a multiplicity of conceptions of separation of powers. Furthermore, in the British context there is, once again, the added layer of complexity, which arises from the evolved, rather than the devised nature of the Constitution. As we saw over the course of Chapters 1 and 2, the balance and concentration of power have emerged organically from centuries of conflict and negotiation between the various players within the system, and not surprisingly the outcome is rather different from that of devised constitutions, where checks and balances on power have been consciously constructed and laid out.

There are even distinguished commentators, such as Marshall, who go so far as to deny the very existence of the doctrine of separation of powers in the British context: 'It may be counted as little more than a jumbled portmanteau of arguments for policies which ought to be supported or rejected on other grounds'.[5]

4 R. Masterman, *The Separation of Powers in the Contemporary Constitution: Judicial Competence and Independence in the United Kingdom* (Cambridge University Press: Cambridge) 2011, 11.

5 G. Marshall, *Constitutional Theory* (Clarendon: Oxford) 1971, 124.

Other voices, such as De Smith,[6] have expressed similar opinions. However, it is beyond doubt that authors like Marshall and De Smith went to the trouble of denying the existence of the principle only because others were equally convinced of its presence and potency. The reality of the doctrine has been affirmed by senior judges such as Lord Diplock[7] and Lord Templeman,[8] and it should also be observed that the notable academic rejections of the separation of powers within the United Kingdom, cited above, both date from the 1970s. As we shall see, the acceptance and application of the separation of powers have been crystallised in the intervening years.

However, it still has to be admitted from the outset that an untutored observer coming from a presidential system of government, such as that of the United States, might imagine the separation of powers in the United Kingdom to be something of a contradiction in terms. At first sight, the various forms of constitutional power in the American system are separated by bright and clear lines;[9] in stark contrast, in the United Kingdom the elements are swirled together, like the various ingredients in a trifle. They can be discerned by observers, but not separated without the destruction of the whole.

For example, in concrete terms, the US Constitution clearly states that legislative power shall vest in Congress,[10] and that executive power shall be vested in the President,[11] who may not be a member of Congress. Consequently, there is a formal and absolute divide between legislative and executive power. In contrast, in the United Kingdom, the Prime Minister is by convention a member of the House of Commons[12] and, therefore, invariably part of the legislature.

Yet, not having a system akin to that of the United States does not mean that the United Kingdom does not have a separation of powers in any functional sense, merely that what exists here is very different from a context such as that in the United States. It is for this reason that the term 'checks and balances' is often usefully employed to describe the regulation of powers in frameworks like the United Kingdom: see, for example, Ginsberg and Versteeg.[13]

There are mechanisms which prevent any one holder of power from exercising it without restraint, but this is not achieved by an impenetrable wall of separation. Seeking to apply the separation of powers in the classic Montesquieu[14] *séparation des pouvoirs* sense is undeniably problematic in the context of the United Kingdom. It is no coincidence that some of the leading undergraduate textbooks

6 S. De Smith, *Constitutional and Administrative Law* (Penguin: Harmondsworth) 3rd edn, 1977, 36.
7 *Duport Steel v Sirs* [1980] 1 WLR 142, 157.
8 *M v Home Office* [1994] 1 AC 377, 395.
9 N. Jayapalan, *Modern Governments* (Atlantic: New Delhi) 1999, 23.
10 Constitution of the United States of America, Art. 1.
11 Ibid., Art. 2.
12 D. Feldman, *English Public Law* (Oxford University Press: Oxford) 2009, para 2.39.
13 T. Ginsberg and M Versteeg ,'Why Do Countries Adopt Constitutional Review?, *Journal of Law, Economics and Organizations*, Vol. 30, No. 3 (2014) 587–622, 591.
14 See the discussion below.

on constitutional law elect to give the relevant chapter a neutral title, avoiding the phrase altogether. For example, Bradley and Ewing refer to '[t]he relationship between legislature, executive and judiciary'.[15] They also correctly acknowledge at the outset that some of the classic constitutional writers on the UK context have regarded the doctrine with some suspicion, citing Dicey[16] and Jennings.[17]

Interestingly, however, Dicey is perhaps more nuanced than Bradley and Ewing suggest. They quote his dismissive observation that the separation of powers was 'the offspring of a double misconception'.[18] Read in context, Dicey's exact words were that the doctrine was '*in some sort* the offspring of a double misconception' (emphasis added). In his view, this two-fold misunderstanding is based upon Montesquieu himself having misconstrued some aspects of the English[19] Constitution, and the theories of Montesquieu themselves subsequently having been distorted and misapplied by the French statesmen of the Revolution.

Furthermore, at other points in his work, Dicey effectively acknowledges the merits of governmental systems operating a very different model of relations between executive and legislature. He expressly admits that there are pros and cons with both kinds of structure:

> The merits and defects of a non-parliamentary executive are the exact opposite of the merits and defects of a parliamentary executive. Each form of administration is strong where the other is weak, and weak where the other is strong. The strong point of a non-parliamentary executive is its comparative independence. Wherever representative government exists, the head of the administration, be he an Emperor or a President, of course prefers to be on good terms with and to have the support of the legislative body. But the German Emperor need not pay anything like absolute deference to the wishes of the Diet; an American President can, if he chooses, run counter to the opinion of Congress.[20]

Obviously, Dicey was writing in his own historical context, and his views reflect the concerns of his contemporaries and the political systems of the world as they existed in the early twentieth century. Nevertheless, if Dicey's work is taken in the round, it is clear that his objection was to *some aspects* of Montesquieu's theory and the way in which they had been applied. For this reason, the *label* 'separation of powers' evidently did not appeal to him. Nevertheless, he very clearly acknowledged that there was a conversation to be had about the appropriate

15 A. Bradley and K. Ewing, *Constitutional and Administrative Law* (Pearson: London) 2014, Ch. 5, 78.

16 Ibid., footnote 2.

17 Ibid., footnote 3.

18 A.V. Dicey, *Introduction to the Study of the Law of the Constitution* (ed. R. Michenor, Liberty Fund: Indianapolis) 1982, 328.

19 The national terminology here belongs to Dicey.

20 Dicey, n. 18 above, Appendix, note 3, 428: 'Distinction between a Parliamentary Executive and a Non-Parliamentary Executive'.

relationship between the different organs of state, and the separation or mingling of both persons and functions. Not surprisingly, Dicey was not alone in this view, and the conversation in question has very much been taking place over the last hundred years.

As indicated above, the label '*séparation des pouvoirs*' to which Dicey took exception, and of which Jennings was suspicious, originally came from the writing of Montesquieu in his *De l'Esprit des Loix*.[21] In essence, the theory argues that the principal institutions of the state (executive, legislature and judiciary) should be kept separate in terms of both their functions and the individuals within them:

> When the legislative and executive powers are united in the same person, or in the same body of magistrates, there can be no liberty ... there can be no liberty if the power of judging is not separated from the legislature and executive ... there would be an end to everything if the same man and the same body were to exercise those three powers.[22]

As can be observed from the contemporary world, these ideas were crucial in shaping the United States of America, as well as many continental jurisdictions, in the drafting and development of their Constitutions. It should also be remembered that the doctrine of separation of powers has undeniably influenced the United Kingdom, even though Montesquieu's work was in a sense a critique of the system in the British context, and could not be accepted wholesale without effectively dismantling the current arrangements and beginning again.

Furthermore, as we have seen, even traditional commentators such as Dicey and Jennings, who were not enamoured with the label 'separation of powers',[23] nevertheless acknowledged that there was scope for debate in relation to the mischief which the doctrine addressed, and it has never been denied that the proper regulation of power by state authorities is a necessary facet of *any* fit-for-purpose constitutional settlement in a liberal democracy.

It is also incontrovertible that the doctrine of separation of powers has played a key part in constitutional debates within the global academic community.[24] As a natural and inevitable consequence, dialogue within the United Kingdom has been bathed with this intellectual tide.

It is possible to accept that in *general* terms a strong degree of separation between the three key forms of state power is a highly desirable outcome, and yet still reject the necessity and desirability of moving towards a system of complete separation. It is reasonable to describe this philosophy as *a* concept of separation of powers, even though it is clearly distinct from the rigid North American understanding of the doctrine.

21 The contemporary spelling is '*lois*'.

22 C. Baron de Montesquieu, *The Spirit of Laws*, (c1748) (translated by A. Cohler, B. Miller and H. Stone (eds), Cambridge University Press: New York) 1989, 157.

23 Bradley and Ewing, n. 15 above, Ch. 5, 78.

24 W. Bondy, *The Separation of Governmental Powers: in History, in Theory and in the Constitution* (The Law Book Exchange: New Jersey) 2004.

Ultimately, we would concur with Masterman's assessment:

> It is more realistic to refer to the idea of separation of powers as being more like the many-headed hydra. And the malleability which has been the result of the multifaceted nature of separation of powers, although clearly responsible for continued doctrinal uncertainty, has also been central to the longevity of the theory.[25]

The precise meaning of the term 'separation of powers' in the United Kingdom has been and remains plastic, but this characteristic confers upon it adaptability rather than weakness, and certainly does not negate its existence. A cynic might argue that Masterman's concession about its uncertain scope and content is in reality an unconscious affirmation of Marshall's dismissal of the doctrine as nothing more than a loose collection of ideas, which should not properly be brought together.[26] However, we would assert that a malleable definition of a term by no means equates to an absence of meaning, and would further endorse Masterman's contention that 'the more definite aims and characteristics of the doctrine, the avoidance of concentrations of power, the preservation of individual liberty, the independence of the judiciary, and so on reflect values and aspirations that, to varying degrees, are to be found in our contemporary constitution and, of course, in many others'.[27]

In other words, Marshall was right to observe that it is a portmanteau term, but this is not a negative feature. Rather, it is a doctrinal concept which holds together and explains a number of features key to the functioning of our contemporary state.

This is not to say that the doctrine is or should be immune from criticism. Carolan[28] makes a sophisticated case for suggesting that the theory was, and always has been, both a myth and an oversimplification and, although it has achieved totemic status, it would be better to depart from the threefold tripartite framework and adopt instead a separation of constituencies. In Carolan's proposed paradigm, power would be distributed between institutions according to their capacity to represent those interests which comprise the key constituent elements of the constitutional order.

Two points should be noted in relation to this. First, even in Carolan's revised order, the state is still pursuing the same goal of managing the exercise of governmental power, so that it is not abused but applied for the common good. Second, in admitting that a 'myth' which is an expression of constitutional doctrine is widely believed and acted upon, Carolan is logically conceding that it has both existence and traction. Judges and academics do not simply believe

25 Masterman, n. 4 above, 16.

26 Marshall, n. 5 above, 124.

27 Masterman, n. 4 above, 16.

28 E. Carolan, *A New Separation of Powers: A Theory for the Modern State* (Oxford University Press: Oxford) 2009.

in the fairy of separation of powers; they continue to clap and, therefore, give it life. Were this not the case, Carolan's arguments for reform would themselves not make sense. Therefore, while we acknowledge the intricacy of Carolan's critique, we remain unpersuaded that it provides a reason not to engage with separation of powers, as it presently exists within our legal framework. Although we accept that the term has a unique and valuable meaning in the UK context, we would still sound a note of caution. The suggestion is *not* that a complete and uncompromising version of the doctrine would be the ideal, but that a modified form is all that can be made compatible with the aged and rickety UK Constitution. It is important to emphasise that the function and understanding of the concept is radically different in the United Kingdom from a system like that of the United States. The UK concept of the separation of powers is not a watered down version of its American counterpart. It is a different phenomenon to fit a different paradigm.

In the United States, separation of powers is a *necessary and deliberate construction*, which must be maintained if the Constitution is to survive in its existing form. Without this status quo, the US Constitution would be something fundamentally different, as an absolute separation of powers is one of its *defining characteristics*; because it is absolute in nature; separation of powers in the American sense must either be present or absent. Its presence cannot be a question of degree. In sharp contrast, separation of powers in the United Kingdom is one of the instruments that contributes to the constitutional symphony. Generally speaking, separating both functions and persons is desirable, but there are circumstances when considerations such as efficiency might outweigh this. It is part of a *system* of checks and balances. In the United Kingdom, the separation of powers is not a goal in itself, but one of the means employed to attain the goal of regulating the proper use of power. *It is neither absolute nor definitional in nature.*

There is little doubt that a concept of separation of powers does exist within the modern Constitution, but it must be borne in mind that it is considerably different from the models in other contexts, and certainly from that which Montesquieu originally had in mind. The spirit of a United Kingdom understanding of the doctrine is expressed eloquently by a House of Commons Library Standard Note:

> In early accounts, such as Montesquieu's *The Spirit of Laws*, the separation of powers is intended to guard against tyranny and preserve liberty. It was held that the major institutions should be divided and dependent upon each other so that one power would not be able to exceed that of the other two. Today, the separation of powers is more often suggested as a way to foster a system of checks and balances necessary for good government.[29]

29 R. Benwell and O. Gay, 'The Separation of Powers', Library of the House of Commons, Standard Note SN/PC/006053, 1.

Lord Mustill also affirmed the existence and importance of the constitutional principle in the *Fire Brigades Union* case:[30]

> It is a feature of the peculiarly UK conception of the separation of powers that Parliament, the executive and the courts each have their distinct and largely exclusive domain. Parliament has a legally unchallengeable right to make whatever laws it thinks right. The executive carries on the administration of the country in accordance with the powers conferred on it by law. The courts interpret the laws and see that they are obeyed.

As we have seen in previous chapters, the account of parliamentary sovereignty and executive authority in this passage must be read in light of the Human Rights Act 1998, evolving ideas about the rule of law, the European Union treaties and whatever international instruments prove to be their successors. As Bogdanor notes, there has been an observable shift flowing from the international treaty obligations of the United Kingdom; having been imported into domestic law the result is that some matters which were once exclusively for ministers to decide, subject to their accountability to Parliament, now in contrast fall to be determined by judges.[31] Although there remains scope for skirmishes around the borderlands of their respective territories in terms of decision-making, there has undoubtedly been a change in expectations.

Nevertheless, Krotoszynski's argument that the United Kingdom is a system which 'intentionally promotes efficiency over abstract concerns about tyranny'[32] still holds good. It is true that a framework within which the legislature and executive are comingled, and the judiciary is confined to its clearly delineated sphere of responsibility, is less likely to breed situations in which policies are tugged and squabbled over by the different organs of the state. The United Kingdom is less prone to the kind of political impasse that can ensue in systems with a rigid separation of powers, especially when this is coupled with a presidential mode of government. As Thakur[33] argues, it is beneficial in many respects to have democratic legitimacy concentrated in one place and this is a strong reason for retaining parliamentary democracy. Furthermore, it should not be forgotten that any attempt to introduce a rigid separation of powers would inevitably necessitate the abandonment of parliamentary sovereignty in its current form, another fundamental pillar of the Constitution.

30 *R v Secretary of State for the Home Department, ex parte Fire Brigades Union* [1995] 2 AC 513, 567.

31 V. Bogdanor, *The New British Constitution* (Hart: Oxford) 2009, Ch. 3: 'The Human Rights Act: Cornerstone of the New Constitution'.

32 R. Krotosynski, 'The Separation of Legislative and Executive Powers', in T. Ginsburg and R. Dixon (eds), *Comparative Constitutional Law* (Edward Elgar: Cheltenham) 2011, 248.

33 R. Thakur, 'Parliamentary Democracy Isn't Perfect but It Is the Best Form of Government We Have', *The Japan Times* (24 Apr 2001), http://www.japantimes.co.jp/opinion/2001/04/26/commentary/world-commentary/parliamentary-democracy-isnt-perfect-but-its-the-best-form-of-government-we-have/#.WQYin4VOJuk.

Nevertheless, equally there has been an increasing awareness of the safeguards offered by the principle. As a result, in the last two decades, there has been what might be described as a 'conscious uncoupling' between the three key seats of state power. There is no suggestion that this could or should be seen as a development towards the adoption of an American or continental model of separation of powers; rather it has been a deliberate strengthening of the doctrine as it exists in the United Kingdom.

In relation to the executive and legislature, the Backbench Business Committee was created in 2010. Prior to this, the Government effectively had complete control over the parliamentary agenda, so the freedom of the legislature to examine and debate issues was determined largely by the executive. Now the Backbench Business Committee has a specific allocation of time outside government control, during which it can schedule matters for debate. As advertised on the Parliament's publicly accessible website:

> The Committee can consider any subject for debate. This includes subjects raised in national or local campaigns, reports by select committees and other groups and issues suggested by constituents, including by people who have signed an e-petition or a traditional paper petition (there is no restriction on the number of signatures required).[34]

Although more narrow in some respects, this innovation has undoubtedly been of practical benefit, and should not be dismissed as merely symbolic in nature. It has meant that the executive has less capacity to act as a gatekeeper in connection with matters admitted for debate.

The meetings of the Committee are held in public and featured on parliamentary television.[35] Thus, not only does the Committee bolster the capacity of the legislature to monitor the executive on its own terms rather than those of the executive itself, it also encourages participation in the process by the general public. Groups and individuals who have engaged with and persuaded their MP to take an item to this Committee can see the issue debated, and understand why it is or is not given parliamentary time. Consequently, the separation of powers and the wider democratic process are both strengthened.

The separation between the judiciary and the legislature is another aspect of the Constitution, which has advanced in recent times. There is a well-established statutory prohibition on judges standing for election as Members of Parliament,[36] so an individual may not join the legislature in this way. Furthermore, the Constitutional Reform Act 2005 removed the Lords of Appeal in Ordinary from the legislature and created an independent Supreme Court. It also removed the

34 UK Parliament, Commons Select Committee, Backbench Business Committee, 'How the Committee Works', http://www.parliament.uk/business/committees/committees-a-z/commons-select/backbench-business-committee/how-the-backbench-business-committee-works.

35 Parliament Live TV, http://www.parliamentlive.tv/Commons.

36 House of Commons (Disqualification) Act 1975.

judicial aspect of the role of Lord Chancellor and transferred the position as head of the judiciary to the Lord Chief Justice. Although intended to further the separation of powers, removing the Lord Chancellor as the voice of the judiciary in Parliament was not an uncontroversial step, and some argued that the presence of this individual there could facilitate relations between the different branches of the state.[37] There remain arguments that too much rigidity in the separation of powers is apt to prioritise abstract concerns over the smooth running of government and the collective good.

The changed role of the Lord Chancellor also meant that a government minister was no longer responsible for the appointment of judges; this function is now fulfilled by an independent Judicial Appointments Commission.

Much of the thrust of the Constitutional Reform Act 2005 was towards ensuring that justice and independence were seen to be done. Judicial independence was by no means a new concept for the British Constitution. However, in recent years the Government has done more to publicise this, explaining the position on an official internet site and promoting awareness of the safeguards of judicial independence.[38] It is important to understand that it is not sufficient for the judges to simply be independent: they must also be seen to be independent. There is universal agreement from commentators across the political and academic spectrum that the judiciary, like Caesar's wife, must be beyond reproach, and the strength of feelings displayed in the controversy over the litigation surrounding the triggering of Article 50 provided a powerful illustration of this.[39] Those who believed that the judges involved had had their integrity unjustly questioned felt that unsubstantiated allegations against those in judicial office could undermine public faith in the justice system, as well as damage the reputation of innocent men and women. On the other hand those who felt that the individual judges had acted unwisely were equally angry that the impartiality of the judiciary was now called into question. All parties agreed that without a reliably impartial judiciary the system could not function.

An important dimension to the long-established tradition of judicial independence is that judges effectively have lifetime tenure, which helps to secure their freedom from coercion.

37 Benwell and Gay, n. 29 above, 8.

38 Courts and Tribunals Judiciary, 'About the Judiciary, Independence', https://www.judiciary.gov.uk/about-the-judiciary/the-judiciary-the-government-and-the-constitution/jud-acc-ind/independence.

39 C. Mortimer, 'Brexiteers Urge Supreme Court Judge to Stand Down from Article 50 Hearing over Wife's Pro-Remain Tweets', *The Independent* (19 Nov 2016), http://www.independent.co.uk/news/uk/politics/brexit-latest-supreme-court-article-50-hearing-judge-lord-neuberger-wife-tweet-impartiality-a7427511.html; B. Riley-Smith, 'Liz Truss Breaks Silence over Article 50 Row to Defend Judiciary', *The Telegraph* (5 Nov 2016), http://www.telegraph.co.uk/news/2016/11/05/tory-mps-and-ex--ministers-call-on-government-to-defend-judiciar; 'Any Wonder Remainers Won? Article 50 Judge Founded EU Integration Group', *The Sunday Express* (5 Nov 2016), http://www.express.co.uk/news/uk/728460/Article-50-three-judges-blocked-Brexit.

The removal of High Court and more senior judges requires both Houses of Parliament to petition the monarch. Although this is now dealt with by modern legislation,[40] the arrangement dates back to the Act of Settlement 1701. The power has never been exercised in respect of a judge in England or Wales, and in fact has only ever been invoked once when an Irish High Court Judge of Admiralty was removed in 1830.[41] Circuit and District judges may be removed after disciplinary proceedings, but again this is a rare occurrence, having taken place on two occasions only.[42]

As has been discussed in great detail in the preceding chapters, the judiciary is subordinate to the legislature in terms of being bound to accept the legal will of Parliament as expressed through legislation.[43] However, the European Community statutes and the Human Rights Act have given them power to scrutinise certain pieces of legislation in particular circumstances, and treat the legislative capacity of Parliament as being kept within the boundaries that the legislature has set for itself until such time as it should decide to alter the position.[44]

In terms of relations between the legislature and the judiciary, the *sub judice* rule exists to try to strike a balance between the right of the citizen to a fair hearing and the general principle that debate in Parliament should be unfettered by the threat of sanction from the courts.[45] The *sub judice* rule is effectively a voluntary compromise of parliamentary privilege, and amounts to a principle that where a matter is awaiting a judicial determination it will not be discussed in either House for fear of prejudicing the outcome. It is not absolute: the chair of proceedings in either House has the freedom to waive the ban and allow matters to be discussed, and the rule does not affect the freedom of Parliament to legislate.

A related development has taken place in respect of the introduction of 'super injunctions'. Some commentators have attacked this development in the strongest possible terms – for example Zuckerman:[46]

> It is possible that the long overdue reform of the rules of costs will make it easier for respondents to mount a more effective resistance to super injunctions, but in the meantime we should not tolerate the undermining of the rule of law by a Kafkaesque process that is inimical to the rule of law and contrary to democratic principles.

40 Senior Courts Act 1981, s. 11(3).

41 Courts and Tribunals Judiciary, 'About the Judiciary, Judges and Parliament', https://www.judiciary.gov.uk/about-the-judiciary/the-judiciary-the-government-and-the-constitution/jud-acc-ind/judges-and-parliament.

42 Ibid.

43 *Pickin v British Railways Board* [1974] AC 765.

44 D. Feldman, 'The European Court of Human Rights and the UK – Why Should Strasbourg Decide on Our Human Rights?', *UK Constitutional Law Association* (7 Dec 2012), http://ukconstitutionallaw.org/2012/12/07/david-feldman-the-european-court-of-human-rights-and-the-uk-why-should-strasbourg-decide-on-our-human-rights.

45 Benwell and Gay, n. 29 above, 7.

46 A. Zuckerman, 'Super Injunctions – Curiosity-Suppressant Orders Undermine the Rule of Law', *Civil Justice Quarterly*, Vol. 29, No. 2 (2010) 131–8, 138.

Effectively, these orders not only prohibit certain facts, identities and allegations from being disclosed (in the manner of a standard injunction), but also provide for anonymity and a prohibition on disclosing the very existence of the order itself. Concern has been expressed that the development of super injunctions has been detrimental to the functioning of the separation of powers on the basis, first, that their creation has involved judges exceeding their powers and effectively taking on the role of Parliament and, second, that their secret nature makes it almost impossible for the executive and the legislature to monitor the conduct of the judiciary.[47]

In addition, there is the anxiety that in stifling the free flow of information, they will reduce the transparency of the state machinery, thereby limiting the opportunities for scrutiny and hampering the system of checks and balances on the uses to which power is being put. We acknowledge the legitimacy of these questions, but would argue that the purpose and application of super injunctions does not bear out such fears. In practice, courts promote openness wherever possible, and carefully explain why they have recourse to these devices when they are employed. If invoked wisely, super injunctions are a mechanism for the various branches of state to protect people who are at serious risk, and who would be endangered by publicity.

Much of the controversy has revolved around stories about celebrity gossip. A recent case in the Family Division has highlighted an instance of a more demonstrably pressing need for such an order. As Miller[48] discusses, Mr Justice Munby released his judgment once it was safely possible to do so, precisely because the case raised important questions about the proper use of the wardship jurisdiction, and 'so-called super injunctions'.

The case of *Re M (Children)*[49] concerned minors whose parents were trying to travel with them to join IS, and taking them into the midst of a war zone. The children were saved as a result of co-operation between the British and Turkish authorities, but the issuing of a court order in the United Kingdom was a key step in the process. At the time, the utmost discretion was required if there was to be no risk of friends or family members of the parents learning what was afoot and thwarting government efforts to keep the children safe. In the worst case scenario, any mistake or disclosure could have cost the lives of the children, and the judge was at pains to demonstrate in the judgment how he had dealt with the press, and the way in which the reporter involved had co-operated with this.

In many respects this is an instance of the practical functioning of the separation of powers. The court was acknowledging the limits to its authority, the reasons for acting as it had done and the appropriateness of being open to parliamentary and public scrutiny, in so far as this did not compromise the rule of law

47 'Privacy Injunctions Unsustainable Says Cameron', *BBC News* (23 May 2011), http://www.bbc.co.uk/news/uk-13498504; D Casciani, 'Q & A Super-Injunctions', *BBC News* (20 May 2011), http://www.bbc.co.uk/news/uk-13473070.

48 J. Miller, 'Court Protects Children from IS', *New Law Journal*, Vol. 165, No. 7670 (2015) 5.

49 *Re M (Children)* [2015] EWHC 1433 (Fam).

or citizens' human rights. The debate about the future of super injunctions will doubtless continue, but the very existence of this dialogue shows that the checks and balances within the constitutional system are operational. The presence of this legal device and the way in which it is employed are matters of public record and critique.

Not only are there the checks within the system itself, there is also the informal but very powerful influence of debate in the public sphere, as the news stories cited indicated. It is reasonable to infer that the public controversy around super injunctions was one of the factors in the judicial decision to lift reporting restrictions and give a detailed account of the case as soon as it was possible to do so.

Equally, the fact that this use of an injunction generated little media interest, and that the press focused on other aspects of the case, demonstrates why freedom of debate in the public sphere *alone* is not a sufficient safeguard. Like all checks and balances, it needs to function as part of a package. Inevitably, journalists cover stories which they believe can be spun to be provocative; they have a vested interest in protesting if they cannot publish accounts of the marital problems of footballers or pop stars. They have less motivation to write about how courts may sometimes need to carry out proceedings behind closed doors in order to protect vulnerable children, while giving adult family members a fair and balanced hearing.

This also illustrates both the importance and limitation of freedom of the press within a framework of constitutional checks and balances on the use of power. On the one hand, it is vital as the ability of those exercising power to suppress information can effectively disable other brakes on their action – for instance, the legislature cannot scrutinise decisions by the executive if its members are unaware that such decisions have ever been made. However, because the press is heavily influenced by commercial pressures, journalists cannot be relied upon to make their professional decisions on the basis solely of the public good.

In addition to its interaction with the legislature, the judiciary also has a scrutinising role in respect of the executive, and once again this area has expanded considerably. Courts must ensure that delegated legislation is made within the bounds set by the parent primary legislation, and act as guarantor of the lawfulness and propriety of the actions of public bodies by means of the judicial review procedure.[50] Although the procedure has long since taken root,[51] and is frequently invoked when neither human rights issues nor matters relating to European law are at stake, these two circumstances provide increased potential for applicants to seek damages for government breaches.

In normal circumstances, the remedies in judicial review actions are focused around addressing the faulty decision-making process applied by the public body.[52] The circumstances in which damages are available are quite limited.

50 Courts and Tribunals Judiciary, 'You and the Judiciary, Judicial Review', https://www.judiciary.gov.uk/you-and-the-judiciary/judicial-review.

51 See, e.g., *Anisminic v Foreign Compensation Commission* [1969] 2 AC 147.

52 Courts and Tribunals Judiciary, 'You and the Judiciary, Judicial Review', n. 50 above.

In pragmatic terms, the warm glow of moral vindication is more satisfying when accompanied by financial rewards, and applicants are more likely to go to the time and trauma of litigation if there is a potential financial benefit in taking this course. Therefore, in increasing the incentive for judicial review actions, these legislative developments have strengthened the functioning of the separation of powers and checks and balances, which the system provides.

In conclusion, it is appropriate to acknowledge separation of powers as a key constitutional principle within the United Kingdom model, even though its form and understanding are radically different from those found in strict separationist regimes. In recent years, the British conception of separation of powers has been consolidated and has become more self-conscious, a development which has had, and continues to have, a beneficial impact upon the functioning of checks and balances on the exercise of power.

For our present purposes, however, we are left with the question of how the religious dimension of the Constitution relates to this doctrine, and it is this matter to which we now turn. Does the religious character of the Constitution and wider legal framework support and enhance the separation of powers?

6.3 Does the tripartite religious character of the legal and constitutional system enhance checks and balances and separation of powers?

6.3.1 Separation of powers and the House of Lords

One of the self-stated functions of the House of Lords is to keep a check on executive power.[53] We have already discussed the place of the Church of England bishops in the House of Lords, and will not at this point focus on the debate about the appropriateness of this. For immediate purposes, we will accept the current reality of their presence in the Upper Chamber and assess the value of its contribution to the separation of powers. In order to do this, we need to understand the composition and role of the House of Lords, so that we can assess how the Lords Spiritual fit into this framework and what they are in a position to contribute.

Although the House of Lords functions on party political lines, in general terms the political affiliation of members is looser than it is in the House of Commons, and the members are, of course, not at risk of losing their seats should there be a change of political climate at election time. Furthermore, a significant number of the peers are 'crossbenchers', describing themselves in the following terms:

> Crossbenchers are members who have no party-political affiliation and participate in parliamentary proceedings independently. They do not adopt collective policy decisions, but rather speak and vote as individuals.

53 UK Parliament, House of Lords, 'Checking and Challenging Government', http://www.parliament.uk/business/lords/work-of-the-house-of-lords/checking-and-challenging-government.

> For administrative purposes all crossbenchers are part of the crossbench group. The group elects a Convenor whose role it is to provide information to crossbenchers and represent their interests in the House.[54]

The crossbenchers have an impressive list of interests and expertise,[55] and a number of them include 'religious affairs' in their interests. Of course, declaring an interest in religious affairs does not necessarily equate to being a member of a faith, although a number of them are high-profile figures from the religious world (such as former Chief Rabbis or Archbishops of Canterbury) and are publicly known to have such beliefs.

Arguably, the distance between the legislature and the politically elected executive is greater in the Upper than it is in the Lower Chamber even though there are political peers and members of the House of Lords can be cabinet ministers.[56] As Rush[57] argues, its role as a revising chamber has traditionally been seen as one of the key functions of the House of Lords. Parliamentary time being short in the Commons, the Lords often has an opportunity to scrutinise and tidy up legislation, ironing out potential problems in bills before they can pass into law. However, as Rush also notes, the House of Lords has sometimes been characterised as a 'wrecking' rather than a revising chamber. Clearly, improvement can be a subjective matter. The government is sometimes equally unenthusiastic about purported improvements by the Commons. Nevertheless, given that the Parliament Acts ensure that the power of the House of Lords is ultimately one of delay rather than veto, its capacity to act as a wrecking chamber is limited by the Constitution

Brazier is perceptive in his observation that the role of the House of Lords as a revising and, indeed, a delaying chamber is, by its very nature, paradoxical.[58]

54 The Independent Crossbenchers, 'Who Are the Crossbenchers?', http://62.32.116.90/who.html.

55 The Independent Crossbenchers, 'A List of Cross Bench Special Interests', http://62.32.116.90/interests.html: agriculture animal welfare, archives, arts and culture, asylum and immigration, charities/voluntary sector, children, citizenship, climate change/environment, Commonwealth, community relations, constitutional affairs, consumer affairs, counter terrorism/intelligence, countries of the world, countryside/rural issues, criminal justice, defence, disability, economic policy, education and training, equal opportunities/equality, employment, ethics, European union/affairs, family, finance, financial services, fisheries, government/citizenship, health, heritage, human rights/civil liberties, international relations, international development, law, lighting, medicine, media/broadcasting, policing, Post Office, public services reform, regeneration, religious affairs, research and design and innovation, science and technology, social policy/welfare, sport, third age, tourism, trade and industry, transport, UK regions, women's issues, world regions, young people

56 This is an accepted reality of the present Constitution, although not uncontroversial. It is also the case that in strict constitutional theory, a government minister need not be a member of either House of Parliament: see further K. Parry and L. Maer, House of Commons Library Standard Note SN/PC/05226, 'Ministers in the House of Lords' (15 Nov 2012).

57 M. Rush, 'The House of Lords: The Political Context', in P. Carmichael and B. Dickson (eds), *The House of Lords: Its Parliamentary and Judicial Roles* (Hart: Oxford) 1999 7–28, 19. Although there have been some important changes to the House of Lords since the time Rush wrote this piece, the relevant points remain applicable.

58 R. Brazier, 'The Second Chamber: Paradoxes and Plans', in Carmichael and Dickson (eds), ibid., 53–66, 54–55.

He points out that, unicameralists aside, there is a general consensus that it is desirable that the House of Lords has the capacity to delay Commons bills in some circumstances, so that public opinion can be sounded. However, this effectively means that reliance is being placed on the unelected and unrepresentative House to relate Parliamentary action to public opinion, by frustrating the wishes of the democratically elected chamber to represent that very opinion. Put in those terms, the logic behind it does seem to be worthy of *Alice in Wonderland*. Furthermore:

> Oppositions want the House of Lords to act against legislation passed by an elective dictatorship, but do not want peers to interfere with their legislation when they are in office. Many Members of Parliament would like to see a reformed second chamber, provided that it did not exercise powers as a rival to the House of Commons; but a newly created second chamber would fairly assume that it had been given powers in order to use them from time to time.[59]

While it must be acknowledged that the role of the present House of Lords as a revising chamber is controversial in some quarters, it has survived more than a century of attempts to devise a better system and it remains an important limb of the current model of separation of powers. Were the United Kingdom ever to move to a unicameral system, the separation of powers would be seriously weakened if the relationship between the legislature and the executive was not drastically revised at the same time. As it stands, the House of Lords' greater detachment from the elected executive places it in a position to check its activity more effectively than the Commons.

Turning now to the Lords Spiritual, it can be seen that they currently play a unique role in this process. Contrary to popular opinion, the Church of England bishops are *not* crossbenchers, although, as the Church itself comments, they do have much in common with them in the sense that they do not take the party whip.[60] Technically, there is nothing to stop them from being appointed cabinet ministers and exercising a political role in that capacity, although it seems abundantly clear that neither the Church of England nor the House of Lords expects this to happen in reality.[61] The House of Lords cites the diversity of thought among the peers as a strength, and positively references both the crossbenchers and the bishops in the composition which allows for this.[62]

59 Ibid.

60 The Church of England, 'Bishops in the House of Lords: The Lords Spiritual', https://www.churchofengland.org/our-views/the-church-in-parliament/bishops-in-the-house-of-lords.aspx.

61 No bishop has been a cabinet minister in modern times and, although it is not expressly prohibited by canon law, it is hard to see how such a move would be compatible with running a diocese and carrying out the functions of their office appropriately; it would, therefore, effectively contravene the Clergy Terms of Service.

62 UK Parliament, House of Lords, 'Who's in the House of Lords, Members and Their Roles, Diverse Experience', http://www.parliament.uk/business/lords/whos-in-the-house-of-lords/members-and-their-roles/diverse-experience.

The bishops, however, do have some characteristics that distinguish them from the crossbenchers, and it is to these that we now turn our attention. We shall look at the unique role of the bishops in strengthening the functioning of the Upper Chamber and thereby the operation of the separation of powers, as the House of Lords exists in part to prevent an over-mighty executive from dominating the legislature.

The special role of the bishops in the House of Lords can be characterised in two distinct, but related, respects. First, they are a guaranteed contingent in the Chamber speaking for the interests of the weak and vulnerable. They are in a position to be advocates for the marginalised, even when the groups in question will not garner much public attention or sympathy. As their presence is as a result of the establishment framework they have no need to court popularity. They also have the liminal dimension to which we referred earlier, being both within and without the focal point of power. Second, they are able to present arguments from a faith perspective – in particular, from a Christian stance, which ensures that such a perspective is heard. Where this viewpoint does not carry the day, its proponents can, at least, be assured that it has received appropriate consideration and respect. This can only strengthen the legitimacy and effectiveness of the checks and balances and the wider democratic process.

As was noted above, of the life peers[63] a significant number have a special interest in religious affairs and may combine this with the neutrality of being a crossbencher. Some are even selected by the House of Lords Appointments Commission[64] in recognition of the skills, experience and contribution to society evidenced by their role within a faith community, but there is no guarantee that any particular number of individuals from other faith traditions or backgrounds will be there at any given time.

We are certainly not suggesting that a strong case could not be made for guaranteed places for members of other religious groups in a future and reformed Upper Chamber, but at present we are addressing the House of Lords *as it currently functions.* Similarly, we are not discounting the religious perspective of some members of the House of Commons, but obviously recognise that this comes about by virtue of the individuals elected, rather than a structure permanently embedded within the Constitution.

Furthermore, as we have discussed, many individuals from across the spectrum of religious positions will concur with the need to regulate the exercise of power to take into account the needs of the vulnerable as well as the interests of religious citizens. There may be disagreement about how far these abstract priorities should go in the hierarchy of decision-making factors. However, for the bishops, these factors should *always* be at the top of the consideration hierarchy, because they should be driven primarily by Christian doctrinal principles rather than economic considerations, Realpolitik, the advancement of scientific knowledge, caring for the interests of the farming community or any of the myriad of

63 There are currently around 700 life peers, ibid.

64 House of Lords Appointments Commission, http://lordsappointments.independent.gov.uk.

other issues which might (entirely reasonably and properly) trump these points for other specific peers, based on their individual outlook.

This is not to suggest that this makes the bishops' contribution superior to that of any other peer, but it is certainly distinct in terms of its emphasis. There is great scope for disagreement among the bishops themselves, and indeed between the bishops and members of other faith communities, when it comes to the determination of specific questions. Nevertheless, the prioritisation of these guiding light principles (protection of the vulnerable and representation of faith interests)[65] should remain constant for the episcopal peers.

This can be seen in relation to some of their contributions to parliamentary dialogue. For example, in a discussion about the new Government in India (which has obvious relevance for British foreign policy and overseas development strategy),[66] Lord Harries[67] instigated the debate and also raised the plight of the millions living in extreme poverty within that jurisdiction, including the *Dalits*, who comprise the most socially excluded group.[68] The Bishop of Carlisle then proceeded to voice concerns about gender inequalities, the gender pay gap and the health and safety of women and girls.[69]

Of course, it is almost too obvious to need stating that there were other, non-episcopal members of the House of Lords who made equally valuable contributions to this debate. Our point is not that the bishops were lone voices, quite the reverse; rather, it is that they raised ethical issues which were in harmony with the concerns of their fellow peers. See, for instance, Lord Patel's contribution to that same discussion.[70]

65 A. Harlow, F. Cranmer and N. Doe: 'Bishops in the House of Lords: A Critical Analysis', *Public Law* (2008) 490.

66 *Daily Hansard* (17 Jul 2014), 'India', col. 691, http://www.publications.parliament.uk/pa/ld201415/ldhansrd/text/140717-0001.htm.

67 Formerly Richard Harries, a retired bishop of Oxford who continues to sit in the House of Lords by virtue of having been given a peerage.

68 *Daily Hansard* (17 Jul 2014), 'India', n. 66 above, col. 691: 'As she knows, poverty in India is on an enormous scale. It has one-third of the world's poor and more poverty than the whole of Africa put together. Is she aware that of the 320 million people living below the poverty level, 200 million are Dalits, 50% of Dalit villages have no clean water and 75% of Dalit women are illiterate? In her discussions with the Indian Government on this issue, will she press home the fact that tackling poverty on such an epic scale is integrally linked to tackling also a system that leaves the Dalits and other scheduled castes trapped at the bottom of an oppressive pile?'

69 *Daily Hansard* (17 Jul 2014), 'India', ibid., col. 692: 'My Lords, does the Minister agree that while the gender gap in employment and political participation is narrowing in India, there is still much that needs to be done by the Government for the health and safety of girls and women? If that is the case, can the Minister assure us that this matter will be given the attention it deserves at the Girl Summit being hosted by the UK Government next week?'

70 *Daily Hansard* (17 Jul 2014), 'India', ibid., col. 693: 'I return to the point that my noble and right reverend friend Lord Harries of Pentregarth made. The poverty is related significantly to discrimination against a group which is a minority but is comprised of a large number of people: the Dalits. What will the British Government do to help India understand that and reduce the poverty among this group of people?'

A similar pattern emerged in a debate on fuel poverty later that same morning, when the Bishop of St Albans was one of several peers to raise concerns about the impact of electricity and gas prices on the poorest members of society.[71] Once again, this is just a snapshot of parliamentary life, but it shows how the bishops in the House of Lords work alongside their colleagues to keep a check on the way in which governmental power is being exercised, and encourage it to be applied for the benefit rather than the detriment of the weak and vulnerable.

Arguably, those without voices to represent them are most in need of advocates in the House of Lords. The economically and socially excluded are not well-equipped to mobilise to lobby the House of Commons, and their cause may not be popular in terms of winning votes. Certainly, a baby girl from a Dalit family clinging to life in the slums of Mumbai will not be voting in British elections (at least in the short or medium term), yet decisions of the British public authorities to act or not to act in various situations may have a direct impact upon her future prospects. It is, therefore, immensely positive that there are members of the House of Lords, including but by no means limited to the bishops, who believe that her interests (and those of people like her) are of relevance for the UK Government.

Nevertheless, it cannot be denied that there are some occasions when the Anglican bishops in the House of Lords do essentially put forward a Church of England perspective. This may be controversial where the debate is of a sensitive nature, arousing strong feelings on all sides. If the Church of England has a particular line, it is likely to be met with opposition and perhaps even hostility from those who take the contrary view, and it does raise a legitimate question about the appropriateness of privileging the status of Anglican views by permitting bishops to sit in the Upper Chamber. We do not deny that this is a thorny issue. However, we would put forward two contrasting instances where this has been the case, with two distinct perspectives on why there is a positive dimension at least to the bishops' presence in the House of Lords, strengthening that chamber and its role in the separation of powers. First, there is the vexed question of assisted dying. The Church of England opposes this, essentially on the basis that its introduction involves *third parties* accepting that some lives should come to an end. Although at times this point is obscured by voices protesting about individual autonomy, the reality is that not everybody requesting help in the ending of their own life would lawfully receive it. Therefore, there is always a third party value judgement being made. Furthermore, the Church is unconvinced that there are, or could ever be, adequate safeguards to prevent individuals from

71 *Daily Hansard* (17 Jul 2014), 'Fuel Poverty', ibid., col. 694: 'My Lords, those who keep a close eye on this area point out that issues of fuel poverty depend on which groups you look at. Clearly, in some groups this is a growing area. Indeed, they assert that there is a connection between the increase in fuel poverty of certain groups and the increase in the number of pre-paid meters that have been installed, partly because it is believed that they are the most expensive way to pay for fuel. In the light of that, can my noble friend tell us what consideration Her Majesty's Government have given to promoting the five principles on the use of pre-paid meters which were agreed between Consumer Focus and the big six energy companies back in March 2011, to ensure consistency in their installation and use?'

feeling a sense of pressure or obligation to bring their life to an end,[72] and this has been expressed by bishops in the House of Lords.[73]

There are no easy answers to the question of how legal systems should respond to individuals who demand at least the possibility of assistance in ending what they regard as an intolerable life. It is a subject beyond the scope of this book and we will not attempt to grapple with its complexity here. However, we do suggest that it is a debate in which all sides should be carefully heard if society is to have any hope of finding a satisfactory way forward.

Several high-profile individuals have campaigned for the introduction of voluntary euthanasia, often in the most tragic of circumstances. Consider, for instance, Sir Terry Pratchett, who publicly allied himself to the Dignity in Dying campaign as his own terminal illness of Alzheimer's gradually progressed.[74] He was a beloved author with an immense worldwide fan base, an incredible gift for the use of language and a huge media presence, as he took part in televised documentaries or gave speeches. He was also dying from a cruel illness which most people justly fear, and which many have seen gradually steal the minds and bodies of their loved ones. There is no doubt that the voices in support of assisted dying are powerful and their arguments are well made. In declining to introduce it as a society, we are condemning some individuals to a slow walk to a death which they do not choose, imprisoned by pain, robbed of joy and in some cases denied even their own personality.

Yet, there is another side to the coin. In agreeing to introduce it, our society would not only place the burden of deciding who should live and who should die on other human beings, but we would also risk condemning vulnerable and frightened people to end their own lives or being tortured with guilt for refusing to do so. By definition, these are people who often do not have anyone to plead their cause.

What about the position of elderly individuals in residential care homes who are acutely aware that their children's inheritance is slipping away, and who do not feel wanted and cherished? These people do not have celebrity advocates. What about those who feel that they have nothing to contribute and are no longer wanted in the world? Tragically, many older people in the United Kingdom do feel lonely and utterly unwanted. Consider the moving 2015 campaign by Age UK 'No-one should have no-one at Christmas'.[75] More than a million older people say that they go over a month without speaking to a friend, neighbour or family member.[76]

72 The Church of England, 'Assisted Dying Bill 2015', https://www.churchofengland.org/our-views/medical-ethics-health-social-care-policy/assisted-suicide/assisted-dying-bill-2015.aspx.

73 *Daily Hansard* (18 Jul 2014), 'Assisted Dying Bill', https://www.publications.parliament.uk/pa/ld201415/ldhansrd/text/140718-0001.htm, cols 805–6, Lord Harries: 'Certainly, if I knew that I had an illness of body or mind that would make me totally dependent on others, I would seriously ask myself whether it would not be better for them if I died. We must ask ourselves whether we really want to put people in a position where they will inevitably be tempted to seek an early way out, rather than become an increasing burden on those they love'.

74 'Dignity in Dying Sir Terry Pratchett Dies' (12 Mar 2015), https://www.dignityindying.org.uk/news/dignity-dying-patron-sir-terry-pratchett-dies.

75 Age UK, http://www.ageuk.org.uk/no-one.

76 Age UK, 'Campaign to Tackle Loneliness', http://www.ageuk.org.uk/no-one/campaign-for-age-uk.

Declining to introduce euthanasia comes at a cost to those who must live out lives they do not wish to endure, but introducing it comes at a cost to those who may be made to conclude that they *should* end their lives. This cost is rarely talked about by those pleading the case for assisted dying, and even provisions restricted to the terminally ill could result in individuals ending their lives far sooner than they would otherwise have done.

Of course, the neglect and social isolation of many elderly people in the United Kingdom is a separate issue from assisted dying, but with such troubling statistics the link that the Church has put forward cannot be lightly dismissed. As stated above, this book does not seek to address the question of whether this consideration should carry the day, or is outweighed by arguments in favour of assisted dying. The point in issue is that in providing the perspective of an often voiceless group, the Church is making a valuable contribution to the debate. Furthermore, it is expressing a point of view which many will regard as uncomfortable, because it is unpalatable to acknowledge as a society that we let our elderly population down to such a shocking degree. In addition, questioning the heart-rending arguments of the terminally ill and often courageous campaigners for assisted dying is not an easy or popular thing to do. Nevertheless, it is in the common interest that such arguments are examined before they are acted upon. The Church, partly through the medium of its bishops in the House of Lords, has the capacity to do things which are socially useful, but are neither easy nor popular. It is worth asking which other interest groups in Parliament would take on that mantle in their absence.

The second example relates to the Church of England's approach to the Marriage (Same Sex Couples) Act 2013 before the bill became law. The Church opposed this legislation on a number of grounds, and the Archbishop of Canterbury argued that it would effectively mean the abolition of marriage as it had previously existed.[77] Again, it could be suggested that the Church strengthened the legislation by ensuring that all sides were considered in the debate beforehand. On this occasion, the bishops could be cast in the light of speaking against, rather than for, a vulnerable group in society. Nevertheless, the opposition to same-sex marriage and the reasons given do reflect a point of view which was entitled to consideration. Given that some Christians are claiming that they are now a persecuted minority in the United Kingdom,[78] and enjoy the backing of a former Archbishop of Canterbury, it can only strengthen the credibility of the democratic, legislative process if their views can be shown to have been heard, and addressed, before being dismissed.

As was discussed in Chapter 5, for legislation to be effective in practical terms it must be accepted and implemented by people outside the confines of

77 *Daily Hansard* (3 Jun 2013), 'Marriage (Same Sex Couples) Bill, Second Reading', https://www.publications.parliament.uk/pa/ld201314/ldhansrd/text/130603-0001.htm, col. 954., Archbishop of Canterbury: 'The result is confusion. Marriage is abolished, redefined and recreated'.

78 'Lord Carey Attacks PM over Christian "Support"', *BBC News* (30 Mar 2013), http://www.bbc.co.uk/news/uk-21979034.

Westminster. Where there is no consensus on a difficult question, the majority view must prevail in a democratic society, but it is important that those who espouse minority opinions are aware that they have been neither ignored nor treated with a lack of respect. The knowledge that those with dissenting opinions have been given a voice can only help to strengthen general perceptions of the legitimacy of legislation and a willingness to implement it.

Furthermore, there was no doubt that the impetus for the same-sex marriage bill came from the executive, as the Prime Minister himself was ideologically committed to this cause.[79] The extensive debate and robust opposition within Parliament demonstrated the operation of the separation of powers or checks and balances in the UK context. It would be difficult now for anyone to argue that same-sex marriage became lawful only because an over-mighty executive forced it through without the consent of the elected legislature.

Moreover, the case of same-sex marriage is crucial for our present purposes because it illustrates that the presence of bishops in the House of Lords does not permit the Church to halt legislation where it is out of step with the majoritarian consensus. Had the Church been making the decision, same-sex marriage would not have been introduced, but the Lords Spiritual in no way hobbled Parliament from enacting legislation which the Church opposed.

In conclusion, the Lords Spiritual enhance the functioning of the Upper House as it is currently constituted, and thereby actively further the operation of the system of checks and balances within the British Constitution.

6.3.2 Child exorcism

In addition to the constitutional and establishment dimension that we have just explored, there are some aspects of the workings of the wider legal framework relating to religion which can be seen to further the functioning of separation of powers. The way in which the law deals with the 'exorcism' of children is one illustration of this.

In order to explore the point, it is necessary first to establish what is meant by the exorcism of children and the serious social problems to which it is linked in some cases. Exorcism has no single or easy definition: it relates to a plethora of practices derived from various cultural and religious beliefs. The Stobart Report was commissioned by the Department for Education and Skills in the wake of two cases in which the deaths of children were connected with beliefs in evil spirits and the perceived need to expel them.[80] The Report observes that '[c]olloquially "exorcism" was the most all-encompassing term understood by most people we spoke to during our research'.[81]

79 See, e.g., C. Hope, 'David Cameron: "I Want to Export Gay Marriage Around the World"', *The Telegraph* (24 Jul 13), http://www.telegraph.co.uk/news/politics/10200636/I-want-to-export-gay-marriage-around-the-world-says-David-Cameron.html.

80 E. Stobart, 'Child Abuse Linked to Accusations of "Possession" and "Witchcraft"', Department of Education and Skills, Research Report RR750 2006, 4, http://dera.ioe.ac.uk/6416/1/RR750.pdf.

81 Ibid., 5.

Like Stobart, we will adopt the term, because it is an accessible and convenient label to use in this context. In doing so, we are certainly not seeking to downplay the diversity of issues involved in contrasting social and cultural contexts. However, as is demonstrated by the response of the Metropolitan Police[82] and other state bodies,[83] as well as highly regarded third-sector organisations such as UNICEF,[84] there are very real issues for contemporary society to address in relation to the abuse of children in the context of perceived spirit possession. It is necessary to adopt some working vocabulary to discuss this. Furthermore, as Government guidance states: 'Child abuse is never acceptable in any community, in any culture, in any religion, under any circumstances. This includes abuse that might arise through a belief in spirit possession or other spiritual or religious beliefs'.[85]

However difficult grappling with the problem might be, the obligation which the state has to protect vulnerable minors[86] means that it cannot be swept under the carpet. Nevertheless, addressing the situation is a delicate and complicated challenge, as by its very nature the task involves balancing the autonomy of individuals and communities against the legitimate needs and duties of the state. There is no doubt about the necessity of upholding the right to private and family life[87] or the right to hold and manifest a religious belief.[88] Furthermore, understanding the experiences and perceptions of individuals with a different cultural heritage from their own can be a challenge for those such as judges, social workers and teachers who are acting on behalf of the state.[89]

There is a risk of misconstruing statements or actions in an unduly negative light because the state representatives involved do not have a sufficiently nuanced understanding of the relevant cultural paradigm. For instance, whether repeatedly directing a particular term at a child is emotionally abusive depends upon the social context as well as the tone of voice.

When the terms being directed at children relate to religious and folk beliefs, it can be very difficult to sift the benign from the dangerous. Is a label one which

82 Metropolitan Police, 'Project Violet: Metropolitan Police Service Response to Abuse Linked to Faith and Belief', https://beta.met.police.uk/advice-and-information/child-abuse/faith-based-abuse.

83 See, e.g., HM Government, 'Safeguarding Children from Abuse Linked to a Belief in Spirit Possession', Non-Statutory Guidance, http://oxfordshirescb.proceduresonline.com/pdf/sg_ch_a_belief_spirit.pdf.

84 A. Cimpric, 'Children Accused of Witchcraft: An Anthropological Study of Contemporary Practices in Africa', UNICEF, Dakar, (Apr 2010), https://www.unicef.org/wcaro/wcaro_children-accused-of-witchcraft-in-Africa.pdf.

85 HM Government, n. 83 above, 2.

86 Up to and including the duty to safeguard their right to life under Art. 2 of the European Convention on Human Rights (ECHR).

87 Art. 8 ECHR.

88 Art. 9 ECHR.

89 See, e.g., S. Jivraj and D. Herman, 'It is Difficult for a White Judge to Understand: Orientalism, Racialisation and Christianity in English Child Welfare Cases', *Child and Family Law Quarterly Review*, Vol. 21, No. 3 (2009) 283–308.

will damage self-esteem and lead to an individual being ostracised, or simply a colourful term of exasperation or endearment? Or even if a word like 'witch' is meant in the *literal* sense, what does that imply within that particular family or cultural world? Is the suggestion that the child is wilfully and permanently 'evil', a slave to dark spiritual powers, or someone suffering from a temporary and morally neutral affliction which can be cured?

Unfortunately, the complexity of these questions can lead to *under* as well as overreaction from teachers and social workers. Sometimes clues to the beginnings of serious abuse can be missed and, as the Stobart Report highlights, early intervention is key to attaining the optimal outcome for children.[90]

The delicacy of the balance explains why the concept of separation of powers, as well as a juridical system with a nuanced approach to religious beliefs, are so critical in this context. All three elements of state power (legislative, administrative and executive) must necessarily be exercised in the defence of vulnerable children, but not in a manner which damages those children more than it helps them, or unjustifiably infringes their rights or the rights of other citizens. Checks and balances exist within the system not only to prevent the cynical and deliberate misappropriation of power, but also to guard against inadvertent misapplication. The functioning of checks and balances and separation of powers in a broad way can be seen in the general approach to the problem of abuse related to child exorcism.

First, it is an area on which the legislature has more than once debated taking specific action, but has to date declined to enact any statute seeking to regulate or outlaw these practices.[91] Yet, the problems associated with abuse linked to child exorcism, and possible ways of responding to them, are addressed by a range of legislative instruments, including the Children Act 1989.

The legislature has effectively set the child protection framework within which the judiciary and executive must operate. In their turn, the executive has the task of implementing legislative provisions in a wide variety of practical ways. For example, all police forces have child abuse investigation units or teams, and cases of abuse linked to exorcism would ordinarily be dealt with by these designated teams. All providers of NHS-funded services are required to have a named doctor and a named nurse with responsibility for safeguarding.[92] Again, cases of child abuse linked to exorcism are among the issues these safeguarding officers are required to address. (While health providers might not generally be thought of as exercising executive powers, in this context they are key in detecting and instigating action on breaches of criminal law.

90 Stobart, n. 80 above, 26.

91 See, e.g., the debates during the passage of what is now the Children and Families Act 2014: *Daily Hansard* (13 Nov 2013), 'Children and Families Bill', http://www.publications.parliament.uk/pa/ld201314/ldhansrd/text/131118-gc0001.htm, col. GC 325; and the Exorcism of Children (Prohibition) Bill presented to the House of Commons (15 Feb 2001), http://www.publications.parliament.uk/pa/cm200001/cmbills/033/2001033.htm.

92 Metropolitan Police, n. 82 above.

Health visitors and GPs are in most instances more likely than police officers to observe and act upon signs of abuse.)

However, just because cases of abuse linked to exorcism are dealt with by the wider arrangements in place in respect of child protection and safeguarding, it does not mean that the executive has failed to specifically address the issues which arise in relation to this particular kind of abuse. For instance, the Metropolitan Police has launched 'Project Violet' in order to:

- develop prevention strategies and initiatives;
- educate and raise awareness among professionals, communities and faith leaders;
- provide advice, support and guidance for referrals and investigations; and
- develop intelligence opportunities.[93]

There is a clear acknowledgement that (i) the religious and cultural factors at play within this type of child abuse require state representatives to operate differently from the way in which they would in cases where beliefs about spirit possession were not a factor, and (ii) having a legal framework which treats religion as a distinct and significant phenomenon encourages particular sensitivity to this type of context. It must be understood that there are considerable challenges in these cases in terms of assessing the causes underlying the problems, and the motivations driving the parties' behaviour, as they are likely to be very different from many other contexts in which child abuse or neglect occurs.

Depriving a child of adequate food, warmth and emotional security is utterly unacceptable and rightly unlawful, whatever the internal narrative of the adults responsible. The optimal strategy for identifying and dealing effectively with this will be very different in a case where parents lack the skills or inclination to provide adequate care from that of a situation in which the abusive adults believe that they are punishing an evil spirit occupying the body of a human child.

This is certainly not to suggest that religious motivations make the criminal behaviour in any way less heinous, or that they should automatically provide evidence of mitigating circumstances, but a different context requires a different response in order to effectively address it. There are circumstances, such as this one, in which a religious dimension to a situation adds *difference* rather than positivity. Nevertheless, it is a strength of the constitutional and legal framework that it is able to be sensitive to this difference at the level of its executive response.

In addition, the judicial task of keeping in check executive action ensures that while the police and other branches of the executive may rightly adopt a tailored strategy to the particular problem, the overarching standards are adhered to in accordance with statutory provisions such as the Human Rights Act 1998, the Police and Criminal Evidence Act 1984 and the Children Act 1989, as well as common law mechanisms such as judicial review. The executive approach can be

93 Ibid.

targeted, but must remain within the parameters set by the legal framework. This will continue to be the case unless and until the legislature revisits its previous decisions not to enact special legislation to apply specific provisions in this area.

Thus, considered in the round, the way in which the current legal framework deals with child exorcism can be seen to both facilitate and demonstrate the functioning of the separation of powers model.

6.3.3 Planning law and the public sector equality duty (PSED)

The Equality Act 2010, which covers England, Wales and Scotland, imposed a general equality duty on public bodies.[94] The way in which this has been implemented in Scotland reflects both the religious character of the Constitution, and also the way in which this dimension enhances the functioning of separation of powers. The Equality and Human Rights Commission in Scotland[95] summarises the duty as follows: Those to whom the duty applies must have due regard to the need to:

- eliminate unlawful discrimination, harassment and victimisation;
- advance equality of opportunity between different groups; and
- foster good relations between different groups.

The duty applies to those with 'relevant protected characteristics': age, disability, gender, gender reassignment, pregnancy and maternity, race, religion or belief, and sexual orientation. It also imposes a requirement to have due regard to the need to eliminate discrimination linked to marriage and civil partnerships in relation to employment issues.

As McColgan's analysis demonstrates,[96] the PSED applies in the context of decisions made in relation to planning law, and may be of great importance in applications for judicial review of planning decisions. The appellate courts have considered the duty in a planning context in cases such as *R (Baker & Others) v SSCLG*[97] and *R (Harris) v LB Haringey*.[98] Although, as McColgan argues, the way in which the courts interpret this duty is still evolving, it is clear from judicial pronouncements in *Harris* that a failure to factor the PSED into the decision-making process will almost inevitably lead to successful applications for judicial review. There is room for debate on how much regard is 'due regard', but if all consideration is absent it is clear that the threshold has not been met.

94 Equality Act 2010, s. 149.

95 Equality and Human Rights Commission Scotland, 'Public Sector Equality Duty FAQs', https://www.equalityhumanrights.com/en/public-sector-equality-duty-scotland/public-sector-equality-duty-faqs.

96 A. McColgan, 'Litigating the Public Sector Equality Duty: The Story So Far', *Oxford Journal of Legal Studies*, Vol. 35 (2015) 453–85.

97 *R (Baker and Others) v Secretary of State for Communities and Local Government* [2008] EWCA Civ 141.

98 *R (Harris) v London Borough of Haringey* [2010] EWCA Civ 703.

Arguably, the awareness that local authorities now have of the possibility of judicial challenge on these grounds may both encourage and empower them to take into account issues relating to religion and belief in a planning context. This is especially relevant where beliefs are at play in circumstances in which such beliefs might not be widely understood and accepted by the majority of the population as being of importance.

A dispute in the Scottish Highlands, reported in *The Times* in 2005,[99] provides a powerful example of such a situation. A housing developer wished to move a large rock in the course of constructing a new estate, but many of the local community of St Fillans were concerned that this would cause injury or offence to the fairies living there. At first the property developer involved assumed that these objections were light-hearted, but it became apparent that the beliefs in fairies associated with that rock were deep-seated and genuine. In this instance, the problems were resolved through dialogue. A meeting of the local community council looked likely to raise a complaint about the proposed building work, and the Planning Inspectorate indicated that it had discretion to take into account local customs and beliefs in reaching a decision.[100] Given that the proposed development was in a National Park, objections from the community council would have had a serious and probably fatal impact on the chances of the application succeeding.[101] An alternative arrangement was reached, and it was agreed that a park would be placed in the centre of the new estate, and the fairies' rock could remain undisturbed.

In that instance, the systems in place appear to have functioned very well and a compromise solution, acceptable to all parties, was achieved. However, it is possible to imagine similar situations arising in which public authorities would not demonstrate comparable sensitivity, and in which the PSED in relation to religion and belief could be used to require decision makers to take into account the deeply held beliefs of local communities.

Ancient beliefs about fairies or nature spirits dwelling in the landscape do persist in many parts of northern Europe. For example, in 2013 concerns about elves were a factor in blocking a project to construct a new road in Iceland.[102] There have also been a number of controversies in Ireland in the twentieth and twenty-first[103] centuries concerning fairy rocks and trees.[104] It is true that some voices argue that, at times, fairies and elves have been used by environmentalists

99 W. Pavia and C. Windle, 'Fairies Stop Developers Bulldozers in their Tracks', *The Times* (21 Nov 2005), https://www.thetimes.co.uk/article/fairies-stop-developers-bulldozers-in-their-tracks-dhk3qfz3rr7.

100 Mysterious Britain & Ireland, 'Fairies of St Fillans' (2005), http://www.mysteriousbritain.co.uk/scotland/perthshire/folklore/fairies-of-st-fillans-2005.html.

101 Scottish Government, 'Building, Planning and Design Policy', http://www.gov.scot/Topics/Built-Environment/planning.

102 Associated Press, 'Elf Lobby Blocks Iceland Road Project', *The Guardian* (22 Dec 2013), https://www.theguardian.com/world/2013/dec/22/elf-lobby-iceland-road-project.

103 J. Walsh ,'John Walsh on Monday: Irish Road Side-Tracked by the Fairies' Right of Way', *The Independent* (19 Nov 1999), http://www.independent.co.uk/news/john-walsh-on-monday-irish-road-side-tracked-by-the-fairies-right-of-way-1120744.html.

104 P. Coulter, 'Fairy Tales: Finding Fairy Bushes Across Northern Ireland', *BBC News* (13 Feb 2015), http://www.bbc.co.uk/news/uk-northern-ireland-31459851.

and others as a device for pursuing their own agendas to prevent building work, but it is incontrovertible that there are those who do believe sincerely.[105]

Whether or not these beliefs could or should be categorised as 'religious' in nature, the PSED is drafted widely enough to encompass them, and to ensure that holders of beliefs should not be subjected to less favourable treatment or be denied respect and dignity. In our view, this is highly positive, especially in light of the humorous tone which journalists are apt to take in reporting stories about fairy-based protests. Minority beliefs which conflict with the majoritarian world-view are especially vulnerable, and therefore arguably need to be treated with particular sensitivity. Given that the nature of many fairy and elf beliefs is such that they are often associated with features of the landscape – such as rocks, trees, pools and waterfalls – there is inevitably potential for conflict when commercial or other interests seek to develop formerly wild areas.[106]

In addition, because these beliefs are marginalised and even ridiculed in some quarters, there is scope for their adherents to feel disempowered and hostile if their views are not adequately heard and, where appropriate, accommodated. As we discussed in relation to parliamentary sovereignty, legislation can be fully effective only if citizens are prepared to accept and co-operate with its aims and implementation. Providing groups and individuals with minority views the opportunity to challenge decision-makers who ignore their perspective is not only positive in terms of the separation of powers, it also promotes parliamentary sovereignty and the rule of law.

Added to this, picking up on a theme from Chapter 3, it is not clear whether a belief in fairies would meet the *Williamson*[107] test and qualify for protection under Article 9 of the European Convention on Human Rights. Like the fairies themselves, such a belief is of an uncertain nature and might or might not be interpreted as religious or relating to some fundamental question. Consequently, the operation of PSED and a willingness to accept deeply held beliefs which are not necessarily caught by Article 9 is highly positive.

For all of the reasons outlined, it is beneficial that the PSED is broad enough to afford beliefs in elves, fairies and nature spirits recognition and protection, and the fact that the significance of PSED in a planning judicial review context is now well established strengthens the separation of powers.

6.3.4 Overview

It can be said that separation of powers is enhanced by the religious character of the Constitution and wider juridical system in two ways. First, it allows for a spiritual perspective to be fed into the collective dialogue on the exercise of power

105 B. Radford, 'Elves (Yes, Elves) Spark Road-Building Protest in Iceland', *Live Science* (14 Jan 2014), http://www.livescience.com/42547-elves-spark-environmental-protest-iceland.html.

106 T. Bane, *The Encyclopaedia of Fairies in the World of Folklore and Mythology* (Jefferson: North Carolina and London) 2013.

107 See further Ch. 3, and *R (on the application of Williamson) v Secretary of State for Education and Employment* [2005] UKHL 15, [2005] 2 AC 246.

and the management of the same by the legislature. Second, and arguably more importantly, it ensures that faith-based issues relating to separation of powers are effectively and sensitively managed. In the case of child exorcism and, the PSED and planning law in Scotland, there is a balance to be struck between the legitimate and necessary action of the state in protecting the vulnerable and managing the use and development of land, and the freedoms and needs of individuals and faith groups on the other.

This effective functioning encourages faith groups, and indeed other sectors of society, to see that state power is being exercised appropriately, and to challenge it where they have grievances and concerns. This bolstering of legitimacy assists the separation of powers, as it increases the likelihood that citizens will engage with lawful forms of protest and challenge when they are dissatisfied with governmental decision-making. A greater number of parties who are willing to actively participate in watching and questioning the exercise of power can only help to drive forward this constitutional pillar.

In addition, it reduces the likelihood of the frustrated and marginalised resorting to unlawful tactics to make their voices heard, thereby supporting the rule of law. The constitutional pillars are all part of the same structure, and if one topples it will inevitably risk bringing the others down with it.

6.4 How do the perspectives and teaching of different religious belief groups influence perceptions of separation of powers and checks and balances?

Having examined how the religious dimension of the Constitution enhances the separation of powers, we now turn our attention to the question of how the teaching and ideas of faith groups might influence the thoughts of their members in relation to the monitoring and exercise of worldly power.

6.4.1 Christianity

As might be expected, Christianity has a complex approach towards questions of power and authority. There are many layers to the overall picture that emerges. In part, it is difficult because the faith emerged as an apocalyptic movement, and many of the Scriptures of the New Testament were not centred around planning a society for the long term. It was only gradually that the realisation dawned that the Second Coming might take some time, and that teaching about governance in the present world could not be based on the assumption that it was temporary and transitory.[108] Furthermore, the faith had to make the transition in many contexts from being a persecuted minority cult to the religion of princes and rulers.

There are some unambiguous statements from Christ, however, about how power is to be wielded. For example, Luke 22:24–27:

108 R. Daly, *Apocalyptic Thought in Early Christianity* (Baker Publishing: Grand Rapids) 2009.

> 24. A dispute also arose among them as to which one of them was to be regarded as the greatest. 25. But he said to them, 'The kings of the Gentiles lord it over them; and those in authority over them are called benefactors. 26. But not so with you; rather the greatest among you must become like the youngest, and the leader like one who serves. 27. For who is greater, the one who is at the table or the one who serves? Is it not the one at the table? But I am among you as one who serves.[109]

The theme of humility and 'servant leadership' became and remains an important strand within Christian thought. Power is to be exercised not to exploit the vulnerable, but to protect and nurture them.[110] Nevertheless, this is a vision of power from the inside looking out. What about power from the outside looking in? What is the appropriate response from a Christian who sees an authority figure abusing his or her position?

Again, there is more than one strand to the philosophy, and it has suited different people down the ages to emphasise different aspects of Christian thought. There has always been the prophetic tradition, with strong biblical foundations, in which the righteous reproach kings and leaders. For example, Nathan shames King David for having taken Bathsheba, the wife of Uriah the Hittite.[111] David spied on Bathsheba while she was bathing, arranging to commit adultery with her, and then attempted to cover up an embarrassing pregnancy scandal by engineering her husband's predictable death in battle.

David, at least, has a conscience and listens to the prophet with due contrition. There are other stories which suggest that, at times, there may be a moral imperative to speak out against unjust rulers, even when the consequences are predictably dire. John the Baptist took Herod to task for (among other things) his unlawful relationship with his sister-in-law, Herodias.[112] This not only resulted in him being thrown into prison, it eventually led to his death, as Herodias did not take kindly to John's interference and, with the help of her daughter, ultimately acquired his head on a plate.

This honoured prophetic culture of speaking out against tyrannical or even inappropriate royal actions continued, and was celebrated in saints like Hugh of Lincoln, who was a friend but also vocal critic of three Angevin monarchs.[113] In more recent times, Christians have continued to honour individuals who have spoken the truth to criticise those exercising lawful or unlawful power in oppressive ways, regardless of the personal cost. For example, Dietrich Bonhoeffer[114]

109 The Holy Bible, New Revised Standard Version (NRSV), Luke 22:24–27.

110 A. Lindzey, *Animal Theology* (SCM Press: London) 1994.

111 NRSV, 2 Samuel 12.

112 NRSV, Luke 3:19.

113 D. Farmer, *The Oxford Dictionary of Saints* (Oxford University Press: Oxford), 5th edn, 2003, 257.

114 Bonhoeffer was a Lutheran pastor who opposed the Nazi regime in Germany and was ultimately executed in a concentration camp, just two weeks before it was liberated: see further E. Metaxas, *Bonhoeffer: Pastor, Martyr, Prophet, Spy* (Thomas Nelson: Nashville) 2011.

and Oscar Romero[115] both paid with their lives for speaking out with integrity, and are commemorated by Christians across the doctrinal spectrum, not merely within their own respective Lutheran and Roman Catholic traditions. For example, the Anglican Westminster Abbey includes them both in its ten statues of twentieth-century martyrs.[116]

It is only fair to acknowledge that there have been contrasting aspects of the Christian tradition. The principle of respect for authority and submitting patiently in this life, even to the point of enduring oppressive behaviour, has also been a factor. Again, there are passages in the Christian Scriptures which support this:

> Let every person be subject to the governing authorities; for there is no authority except from God, and those authorities that exist have been instituted by God. Therefore whoever resists authority resists what God has appointed, and those who resist will incur judgement.[117]

There was also a related concept that human beings were placed in a particular position within the social hierarchy according to divine will, and that individuals should embrace and accept this, along with whatever conventional limitations were expected to come with their economic status, gender or racial group. The original version of the popular hymn 'All Things Bright and Beautiful' is a classic illustration:

> The rich man in his castle,
> the poor man at his gate,
> God made them high and lowly,
> and ordered their estate[118]

However, it is also highly relevant to note that this notorious verse is omitted from most modern hymn books. The centre of gravity of mainstream Christianity has long since moved away from this pattern of thought, and down the ages there have always been many spiritual preachers and teachers who strongly disavowed it. Figures as diverse as John Wesley, Cardinal Manning,[119] Oscar Romero, Martin

115 Romero was Archbishop of San Salvador and campaigned against poverty, social justice and the gross human rights abuses which were taking place; he was assassinated while saying mass: see further I. Hodgson, *Archbishop Oscar Romero: A Shepherd's Diary* (St Anthony Messenger Press: Cincinnati) 1993.

116 'UK Martyrs of the Modern Era', *BBC News* (9 Jul 1998), http://news.bbc.co.uk/1/hi/uk/129587.stm.

117 NRSV, Romans 13:1–2.

118 C.F. Alexander, 'Hymns for Little Children' (1848), http://www.cyberhymnal.org/htm/a/l/allthing.htm.

119 The Roman Catholic Archbishop of Westminster, who was a key player in conciliating the London Dock strike of 1889 and who championed the right of all workers to be treated with dignity and paid a fair wage: see Caritas Anchor House, 'Celebrating the Life and Legacy of Cardinal Manning' (11 Jun 2014), http://caritasanchorhouse.org.uk/blog/2014/06/11/

Luther King and Anne Hutchinson[120] testify to the longstanding and continuing capacity for spiritually inspired protests from Christians about systemic injustices.

However, it is also both fair and important to note that there is another dynamic to both Christian thought and social reality. There are instances of tyranny and abuse so extreme that most individuals of conscience, regardless of faith or place on the political spectrum, would affirm the need to oppose them. The regime in Nazi Germany is an obvious and tragic example of this. Most of the time, however, society and politics function in a way which is more collaborative than oppositional. Although there are different points of view on political questions, and specific issues which might be the subject of protest, the debate and challenge takes place within an accepted system.

In other words, most Christians, and indeed most citizens, would probably not see themselves as being locked within a Harry Potteresque battle between good and evil in terms of the UK Constitution and legal system. Most people would not identify those with a different political opinion from themselves with (in Christian terms) the Anti-Christ, but understand that they have the opportunity to participate as citizens in a functional, if imperfect system, and attempt to work collectively for the common good. The system itself contains checks and balances and the capacity for reform.

In reality, it is only in extreme situations that there is a polarised choice between critiquing authority figures and their decisions, and between willing to support and collaborate with the power structures in question. For instance, most individuals would not deny the legitimacy of the Westminster Government, nor refuse to engage with public bodies, simply because they voted for a losing party in a General Election and also believe that the voting system should be reformed.

In conclusion, there is a strong Christian tradition for speaking out against the wrongful use of power, but this should not be set up as being in opposition to working within the political system to change it.

6.4.2 Judaism

Judaism is the faith from which Christianity developed, and it is almost too obvious to need stating that the prophetic tradition referred to above runs equally through Jewish thought. There are occasions when the righteous are required to stand against the abuse of power by earthly rulers.

However, the motif of bringing constructive (rather than destructive) criticism where possible and working collaboratively to build a better a world also runs

celebrating-the-life-and-legacy-of-cardinal-manning; see also J. Pereiro, *Cardinal Manning: An Intellectual Biography* (Clarendon: Oxford) 1998.

120 Anne Hutchinson was a leading figure in political and theological controversies in colonial New England, and is sometimes described as a 'proto-feminist'. While scholars and critics are divided about her legacy, she is certainly a clear example of a committed Christian who rejected the idea that women should be silent and submissive: T. Hall, *Anne Hutchinson: Puritan Prophet* (Pearson: Cambridge) 2010.

through Judaism, as well as Christianity. There is a specific duty to address concerns with other Jews when they are acting wrongly, *toch'acha*,[121] but also a strict prohibition on the malicious use of language, particularly to third parties.[122] Criticism of anyone, high or low, Jew or Gentile, must be raised in the proper manner for righteous motives if it is not to be categorised as a sin. Therefore, those exercising power should be held to account, but in a just and a proportionate manner.

Community is also an extremely important concept within Jewish spirituality. The words of the teacher Hillel (a figure roughly contemporary with Christ) are often quoted: 'If am I not for myself, then who will be for me? If I am only for myself, then who am I? If not now, when?'[123]

Self-respect and self-care are important duties within Judaism. Deliberate punishment or harming of the body do not form part of the tradition and would, in fact, be prohibited in the eyes of most Jewish theologians.[124] However, this does not equate to opting for a self-centred approach to life, and compassion and generosity towards all humankind are non-negotiable requirements. For example, it is written in the Talmud: 'The world rests upon three things, the Torah, service to G-d and showing loving kindness'.[125]

In addition to the commandment to treat all people with compassion, there is the huge emphasis that is placed upon justice: 'Rabbi Shimon the son of Gamliel would say: By three things is the world sustained: law, truth and peace'.[126] Therefore, if the actions of authority figures are causing suffering, especially to the vulnerable, then the requirements of justice and compassion mean that observant Jews should not ignore the situation.

It is also striking that one of the seven universal laws of Noahides is to establish courts of justice.[127] These laws were given to Noah after the flood, and are believed to apply to all humanity rather than simply the Jewish people. Righteous Gentiles who keep them will be granted an equal place in Heaven. In fairness, the content and meaning of these laws is open to debate, but for present purposes it is sufficient to observe that the requirement of a legal justice framework is believed by Judaism to be so fundamental as to be required of Gentiles as well as Jews.

121 See, e.g., NRSV, Leviticus 19:17: 'You shall not hate in your heart anyone of your kin; you shall reprove your neighbour, or you will incur guilt yourself'.

122 See, e.g., NRSV, Jeremiah 9:2–4. There are also complicated rules within Judaism about the proper and improper use of speech, and a highly developed understanding of the damage which misuse of the tongue may cause.

123 Chapters of the Fathers 1:14 (the Chapters of the Fathers, or Pirkei Avot, are a collection of ethical sayings which form a component of the Talmud, or Oral Torah).

124 In contrast to some strands within both Christianity and Islam. Religious mortification of the body is a sufficiently recognised part of religious practice within the Christian tradition that the House of Lords has acknowledged it as one of the known exceptions to the general prohibition on consent to actual bodily harm: *R v Brown* [1994] 1 AC 212.

125 Chapters of the Fathers, 1:2 (this reflects the spelling in the original text).

126 Chapters of the Fathers, 1.18.

127 J. Abramowitz, 'Seven Universal Laws (of Noahides)' *Jew in the City* (20 Nov 2013), http://jewinthecity.com/2013/11/seven-universal-laws-of-noahides.

In other words, there is a requirement built into the Jewish worldview that all human societies should have structures whereby justice can be dispensed through formal processes. Holding the powerful to account and preventing them from oppressing the weak is clearly central to this understanding. Courts effectively prevent those with the biggest sticks, swords or guns, and the most wicked and menacing supporters to wield them, from running the world however it suits them. Taken together, the following themes can be drawn out:

1 Observant Jews are required to pursue the ways of justice and compassion. This, combined with the prophetic tradition of challenging wrongdoing, necessitates that the faithful speak out on behalf of victims of the abuse of power, and also in relation to practices which are damaging for society as a whole.
2 Community, peace, justice and the legal framework are all important values within Judaism. Therefore, it is reasonable to suggest that the overall outlook encourages individuals and groups to participate positively in discussions which further the common good, and to have recourse to courts of law where this is appropriate.

6.4.3 Islam

Once again, it is important to observe that Islam is in a very different position from the other Abrahamic faiths, and particularly Christianity, because in the conventional Muslim paradigm there is no distinction between secular and sacred authority.[128] Therefore, the dialogue about engagement with authority figures which may be derived from scriptural sources is taken from a very different context. There is no space for dialogue between the temporal and the spiritual, because the two are indivisibly enmeshed.

Nevertheless, it is helpful to notice that within Islam, the concept of *adl* (translatable loosely as justice) is regarded as a supreme value:[129]

> Muslim scholars have argued that the main purpose of revelation and the basic task of the prophets is to bring justice on earth … At a communal level, justice demands that one fulfils one's social obligations and responsibilities. It is the duty of a Muslim to stand up against all sorts of oppression, even if this involves one's own blood, society or country.

Once again, oppression, particularly of the weak and vulnerable, is condemned. It is also striking that the teachings of the Prophet include an instruction to '[h]elp your brother, whether he is an oppressor or an oppressed one'.[130]

128 C. Joppke, *The Secular State under Siege: Religion and Politics in Europe and America* (Polity Press: Cambridge) 2015, 137.
129 Z. Sardar and Z. Malik, *Introducing Islam* (Totem Books: Royston) 2004, 57.
130 Sahih Bukhari ,Vol. 3, Book 43, Number 623 (Sahih Bukhari is one of the collections of hadith, or sayings of the Prophet, from the Sunni tradition).

When asked for clarification about how faithful Muslims striving to do good should help the sinful oppressor, the response came back: 'By preventing him from oppressing others'.[131] Consequently, there is a spiritual mandate for active engagement not only with the individuals and groups who might be suffering the consequences of injustice, but also active engagement with the perpetrator.

As with Christianity, Judaism and all of the faiths being discussed, we are not suggesting that there can be a single Islamic perspective on justice or oppression in terms of what constitutes oppressive behaviour, by whom, and what means are legitimate in tackling it. Nevertheless, the requirement from a sense of justice infusing all actions and thoughts, *adl*, is undoubtedly a core component of the faith.

While, as has been noted, there are complex issues about the interface between the sacred and the secular for Muslims living as a minority in a predominantly non-Muslim culture, Joppke raises a key point in this context:

> Cadwell argues that 'in the case of Muslims and Islam in Europe one is not dealing with an ordinary immigration problem … but with an adversary culture' which threatens nothing less than the 'essence of Europe'. In the following, I will argue that there are elements of an 'adversarial culture' but only at the level of Islamic elite discourse. By contrast, ordinary Muslims hold views that are not that different from those of average Europeans or, at worst, similar to those of other religious conservatives.[132]

As we have discussed at length above, the purpose of this study is not to look at the compatibility of Islam with European legal models and culture; that is a complex socio-political dialogue beyond the scope of this book. Nor do we wish to gloss over the reality that there are particular issues with current interaction between Islam and contemporary 'Western' culture at this point in history. However, it is the case that the majority of Muslims living in the United Kingdom see themselves as belonging to the collective project of British society. Like their non-Muslim neighbours, they have a range of opinions on political questions, and are in general willing to participate in the system on the same basis.

The current point is that the underlying emphasis on justice, which Muslims are tasked with allowing to suffuse their thought and action, should be a positive factor in dealing with authority figures. Again, it should encourage a response where authorities are seen to be acting inappropriately, but within the context of trying to relate positively towards others, and assisting those in positions of power to improve their practice where possible. As with the Judeo-Christian model, addressing issues with authority can be couched in collaborative, rather than oppositional terms much of the time.

131 Sahih Bukhari, Vol. 3, Book 43, Number 624.
132 C. Joppke, n. 128 above, 138.

6.4.4 Hinduism

Once again, stepping from the Abrahamic religions into the Eastern religions involves walking into a very different paradigm. The distinction between religion and lifestyle, orthodoxy and orthopraxy begin to mingle. However, a useful starting point for this discussion must be some of the ideas contained within the concept of *dharma*, which might be broadly thought of as a religious duty or pathway. Dwivedi quotes one observation on dharma from Hindu sacred writings: 'Dharma exists for the welfare of all living beings, that which sustains the welfare of all living beings is unquestionably dharma'.[133]

Hinduism commends mercy to all creatures, including fellow human beings, an approach of gentleness and compassion, and a positive affirmation of all that is life-affirming for others. It is true that, as Singh acknowledges, 'there exists a deep gulf between Hindu philosophy interpreted from a variety of ancient Hindu scriptures, and the on-the-ground realities of Hindu practices and social rituals'.[134]

Singh is writing from a perspective shaped by the contemporary Indian experience and the challenges currently faced by that nation. She points out that Hinduism has not wholly escaped the evils of 'casteism, untouchability and bride burning'.[135] Yet, she also emphasises that the strides in the direction of human rights and great social justice which India has made in the last 60 years have been possible because of the 'high sense of justice among average Hindus'.[136]

The interplay between the ancient and the modern is extremely complex within Hinduism, and the relationship between religion and culture is an intricate one in all contexts. It is important to remember that faith-based teaching is not necessarily political philosophy, although it can be, and it is wise to guard against treating the politically orientated aspects of some faiths as templates for examining others. Singh's argument is essentially that Hinduism is a framework within which many different social and political institutions have developed over the course of thousands of years. Some of these have grown directly out of Hindu thought patterns, others have been compatible with them, while still others have been logically incompatible but have nevertheless flourished within majority Hindu societies at different times and places. Disentangling Hinduism from the cultural evolution, which has taken place around it and within it, is by no means easy, nor is it necessarily even *appropriate* as far as many Hindus are concerned, as much as some occidental scholars might pine to attempt it. Singh's observation is that the majority of Hindu society of India has adapted, and is adapting, in ways which are positive in so far as human rights and equality of opportunity are concerned, and that the Hindu tradition has been the intellectual and cultural

133 O. Dwivedi, 'Hinduism: Historical Setting', in M. Palmer and S. Burgess (eds), *The Blackstone Companion to Religion and Social Justice* (Blackstone: Oxford) 2012, 110, 114.

134 A. Singh, 'Hinduism: Contemporary Expressions', in Palmer and Burgess (eds), ibid., 122, 122.

135 Ibid.

136 Ibid.

setting for this paradigm shift. What to many eyes are regressive trends within Hinduism undeniably do exist – for example, support for right wing political parties in India with an agenda that is hostile towards minorities,[137] – but these must be set against the progressive moves that a majority Hindu nation has taken.

Furthermore, the thrust of *dharma* towards compassion for all life, set out above, inclines towards social justice and, therefore, engagement with issues stemming from abuses of power and authority. If individuals and communities are angled towards fostering the well-being of all, then there is motivation to oppose injustice or oppression. This outworking of Hinduism was apparent in the life and teachings of figures such as Gandhi, and has the capacity to motivate Hindus in Great Britain to address injustices where they perceive matters of concern. The pattern of social and political engagement stemming from a call for compassion is common to Hinduism as it is to some of the religions previously discussed.

6.4.5 Buddhism

The Buddhist tradition contains the *Dasavidha-rājadhamma*,[138] the ten-fold virtues which kings – or, in the modern age, other leaders in politics or commerce – should attempt to cultivate. These are charity, morality, altruism, honesty, gentleness, self-control, rejection of anger, rejection of violence, patience and respect for others (including their opinions). Clearly, were this followed, it would be a good blueprint against the misuse of power. However, again this is a view of authority from the inside looking out, and it leaves open the question of how to respond when those who wield power do not display these ten-fold virtues. This is a complicated question, because Buddhism is a pathway which focuses on individual transformation. The emphasis is upon inner change, although of course if individuals are successful in this, collective benefits arise. As a lifestyle it is not selfish, but is centred upon self.

A beautiful illustration of this is to be found in the *Jataka Tales Volume* (Tale 316).[139] On the Holy Day of the full moon, four animals decided to do something charitable in the hope of gaining reward for their goodness. They met an old man begging for food and seized their opportunity to be charitable. The monkey picked fruit from the trees, the otter caught fish and the delinquent jackal went out and managed to thieve a lizard and a pot of milk curd. However, the poor little rabbit knew only how to nibble grass, which was no use to the beggar man to eat, so she threw herself onto the fire so that he could have a supper of roast rabbit. However, the brave rabbit did not burn; the old man was really Sakra[140] and he was

137 See, e.g., D. Ayra, 'Are Hindu Nationalists a Danger to Other Indians?', *BBC News* (12 Sept 2015), http://www.bbc.co.uk/news/magazine-33241100.

138 A. Dharmapala, *The Maha Bodhi, Volume 105* (Maha Bodhi Society of India: Gaya) 1997, 12.

139 See, e.g., E.C. Babitt, *The Complete Jataka Tales* (Jazzybee Verlag Jurgen Beck: Atenmunster) 2012.

140 Or, in Chinese tradition, Dishitian; in Japanese tradition, Taishakuten. He is lord of one of the High Heavens, and he is distinct from the Vedic god, Indra.

so touched by the rabbit's actions that not only did he save her life, he put an image of her on the moon for all to see, still wrapped in smoke.[141]

Stories are as important as doctrine in religious thought, and the tale of the moon rabbit demonstrates well the Buddhist concept that, in addressing a situation, we should look within rather than without. Therefore, there is guidance on how rulers should behave and order their own lives and conduct. There is less, in general terms, about forms of engagement with government, politics or others wielding power.

Of course, this whole analysis is being drawn in incredibly broad brush strokes. There are many Buddhist traditions, some of which contain more structured ideas about models for human society, others would encourage followers to try to eschew entirely all worldly concerns. However, viewed from a distance, the centre of gravity is on inner transformation rather than communal action. Yet, as the story of the moon rabbit reminds us, this does not translate into an isolationist approach to life or indifference to the suffering or problems of others. Therefore, Buddhists may have a strong interest in social dialogue which involves a reduction of suffering or the promotion of harmony, and it is fair to say that implicit within the ten-fold virtues of kingship is an assumption of discussion and collaboration. How is a king supposed to respect the views of others unless people (even if only the elite) are actually talking to him?

In consequence, there is an impetus from a Buddhist perspective to address power in society and the way it is being used or misused, but from a position of collaboration and self-awareness. The drive is to strive for peace, harmony and the well-being of all, and this will spill over into social and political action.

6.4.6 Sikhism

As we have seen in earlier chapters, Sikhism is a faith which stresses the importance of community, working alongside others and addressing issues of social and political justice. This is significant in understanding how the faith group approaches issues of managing and interacting with the holders of temporal power.

It is striking that there have been expressions of disappointment from the Sikh community that, following the 2015 General Election, there are no Sikh Members of the House of Commons. However, a spokesman for Sikhs in England affirmed his confidence that Sikh issues would not be lost, and that the Sikh community could, and would, use other political mechanisms to get issues examined: 'I do not believe that because there are no Sikh MPs that Sikhs' issues will be lost', he said. 'There are appropriate political mechanisms to get all issues examined'. He added: 'I think all MPs are swayed by party issues, but on a personal basis they take all constituent issues importantly. I am not dismayed by the lack of Sikh MPs in Parliament'.[142] This response reveals an important facet of the community

141 There are many slight variations of this basic tale throughout Asia and East Asia.

142 D. Talwar and B. Mostyn, 'No Sikhs in New Parliament', *BBC News* (12 May 2015), http://www.bbc.co.uk/news/uk-politics-32696615.

outlook, even though happily post the 2017 election, there is once again Sikh representation in the House of Commons.

This affirmation of a continuing intent to engage with matters in the public forum, and also a sanguine attitude towards taking matters to non-Sikh constituency MPs, are in keeping with the general Sikh worldview. Sikhism actively embraces interfaith collaboration and acknowledges the validity of other religious pathways. For example, the Sri Guru Granth Sahib (the holy book which Sikhs revere as a living guru) states: 'The person who recognises that all spiritual paths lead to the One shall be emancipated'.[143]

Therefore, working with non-Sikh individuals and institutions with authority is not problematic for Sikhs. In addition, the Sikh emphasis on justice and community action promotes an active stance towards issues that are perceived to be problematic. So there is another instance of a worldview which would encourage engagement and challenge where appropriate, but would also see collaborative action as preferable to confrontational approaches where possible.

6.4.7 Zoroastrianism

Again, as we have seen in earlier chapters, this is a faith tradition which promotes compassion and justice, and therefore would see working to address issues of inappropriate action by authority figures and structures as part and parcel of this holistic outlook. Zoroastrianism teaches that there are opposing forces in the universe, consciously embracing the dualism which Christianity and Judaism at times flirt with, but doctrinally firmly reject. Not only do human beings personally have two inclinations, for evil and for good, there is also an ongoing cosmic battle between good and evil. Individuals have a duty to join in on the side of righteousness, order, harmony, compassion, a concept encapsulated in the word *asha*. Ensuring that society is well ordered, but also just and caring, is a part of the struggle to promote *asha*.

Therefore, although on one level the focus of the core teaching of the faith is not overtly political, living out the ideals of the faith require an engagement with the world and society. Zoroastrianism is not an aesthetic religion, which seeks escape or distance from the material or temporal. These traits have led to high levels of political engagement by members of the Zoroastrian community. As discussed, the first British Asian MP was a Parsi,[144] and was followed by a variety of other prominent British Asian politicians in the late nineteenth and twentieth centuries. The same ideological trends which promote active political participation would encourage vigilance in terms of the exercise of authority by temporal leaders and a preparedness to be active in responding to issues seen as problematic.

6.4.8 Paganism

As noted earlier, those who self-identify within modern Paganism are bound together by commonly agreed doctrines. Nevertheless, the Wiccan Rede is

143 Sri Guru Granth Sahib, 142.

144 S. Mistry, 'Naorojiin, Dadabhai', in D. Dabydeen et al. (eds), *The Oxford Companion of Black British History* (Oxford University Press: Oxford) 2007, 336–7.

adopted by many, and in its full version stresses the importance of love, trust and fair dealing with all.[145] To misuse power would be contrary to the spirit and word of the Rede, and invite the dark consequences of the 'three-fold law'. Both good and evil deeds alike are revisited upon the doer with triple strength. Personal responsibility is a key element of Wicca and many other branches of Neo-Paganism.

However, there remains the question of how this rejection of any abuse of power might translate into the collective context. Certainly, the implicit mandate to do good deeds inspires individuals and groups to speak out against injustice and oppression. There is ample evidence of this ideology being put into practice in contemporary Great Britain, especially in relation to issues which are of particular importance for the Pagan community. For example, many Pagan groups have engaged in peaceful protest and awareness-raising in relation to fracking and other environmental issues, as well as trying to combat in a spiritual manner what they perceive as harmful developments.[146]

6.4.9 Common themes

Drawing the above threads together, some common patterns emerge. While the different religious traditions view the material, and even the secular world, in different ways, and have different teachings on the appropriate way for individuals and communities to respond, there are a number of themes that recur in different guises, in particular:

- the importance of justice and order;
- the significance of compassion, and the need for this to be displayed through practical action;
- the importance of rulers and society operating in accordance with justice and kindness;
- the need to challenge injustice and alleviate suffering;
- a sense of personal responsibility, and a preference for dialogue and collaborative action over confrontation, where there is possible, in order to challenge injustice and alleviate suffering.

6.5 Do faith communities make a practical contribution towards the functioning of checks and balances and separation of powers? Lobbying, campaigning and litigation – turning the mill wheels

The elements of the separation of powers concept described above could be compared with the gears of a mill. They are of very little use without either wind or water to push them around. As well as the engagement from within the system,

145 The Celtic Connection, 'The Wiccan Rede', http://wicca.com/celtic/wicca/rede.htm.

146 L. Thorp, 'Pagans Gather in Moss Bank Park for Anti-Fracking Ritual', *The Bolton News* (30 Sept 2013), http://www.theboltonnews.co.uk/news/10706465._/

religious communities have an important part in ensuring that the separation of powers functions from without, making the gears turn. Many religious groups are actively involved in lobbying members of the legislature when they are concerned about actions by the executive. This pressure encourages Members of Parliament to question and scrutinise executive plans and action.

For example, a recent government bill to reintroduce fox-hunting was met with opposition campaigns from groups such as the Anglican Society for the Welfare of Animals[147] and the Animal Interfaith Alliance.[148] While opinion may vary about the arguments put forward by these groups, the engagement and demand for scrutiny, in and of itself, furthers the doctrine of separation of powers.

In addition to concerted lobbying, the principles discussed above in relation to the proper use of power and social justice prompt religious spokespeople to condemn government action where this is deemed to be inappropriate. For example, Roman Catholic and Anglican clergy attacked the Government policy decision not to back rescue missions for refugees drowning in the Mediterranean:

> Bishop Patrick Lynch, who speaks for the Roman Catholic Church in England and Wales on migration, said the decision not to support rescues was 'a misguided abdication of responsibility' to thousands of desperate people fleeing war and persecution in the Middle East and Africa. He said that as Europe's 'leading naval power' the UK has a moral responsibility to step in to save those risking death in attempting to reach Europe.
>
> The Anglican Bishop of St Albans, the Rt Rev Alan Smith, said the decision was one he would 'lament'.[149]

Once again, the validity of this criticism is, of course, a moot point. This will always be true in relation to the validity of the contribution made by *any* party to *any* debate, and the criticism given by any party to any debate may be open to question. The crucial point is that the willingness of these groups to engage helps to ensure full and open discussion and scrutiny of policy decisions, and such engagement itself is of value.

Furthermore, although in this instance the faith groups concerned felt morally obliged to simply condemn what was being proposed, in many other instances the object is to contribute to or foster dialogue, rather than to take an oppositional

147 Anglican Society for the Welfare of Animals, 'Campaigns: Threat to Hunting Bill', http://www.aswa.org.uk/page/campaigns/threat_to_hunting_bill/.

148 Animal Interfaith Alliance, 'Interfaith Celebration for Animals and AGM 2015' (13 Jul 2015), https://animal-interfaith-alliance.com/?s=AGM+2015.

149 J. Bingham, 'Church Condemns Government as Un-Christian over Stance on Drowning Migrants', *The Telegraph* (30 Oct 2014), http://www.telegraph.co.uk/news/uknews/immigration/11198140/Church-condemns-Government-as-un-Christian-over-stance-on-drowning-migrants.html.

stance. For example, in 2013, a number of Christian Churches (the Methodist Church, Baptists Together, Church of Scotland and the United Reform Church) came together to publish a report entitled 'Truth and Lies About Poverty', and urged individuals to take the following steps:

> *Tell your MP*
>
> Let your MP know that you care. We have sent a copy of this report to every MP in the country. Now they need to know that their constituents care about this issue. We want you to write to your MP – ask them to ensure that they read the report and listen to its recommendations. Email your MP now!
>
> *Tell your local newspaper editor*
>
> Use Church Action on Poverty's web tool to ask the editor, journalists and readers of your local newspaper to think carefully about the labels they use – and the people behind those labels.
>
> *Meet your MP*
>
> Set up a meeting with your MP to talk about the issues raised in the report, and to ask them to help stop lies about poverty permeating public debate.[150]

Although this was very clearly a campaign with a strong agenda, it was one which sought to engage people in well-informed and constructive dialogue, rather than simply criticising and moving on. This kind of action does not merely hold those who wield power to account in the sense of catching and restraining misuse of that power, but provides suggestions on how power could be redirected and reapplied. Of course, other parties may legitimately disagree about the merits of the arguments being put forward, but whether or not the points made are ultimately accepted and adopted, it is positive that another reasoned perspective is fed into the dialogue for discussion and consideration. This kind of model of engagement treats separation of powers like the gears of a mill wheel which need to be moved in order for the Constitution to function; the opposing forces and energy feed into a collective and productive action. This is in harmony with the five principles set out above, and is also to the overall benefit of society.

There are times, however, when a more confrontational stance is deemed appropriate and when litigation may be resorted to. The role of the judiciary in the separation of powers cannot be performed unless citizens or groups of citizens bring cases into the arena of the courts. In this area, the cases will generally be in relation to matters concerning the faith groups themselves rather than

150 Churches Working Together, Joint Public Issues Team, 'Truth and Lies About Poverty' (1 Mar 2013), http://www.jointpublicissues.org.uk/truthandliesaboutpoverty.

society as a whole. In pragmatic terms, parties will usually have neither the legal standing nor the inclination to litigate matters that do not concern them directly. Nevertheless, this in no way invalidates or downgrades the importance of this in relation to the functioning of the separation of powers. The role of the judiciary in this would be highly ineffective if parties did not come to the courts and enable the judiciary to perform its constitutional function. The UK system does not empower judges to instigate investigatory measures of their own volition, so the judicial input into separation of powers requires some form of external instigation if it is to be exercised.

The type of action may vary depending upon the nature of the case. It may be founded in administrative law. It could equally well commence in a private law field such as employment, where an individual backed by a faith group (or groups) brings a claim in the Employment Tribunal, arguing that there is a human rights dimension to the case. This may directly call into question the decision-making and policies of a public body where the employee works in the public sector, or the adequacy of legislation or policy where the employee works in the private sphere, but the employee is unable to obtain protection or vindication of his or her rights on the basis of the current legal framework.

The case of Nadia Eweida is a good example of this. She initially sued her employer, British Airways, in the Employment Tribunal for refusing to pay her for a period of semi-voluntary suspension.[151] She had presented at work wearing a cross, contrary to uniform policy, and refused to perform a non-public facing role while the matter was investigated. Having taken her case through the domestic courts in the United Kingdom, she ultimately ended up in Strasbourg, proceeding against the state for failing to provide her with a remedy.[152]

The case gave the courts an opportunity to consider the legislative framework and its compliance with the European Convention on Human Rights; the fact that Ms Eweida did not obtain the outcome she desired at the domestic level does not detract from this dimension. Furthermore, the case also indirectly contributed to the separation of powers in relation to the considerable amount of academic and popular debate that it generated. This gave other groups with an interest, faith-based or otherwise, an opportunity to air their views in relation to the collective dialogue.

A vast array of other issues have been litigated and continue to be brought before the courts, either directly by faith groups or through religious organisations providing financial assistance and moral support to individuals who wish to bring claims. The facts at issue have covered a vast spectrum of concerns, from corporal punishment in schools[153] to reasonable professional requirements for sex

151 *Eweida v British Airways plc* [2010] EWCA Civ 80.

152 *Eweida and Others v United Kingdom* [2013] ECHR 37.

153 *R (on the application of Williamson) v Secretary of State for Education and Employment*, n. 107 above.

therapists.[154] Equally, at times faith groups have intervened to help a defendant in a case, and have provided input into the judicial process and public debate from the other side of the fence.

6.6 Conclusion

As we have seen, the religious dimension of the Constitution and legal framework enhances separation of powers in two key ways: (i) it supports the role of faith communities as active participants in the system, challenging and questioning the exercise of state power; and (ii) it strengths the capacity of the legal machinery to deal appropriately with conflicts around the use of state power, and the practice of religious faith.

In terms of the first aspect, separation of powers can only function fully, and the judicial aspect of it can only function at all, with external as well as internal input. The concern for furthering the values of compassion and justice, which span all of the mainstream religious traditions we have examined, provides impetus for both individuals and groups to engage with this and participate in ensuring that the checks and balances on the exercise of power are effectively maintained. In supporting faith groups and enabling them to participate in the life of the state, the legal framework enhances separation of powers.

Clearly, the role of religious bodies is very different from that of the Church in the Middle Ages, when all temporal power (legislative, executive and judicial) was acknowledged to reside with and flow from royal authority, and spiritual power was the only systemic and official force to counterbalance it – although, as King John could testify to his chagrin, other temporal interests could and did push back against the exercise of this authority when they deemed it was being abused. However, even in the case of the baronial rebellion, it was no accident that the Church, both domestically and internationally, was a key player in the renegotiation of the balance of power.

Nevertheless, religious groups do still have a key part to play. Just as the octopus is not defenceless without the hard shell of its ancestors, faith bodies have evolved new and more diverse ways of acting as a counterbalance on the exercise of temporal power. As would be expected given the liminal nature of the established Churches, they fulfil this function from both within and without the organs of state authority. The Church of England participates in the House of Lords, bolstering the capacity of the legislature to respond to and scrutinise executive action.

In addition, even more importantly, there is the second consideration outlined above. The religious dimension of the legal framework enables issues that

154 *Eweida and Others v United Kingdom*, n. 152 above; see the element of the case concerning one of the claimants, Macfarlane, a sex therapist who objected to counselling same-sex couples.

directly concern a clash between the outworkings of faith and the legitimate exercise of state power (for example, in responding to child exorcism abuse cases or dealing with planning applications contested on spiritual grounds) to be dealt with sensitively, and therefore, effectively. This increases the willingness of citizens to trust and participate in the system of checks and balances on the exercise of power in a way that promotes both their legitimacy and effectiveness.

In terms of participation from outside state organs of authority, religious groups make a vital contribution in their support and driving of lobbying, campaigning and litigating. Without this injection of external power, the gears driving the mechanisms of the separation of powers simply will not and cannot turn. Faith groups are not unique in engaging in their activities; many other special interest and pressure groups do so. However, like the bishops, faith groups are driven to pursue this course by the guiding principles set out above, which help to foster a benign and constructive manner of participation. It should be emphasised that without the participation of external actors like them the legal and political checks and balances within our Constitution cannot operate.

Chapter 6 appended interview material

The Most Reverend Dr Barry Morgan

What does your faith teach about people with power, and the ways in which they should be held accountable?

Power should only be used to serve people and should be exercised with humility. In the end, we are all accountable to God and one another. Some people in the Church in Wales think that bishops have great power and that the archbishop has absolute power to do what he wants. In fact, the only power one has is influence. If you are in a position of authority, you have to be careful that you don't abuse it. In the end, bishops are accountable to the Church which appoints them.

Dominic Grieve QC MP

What does your Anglican faith teach you about people who exercise power?

This country has never really believed in the separation of powers. Poor old Montesquieu came over and found that the judiciary were independent, which was astonishing, because in France they were the mere creatures of the administration and he was so shocked by this that he thought there was a separation of powers, but actually, in many respects there isn't. Although in reality . . . is our judiciary independent? Well . . . yes, of course, it is, but judicial appointments are subject to a level of parliamentary scrutiny or approval, and power is ultimately wielded by the Queen in Parliament. In terms of religion and the state, is there a separation of powers? Well . . . yes, in practice, but not in theory because of the things we were talking about.

Dr Hilary Firestone

What do you think that Judaism teaches about people with power and how they should be held accountable?

During the Yom Kippur (Day of Atonement) prayers we ask for forgiveness for the sins we have committed in business, man against man, in terms of any economic or political or personal relationships where we have not treated them appropriately. Judaism promotes fairness, honesty and ethical handling.

The Rt Rev'd James Jones

What does your faith teach you about people with power? How should they be held accountable?

That is a brilliant question and I could talk for ever on this. First of all, I think the Church has made a fundamental mistake of making powerlessness a virtue, and not understanding the virtue of power. We talk about Jesus as a powerless person, but in fact he wasn't. In terms of personal charisma, he was immensely powerful. He could silence people by his own power, he could get the attention from the crowds . . . He was immensely powerful and we need in the Church a theology of power. Life is power. Power can be abused, but we need to recover a sense of the goodness and virtue of power. We also need to recover a sense of power originating from God himself. Energy that comes from God.

Can power be corrupting? Can it be corrosive? Yes. Should power be held to account? Yes. That is why I think Christians must be involved in the whole democratic process, because that is a mean to hold powerful people to account. This patronising disposition of unaccountable power needs checks and balances, which is an important feature of our democracy.

Kimberley Long

What does your faith teach you about people with power?

Jesus was a servant, that is the example we are given, he gave up power. He was born as a baby, dependent on others, as a refugee to an unmarried teenage woman. God's bias is towards the poor and not the powerful.

Professor Dame Jocelyn Bell Burnell

What does your faith teach you about the exercise of power and accountability?

[. . .] I think one or two Quaker practices can be useful to wider society . . . in the court of law Quakers ask not to swear an oath, but to affirm, because we argue that swearing an oath implies two standards of truthfulness . . . That must make some people stop and think.

Naveed Choudhry

What does Islam teach you about people with power? How should they be held accountable? By human beings or is it a matter for God? What does Islam have to teach wider society?

The main thing with Islam is, yes . . . we shall be judged by God, especially if you are put in a position of power, and then you have the opportunity to help the world, I think God will judge you for that.

Professor Robert Winston

What, in your view, does Judaism teach about controlling people with power and keeping a check on abuse of power by rulers?

Well, Judaism is very strong on that. Judaism argues in the Talmud – which, after all is a second-century document but it goes back to Biblical exegesis, which is much earlier – that you don't put your trust in princes . . . okay. What it says in the sayings of the Fathers (Pirkei Avot) which is part of the Mishnah, is be on your guard against ruling power, but support it. So, there's a notion that you support the status quo, but be aware that you don't necessarily want to imitate it, okay.

Dr David Perfect

What does Anglicanism teach about the exercise of power?

Anglicanism has a lot to teach the rest of society in terms of separation of powers. The Churches as a whole have a requirement to speak publicly on key moral and social issues, and that has often been seen as overtly political. The classic example for Anglicans is Faith and City in 1979. That report was seen as basically anti-Tory and anti-Mrs Thatcher, but I think the principle was that the Church saw a great increase in social division, and a lot of problems in the urban areas, and it spoke up. It is related to what I said earlier. I think the bishops must speak out; as an institution the Church should do that.

Ioannis Stylianou

What does your faith teach about people with power and how they should be held to account?

Christianity basically says that you will be judged on your actions. So, if someone is in power and acts immorally, affecting people's lives negatively, then he/she will be judged by God. Nevertheless, in my opinion, you should also be judged by the law and the society.

Rev John Chalmers QHC

What does your faith teach about people who exercise power? How should they be held accountable?

I had an extraordinary experience in Nigeria last week, where the state Governor turned up at church and the Moderator of the East Central Synod asked me to pray for the Governor and for success in the election. And he had cornered me in front of a congregation of 1,000 people; it wasn't on the order of service that I was to do this. I knew that in all conscience (and everything which I had learned theologically about the way in which Church and state remain separate) that I wasn't going to pray for his success in the election, but for humility for those who have great power, honesty for those who handle great resources, integrity and wisdom for those who will be voting. I don't think he liked the prayer but that is what he got.

Professor David Feldman

What responsibilities does your faith tradition teach come with power and its exercise?

I think the lesson is that power is dangerous, but sometimes necessary, and usually inevitable. So, if you accept the viability of people having power, you have to think seriously about who has what power.

So, my instincts, when it comes to separation, is that one wants to give as little power to any one person, whether religious or secular, as you can except insofar as is absolutely necessary in order to enable them to do fulfil the task which they have been given.

Chikwan Nam

How should society hold people with power to account and monitor what they do?

[. . .] I do believe in freedom of the press, but again . . . I am a member of Amnesty International and I suppose you do need these groups to say that the public is watching you, watching what you are doing. But do they actually work? I'm not sure. I don't know what the answer is to make it better.

The Rev'd Professor Thomas Watkin

How should society hold people with power to account?

[. . .] I am currently worried that the press and public opinion is becoming too strong in relation to issues which it should not seek to determine. For instance, the issue of a professional footballer being signed up to play football after a rape conviction. There is a very real question about whether a person convicted of that sort of offence should be allowed to resume their career, but it shouldn't be answered by popular clamour. We shouldn't have mob rule; the question should be answered judicially, in a disinterested manner. It should be settled by the court at the time of sentencing. I don't like the press taking on any more than saying that this is a question that needs answering, I find press-led lynch law disturbing. Similarly, I don't like seeing the press hounding someone out of office.

Professor Grace Davie

What mechanisms should we employ to ensure that those who exercise power are accountable? Is the current system functioning effectively?

A free press is crucial, but it is all too often abused. A good example is what has happened recently (May 2015) with Chuka Umunna. I was disturbed by that, because I thought he was the sort of person who could make a very positive contribution to political debate. I don't really know why he withdrew from the leadership contest in the Labour Party, but I did think that the level of media intrusion was unacceptable. We get what we deserve though! If we read the papers, we will encourage the trend . . .

Rabbi Reuven Silverman

How should those with power be held accountable?

You have to realise that Jewish law is a self-contained thing and it is about self-governing the Jewish community, and our approach to the law of the state is that unless the law radically conflicts with Jewish law, then the law of the land must be respected.

Jessica Morden MP

What responsibilities come with power?

I think people with power have a responsibility to speak for those who don't have a voice in our society.

Lucy Gorman

What responsibilities come with power in your faith and understanding?

I think we all have a certain amount of responsibility . . . responsibility to recycle, to be more eco-friendly, to welcome each other into places . . . I don't want to use the word tolerance . . . to make an effort to welcome others, regardless of our backgrounds, and I feel we have that responsibility to others, whether or not we have powers.

Wendy Huggett

How should we hold people with power to account?

Power corrupts and absolute power corrupts absolutely. This is an ethos in which I totally believe.

Shaina Huleatt

What does your faith/ideology teach about people with power? How should they be held accountable by human beings, or is that primarily a matter for God? Does this religious/ideological understanding have anything to teach wider society?

[. . .] While the state has God-given authority to promote peace and order, its commands are backed by coercive force and, as a result, participation in government is antithetical to a Christian life based on love and forgiveness. Therefore, members of the Bruderhof would never hold government office or accept a role (such as a juror) that involves having power over the rights and freedoms of others.

The Rev'd Dr Will Adam

What does your faith teach you about people who exercise power and the responsibilities which come with that?

The New Testament talks about the exercise of authority and the imperative of love. The exercise of any power has to be based on the recognition of the other's human dignity and the common good. Both are things which you can hear very strongly within the Christian tradition.

Dr Myriam Hunter-Henin

What does your Catholic faith teach about people with power? How should they be held accountable? By human beings or is that primarily a matter for God?

Big question! I think they are accountable to God, but I am also a lawyer . . . obviously they should also be accountable to human beings through the right procedures.

Baroness Elizabeth Berridge

How should people who exercise power be held accountable? What responsibilities come with power?

[. . .] This was dealt with by the Old Testament, that power was not to be vested in one person. Power had to be held . . . Judges have to be elected by the seven, the seventy . . . then you had a role for the prophets, the priests and the kings . . . When you look at the Old Testament, it is interesting to see that separation of powers was even recognised then.

Una Mary Parker

What does your faith teach about power and the responsibilities it brings?

I think the Church of England says that we have to be generous to others that haven't got what you have, but they are more interested in individual beliefs rather than they are about how to behave with people who are less privileged. I have never had a conversation with a clergyman that pointed out that I was luckier than other people.

We are all equal before God . . . that's the point, but the CofE doesn't make an issue of that. They don't grudge the rich in the CofE. They are interested in the spiritual side. A very rich man can be very unhappy and need help, whilst the butcher round the street is fine. It is the soul of the person what they are really interested in.

Frank Cranmer

What does your faith teach about power and responsibility/accountability?

[. . .] The Quaker take is that it is the job of right-thinking people to tell people in power when they are wrong and, if necessary, hammer away at them until they do the right thing.

Shaun Wallace

What responsibilities does your Christian faith teach about the exercise of power?

With power comes responsibility and it should be used responsibly. Living in a democratic society, people in power have a responsibility to use it not for their own selfish gain, but for the common interest.

Roque Santa Cruz

What responsibilities do leading sportspeople owe to society as role models? Is their behaviour 'off the pitch' important? Is it appropriate for sports regulators to police/

sanction behaviour which happens outside of the sport (e.g. unrelated criminal offences, drink driving, assault). Why/why not?

I think that it is very important the role model presented by sportspeople, public persons that are seen as role models and, for this reason, there is also a need to be specially hard in sanctioning misbehaviours of these persons. Everybody looks at what famous athletes and public persons are about, a good example is clearer than a million words.

Sir Mark Hedley DL

What duties do all citizens owe society?

All citizens owe to the rest of society compliance with criminal law. Let's start with the fundamentals. Second, there are civil duties which the law of torts provides, which are imposed on us, and, third, effectively duties when we decide to have children, and the care and upbringing of children and so on . . . Beyond that I am a believer that the law has powers to constrain wickedness, but very few powers to make us good . . . the whole essence of good is that we choose it.

Lucy Skilbeck

What do all citizens owe to the rest of society?

[. . .] responsibility to behave as a member of society rather than sitting outside in an individualistic way is fundamental to society working.

Sarah Miles

What responsibilities do all citizens owe to society in general? Do you think that people are comfortable being open about their atheism?

You can't have peace without justice. You can't have justice without sharing. It is as simple as that. No more, no less. You can't have peace without justice, and you can't have justice without sharing. And until that 2,500 pounds handbag goes to someone in need, we are never going to heal the human race. We have to stop this ridiculous nonsense. We have to share equally, all of us. My home has no barriers, everybody is welcome here. I do meditation for people, they don't pay, they just come. No charges, just love!

Eamonn O'Brien

What duties do all citizens owe to the rest of society?

For me, it is always about sharing as much as possible on different levels, not just financially. Sharing resources, time and skills. I found through my limited experience at university that people could help you a lot without giving you money, giving you a book that they've read or emotional and spiritual support. That is difficult to quantify in terms of money and we don't tend to think about it as much; some things we are taught in a religious sense are different from what society expects. Things that we can consume are not always the most important thing; solidarity and support can contribute more.

The Rev'd Professor Martin Henig

What duties do all citizens owe to the rest of society?

They have a duty to make things run more easily, and I think that everyone can make personal judgments which make life for others better, whether that is picking up litter in the street or trying to assist individuals with problems. It's simply a matter of neighbourliness.

Gurd Kandola

What duties do people with power owe to the wider society?

Yes, you know, big corporations and certainly people with that power have greater responsibility to society. It also makes commercial sense actually. I think this is an element that probably draws upon my understanding of Sikhism, the sense that the philosophy that draws on this emphasis on equality . . . there is no shame in the recognition that hard work is important, as well as making your own way, but when you get to a comfortable point, you must also give something back to society: the Sikh concept of *Seva*, being selfless service to the community, is at the core of Sikh belief. So, in a nutshell, yes, there is responsibility towards society. You can't continue down a path totally ignoring and not considering the impact of your actions, individually or collectively. It would be a self-defeating practice indeed.

Lady Brenda Hale

What responsibilities do the judiciary have in relation to society and the exercise of power?

[. . .] I agree to meet groups of schoolgirls, and so on. I think it is important and we learn from it too. It is learning from other people. I think that is a moral responsibility too [. . .] They do know about the Tudors, and they do know about the Second World War, but the Tudors are nothing like as important as what went on in the XVII century. The XVII century is exciting! Yes, Henry VIII and the Reformation, that is quite important, it is nice to know, but what went on throughout the XVII century is what has made this country what it is, religiously, as well as politically, and I find it staggering that it seems not to be taught. When I ask grandchildren if they have studied this or that, they very rarely have.

Jenny Hodge

How well do you think leaders in society reflect the composition of our society?

I gather that they are mostly white men, which isn't very representative of the country as a whole. I think that we should try and change it. A lot of them are privately educated, come from quite well-off backgrounds, don't really understand the poverty of others. People from a poor background will understand more of what needs to be done. I think that education is important; the rich parents have children who go to private schools, they have the best facilities and chances and they become rich and send their children to private schools. Everyone should have the same beginnings in life.

Faisal Khan

Are politicians representative of wider society?

I don't think our politicians represent society. I think they represent rich people. They don't represent the working class people; they don't know how much the food costs for a week. I think the average politician is an upper class man, with a good background, private education, and things like that. I think they are all like that.

I would like to see more people of working class background getting into politics, to top jobs, in order to represent people who don't have a say.

Shaun Wallace

Would you say that our politicians reflect society as a whole in terms of gender, age, sexuality, race, social class, etc? If not, is there anything which can or should be done about it?

It is better now than 40 years ago. There is one thing that I am personally pleased with is that women are at the top of most civilised, democratic societies in the world.

Danny Batth

Do you think that our politicians are representative of society?

I think our politicians are mainly London-based. They are not paid ridiculous amounts of money, are they? So, if the money were better for politicians, you would find that the chief executives of all banks would want to be politicians, but because the money is not as good, a lot of our people go into banking, corporate . . . maybe that is why there is only a type of person who goes for the job as Prime Minister or to work in the House of Commons.

A CEO makes £66,000 (the annual salary of an MP) in a week. Politicians have studied, they have gone through university, and what they get in terms of money is probably not what they deserve.

I think our politicians are not sufficiently representative of our diversity in terms of race, social class, gender, etc, but at the same time if you are good in what you are . . . if you are a woman, black, etc, it shouldn't be relevant . . . It shouldn't be a case about letting someone in just because they are different. I think it should be the best people to get the job.

Patricia Travis

Do you feel that our leaders represent the population as a whole?

[. . .] I don't feel represented by politicians. I feel detached from them. I feel more connected with the Royal Family and I feel very proud of them. It is because she is the Queen. I don't know what is going to happen with Charles . . . He is changing, the Royal Family is changing.

Professor Dame Nancy Rothwell

Are Agnostics proportionately represented in Parliament?

I wouldn't necessarily know and I don't need to know. I think the belief of my MP is irrelevant. I think it is their principles, rather than their adherence to a particular religion, that is important.

Dr David Perfect

Do you think that there is an adequate understanding of Anglicanism in society?

[. . .] In terms of the health sector, again some of our work shows that in some contexts there is a lack of understanding of people's Christian beliefs; I would say Christian rather than Anglican, in terms of ridiculing people who pray in hospital or want to read the Bible . . . I think universities are also an interesting area. There is obviously not one model of universities, but there are some universities which think that religion has no place on campus and that the university should be a completely secular place. There are others which have a completely different view.

Imam Irfan Chishti MBE

Do you think that Muslims are appropriately and proportionately represented in public life?

My view is that we are not fully represented in public life, but it is brilliant that we have a Muslim Mayor of London, who is a great inspiration. But I want to give you a much more worrying statistic. As a Muslim populace we are over-represented in one area and under-represented in all other key areas of life – I think we are something like 2.4% of the population but we make up 12.3% of the prison population. I am sure you have seen the stats. It makes me annoyed, my dad used to teach us as children, education, education, education . . . Through that education we can get into positions of responsibility and help, hopefully, the wider society and community. We have not taken up those opportunities ourselves in many ways.

Constance Jackson

Do you think that Protestant Christians are still appropriately and proportionately represented?

Interesting, I'm not sure of the make-up . . . because religion plays such a small part, the Protestant religion here. [. . .] remember the whole debate with Tony Blair's spin doctor, Alistair Darling, saying 'We don't do God.' Here I find there's not a lot of discussion about religion, unless it's anti-Islam. Spirituality seems to be very personal here . . . little 'p' Protestant, but the funny thing is that the Protestant church in Europe was founded by the protesters – the people who didn't want to go along with the orthodoxy of the time. But here in the UK *it is* the orthodoxy, so you know it's not probably as true to its Protestant roots, when it becomes the religion of the establishment.

Professor Ronald Hutton

Do you think that Pagans are appropriately and proportionately represented in public life?

I think that the insights of Pagans do have a particular contribution to make to modern society, if only because Pagans are acutely interested in the female side of the divine and the inherent divinity of nature, which are less well explored, if at all, in other religions. Pagans are at present not represented in the political system at all. I don't know of a single Pagan MP and if there is a Pagan member of the House of Lords then their views are strictly private. This is a weakness of modern Paganism and one of its striking features is the lack of a representative in any powerful position. We do not seem to have a single leading industrialist, leading business person, or leader of the judiciary or the medical system who openly professes Paganism.

Professor Steven Jones

Are Atheists proportionately represented in Parliament and public life?

There is always Richard Dawkins. I think they are implicitly voiced; most MPs especially Tories will claim to be Christian, but in reality they are probably Atheists a lot of the time. Because there isn't really a penetrating religious voice in society any more, you don't really need a penetrating Atheist voice.

Dr Tobias Lock

Do you feel that Atheists and Agnostics are proportionately and appropriately represented in public life?

[. . .] Some Atheists may think religion is completely irrational, because their own decisions are based on rational values . . . but these would be radical Atheists. Liberal Atheists would not rule out religious people like that. The Atheist approach could also work to the benefit of minority religions too, as it would bring a liberal outlook to the public arena and would prevent them from being subject to some hard religious rules.

Ruth Jenkins

Are Catholics appropriately represented in public life?

I don't think people bring their faith into their public life. When Tony Blair became a Catholic, it was made public . . . I do wonder . . . I don't really know the reasons why it was disclosed then. I think religion is a very private matter for lots of people, but I am not frightened to say who I am at all. I think you can show the type of person you are just by your behaviour . . .

David Harte

Do you think that Christians are appropriately and proportionately represented?

No, but I think that is their fault rather than that of society; more should feel a responsibility to play a part in Parliament. I don't know . . . I would want to do a statistical study before reaching a conclusion, but I think that all Christians should seriously consider whether they have a calling to play a part in democratic government. It is a calling. As far as the law is concerned, I have a bit of a beef, because those who are most concerned with promoting Christian beliefs through the law do it in a negative way. You get groups who join battle and see the law as something oppressive which they have to fight, instead of something enabling in which they should participate for the good of society.

Wendy Huggett

Do you think that Atheists are proportionately represented in public life? Do you think that people are comfortable being open about their atheism?

[. . .] It is interesting even when I go to court, the question is whether to swear on the Bible . . . and most people still swear on the Bible rather than affirming. I think that is still seen as the norm. I think most people would still go for it as it is the norm. The same when it comes to the census and you have to tick a box. Most people would probably go with the Protestant or Christian box. You will be more likely to tick the box which says you are religious as opposed to non-religious.

Mona Bayoumi

Are Muslims proportionately represented in public life?

Probably the first answer to whether Muslims are appropriately and proportionally represented in different institutions is 'no', but it is not a process that can happen overnight. I am not a fan of positive discrimination and I don't believe that you should fill a quota for the sake of numbers, because the risk then is that you don't put the right people . . .

Dr Elizabeth Healey

Are Roman Catholics appropriately and proportionately represented in public life?

I don't have any idea about how many Catholics we have in public bodies, and I think it shouldn't matter . . . I don't elect my MP because he/she is Catholic . . . I think that would be irrelevant . . . I elect them because they have the good of the community at heart, and are effective in making change happen. But if there were two or three candidates on an equal footing, that could be a reason to choose the Catholic one . . .

Jon Nott

Do you think that Humanists have a contribution to make to public life? Are they appropriately and proportionately represented in Parliament, local authorities, the judiciary, etc?

I definitely think that Humanists have a contribution to make. I think there probably are a reasonable number of them in public life, and whether it is directly proportional I've no idea. I don't know whether I think there would be areas where it would be a challenge. I don't know enough about the appointment of magistrates and judges, and whether being a Humanist would be an issue. I certainly don't think that it would be a problem for parliament or local authorities – it's more of a problem to be a Republican. You don't have to swear loyalty to God but you do to the Queen. I don't think that there is any systematic oppression of Humanists.

Nico McNenzie-Juetten

Do you think that non-religious people are proportionately represented in public life?

I really don't know. There are some very outspoken Atheists and secularists around in the Parliament. I am reasonably happy to be claimed by some of the secularist groups, but not the Atheists. I think that secularism is on the rise.

Sam Dick

Are LGBT citizens appropriately represented in public life?

I don't think LGBT citizens are appropriately represented in civil life for a number of reasons. For historical reasons, they couldn't be open and they could not reach certain positions. Furthermore, there is still active discrimination against LGBT people in some contexts. I think there are many gay people in public life, but not proportionately represented, I would think. There are only a small number of parliamentarians who are openly LGBT and, within that, you only have one or two openly lesbian MPs. So even within that small percentage, there are differences.

Jessica Morden MP

Does our system of checks and balances work effectively at present?

I think now, even at constituency level, scrutiny has increased . . . people know what you are doing every day.

I think as an MP scrutiny and accountability really work and are efficient. You are definitely held to account. Social media, for instance, plays a key role . . . I think people are now more aware than ever before. This morning, for instance, I may have had 14 emails from anti-fracking groups, and you are very aware that you are scrutinised. It is certainly much more open than it was.

Philip Bird

Is there enough distance between politicians and the judiciary in this country?

Yes, it is Shell, Mobil and Exxon which worry me.

Fr Ian Paton

Would you say there is enough distance between the executive and the judiciary?

In Scotland there seems to be; that is partly because devolution came after . . . the judiciary never ceased to be independent. For a long time the government were in Westminster and the Scottish judiciary were here getting on with being the Scottish judiciary. There was a literal distance. So the devolved administration came into this context.

Professor John Healey

Do you feel that the judiciary are sufficiently independent?

I think our judiciary are sufficiently independent. There was a time in the 1950s and 1960s in which some of those networks, including the legal profession, would have regarded Catholics as outsiders, but I think that has gone now. I have been at dinner parties with lawyers and barristers. You sit next to a Catholic barrister or a Jewish barrister or Muslim barrister. Until the 1970s there was in Britain a certain amount of anti-Catholicism, but that has almost completely gone now.

David Harte

Do you think that the judiciary are sufficiently independent?

I think they are. Whether they are perceived to be is another matter. Look at the difficulty there was in finding someone for the child abuse investigation . . . but that was exceptional and they found a good solution in getting a senior judge from another jurisdiction. Other than that, moving from the House of Lords to the Supreme Court seems to have been a matter of window dressing, and perhaps getting better premises, than a matter of real substance.

Joanna Griffiths

Are the judiciary sufficiently independent?

I don't think our judiciary in the UK are completely independent. In principle, magistrates are independent and are supposed to be independent, but we do have a lot of guidance. We have to work within the guidance and give reasons for our decisions. Sometimes, however, we need to exercise a little common sense!

The Rt Rev'd Dominic Walker OGS

Is there enough distance between Parliament and the judiciary?

Yes, the judges are independent, and they rightly value their independence. It is Parliament's job to create the laws but not their job to tell the judges how to go about their business. It is important that there is 'separation of powers'. Sometimes laws are poorly or quickly made by Parliament, like for example, the Dangerous Dogs Act, and then judges have to decide how to apply the legislation.

Fr Paul Stonham

Is there enough distance between the legislature and judiciary?

I really don't know.

Professor John Healey

Do you think that the current system of checks and balances between the legislature and executive are effective?

[. . .] was the whole question of pollution levels in streets in our cities. There is a government decision to reach a certain air quality by 2030, but local authorities are being very slow about this, because of the impact that it has on other concerns they have. There are tensions there and there must be someone to make sure that things which are decided by Parliament are really implemented.

Professor Steven Jones

How do you think the exercise of power by Parliament and the Government should be regulated?

The big mistake would be to write it down; if you have a Constitution with written checks and balances it tends to freeze up. You have to be pragmatic. The ultimate check comes from the mob. When you saw the Poll Tax riots, it is clear that the streets won the Poll Tax debates.

Lord Richard Harries of Pentregarth

What mechanisms are important for society to monitor and respond to use of Parliamentary and government authority?

I'm a great believer in citizenship studies in schools, which I'm afraid don't get the importance attached to them which they ought to have. There should be proper courses in schools where people learn what democracy is about, how to participate, why it is important.

Baroness Elizabeth Butler-Sloss

How do Anglicans challenge decisions which they perceive as problematic?

We have to be very careful about challenging decisions which are problematic for Christians. We have a wide range of Christian branches in this country, not all of them agree with each other . . . Issues which are important to Christians are also important to Jews and Muslims, and Hindus . . . Jews, Christians and Muslims are people of the Book, although some Muslims don't recognise it. We are people of the Book and so our background is likely to be very similar about welfare issues, for example.

Lucy Powell MP

How do Atheists help to challenge decisions which they perceive as problematic, either for their members or for society as a whole?

I don't think I have really made a decision as an Atheist. I never have thought this was a problem. And, anyway, our society is more liberal . . . So, I think my views are the views of mainstream society. If you think of big issues like gay marriage, for example, there were religious groups which had concerns about that legislation. Their views did not prevail.

Frank Williams

How do Anglicans challenge policies which they see as problematic?

The CofE must make some fuss from time to time and I think it does it. There are occasions in which some people like the Archbishop of Canterbury can tell the Government that they think that a particular piece of legislation is wrong, because it is actually doing something which is against humanity and certainly against Christian principles; and also through its spokepersons in the House of Lords.

I think that people of other faiths and none have absorbed important Christian principles. So, I think, interestingly, I belong to an organisation called Theatre Chaplaincy UK and I think we have found recently that there was a time when some theatres would say they didn't want to have a chaplain there and that if they had an Anglican chaplain, they would need to have a Rabbi, an Imam, and so on, but lately it seems that theatres are more accepting of having chaplains. Speaking personally, I have found that the fact that a theatre has a chaplain is seen as a positive thing by all sorts of people.

Fr William Pearsall

How does the Roman Catholic Church seek to challenge issues which it perceives as problematic?

There is a wider issue that the Roman Catholic Church being universal is aware of the persecution of Christians in countries where there is no rule of law, or gender equality. I can think of several couples I have prepared for marriage where I had to do some teach-in that male and female were equal in partnership, because their culture hadn't reached that stage. The Roman Catholic Church, because it is universal, can promote HR on a universal scale.

Dr Hilary Firestone

How does Orthodox Judaism seek to challenge decisions which it perceives as problematic?

We came here as refugees, so most of the Jews living in this country were refugees one or two generations back. I've always believed that we are in no position to be anti-refugee. You can be integrated, without being assimilated. It is about mutual respect. You respect society and they will respect you back.

Baroness Elizabeth Berridge

How do Christians seek to challenge decisions which they see as problematic?

Christians can come across sometimes as quite a complaining group of people. They should commend what is good and critique what is bad. Christians do sometimes seem to act out of anger and complaint, instead of doing it out of love and thorough understanding.

I think we have a problem of religious literacy. Public authorities really don't understand, not just Christianity but religions in general, and they tend to think this is something that people can just really take off. We have lost a grounded concept of conscience and I don't think people can really understand why it is so important for some religious people not to breach their conscience . . . There is very little understanding of it.

Dr Adrian Crisp MD

Have you ever felt so strongly about a social or political situation that you have done something to try to change it, and if so what?

[. . .] I believed strongly that the hospital should be smoke free. Nobody should smoke on site. When I was up for election, my platform was that within my three stints Addenbrooke's would be a smoke-free zone. We initially won, but the protests were immense, the nurses, the visitors, there was huge trouble. So management caved in and appeased the smoking lobby. More recently, of course, it has become standard practice, but I did stand up and it did make a difference. In the long term we won the battle.

Again, freedom without responsibilities . . . We've become a liberal society, but individuals have responsibilities. By smoking they are doing harm to those around them.

Baroness Ros Altmann

Are there any issues which you have felt so strongly about it that you personally wanted to campaign to change them?

I've spent much of my life in recent years campaigning against government and businesses to try and help those affected by injustice and achieve recompense for them or to achieve change so that the injustice stops.

The campaign that I was involved in was to restore pensions to the 160,000 workers and their families whose final salary pensions were taken away from them by flawed law. The Government tried to deny all responsibility when they clearly were responsible, and these people were in desperate straits, their whole life savings and part of their state pension were in there. They were told tough luck, it's gone, but it will be okay in future. But your money has gone to pay your big bosses who saw what was coming when they were in their early 50s whilst you are 64 and have nothing left, even some of your state pension. The law which they were told would protect them didn't work properly, they were misled [. . .]

It was a real eye-opener to me how the ordinary person can just get completely ignored, forgotten, overlooked and treated with disdain and injustice, and the Government just turns its back because it has the power. It is one thing when it's just one word against another, but when all the verdicts have gone against and you still say tough luck there is nothing you can say.

Samantha Chandler

Have you ever felt so strongly about a political or social situation that you personally wanted to campaign to change it? If so, what did you do and why? (e.g. writing to your MP, joining a demonstration)?

Yes, often animal related. I've written letters, signed petitions etc. I'm involved with a planning application in the village where I live where they are threatening to build 5,000 houses on a greenfield site. It is a part of the government drive for more houses and whilst I acknowledge that there is a desperate need for more housing and the problem must be addressed, it should not be at the expense of the countryside. It should be on brownfield sites or areas where it doesn't impact on wildlife. My campaigning has only ever gone as far as attending meetings, writing letters and signing petitions.

Dr Catharine Morgan

Have you ever felt so strongly about an issue that you have wanted to campaign to change it?

The only situation that comes to mind is, as a medical student, there was animal experimentation . . . and again nobody was forced, but one or two people said that they were not prepared to do it . . . I didn't say 'no' at that point, but I actually felt compromised afterwards. So, my belief system was compromised.

Anne Duddington

Have you ever felt so strongly about a political situation that you have wanted to campaign to change it? If so, what did you do?

[. . .] In relation to hospitals, I have found them at times very insensitive and at times very anti-Catholic. 'Are you one of them?' I have been asked a few times. It is that kind of approach . . . You have to justify being a Catholic when you are feeling unwell . . . that is the worst time to be challenged.

Keith Porteous Wood

Have you ever felt so strongly about a political or social situation that you personally campaigned to try to change it? If so, what did you do?

One of the things I have worked hard on, one of the reasons I do this job is that I agree passionately with the NSS objectives set out in its Secular Charter [http://www.secularism.org.uk/secularcharter.html], so my personal objectives are closely matched to the organisation's.

One area in my own life where I have campaigned strongly is on gay rights. I feel very strongly and positively about the change, in encouraging moves forward from decriminalisation to equal ages of consent to civil partnership to marriage. I have used every possible avenue to promote this. And that is probably one of the most positive stories that you could tell about the change of attitude to gay people and the pace it has happened throughout the world. Having said that, there is still a lot of homophobia, a high suicide rate amongst younger LGBT people. And one of the problems with becoming a multi-religious country is that the attitude to gay people is less positive among those in minority religions, and that is echoed in the EU. The accession of more countries from the east is reducing the acceptance of homosexuality, and some women's rights issues such as abortion. Opposition of the scale seen now in the European Parliament on both fronts would have been unthinkable 10 years ago.

Philip Bird

Have you ever been involved in any campaigns on issues you have felt strongly about?

I marched for CND back in the 1980s, and my mail started getting opened, which I was very upset about. I write to my MP about fracking, about the Greenpeace guys in the Arctic; generally about environmental issues when they come up against economic ones – energy, solar vs oil; wildlife vs GM crops. It's generally future of the planet stuff. But I also write letters to my local council and MP about the 'Tescofication' of the village. I belong to various charities in the kind of Soil Association, Greenpeace type area. I really don't think that man is the most important species on this planet; I think that we are all in it together. If we lose birds, worms or bees, we are in trouble.

Jim Sutcliffe

Have you personally ever felt so strongly about a particular political or social problem that you've done something about it, and if so what?

Yes, lots of times. Well, like car parking in the town. They decided to do away with the free car parking and put the parking charges up, and lots of people just wanted to brush it under the carpet and say that this kind of thing happens. But I managed to get on the radio and television and various other things and preach on my soapbox. Actually, what they should have done was the other way around, to try and get people into the town. The car parks make X amount of money and they waste it up at the council; it is a tiny drop in a big ocean. If they did away with the charges altogether people would come and spend money locally, which would recycle itself locally, which then means that there is less need for housing benefit and all the other bits that come from the council [. . .]

It's like education, we take kids every year for work experience. Last year they sent a girl who was interested in cookery. When she got here she couldn't read the face of a clock, she couldn't do basic maths, she couldn't spell and her writing . . . my niece who is three-and-a-half could do better, and I felt really sorry for her because the school failed her, she was 11 months off leaving education and I thought there was something wrong. So I wrote a letter to them at school and told them that I was appalled at the state she was in as far as readiness for work. Reading, writing and mathematics have to be important for everyone whatever you do.

Dr Hema Radhakrishnan

Do you think that public authorities have a good understanding of the needs of Hindu citizens?

Probably not . . . I'm not sure that they can even distinguish it. Most of the time I am seen as brown-skinned, so people think that I must be a Muslim. The other day I was dropping my son at the nursery and the lady told me that they were doing Halal meals from next week, and I thought, how does that affect me? Because we are more of a minority than other groups, people are less aware.

Ruth Jenkins

Have public bodies shown an understanding towards the needs of your faith?

I have been in situations where my Catholic faith had to be catered for. My experience in hospitals was excellent. I had a very small premature baby boy, whom we named Andrew, baptised the day he was born, and it really didn't matter what your creed was. I know people of other faiths would have also received excellent treatment.

Dominic Dyer

In your experience of dealing with public authorities, have your beliefs been appropriately understood and respected?

[. . .] There have been times when I have thought that 'hey, this isn't fair' when it came to charity law on charities lobbying; for example, during the election campaign I fell foul of that, because the Conservatives wanted to continue with badger culling and Labour had agreed to support it in their manifesto. I was seen as taking sides and had various people in the Charity Commission and ministers and others weigh in, and there was a debate in Parliament. And when I read about that I felt . . . 'well, hang on a minute, that isn't what actually happened', but there were certain people who wanted to portray it as such to make an example of me to then try and force broader change on charities to restrict their ability to speak out.

The Most Reverend Peter Smith

Do you think that public authorities have a good understanding of the needs of Roman Catholic citizens?

My honest answer is 'no'. As we've become a more secular society, many young people have no understanding of religion. If they have any perception it is from press conferences where religious people are made out to be fanatics. It is a difficulty we do find in negotiating with the Government. We find this with foreign priests coming here for experience, getting them a visa is difficult. Visa forms are for general employment. They have a category for minister of religion. They treat priests as employees. It isn't prejudice, it is ignorance. They have no understanding of the Church.

Fr Roddy Johnston

Have public authorities shown an appropriate level of respect towards your beliefs?

I have found that people have, without exception, been very professionally courteous. I do know of priests and ministers who have difficulty with hospitals or councils or whatever, but usually there are reasons for it. It may be down to them!

Lady Brenda Hale

In your own experience of dealing with public authorities, have any needs relating to your faith been dealt with appropriately?

There is only one situation in which I can recall my faith was relevant. That was when my daughter was born prematurely, unexpectedly, and almost the first thing they asked after asking me what her name would be was 'would you like her baptised?', and I think that is a standard question, they do it all the time.

Whether they do it appropriately for non-Christians, I don't know. I may have been asked my religion before having been admitted to hospital, and I would have said 'Church of England'. That is the only example which I can think where my faith was relevant, and it was handled in my view entirely appropriately.

Professor Ronald Hutton

Would you say that public bodies have a good understanding of the needs of Pagans? Is the understanding better in some areas than others?

[. . .] The caring services which, when a Pagan is sick and disempowered in hospital, can make them feel supported or persecuted in their religion . . . the education system, which can treat Pagan children equally or make them feel different . . . These are the vital groups and, on the whole, they pay very little attention to the judiciary, legislative and the executive and operate much as laws unto themselves.

The Rt Rev'd Tim Thornton

Do you think that public authorities (NHS, local authorities, etc) understand the needs of practising Anglicans? Is the understanding of any of these bodies better or worse than the understanding of others?

I think it is a mixed answer. More or less, on the whole, I think people understand. There was a governance review of the Cornwall local council and I was asked to be one of the three people who did it. I think local authorities and public bodies hold the Church in high esteem and ask us to do things. I think sometimes some parts of some public have some neuralgia about faith groups and I am not sure where it comes from. I think it is about fear of proselytism. So, it is interesting that some of the publicly funded bodies are at times quite resistant to faith-based organisations.

Rev David Robertson

Do you think that public authorities (e.g. local authorities, NHS, courts etc) really understand the needs of evangelical Christians? Do you think the understanding of any of these bodies is better or worse than others?

I think that there is a tendency to marginalise, to ridicule and a confusion which means that many people are unable to distinguish between an ISIS terrorist, a normal Muslim and an evangelical Christian. They lump all religions together and, in my view, they end up unfairly discriminating. My view would be that there is a considerable lack of understanding.

In hospitals there is a chaplaincy system and there is not a particular problem. My concern about the NHS is the different levels of treatment, not because of religion, but because of wealth, and at the moment you are meant to receive the same treatment for all, but I think that will change.

Dr Tobias Lock

Have your beliefs been understood and respected when you have had dealings with public bodies?

I can't really imagine in what situations my Atheist beliefs would have to be catered for by public bodies such as hospitals or schools.

Rabbi Jonathan Sacks

Do you think that public authorities understand and respond appropriately to the needs of the Jewish community in Britain?

[. . .] But what I do worry about is the hijacking of certain civic occasions for political ends: Holocaust Memorial Day, for instance. This was boycotted by at least one well-known Muslim group on the grounds that it did not make reference to the ongoing events in the Middle East. Holocaust Memorial is a civic occasion and stands above party political divisions on matters relating to contemporary politics. Whenever you politicise a civic occasion you begin to kill it [. . .] I am worried about the civic space that we call a university. There are campaigns that enter the campus that have a seriously corrosive force on freedom of speech and intellectual freedom. I regard it as an absolute principle. Roman law, I'm not quoting Jewish law here, I'm quoting Roman law, holds as a condition of justice: *audi alderam partem*, hear the other side. I think on many issues today the other side is not heard. The area where I would raise most concern is university campuses, an area where local and central government have limited control, but I do see this as a threat to the continued health of British civil life. We are in some danger in some universities of encountering the intellectual organisation of political hatred, which is a huge danger to the future of British civic life.

Thomas Haines

Have your beliefs been understood and accommodated by public bodies?

Atheists have very different beliefs but I think they are properly catered for by public bodies. Of course, it is not 100%, but everyone is reasonably well catered for.

I think Atheists have similar views or morals, but there is no kind of group mentality, only in big issues which really bring people together.

David Harte

Do you think that public authorities understand the needs of Christians?

[. . .] My main reservation about Christian religious voices in society is that they are not allowed sufficiently by the media. We talk about freedom of the press, but the press itself is very good at censoring views which it doesn't want to promote.

Faisal Khan

Do public authorities (e.g. local authorities, NHS, the police, etc) have a good understanding of your needs?

I think the NHS treats everybody the same. In schools . . . schools where I went to were mainly Asians. So, the schools were fine . . . We had no problem at all. I think the police can be racist. I don't really trust the police, just with the whole . . . The police are in the middle, between the judges and the politicians. The police are not all that bad, but some of them are intimidating; they are not that friendly when you need help. Once I got burgled, they were like . . . 'well, sort it out yourself' . . . and I think it is because we are Asians, and where we live really . . . I lived then with my mum . . . I live on my own now and my mum with my sister.

I have never been taken into hospital, but my mother was. It is good that they have Halal meat. Her requests were accommodated in the NHS hospital and I think that is really nice. I wouldn't say they have to do it . . . because we could still have a vegetarian option, which I think it is fine . . .

Fr Paul Stonham

Do public bodies have an understanding of practical needs of Roman Catholic citizens?

[. . .] My experience certainly locally is that if someone does ask for a priest they're on the 'phone straight away, so they're pretty quick. There is a kind of advantage for Catholics, as many nurses are Filippino, Indian from Kerala or east Europeans, who happen to be Catholics, and a surprising number of surgeons are also Catholic, like doctors were in the old days when they were mostly Irish.

Gurd Kandola

Has your Sikhism been ever relevant in your dealings with public authorities such as hospitals, schools, etc?

[. . .] We were made aware of one particular lunchtime in school where there was an instance where my son appeared to have been denied a meal choice which contained pork, which he is permitted to consume, and the only apparent reason for this appears to be because he was confused with a child who shares a similar sounding name to my son who is Muslim and therefore understandably may not consume meals containing pork. That is the only instance in which I thought . . . 'is this a race issue?' Is it because the names are similar or is it because the names are not European or English names? That made me question things with the school . . . would the same situation arise if there were two fair-haired boys called James and one was vegetarian? Would the same issue have occurred? Is this another case of the old 'they all look similar'? That was the only time I questioned it – was this an issue which is related to religion and my child's appearance? And was this issue taken seriously by the school?

Chris Morris

Do you think that public bodies have a good understanding of the needs of practising Anglicans? In your personal experience, have your beliefs been understood and respected?

Personally, yes. I suppose two points arise from that. Again, I find it difficult to identify public agencies with a unified approach towards different religious groups. Having said that, most of the public authorities I come into contact with are, whether they know it or acknowledge it or not, built on deep-seated societal, Christian frameworks.

Daisuke Miura

Whenever you've had any reason to deal with public bodies, schools, hospitals etc, have you felt that your views and beliefs have been treated with appropriate respect by people in authority?

Let me think . . . I always, because it's my personality, feel that if something needs to be changed, I need to do something about this. So I will ask: could you provide this for my students, could you do this for me? But I always want to believe that people are doing their best. If things are not happening, it's likely there's a problem in the system, it's not that the individuals involved don't want to help. Obviously, if they don't have money, they cannot use money they do not have. Obviously, everyone wants to provide the best possible quality of education, but realistically we always have to do the best with what we have.

I don't see this as a limitation as such, I just try to do things to make the best out of what I do have. I don't feel like I've ever been treated unfairly. Someone said that what you get in your life is exactly equal to how much you choose to put into your life. So if we've not been treated fairly or haven't been given what we deserve, I think it's generally because we haven't given enough or we haven't achieved enough. So in that kind of sense my answer is 'no'. Possibly, maybe, but I believe this whole system works very fairly, but not just fairly for one person, fairly for whole world's benefit. So therefore I have never felt that I have been treated badly or unfairly.

Aled Griffiths

In your dealings with public authorities, have your faith and the needs arising from it been appropriately respected?

[. . .] Every day we are celebrating a war . . . the battle of Waterloo, the Second World War, the Great War . . . Every day in the last two years we are allowing our society to think only in terms of military solutions and I am finding that very uncomfortable and difficult to accept. When I was young, that was completely different, but even my grandchildren now are being taught that it is normal to shoot people, it is normal to play games with guns . . . In a generation that has happened, and to me Christian pacifism is a deep conviction and

I find that there should be no place for militarism in a civilised society. But it is happening even in Wales.

Elder Clifford Herbertson

Do public authorities understand the needs of Latter-Day Saints?

Again, I think the responsibility of them understanding our needs is up to us to express those needs. I'm a great believer that we can't turn around and expect others to know of our needs . . . we have to be the ones to go out there and help people understand. And my experience when we reach out to organisations and share our needs is that they are respectful and appreciative. There are three main thrusts of community engagement that the Church is involved with in the UK. The first one is blood donation; the Church is one of the largest organisations involved in donating blood. We give to the wider community, for example this meeting house; we allow the NHS blood and transfusion service to come in and use it free of charge, all of our facilities; members of our Church and members of the community come in and donate blood. The NHS BT are so appreciative and respectful of that engagement.

Ian Scott

Do you think that public authorities have a good understanding of the needs of Humanists?

I'd say that in general, no definitely not; there is conflation between Humanist and militant Atheist or militant secularist. The idea that Humanists are negative, and just want to stop other people doing things, stamping out religious rights, that this would ignore all of the stuff about allowing other people having rights which they should have access to, whether this be same-sex marriage or allowing people to end their life. I think that that sort of conflation is unhelpful, often deliberately unhelpful. I think that Humanism has a long way to go to be understood as being separate from or different from Atheism.

Michael Kennedy QC

In your personal interactions with public bodies, do you feel that your personal spiritual needs have been met and respected?

The only people I have come across have been educational. I have been on various things to do with universities. I haven't had any difficulty, but I don't know if they regard me as a barmy old nutter, or whether they take my views seriously. On the whole, I was chairman of a CAB, I had a lot to do with a funding question about a legal help desk at prison, and I found everyone I dealt with first rate, but I have always wondered whether people are nice to me because I am a judge.

The Most Reverend Professor Rowan Williams

Do you think that public authorities have a good understanding of the needs of Anglicans?

I think the understanding of public bodies about the needs and beliefs of Anglicans (and other religious groups) is very uneven indeed [. . .]

I think the judiciary do pretty well in terms of awareness of the needs of the Christian community. There was a notorious episode a couple of years ago . . . Lord Justice Laws, who is an Anglican himself, said in court that the court is not here to uphold Christian doctrine, and there was a certain amount of outrage; but I think he was simply articulating the fact that the role of a court is the interpretation of the law, not primarily the interpretation or the enforcement of religious points of view. Some people thought this meant that the law is now Godless. Personally, I think this is an absurd reaction, but this is one part of the present spectrum. I don't feel that there is the level of disconnection in the courts that you find in local government, and sometimes in employment tribunals and the like.

Gary McFarlane

Are public authorities sensitive to the needs of Christians?

No, public authorities are not sufficiently sensitive towards the needs of Christians and we see it in every level of society. In the last 15 years there has been something of an anti-Christian move in society . . . Whether it has come from a secular humanistic place or not . . . there is now an absolute intolerance . . . not just a preference, but an aggressive intolerance, that is what we face and it is shocking. There is an aggressiveness and intolerance against the Christian faith and it is hard to understand how it came about in just 15 years or so. It is an aggressive attitude of 'you can't and you won't'.

Mona Bayoumi

Do public authorities understand and address any religious needs you have?

Broadly speaking, if I had to compare with other countries, I think that the needs of Muslims are catered for (in hospitals, schools, etc), but there are some issues, for example, in hospitals. As a female, I'd rather be examined by a female doctor if I can. I won't kick up a fuss about it . . . if there is nobody else available, that's it, but if there is a choice, I'd like to be able to exercise that choice without feeling guilty, without feeling that I have been accused of discrimination by doing it.

The Rev'd Dr Jason Bray

Do public authorities have a good understanding of the needs of practising Anglicans?

Probably not. I think that part of it is the general assumption that Anglican is the sort of default, so sticking Church of England on your form at the hospital when actually the Church in Wales hasn't been part of the Church of England for 94 years, it still hasn't cottoned on. They don't take any notice of the needs of practising Anglicans, because so many people are nominally Anglican, but don't actually practise, that when you come across somebody who does actually practise they're not quite sure what to do.

Professor Sheila McLean

Are the needs of Atheists understood and met by public authorities?

I suspect that there is not a community of Atheists in the UK. Atheists don't really feel they have to belong to a community. When my mother goes to church, one of the things she gets out of it is the sense of community. As an elderly lady on her own and an increasingly reduced group of friends, that is crucial. I am not clear that those who don't adhere to a particular faith have the same need or opportunity to affiliate in that way. However, they do it in other ways, of course. They become members of a political party or share a commitment to an ideology, which is not political, but with like-minded people. At the end of the day we are all social animals.

I don't think individual Atheists have needs that people of faith have. For example, I think it is important that in hospitals there are representatives of different faiths and for those who have faith, I would hope, it is very comforting and I have no qualms about it.

Ashley Gilbert

In your experience of dealing with public authorities, do they show an appropriate level of awareness and respect towards Pagan beliefs and needs?

I think that broadly speaking they do. There is a willingness to engage with faith communities and us, as a very fringe faith community. Most human beings, including councils, respond in kind when spoken to reasonably and logically. I am a big supporter of the police, I have found that in any case where there has been any kind of contention, there has been a willingness to talk and find a common-sense solution. My experiences are largely positive.

The Rt Rev'd Christine Hardman

In your personal experience of dealing with public authorities, has there been an appropriate level of awareness and respect demonstrated towards your beliefs and any needs flowing from them?

I suppose I have been quite fortunate in generally having been someone operating with a level of authority within the Church, and with a certain confidence. So I don't think that I will have experienced some of the more difficult responses from institutions. I have generally been working at the level of institution to institution. But there have been occasions when I have felt, particularly around hospitals, that the complexity about being a neutral institution has been a problem. I think that were I taken into hospital, and not well enough to state my request to see a priest, that would not have been easy. The system is geared towards protecting patients and confidentiality, which I understand, but I think that there is not always an awareness on busy hospital wards of a person's spiritual needs. I can think of a few occasions when, as a parish priest, I have had a parishioner taken into hospital as an emergency, where I have not been able to see them, and I know that if they are dying the one thing which they would want is anointing . . . and it is very difficult to do that when the hospital's priority has been to try to resuscitate . . . However, I quite understand that at that point the hospital has no proof of that. So religious needs are seen as secondary by the hospital in a way they are not by the individual.

Carole Emmerson

Would you say that there is sufficient awareness in the healthcare sector of patients' spiritual beliefs and needs?

I would say that there is some awareness in the health system, although it is probably easier to meet specific religious needs, rather than spiritual needs – for example, meeting religious dietary requirements. I think there is a problem with spirituality, what it really means and how to meet those needs.

Maybe the needs of patients of institutionalised religions are better defined and they are easier to be provided. For instance, people who want to get communion on Sundays or if somebody doesn't want his/her body to be touched by anyone outside the family until they die, that is quantifiable and you are able to do that. I think some religious needs are more defined, but spiritual needs are much looser and so often we don't know what we need ourselves.

Patients need compassion and spirituality can bring that. Often we don't have time, I think we need to be with people . . . to listen to them.

7 Human rights and the religious character of the Constitution and the wider legal framework

7.1 Introduction

The preceding chapters have explored ways in which the religious dimension of both the Constitution and the legal framework contribute positively to the juridical system as a whole, and therefore to the freedoms and the welfare of citizens. As we have stressed repeatedly, however, the purpose of this endeavour has been *not* to justify the religious character of the Constitution and legal framework on the strength of a cost/benefit analysis; such an exercise would be mired in subjectivity and inherently unsound, and it would purport to justify an enduring constitutional framework on the strength of a snapshot in time. Even if at the moment under consideration the advantages of the arrangements outweighed the disadvantages, it would not necessarily follow that this would always remain the case.

So, our task emphatically has *not* been to keep a tally of the pluses and minuses contained in the present system, the aim of defending it on the basis of the outcome. Rather, it has been to acknowledge that *all* constitutional systems are essentially co-operationist in nature, and to question the proposition that a move towards the secular end of the spectrum would necessarily lead to a more inclusive and just society. If the present Great Britain is functioning well when tested against our core constitutional principles, the onus is on those calling for change to prove that their reformed framework would achieve this more effectively or reliably.

Furthermore, the present context cannot coherently be either attacked or defended unless it is adequately understood. To this end, we have considered whether the religious elements of the legal framework enhance the pillars of the British Constitution, and we have seen so far that there are a great number of benefits for all citizens in the way in which this religious dynamic has evolved, as well as a strong case to suggest that it is in the collective best interests of society to continue the evolutionary journey without seeking to strip away the religious character that infuses the current juridical system. It is doubtful whether this is even possible, but on the hypothetical basis that it could be at least partially achieved, there is still little convincing evidence that it would actually be desirable.

However, despite having stressed that our concern is *not* to balance the positive and negative implications of a religious as opposed to a secular framework, we are still faced with a unique challenge in relation to the final pillar of the Constitution. Where human rights are concerned, there are those who perceive a direct clash with religious interests, and our intention is to address this head-on, rather than attempt to sweep it under the carpet.

The contemporary British Constitution and legal framework expressly recognise both the existence of human rights and the imperative of safeguarding them. Yet, there are some streams of popular thought within contemporary culture that regard religion as a negative force in this context. For instance, writing in *The Guardian* newspaper, Deborah Orr commented: 'It's significant, of course, that these ideas of common rights flourished in Britain at a time when religious belief was in decline. For many, these days, religious belief is seen as one of the greatest bars to the spread of human rights'.[1]

Clearly, journalists writing opinion pieces (as opposed to news reports) in the popular press are neither required nor expected to back up their assertions with robust evidence and careful citation. Opinions are by definition subjective; sensational opinions sell more newspapers than moderate views, and consequently we should be cautious about building too much of a case upon this kind of journalism.

Nevertheless, Orr is not a lone voice. Other high-profile media figures have expressed similar opinions – for example, the Aslan-bashing[2] Polly Toynbee:

> I pointed out yet again that theocracy is lethal. Wherever religion controls politics it drives out tolerance and basic human rights. The history of Christianity has been the perfect exemplar, a force for repression whenever it holds any political sway. It only turns peace-loving when it is powerless. People led by some unalterable revealed voice of God cannot be tolerant of the godless.[3]

In addition, there are highly respected academic commentators, such as Nehustan,[4] who similarly argue that religion has at least the capacity to be inimical towards human rights. In his view, religious communities which adopt an 'intolerant' worldview in relation to those who do not believe or conform are an inevitable threat to the rights and freedoms of others.

1 D. Orr, 'For Human Rights to Flourish, Religious Rights Have to Come Second', *The Guardian* (27 Dec 2013), http://www.theguardian.com/commentisfree/2013/dec/27/human-rights-religious-rights-come-second.

2 P. Toynbee, 'Narnia Represents Everything that is Most Hateful about Religion', *The Guardian* (5 Dec 2005), http://www.theguardian.com/books/2005/dec/05/cslewis.booksforchildrenandteenagers. Aslan is a character in the Chronicles of Narnia. He is the lion in the most famous of these books, The Lion, the Witch and the Wardrobe, and is the Christ-figure in the Narnia universe.

3 P. Toynbee, 'We Must be Free to Criticise without being called Racist', *The Guardian* (18 Sept 2004), http://www.theguardian.com/world/2004/aug/18/religion.politic.

4 Y. Nehustan, *Intolerant Religion in a Tolerant Liberal Democracy* (Hart: Oxford) 2015.

Nevertheless, this negative perception of religion in relation to human rights is by no means the only viewpoint. The international not-for-profit organisation United for Human Rights exists in order to promote the implementation of the United Nations Universal Declaration of Human Rights.[5] Its website highlights ten outstanding and inspiring human rights champions who have made an exceptional and global impact.[6] Not only does the list include figures such as Mahatma Gandhi who made their spiritual life a matter of public record and stressed its importance as a motivating factor,[7] it also encompasses religious leaders like Archbishop Desmond Tutu and Martin Luther King Jnr. Few people would dispute the honoured place of any of these individuals from the pantheon of renowned human rights activists, a reality that in itself calls into question a straightforward negative association between religion and human rights protection.

Of course, the overarching debate about the general and abstract interaction between human rights and religion is beyond the scope of this book. We are concerned with human rights as they exist within the legal framework of Great Britain, rather than the purely mental space of philosophical discourse, and the way in which the established Churches and other faith groups interact with these. In the case of the constitutional principles previously considered, we have seen that religious bodies are a positive force of advancement and support. Is this equally true of human rights?

In order to address this, we shall begin by considering what is meant by human rights in this particular context as far as the legal system is concerned, before moving on to discuss whether the legal framework concerning religion enhances or weakens religious freedom. We shall then look at the way in which various religious groups view human rights in their understanding. Our discussion of the practical impact of faith communities on human rights, will be subsumed within our assessment of the religious legal framework, for reasons which will become apparent during the course of our discussion.

7.2 What do human rights mean in the context of the UK Constitution?

7.2.1 Preliminary reflections

Human rights law, by its very nature, has an international dimension. As Robertson and Merrills[8] observe, the world has moved a long way from the

5 United for Human Rights, 'About Us', http://www.humanrights.com/about-us/what-is-united-for-human-rights.html.

6 Ibid., 'Champions of Human Rights', http://www.humanrights.com/voices-for-human-rights/champions-human-rights.html.

7 See, e.g., B. Parekh, *Gandhi: A Brief Insight* (Sterling: New York) 2010.

8 A. Robertson and G. Merrills, *Human Rights in the World* (Manchester University Press: Manchester) 1996, Ch. 1 'International Concern with Human Rights'.

position outlined by Oppenheim at the start of the twentieth century, when public international law governed relations between states but did not operate to confer rights on individuals. Although there is still debate about the extent to which it is possible or desirable to limit the autonomy of sovereign states, there is now widespread acceptance of the idea that international instruments can and should invest individuals with rights.

Interestingly, as we saw in Chapter 1, the model of state powers being moderated by international norms was foreshadowed by the Christian medieval West. The state existed as part of a wider community of Christian nations and was expected to adhere to the rules and values of that community, often as adjudicated by the Papacy.

The position was explained most eloquently and dramatically by Sir Thomas More at his trial:

> Forasmuch, my Lorde, as this Indictment is grounded vppon an acte of parliamente directly repugnant to the laws of God and His Holy Churche, the supreeme government of which, or of any parte thereof, may no temporall prince presume by any lawe to take vppon him, as rightfully belonging to the See of Rome, a spirituall preheminence by the mouth of our Saviour Hymself, personally present vppon the earth, only to St. Peter and his successors, Byshopps of the same See, by speciall prerogative guarunted, it is therefore in law among Christien men insufficient to charge any Christien man ...
>
> ... this Realme, being but one member and smale parte of the Church, might not make a particular lawe disagreeable with the generall lawe of Christes vniuersall Catholike Churche. No more than the city of London, being but one poore member in respect of the whole realme, might make a lawe against an acte of parliamente to bind the whole realme.[9]

Of course, Sir Thomas More's argument did not prevail, but there was little doubt that it was toppled by fear and self-interest on the part of his fellow judges, rather than any flaw in legal logic. His words shook the Lord Chancellor Audley into rapidly closing down the debate, after he and the other senior judges failed to find either a crack in More's legal reasoning or a plausible counter-argument.

Moreover, as we know, at this point in history, religious politics in England and Wales changed, and any brake on royal power was rejected. Also, the winds of change were not only felt on British shores: with the coming of the European Reformations in general[10] the shared acceptance (at least in abstract terms) that the Papacy could act as a pan-European arbiter of accepted standards ended, as did the understanding that citizens of neighbouring states were fellow Christians

9 P. Ackroyd, *The Life of St Thomas More* (Vintage: London) 1998, 385–6.

10 See further B. Heal and O. Grell, *The Impact of the European Reformation: Princes, Clergy and People* (Ashgate: London) 2008.

in the West and answerable to the same spiritual and moral authority. For both Catholics and Protestants (and indeed factions with Protestantism) those who chose the 'wrong' side were deemed to be allies of the Anti-Christ.

We are certainly not suggesting that there is any direct continuity, nor obviously that the collective norms enshrined in internal treaties like the European Convention on Human Rights (ECHR) simply stepped into the breach left by the abandoned collective norms of Christendom. Nevertheless, it is interesting that there was an historic model within English legal thought for the freedom for states to be constrained by universal and extra-national moral and legal frameworks, which could not be altered by the will of the legislature. Moreover, it is important to acknowledge that the concepts related to human rights have deep roots within English legal thought, as it is indisputable that the human rights movement in its modern form, and also the legal protection which has developed from it, have both come about as the global community tried to formulate a response to the Second World War, the Holocaust and other atrocities linked to that conflict. The United Nations itself is explicit about this in relation to the Universal Declaration of Human Rights,[11] but it is also true that the concept of human rights as we now know it was constructed from the bricks that our forebears made.

This is a relevant consideration, bearing in mind some of the ideas being fed into the current political debate. The journalist Littlejohn wrote in a newspaper (*The Daily Mail*), which at the time was read by 3,704,000 people in the United Kingdom:[12] 'Britain has no need of laws made by unelected activist judges, based upon a foreign and wholly alien concept of justice and "human rights". That's why we should scrap the [Human Rights] Act and withdraw from the Convention'.[13]

The reality, however, could not be more different. Human rights, as they exist within the British Constitution, are in no way an alien concept in the sense of being imported from an external context. This kind of rhetoric presents them as being some sort of invasive species, like Japanese knotweed[14] or Spanish slugs,[15] doing

11 United Nations, 'Universal Declaration of Human Rights, History of the Document', http://www.un.org/en/sections/universal-declaration/history-document.

12 National Readership Survey, 'Newsbrands, April 2014–March 2015', http://www.nrs.co.uk/latest-results/nrs-print-results/newspapers-nrsprintresults.

13 *Please be aware before accessing this link, that the article contains language which may be found offensive on racial and other grounds. We have included it because it was published in a mainstream national newspaper and reflects a significant section of the debate. We, however, do not condone any discrimination or use of pejorative language, particularly on grounds of race, religion and sexuality.* R. Littlejohn, 'Democracy? No, Britain's Now a Judicial Dictatorship and It's Time for Revolution', *The Daily Mail* (13 Aug 2014), http://www.dailymail.co.uk/debate/article-2723472/Democracy-No-Britain-s-judicial-dictatorship-s-time-revolution-writes-richard-littlejohn.html.

14 Natural England, Department for Environment, Food & Rural Affairs and Environment Agency, 'Environmental Management Guidance – Harmful Weeds and Invasive, Non-Native Plants: Prevent Them Spreading' (23 Sept 2014, updated 16 Jun 2015), https://www.gov.uk/prevent-the-spread-of-harmful-invasive-and-non-native-plants.

15 'Spanish Slugs: Public Urged to Report Sightings', *BBC News* (19 Oct 2013), http://www.bbc.com/news/av/science-environment-24593015/public-urged-to-slug-spot-in-garden.

untold damage to native legal fauna and flora. It is true that, as already outlined, human rights as they exist in twenty-first-century Britain are indeed part of an international, pan-territorial framework. However (i) it is a framework which the United Kingdom played a role in developing; and (ii) human rights protection is applied by, and interpreted within the domestic legal and cultural setting.

As Bates[16] argues, drawing on the work of Ishay,[17] concepts related to human rights – the mud for the bricks – which finally became the building, can be found in the Law Code of Hammurabi, produced in Babylon in the eighteenth century BC. Equally, as Bates also acknowledges, there are provisions in many religious texts, such as the Torah, which made a key contribution. For example, in Genesis 9:6:

> Whoever sheds the blood of a human,
> by a human shall that person's blood be shed;
> for in his own image
> God made humankind.[18]

The command applies in relation to human beings, and does so on the basis that *all* human beings are made in the image of God. Murdering a woman, Gentile or a sick child would infringe this provision just as greatly as murdering a healthy Jewish adult male. The mere fact of being human is sufficient to vest an individual with a sacred status in this sense, and protects their life from being unlawfully taken.

However, the paradoxical flipside of this statement on the sanctity of human life is the *apparent*[19] automatic requirement for capital punishment in the event that this prohibition of murder is transgressed. To say the least, this position does not accord easily with a contemporary understanding of human rights.

The reality is that the road towards the current position on human rights, in Great Britain and globally, has been a long one, and we are by no means at the end of our collective journey. The human rights movement, as it emerged in the mid-twentieth century, was the convergence of many different streams of thought and cultural traditions, some of which spanned the centuries and evolved radically along the way.

As well as the religious and quasi-religious legal texts, Greek philosophy and, in particular, the Stoic school had a key role to play in the development of an idea that human beings possessed natural rights.[20] Yet, it was by no means clear within Greek intellectual circles that the definition of 'human' was broad enough

16 E. Bates, 'History', in D. Moeckli, S. Shah, S Sivakumaran and D. Harris, *International Human Rights Law* (Oxford University Press: Oxford) 2013, 18.

17 M. Ishay, *The Human Rights Reader* (Routledge: Abingdon) 2007, Introduction 'The History of Human Rights from Ancient Times to the Globalisation Era', xxi–xxviii.

18 New Revised Standard Version Bible, Popular Text Edition with Apocrypha (Oxford University Press: Oxford) 1995.

19 The implementation, or deliberate lack thereof, of capital punishment within Jewish religious law in historical times is a complex academic debate. It is clear, however, that the sanctity of human life is a key facet of mainstream modern Judaism.

20 Bates, n. 16 above, 18.

to encompass women, or those unfortunate enough to be slaves. In the view of Aristotle, the 'deliberative' aspect of the female soul was impotent and therefore in need of male supervision.[21] Such a viewpoint was obviously not compatible with according any sort of political rights to the intrinsically incapable female members of society.

Robertson and Merrills correctly observe that different cultures took different routes towards their present understanding of human rights,[22] and Great Britain and its approach to human rights sit within the cultural stream which they term the 'liberal tradition of Western democracies'. According to these commentators, this tradition was built upon Greek philosophy, Roman law, the Judeo-Christian tradition, Reformation Humanism and the Age of Reason. Of course, each one of these individual aspects contains a huge number of contrasting and often contradictory elements, and there is a very complicated interplay between each of these aspects. For instance, the movers and shakers of Reformation Humanism immersed themselves in classical Greek texts. Given Aristotle's enchanting notion of women in biological terms as failed men, misshapen and feeble in body and soul, this did not bode well for the Humanist[23] ideas of the feminine. Nevertheless, as the work of commentators like Allen has revealed, the concept of women during this period was in fact complex and multifaceted.[24] While the classical negativity was one significant strand of thought, it did not eclipse all others.

Consequently, it is not possible to identify a single Renaissance Humanist understanding of women, and thereby straightforwardly address how this may have helped or hindered the development of human rights and notions of gender equality. The picture was more complex and nuanced than that. What is apparent, however, is that the road towards modern human rights, in Great Britain and elsewhere, has been a gradual and sometimes bumpy one. The concept did not mushroom overnight, but grew with the gradual and expansive form of a tree. Sometimes branches stretched in unpromising directions and had to twist again to find the light.

7.2.2 The journey towards modern human rights

There were two streams in the development of legal thought, which have converged into the river of modern human rights. We shall briefly consider each of

21 S. Pomeroy, *Goddesses, Whores, Wives and Slaves: Women in Classical Antiquity* (Pimlico: London) 1994, 131.

22 Robertson and Merrills, n. 8 above, Ch. 1 'International Concern With Human Rights', Section II, 'Different Cultures and Their Approach to Human Rights'.

23 Renaissance Humanism in this context is obviously different from the 'secular Humanism' discussed elsewhere in this book, and refers to the early modern intellectual movement as opposed to the non-religious ideological stance of organisations like the British Humanist Association.

24 P. Allen, *The Concept of Woman, 2: The Early Humanist Reformation, 1250–1500* (Grand Rapids: Eerdmans) 2006.

these in turn, as they will explain how the concept of human rights has evolved organically in Great Britain, and will continue to do so.

First, there is the question of who qualifies for the fundamental rights recognised by the legal system? For instance, Magna Carta[25] famously referred to free men, and thereby excluded far more people than it included. Second, there is the question of which rights the legal system regards as special and fundamental. These have also multiplied over time. For example, the right not to be detained indefinitely without trial was recognised long before the right to vote and participate in the democratic process.

The reality is that as the British legal framework evolved to recognise an increasing number of rights vested in individuals, it also developed to recognise a growing number of individuals in whom such rights were vested. These two processes happened in parallel, but certainly not in synch. In pragmatic terms, therefore, it makes sense to analyse them separately. We will consider how the legal system developed along both of these pathways before meeting at its present understanding of universal human rights.

7.2.2.1 Qualifying for rights: in whom are rights vested?

Clearly, if a modern legal system does not accord a right to all people by virtue of their human status, it is not recognising a human right but privileging one group of people to the detriment of another.[26] It is indeed helpful to consider how rights developed in relation to disempowered groups within society. Admittedly, it would be beyond the scope of this book to address *all* disempowered groups, or to examine the story of any one group in any depth. However, briefly considering the way in which British law has evolved in relation to women as a case study helps to shed light on the broader picture.

We shall avoid couching the discussion in terms of personhood or humanity, except in so far as the historical narrative demands this, because in most cases this would obscure, rather than illuminate, the underlying reality. Before human rights became recognised, lacking rights did not make an individual less than *human* in contemporary eyes. A lawyer in the fifteenth century might well deem that female children had very few rights in law, but would in all probability have been incensed at the suggestion that his six-year-old daughter was not a person made in the image of God, in accordance with the teachings of the Church and the prevailing worldview within his culture.

Nevertheless, as Wiseberg and Scoble argue: 'Philosophically and theoretically, the struggle for the attainment of equal rights for women is an integral

25 British Library, 'English Translation of Magna Carta', https://www.bl.uk/magna-carta/articles/magna-carta-english-translation.

26 Subject to the caveat that some individuals may not have the capacity to exercise certain rights by virtue of a vulnerability of which the legal system needs to take cognisance. For instance, children do not have a present right to marry and found a family (although they do have a right to be safeguarded from treatment which might jeopardise their ability to fully exercise that right later in life).

part of the struggle for the actualization of rights, through both domestic and international procedures and processes'.[27]

Yet, until the nineteenth and twentieth centuries women were disadvantaged in numerous legal spheres, and this inequality was not merely accepted, but actively embraced. If married, women lacked the capacity to hold property independently at common law,[28] as husband and wife were for many purposes a single legal unit.[29] However, Victorian legislation enabled married women first to retain their own earnings[30] and later to own property independently, even if it was acquired after their marriage.[31]

Women were also subject to serious inequalities in relation to family law, and divorce and separation were extremely difficult. In fact, the Matrimonial Causes Act 1857 provided access to divorce for the first time to those[32] unable to afford a private Act of Parliament. Yet the sting in the tail for women was that the legislation treated husbands and wives very differently: husbands could obtain a divorce on the grounds of adultery, cruelty or desertion, whereas wives were required to prove adultery aggravated by one of the specified factors, such as bigamy, incest or desertion. It was not until 1923 that women finally obtained access to divorce on an equal legal footing to men.

There was also a stark contrast in the position of male and female spouses in relation to the custody of young children following divorce or separation. Until the early 1830s, the basic position was that children remained in the control of their father, regardless of the circumstances of the marital breakdown and the characteristics of the children.[33] This changed with the Custody of Infants Act 1839 (Talfourd's Act), which provided that a woman could petition the courts for custody of her children up to the age of seven, and to have access to older children in the event of separation.[34] However, it also specifically provided that no such order could be made in cases where the mother was guilty of adultery.

These developments illustrate well the haphazard nature of the development of rights in relation to women, and more generally. The legislature was not attempting to implement a coherent social policy in respect of gender relations

27 L.S. Wiseberg & H.M. Scoble, 'Women's Rights and International Human Rights: A Bibliographical Note', *Human Rights Quarterly*, Vol. 3, No. 2 (1981) 127–35, 127.

28 It should be noted that although married women could not own property independently from their husbands at law prior to the Victorian legal reforms, they could enjoy an equitable interest in property in certain circumstances. For a fuller discussion of the historical law of equity and its implications see J.H. Baker, *An Introduction to English Legal History* (Oxford University Press: Oxford) 4th edn, 2005.

29 The legal fiction of husband and wife being one person never extended to all aspects of legal personality; for instance, criminal responsibility was never shared.

30 Married Women's Property Act 1870.

31 Married Women's Property Act 1882.

32 Matrimonial Causes Act 1923.

33 A. Bainham and S. Gilmore (with specialist contributions from N. Harris and K. Holdsworth), *Children: The Modern Law* (Family Law: Bristol) 2013, 16–17.

34 N. Lowe and G. Douglas, *Bromley's Family Law* (Oxford University Press: Oxford) 10th edn, 2007, 354–5.

or rights; it was responding to a social problem raised by a series of high-profile cases[35] and campaigners. As a result, there was no holistic consideration of the competing rights of the various parties involved.

In the course of the twentieth century, there were moves towards recognising the right of women to equal treatment in economic and political terms, although the process was by no means always direct and smooth. Ironically, the very legal reforms of the nineteenth century which had sought to increase participation in parliamentary democracy functioned to further exclude women from the political process. Prior to the 1832 Reform Act, voting rights were related to property. Although women were much less likely to inherit or otherwise come into possession of substantial property, there was nothing to prevent them from voting if this happened to be the case. However, this possibility ended with the legislative rationalisation of the system.

Nor were women the only group to be disadvantaged by this Act, which effectively extended voting rights to the middle classes. It also functioned to deprive some economically disadvantaged individuals of their rights, and the famous potwallopers[36] lost the vote. Historically, in some parliamentary boroughs, the franchise had extended to the male head of any household with a hearth big enough to wallop (or boil) a cauldron. This sporadic and partial extension of voting rights to some working people was squashed from on high by the supposedly liberalising measure. The battle for universal male suffrage raged on until the second half of the nineteenth century, while women had to wait even longer to obtain the vote.

The epic struggle for women's suffrage has become an iconic aspect of Edwardian England,[37] as middle and upper-class women mobilised to demand the right to participate as citizens in a democratic nation. A significant proportion of them were prepared to resort to extreme, and at times, even violent tactics. The Government, for its part, was willing to order the brutal force-feeding of suffragettes on hunger strike in prison, and also passed the 'Cat and Mouse' Act 1913,[38] enabling suffragettes on hunger strike to be released from custody and recalled once they had restarted eating and had recovered.

Women were finally granted the right to vote in 1918,[39] but only for those aged 30 and over, and they were not permitted to vote on the same terms as their male counterparts until 1928.[40] Intriguingly, however, the Parliament

35 *R v de Manderville* (1804) 5 East 221; *De Manderville v De Manderville* (1804) 10 Ves 52; and *R v Greenhill* (1836) 4 Ad & E 624.

36 J. Phillips, 'The Structure of Electoral Politics in Unreformed England', *Journal of British Studies*, Vol. 19, No. 1 (1979) 76–100.

37 See, e.g., J. Marlow (ed.), *Votes for Women: The Virago Book of Suffragettes* (Virago: London) 2001.

38 Formally known as the Prisoners (Temporary Discharge for Ill Health) Act 1913: see further, UK Parliament, 'Living Heritage', http://www.parliament.uk/about/living-heritage/transformingsociety/electionsvoting/womenvote/case-study-the-right-to-vote/the-right-to-vote/winson-green-forcefeeding/cat-and-mouse-act.

39 Representation of the People Act 1918.

40 Representation of the People Act 1928.

(Qualification of Women) Act 1918 permitted women aged 21 and over to stand and be elected as Members of the House of Commons. So, there was a period during which young adult women could theoretically participate in the democratic process as candidates, but not as members of the electorate. This is another clear illustration of the unsystematic nature of moves towards legal gender equality: the democratic framework responded to changes in the political and social tide but could not be said to be following any fixed and consistent agenda.

Not only was the journey towards legal gender equality unmapped, external as well as internal pressures were at times important catalysts for change. A further crucial stepping stone across the river of discrimination came with the Equal Pay Act 1970. This was in part the result of industrial relations issues at home – in particular, a strike by female sewing machinists,[41] which became the backdrop for the film and musical *Made in Dagenham*[42] – but it was also a *sine qua non* for the United Kingdom to join the European Economic Community (which would become the European Union after the Maastricht Treaty). As Rubery[43] argues, equal pay was an important principle within even the foundational treaty of the (now) European Union, and Article 141 requires that 'each Member State shall ensure that the principle of equal pay for male and female workers for equal work or work of equal value is applied'.

Furthermore, in 1983 the United Kingdom passed legislation[44] amending the Equal Pay Act to incorporate the principle of equal pay for equal value work into domestic law, in response to a judgment of the European Court of Justice which found the UK framework inadequate in this regard.[45] Thus, international obligations flowing from what were primarily economic, rather than human rights, treaties forced the United Kingdom to move forward on this issue.

One of the most significant developments of the second half of the twentieth century was the passage of the Sex Discrimination Act 1975, which prohibited discrimination in relation to employment, training, education, the provision of goods and services, and the disposal of premises. It covered discrimination on the grounds of sex or marital status, and afforded protection to men, as well as women, in this regard. It also established the Equal Opportunities Commission, which – significantly for our discussion – has now become part of the Equality and Human Rights Commission (EHRC). This direct line of descent demonstrates the relationship between these developments and an evolving dialogue on

41 British Library, 'Sisterhood and After: Timeline of the Women's Liberation Movement', http://www.bl.uk/sisterhood/timeline.

42 D. Cox, 'Made in Dagenham: A Squandered Opportunity', *The Guardian* (30 Sept 2010), http://www.theguardian.com/film/filmblog/2010/sep/13/made-in-dagenham-first-look.

43 J. Rubery, 'Equal Pay and Europe', in *Winning Equal Pay: The Value of Women's Work*, part of the Union Makes Us Strong website, a collaboration between London Metropolitan University and the Trades Unions Congress, http://www.unionhistory.info/equalpay/roaddisplay.php?irn=785.

44 The Equal Pay (Amendment) Regulations 1983.

45 *Commission of the European Communities v United* Kingdom, Case 61/81 [1982] ICR 578.

rights and human rights.[46] It is also important to note that the EHRC now has devolved authorities in Wales[47] and Scotland.[48]

Subject to certain exceptions built into the legislation (for example, to allow religious groups to appoint only men as ministers, or theatre companies to discriminate on grounds of gender when holding casting auditions), it was now essentially unlawful to subject any human being to discrimination on grounds of gender in key spheres of public human activity. In due course the Sex Discrimination Act (along with various other statutes prohibiting distinct forms of discrimination, including the Equal Pay Act 1970) was replaced by the Equality Act 2010. This legislation was passed in response to EU Equal Treatment directives and operated to consolidate, and in certain respects reform, UK discrimination law. Once again, the Act applied to everybody, and thereby affirmed a universal right to freedom from discrimination on the grounds and in the circumstances described.

Of course, in addition to all of this are the provisions of the Human Rights Act 1998 and the ECHR. Article 14 of the ECHR leaves no room for doubt that the Convention applies in exactly the same way to men and women. This provision prohibits discrimination in relation to any of the other rights contained in the Convention. Its basic structure, therefore, is to create a piggy-back rather than a freestanding right. Protocol 12 applies the prohibited grounds of discrimination to the exercise of *any* legal right and to the actions of public authorities, but the United Kingdom is among the states not to have signed up to this new provision.

Thus, in summary, the recognition of human rights vested in women and men equally was not some alien and unfamiliar concept which was imposed upon the UK legal system. As we have seen earlier in this chapter, there are certainly voices in the popular press arguing that the language of rights and human rights is being imposed on Britain by external forces, but in reality the law had been gradually dismantling systemic gender inequalities for the better part of three hundred years, and the provisions of the Human Rights Act in this regard were very much in harmony with the tune which was already being played. A dialogue rooted in rights was a core element of this throughout the process. Consider, for example, the title of Mary Wollstonecraft's great work 'A Vindication of the Rights of Woman'.[49]

Yet, as previously noted, it would be misguided to try to assert that the previous legislative and judicial developments had been in pursuance of any coherent and overarching plan. On many occasions, changes were in response to a very

46 Equality and Human Rights Commission, 'About Us', http://www.equalityhumanrights.com/about-us.

47 Equality and Human Rights Commission, http://www.equalityhumanrights.com/about-us/devolved-authorities/commission-wales.

48 Equality and Human Rights Commission, http://www.equalityhumanrights.com/about-us/devolved-authorities/commission-scotland.

49 M. Wollstonecroft, *A Vindication of the Rights of Men; A Vindication of the Rights of Woman; An Historical and Moral View of the French Revolution* (Oxford University Press: Oxford) 1999, 'A Vindication of the Rights of Woman'.

specific problem, crisis or campaign. Furthermore, because amendments were introduced to address a particular problem or set of problems, there was often no consideration of how expanding rights in one direction might have an adverse impact on rights enjoyed in another, and the development of legal equality for women gradually came to be set within the wider context of ending discrimination based on gender, as the 1975 Sex Discrimination Act demonstrates. It was, in fact, part of a collective legal and social dialogue about rights.

Nevertheless, as will be discussed further below, it was largely the Human Rights Act which placed this dialogue within a structured framework, and allowed for a deliberate and ordered balance of competing rights in a holistic manner.

Different narratives following a broadly similar trajectory can be traced in relation to other legally and culturally disempowered groups in society – for example, children, racial minorities, religious minorities, the mentally incapacitated, homosexual and transgender citizens, as well as the economically disadvantaged. This is not to downplay the profound and continuing differences, as each group has its own story, has faced and continues to face its own challenges. Furthermore, we certainly do not imply that inequality is something which we have successfully consigned to history, but the legal system has transitioned to a position in which human rights are accepted as being exactly that: rights vested in human beings by virtue of their humanity.

7.2.2.2 Recognition of human rights in the United Kingdom

Just as the number of citizens in possession of legal rights evolved over time, so there is an increase in the number of rights. There are now more diners at the table, and the menu has vastly expanded. Nevertheless, despite the journalistic hype cited above, it would be absurd to suggest that human rights had no place within the United Kingdom legal framework until the Human Rights Act was passed by the Blair administration.

In the following brief overview we shall consider: (i) human rights conferred by the United Kingdom legal framework before 1998; (ii) the significance of second and third generation rights; and (iii) the European Convention on Human Rights.

7.2.2.2.1 HUMAN RIGHTS CONFERRED BY THE UNITED KINGDOM LEGAL FRAMEWORK PRIOR TO 2000

As has already been discussed, human rights are ancient in origin, but there are a number of significant legal developments which enshrine certain specific rights within the law of the United Kingdom.

Although it has been accorded talismanic status, the rights conferred by the Magna Carta were very much the stuff of reality as well as legend in the sense that they have functioned to shape legal thinking. Clause 29 remains part of British law:

> No free man shall be seized or imprisoned, or stripped of his rights or possessions, or outlawed or exiled, or deprived of his standing in any other way, nor will we proceed with force against him, or send others to do so, except by the lawful judgment of his equals or by the law of the land.[50]

As Willey observes, members of the Supreme Court recently cited the Magna Carta as the source for the right to a fair trial and due process.[51] Lady Hale, speaking extra-judicially, suggested that it was the progenitor of Article 6 of the ECHR.[52] This is an interesting and pertinent thought, and in reality cultural and legal dialogues tend to be two-way traffic. The Convention emerged from the Western liberal tradition, and the philosophy and jurisprudence of the United Kingdom was one ingredient in this intellectual soup. Ideas can be exported and imported, and some aspects of human rights have moved between the United Kingdom and continental Europe.

Equally, the Bill of Rights 1688 was a significant development, asserting the collective right to regular Parliaments and elections, and freedom of speech in Parliament, as well as limiting the power of the Crown. It is true that it did less towards the advancement of individual rights, but it did set out some personal rights, including freedom from cruel and unusual punishment.

Another key element of human rights protection was the overarching principle of liberty as the default position. As Lester and Pannick[53] argue, the theme running through the common law tradition was that individuals were free to take any action they pleased, provided that the law did not forbid or restrict it. This was bolstered by the *Entick v Carrington*[54] precept: the Crown and its servants must act within the rule of law. In other words, the choices, behaviour and property of private citizens could not be interfered with unless there was some legal basis for the intervention. Feldman describes the position in the following terms:

> Until recently, the general approach to protecting rights in the UK was to think in terms not of liberties or freedoms, but of liberty or freedom. The dominant idea has been that of an undifferentiated mass of liberty.[55]

This idea of a kind of 'liberty ball' could potentially appear unappealing because it conjures up visions of a ball of rights squashed and mingled together.

50 British Library, Learning Timelines: Sources from History, 'The Magna Carta 1215', http://www.bl.uk/learning/timeline/item95692.html.

51 P. Willey, 'Trials in Absentia and the Cuts to Criminal Legal Aid: A Deadly Combination?', *Journal of Criminal Law*, Vol. 78, No. 6 (2014) 486–510.

52 Lady Hale, 'What's the Point of Human Rights?', Warwick Law Lecture (28 Nov 2013), para. 1, http://supremecourt.uk/docs/speech-131128.pdf.

53 A.P. Lester and D. Pannick, *Human Rights: Law and Practice* (Butterworths: Kent) 2000, para 1.02.

54 *Entick v Carrington* (1765)19 St Tr 1030, [1765] EWHC KB J98.

55 D. Feldman, *Civil Liberties and Human Rights in England and Wales* (Oxford University Press: Oxford) 2000, 68.

Certainly, this mass of liberty was not unproblematic, as it did not always lend itself easily to extracting individual 'colours' in terms of particular rights and asserting them. For instance, citizens were free to believe whatever they wished and act upon their beliefs as far as their conduct was not unlawful. However, this would not assist a person to vindicate his or her right to 'manifest' a belief in the same manner as the specific protection conferred by Article 9 of the ECHR and the Human Rights Act. Remarkably, discrimination legislation might be called upon to assist if somebody wished to manifest a belief linked to ethnicity or other protected characteristic, as it was sometimes possible in such circumstances to demonstrate indirect discrimination.

However, looking at the historical legal framework as a whole, it was possible to discern rights now enshrined in the ECHR as having had a prior existence. For instance, although there was no specific right to marry and found a family, the law provided all citizens in England and Wales the right to marry in an Anglican church; for citizens in Scotland there was the possibility of requesting a marriage in the Church of Scotland, while for all there was both the right to marry in a secular service presided over by a registrar, and the right to marry in accordance with another faith tradition willing to perform the service and able to comply with the relevant legislative requirements. Therefore, as marriage was not unlawful, it was contained within this ball of liberties and the state provided a legal mechanism to enable people to take the relevant action to achieve it.

Arguably, as the law developed, it allowed more and more people to draw on the mass of liberties and exercise the rights which it contained, and it would be impossible to argue that the Human Rights Act did not radically alter the position in terms of recognising rights and the avenues by which citizens could enforce them. However, as we have seen in our discussion about the gradual broadening of access to rights, many of the rights themselves already existed implicitly within the body of law, and the state had taken measures to facilitate their exercise. It was not the case that the raft of rights which the Human Rights Act introduced were *in themselves* all new.

7.2.2.2.2 THE SIGNIFICANCE OF SECOND AND THIRD GENERATION RIGHTS

It would also be deeply misguided to assume that the conception of human rights within the United Kingdom legal framework is now *limited* to the rights enshrined in the Human Rights Act. In addition to the positive rights flowing from that legislation the residual liberty ball still exists, as do other rights contained within the legal framework.

The division of rights into three generations, originally proposed by Vasak,[56] may be a helpful tool to introduce at this point. According to Vasak's scheme, first generation rights address civil and political liberty; second generation rights

56 P. Macklem, 'Human Rights in International Law: Three Generations or One?', *London Review of International Law*, Vol. 3, No. 1 (2015) 61–92.

address economic, social and cultural rights; while third generation rights address what are perceived as being more aspirational goals, such as the right to a healthy environment, right of access to natural resources and the right to participate in cultural heritage.

It is true that this structure has been criticised by commentators like Macklem for drawing artificial and unhelpful boundaries between related rights. Although this point is not without some validity, Vasak's division does provide a convenient starting point for analysis. It may not reveal the entire vista, but it is a picture which allows us to see one aspect of reality.

While the ECHR incorporates certain elements of all three generations of rights, it undeniably leans heavily towards the first generation. This is not surprising, given that in general first generation rights are absolute and enforceable, whereas second generation rights are relative and their provision tends to be resource-dependent. With regard to the right to medical care, for example, how much medical care is to be provided, in what circumstances and on what financial basis?

This does not mean, however, that the UK legal framework is hobbled in its progress, and is incapable of pulling rights out of its liberty ball which cover territory not spanned by the Human Rights Act. Importantly, the collective dialogue and movement on rights does go on.

7.2.3 The Human Rights Act 1998

(a) The provision of identifiable rights

We have already looked at the Human Rights Act in the context of parliamentary sovereignty. The statute incorporates most provisions of the ECHR into domestic law and confers positive and distinct rights[57] upon both citizens and others within the jurisdiction of the state.[58] The rights are truly *human* rights, as they apply to all human beings and discrimination in their application is expressly prohibited.[59] Public bodies have a duty to act in accordance with these rights, and there are mechanisms to ensure that the legislature does not inadvertently pass legislation which might infringe them.

57 The core rights are those set out in the ECHR: Art. 2, the right to life; Art. 3, prohibition on torture; Art. 3, prohibition on slavery and forced labour; Art. 5, the right to liberty and security of person; Art. 6, the right to a fair trial; Art. 7, freedom from retroactive criminalisation of acts or omissions; Art. 8, the right to respect for privacy and family life; Art. 9, the right to freedom of conscience and religion; Art. 10, the right to freedom of expression; Art. 11, the right to freedom of association and assembly; Art. 12, the right to marry and found a family; Art. 13, the right to an effective remedy within national law for infringement of convention rights; and Art. 14, the right to freedom from discrimination in relation to Convention rights. There are also a series of Protocols to the Convention, some of which have been ratified by the United Kingdom.

58 Art. 1 ECHR.

59 Art. 14 ECHR. As noted above, we acknowledge that there are complex issues in relation to the application and outworking of certain rights for certain groups.

(b) A framework for ongoing collective dialogue

Not only does it provide individuals with identifiable rights, as opposed to a liberty ball from which they are obliged to pull and mould freedoms, but it also sets the collective dialogue on rights within a known framework. As we have seen, there is nothing new about the collective social dialogue on the rights which citizens should have, in whom they should be vested or the extent to which they should be promoted and defended by the law. However, this conversation currently takes place within the structure set out by the legislation. The impact of any changes on the human rights of all individuals and groups within society must be considered by the legislature and executive, and it is now more difficult for governments to seek to address a deficit of rights in one group and inadvertently oppress another.

For example, in an article that addresses the current legal provisions in relation to domestic violence, Bessant[60] considers the tension between the rights of victims of domestic violence and those of the perpetrators, as well as the challenge for state authorities in appropriately balancing these. She looks at the ECHR, and interestingly also other international obligations which do not form part of domestic law, such as the 1993 UN Declaration on the Elimination of Violence Against Women.[61] As well as being of great interest in terms of the topic being addressed, this piece illustrates two important points.

First, the imposition of the ECHR framework in a United Kingdom context ensures that the human rights of *all* relevant parties must now be included in policy and legal decision-making, even when some of the individuals concerned may not be well placed to attract sympathy. While many people may feel an instinctive repugnance towards the perpetrators of domestic violence, this does not deprive them of their human status nor the rights which flow from it. Given the tendency for the rights of one group to be advanced at the cost of another during the long phase of organic development of rights within the UK context prior to the passage of the Human Rights Act, this requirement to balance competing interests, regardless of political expedience, is important.

Second, it demonstrates that while the ECHR and the Human Rights Act are now central to the way in which the Constitution and the wider legal framework deal with human rights, they are an endoskeleton and not an exoskeleton. In other words, they function like the bone structure of a panther rather than the shell of a prawn.

The whole body of the prawn is contained within its hard outer casing and, by its very nature, the organism cannot grow beyond the armour which holds it altogether. The plating is protective but also, by its very nature, limiting. Even the

60 C. Bessant, ‘Protecting Victims of Domestic Violence – Have We Got the Balance Right?’, *Journal of Criminal Law*, Vol. 79, No. 2 (2015) 102–21.

61 United Nations General Assembly, Declaration on the Elimination of Violence Against Women, 20 Dec 1993, http://www.un.org/documents/ga/res/48/a48r104.htm.

giant, human-sized lobster *Aegirocassis Benmoulae*, which roamed the Ordovician oceans, was entirely contained within its exoskeleton.[62] In contrast, the internal skeleton of a mammal like a panther holds the organism together and protects its delicate parts, but the body grows around, rather than within the framework. The Human Rights Act does not *limit* the expansion of human rights: the residual constitutional and common law liberties remain intact, while the provisions of international law are still key, as are other legislative developments which may confer rights above and beyond those recognised by the Convention. Certainly, the state is free to recognise and promote other human rights, including 'second generation' rights.

By way of example, the National Health Service was founded on three core principles by Aneurin Bevan, and these remain intact:

- that it meet the needs of everyone
- that it be free at the point of delivery
- that it be based on clinical need, not ability to pay.[63]

A commitment to these principles is not required by the ECHR, and indeed many Convention states do not have a comparable public health care system. Nevertheless, the right to clinically required health care, free at the point of delivery, is an accepted part of the present UK political framework, although this is not to suggest that this position will never change or that the statutes upon which the NHS are built are constitutional statutes in the same way as the Human Rights Act.

Furthermore, it is not the case that the right to free medical treatment applies equally to all human beings within the jurisdiction of the United Kingdom, and there are indeed certain circumstances in which charges can be recovered from overseas visitors.[64] However, although second generation rights, such as the right to healthcare, are relative and dependent upon resources, it is also the case that the emergency medical treatment is provided to all visitors to the United Kingdom, regardless of whether their presence is even lawful.[65] Indeed, the culture in public hospitals is undoubtedly to treat first and ask questions later.

Moreover, it is the case that not all forms of legal recognition of human rights take the same form or have the same status. Just because the rights contained in NHS legislation are not isomorphic to the rights recognised by the Human Rights Act, this does not mean that they should not be described as human rights for some purposes. Otherwise, rights contained in international treaties

62 '"Giant Lobster" Ate Like a Whale', *BBC News* (12 Mar 2015), http://www.bbc.co.uk/news/science-environment-31837024.

63 NHS Choices, About the NHS, 'Principles and Choices that Guide the NHS', http://www.nhs.uk/NHSEngland/thenhs/about/Pages/nhscoreprinciples.aspx.

64 UK Government, 'Guidance on Overseas Visitors Hospital Charging Regulations', https://www.gov.uk/government/publications/guidance-on-overseas-visitors-hospital-charging-regulations.

65 Ibid.

such as the UN Convention on the Rights of the Child[66] could not be described as human rights in any sense.

Consequently, the Human Rights Act is enabling, rather than constraining, the general provision of human rights in the United Kingdom, which brings us to the second point arising from Bessant's reflections, and it can be argued persuasively that since the introduction of the Human Rights Act both commentators and judges have shown an increased awareness of international human rights obligations, and their weight as persuasive authority has increased.

Nevertheless, at the time of writing it would be impossible to consider the impact of the Human Rights Act without acknowledging that its future is still uncertain, and the current Conservative Government appears to have put on ice progress on its previous commitment to replace the Human Rights Act with a Bill of Rights.[67] Prior to the 2017 election, the Tory Administration announced that if reelected, it would not allow this debate to be a distraction from Brexit. So although it has been downgraded as a priority, in principle, the Conservative Party remains ideologically committed to it. Before the 2015 General Election, in October 2014, the Conservative Party had produced a document[68] setting out the following points at the heart of its vision for the future:

- The European Court of Human Rights is no longer binding over the UK Supreme Court.
- The European Court of Human Rights is no longer able to order a change in UK law and becomes an advisory body only.
- There is a proper balance between rights and responsibilities in UK law.[69]

Generally speaking, academic reaction to the prospect of scrapping the Human Rights Act has been extremely negative. Lambrecht, for instance, observes that the systemic criticism of the ECHR within the United Kingdom is out of step with the general European context, and queries whether the true agenda behind the planned reforms is to clip the wings of the domestic courts.[70] On the other hand, Sir Francis Jacobs, former Advocate General of the European Court of Justice, criticised a key part of the asserted rationale for the change: 'There is a feeling that issues of human rights should be resolved by parliament. But the problem is

66 United Nations Convention on the Rights of the Child, 20 Nov 1989, https://www.unicef.org.uk/wp-content/uploads/2010/05/UNCRC_united_nations_convention_on_the_rights_of_the_child.pdf (greater steps have been taken to integrate this with the domestic law of Scotland than that of England and Wales).

67 B. Collins and N. Newbegin, 'HRA 1998: The End', *New Law Journal*, Vol. 165, No. 7662 (2015) 11.

68 The Conservative Party, 'Protecting Human Rights in the UK: The Conservatives' Proposals for Changing Britain's Human Rights Laws' (Oct 2014), https://www.conservatives.com/~/media/files/.../human_rights.pdf.

69 Ibid., 5.

70 S. Lambrecht, 'HRA Watch: Reform, Repeal, Replace? Criticism of the European Court of Human Rights – A UK Phenomenon?', *UK Constitutional Law Association* (27 Jul 2015), http://ukconstitutionallaw.org/2015/07/27/hra-watch-reform-repeal-replace-sarah-lambrecht-criticism-of-the-european-court-of-human-rights-a-uk-phenomenon.

parliament is not always a reliable arbiter on questions of human rights', and at the same time expressed concerned about the message which the action would send to the international community.[71] The shape of any new legal framework remains very hazy and, as Collins and Newbegin point out, the implications for other areas of the legal system, such as employment, are far from clear.[72]

In addition, there has been a backlash from some human rights campaign groups. Liberty, for instance, states:

> This would weaken the rights of everyone, meaning less protection against powerful interests. It would also limit human rights to only those cases the Government considers 'most serious'. Can we really trust political elites to decide when our freedoms should apply?[73]

Clearly, this is a political message and does not claim to be coming from a neutral place, but it does evidence the kind of opposition and arguments that moves to repeal the Human Rights Act face from some quarters.

One aspect of the Conservative Party's argument for abolishing the current statutory framework – which is difficult to substantiate logically – is the phenomenon which it describes as 'mission creep':

> The European Court of Human Rights has developed 'mission creep'. Strasbourg adopts a principle of interpretation that regards the Convention as a 'living instrument'. Even allowing for necessary changes over the decades, the ECtHR has used its 'living instrument doctrine' to expand Convention rights into new areas, and certainly beyond what the framers of the Convention had in mind when they signed up to it. There is mounting concern at Strasbourg's attempts to overrule decisions of our democratically elected Parliament and overturn the UK courts' careful applications of Convention rights.[74]

The contrast in the language used to describe essentially the same reality is striking. In our view, the term 'mission creep' has sinister connotations, whereas 'living instrument' implies something vibrant, flexible and subject to organic change. The truth is that the status of the Convention as a 'living instrument' and use of the term is widely accepted and respected by both judges and academics.[75] However, as Letsas argues, there are complications inherent in the idea of treating either national constitutions or international treaties as living instruments:[76]

71 P. Rogerson, 'News: Human Rights Warning from Leading Jurist', *Law Society Gazette*, Vol. 3, No. 1 (22 Jun 2015).

72 Collins and Newbegin, n. 67 above.

73 Liberty, 'Campaigning, Save Our Human Rights Act', https://www.liberty-human-rights.org.uk/campaigning/save-our-human-rights-act.

74 The Conservative Party, n. 68 above, 3.

75 See, e.g., the discussion in G. Bindman, 'Battle of the Giants', *New Law Journal*, Vol. 165, No. 7641 (2015) 8.

76 G. Letsas, 'The ECHR as a Living Instrument: Its Meaning and Legitimacy', in A. Føllesdal, B. Peters and G. Ulfstein (eds), *Constituting Europe: The European Court of Human Rights in a*

> Advocates of the 'living constitution' oppose the idea that present-day conditions should be fully governed by a document whose drafters died decades or even centuries ago. But they are burdened with the difficulty of explaining what kind of pre-commitment the original constitution is meant to express, if its meaning is not treated as frozen.

It is undeniable that the scope of growth on this basis is a controversial issue, and there is debate as to how far courts can, or should, extend the application and interpretation of the principles contained with the Convention framework. Nevertheless, it is equally clear that pan-European norms have altered radically since the Convention was first drafted, and it is inevitable that the understanding of the principles contained within in must evolve with the shifting consensus.

Even if, for some reason, it was thought desirable to freeze our collective interpretation in time, this would not be possible unless it was also within our technological capacity to freeze the judges themselves. Unless the human beings required to apply the law are somehow kept in suspended animation, sealed off from cultural changes and thawed out only to hear cases in a protected environment, they will be influenced by a changing world and understandings will gradually alter over time.

In the 1950s it was normal and acceptable across Europe for children, and especially boys, to be beaten with canes, slippers and other objects, both in school and at home.[77] While not all parents and teachers agreed with the practice, it was regarded as legitimate by society and was even the subject of jokes in popular children's comics like *The Beano*.[78] However, this is now no longer the case, and the European Court of Justice has reflected the changed reality by declaring practices such as beating children with canes and slippers to be inhuman and degrading treatment.[79]

We acknowledge that it would have been grossly inappropriate to try to interpret Article 3 on the basis of what would have appeared to be inhuman and degrading two generations ago. If the contemporary reality was ignored, the Convention would have limited impact within that paradigm, and it is important to emphasise that the Strasbourg Court has *consistently* refused to use the living instrument principle where the collective consensus across the signatory states has not shifted.

An excellent example of this is the Court's treatment of same-sex marriage. As Johnson argues, in recent cases the Court has increasingly adopted a stance which challenges a heteronormative approach to voluntary adult partnerships,

National, European and Global Context (Cambridge University Press: Cambridge) 2013, 106, 124–5 'Introduction'.

77 J. Middleton, 'Spare the Rod', *History Today*, Vol. 62, No. 11 (2012).

78 *The Beano* comic ceased to have scenes of the notorious Dennis the Menace being spanked by his father with a slipper in the 1980s, as it was recognised no longer to be a socially acceptable way to parent: S. Jeffries, 'The Beano – A Happy 75th Anniversary', *The Guardian* (20 Jul 2013), http://www.theguardian.com/lifeandstyle/2013/jul/20/beano-75-year-anniversary.

79 *Costello-Roberts v United Kingdom* (1993) 19 EHRR 112.

but has nevertheless declined to use the living instrument principle to require states to offer same-sex marriage to citizens.[80] This reflects the reality that not only has European society radically changed its attitude towards same-sex relationships in the last half century or so, but also that substantial differences remain in relation to same-sex marriage across the Convention states, as the Court observed in *Schalk*.[81]

The Conservative Party's use of the term 'mission creep' is misguided for two reasons. First, there is good evidence that the Court has been careful only to employ the doctrine where there is an objective reason to believe that the pan-European consensus has shifted; second, the living instrument principle is inevitable with any rights-based document being interpreted by any set of judges. Even if the legislature in the United Kingdom opted for a statutory scheme which wholly ousted both the Convention and the Strasbourg Court, British judges interpreting a British Bill of Rights would still develop a body of case law that would move and change with evolving cultural norms.

To add insult to injury for some, the United Kingdom would still be part of the cultural as well as geographical space that is the continent of Europe. Our intellectual and cultural life would still be influenced by, and contribute to, the life of Europe as a whole and, therefore, the interpretation of a Bill of Rights would still change as Europe changed. The notion of '*sakoku*' or 'locked country' was not wholly successful in seventeenth-century Japan, and it is hardly a probable phenomenon in twenty-first-century Europe. In all fairness, this is not being proposed by even the most vehement Eurosceptics, and the flow of ideas is going to continue in both directions, whatever legislation is passed.

In summary, the story of human rights within the United Kingdom legal system has always been one of evolving understanding and collective dialogue, and this will continue even if the paradigm is fundamentally shifted by the repeal of the Human Rights Act.

The issue to which we are about to turn is how the religious dimension of the Constitution and the wider legal framework influence the manner in which human rights are currently understood and interpreted in the British context. Are there any ways in which it has a positive impact on the functioning of the newest constitutional pillar?

7.3 Does the tripartite character of the legal and constitutional system enhance or weaken human rights?

Are there any specific and tangible ways in which the positive treatment of religion by the current legal framework has a beneficial impact upon human rights more generally? We suggest that a number of examples of this can be identified.

80 P. Johnson, 'Marriage, Heteronormativity and the European Court of Human Rights: A Reappraisal', *International Journal of Law, Policy and the Family*, Vol. 29, No. 1 (2015) 56–77.

81 *Schalk and Kopf v Austria*, App. no. 30141/04, 24 June 2010 (ECtHR).

7.3.1 The Succession to the Crown Act 2013

This legislative development demonstrates how the models of establishment in the United Kingdom are flexible enough to remould themselves around changing understandings of human rights. It also illustrates well that the religious dimension is by no means the only aspect of the Constitution endowed with this plasticity and capacity to evolve. Here, the religious and political aspects of the framework travelled together.

The Succession to the Crown Act 2013 removed the bar upon persons married to Roman Catholics from the line of succession.[82] Although the debate surrounding this was wider than establishment, it nevertheless clearly had great relevance for the monarch's position as Supreme Governor of the Church of England and the Coronation Oath to maintain the established Church.[83] Equally, it was significant in relation to the Oath of Accession, which requires the monarch to 'maintain and preserve the Protestant Religion and Presbyterian Church government' in Scotland.[84]

Importantly, the Church of England was supportive of the reform and eased the passage of the legislation in practical ways. The Parliamentary Unit of the Church of England stated that 'the present prohibition on anyone remaining in the line of succession or succeeding to the Crown as a result of marrying a Roman Catholic is not necessary to support the requirement that the Sovereign join in communion with the Church of England'.[85]

Furthermore, Church of England bishops helped to allay concerns of some peers in the House of Lords about the implications of such a marriage in terms of Roman Catholic and Anglican canon law, and the requirements of the Roman Catholic Church in relation to the bringing up of children from a 'mixed marriage'.[86]

Moreover, representatives of the Roman Catholic Church met with the Advocate-General for Scotland, and assisted in providing clarification about

82 Succession to the Crown Act 2013, s. 2.

83 The Official Website of the British Monarch, Coronation Oath, 2nd June 1953: 'Archbishop. Will you to the utmost of your power maintain the Laws of God and the true profession of the Gospel? Will you to the utmost of your power maintain in the United Kingdom the Protestant Reformed Religion established by law? Will you maintain and preserve inviolably the settlement of the Church of England, and the doctrine, worship, discipline, and government thereof, as by law established in England? And will you preserve unto the Bishops and Clergy of England, and to the Churches there committed to their charge, all such rights and privileges, as by law do or shall appertain to them or any of them?': The Official Website of the British Monarch, Coronation Oath, https://www.royal.uk/coronation.

84 The Church of Scotland, 'How We Are Organised', http://www.churchofscotland.org.uk/about_us/how_we_are_organised.

85 UK Government, Succession to the Crown Bill: Deputy Prime Minister's Opening Statement (at the second reading in the House of Commons) (22 Jan 2013), https://www.gov.uk/government/news/succession-to-the-crown-bill-deputy-prime-ministers-opening-statement.

86 D Pocklington, 'Succession to the Crown Bill Passed', *Law and Religion UK* (26 Apr 2013), http://www.lawandreligionuk.com/2013/04/26/succession-to-the-crown-bill-passed.

the duties of a Roman Catholic married to a non-Catholic spouse. The reassurance that such an individual would not be subject to censure from canon law in circumstances where it was not possible to raise any children in the Roman Catholic religion was also useful in gaining parliamentary approval for the Bill.[87]

Clearly, the willingness of faith communities to work with Parliament and to dispel misunderstandings about their beliefs and position, as well as the support of the Church of England for the introduction of a more inclusive legal framework, were positive forces in the passage of a liberalising Act, which made the Constitution more accommodating of human rights.

Not only was the former position oppressive with regard to the personal freedoms of individuals who were in the line of succession, but it also sent an unwelcome and discriminatory message to all Roman Catholic citizens. Potential heirs to the throne could in principle marry a partner of any other religious or philosophical outlook, and *only* Roman Catholics members of that denomination were expressly prohibited as somehow being particularly dangerous and undesirable.

Undoubtedly, reforming this anachronistic and insulting provision was a step forward. However, as Parpworth argued, the legislation is by no means as comprehensive as it might have been, leaving as it does the prohibition on the monarch actually *being* a Roman Catholic.[88] Morris also observed that the legislation had failed to introduce true religious equality.[89]

At one level, it is impossible to refute these claims. The British Constitution does not operate in a religiously neutral manner, and this has implications for the individuals who are members or potential members of the Royal Family and their rights and freedoms, as well as the wider society.

However, it is important to pause and observe that in this regard the religious dimension is only one aspect of the Constitution against which this charge could be levelled. Indeed, other provisions of, and indeed omissions from the Act were equally troubling in terms of human rights and equality. For instance, as Parpworth noted, although the legislation moved from male primogeniture to absolute primogeniture in relation to the monarchy, it failed to introduce gender equality in relation to hereditary peerages.[90]

Again, the gender discrimination in connection with peerages not only touches the individuals and the families involved. It also means that *all* female citizens have to face some instances in which the legal system treats women less favourably than men, and there is no practical need or justification beyond the fact that it has always discriminated against female children in this regard. Understandably,

87 Ibid.

88 N. Parpworth, 'The Succession to the Crown Act 2013: Modernising the Monarchy', *The Modern Law Review*, Vol. 76, No. 6 (2013) 1070–93.

89 B. Morris, 'Succession to the Crown Bill: Possible Untoward Effects', *Ecclesiastical Law Journal*, Vol. 15, No. 2 (2013) 186–91.

90 Parpworth, n. 88 above.

many feel that this is unacceptable, and there is at present a campaign to change the rules of succession in relation to peerages and other inherited titles.[91]

Similarly, although the Succession to the Crown Act narrowed the powers of the monarch in relation to controlling the marriages of heirs to the throne, royal consent is still required for the six most immediate in the line of succession,[92] and failure to obtain such consent would result in that person and their descendants being disqualified from succeeding to the throne. Again, subjecting individuals to a disbenefit if they marry without the consent of the head of state is difficult to justify in the twenty-first century. The potential for discrimination here goes well beyond the religious, as the monarch may withhold consent on *any* basis which he or she chooses. Once again, this might be thought far from satisfactory in the modern age, and there is certainly scope for conflict with the Article 12 right to marry and found a family.[93]

Considered altogether, two points emerge from the Succession to the Crown Act. First, it can be seen that the models of establishment in England and Scotland are malleable enough to move with the pace of the collective dialogue on human rights, and reshape their institutions accordingly. Indeed, on this occasion the Church of England was not merely responsive to measures strengthening human rights: it actively facilitated their passage.

Second, it must be acknowledged that the collective dialogue on human rights does not always move at the speed which many in society would desire. Where the pace of travel is slow and pockets of inequality exist, it is not necessarily the religious dimension that is causing the delay. There are aspects of the religious equality implications of the Succession to the Crown Act which arguably are less than ideal, but the same point is equally true of non-religious aspects of that legislation. Ultimately, the rate of change is set by the legislature's agenda and can go only as fast as the democratic consensus will allow. Laying the blame for this at the door of establishment would be very unfair. It is now time to turn to other examples within the wider legal framework and beyond the models of establishment in Great Britain.

7.3.2 The Marriage (Same Sex Couples) Act 2013

The original government consultation on the introduction of same-sex marriage had proceeded on the basis of discussing 'equal civil marriage'[94] and religious groups were to be banned from conducting same-sex marriages. However, the feedback from the majority of respondents made it clear that there was a groundswell of opinion in favour of permitting faith groups that supported same-sex

91 'To the Manor Born: the Female Aristocrats Battling to Inherit the Title', *The Independent* (14 Jun 2013).

92 Succession to the Crown Act 2013.

93 Art. 12 ECHR.

94 'Equal Marriage: The Government's Response' (Dec 2012), Executive Summary, para. 1.7, https://www.gov.uk/government/consultations/equal-marriage-consultation.

marriages to do so. Consequently, the statutory regime which was introduced gave religious groups this freedom, while incorporating robust safeguards to prevent any group or individual with conscientious objections from being forced to participate in such practices.

In our view, this arrangement bolsters human rights in two key respects. First, there is the direct benefit in allowing faith communities and believing couples who support same-sex marriage to express this through their actions. In fact, both the right to marry and found a family[95] and the right to manifest religious belief[96] are protected by the ECHR; permitting same-sex couples from religious communities in favour of homosexual unions to marry, while manifesting a religious belief, is arguably very much in harmony with the spirit of the Convention (even though it goes beyond what the Strasbourg Court currently interprets it as requiring). Equally, the protection afforded to ministers and faith groups who do *not* wish to participate is also crucial in safeguarding freedom of religion and belief.

Nevertheless, there is a second and no less important way in which this legal development supports human rights more widely. The legislation recognises the cultural importance of religion, and the accompanying social reality that introducing a secular-only form of same-sex marriage would have left same-sex couples with a different and, in some eyes, lesser legal institution than that afforded to heterosexual couples.

In purely functional terms, the Marriage (Same Sex Couples) Act[97] made little difference. The legal institution of civil partnership[98] had given rise to almost identical rights and responsibilities as marriage, but civil partnership was *not* marriage; if it had been, the Marriage (Same Sex Couples) Act would not have been so fiercely controversial. Some same-sex couples wanted to be married, and did not wish to enter into an institution which was a marriage substitute or marriage-like partnership for gay people. Crucially, legal provisions have the potential to carry significance far beyond their functional impact, and they are important in terms of the collective values which they enshrine and the messages they convey. This is why, for example, pardoning long-dead individuals like Alan Turing[99] or traumatised soldiers from the First World War[100] is by no means a futile action. It matters profoundly what our law says and symbolises.

Considered logically, had 'equal marriage' meant 'equal *civil* marriage', same-sex couples would still have been granted only a parallel legal institution to that available to opposite-sex couples, and this would have been disadvantageous to

95 Art. 12 ECHR.

96 Art. 9 ECHR.

97 Marriage (Same Sex Couples) Act 2013.

98 As introduced by the Civil Partnership Act 2004.

99 'Royal Pardon for Codebreaker Alan Turing', *BBC News* (24 Dec 2013), http://www.bbc.co.uk/news/technology-25495315.

100 '300 WWI Soldiers Receive Pardons', *BBC News* (16 Aug 2006), http://news.bbc.co.uk/1/hi/uk/4796579.stm.

all same-sex couples wishing to marry. Even where both parties were vehemently Atheist and firm in their desire for a civil ceremony, they would still be undeniably entering into a legal institution which differed from that of their heterosexual counterparts. It is one thing to opt for a civil ceremony; it is quite another to be told *by the state* that nothing else is available to people like you and your fiancé(e). This is as far as the state's position is concerned.

With regard to religious communities, many of them, when performing legally recognised marriage, are selective about who may receive these services, and because their grounds for selection are based on religious doctrine, they are not required to be logical or fair. Nor are they generally subject to judicial review when making decisions based purely upon religious doctrine.[101] An individual might be deemed (formally or informally) ineligible for religious marriage by or within a particular faith group because the individual is not regarded as having satisfied, or even be capable of satisfying, the criteria for membership of the group or matrimony within it.

The reasons might relate to being divorced and having a former spouse still living, having undergone gender reassignment or ritual male circumcision (even as an infant, without having been given an opportunity to object), or simply not having been born into the group in question. Many or all of these reasons might appear arbitrary to outside observers who do not accept the tenets of the faith involved.

Thus, *all* citizens are effectively at risk of being refused a religious marriage in a particular faith tradition on grounds which appear to them unjust or irrational and, in this regard, homosexual citizens are in no different a position from anybody else. However, in granting them the freedom to be married by religious organisations and ministers who deem them appropriate candidates, they are placed in the same position as other all members of society as far as the secular legal regime is concerned. Anyone can seek a religious marriage from groups which perform them, but it is up to the group in question to decide upon the suitability of *any* given couple or individual.

Consequently, the current legal framework on marriage treats citizens equally regardless of their sexuality, something which has implications for gay, lesbian and bisexual people, whatever their view on spiritual matters. It is also an important consideration for many heterosexual citizens, who are either married or considering marriage, as they may prefer to participate in an institution which does not discriminate against others on grounds of their sexuality as opposed to one tainted by intrinsic prejudice.[102]

101 See further the discussion below on the right to a fair trial. Also *R v Chief Rabbi, ex parte Wachman* [1992] 1 WLR 1036 and *Shergill and Others v Khaira and Others* [2014] UKSC 33. While the Supreme Court was critical of the way in which *Wachmann* was interpreted in the intervening cases, and indicated that a religious dimension to a case would not, in and of itself, render it non-justiciable, there are still clear limits to the willingness of the courts to intervene in spiritual affairs. There must be an issue of secular law at stake and the disputed matter must be capable of objective determination.

102 'Kylie Minogue Wedding Waits for Australian Marriage Equality', *BBC News* (6 Oct 2016), http://www.bbc.co.uk/news/world-australia-37548760.

To sum up, the recognition of the importance of the religious dimension of marriage for many people, and the freedom granted to faith groups in favour of same-sex marriages to perform them, have positive implications for the human rights of everyone, regardless of religion or sexuality.

7.3.3 The right to a fair trial[103]

It was until recently considered well-established doctrine that the secular courts would not adjudicate on religious matters.[104] In *R v Chief Rabbi, ex parte Wachman* an application for judicial review against a rabbinical decision was robustly rejected by the court.

This apparent principle of non-justiciability of religious matters was taken up and well-illustrated by the attempt of a former Church of England clergyman to sue *The Daily Mail* for defamation over the assertion that he was 'self-styled' and therefore, by implication, a fake bishop.[105] The court refused to allow the claim to proceed on the grounds that it would be impossible for a secular judge to determine whether an individual was in fact a genuine bishop.

However, in a somewhat surprising decision, the Supreme Court in *Shergill v Khaira*[106] asserted that *Wachman* had been misinterpreted. The ratio of the case was based not upon the religious subject matter, but upon the conclusion that the Chief Rabbi's decision did not involve any element of 'public law' and for that reason was not reviewable. In other words, the Court at the time did not wish to extend the '*Datafin* principle'[107] (that a private body exercising public law functions may be subject to judicial review), which was then still quite new and controversial. In *Shergill*, the Court stressed that religious matters are not, per se, non-justiciable, but it made clear that secular courts would only adjudicate on matters which could be subjected to objective analysis and consideration.

Having said that, it remains the case that secular courts could never determine purely spiritual and subjective matters. The caution with which the courts treat religion in relation to litigation, and the fine balances which are struck, does (and always has) helped to further the right to a fair trial. Even at the high watermark of the non-justiciability doctrine, the courts did not allow it to shield religious organisations from claims relating to worldly rather than spiritual matters, such as debt[108] or vicarious liability for assaults by ministers.[109] Equally, however, now that the Supreme Court has relaxed its stance on considering cases with a religious dimension, it remains beyond doubt that only matters capable of objective

103 As is recognised by Art. 6 ECHR.

104 *R v Chief Rabbi, ex parte Wachman*, n. 101 above.

105 *Blake v Associated Newspapers Ltd* [2003] All ER (D) 571 (Jul).

106 *Shergill v Khaira*, n. 101 above.

107 *R (Datafin plc) v Panel on Take-overs and Mergers* [1987] QB 815.

108 *Percy v Church of Scotland Board of National Mission* [2005] UKHL 73. Although obiter, the House of Lords was in no doubt that a Church of Scotland minister could claim in debt for monies due to be paid by the Church, and also allowed a claim for sex discrimination on the facts.

109 *JGE v English Province of Our Lady of Charity and Another* [2011] All ER (D) 50 (Nov).

analysis will be tried in state courts. The right to a fair trial is, therefore, protected by both the limit and extent of the principle that secular courts will not adjudicate on spiritual matters.

7.3.4 Parental responsibility and child autonomy

As we have already seen, the law recognises the importance of faith, and grants parents exceptional latitude in terms of making choices for their children, from permitting them to consent to irreversible surgical intervention which is not medically required in the case of male circumcision, to allowing them to withdraw their child from some aspects of the school curriculum. However, the weight that is placed upon faith matters also means that courts are extremely cautious in proceeding where there is any disagreement between adults with parental responsibility, or between parents and children.

Therefore, while parents have greater scope in their decision-making where there is consensus in faith-based matters, where there is disagreement their freedom, and to a considerable extent the freedom of minors also, is considerably restricted. Ritual male circumcision is a classic example of this. Parental consent is effective only in those situations in which there is consensus among the parties with parental responsibility or a court order is in place (and courts have been consistently unwilling to grant this on grounds of best interests where close family members are opposed).[110]

Equally, in the case of *Re C*[111] a minor and her father were neither permitted to give consent for her baptism into the Anglican faith until certain conditions had been met, nor to her confirmation until she had attained a higher age, in the face of opposition from her mother and both sets of grandparents. In contrast to the male circumcision cases, there was no element of physical risk involved in the ritual; the court's concern related to the emotional, social and cultural consequences of the decision, and how this would affect the child's developing sense of identity and place within her family and the various communities of which she was a part.

Once again, in treating religious matters as special or different from other issues, the courts are not privileging religious citizens above non-religious ones. They are effectively recognising that all human beings have a religious identity[112] and that it is not for the state to interfere with this without good reason. Equally, where there is disagreement involving vulnerable minors, it is not appropriate for one adult party to impose his or her will unless there are very strong, objective grounds relating to the child's welfare which justify this.

110 See, e.g., *Re J (Specific Issue Orders: Child's Religious Upbringing and Circumcision)* [2000] 1 FLR 571 (CA) 307.

111 *Re: C (A Child)* [2012] EW Misc (CC).

112 As discussed in Chs 2, 3 and 4, for some individuals this may be an identity which rejects non-rational, faith-based belief such as Humanism, or any concept of Divinity such as Atheism. It may also be complex, multifaceted and subject to change.

There is clearly a direct benefit to all citizens, in that this approach safeguards personal autonomy without favouring one religion or ideology above another. Humanist, secular or religiously neutral parents receive just as firm protection as religious parents in making spiritual choices for their children.

There is also arguably an indirect benefit for human rights, which is in the process of emerging and which we touched upon in Chapter 3. Religious matters are recognised as special and necessitate special protection, but by analogy other matters of deep conscience (not relating to spirituality or belief in or rejection of the divine) are being approached with equal caution.

In *F and F*[113] the issue of child vaccination was considered in a context where veganism and the rejection of animal products was one basis for refusal. The children were of an age to have opinions on the matter and to express them, although it was found on the facts that they lacked *Gillick* competence[114] and the necessary information to make a balanced judgement. The decision was made on the basis of the clinical best interests of the children, but their ideological concerns were given careful consideration.

In our view, the body of case law and judicial skills built up in the religious upbringing cases are of great value in addressing other issues of conscience which arise in relation to minors. Moreover, there is a clear recognition, highlighted and affirmed by the religious upbringing cases, that children have a developing identity with their family and community, as well as a growing individual, moral and ethical outlook (which may or may not involve a religious faith). These should be respected and nurtured, but it must also be understood that these facets are inchoate in a minor, and a child should be protected from manipulation or damaging influences.

Thus, the approach taken in the religious upbringing cases provides helpful foundations for negotiating the minefield of other contentious matters of conscience involving minors, and bolsters human rights beyond the religious or quasi-religious field. It is perfectly possible to imagine, for instance, parents in agreement about their attitude towards religious belief, but in bitter disagreement over veganism, gender roles or other matters affecting their children. As our collective awareness of human rights and child rights grows, there may well be more such cases and the path forged by religious upbringing issues may be very valuable in other contexts.

7.3.5 The status of the United Nations Convention on the Rights of the Child (UNCRC) in Scotland

Another instance of the religious character of the legal framework being beneficial for human rights relates to the rights of minors in particular. As in England and Wales, the UNCRC[115] is not fully incorporated into Scots law, having been

113 *Between F and F* [2013] EWHC 2683 (Fam)

114 *Gillick v West Norfolk & Wisbech Area Health Authority* [1986] AC 112.

115 United Nations Convention on the Rights of the Child (20 Nov 1989).

criticised by the Children and Young People's Commissioner of Scotland.[116] Nevertheless, the devolved Scottish Government has sought to take strategic action to implement the provisions of this Treaty in Scotland,[117] and the Children and Young People (Scotland) Act 2014 has imposed duties on ministers and public bodies in respect of children's rights. Ministers have a duty to further the UNCRC and to promote public awareness and understanding of it;[118] there is also a duty imposed on public bodies to report on their progress in furthering the rights contained in the UNCRC. Voluntary organisations, such as Together Scotland (formerly known as the Scottish Alliance for Children's Rights), have expressed disappointment that the duty was merely to give information on progress rather than to actually implement the provisions.[119] Nevertheless, despite this weakness, it has considerable importance in relation to human rights and religion. Article 14 of the UNCRC gives children and young people the right to choose their own religion and beliefs;[120] Article 30 provides children and young people from minority groups with the right to enjoy their own culture, practise their own religion and use their own language.

Public organisations, and particularly the Children and Young People's Commissioner in Scotland, have taken steps to actively promote the rights contained in the UNCRC in an effort to empower young people – for example, by giving voice to young Muslims about their experiences of practising their faith in contemporary Scotland, and seeking their views on what could be done to break down barriers between communities.[121]

The way in which the rights provided by the UNCRC are being addressed by the devolved Government in Scotland demonstrates that where there is a political will, even rights which are not fully enshrined in domestic law can be something more than simply aspirational. It also illustrates how, as discussed above, the rights contained in the ECHR should not be seen as limiting the conception of human rights within the juridical framework of Great Britain. They are a scaffolding over which a greater structure has room to grow.

7.3.6 Enabling the practical contribution of religious belief groups

The final, the broadest and perhaps most significant way in which the current legal structure on faith bolsters human rights relates quite simply to the

116 Children and Young People's Commissioner Scotland, '5 Concerns about Children's Rights in Scotland' (8 Apr 2015), http://www.cypcs.org.uk/news/in-the-news/5-concerns-for-childrens-rights-in-scotland.

117 UNCRC and the Scottish Government, 'Do the Right Thing: Progress Report 2012', http://www.gov.scot/Resource/0039/00392997.pdf.

118 Children and Young People (Scotland) Act 2014.

119 Together (Scottish Alliance for Children's Rights), 'State of Children's Rights in Scotland' (Nov 2014), 3, http://www.togetherscotland.org.uk/pdfs/SOCRRTogetherReport2014.pdf.

120 The Scottish Government, 'The UN Convention on the Rights of the Child: A Guide for Children and Young People', Art. 14, http://www.gov.scot/Resource/0048/00486690.pdf.

121 Children and Young People's Commissioner Scotland, n. 116 above: 'People have said to me, when you leave school are you going to join ISIS?' Young Muslims talk about their right to practice religion' (9 Dec 2015).

direct contribution which faith groups themselves make. In having charity law, education law and other aspects of the legal system geared towards enabling faith groups to be socially engaged, countless religious and quasi-religious organisations are able to assist in providing education for children and adults, meals for the hungry, shelter for the homeless, advocacy services for the vulnerable, practical assistance for those who have been the victims of human trafficking, and many other services which further human rights in the widest sense. Although arguably more social than legal, faith groups could not make these practical contributions, or at least could not do so as effectively, if the legal framework did not provide a supportive environment for them.

7.4 How do the perspectives and teaching of different religious belief groups influence perceptions of human rights?

Having stated that faith groups contribute in a practical way to the promotion of human rights, we are still left with the question of how their teaching might influence their members' views on the subject. As we acknowledged at the beginning of this chapter, there are those who see clashes between faith communities and the legal system in cases like *Eweida* as indisputable evidence of an inherent conflict between religion and human rights. We wonder if this perception is justified and we shall explore, in turn, each faith tradition being examined before moving on to assess the bigger picture in this regard. Are these criticisms justified?

7.4.1 Christianity

Much of the teaching and heritage on human rights is shared by different Christian Churches. For this reason, we will look at the common Christian perspectives on this issue, following the approach adopted in the chapters on parliamentary supremacy and separation of powers.

As some of the quotes with which we opened this chapter would suggest, the relationship between Christianity and human rights has, in some ways, been an ambiguous one down the centuries. Villa Vicencio argues:

> The affirmation of human rights emerged painfully and belatedly in the Christian church. The 'deep biblical roots of human rights ideals' have, however, been periodically acknowledged and retrieved throughout the history of the church in an attempt to correct wrongs, repudiate theological support for abuses and to pursue a more humane society.[122]

In other words, at times there has been an undeniable dissonance between the principles of human equality and dignity to be found in the Christian Scriptures and the way in which 'Christian' societies have operated. As we have seen, the

122 C. Villa Vicencio, 'Christianity and Human Rights', *Journal of Law and Religion*, Vol. 14, No. 2 (1999–2000) 579–600, 579.

interplay between religious and secular power has been complex and fractious in the history of the British Isles; religious authorities have, on occasions, been the ones controlled and manipulated by secular power, and the behaviour of some of the clergy prepared to collude with Henry VIII and other oppressive Tudor regimes is not especially edifying. Needless to say, it is easy to condemn from the safety and comfort of the twenty-first century, secure in the knowledge that we are not at risk of being either burnt at the stake or dragged through the streets behind a horse, partially asphyxiated, dismembered and eviscerated. Unfortunately, we do not all have the heroism of Sir Thomas More.[123]

Yet, it would be wrong to allow the considerable negative elements of the European historical experience to completely obscure the positive contribution that Christian doctrine has made in relation to the development of rights within the juridical system. At the very heart of Christian teaching is the Scriptural passage, already alluded to, in which all human beings are said to be made in the image of God.[124] This has not prevented some traditions within Christianity having legitimated, and in some cases continuing to legitimate, the different categorisation of some human beings depending on their gender, race or social status, but there is an overarching understanding of *all* people being created in the image of the Divine. All people have the right to life, compassion and assistance when required.

For instance, although the direct causal link between the rise of Christianity in the Roman Empire and the decline of gladiatorial combat and other brutalities of the amphitheatre is disputed by modern historians,[125] there is still a consensus that Christian moralists condemned such practices.[126] Christianity was part of the intellectual ferment which came to reject the taking of human life as part of the entertainment industry. While public executions remained a popular spectacle until the nineteenth century,[127] the underlying *purpose* of the event was punishment rather than sport. The societal adoption of Christianity did not lead to the recognition of an inviolable right to life, but a Christian understanding of the sanctity of life did at least mean that individuals could be deprived of their lives only for criminal transgressions by a due process of law.

This is further evidenced by the rejection of infanticide with the advent of Christianity.[128] A human life was a human life, and a baby girl from a peasant family was as much possessed of an immortal soul as a ruling king. This concept is reinforced by the universal recognition of the nature of the baptism as the

123 Although in the event he was beheaded, at the time of making his fateful decision, More could have had no way of knowing that he would not face the full force of the law.

124 Genesis 1:27 (see Ch. 5, n. 126).

125 E. Rubin, *The Soul and Society: The New Morality and the Modern State* (Oxford University Press: Oxford) 2015, 143.

126 D. Bomgardner, *Roman Amphitheatre* (Routledge: Abingdon) 2000, 207.

127 J. Hostettler, *A History of Criminal Justice in England and Wales* (Waterside Press: Sheffield) 2009, 185.

128 N. Berend, *Christianization and the Rise of Christian Monarchy: Scandinavia, Central Europe and Rus' c.900–1200* (Cambridge University Press: Cambridge) 2007, 63.

Christian rite of initiation. It was, and is, available and required regardless of age, status or gender.

Despite the fact that it cannot be said that the Christianisation of European and other societies led instantly towards a fully fledged recognition of the right to life, it was undoubtedly one force that drove some of the key steps in the journey towards our contemporary interpretation of Article 2.[129]

Equally, concepts about rights to property can be found within Christian-Judeo teaching (see the discussion below in the context of Judaism), and the idealisation of poverty was not accepted as a mandate within mainstream Christian societies for depriving individuals of their rightful ownership. Again, ideas about the sanctity of personal property can be found in the Magna Carta.[130]

Christianity conceives of human beings as individuals, with an immortal soul, made in the image of the Divine and in possession of certain God-given rights. This, combined with the teachings of Christ to care for the poor, the weak and the vulnerable, and to see the presence of God in the face of those in need,[131] have inspired members of this faith to advocate and assist other fellow beings in all circumstances down the ages. Anti-slavery campaigners such as William Wilberforce,[132] prisoner reformers like Elizabeth Fry,[133] and civil rights activists like Martin Luther King[134] were all driven by their Christian principles.

Consequently, Christianity as a worldview is likely to dispose its adherents to the idea of human rights, broadly understood. It is undeniable that the very concept of human rights as recognised by our legal system has grown up in a cultural paradigm heavily moulded by Christian thoughts and ideas, and the notion that the very fact of a person's humanity gives him or her inalienable rights and dignity is a profoundly Christian view. More problematic, however, is the extent of the canon of these rights. It is here where some groups and individuals who identity as Christian have come into conflict with modern law in relation to human rights and equality. How do human rights relate to sexual conduct, and how can conflicts of rights be resolved where the exercise of one person's liberties appears to clash with another's right to freedom of conscience?[135]

There is also the vexed question of what constitutes human status and, therefore, the gateway to human rights. Again, some Christian groups take a different

129 Art. 2 ECHR.

130 British Library, 'English Translation of the Magna Carta', n. 25 above.

131 NRSV, Matthew 25:37–40 : '[37] Then the righteous will answer him, "Lord, when was it that we saw you hungry and gave you food, or thirsty and gave you something to drink? [38] And when was it that we saw you a stranger and welcomed you, or naked and gave you clothing? [39] And when was it that we saw you sick or in prison and visited you?" [40] And the king will answer them, "Truly I tell you, just as you did it to one of the least of these who are members of my family,* you did it to me".'

132 S. Tomkins, *William Wilberforce: A Biography* (Lion: Oxford) 2007.

133 J. Hatton, *Betsy: The Dramatic Biography of Prison Reformer Elizabeth Fry* (Monarch: Oxford) 2005.

134 R. Bruns, *Martin Luther King Jr.: A Biography* (Greenwood: London/Connecticut) 2006.

135 See, e.g., the litigation in cases such as *Bull and Another v Hall and Another* [2013] UKSC 73.

approach from the law of a secular state. If an individual has human status from the moment of conception, for example, the balance of rights between a foetus and the mother is likely to be weighed differently from the position where human status is acknowledged after birth.[136]

7.4.2 Judaism

Again, in Judaism a key precept is the notion that all human beings are made in the image of God – in Hebrew אֱלֹהִים צֶלֶם (*B'tzelem Elohim*). Some of the outworkings of this concept are expressed poetically in a popular song in the Reform tradition by Dan Nichols:

> When I reach out to you and you to me
> We become B'tzelem Elohim
> When we share our hopes and our dreams
> Each one of us B'tzelem Elohim.[137]

It encapsulates the Jewish understanding (retained, as discussed above, by the Christian faith) that each person is a unique individual, known to God before time and the universe began, imbued with a touch of God's creative capacity, and equipped with his or her own special and particular gifts.[138] Although this song is taken from the Reform tradition, there is nothing in it that would be incompatible with the views of mainstream Orthodox Jews. To state that all human beings are made in the image of God is not to assert that all human beings have the same characteristics or duties, as it allows for distinctions to be made between men and women, Jews and Gentiles, and so on. Nevertheless, it once again affirms the preciousness of each human person, and their unique place within God's creation.

The importance of compassion and helping others are indeed key spiritual values within Orthodox Judaism, because individuals made in the image of God have a need and a right to be cared for. Almost all commandments can be set aside in the interests of preserving human life and bringing help to those in need. For example, religious Jews who volunteered to go to Haiti following the devastating earthquake were 'proud' to break the Sabbath in order to assist fellow human beings in dire distress.[139] Similarly, many synagogues and other Jewish organisations involve themselves in community work to serve all human beings in need.

Nevertheless, in addition to these general ideas about the nature of human beings and the overriding requirement for compassion, Judaism has a sophisticated system

136 See, e.g., the Society for the Protection of Unborn Children, https://www.spuc.org.uk.

137 B'tzelem Elohim © 1999 words and music Dan Nichols, E18hteen and Rabbi Mike Moskowitz. For a live version of the author singing this song (accompanied by a mixed gender audience) see https://www.youtube.com/watch?v=vky2vjnvF2Q.

138 See, e.g., Psalm 139 and the commentary by Rashi on the same: The Complete Jewish Bible (with Rashi Commentary), Tehillim, Psalms, Chapter 139, http://www.chabad.org/library/bible_cdo/aid/16360/jewish/Chapter-139.htm#showrashi=true.

139 A. Levy, 'ZAKA Mission to Haiti "Proudly Desecrating Shabbat"', *Ynet news.com* (17 Jan 2010), http://www.ynetnews.com/articles/0,7340,L-3835327,00.html.

of law codes which recognise tangible and specific rights, and an understanding of rights in relation to property has an extremely long heritage. For example, Jewish Scriptures contain the story of Naboth's vineyard.[140] A king offers to buy a plot of ground from a man who does not wish to sell; initially he responds to this refusal with a bout of depression. However, his wife Jezebel shakes him out of this, and contrives a way to take the property by force, having Naboth falsely accused of blasphemy and stoned to death. It is striking in the story that even the monarch had no power to force an individual to part with his property against his will, and that even the villainous Jezebel chooses to abuse the judicial process, rather than simply sending soldiers to seize the property.

Principles relating to identifiable rights are deeply embedded within Judaism, and have been applied by Jewish courts from antiquity[141] to the present day. Many of these principles, such as individual rights to property, are entirely in harmony with ideas embedded in secular human rights doctrine, whereas others are not. For instance, women are subject to certain disadvantages in relation to matrimonial law[142] and in terms of their capacity to act as witnesses in some Jewish courts.[143]

In relation to the legal values which are not at first compatible with secular notions of human rights, essentially the same principle discussed in Christianity applies here. The issue is not so much one of disagreeing with the notion of rights per se as dissension as to what should be designated and understood as a right.

Furthermore, while we do not deny that there is a clash in many cases, it should also be noticed that Judaism (like other religions) is a dynamic and organic force. There are moves to reconsider whether some laws which appear to infringe modern theories of gender equality are, in fact, eternal laws at all, and interestingly some groups argue that there is a need for reconsideration and reinterpretation of fundamental Jewish principles.[144]

At the same time, others seek to mitigate the practical impact of what they see as unchangeable law. The most obvious example of this relates to 'chained wives' and the refusal of some bitter husbands to grant their spouse a religious divorce. This is widely acknowledged to be a serious problem, and across Orthodox Judaism a number of solutions are being proposed.[145]

Thus, again, the presentation of the religion as antipathetic towards human rights is distorted.

140 The story can be found in 1 Kings 21.

141 D. Daube, 'Jewish Law in the Hellenistic World', in B. Jackson (ed.), *Jewish Law in Legal History and the Modern World* (Brill: Leiden) 1980, 45.

142 M. Broyde, *Marriage, Divorce and the Abandoned Wife in Jewish Law: A Conceptual Understanding of Agunah Problems in America* (Ktav: New Jersey) 2001.

143 Although within Orthodox contexts women may generally not act as witnesses, this is not the case in Reform Judaism – see the statement by the Rabbinical Assembly (an association of Conservative and Masorti Rabbis in the United States): A. Mackler, 'Edut Nashim K'Edut Anashim: The Testimony of Women is as the Testimony of Men' (Nov 2004), https://www.rabbinicalassembly.org/sites/default/files/public/halakhah/teshuvot/20052010/mackler_women_witnesses.pdf.

144 L. Levitt, *Jews and Feminism: The Ambivalent Search for Home* (Routledge: New York and London) 1997.

145 In the UK, secular law may be used to apply pressure to recalcitrant husbands: see the Divorce (Religious Marriages) Act 2002.

7.4.3 Islam

It is a core tenet of Islam that the religion is open to all humankind. Therefore, all human beings – regardless of gender, ethnicity, social and educational background – have the same opportunity to serve and accept Allah. Moreover, all human beings enjoy the right to life, their property and their honour, and should not be deprived of any of these things except by due legal process.[146] It is good and appropriate to assist non-Muslims who are in need in a practical way, and be permitted to pray for a known non-Muslim in distress.[147]

Practical manifestations of this commitment to fellow human beings can be seen in charitable organisations such as Muslim Aid, which has an express commitment to 'serv[e] humanity' and work with 'all in need, regardless of race, religion, gender, nationality or political opinion'.[148]

Again, many of the ideas and values which are core aspects of human rights as understood in Great Britain can be identified within Islamic law and thought, although it cannot be denied that 'Western' human rights have effectively clashed with some interpretations of Islam on the world stage. A number of Islamic states regarded the UN Universal Declaration of Human Rights[149] as problematic, and Saudi Arabia[150] declined to sign it. As Arzt[151] points out, however, it should be recognised that Saudi Arabia was at least honest in expressing its dissent, while many states (Muslim and non-Muslim alike) willingly signed the Declaration, but have since flagrantly ignored its provisions in the intervening decades.

The concern that the Declaration is unsuitable in an Islamic context has remained, and in 1990 a group of states issued the Cairo Declaration on Human Rights in Islam.[152] The document is rooted in Sharia law, and rejects freedom in relation to religious conversion, conscience, gender equality and sexuality. It also effectively subjugates the rights of children to the religious status of their parents. Consequently, fathers are accorded greater rights than mothers in relation to the custody and control of children, regardless of whether this is in the objective best interests of children.

It should be noted, of course, that not all Muslim states, groups or individuals would endorse the Cairo Declaration or the thinking behind it. For example, An-an'im[153] cogently argues that in 'modern circumstances of permanent

146 S.H. Al Aayed (translation A. Alosh), *The Rights of Non-Muslims in the Islamic World* (Dar Eshbelia: Riyadh) 2002, 40.

147 C.T. Jaleel, *On Entering Deen Completely* (Google Books, July 2015) 267.

148 Muslim Aid, 'What We Do', https://www.muslimaid.org/what-we-do.

149 United Nations Universal Declaration of Human Rights 1948, http://www.un.org/en/universal-declaration human-rights.

150 D. Arzt, 'The Treatment of Religious Dissidents under Classical and Contemporary Religious Law', in J. Witte and J. Van de Vyver (eds), *Religious Human Rights in a Global Perspective: Religious Perspective* (Martinus Nijhoff: Leiden) 2000, 387, 425.

151 Ibid.

152 Cairo Declaration on Human Rights in Islam (5 Aug 1990).

153 A. An-an'im, 'Islamic Foundations of Religious Human Rights', in Witte and Van de Vyver (eds), n. 150 above, 341.

religious and other pluralities, national and international political communities require equal respect for the religious human rights of all members of the community as the basis of the demand of Muslims themselves to those rights', and many Muslims would no doubt agree with this assessment. In having chosen or inherited life in a pluralistic context, many of its realities are both pragmatically advantageous and ideologically desirable. No human being forms their religious beliefs in a cultural or social vacuum.

The fact that there are aspects of mainstream human rights – such as freedom of speech and the resulting right to offend – which a very significant number of Muslims find problematic, even when living in non-Muslim majority societies like Great Britain, should not be underestimated.[154] However, it should also be emphasised that there are many points where Islam, like Judaism and Christianity, is absolutely in conformity with core principles of human rights as they are understood within our juridical system. It should also be noted that where there is a dissonance, individuals and communities frequently find ways of reconciling the clash, which make sense within their context, or else live together while holding the opposing perspectives. As we saw in the context of the rule of law, many Muslims living in contemporary Britain seek from *within* their faith answers to tensions between their multiple identities. The question here is not how 'Islam' views human rights, but how individuals embracing Islam may be influenced by their faith to regard that concept, and this will depend hugely on how those individuals interpret and understand their religion. There are many who choose to focus on the beliefs outlined at the start of this section, and who would agree with An-an'im's[155] assessment that in this life, at least, the faith can be viewed only through the filter of cultural and communal context and experience.

Clearly many individuals and groups draw from their Islamic faith inspiration for supporting the rights of all people to compassion, dignity and respect.[156] It is significant that even the group of Muslim regimes which found the United Nations Universal Declaration on Human Rights problematic wanted an Islamic version in the Cairo Declaration, and they did not wish to reject human rights. Once again, there is undoubted support for the notion of human rights, but debate as to which rights this understanding should encompass.

7.4.4 Hinduism

It is undeniable that Hinduism approaches questions of humanity and human nature in a very different manner from that of the 'Religions of the Book' and, as we have explored in previous chapters, it operates within a fundamentally

154 A. Bland, 'Freedom of Speech: Is It My Right to Offend You?', *The Independent*, (2Feb 2014), http://www.independent.co.uk/news/uk/politics/freedom-of-speech-is-it-my-right-to-offend-you-9101650.html.

155 An-an'im, n. 153 above.

156 See, e.g., the Holy Quran, Verse 2:195: 'Surely Allah loves those who do good to others'.

different paradigm. Naïve attempts to map Western concepts directly onto Hindu thought tend to breed misunderstandings rather than clarity.

As Sharma argues, Hinduism does not operate in terms of particularistic ethics or specific moral edicts in the same way as Christianity, Judaism or Islam. Instead, its approach to moral dilemmas is frequently through narrative: what stories are there about people faced with similar dilemmas?[157] Consequently, the kind of guidance which is available on appropriate treatment of human beings is qualitatively different from that of the Torah, the Bible and the Quran. Nevertheless, it should be noted that even among those three religions, there are crucial differences both within and between the faiths in terms of how they use and interpret holy texts.

It is also the case that for the majority of its adherents, Hinduism is a religion of orthopraxy rather than orthodoxy. Trying to approach the question on the basis of 'we believe X about human beings, so we must do Y' is to try to impose an incongruous Western intellectual framework in a Hindu context.

There are, in fact, numerous strands of tradition in relation to the way in which Hindus should treat and perceive their fellow human beings. Some of them are at odds with the dominant themes of equality and universality within the modern human rights movement – for example, in relation to gender roles and residual ideas about social placement or caste – which have by no means wholly died away.[158] Yet, equally, Gandhi criticised the injustice of discrimination in the caste system from a perspective fully immersed in and committed to the Hindu faith, comparing it with an infection, like tuberculosis, in the body of faith.[159] Many others are in agreement, and have echoed his emphasis on fairness, love, compassion and peace towards all people.

Also, in a religion more rooted in practice than doctrine, it is important to note the number of Hindu charities working towards positive social change, and thereby the advancement of all three generations of human rights.[160] Sewa, for example, is an international charity based in the United States, which makes the following statement about its work and motivation: 'In the ancient Indian language of Sanskrit, Sewa means Service – a unique concept of Service – Selfless Efforts for Welfare of All'. Their stated motto is 'Nar Sewa Narayan Sewa' – 'Serving Humanity is Serving God'.[161]

Although inspired by the duty to act, rather more than an abstract idea about the nature of humanity, this nevertheless demonstrates a firm commitment to human rights.

157 A. Sharma, *Hindu Narratives on Human Rights* (Greenwood: Santa Barbara) 2010, ix.

158 'What Future for India's Caste System?', *BBC News* (22 Jun 2013), http://www.bbc.co.uk/news/business-22724831.

159 M.K. Gandhi, *Hindu Dharma* (Orient Paperbacks: New Delhi) 2005, 74.

160 M. Balaji, 'Let's Not Forget These Hindu Voices in the World of Social Uplift', *Huffington Post* (20 Jun 2014), http://www.huffingtonpost.com/murali-balaji/lets-not-forget-these-hin_b_5514768.html.

161 Sewa International USA, 'About Us', http://www.sewausa.org.

7.4.5 Sikhism

Sikhism has a strong commitment to the equality of all human beings and places much stress on the duties of its followers to work for the common good:

> Sikhism lays emphasis on man's social obligations. Man is part of society and has to work for its uplift. That is why social reform is a strong point in the Guru's teaching. The Gurus rejected the caste system, untouchability, taboos against women, good and bad omens and the worshipping of graves, idols and mausoleums. Sikhism believes in the equality of man, which is practically demonstrated through the institution of *Langar* (the Temple of Bread) where all dine together in a single line or *Pangat*. Inter-caste marriages and mixing of persons of diverse faiths and nationalities is the norm.[162]

This essential position does not really require much commentary or gloss as far as the treatment of human beings is concerned. As with other faiths, at times its abstract ideals have been (sometimes very badly) let down by human frailty and ambition in the course of history, but the fundamental compatibility between Sikhism and human rights is not in doubt. It is also the case that Sikhism teaches that individual souls have been through many incarnations before achieving human status and capacity:

> For many births you have become a worm or moth, an elephant, a fish or a deer. In several births you may have become a bird or a snake or may have been yoked as a horse or an ox. Meet the Lord of the universe. Now is the time for you to meet him; after a long time you have been given human form.[163]

Human life is treated as being de facto better than other forms of existence, because of the spiritual and moral capacity with which human beings are seen to be uniquely invested. Therefore, as all humans have these distinctive characteristics, their inherent dignity and potential should be recognised. Furthermore, there are a number of Sikh charities which put this belief into practice, and seek to provide assistance for those in need both in the United Kingdom and on an international basis.[164]

7.4.6 Buddhism

As with Hinduism, we are faced with a challenge before we even begin our consideration of human nature and human rights from a Buddhist perspective.

162 G.S. Mansukhani, *Introduction to Sikhism* (Hemkunt Press: New Delhi) 14th edn, 2007, 21.
163 Adi Granth, 176.
164 See, e.g., Khalsa Aid, 'Recognise the Whole Human Race as One', http://www.khalsaaid.org; the City Sikhs Volunteering Initiative, http://www.citysikhs.org.uk.

To attempt this is almost inevitably to try to transfer concepts from one cultural and intellectual tradition into another. Buddhism has no language of rights, it just does not.[165] As Epstein describes it:[166]

> Unlike the Judeo-Christian tradition, Buddhism affirms the unity of all living beings, all equally possess the Buddha-nature, and all have the potential to become Buddhas, that is, to become fully and perfectly enlightened. Among the sentient, there are no second-class citizens.[167] According to Buddhist teaching, human beings do not have a privileged, special place above and beyond that of the rest of life.

Yet, Keown argues that not having a word for a concept, it is possible for a society to have a concept without the language to describe it.

Ihara provides a cogent counter-argument, however.[168] He begins by drawing an analogy with the world of ballet, observing that in most productions the male lead will be required to pick up or catch the prima ballerina. However, should he fluff this in some way and miss the catch, or stumble and drop her, it is unlikely that the choreographer or the prima ballerina would employ the language of rights in their reaction. Ihara's point is that all kinds of angry and graphic things which might be said by the ballerina would certainly not include 'You have infringed my *right* to be caught'. Ballet is a collaborative endeavour; people have roles and with these come responsibilities.

Ihara challenges Keown's assertion that a responsibility vested in one individual *necessarily* generates a corresponding right in a third party. For Ihara, rights are not implicit within classical Buddhism, and the better question is whether they are in fact compatible with it, in the sense that they could be introduced without transforming the nature of Buddhism. His conclusion is in the negative.[169] The Buddhist understanding of 'dharma' in the sense of a universal dance in which all sentient beings have defined roles and responsibilities would be undermined if the parties were not engaged in the common enterprise of dancing, but were individuals in fact tied together by reciprocal duties and rights. In Ihara's view, the dynamic would have fundamentally changed.

However, he does not conclude from this that the introduction of rights into classical Buddhism is automatically a misguided way to proceed. This commentator

165 D. Keown, 'Are There Rights in Buddhism?', *Journal of Buddhist Ethics*, Vol. 2 (1995) 3–27.

166 R. Epstein, 'A Buddhist Perspective of Animal Rights', based on a presentation given at San Francisco State University Conference 'Animal Rights and Our Relationship to the Biosphere' (29 Jan 1990).

167 Many would argue that this is a stereotyped distortion of the Judeo-Christian tradition, and that it does recognise a unity of animal life (including human animals) as creatures from the same loving Creator. In this view, in so far as human beings are different, they have greater responsibility, rather than greater privilege, being charged with a duty to take care of other life on Earth: see A. Linzey, *Animal Theology* (University of Illinois Press: Illinois) 1995.

168 C. Ihara, 'Why There Are No Rights in Buddhism – A Reply to Damien Keown', in D. Keown, C. Prebish and W. Husted (eds), *Buddhism and Human Rights* (Curzon Press: Padstow) 1998, 43.

169 Ibid., 47–8.

argues that it sets up a rebuttable presumption against making such a change, but maintains that Buddhism has 'never been so wedded to Scripture, tradition, doctrine or language that it could not adopt news of reacting to those in need of help'.[170] If introducing this concept would enable practitioners of Buddhism to progress the elimination of suffering or the advancement of social justice, for example, by enabling them to engage in rights-based dialogue, then it would be appropriate to facilitate such a transformation.

Ihara's argument is attractive, and of significance whether or not it is accepted. It demonstrates that a religious system which does not encompass a concept of human rights in the way in which Western religions might may still engage positively within a rights-based paradigm, as it may well be the case that the goals being pursued by individuals within that faith tradition, and the prescribed manner of pursuing them, will lead to support for the defence of the human rights and freedoms of others. Thus, religions which are not orientated towards rights may nevertheless contribute positively to them. For example, unjustly imprisoning an individual would lead to suffering; Buddhism would, therefore, have an ethical objection to such a phenomenon. To return to Ihara's image, the lead man will have an equal interest in catching the ballerina as she leaps, even if his motivation and perhaps even method of getting on stage differ from that of the other dancers.

This theory has been seen to have had a practical outworking in many Buddhist contexts. For example, in historic times, Buddhist priests and theological arguments were significant in condemning the practice of infanticide.[171] Although this was not couched in terms of a right to life vested in the female baby, the trajectory of the ethical argument moved in the same direction.

7.4.7 Zoroastrianism

Following on from the previous discussion, it again must be acknowledged that this faith in its ancient form did not have a highly developed doctrine of human rights, or indeed highly developed *doctrines* of any sort. However, its core philosophy of 'Good thoughts, good words, good deeds'[172] would lead to an approach to life which would support the nurturing of human rights. Nor is it a surprise that a modern group of Zoroastrians have explicitly affirmed their faith-based commitment to human rights:

> Zoroastrianism is the first religion that has taken a doctrinal and political stand on the subject of human rights and has condemned the limitation or curtailment of those rights under any pretext.
>
> Although it is a modern legal coinage not used in religious literatures of the past, the concept of human rights as a system of values and ideas is ingrained in Zoroastrianism. In Zoroastrianism the idea of human rights

170 Ibid., 50.

171 F. Drixler, *Mabiki: Infanticide and Population Growth in Eastern Japan 1660–1950* (University of California Press: Berkley) 2013, 55.

172 Zoroastrian Online, http://zoroastrianonline.com.

> stems from the principle that man is created to be a co-worker with God and as such ought to try to emulate the master of the craft. Being only a good creator, God has created the Universe and man as essentially good.[173]

While the statement that Zoroastrianism is or was the first religion to do this is by no means uncontroversial, and the authority of one group to speak for the global Zoroastrian community is also open to challenge – this willingness to make the leap between the doctrines of the faith and the modern legal concept of human rights is, in itself, highly significant. The outlook which the faith encourages its followers to adopt is one that is intrinsically supportive of the defence of common rights vested in all humankind.

7.4.8 Paganism

Although, as we have discussed in earlier chapters, Paganism is an umbrella term for a number of spiritual pathways and creedal generalisations cannot be made, the essential features of human rights are very much in line with the shared outlook held by many within the Pagan community. For instance, the Pagan Federation International includes the following in its common shared essentials: 'A positive morality, in which the individual is responsible for the discovery and development of their true nature in harmony with the outer world and community. This is often expressed as "Do what you will, as long as it harms none"'.[174]

This affirms not just the freedom and dignity of individual human beings, but also their wider responsibilities. Liberty should be enjoyed and exercised, but not in manner which has a negative impact upon others. There is also a robust rejection of isolationism in this statement. Further evidence of active support for human rights is provided by the way in which Pagan organisations like Pagan Federation International, as well as Pagan individuals, use human rights law to protect or advance their needs and concerns. For example, three worshippers of Norse gods, who were in a sexual relationship together, successfully relied on human rights arguments to prevent the deportation of one of their number.[175] There was a significant religious dimension to the case, as one issue was the apparently polygamous nature of the union. The married couple involved argued that they could not divorce as their allegiances to the same gods meant that it would be against their religion to do so.

Perhaps the greatest difficulty that a Pagan outlook might have towards human rights is irredeemably its anthropocentric nature. In other words, many

173 F. Mehr, 'Human Rights in Zoroastrianism', Association for the Revival of Zoroastrianism, https://www.causes.com/causes/566882-association-for-revival-of-zoroastrianism/updates/504963-human-rights-in-zoroastrianism.

174 The Pagan Federation International, 'Three Principles of Membership', http://www.paganfederation.org/about-the-pf/#Functions.

175 D. Barrett and C. Duffin, 'Pagan Wins "Family Life" Human Rights Case', *The Telegraph* (18 Dec 2011), http://www.telegraph.co.uk/news/uknews/immigration/8963019/Pagan-wins-family-life-human-rights-case.html.

Pagans would argue that respecting the needs and dignity of humans is not sufficient, as they are not the only beings and entities who should be valued and cared for. The Pagan Federation's Code of Conduct expressly lists animal cruelty and environmental damage[176] as matters which will lead to disciplinary action by the society.

Yet, despite the caveat, we are not suggesting that Pagan ideas would be inclined to lead individuals to reject the concept of human rights. On the contrary, it is the case that many strands of Paganism would encourage followers to desire that fundamental rights be extended and adapted to encompass non-human life.

7.4.9 Humanism (as expressed by the British Humanist Association)[177]

At one level, the furtherance of human rights could be said to be quintessential for the Humanist worldview. In the definition of Humanism put forward by the British Humanist Association (BHA), it is stated that '[t]hey [Humanists] have trusted to the scientific method, evidence, and reason to discover truths about the universe and have placed human welfare and happiness at the centre of their ethical decision making'.[178]

Moreover, a Humanist is someone who:

> trusts to the scientific method when it comes to understanding how the universe works and rejects the idea of the supernatural (and is therefore an atheist or agnostic)
>
> makes their ethical decisions based on reason, empathy, and a concern for human beings and other sentient animals
>
> believes that, in the absence of an afterlife and any discernible purpose to the universe, human beings can act to give their own lives meaning by seeking happiness in this life and helping others to do the same.[179]

Generally speaking, therefore, this is a philosophical (or, for our purposes, religious) position that will naturally be in harmony with human rights, as it seeks to promote human welfare, happiness and respect for the autonomy and dignity of persons. Yet, there are two related points which do have the potential to muddy the water, namely (i) the absence of any *necessary* concept of absolute ethical values; and (ii) the lack of any guiding principles by which clashes between opposing rights may be resolved.

176 The Pagan Federation International, 'Code of Conduct', https://paganfed.org/index.php/federation/pagan-federation-code-of-ethics/code-of-conduct#8_-_Animal_cruelty__

177 As we discussed at length in Chapters 3 and 4, for our current and specific purposes the BHA may appropriately be dealt with a 'religious belief group' and is therefore included in this chapter as such.

178 British Humanist Association, 'Humanism', https://humanism.org.uk/humanism.

179 Ibid.

Individual Humanists may or may not personally adhere to absolute moral values with a non-religious basis, but they are not a required part of Humanism. Consequently, from a Humanist perspective, there would be no fundamental objection to resolving the classic 'ticking time-bomb' moral dilemma by advocating torture, or even killing as a means to an end. In this scenario, a criminal has planted a time-bomb set to explode, inevitably killing and injuring many people. He is refusing to disclose its whereabouts to the authorities, and the question is whether it could ever be legitimate to beat, water-board or otherwise abuse him until he reveals the information.

In a straightforward utilitarian calculation, the greatest happiness of the greatest number might be achieved by permitting the police to take such action. Some, undoubtedly many, Humanists would reject this position, either finding some non-religious reason to argue for abstract ethical values, or by maintaining that living in a state which practises torture would not in the long term be the optimal path towards maximising human happiness and welfare. However, this response is not required by the Humanist doctrines, as the BHA formulates them.

There is also the related difficulty of how to resolve dilemmas where opposing rights are in conflict, or appear to be in conflict. At one level, it might be argued that the solution adopted should be that which most effectively promotes human dignity and human welfare, but how is this to be ascertained?

In addition, if rationalism should be prioritised, how are views which might be termed 'suprarational'[180] to be factored into the calculation? Inevitably, in balancing needs which are at odds, Humanism in practice imports a rationalist perspective into determining the hierarchy of need. See, for example, the BHA's comments on 'conscientious objection' and the concern expressed about any further accommodation of religious exemptions from general legal obligations.[181]

So, while there is ultimately no single clear way to resolve dilemmas caused by clashing rights in a Humanist paradigm, there is a favouring of Humanist values in attempting to balance competing interests, which if applied would potentially disadvantage those whose worldview was incompatible with the non-religious, rationalist dimension of Humanism. Essentially, the dilemma mirrors that of many faith groups, and indeed society at large. It is part of the ongoing questions around which rights are accepted as fundamental human rights and how we resolve conflicts of rights. All religious belief groups, whether Humanist and rationalist or faith-based in nature, will advocate a resolution which is in line with their values and outlook.

In common with many faith traditions, the underlying philosophy of Humanism is, in the majority of instances, supportive of, and even coterminous with, the values of the human rights movement in the liberal Western tradition.

180 See, e.g., the discussion by R. Domingo, *God and the Secular Legal System* (Cambridge University Press: Cambridge) 2016, 84.

181 British Humanist Association, 'Conscientious Objection', https://humanism.org.uk/campaigns/human-rights-and-equality/conscientious-objection.

However, like many of the faith paradigms, it is not of necessity compatible with widely accepted notions of human rights for all adherents and in all circumstances.

A final point to note before moving on is that the BHA is expressly supportive of one major element within the current legal human rights framework: it is passionately campaigning for the retention of the Human Rights Act.[182]

7.4.10 Overall reflections on religion and human rights

Based on the discussion above, there is good reason to be highly positive about the attitude of religious individuals and groups towards the basic concept of human rights. Despite the multiplicity of doctrinal differences, there is an overarching respect for the dignity of human beings and a mandate for compassion and advancing their welfare.

Strikingly, Allison Josephs – a well-known advocate for Orthodox Judaism, who emphasises the capacity of Orthodox Jews to contribute positively to society as a whole – recently observed that there is more which unites than divides human beings. She quotes with approval the words of the well-known Atheist John Lennon, and argues that rather than seeing human beings in different categories when it comes to religious belief, we should see ourselves as all having a place on a spectrum of faith and outlook. [183]

The idea of conceptualising human beings of all shades of faith-based opinion as being on a shared journey towards a better collective future, with more values uniting than dividing them, is in harmony with many of the themes of earlier chapters. In addition, the notion of a spectrum reflects the anthropological reality which we have seen in terms of individuals who often have multiple religious identities and moving between them in different contexts, as well as reflecting similar goals and concerns for our collective life together.

It fits well with the image of different faith groups moving collectively as part of the wings of the penguin, while taking advantage of the structures put in place by the establishment frameworks in order to engage in social and political dialogue. When there is a shared project, which involves all of society, and when there are shared values driving it forward, it makes no sense to suggest excluding religious voices.

In no context is dialogue more important than in the realm of human rights. As we have seen, they exist in the current legal framework by virtue of dialogue. The categories of rights-holders and the rights which the law recognises have evolved over time. The Human Rights Act 1998 has created a category of positive rights and a framework for balancing conflicting rights when they collide,

182 British Humanist Association, 'Humanists and Civil Rights Groups Rally to Defend Human Rights Act' (10 Dec 2016), https://humanism.org.uk/2016/12/10/humanists-and-civil-rights-groups-rally-to-defend-human-rights-act.

183 A. Josephs, 'Shabbos Chazon: Why John Lennon's "Imagine" is Messianic', *Jew in the City* (24 Jul 2015), http://jewinthecity.com/2015/07/shabbos-chazon-why-lennons-imagine-is-messianic.

but this has, by no means, closed down or restricted the growth of human rights around and beyond those provided by the ECHR. As we explained thoroughly in the second section of this chapter, the 1998 Act has simply put in place a structure to support their development.

The movement and future of human rights within the legal framework is dependent upon collective dialogue and citizens engaging creatively in this. Unquestionably, some religious groups and individuals resist the advancement or exercise of some specific rights by some specific individuals, but this is all part of the collective dialogue. Where specific rights conflict, it is necessary for all parties with an interest to have their say and put forward their case before judges or administrative decision-makers to decide which rights to prioritise and when. This is helpful in ensuring that justice is visible, and even objections which do not carry the day can be beneficial in generating good legislation and policy. Proposals that are subject to scrutiny and require robust justification are likely to be more solid than those that sail through without question.

Furthermore, there is a vast difference between some religious people and groups objecting to some developments or manifestations of some human rights, and the asserted position of religious people in general being a negative force where human rights are concerned. All of the major religions based in Great Britain and which we have considered would encourage their followers to support the institution of human rights as a whole, and to debate the place and nature of specific rights in specific contexts. Given that rights are frequently in conflict, it is a logical impossibility to support all rights all of the time.

Furthermore, it must be acknowledged that societal understanding of what constitutes 'human rights' shifts, as cultural and moral norms evolve. Society as a whole, as well as its secular and religious component parts, undergoes constant change, and this has a dramatic impact on our collective conception of human rights. In light of the evolving nature of our society, objecting to or debating some rights in some contexts, by different actors (including religious actors), does not equate to opposing rights.

Human rights can function in a legal system and society only where there is a good dialogue, from a variety of perspectives, and religious communities have a vital role to play in enabling this to happen.

7.5 Conclusion

It can be seen that in the broadest sense, human rights are not merely supported, but actively furthered by the Constitution and the wider legal framework on religion. This happens in two ways.

First, the nuanced approach towards religion is conducive to dealing effectively and appropriately with faith issues that intersect with secular law. It encourages judges and legislators to adopt a positive and empathetic approach to individuals and communities. This is beneficial when it comes to recognising and safeguarding human rights, especially when there is conflict between a number of rights that may be at play. A variety of examples of the law in England, Wales and

Scotland have illustrated the findings of the key part of our chapter. It allows for needs and objectives stemming from faith to be accommodated where possible, but it also helps to prevent them from overshadowing other considerations and taking precedence when this would be inappropriate. The more sophisticated the treatment of religion, the more probable it is that the correct outcome will be achieved when it comes to balancing conflicting rights. Furthermore, on the occasions where the case or objectives of religious citizens do not prevail, they are more likely to feel that they have received a just and comprehensive hearing.

In addition, having a supportive framework where religion is concerned allows faith groups to contribute in practical ways to the furtherance and implantation of human rights. This is true of the established and quasi-established Churches, but is by no means limited to them; citizens of different religious traditions are equally willing to join the collective human rights journey which is guiding our twenty-first-century society. This journey encompasses both giving effect to the rights that we recognise, as well as negotiating which rights should be added to the accepted canon of fundamental human rights and how these might be interpreted.

Furthermore, we suggest that the objection by some religious groups to some expressions of some rights should not be presented as evidence of human rights and religion being in opposition by their very nature. Debate about the appropriateness of a particular aspect of a societal project does not amount to rejection of the project itself.

Chapter 7 appended interview material

Baroness Elizabeth Butler-Sloss

Has the Human Rights Act been positive for British society?

[. . .] Sitting as a family judge, which I did for very many years, I was very much supportive of children and I believe children have rights and they have a right to be treated as people and not just as objects [. . .]

[. . .] These are difficult decisions. There was a 15-year-old who refused to have a heart transplant because she claimed she wouldn't be herself, and then she was persuaded to change her mind and she lived. So, it is a very difficult balance for the teenage child . . . how much they know, how much they understand, and it is a question of the degree of capacity to make that decision, which is different from the adults.

Lady Brenda Hale

What has been the impact of the HRA on the legal framework, especially in relation to religion and belief?

The HRA has made a huge difference to the work of the courts, because there are issues which we can now analyse in a different way from how we could have analysed them in the past. Religion is a good example of that, because the non-discrimination cases in Employment Tribunals were not analysed in terms of Article 9 as well as in terms of the non-discrimination laws.

Sir Mark Hedley DL

Has the Human Rights Act been positive for our society?

[. . .] At the moment, the statute and the Convention provide no means for redressing conflicts between rights. They don't articulate any positive means for doing it, so people who have done it might use the qualifications of Article 8 and Article 10 and the other qualified rights, and that is where proportionality comes in, as far as I understand it. Being a family lawyer, I am instinctively at ease with the concept of dealing with things on a case by case basis and finding a solution that suits the facts of your case, but in strict human rights terms, it has the huge disadvantage of making the outcome unpredictable, and therefore it is difficult to advise people of their rights if you don't actually know the extent to which they are going to be upheld if they are found to be in conflict with other human rights. I am not sure there is a way around that.

Professor Imre Leader

How do you regard human rights? Has the Human Rights Act been a positive development for our society?

Too much interference. The way Britain was pre-EU, pre human rights, was a much better thing. Everything was fully safeguarded. I don't think that the

Human Rights Act adds to anything, in fact it detracts because there is now a whole nasty culture of making spurious claims. In the past if a warder attacked a prisoner then they could sue the prison warden, and that was correct. But now the prisoner can sue because he can't vote, or because his right to get books out of the library is curtailed. That is the kind of culture which the Human Rights Act has generated and that is a very bad thing.

Daisuke Miura

Do you think that Great Britain is an equal and a tolerant society?

I think the British Government tries very hard to make everything equal, and to show respect for minority religions. Compared to France it isn't doing too badly. If you go to France, Islamic people aren't allowed to put the veil on and stuff like that.

Really, though, I'm not sure what the best approach is. Again, for example, if you go to someone else's house . . . like, say in my country [Japan] you always, always take your shoes off, that's their idea of respect. But because in Europe you normally go into the house without taking your shoes off, when I'm here that's how I do it. The point is, even though it seems strange and wrong to me, if I visit your house in Europe I'm going to keep my shoes on, because it is the done thing here . . . there's a possibility that they're going to make a mess on your carpet, but I believe that following the rules here is the right thing to do, so if there is mess, so be it. The British Government is doing the opposite: saying that everyone is different, so if that is what you believe, I will let you do it. I think the British Government is trying very hard, but they don't necessarily have the right approach.

Sarah Miles

Would you describe Great Britain as an equal and tolerant society, especially in relation to religion and belief?

I think it tries. I think it is not there yet, but I think our heart is in the right place, and most of us are really completely oblivious to colour and race, especially when it comes to parts of London, where you have all religions and races very happy . . . as part of a team. I think social media has exaggerated the problems . . . we see things from a different perspective as a result. I think we are pretty good as a society towards that end of no prejudice.

The Rt Rev'd Dominic Walker OGS

Is Great Britain an equal and tolerant society, particular in relation to religion and belief?

I think that it is generally getting better. We are becoming a more tolerant society. In the past, it was argued that legislation wouldn't make us more tolerant, and having laws about racial discrimination would not work, but I think that it has and good legislation can be educational. People are more tolerant of other races, homosexuality and unmarried parents; today the majority of children are born out of wedlock. People are more tolerant about divorce and the Church of England now permits the remarriage and ordination of divorced people, whereas people in general are less tolerant of religious extremists and hypocrisy.

Frank Williams

Is Great Britain an equal and tolerant society, especially in relation to religion and belief?

I think Great Britain is a tolerant and equal society in relation to religion and belief. Well, it is the only society I have really experienced in depth, but it is to me religiously tolerant, and from what I hear from the news I think it is much more tolerant than many other places. The place I grew up in . . . which had a very large Jewish population. My closest friend next door was Jewish, and quite often I'd be in there when his father would do the Friday night prayers and lit candles, and so on. I certainly grew up with an understanding of Judaism and Christianity, and I think now we have become much more multi-faith. I think we are tolerant to each other and we actually care for each other, and the other thing I have noticed is that Jewish people are much more prepared to declare their identity as Jewish people in a way they wouldn't when I was growing up.

Anne Duddington

Do you think that Great Britain is an equal and tolerant society, especially in relation to religion and belief?

In some respects Great Britain is an equal and tolerant society in relation to religion and belief, but in other respects it is not. In particular, on occasions I feel marginalised as a Catholic. I can remember, for example, doing some training at university to do with equality, and I remember the person from HR giving Catholics as an example, and I remember feeling very marginalised by that. There is intolerance towards some religions, and that very much depends on the way the media portray them. Technically there should be freedom to practise any religion and belief, but as a Catholic I certainly feel there are times in which I have been marginalised, especially in schools. I have a disabled son. He lacks mental capacity, he doesn't have any speech, but he has been baptised as a Catholic and he is extremely spiritual. He really participates in services in church. I have absolutely no doubt that in his ways he is a better Catholic than I am, but when he went to his special school, we had to follow the agreed syllabus for religion, and when I asked if I could take my son out of school to go to mass on Tuesdays, I got comments from the teacher suggesting that he was 'skiving again . . .'. I think there are lots of hidden prejudices . . . which prevent us from practising freely. That is my experience.

Dr Elizabeth Healey

Would you describe Great Britain as an equal and tolerant society, especially in relation to religion and belief?

I would like to think so, and compared to many countries it is, but in reality we can be extremely and embarrassingly prejudiced (as the discussion about immigration and Brexit has demonstrated). We tend to be wary of people that are different in some way, whether in religion, race or language. Catholics or left footers are often seen as rather strange people, slightly suspect, perhaps a bit of an embarrassment, though not to be laughed at either . . . There is always a surprise, not in a particularly nasty way, when someone discovers that you are a Roman Catholic and the conversation usually ends there. I don't think people are generally nervous about Catholics as long as religious beliefs are kept at arm's length and I think that goes for most other Christian religions as well. In that respect Britain is tolerant (if somewhat ill-informed), but probably not open. You can think and believe what you like as long as you don't talk about it.

In academic circles I wouldn't start a conversation about religion unless there was a really good reason. Most people simply don't talk openly about their faith and religion.

Wendy Huggett

Would you describe Great Britain as an equal and tolerant society, especially in relation to religion and belief?

[. . .] I view my position as being relatively lucky. You can see that the Church still carries resonance, but it is more traditional than real powers nowadays . . . this is very different, needless to say, from Henry VIII's times. Nowadays I don't feel obliged to follow the Church's views and that is very positive. I have never felt compelled, indeed. Sometimes in a way it would make my life easier to be a believer . . . having that thought that there is something else . . . particularly when things go wrong. That reassurance that everything will be all right is important. I see how people who are religious, when they go through traumatic and devastating experiences, they take a massive comfort from religion. In that sense, I would like to have that. I can see how much religion comforts other people and undoubtedly I would like that, but I don't have it.

Jeff Tyldesley

Is Great Britain an equal and tolerant society, especially in relation to religion and belief?

In Great Britain there are lots of people who are tolerant (in terms of religion and belief). It depends on the person you speak to. Academics are tolerant, with a worldwide view . . . but there are lots of ignorant people out there too. I speak to a few of them in my job. There is a lot of racism and a lot of intolerance, particularly towards Muslims. It is noticeable. So, I wouldn't say Great Britain is, generally speaking, tolerant. I would say that there are many people who are tolerant and open-minded, as well as intelligent, but many other people aren't.

Gary McFarlane

Is Great Britain an equal and tolerant society, especially in relation to religion and belief?

Great Britain is not a tolerant and equal society in relation to religion and belief.

Kimberley Long

Would you say that Great Britain is an equal and tolerant society, especially in relation to religion and belief?

I don't think it's possible to assess Great Britain as a whole, because there are marked differences in legislation and attitude between Scotland and the rest of the UK. Scotland seems to be more progressive and tolerant – obviously as a Scot I have a bias, but for example, we have a First Minister who not only describes herself as feminist but has put this into action with a gender balanced cabinet and money towards domestic violence prevention strategies. Another example would be that the Scottish Government has a positive and welcoming stance on immigration – so different from Westminster. When you listen to Radio 4 in the morning you get a real sense of how vastly different the political climate is down there.

Imam Irfan Chishti MBE

Do you think that Great Britain is an equal and tolerant society, particularly in relation to religion and belief?

I would say that there have been some mistakes surrounding multiculturalism. I realise this is perhaps a little controversial for someone of my standing to say this, so I shall illustrate it with an anecdote. A few years ago, I was in a church interfaith gathering, and an elderly Christian lady remarked 'I really don't understand our country any more'. I quizzed her: 'What do you mean?', and then she said 'We can't even have hot cross buns at Easter time anymore'. 'Why can't you?', I challenged, 'It is a tradition of this country, and England . . . Britain . . . is a Christian country in the main' . . . She said that the council had given advice to its local schools that it couldn't do it anymore because it could be offensive to Muslims. You know what I said? 'That is an absolute joke'. As the only member of the Muslim community present, I could see visibly the Christian audience was shocked at my comment. I further remarked, 'It is a joke and it is political correctness going wrong'.

This is what I mean when I say in terms of this debate on tolerance and multiculturalism. Another more serious example of this is the recent case of Rotherham, where we know that the sexual exploitation of minors was not immediately and appropriately dealt with. There was a clear failure of officials, who had responsibility in these matters because they did not act. This failure to act was purely because of the perceived fear of how communities would react. For crying aloud, you are in a position of responsibility and authority . . . people haven't put you there to be pandering to perceptions and political correctness . . . there are peoples' lives at stake!

Baroness Haleh Afshar

Would you describe Great Britain as an equal and tolerant society, especially in relation to human rights?

There is no way that I would talk of Great Britain as a single category [. . .] it's a question of locality and social construct of the groups, rather than a matter of faith.

Professor Lord Robert Winston

Do you think that Great Britain is an equal and tolerant society, particularly in relation to religion and belief systems?

In my view, the irony in Britain is rather well illustrated by the extraordinarily forthright assertions of my friend and colleague, Richard Dawkins, who is almost virulently anti-religious and who is, if you like, religiously Atheist. Much to his irritation, I've called him publicly one of the great religious leaders of our age. With my tongue in my cheek, he didn't like that (*laughter*) but the reason why I start off like that is what is ironic about Richard Dawkins sums up the answer to your question. Richard in a sense rails against the very beliefs which in my view have shaped British democracy. The reason why British democracy is fundamentally different from what happened in 1681 [. . .] is that already by that time there was a starting of the ascent of Anglicanism.

Rev John Chalmers QHC

Would you say that Great Britain/Scotland is an equal and tolerant society, especially in relation to human rights?

[. . .] There was, for instance, in some law firms the exclusion of Catholic employees or in some of the gentlemen's clubs. It was a long time before they entertained membership from Catholics. It would have to be said that now we're getting on top of that, but it's not completely gone. I have heard that even one of the big employers, not far from here, is a mixed employer, but to make life easier choose not to mix employees. So they have a shift of Catholic workers and a different shift of Protestant workers. As a result, in 2015 there is still a little bit of that. It's isolated now, but it's around.

Zerbanoo Gifford

Moving on to questions specifically about human rights, do you think that Great Britain is an equal and tolerant society, particularly in relation to religion and belief?

What is missing in Britain is a lack of curiosity and the willingness to engage with other people not of your community. You're allowed to do whatever you want to do behind closed doors, consenting adults . . . but there isn't that sort of joyfulness, of seeing what the connections are and what the shared heritage is. That's what I'm interested in. We share so much, yet we concentrate on what divides us all the time.

Professor Norman Doe

Do you think Great Britain is an equal and tolerant society, especially as to religion and belief?

Personally, I think people are equal in dignity. But it is self-evident that people are not equal in the sense of exact sameness. They are different. They may be created in the image of God, but they have different talents, abilities, prejudices, relationships with people. So, if they are equal in dignity, which I accept, they are unequal in thoughts, goodness, badness, actions, and so on. And both this equality and this diversity should be taken into consideration when action is required towards them – and by them.

Faisal Khan

Is Great Britain an equal and tolerant society?

Parts of Britain are tolerant in relation to religion and belief. The big cities are. In places where there are not many Asians, people tend to be wary. In white areas, people are still surprised to see Asian people there . . . It is hard to explain and you wouldn't really understand it if you are born here in Manchester . . . but I would say 90% of the country is tolerant.

Dominic Grieve QC MP

Do you see Great Britain as an equal and tolerant society?

[. . .] I think Great Britain has historically been very tolerant, and I think that tolerance has almost been imprinted into its DNA. That isn't to say that there hasn't been discrimination against people with differing views. You only have to go back 60 or 70 years and Catholicism was seen as being at least a minority, and probably a suspicious activity, even though there were lots of Catholics who were leading members of British society. And similarly there was undoubtedly discrimination against Jewish immigrants in the nineteenth century, and some of my forebears are Jewish. But when that's been said and done, I think that because of our history, and the need to accommodate people who came out of our religious strife in the sixteenth and seventeenth century, there has been a huge level of tolerance and acceptance. I don't think it's for nothing that a lot of pubs are called 'The Live and Let Live', but that's what it's all about. There has been a long tradition of equality. There has also always been an attitude of suspicion towards overt displays of religious enthusiasm. You can see that in the attitude which Anglicans took to Orangemen in the nineteenth century. They thought that they were disturbers of the peace in the context of Ireland. In general most people in Britain are quite comfortable with other people's views. On the other hand, you tend to get quite uncomfortable when they have excessive amounts of religion or religious views spouted to them. Now other countries in Europe will have different traditions. But here I think that tolerance is well ingrained.

Don Horrocks

Do you think Great Britain is an equal and tolerant society in relation to religion and belief?

Our perception (that it is not equal and tolerant), in my view, is backed up by evidence that there is an understanding that there is a hierarchy of rights, and religion and belief are at the very bottom of that hierarchy . . .

There is case after case on the legal front affecting Christians who are not freely able to live their ordinary lives.

Dr David Perfect

Is Great Britain an equal and tolerant society, especially in relation to religion and belief?

I think there is a lot of intolerance towards people who hold Pagan or Wiccan beliefs in the workplace, because they are seen as something strange, and people don't understand and they don't really want to understand. So, yes, generally there is a lot of tolerance, but in places it is a bit qualified.

Sir Gareth Edwards CBE

Would you say that this country is a fairly equal and tolerant one with regard to religion?

I think it is relatively. It is very tolerant of different people's views, extremely so, whereas compared to other parts of the world you don't have the choice or desire to let others have thoughts. There is always a danger of taking one exception or situation, say in the Middle East or the Far East. I have travelled . . . usually to British . . . parts of the old Empire where religion has been fairly standardised, but I think that we are tolerant.

Maybe this was part of going away to Millfield School and the mixture there, lots of nationalities and religions and backgrounds without question. You had all extremes, which is what the basis of the school is all about. And now they have all kinds of people who come together, and they help each other. When you think of where I came from with a scholarship from my mining village at 16, thrust into a melting pot of different people from all over the world, it was a quick step forward. It was a fast track to take it all on board and be aware of it. It made me aware, it gave me first-hand information. It wasn't like now when we have media and we are aware. At that time I met boys from Asia or Africa, I learnt about problems in their area that I would never have known otherwise. I quickly became aware that things were different in different places, and that things happened to individuals that you knew. I became aware that you had to be tolerant because certain people had strong views; I am fairly easy going.

Frank Cranmer

Is Great Britain an equal and tolerant society, especially in relation to religion and belief?

Yes, I think Great Britain is as tolerant as you can get (in terms of religion and belief). Clearly, there are signs of intolerance in some quarters. This is evident in terms of anti-Semitism. There are also signs of Islamophobia in some quarters, but on the whole, although not without blemish, I think as far as religious tolerance in Western societies is concerned, the UK is pretty good.

Professor Linda Woodhead

Is Great Britain an equal and tolerant society, particularly in relation to religion and belief?

I think Britain is an equal and tolerant society, not perfection obviously, but it is in general, and also a meritocratic one, and I think it has quite a strong legal basis to support it. I think that there is a fair degree of religious freedom and I worry, this is quite ironic, that religious individuals don't have a great deal of freedom because there is an 'unfreedom' imposed on them more by their Churches than by the state. At the moment, for example, my Church is insisting against a majority of its members' consciences on not performing same-sex marriage.

Dr Hilary Firestone

Do you think that Great Britain is an open and a tolerant society, particularly in relation to religion and belief?

Probably the answer is 'no', but I have never encountered any problem. So if you are asking me from purely personal experience, no. Having said that, I have always bent over backwards. If I have taken a day off I have paid it back. With my son who is at a non-Jewish school, I have always asked for permission to take him out and it is on the proviso that he catches up with the work and hands it in by the right time. So it is give and take.

Dominic Dyer

Would you say that beliefs in relation to religion and animal welfare are taken seriously and given respect in contemporary Great Britain?

I feel that there are difficulties with religion and animal welfare because of some of the difficulties around Halal and Kosher slaughter requirements, and you know there is quite a significant debate going on in animal welfare circles around those issues. I can appreciate the sensitivities on both sides in relation to the religious and historical significance, but also the nitty gritty of what happens when you kill an animal and the fact that you are not stunning it before you slaughter it. So I think that in those areas religion and animal welfare can be quite difficult, but in other areas I have spoken to the Quaker animal welfare group and have had contact with other groups with religious connections that are very much involved in raising concerns about animal welfare and wildlife protection, and have some very good individuals involved in terms of what they are trying to achieve.

Rabbi Lord Jonathan Sacks

How easy is it for you to live in accordance with your beliefs? Are there any challenges and, if so, are they social, legal or political in nature?

[. . .] Challenges? Of course . . . there are some specific ones. Periodically, challenges are raised against some very, very ancient religious practices that Jews have . . . specifically *shechita*, which is the Jewish way of killing animals for meat, which we believe is as humane as the most humane method available. And Brit Milah, the circumcision of males, usually at the age of eight days or when they are healthy enough to do so, both of which go way, way back. Circumcision goes back to Abraham, the dietary laws to Moses, and they are challenged from time to time. Those are legal risks. There is a cultural risk: the return of anti-Semitism to Europe within living memory of the Holocaust, the one thing none of us born after the Holocaust thought was possible. That is of great concern to Jews in Britain and Jews in other European countries.

Professor Dame Nancy Rothwell

Are there any challenges to living in accordance with your convictions in Great Britain? If so, are they social, legal or political in nature?

I can see that to some it may be considered that an Atheist MP might not uphold the Christian principles of the United Kingdom. To me, Atheists can uphold those principles just as well, without being religious.

The Rev'd Dr Jason Bray

How easy is it for you to live in accordance with your faith in Wales? Are there any challenges?

Challenges to Anglicanism in Wales? The Anglican Church in Wales has got a particular history where it is associated with landowners and effectively foreigners and middle classes. One of the difficult things about being an Anglican in Wales is that Welsh cultural identity is traditionally vested in the Non-Conformist chapels and we're sort of fighting against that, but we're also unfortunately inheriting the historical difficulties that they had. So, for example, in my own community, people will tell me that they don't go to church or chapel because the chapels didn't support the working men during the strikes. Despite the fact that, actually, as the vicar I'm interested in social justice and they commend me for that; they won't come to church because we are tarred with the same brush as the traditional Non-Conformists.

Anglicanism is also in a relatively strong position, though, because we are still represented in every community or everybody is at least within driving distance of an Anglican church.

Ian Scott

How easy is it for you to live as a Humanist? Are there any challenges and, if so, are they social, political or legal in nature?

Social, in Scotland no; in England and Wales you are still barred from having Humanist marriage, but we have had Humanist weddings in Scotland for over 10 years. We have more weddings than the Roman Catholic Church and expect to have more than the Church of Scotland by the end of the year. I don't have any issues identifying as a Humanist. I've never experienced any social backlash other than from people who think that you identify as Humanist to avoid identifying as feminist. Legally, there are still issues regarding opt-outs from schools etc, which can discriminate against you from teaching in particular schools. If you are the child of Humanist parents you can be discriminated against by schools: state-funded schools can choose to give you a less than adequate sex education.

The Rev'd Dr Will Adam

How easy do you find it to live in accordance with your beliefs and identity in this country? Do you find that there are challenges and, if so, are they social, legal or political in nature?

I can't say I have had much difficulty being me in my life, whether that would have been the same had I not been white, male, educated etc, so able to fit into stuff, I don't know. Sometimes you do get professional issues as the public minister rather than just as a Christian. A supposed equality agenda does lead to you being less welcome than you would have been 20 years ago in the public square.

Chris Morris

How easy it is for you to live in accordance with your personal beliefs in this country? If so, are they social, legal or political in nature? Are there any challenges?

Purely social. But when I say social, I perhaps don't mean as a result of direct societal pressure to live in a different way from how I live. It's more sort of the norm of the rat race. I feel to a certain extent in the UK this is a generalisation, so probably unfair, but many people I speak to feel that they've been brought up to work in a secure professional job, to buy a house and save enough for retirement and make oneself materially comfortable.

And that's a counter Christian norm?

Not so much directly, but it can make one reasonably insular in terms of perspective, so that would be counter Christian in terms of feathering one's own nest before looking after others. I think increasingly the problem is one of a pull on time and the pressures of an open all hours society.

Dr Hema Radhakrishnan

How easy is it for you to live in accordance with your faith? Are there any challenges and, if so, are they social, legal or political?

I don't really know much about the legal aspects, it has never come up. Politically I don't see much of a challenge. If anything, Britain is more tolerant politically in trying to accommodate everybody than other countries. For example, I come from India, and there are no shopping malls with praying facilities, although the vast majority of our population is very religious, either Hindu or Muslim. But all the same, the ethos in most other countries is that if you are going to pray, you shouldn't be in a shopping centre; you should be in a temple or a mosque, and that is the ideology of politicians in India. But here it is different, and because people are given more they sometimes start expecting more. Sometimes this is feasible and sometimes not. Generally, I think that the society is very inclusive.

Samantha Chandler

How easy is it for you to live in accordance with your personal beliefs in this country? Are there any challenges and, if so, are they social, political or legal?

I don't feel persecuted. I think that to be a Christian is sometimes thought of as slightly twee in this country now and a little bit eccentric.

Professor Grace Davie

Are there any challenges for you to live in accordance with your beliefs in this country? If so, are they social, legal or political in nature?

[. . .] I am very, very irritated by Christians in this country who claim that they are being persecuted. They don't understand the meaning of persecution. I only have to read the newspapers to realise how lucky I am.

The Most Reverend Dr Barry Morgan

How easy is it for you to live in accordance with your faith? Are there challenges?

Obviously there are no legal obstacles and everyone in Britain is free to practise their faith. Trying to live out the Gospel values, of course, is never easy. Although the Church in Wales is a disestablished Church, there are vestiges of establishment left. All our clergy are registrars for marriages, but we are excused by law from marrying same-sex couples unless the Church in Wales' Governing Body passes a canon enabling that to happen. As registrars for marriage, we also have to follow Home Office regulations to make sure people are not entering sham marriages. In Wales as in England, everyone who lives in a parish has the legal right to be baptised in that parish, to be married in the parish church and to be buried in the parish churchyard if it is not full. When churchyards are full, however, they cannot be handed back to the state as they are in England, but have to continue to be maintained by the Church. In terms of the challenges we face as a Church, we are declining in membership, and although we are present in every community and do excellent community work, that is certainly not reflected in attendance at Sunday worship. We are an ageing Church, although a quarter of the pupils in Wales attend faith schools.

The Rev'd Professor Thomas Watkin

How easy is it for you to live in accordance with your personal beliefs?

[. . .] I tend to feel that in the media, in particular, there is a slight bias against the holding of religious beliefs. I think that might be about to change, because we are becoming more sensitive to the respect which we have to show to other faiths like Islam. I think that the pay-off might be greater respect for the more established faiths in this country, Christianity and Judaism.

Dominic Grieve QC MP

How easy is it for you to live in accordance with your faith in Great Britain?

[. . .] And nor do I share this gloom which I sometimes feel is felt my some sections of the Christian community in Britain that Britain is losing its identity. Its identity is undoubtedly evolving, but the freedom to worship, the freedom to have your beliefs, the freedom to bring up your children in the beliefs which you have, subject to their freedom to have their own beliefs which will evolve with time, have never been obstructed in any way. So I am very comfortable.

Gurd Kandola

How easy is it for you to live in accordance with Sikhism in this country? Are there any challenges and, if there are, are they social, political or legal in nature?

I don't think there are significant challenges. I believe Sikhs in Britain are able to practise their faith and on the whole are quite content. In my view Sikhs have an openness and tolerance which allows them to be able to assimilate whilst retaining their belief and ideology. This ability to successfully integrate and happily co-exist in society outside of the Punjab has led to Sikhs creating prosperous communities, which in turn make valuable contributions to wider society all over the world. In the working environment, major organisations have developed policies to adhere to employment law around respect for employees from minority groups, including their religious backgrounds. I personally don't have experience of any significant particular issues or challenges. Perhaps, I would have a different outlook if I were a Sikh wearing a turban . . . there have been reports in the media of more frequent attacks on Sikhs by individuals who, through ignorance, confuse the appearance of a Sikh with that of images of extremists and terrorists, and reports of a high-profile Sikh who was not allowed to board a flight wearing his turban.

Rev David Robertson

How easy is it for you to live in accordance with your Presbyterian faith in Scotland? Are there any challenges and, if there are, are they social, political or legal in nature?

Growing up, virtually no challenges, other than it is becoming more difficult. Because of the default position of the established Church, there is secular liberalism and that is becoming increasingly intolerant and illiberal. Although I don't experience persecution, I am used to receiving a significant amount of discrimination and abuse because of my beliefs. I think we have a Scottish society which includes a significant principle of equality and diversity, which was largely founded upon Christian principles. As we have taken away the roots, we are in danger of losing some of the fruits. We are becoming a more intolerant society.

Ashley Gilbert

How easy is it for you to live in accordance with your beliefs?

So I consider myself very lucky personally; by and large I don't encounter the kind of bigotry which I know that other people do encounter. And I think that has helped me to do what I do, and be part of the Pagan community and help other people stand up when necessary. I am a member of the interfaith council, I am on the Nottinghamshire SACRE and I've kind of involved myself in, not so much being an activist and fighting causes, but standing up for what is right when it needs to be done.

Andrew Copson

How easy is it to live in accordance with your beliefs?

For me it is very easy, because I am middle class, comfortable and don't have children. But were I not in those three categories it would be different. Thinking of friends who have children, it is very difficult for them in terms of what their children are going to encounter at school, for instance, prayers. They experience this and then come home and ask 'what's this about Jesus?'. And because these things are compulsory they can't take their children out of them without having them essentially marginalised in some sense from the school setting. Getting them into school in the first place is hard because so many schools are run by Churches. If I was unemployed or reliant on social services or welfare services it might be difficult. A lot of the cases we have had are where their welfare programme has been contracted out to a religious organisation and they find themselves in a setting where they are very uncomfortable. There are obviously employment restrictions on non-religious people if they are in the education sector or contracted-out public services.

Can you give some examples of the kinds of case you were referring to in which people had had their rights infringed by receiving services from providers with religious links?

Yes, so a woman who was long-term unemployed and got shifted onto a new welfare to work-type stuff, which had been contracted out to a multifaith, but faith-based organisation. The sessions were held in rooms with things on the walls, which were offensive in her eyes, particularly to women. The actual trigger for her getting in touch with us was that there was a lot of homophobia. She had a gay son, and so the sessions which were being run, largely on things like how to write your CV etc., were being run by people from religious organisations, and they were saying things about gay marriage being introduced, joking and saying it won't be long before you can marry a pig. These and similar unsavoury things were being said, and as a result she had refused to attend the sessions and had her benefits stopped. The Job Centre which was contracted with this organisation were not sympathetic.

Professor Dame Jocelyn Bell Burnell

Are there any challenges to you living in accordance with your beliefs? If so, are they social, political or legal in nature?

Sometimes they are legal [. . .] probably the biggest challenge remembered particularly this year in which we are marking the centenary of the First World War, is that many Quakers are pacifists, and we see a rise in militarism in Britain now, maybe generally . . . That is partially ethical, partially political . . . I don't know where the divide is, to be honest.

Una Mary Parker

Are there any challenges in living in accordance with your beliefs? If so, are they social, legal or political in nature?

It is completely fine to be Anglican in the UK. The UK is basically Church of England and there are some Roman Catholics who resent that fact, that Eton and Harrow are the top, smartest schools, and they are both Church of England . . . Catholics are relegated to a second place. That is lessening now, that division of Catholics living in this country. We are all becoming, hopefully, more tolerant of that religion. I think it is difficult with some other religions, because they seem to us to be two thousand years out of date . . . when you get these Arab ladies, covered in black, walking behind their husbands, not allowed to drive their cars . . . it is not for us to criticise or to make a fuss about it, but I do think the time has come to move with the times for lots of the world that is sticking to two thousand-year-old customs.

Lillie Flynn

Are there any challenges to living in accordance with your beliefs? If so, are they social, political or legal in nature?

In my industry, acting, I don't come across many people who think the way I do. As I said, I am one of those spiritual persons, and in the acting industry there are not many.

Rabbi Reuven Silverman

Are human rights enshrined in law positive for our society?

Asking that question is like asking whether air is good for people! They are unquestionably good for society.

Elder Clifford Herbertson

Are human rights applied to all people in our society a good or a bad thing?

It can only be a good thing for British society for us to have that, because it's about respect. If we respect each other, we seek to understand why they do things, why they behave in a certain way, and I think as long as we are open to understanding, accepting and respecting other people, we will be able to live in a much more comfortable society.

Keith Porteous Wood

Do you think that human rights which apply to everyone are a good or a bad thing for British society?

Human rights must apply to everyone, they must be universal or they are of no value. The ideal of human rights being something over which all of mankind, believers or not, can agree in the furtherance of our common humanity seems, sadly to be receding. I am very worried about the growing attempts to undermine universal human rights by, for example, the Cairo Declaration – the attempt by the Organisation of Islamic Co-operation to have an alternative human rights declaration, subject to Sharia. That, I think, is a key example of the worrying and growing dismissal of human rights as a 'Western construct'. This was not the case fifty or even twenty years ago. The problem is primarily, but not exclusively, from Islam, but almost all of the attacks on human rights are religiously based and could eventually lead to their destruction. There should be only one set of universal human rights, and they shouldn't be exemptions for anything, whether that is Sharia or anything else.

Mark Gifford

How does your religion regard human rights, and how has it contributed to or influenced the world's understanding of human rights?

The ancient Zoroastrian scriptures are very interesting. They're one of the earliest pieces of literature that we still have . . . they're from the Bronze Age and they talk about the conscience of each man and woman, and that religious belief should be pursued as a result of each man and woman considering in their conscience what they believe to be the right thing. So, even from the really earliest period it looks as though there's an emphasis on autonomy, but also personal responsibility, and that has kind of percolated down through the centuries in Zoroastrianism. So there's always been an emphasis, I think, on people doing the right thing out of their own conviction.

Baroness Kathleen Richardson

How does your faith regard human rights?

I think my understanding of Creation is that everybody is born with the right to life and well-being, but my Methodist upbringing will tell me that has to be limited if my freedom infringes somebody else's freedoms or rights.

The Most Reverend Professor Rowan Williams

Are there any ways in which your group has a practical influence on human rights in contemporary Britain? For example, does it actively campaign on any issues which you can think of?

I am, right at the moment, looking at the work which my successor is doing with the Pope and other religious leaders on human trafficking, a new form of slavery. That's certainly been quite a focus in recent years. There has been a strong emphasis in many Church related bodies on the rights of children. The extremely important work which the Children's Society (a body with strong Church links) did a few years ago on the idea of 'A Good Childhood' was about the fundamental rights of the child. Many Christians have been involved in debates about penal reform, the rights of prisoners, refugees and detainees.

Professor Sheila McLean

Would you say that Atheists have contributed to our collective understanding of human rights?

[. . .] Oddly enough, our contribution (as Atheists) to the human rights debate in Scotland hasn't been massive. Maybe what we do is replace some sort of faith with another. We don't believe in a God but we believe in fundamental ethical principles [. . .] For some reason people tend to think that political correctness is a tool of the left, but in fact it is a tool of the right imported from the USA and it was, in my view, a conscious attempt to restrict freedom of speech, for example. It has done that not just in terms of stopping people from saying what they think about particular groups or protected ethnicities (and I don't say this in a hostile way), but it has also resulted in serious inflictions of harm (as in Rotherham) on vulnerable people.

Thomas Haines

Have Atheists contributed to the development of human rights in Great Britain?

Atheist voices, such as Fathers for Justice, have contributed immensely to the human rights debate in contemporary Britain. There must be other bodies. Fathers for Justice must be effective, and I don't think they are aligned to any particular religion. They just want to be around their kids.

David Pollock

Does Humanism have a practical influence on human rights at present?

[. . .] Otherwise, in the BHA we continue to take a keen interest in cases that raise matters of religion and belief, and we use the HRA in a lot of our arguments when the BHA goes to court, as we did, for example, in the Nicklinson case on assisted dying in the Supreme Court . . . Our case was based entirely on human rights. In fact, we are generally very active indeed in our use of the Act.

Jessica Morden MP

Do Christians make a practical contribution to human rights?

I think there are examples of bishops contributing to the human rights debate, whilst bringing people together. More generally, from my constituency we can see the work that the Churches are doing . . . running food banks in Newport, helping homeless people . . . It is just a phenomenal amount of work and probably the most difficult tasks. It is quite amazing.

Professor Lord Robert Winston

How does Judaism regard human rights? Has it contributed to or has it influenced the world's understanding of human rights?

Well, Judaism is about human rights. I mean Judaism almost founded human rights. The notion was from very early on Mosaic law argued that kings weren't the appropriate way forward, that actually you had to have representative government. So, of course, right back from the . . . Judaism is about freedom. That's why the celebration of the Passover, the leaving of Egypt is so important, because it's essentially about release from slavery. And that actually meant that you had to have a people who, whatever their faults, showed respect for the rights of everyone, even fugitives from justice, so cities were designated as safe places for them. And although there was a death penalty, what is remarkable in Judaism is that the Sanhedrin, the great court of Israel, only actually condemned one individual to death ever, although there were penalties like stoning, hanging and the rest of it. There was only individual who was ever actually condemned to death until Adolf Eichmann was condemned to death, much against the will of very many Jews actually.

Professor Dame Jocelyn Bell Burnell

Has Quakerism contributed to our collective understanding of human rights?

Human rights are very, very important to Quakers, because of that tenet that there is something good, something of God is in everybody. Quakers, for instance, in Britain, were the first Church to agree to have same-sex marriage.

Professor Steven Jones

Has Atheism contributed to human rights in your view?

[. . .] I am not aware of any schisms within Atheism where people are saying you are this particular type of Atheist, therefore I will kill you. I think that Atheism is more open to equal rights than religion. Some religions may preach human rights, but if you look into the background, very few of them practise it.

Professor Linda Woodhead

Has Anglicanism had an influence on human rights?

[. . .] To give you another example, in the 1970s Anglicans were at the fore in arguing for the liberalisation of abortion, divorce, and changes of the law in relation to homosexuality. There were powerful Anglican voices in support of those causes, and it is sad that the official leaders went back on all those things, but the majority of Anglicans have been and remain supportive of those changes. Many ordinary Anglicans have defended liberal causes, greater equality and human rights – including many in the legal profession who are Anglican – but they are lay Anglicans who do not advertise their religious identity, and are not given authority in their Church. That is the problem.

Jenny Hodge

Can you think of any way in which the Catholic Church has a practical influence on human rights in this country?

In small senses, I am currently president of the St Vincent de Paul Society; we work with the homeless, and with older people and children . . . we believe that everyone should have these rights. We chat to homeless people, give them food and chat to them because we believe that they are equal members of society. So we do contribute, but not in a big way as we are not the main religion of this country.

The Most Reverend Peter Smith

Can you think of any ways in which the Church has a practical influence on human rights in contemporary Britain?

Yes, a good example, human trafficking. My auxiliary bishop here, Pat Lynch, has been one of the prime movers in that when we became aware that young women, in particular, were being trafficked. I suppose we all knew vaguely that it was going on, but it was coming to light. Pat looks after the migrants' office in the Bishops' Conference. We have always supported the freedom of people in this country and have had a good record of welcoming people. This came up and the Bishops' Conference supported Pat, he got very involved with the Met Police. What developed from something reasonably local became an international thing; it went to the Vatican. Kevin Highland was the police representative at a conference here with police chiefs from all around the world. Our women religious congregations have got very involved in providing safe houses. Now the police, when they have identified what they believe to be a house used for trafficking, will not go in unless they have two religious sisters with them. Because these poor lasses come from countries where nobody trusts the police, their view of a police raid is that they are as bad as the lot keeping them there. They are more open to the religious sisters. That to me is a magnificent input by the Catholic Church.

Thomas Nichols

What contribution can the world of sport make to human rights – for example, in terms of role models and discrimination concerning race, sexual orientation, gender, etc?

Probably the response of sport authorities to practices such as homophobia is lukewarm. The only area which I have looked into is the football's sport bodies, because that is really the sport I am interested in. I think the response has been lukewarm, indeed. Homophobia is rooted in football, but I wouldn't say racism is. I have been in many games and it was not an issue. I know there have been incidents, but isolated. Xenophobia? I don't think so. In Man United the opposite is true.

Professor Sir John Sulston

Have you personally ever campaigned on a human rights related issue?

Yes, in all sorts of ways, though not major ones. I suppose that my biggest contribution in this regard was in relation to the human genome, making sure that it progressed and that information was available to the public. This activity was written up (with Georgina Ferry) in our book *The Common Thread*. This led to many talks about affordable medicine and other aspects of scientific responsibility.

I support a number of campaigning organisations including Liberty, Amnesty, British Humanist Association, American Civil Liberties Union (on their gene patent case). I was a member of the Human Genetics Commission for a number of years, and that involved a lot of human rights issues.

Bharti Tailor

Do you think that public authorities generally respect human rights?

I think in comparison with continental Europe, in Britain human rights are legislated for and adhered to, more than in other countries, I would say. I think we have actually activated equality legislation, which is part of this human rights agenda, when many countries in Europe have not. They know it is good, but they have not necessarily enacted it, but we have in Britain. In general, I think we do quite well in human rights in Britain. I can't think of any particular aspect where the Government doesn't cater for or adhere to.

Dr Tobias Lock

Do you think that public bodies generally respect human rights? How does it compare with other jurisdictions?

[. . .] The basic German outlook is less liberal than Great Britain, when it comes to liberty as a concept, but on the whole, I think, human rights are not violated [. . .] In Germany you hear language which is discriminatory. It is not just the linguistic element. You never know what people may think because we are in a very politically correct culture. Overall, however, when it comes to human rights and liberty, there are not many differences between Germany and the UK.

Professor Ronald Hutton

Do you think that the state intervenes too much or not enough in the lives of citizens?

[. . .] Until recently if a Pagan was accused of a crime, which fortunately was rare, the police would automatically search their home and seize all of the books and equipment related to their religion to be presented in court as evidence of their bad character. Now usually when a Pagan is accused of a crime, the police bring in an expert witness to reassure the public that Pagans are not inherently criminal.

Dr Myriam Hunter-Henin

Do you think that public authorities intervene too much or not enough in the lives of individuals and groups specifically in relation to freedom of religion and belief, or they take the right stance in your view?

In England, when public authorities intervene, they will intervene for bureaucratic reasons . . . like charities will have a lot of hassle to go through for tax purposes, filing exemptions, etc. You need to be a lawyer to be able to follow it! But in substance, these administrative burdens will not attack the right in question.

Wendy Huggett

When should the state intervene in the expression of religious beliefs?

Needless to say, Islam does not amount to terrorism, but if someone has a belief that has an impact on other people's human rights and they do something which evokes hatred towards other people and incites hatred, I think the state has an obligation to protect human rights, and when it comes to those situations I wouldn't want the state to sit back. I don't want a Big Brother state, but at the same time I wouldn't want the state to sit back. There are malignant groups which think they should have a free ride because they are religious bodies, but that is simply wrong.

David Harte

Do you think that the state gets the balance right between protection and freedom when it comes to intervening in the lives of citizens, especially in relation to religion?

The secular state is not prepared to distinguish between religious viewpoints. That is unrealistic, because some of them are supporting the liberal traditions which are supportive of social order and co-operation, whereas others are not. And treating them all the same actually puts the beneficial religious traditions at a disadvantage and is harmful for society.

Lucy Powell MP

Do you think in Great Britain public authorities intervene too much or not enough in the lives of individuals and groups, both in general and specifically in relation to freedom of religion and belief?

I think it is different in different places. So much of these issues depend . . . in fact, I was talking earlier about the Prevent Programme, which tries to flag up at an early stage warning signs . . . The principles of that programme are very good indeed, but how they actually operate is very difficult, and a lot of the time it is about training individuals, how they understand these programmes, how they understand their roles, and too often the interpretation of these, either programmes or policies, is left too open at grassroots level. We can do a lot about building awareness. The framework is often there. You can come across examples where the balance is too much one way, or too much the other way.

Professor Dame Jocelyn Bell Burnell

Does the state achieve the right balance between freedom and protection when it comes to intervening in the lives of citizens?

I suspect the state interferes too much in the lives of poor people, people with disability . . . There has been a certain amount of legislation and changes of practice in this country in the last few years, which has made life much more difficult . . . Things such as the bedroom tax, which I don't think is fair, generous or ethical, or any of those things.

Baroness Elizabeth Berridge

Do public authorities achieve the correct level of intervention in the lives of citizens in relation to the expression of religious beliefs?

[. . .] the state doesn't intervene here. It doesn't tell people what to teach, and what is said in the pulpit or by the Iman is governed by the same laws as it is set in Hyde Park Corner. So, it is just the criminal law and, aside of that, you are free to preach.

Nico McNenzie-Juetten

Do you think that there has been enough perception that human rights include children?

Many politicians and practitioners don't realise that children are rights-holders or fully appreciate what that means. There is more awareness, but I think that people still find it difficult at root to see children as people in their own right and with their own rights, rather than in the sense of having rights which flow from their parents' rights and are secondary to those. Interestingly, that can be a particular problem in relation to education, in my view.

Sir Mark Hedley DL

How should the state balance the rights of parents and children in relation to religious education and upbringing?

I think part of the problem is that English law still wrestles with the concept of children rights. The academics are extremely hot on it, and the culture within English society maybe is changing, but traditionally it was very paternalistic. So, religious education was regarded as the responsibility of the parents to decide.

[. . .] There is a fundamental conflict within family law between the need to protect children and the respect for the autonomy of the family, and that will apply to this particular issue as well. We have not, I think, finally addressed conflicts . . . nor I do believe we shall be able to . . . because children – in fact, the younger they are the truer this is, but it is true all the way up – don't survive independently outside a relationship with a parent, or a carer rather, or carers, and therefore, you can't force the distinction between family autonomy and children rights to its logical conclusion . . . You live permanently in a state of tensions in which you try to respect the one against the other [. . .] The judge who may have personal reservations about . . . shall we say male circumcision, he/she is dealing with a Muslim family, it is not likely that he/she will impose his/her views, because of the impact on the child, that may drive him outside of his own community . . . It is not consistent with child welfare. So, in that set up the family views prevail.

Lady Brenda Hale

When is it appropriate/necessary for the state to intervene in citizens manifesting their religious beliefs – for example, to protect the vulnerable, including children?

The question concerning potential conflicts between parents and children in terms of religion is a very interesting one. This answer is very much off the top of my head to what is a very difficult question. There isn't a lot of law in this country. It has been confronted in the United States, with cases like *Wisconsin v Yoder*, where the Amish community said that they didn't want their children to be educated beyond the age of 14, I think it was, as they would be contaminated with modern life if they went any further. That is the perpetual tension between the child's rights to be exposed to the same level of education as any other child in the country versus the parental view that this is damaging from a religious point of view. There could be lots of examples like that in this country at the moment.

Lord Richard Harries of Pentregarth

When do you think public authorities should intervene to limit practical expressions of religious belief by citizens?

[. . .] Public money has been made available at a local level to support interfaith work because it is felt that that builds up community cohesion, and that's absolutely right. And I would also support public money for training imams to make them conversant with English culture and way of life. What's interesting is that there is good historical precedent for this. The government in the early nineteenth century gave government money to support the Roman Catholic seminary at Maynooth because they realised that Roman Catholic clergy then needed a rather better education than they were getting with their own authorities. So, in those kind of positive ways, when it serves the common good not to promote any one faith or denomination, but when it serves the common good there is a case for the state . . . in exactly the same way it supports faith-based social organisations, provided that they are not partisan or only serving members of their own faith or anything like that.

Grace Hatley

How should we respond to challenges to freedom of expression?

[. . .] From a legal point of view, if you are going to find something offensive don't go and watch it, but that play must go ahead. There are always going to be conflicts and arguments, but that does not mean . . . it is important that people have their right to voice their opinions. So, the limits are social, not legal. The legal dimension only comes when there are dangers or threats.

Naveed Choudhry

As an actor, what are your views about the ongoing tension between freedom of speech and protection of religious feelings? Should there be limits?

I think there should be a level of respect. I think that people know when they draw a certain cartoon, people know the message which they are trying to spread with certain material . . . In the editing, etc, the media have a vision, and they know what they want to say, and drama sells, and the more people talk about it . . . if you create something controversial, there will be more media coverage, and people will be intrigued. People will wonder 'what is there in that film? I wanna see' . . . So, selfishly, as a film maker, I could say 'let's produce a reaction, let's see what happens, let's make more money', but then the respect (for me) means that I don't want to offend people [. . .]

Oh dear . . . it is a tricky one. My heart tells me that there should be limits . . . If you are going to attack, people will attack back. My head, however, as an actor and a film maker, tells me something different. I could respect someone's imagination . . . It is a very thought-provoking question, Javier, with the whole freedom of speech in Paris, etc. I have to say that all the controversy with the cartoons, as a Muslim, it does not affect me, because I know that my faith is much bigger than a cartoon, but then you are going to get people who are maybe angry at the world, you give them an excuse, a reason to fight . . . Those things give negative powers to those extremists.

Stephen Castle

Have the events in Paris with the Charlie Hebdo murders had an impact on freedom of expression?

With issues like Charlie Hebdo the British media were actually quite mature. They took the view that freedom of expression was something very important. If one person wanted deliberately to offend others, that was up to them and was their right, but the media didn't all have an obligation to do the same and reprint it. It was a question of editorial judgment.

I think journalism is essential for a democracy and a free media is an underrated element in democracies.

Joe Ahearne

Would you say that there have been any negative developments in relation to freedom of expression in recent years, taking into account the geopolitical climate and Je Suis Charlie etc?

Yes, I would say there are in relation to religion, censorship on that ground has grown, yes. I made a drama series a number of years ago on issues within Catholicism and it was censored on grounds of blasphemy.

It is a difficult line to draw, because if you are talking about the Mohammed cartoons, then racism and Islamophobia get mixed in with issues about freedom of expression. It has become more difficult in the last 20 years though.

Philip Bird

What role do the arts have in defending freedoms and pointing out injustice?

[. . .] Theatre is unique in the sense that it is using something live, where you can give a voice to someone who doesn't normally have a voice and bring something into focus which would have got buried on page 14 of the newspaper or never even been properly publicised. It is invaluable for airing problems or paradoxes in society.

Alison Steadman

Would you say that the arts have a role in building a more cohesive and empathetic society?

Oh, absolutely. On the stage you can say and do things that you never would in a one-to-one with somebody; you can express and show people things in films and plays, which explains things more clearly; you can show human life and all of the sides of it. It's so important that we keep that freedom of speech. I wouldn't want someone to say that we don't do this play because it says this or that. This will help people to understand someone else's point of view and have empathy for their situation.

Joe Ahearne

Do you see the arts as having a particular contribution to make to society, especially when it comes to the collective dialogue on human rights?

Yes, they do. It's difficult to pursue certain changes in human rights or the status of certain groups without seeing those groups represented. Representation only happens in two spheres, media and the arts. So the arts have a strong influence on the progress of things.

Daisuke Miura

How can the arts positively contribute to society, especially in terms of freedom?

Through the arts I believe that it will open our eyes and make us realise what kind of feeling and opinion we truly have. And I would like to . . . I believe in using the arts as a tool to connect with the others and I think that's the answer. It is a tool to connect and try to transfer, to make other people understand the message you are trying to give, and thereby influence other people's opinions or theories or principles. If it works, it will help other people to grow for themselves. It is achieving something by not doing something . . . you try to do some kind of difficult step; once you have achieved it you feel like, suddenly feel like a different person, reborn. I think the arts have the power to do that, the power to make you suddenly grow and mature. It makes other people happy, enables you to connect with people. That's my programme.

The Rev'd Professor Martin Henig

How do you regard religious bodies being permitted certain exemptions from discrimination law?

I think that this is thoroughly wrong. Jesus was quite clearly against discrimination and I don't think that any religion should claim an exemption from what are in reality the human rights of others. It seems to me to be a contradiction of what religion should be about.

Dr Martin Clarke

What is your feeling towards religious groups who want greater exemptions from general legal rules? Things like the 'cake case'?[184]

I think my instinctive reaction as somebody who is theologically and socially inclined to a reasonably liberal point of view, would be tough! Get on with it! You are restricting somebody else's rights and freedom. In the cake case, is that such a fundamental aspect of Christian faith as some groups make out? No . . . On the other hand, having a friend who is a senior Methodist minister in a multicultural part of Birmingham, he is concerned that whilst a liberal Christian viewpoint would be as I suggest, that has difficulties in interfaith relations. I'm not sure . . . in some cases I think I would rather see engagement with points where the religious belief comes into conflict with the law of the land, say on gender equality, to be debated from the theological perspective of that particular religion, than recourse to secular law. But my own liberal inclinations would be to go with secular law.

Jim Sutcliffe

How do you feel about religious individuals being allowed exemptions from discrimination law when dealing with the public?

I don't know. If you run a bed-and-breakfast you go into that with your eyes open. In this profession, I had people in the shop who aren't necessarily the kind of people I'd socialise with, but their money is as good as anybody else's. Providing that they don't give me any issues as far as violence or rudeness, I don't see any problem with it [. . .]

184 The 'gay cake' case: see 'Belfast Gay-Themed Cake Case will not go to the UK Supreme Court', *The Guardian* (21 Dec 2016), https://www.theguardian.com/law/2016/dec/21/belfast-gay-themed-cake-case-will-not-go-uk-supreme-court.

Obviously, being a business we have all kinds of people come through the door – gay, transgender, all kinds of ethnic origin – and to be honest there's good and bad among them all. The homosexual sector is probably one of our most profitable; they enjoy nice things, they don't have any kids to spend money on, so they spend more on themselves.

Anyway, if you open a bed-and-breakfast you have to take whoever comes. What if someone didn't like ethnic minorities? There's no way on earth you could run a bed-and-breakfast and say 'I don't like black people so I'm not letting them stay'. Where would you draw the line if you allowed discrimination? Where do you say what's right and what's wrong. There are all sorts of things that people believe in or don't believe in. If you don't like that kind of thing, don't open a bed-and-breakfast.

Joanna Griffiths

Should religious businesses be allowed exemptions from discrimination law?

I think that some religious people discriminate against people and I don't think religious views give you the right to basically abuse other people, because that is what the owners of the hotel were doing. I don't know where in the Bible it is said that they should not admit people into their hotels because of their sexual orientation. So, I concur with the judicial decision.

Rev David Robertson

Some commentators have stated that increasingly we are witnessing a hierarchy of rights when it comes to freedom of religion and belief and prohibition of discrimination on different grounds, including sexual orientation. Do you think that is happening in Great Britain, although theoretically there is not such a hierarchy?

Absolutely! There is a hierarchy of rights, and many of the rights . . . what bothers me is the lack of basis. So, if someone says, for example, 'there must be a right to same-sex marriage', my view is that same-sex marriage is an oxymoron . . . it is like arguing for a square circle. My view would be that human rights . . . homosexuals should not be discriminated against and homophobia is wrong, but if you redefine marriage for everybody, then to me, I don't accept that definition and I reserve the right to disagree with it. One of my concerns is that human rights are being taught as obvious . . . and I don't like that sense of 'obvious'. That is a sort of fundamentalism. I warned a few years ago that if we followed the route of same-sex marriage, we would have to end up discussing polygamy. I was told not to be ridiculous, but that is certainly the case now. Or something as complex as transgender, I have done a lot of work with transgender people. It is very complex, very difficult, but all of a sudden in our media people just say that you can change sex if you want it. No, no . . . it is more difficult than that. And immediately people jump to your throat and they accuse you of being unloving or whatever . . . So what bothers me is that morality and ethics and rights are not thought through. They have put in an emotive or media level, which later on politicians catch up with, if you like. But I am concerned about the basis in law of human rights. That is my main concern.

Joe Ahearne

So you would say that religion has generally been a negative force when it comes to human rights?

Absolutely, in terms of my rights as a gay man.

Roque Santa Cruz

Do you think that within the world of sports there is enough respect for individuals in relation to their personal beliefs? Do you think that there are challenges for sports people who are openly religious?

I have played in Germany, England, Spain, Mexico and in Paraguay, and I have never experienced a single problem in relation to personal beliefs. To the contrary, I found that sports were so multicultural, so universal, a big window of understanding and such an open-minded subject, that they enabled you to compete, work hard and respect others' efforts, to achieve friendship through sports, to celebrate victories and suffer losses with different kinds of people, no matter colour or religions. It should be seen as a way to fight those differences.

Danny Batth

Are there challenges for religious people in the field of sports?

I think sports are a difficult world for religious people. Obviously in England Christianity is the majority, and if you are anything else, Jewish, Sikh, Muslim, whatever . . . obviously it is more challenging. The Ramadan period for Muslim . . . if you are fasting, you just have to get on with it. You really don't have an option to get a special treatment really. So, I think being openly religious in sports is challenging. Of course, it depends on the person. If you are confident and can take a bit of banter, you are fine . . . but I think people who are a bit quiet, they are not so sure and they don't talk about it, they may find it difficult.

Joaquin Acedo

Do you see problems in football involving discrimination based on race, sexual orientation, etc?

You clearly see in the world of football that there is a problem with racism in some areas, especially in certain stadiums in Britain, Spain and Germany. Above all, black players are treated quite badly.

Dr Catharine Morgan

Do you think that state-sponsored chaplains are appropriate?

There is a role for spirituality in hospitals, hospices and prisons, and my strongest example of that is working in a hospice where we had a chaplain who came every day, saw all the patients, and it didn't matter at all what religion they followed or none, because they knew they could talk about anything, their pains, their worries . . . she was someone with whom they could discuss the meanings of their lives, and I think there must be a space to do that; I think it should be paid for by the state . . . you could say that the Church could send someone for free, and some people would argue that spiritual care is not part of healthcare, but I think it is.

Carole Emmerson

Should there be a universal right to free medical care?

There is a financial limit for a universal right to free medical care. It would be great if there were an open door policy for anyone from the world who came for treatment here, but you know there are financial restrictions. I am afraid it is not a realistic one, perhaps in an ideal world. There must be a limit, drugs for cancer and stuff like that . . . there are limited pots, and I think people have responsibilities. We talk about rights, but people also have a duty to look after themselves. Many people don't, but still expect excellent medical care, when actually they are contributing to their situation.

Professor Sir John Sulston

What do you think about faith schools?

There is a very clear distinction in my mind between state-funded schools, which should teach the curriculum especially in relation to science, and other types of school. I think that there are different issues with privately funded schools. I do think personally that it is wrong, morally wrong, that parents should try and influence their children by denying them information. But I think that on the whole it is probably better to try and persuade people rather than force them in terms of how they bring up their children.

Joanna Griffiths

How do you feel about faith schools?

Faith schools are a source of segregation in my view. Probably not the Church schools as they take children from all or no religious backgrounds, but certainly what is happening in Britain at the moment is that the Muslim community is being given the opportunity to educate their children separately from other children. I don't think that is right, as it can lead to segregation and to a lack of understanding of all religions. If you have all children together in one place and you talk about all religions, that would enhance cohesion, understanding and a much better relationship among people of all faiths.

Sir Gareth Edwards CBE

Do you think that faith schools are a good or a bad thing for British society?

Because of the background I had, I think that you are better to have a mixture and benefit from other people's views. You have to be able to understand and compromise. One of the most difficult things for human beings is to understand each other. And there is a danger in religion of the extremist view. It's all right having strong views and a belief, but quite often believing that you are right causes grief to other people.

Lucy Skilbeck

How do you feel about faith schools?

If you have a school of any complexion whether it's a faith school or a free school or whatever, but if you have a school that limits the children's education and denies them access to things that we understand as a society to be useful things for children to learn about and children in the mainstream are being taught about, including things like evolution, gender equality and sex education then I think that's really problematic. I think that a good social education is important, a good scientific education is important, a good cultural education is important, a good personal education is important. I don't share concerns about faith schools per se indoctrinating or inculcating a certain kind of belief system – in part because in my son's experience it didn't do that (he went to a very diversely mixed C of E school), which is obviously purely anecdotal. But where schools are teaching a narrow doctrine and not a pluralist curriculum I have serious concerns, whether they are faith schools or free schools or independent schools or any other kind of schools.

Lucy Gorman

How do you feel about faith schools?

I think faith schools are, generally speaking, good. To a certain extent, parents have the right to have their children educated according to their beliefs, but at the same time children cannot be ignorant about some issues; they need to have knowledge about some matters, including sexual education, as well as education on other religions . . . When I was in school I was never given any type of relationship education; I didn't know if my sexuality was normal or not . . . if we include it in the education system, the child will know that is normal . . .

Aled Griffiths

How do you regard faith schools?

I am not a particular fan of faith schools. Having said that, my upbringing was in non-faith schools, but it had a Christian orientation. What has happened in Wales is that there is very little religious education in Welsh schools and I find that strange for two reasons: (i) I don't think that values which I hold dear emerge unless they are taught; (ii) the only reason we have our language in Wales is that it was preserved by the chapels, and religion will still play an important role in this. Most Welsh people of my generation were happy to talk about religion in Welsh, because that was our upbringing. I think theologically in Welsh, and I would find it difficult in English, but I would talk about mathematics in English. The Welsh language is a crucial part of our culture.

Conclusion

We began our study with the intention of bringing into the foreground an aspect of the constitutional framework which is often relegated to the periphery of academic discussion, namely its religious dimension. Generally speaking, this is only brought into the limelight in order to be critiqued at the level of abstract principle, or when some very particular elements of its structures are creaking under the strains of twenty-first-century social and political pressures (for example, the compulsory daily act of worship within state schools without a religious character).

We sought to break this mould, and ask what it means for Great Britain, in practical legal terms, to operate its unique brand of Church/state relations in the modern era. Are the models of establishment in England and Scotland anachronistic, or even actively damaging in terms of the rights and freedoms of citizens and the cohesion of society as a whole? Rather than commencing with theoretical debates about the benefits and pitfalls of establishment in the realm of abstract ideas, we sought to uncover what establishment means when earthed in the particular setting of Great Britain. We started by tracing its historical development in England, Wales and Scotland – the three nations under consideration – and examining what this evolutionary process has left behind. We then moved on to assess the implications this has for citizens with religious beliefs, and also with strong beliefs not of a religious nature, before finally questioning how the religious character of the Constitution interacts with its foundations: the rule of law, parliamentary supremacy, checks and balances and separation of powers, as well as human rights.

In the course of this journey, we came to a number of striking and, at times, surprising conclusions.

Importantly, the process of legal evolution in relation to religious and secular power has left behind something far more nuanced than an establishment pattern of Church/state relations. The momentous events of the era of European Reformations forged in England, Wales and Scotland formed ties between national Churches and the state, as a variety of primary legislative instruments attest. Yet, the story by no means ended at that point, and both legal and political history continued to unfold. The consequences of being a self-consciously Christian state, with explicit national understandings of Christianity, diffused their way through the legal system as a whole, and the effects of establishment were not confined to constitutional law (even allowing for the fairly porous relationship between public and private law in a context without a codified Constitution).

It was axiomatic for both judges and the legislature that the official religion should be supported and advanced, and there were several respects in which the legal system as a whole actively sought to promote and facilitate the practice of Anglicanism, and to a lesser extent Presbyterianism in Scotland. Furthermore, there were a significant number of disadvantages for citizens who did not adhere to Anglicanism, such as bars to studying at Cambridge or Oxford, or becoming a Member of Parliament. Thus, there was positive support for individuals to remain within, or convert to, the state-endorsed faith on the one hand, and strong disincentives against leaving on the other.

As the nineteenth century progressed, however, it became increasingly unacceptable for the legal machinery of the state to practise coercive discrimination, and religion came to be perceived more and more as a matter of private conviction, rather than concern for the body politic. Moreover, in tandem with this development, there was a burgeoning discourse in relation to what would ultimately become the arena of human rights, and a gathering sense that individuals had a *right* to choose their own spiritual identity. A convergence of these two streams meant that the systemic privileging of Anglican citizens to the detriment of others was addressed, albeit in a piecemeal and haphazard fashion. Crucially for our purposes, the preferred approach was generally not to strip Anglicans of the legal benefits which they enjoyed, but to open them up to citizens of other faiths.

It is important to appreciate that the movement was not one which problematised religion in any way – quite the reverse. The juridical system shifted from treating the practice of established religions as a positive phenomenon to regarding the practice of other Christian denominations, and later all faiths, as positive. This was reflected, for example, in charity law, which gradually came to support the advancement not just of Anglicanism but of *any* religion.

Effectively, these developments generated a tripartite structure, which we have likened to a Russian doll. On the inside, we have the formal ties between Church and state, which are the embodiment of the establishment relationship. Next, we have a systemic support for the Christian religion in general terms, and finally we have the outer layer of positivity towards the practice of religion.

There is, we have suggested, a perception of religious faith as a phenomenon, which the legal system supports, and therefore a soft presumption in favour of enabling and facilitating its practice where possible. We characterise the presumption as soft, because although the starting point for both the courts and the legislature is that of supporting religion, this stance will readily give way if there are factors that push against it, ordinarily harm to society or identifiable risks for vulnerable individuals. For instance, religious convictions will not permit citizens who wish to run a business to discriminate against others on the basis of protected characteristics. In addition, the systemic approach is frequently nuanced when it comes to a balancing of rights. For example, ritual male circumcision is at present accepted as lawful, but it is treated as an exemption from the general criminal law, which rejects the possibility of consent as a defence for actual bodily harm. In recognising that the behaviour would ordinarily be criminal, the courts have effectively kept this practice in an amber zone. It is a clear signal that it is at the outer margin of what the law will tolerate in the sphere of parental religious choice, and there is clear scope for further differentiation. Although the point has not been tested, it is very possible, for example, that circumcision carried out on minors in the absence of pain relief is outside the scope of the exemption. While male children may be lawfully circumcised for religious reasons, faith communities have not been given *carte blanche* in this arena.

Thus, we draw two key conclusions, the first of which is that establishment cannot be addressed in isolation. It is, by no means, the only feature which justifies the characterisation of the present Constitution and surrounding legal framework as religious. As stated, it must be understood as part of a tripartite suite of characteristics, the most significant of which is the treatment of religion as a positive phenomenon and the soft presumption in favour of facilitating its practice. In light of this essential trait (and the plethora of legal provisions which it has generated), we would go as far as to assert that even if an Act of Parliament were to disestablish both the Church of England and the Church of Scotland, it would still be both appropriate, and indeed necessary, to characterise the legal framework as religious. Second, this religious legal framework does not just benefit members of the established Churches, it supports *all* citizens who have religious convictions.

For most purposes, religious convictions in this setting include all convictions on religious matters – Atheism, Humanism and all other conscious ideological standpoints on faith matters. It may be counterintuitive to assert that Atheists and Humanists benefit from a religious legal paradigm, but as citizens who own and assert a conscious position on faith-based matters, they are beneficiaries of the support and recognition which the juridical system affords to *all* identifiable positions in relation to faith.

The explanation for this lies in the outworking of our tripartite model. While establishment is the smallest, innermost doll, and in some respects the least important of the three characteristics in the suite, it is by no means insignificant. It provides structures and a template into which other groups defined by their convictions on religion can step and participate. This applies to all faith groups, but equally to Humanist or Atheist organisations. For example, representatives can offer to contribute to school assemblies in state schools without a religious character, and this will frequently be taken up as there is a precedent and understanding of this role. Other groups can and do provide speakers and an official presence for civic occasions such as Remembrance Sunday. Rather than hampering the participation of other faith and religious conviction groups in public life, establishment has the capacity to facilitate it.

We do not, of course, claim that the system is perfect or that all groups always participate in the same manner. So, for example, citizens of some Pagan traditions, which would reject the hierarchical or organised religious practice, might find it more challenging to enter arenas which are geared towards dealing with formal, recognised groups such as the Methodist Church or the British Humanist Association. Equally, at times, Atheist or Humanist groups might feel marginalised in fora where there is a consciously religious (as opposed to religious conviction) dynamic. Different groups face different internal and external challenges in managing their levels and styles of participation, and at times the legal system could do more to facilitate this, for example, by providing Humanist celebrants with a mechanism to carry out legally recognised marriages in England and Wales.

Nevertheless, one strength of the current establishment model is that it is flexible and adaptable, and in general terms has a malleability which enables it to fit around changing and competing needs and expectations. The reality is that no alternative model, whether towards the religious or secular end of the Church/state relationship spectrum, could hope to provide a one-size-fits-all solution which would satisfy the desires of all citizens in all contexts. Ultimately, establishment in Great Britain is an embodiment of the notion that faith and religious convictions are valued and supported by society, and this principle is one that a wide range of people from diverse background warmly endorse.

We do not, however, dismiss the perspective of citizens without strong religious convictions of any sort. Indeed, our next finding was to suggest that the religious character of the legal framework benefits citizens who hold profound beliefs on matters unrelated to religion. We would suggest that while the religious legal framework *directly* benefits citizens with non-Anglican/Presbyterian religious convictions (including those of an Atheist or Humanist nature), it *indirectly* benefits citizens who have other types of profound belief. This happens in three ways, and such beliefs receive protection and recognition by (i) association with religious groups/beliefs; (ii) analogy with religious beliefs; and (iii) support for personal convictions which goes beyond the parameters of Article 9 of the European Convention on Human Rights.

In concrete terms, as we have seen, the first pacifists to receive legal exemptions were religiously motivated, but citizens who identified as pacifists for other reasons came very properly to enjoy equal recognition and respect by the twentieth century. Furthermore, the movement towards freedom of religion flowed naturally into the crystallisation of freedom of conscience as a concept and we suggest that one factor in this at times has been an analogy with religion. In certain instances, courts have understood and protected an expression of freedom of conscience because the issue has been likened to a religious principle in qualitative terms. This has been seen in relation to convictions concerning alternative medicine, for example. Finally, because a respect for religious faith has over time engendered a systemic respect for belief more widely, the legal system also demonstrates protective regard towards beliefs which are not necessarily capable of satisfying the criteria for protection under Article 9 of the Convention. A belief in fairies or nature spirits of the landscape is one instance of this, and there is evidence that British authorities have taken cognisance and accommodated such beliefs, even though it is by no means clear that they are required to do so, based solely on case law relating to the types of belief that trigger Article 9. We suggest that this openness is highly positive, because the further a belief is from mainstream thought, the harder it may be for an applicant to show that it is serious and worthy of respect. Going beyond the boundaries of Article 9 potentially provides an additional layer of protection for those who hold ideas which are out of sync with the majority outlook.

Having reached this point, we then moved on to our focused constitutional discussion. We tested the functioning of our religious legal system against the pillars of the Constitution: the rule of law, parliamentary supremacy, separation of powers and checks and balances, and human rights. In each case we looked at relevant manifestations of the religious dimension of the legal framework, and discovered that they were not merely compatible with these principles, but positively enhanced them.

So, for example, in placing some consensual physical assaults (ritual male circumcision and religious mortification) in the category of exemptions from the general criminal prohibition on assault occasioning actual bodily harm, the courts have effectively kept such conduct in an amber zone. This approach effectively supports parliamentary supremacy. It recognises that Parliament has repeatedly declined to pass legislation in numerous statutory overhauls of the law on assault to criminalise what are frequently open and widely known practices. At the same time, it makes it clear that this behaviour is close to the frontier of criminal conduct, and is apt to be publicly examined. This assists in flagging up potentially problematic situations for Parliament to revisit if necessary.

Equally, in developing a chameleon character of religious ministers when it comes to employment status, the legal system has bolstered the rule of law. On the one hand, respect for religious convictions has been a longstanding factor in the consistent judicial refusal to infer an employment contract for employment law purposes where an intent to create legal relations in secular terms would have been incompatible with the doctrines of the relevant faith. Yet, at the same time, a willingness to treat religious ministers as quasi-employees for the purposes of vicarious liability has prevented victims of tortious conduct being denied the same avenues for recourse which would be open to them in a non-religious setting.

Nor is the enhancement of constitutional principles a phenomenon confined to the judiciary. In relation to child exorcism, the legal system as a whole can be seen to be working in concert in order to balance conflicting goals (respect for freedoms in relation to religion and family life on the one hand, and the imperative to protect vulnerable minors from grave harm on the other), and consequently this supports the principle of separation of powers. Parliament has considered the matter on several occasions and decided not to pass specific legislation prohibiting child exorcism, but a number of manifestations of the executive (such as government ministers and police forces) have developed guidance to assist in protecting children, while respecting the autonomy of faith communities. Furthermore, the judiciary oversees the use and implementation of executive power in this regard, and ensures that statutory agencies meet the general duties and standards set out in legislation such as the Children Act 1989. A sensitivity towards religious needs from all branches of the state, combined with a robust rejection of unconditional support for faith-based practices, has been beneficial in creating a context in which damaging behaviour can be addressed without an undue restriction of liberty. These two distinct aims guide the application of checks and balances in the interaction between the various organs of state in this arena.

All in all, in juridical terms, we suggest that the religious dimension of the legal framework is an asset for our Constitution. We do not assert that it is one which would necessarily translate to another context, but in Great Britain, with its particular history and dynamics, it functions in a beneficial manner. Inevitably, there are some specific elements of it which are ripe for reform and renegotiation, but the system as a whole is fit for purpose. We maintain that this should be recognised and celebrated, rather than side-lined or viewed through a negative prism. Too many commentators have assumed that establishment is anachronistic, or have attacked it from an ivory tower of abstract theory, without examining how it actually functions in Great Britain specifically and the tangible positive contributions which it brings to the table in terms of the Constitution and legal framework.

In the course of our analysis, we have also taken time in each of the chapters that examines a constitutional pillar to consider how the ideas and teachings of various faiths might influence adherents in relation to that pillar. We do not ask what a particular denomination teaches about the principle as, for reasons explained, that would frequently be neither a meaningful nor a fruitful question, but we do explore what building blocks each faith tradition gives followers when it comes to constructing their own perspectives. The purpose of these passages has been to challenge the tendency for religious outlooks to be uncritically problematised. It can be seen that, in most cases, the ideas provided by the faith lend themselves naturally to building a positive and supportive stance towards the foundational principles of our Constitution. Not all individuals will necessarily form such an opinion, but it is misguided to cast religion as a phenomenon in a negative light in relation to ideas such as human rights or the rule of law.

We also note that the positivity shown towards belief more widely enables many conviction-led groups, which are not religious in nature, to foster positive approaches towards constitutional principles and the legal system more widely. We considered, for instance, how groups like the Badger Trust and Stonewall enhance the application of the rule of law (in the former case by facilitating the prosecution of illegal harm to wildlife, while condemning and rejecting criminal tactics for protecting the UK badger population) and human rights (in the latter cases by promoting equal and positive treatment for all citizens, regardless of their sexual and gender identity). Again, we clearly acknowledge that by no means all beliefs which bind groups of citizens together are beneficial to social cohesion or the operation of the Constitution. However, many conviction-led groups do enhance the social, legal and environmental landscape of Britain.

Often, criticism is the bread-and-butter of academic discourse, and being academics we have naturally found aspects of our legal and constitutional system to critique along the way. However, our fundamental conclusions are, in the main, positive. Our study has shown us that the religious dimension of our juridical system is not an encumbrance in the twenty-first century, and it is in fact an asset. It provides direct benefits for all citizens with religious convictions and indirect benefits for those with non-religious convictions. It enhances the pillars of our Constitution and gives us a gateway for inclusion and diversity. It is necessary that the flaws in any legal system are identified and reformed, but it is equally vital that the positive elements are recognised. If commentators fail to do this, there is a constant risk of throwing the baby out with the bathwater, and losing characteristics which greatly benefit our society.

As a final note of positivity, we should stress once more that the interview material included in this book has not been inserted to drive or prove our conclusions. Our legal analysis has been entirely separate from this. Nevertheless, we are convinced that this work is a far richer resource for its inclusion. The perspectives and insights of our interviewees remind us that, while opinions vary greatly on the questions we have been considering, they are of relevance and importance to us all, regardless of religious or professional background, age, gender, race, or any of the other categories into which human beings so often divide themselves. We are all part of a collective project while living together as a society, and all have a stake in our Constitution and legal system, and specifically in their interaction with religion and belief.

References

Chapter 1

Books

American Missionary Fellowship, *The Life of John Knox* (Attic Books: Green Forest, Arizona) 2011.
Aylett, J.F., *In Search of History 1485–1715* (Hodder & Stoughton: London) 1984.
Baker, J.H., *An Introduction to English Legal History* (Butterworths: London) 3rd edn, 1990.
Barrow, G.W.S., *R. Bruce and the Community of the Realm of Scotland* (Edinburgh University Press: Edinburgh) 1988.
Bede, *The Age of Bede* (Penguin: London) 1998.
Bennett, M., *The Civil Wars in Britain and Ireland: 1638–1651* (Wiley: Chichester) 1997.
Bonner, G., D. Rollason and C. Stancliffe, *St Cuthbert, His Cult and His Community to AD 1200* (The Boydell Press: Woodbridge) 1989.
Boswell, J., *The Life of Johnson* (Westminster, A. Constable & Co: Philadelphia) 1901.
Brown, C.G., *The Social History of Religion in Scotland since 1730* (Methuen: New York) 1987.
Burgess, G. & M. Festenstein, *English Radicalism 1550–1850* (Cambridge University Press: Cambridge) 2007.
Cavill, P., *Anglo-Saxon Christianity* (Fount: London) 1999.
Chamber, P., *Religion, Secularisation and Social Change in Wales: Congregational Studies in Post-Christian Society* (University of Wales Press: Cardiff) 2005.
Chapman, H.W., *Lady Jane Grey* (Pan Books: Bucks) 1962.
Cheyne, A., *The Transforming of the Kirk: Victorian Scotland's Religious Revolution* (St Andrews Press: Edinburgh) 1983.
Cowan, E.J., *For Freedom Alone: The Declaration of Arbroath 1320* (Tuckwell Press: East Lothian) 2003.
Devine, T.M., *The Scottish Nation 1700–2000* (Penguin: London) 1999.
Driscoll, S., *Alba: The Gaelic Kingdom of Scotland AD 800–1124* (Birlin: Edinburgh) 2002.
Duffy, E., *Fires of Faith: Catholic England under Mary Tudor* (Yale University Press: New Haven and London) 2010.
Duffy, E., *The Stripping of the Altars: Traditional Religion in England 1400–1580* (Yale University Press: New Haven and London) 2005.
Duffy, E., *The Voices of Morebath* (Yale University Press: New Haven & London) 2003.
Garbett, C. (Archbishop of York), *The Claims of the Church of England* (Hodder & Stoughton: London) 1947.

Gilley, S. and W. Sheils (eds), *A History of Religion in Britain: Practice and Beliefs from Pre-Roman Times to the Present* (Wiley Blackwell: Oxford) 1994.

Guy, J., *Queen of Scots: The True Life of Mary Stuart* (HMH: Boston) 2005.

Fissel, M., *The Bishops' Wars: Charles I's Campaigns against Scotland, 1638–1640* (Cambridge University Press: Cambridge) 1994.

Fletcher, R., *The Conversion of Europe: From Paganism to Christianity 371–1386 AD* (Fontana Press: London) 1998.

Fraser, A., *Cromwell, Our Chief of Men* (Mandarin: Reading) 1993.

Fraser, A., *Mary Queen of Scots* (World Books: London) 2nd edn, 1971.

Hadley, D., *The Vikings in England* (Manchester University Press: Manchester) 2006.

Hall, D., *Muscular Christianity: Embodying the Victorian Age (Cambridge Studies in Nineteenth-Century Literature and Culture)* (Cambridge University Press: Cambridge) 1994.

Hempton, D., *Religion and Political Culture in Britain and Ireland* (Cambridge University Press: Cambridge) 1996.

Hill, C., *The World Turned Upside Down: Radical Ideas During the English Revolution* (Penguin: London) 1991.

Johnston, A., *The British Empire, Colonialism, and Missionary Activity* (Cambridge University Press: Cambridge) 2003.

Kent, J., *Wesley and the Wesleyans: Religion in Eighteenth Century Britain* (Cambridge University Press: Cambridge) 2002.

MacDougall, N., *An Antidote to the English: The Auld Alliance 1295–1560* (Tuckwell Press: East Lothian) 2001.

Munsey Turner, J., *John Wesley: The Evangelical Revival and the Rise of Methodism in England* (Epworth Press: Peterborough) 2002.

Nicholson, A., *Power and Glory: Jacobean England and the Making of the King James Bible* (Harper Perennial: London) 2003.

Nockles, P.B., *The Oxford Movement in Context: Anglican High Churchmanship 1760–1857* (Cambridge University Press: Cambridge) 1994.

Oakley, F., *Empty Bottles of Gentilism: Kingship and the Divine in Late Antiquity and the Early Middle Ages (to 1050)* (Yale University Press: New Haven) 2010.

Patterson, W., *James VI and I and the Reunion of Christendom* (Cambridge University Press: Cambridge) 2000.

Pope, R. (ed.), *Religion and National Identity: Wales and Scotland c1700–2000* (University of Wales Press: Cardiff) 2001.

Rack, H.D., *Reasonable Enthusiast: John Wesley and the Rise of Methodism* (Epworth Press: London) 2002.

Ridley, J., *Bloody Mary's Martyrs* (Constable and Robinson: London) 2001.

Russell, C., *Causes of the English Civil War* (Oxford University Press: Oxford) 1990.

Russell, F.H., *The Just War in the Middle Ages* (Cambridge University Press: Cambridge) 1976.

Sampson, F., *Visions and Voyages: The Story of Our Celtic Heritage* (Triangle: London) 1998.

Sandberg, R., *Law and Religion* (Cambridge University Press: Cambridge) 2011.

Sheldrake, P., *Living Between Worlds: Place and Journey in Celtic Spirituality* (DLT: London) 1995.

Shelton Reed, J., *Glorious Battle: The Cultural Politics of Victorian Anglo-Catholicism* (Vanderbilt University Press: Nashville) 1996.

Stephen, J., *Presbyterians and the Act of Union 1707* (Edinburgh University Press: Edinburgh) 2007.

Stockwood, M., *Chanctonbury Ring: The Autobiography of Mervyn Stockwood* (Hodder & Stoughton: London) 1982.
Turner, R.V., *King John* (Longman: London and New York) 1994.
Wood, M., *In Search of the Dark Ages* (Ariel: London) 1981.
Yorke, B., *The Conversion of Britain 600–800* (Pearson: Edinburgh) 2006.

Articles, book chapters and conference papers

Ames, R.A. & H.C. Montgomery, 'The Influence of Rome on the American Constitution', *The Classical Journal*, Vol. 30, No. 1 (1934) 19–27.
Barnes, R.P., 'Scotland and the Glorious Revolution of 1688', *Albion: A Quarterly Journal Concerned with British Studies*, Vol. 3, No. 3 (1971) 116–27.
Brown, R.L., 'In Pursuit of a Welsh Episcopate', in R. Pope (ed.), *Religion and National Identity: Wales and Scotland c.1700–2000* (University of Wales Press: Cardiff) 2001, 84–102.
Burgess, G., 'Introduction', in G. Burgess & M. Festenstein, *English Radicalism 1550–1850* (Cambridge University Press: Cambridge) 2007, 1.
Burgess, G., 'Radicalism and the English Revolution', in G. Burgess & M. Festenstein, *English Radicalism 1550–1850* (Cambridge University Press: Cambridge) 2007, 62.
Burgess, G., 'The Divine Right of Kings Reconsidered', *The English Historical Review*, Vol. 107, No. 425 (1992) 837–61.
Chibnall, M., 'The Empress Matilda and Church Reform', *Transactions of the Royal Historical Society*, Vol. 38 (1988) 107–30.
Doe, N. & R. Sandberg, 'Church-State Relations in Europe', *Religion Compass*, Vol 1, No. 5 (2007) 561–78.
García Oliva, J., 'The Denominational Teaching of Religion in Spanish State Schools', in M. Hunter-Henin (ed.), *Law, Religious Freedoms and Education in Europe* (Ashgate: Surrey) 2011, 183–206.
Graham, F.M., 'Conflict and Sacred Space in Reformation-Era Scotland', *Albion: A Quarterly Journal Concerned with British Studies*, Vol. 33, No. 3 (2001) 371–87.
Gray, J.W., 'The Problem of Papal Power in the Ecclesiology of St Bernard', *Transactions of the Royal Historical Society*, Vol. 24 (1974) 1–17.
Hamburger, P.A., 'Natural Rights, Natural Law, and American Constitutions', *The Yale Law Journal*, Vol. 102, No. 4 (1993) 907–60.
Harris, B., 'The Anglo-Scottish Treaty of Union, 1707 in 2007: Defending the Revolution, Defeating the Jacobites', *The Journal of British Studies*, Vol. 49, Special Issue 01 (2010) 28– 46, 35.
Helmholz, R.H., 'Magna Carta and the Ius Commune', *University of Chicago Law Review*, Vol. 66, No. 2 (1999) 297–371, 301.
Howe, D.W., 'Why the Scottish Enlightenment Was Useful to Framers of the American Constitution', *Comparative Studies in Society and History*, Vol. 31, No. 3 (1989) 572–87.
Hutton, R., 'How Pagan Were the Medieval English?', *Folklore*, Vol. 122, No. 3 (2011) 235–49.
Hyman, E.H., 'A Church Militant: Scotland, 1661–1690', *The Sixteenth Century Journal*, Vol. 26, No. 1 (1995) 49–74.
James, E.W., 'The New Birth of a People: Welsh Language and Identity and the Welsh Methodists c1740–1820', in R. Pope (ed.), *Religion and National Identity: Wales and Scotland c1700–2000* (University of Wales Press: Cardiff) 2001, 14.
Kelsey, S., 'The Trial of Charles I', *The English Historical Review*, Vol. 118, No. 477 (2003) 583–616.

Kennedy, A.D., 'Reducing that Barbarous Country: Center, Periphery, and Highland Policy in Restoration Britain', *Journal of British Studies*, Vol. 52, No. 3 (2013) 597–614.

Macdonald, A.R., 'James VI and I: The Church of Scotland and British Ecclesiastical Convergence', *The Historical Journal*, Vol. 48, No. 4 (2005) 855–903.

Mackillop, A., 'The Political Culture of the Scottish Highlands from Culloden to Waterloo', *The Historical Journal*, Vol. 46, No. 3 (2003) 511–32.

Marshall, P., 'The Greatest Man in Wales: James Ap Gruffydd Ap Hywel and the International Opposition to Henry VIII', *The Sixteenth Century Journal*, Vol. 39, No. 3 (2008) 681–704.

McLynn, F., 'Issues and Motives in the Jacobite Rising 1745', *The Eighteenth Century*, Vol. 23 No. 2 (1982).

Nederman, C.J., 'The Liberty of the Church and the Road to Runnymede: John of Salisbury and the Intellectual Foundations of the Magna Carta', *PS: Political Science and Politics*, Vol. 43, No. 3 (2010) 456–61.

Parry, K., 'Constitutional Change: Timeline for 1911: House of Commons Background Paper, Standard Note SN/PC 06256', *Parliament and Constitution Centre* (21 Dec 2012).

Robbins, K., 'Religion and Community in Scotland and Wales since 1800', S. Gilley and W. Sheils (eds), *A History of Religion in Britain: Practice and Belief from Pre-Roman Times to the Present* (Wiley Blackwell: Oxford) 1994, 363.

Veitch, K., 'The Alliance between Church and State in Early Medieval Alba', *Albion: A Quarterly Journal Concerned with British Studies*, Vol. 30, No. 2 (1998) 193–220.

Warren Hollister, C., 'Courtly Culture and Courtly Style in the Anglo-Norman World', *Albion: A Quarterly Journal Concerned with British Studies*, Vol. 20, No. 1 (1988) 1–17.

Williams, C., 'British Religion and the Wider World: Mission and Empire 1800–1940', in S. Gilley and W. Sheils (eds), *A History of Religion in Britain: Practice and Beliefs from Pre-Roman Times to the Present* (Blackwell: Oxford) 1994, 381.

Zuckerman, C., 'The Relationship of Theories of Universals to Theories of Church Government in the Middle Ages: A Critique of Previous Views', *Journal of the History of Ideas*, Vol. 36, No. 4 (1975) 579–94.

Websites

Ascribed author

Chesterton, G.K., 'Antichrist, or the Reunion of Christendom: An Ode', http://www.cse.dmu.ac.uk/~mward/gkc/books/smith.txt

Handwerk, B., 'Why Did Penguins Stop Flying? The Answer is Evolutionary', *National Geographic* (May 2013), http://news.nationalgeographic.com/news/2013/13/131320-penguin-evolution-science-flight-diving-swimming-wings

Mueller, T., 'Whale Evolution', *National Geographic* (Aug 2010) 7, http://ngm.nationalgeographic.com/2010/08/whale-evolution/mueller-text

Weeks T.H. (translation), The Pictish Chronicle MS. COLB. BIB. IMP. PARIS, 4126. 'The Chronicle of the Kings of Alba, Constantine II 900–943', http://www.kjhskj75z.talktalk.net/pictish.html#third

No ascribed author

The Anglo-Saxon Chronicle, Year AD 1072 (The Project Gutenberg ebook of *The Anglo-Saxon Chronicle*) http://www.gutenberg.org/cache/epub/657/pg657.html.

The Antonine Wall, 'The Antonine Wall: Frontiers of the Roman Empire', http://www.antoninewall.org

BBC History Home, Wales History, Ch. 16, 'Religion in the Nineteenth and Twentieth Centuries', http://www.bbc.co.uk/wales/history/sites/themes/guide/ch16_religion_19th_and_20th_centuries.shtml

British Humanist Association, 'Campaigns, Constitutional Reform', https://humanism.org.uk/campaigns/constitutional-reform

British Library, 'English Translation of the Magna Carta', http://www.bl.uk/magna-carta/articles/magna-carta-english-translation

Cabinet Office, 'The Cabinet Manual: A Guide to the Laws, Conventions and Rules on the Operation of Government' (Oct 2011), https://www.ppforum.ca/sites/default/files/uk_cabinet_manual.pdf

City of the Dead, Haunted Graveyard, 'The World Famous Edinburgh Ghost and Graveyard Tours', http://www.cityofthedeadtours.com/tours/city-of-the-dead-haunted-graveyard-tour

Constitution Society, King James, *The Trew Law of Free Monarchies*, http://www.constitution.org/primarysources/stuart.html

'Constitutional Change Necessary to Protect Japanese Citizens: Abe', *The Japan Times* (3 Feb 2015), http://www.japantimes.co.jp/news/2015/02/03/national/politics-diplomacy/constitutional-change-necessary-protect-japanese-citizens-abe

House of Lords, 'Constitution Committee – Fifteenth Report: The Process of Constitutional Change' (11 Jul 2011), http://www.publications.parliament.uk/pa/ld201012/ldselect/ldconst/177/17702.htm.

Nash Ford Publishing, Royal Berkshire History, 'The Vicar of Bray', http://www.berkshirehistory.com/legends/vicarofbray_bal.html

The National Library of Wales, 'Collections, Welsh Bible 1588', http://www.llgc.org.uk/index.php?id=292

Offa's Dyke Association, 'King Offa and the Dyke', http://www.offasdyke.demon.co.uk/dyke.htm

Project Canterbury, 'Legislation related to Liturgy in the Church of England, Public Worship Regulation Act, Report of the Royal Commission on Ecclesiastical Discipline', presented to both Houses of Parliament by Command of His Majesty' (1906), http://anglicanhistory.org/pwra

Project Canterbury, 'Second Report of the Commissioners Appointed to Inquire into the Rubrics, Orders and Directions for Regulating the Course and Conduct of Public Worship, &c.', (1867), http://anglicanhistory.org/pwra

The Scotsman, 'Sawney Bean the Cannibal: All the Product of English Propaganda', (30 Jan 2008), http://www.scotsman.com/news/sawney-bean-the-cannibal-all-a-product-of-english-propaganda-1-1076320

Scottish Covenanters Memorial Association, 'Who were the Covenanters', http://www.covenanter.org.uk/whowere.html

'Visit Hadrian's Wall, Why was the Wall Built?', http://www.visithadrianswall.co.uk/hadrians-wall/about-hadrians-wall/why-was-the-wall-built

Chapter 2

Books

Ahdar, R. and I. Leigh, *Religious Freedom in the Liberal State* (Oxford University Press: Oxford) 2005.

Alridge, A., *Voltaire and the Century of Light* (Princeton University Press: Princeton) 1975.

Anderson, J., *Religion, State and Politics in the Soviet Union and Successor States* (Cambridge University Press: Cambridge) 1994.

Beaman, L., *Religion and Canadian Society: Context Identities and Strategies* (Canadian Scholars Press: Toronto) 2005.

Beckford, J.A. and S. Gilliat-Ray, *Religion and Prison: Equal Rites in a Multi-Faith Society* (Cambridge University Press: Cambridge) 1998.

Buchanan, C., *Cut the Connection: Disestablishment and the Church of England* (DLT: London) 1994.

Carling, A., (ed.), *The Social Equality of Religion or Belief: A New View of Religion's Place in Society* (Palgrave Macmillan: Basingstoke) 2016.

Doe, N., *The Legal Framework of the Church of England* (Oxford University Press: Oxford) 1996.

Elver, H., *The Headscarf Controversy: Secularism and Freedom of Religion* (Oxford University Press: Oxford) 2012.

Ferguson, P. and C. McDiarmid, *Scots Criminal Law: A Critical Analysis* (Edinburgh University Press: Edinburgh) 2nd edn, 2014.

Hill, M., *Ecclesiastical Law* (Oxford University Press: Oxford) 2007.

Hirsi Ali, A., *Heretic: Why Islam Needs a Reformation Now* (Harper Collins: Glasgow) 2015.

Jones, G.E., *Modern Wales: A Concise History* (Cambridge University Press: Cambridge) 1994.

Lowe, N. and G. Douglas, *Bromley's Family Law* (Oxford University Press: Oxford) 10th edn, 2007.

Morris R. (ed.), *Church and State in 21st Century Britain: The Future of Church Establishment* (Palgrave McMillan: London) 2009.

Nadler, S., *Spinoza: A Life* (Cambridge University Press: Cambridge) 1999.

Ono, S., *The Kami Way* (Tuttle Publishing: Singapore) 1962.

Rivers, J., *The Law of Organised Religions: Between Establishment and Secularism* (Oxford: Oxford University Press) 2010.

Russo C. (ed.), *International Perspectives on Education, Religion and Law* (Routledge: Abingdon) 2014.

Trigg, R., *Religion in Public Life: Must Religion be Privatised?* (Oxford University Press: Oxford) 2007.

Vazquez Alonso, V., *Laicidad y Constitución* (Centro de Estudios Políticos y Constitucionales: Madrid) 2012.

Von Leyden, W. (ed.), *Essays on the Law of Nature and Associated Writings* (Clarendon Press: Oxford) 2002.

Watkin, T.G., *A Legal History of Wales* (University of Wales: Cardiff) 2007.

Weatherall, D., *D. Ricardo: A Biography* (Martinus Nijhoff: The Hague) 1976.

Articles, book chapters and conference papers

Bakalis, C. and P. Edge, 'Sentencing the Religious Defendant: The Constraints of the European Convention on Human Rights', *European Human Rights Law Review*, Vol. 5 (2009) 659–69.

Baldry, T., 'Parliament and the Church', *Ecclesiastical Law Journal*, Vol. 17, No. 2 (2015) 202–14.

Barber, P., 'State Schools and Religious Authority – Where to Draw the Line?,' *Ecclesiastical Law Journal*, Vol. 12, No. 2 (2010) 224–8.

Bhandar, B., 'The Ties That Bind: Multiculturalism and Secularism Reconsidered', *Journal of Law and Society*, Vol. 36, No. 3 (2009) 301–26.

Bix, B.H., 'Assault, Sado-Masochism and Consent, *Law Quarterly Review*, Vol. 109 (1993) 540–4.

Bonney, N., 'Established Religion, Parliamentary Devolution and New State Religion in the UK', *Parliamentary Affairs*, Vol. 66, No. 2 (2013) 425–42.

Carr, W., 'A Developing Establishment', *Theology* (Jan 1999) 2–10.

Cobb, N., 'The Church of England's Hold Over Marriage: The Queer Case for Disestablishment', in A. Carling (ed.), *The Social Equality of Religion or Belief: A New View of Religion's Place in Society* (Palgrave Macmillan: Basingstoke) 2016, 200–15.

Cohen, J., 'The Politics and Risks of the New Legal Pluralism in the Domain of Intimacy', *International Journal of Constitutional Law*, Vol, 10, No. 2 (2012) 380–97.

Cranmer, F., 'Human Sexuality and the Church of Scotland: Aitken et al v Presbytery of Aberdeen', *Ecclesiastical Law Journal*, Vol. 11, No. 3 (2009) 335–39.

Cranmer, F., 'Judicial Review and Church Courts in the Law of Scotland', *Denning Law Journal*, Vol. 13, No. 1(1998) 49–66.

Cumper, P., 'Multiculturalism, Human Rights and the Accommodation of Sharia Law', *Human Rights Law Review*, Vol. 14, No. 1 (2014) 31–57.

Derr, B.W., 'Implications of Menstruation as a Liminal State', *American Anthropologist New Series*, Vol. 84, No. 3 (1982) 644–5.

Domingo, R., 'The Constitutional Justification of Religion', *Ecclesiastical Law Journal Vol.* 18, No. 1 (2016) 14–35.

Domingo, R., 'Religion for Hedgehogs? An Argument against the Dworkinian Approach to Religious Freedom', *Oxford Journal of Law and Religion*, Vol. 2, No. 2 (2013) 371–92.

Dowling, G., 'The Liminal Boundary: An Analysis of the Sacral Potency of the Ditch at Ráith na Ríg, Tara, Co. Meath', *The Journal of Irish Archaeology*, Vol. 15 (2006) 15–37.

Durston, C., 'The Puritan War on Christmas', *History Today*, Vol. 35 (12 Dec 1985).

Edge, P., 'Religious Remnants in the Composition of the United Kingdom Parliament', in R. O'Dair and A. Lewis (eds.), *Law and Religion: Current Legal Issues*, Vol. IV (Oxford University Press: Oxford) 2001, 443–55.

Engelke, M., *God's Agents: Biblical Publicity in Contemporary England* (University of California Press: California) 2013, Ch. 3 'Kingdom and Christendom'.

Evans, C., 'Religious Education in Public Schools: An International Human Rights Perspective', *Human Rights Law Review*, Vol. 8, No. 3 (2008) 449–73.

Falsone, A., 'Redundant Crimes of Blasphemy in Scotland', *Ecclesiastical Law Journal*, Vol. 16, No. 2 (2014) 190–7.

García Oliva, J., 'The Favourable Legal View of Religion in England in the XXI Century', *Derecho y Religión*, Vol. X (2015).

García Oliva, J., 'Church, State and Establishment in the United Kingdom in the 21st century: Anachronism or Idiosyncrasy?', *Public Law* (2010) 482–504.

García Oliva, J. and H. Hall, 'Same-Sex Marriage: An Inevitable Challenge to Religious Liberty and Establishment?', *Oxford Journal of Law and Religion*, Vol. 3, No. 1 (2014) 25–56

Gibson, M., 'The God "Dilution" of Religion, Discrimination and the Case for Reasonable Accommodation', *Cambridge Law Journal*, Vol. 72, No. 3 (2013) 578–616.

Giles, M., '*R v Brown*: Consensual Harm and the Public Interest', *The Modern Law Review*, Vol. 57, No. 1 (1994) 101–11.

Hale, Baroness., 'Secular Judges and Christian Law', *Ecclesiastical Law Journal*, Vol. 17, No. 2 (2015) 170–81.

Hall, H., 'Exorcism, Religious Freedom and Consent: The Devil in the Detail', *Journal of Criminal Law*, Vol. 80, No. 4 (2016) 241–53.

Harlow, A., F. Cranmer and N. Doe, 'Bishops in the House of Lords: A Critical Analysis', *Public Law* (2008) 490–509.

Harris, N., 'Local Authorities and the Accountability Gap in a Fragmenting Schools System', *The Modern Law Review*, Vol. 75, No. 4 (2012) 511–46.

Harris, N., 'Playing Catch-Up in the Schoolyard? Children and Young People's "Voice" and Education Rights in the UK', *International Journal of Law, Policy and the Family*, Vol. 23, (No. 3 (2009) 331–66.

Harris, N. and J. García Oliva, 'Adapting to Religious Diversity: Legal Protection of Religious Preference in State Funded Schools in England', in C. Russo (ed.), *International Perspectives on Education, Religion and Law* (Routledge: Abingdon) 2014, 134–54.

Hwangpo, M.C., 'El Compadre: Un tipo porteño liminal y espacial', *Revista de Crítica Literaria Latinoamericana*, Año 35, No. 70 (2009) 257–72.

Jeremy, A., 'Practical Implications of the Enactment of the Racial and Religious Hatred Act 2007, *Ecclesiastical Law Journal*, Vol. 9, No. 2 (2007) 187–201.

Knight, J., Schools Minister, *House of Commons Debates*, Vol. 451, col. 502 (2 Nov 2006).

Laborde, C., 'Equal Liberty, Non-Establishment and Religious Freedom', *Legal Theory*, Vol. 20, No. 1 (2014) 52–77.

Leigh, I., 'By Law Established? The Church of England and Constitutional Reform', *Public Law* (2004) 266–73.

Long, R. and P. Bolton, 'Faith Schools: Frequently Asked Questions House of Commons Library Briefing Paper' (14 Oct 2015).

Lundy, L., 'Family Values in the Classroom? Reconciling Parental Wishes and Children's Rights in State Schools', *International Journal of Law, Policy and the Family*, Vol. 19, No. 3 (2005) 346–72.

Lundy, L., '"Voice" is Not Enough: Conceptualising Article 12 of the United Nations Convention on the Rights of the Child', *British Educational Research Journal*, Vol. 33 (2007) 927–42.

Lyall, F., 'Church and State (Legal Questions)', in *Dictionary of Scottish Church History and Theology* (T&T Clark : Edinburgh) 1993.

McClean, D., 'The Changing Legal Framework of Establishment', *Ecclesiastical Law Journal*, Vol. 7, No. 34 (2004) 292–303.

McClean, I. and S. Peterson, 'Entrenching the Establishment and Free Exercise of Religion in the Written U.K. Constitution', *International Journal of Constitutional Law*, Vol. 9 (2011) 230–50.

MacLean, M.A., 'The Church of Scotland as a National Church', *Law & Justice*, Vol. 149 (2002) 12.

Modood, T., 'Establishment, Multiculturalism and British Citizenship', *The Political Quarterly*, Vol. 65, No. 1 (1994) 53–73.

Monk, D., 'Challenging Homophobic Bullying in Schools: The Politics of Progress', *International Journal of Law in Context*, Vol. 7, No. 2 (2011) 181–207.

Monk, D., 'Out of School Education and Radicalisation: Home Education Revisited', *Education Law Journal*, Vol. 1 (2016) 17–31.

Morris, R.M., 'Towards a New Balance', in R. Morris (ed.), *Church and State in 21st Century Britain: The Future of Church Establishment* (Palgrave McMillan: London) 2009, 226–41.

Munro, C., 'Does Scotland Have an Established Church', *Ecclesiastical Law Journal*, Vol. 4, No. 20 (1997) 639–45.

Nieuwenhuis, A.J., 'State and Religion, a Multidimensional Relationship: Some Comparative Law Remarks', *International Journal of Constitutional Law*, Vol. 10, No. 1 (2012) 153–74.

Petchey, P., 'Legal Issues for Faith Schools in England and Wales', *Ecclesiastical Law Journal*, Vol. 10, No. 2 (2008) 174–90.

Rickett, C.E.F., 'An Anti-Roman Catholic Bias in the Law of Charity', *Conveyancer and Property Lawyer* (1990) 34–44.

Rivers, J., 'The Secularisation of the British Constitution', *Ecclesiastical Law Journal*, Vol. 14, No. 3 (2012) 371–99.

Rosenberg D. and R. Desai, 'The Admissions Arrangements of Faith Schools and the Equality Act 2010', *Ecclesiastical Law Journal*, Vol. 14, No. 2 (2013) 93–9.

Rudwick, M., 'Geological Travel and Theoretical Innovation: The Role of "Liminal" Experience', *Social Studies of Science*, Vol. 26, No. 1 (1996) 143–59.

Sample, I., 'Martin Rees – I've Got No Religious Beliefs at All', *The Guardian* (6 Apr 2011), https://www.theguardian.com/science/2011/apr/06/astronomer-royal-martin-rees-interview

Sandberg, R., 'Defining the Divine', *Ecclesiastical Law Journal*, Vol. 16, No. 2 (2014) 198–204.

Sandberg, R., 'Church-State Relations in Europe: From Legal Models to an Interdisciplinary Approach', *Journal of Religion in Europe*, Vol. 1 (2008) 329–52.

Shelley, C., 'Beating Children Is Wrong, Isn't It? Resolving Conflicts in the Encounter between Religious Worldviews and Child Protection', *Ecclesiastical Law Journal*, Vol. 15, No. 2 (2013) 130–43.

Smith, R., 'Caesar's Palace, not Lambeth's', *New Law Journal*, Vol. 158, No. 7348 (2008) 229.

Streets, S., 'S&M in the House of Lords', *Alternative Law Journal*, Vol. 18, No. 5 (1993) 233–6.

Taylor, R., 'Responsibility for the Soul of the Child: The Role of the State and Parents in Determining Religious Upbringing and Education', *International Journal of Law, Policy and the Family*, Vol. 29, No. 1 (2015) 15–35.

Temperman, J., 'Are State Churches Contrary to International Law?', *Oxford Journal of Law and Religion*, Vol. 2, No. 1 (2013) 119–49.

Tolmie, J., 'Consent to Harmful Assaults: The Case for Moving Away from Category Based Decision Making', *Criminal Law Review* (2012) 656–71.

Twomey, A., 'Changing the Rules of Succession to the Throne', *Public Law* (2011) 378–401.

Vickers, L., 'Twin Approaches to Secularism: Organized Religion and Society', Oxford Journal of Legal Studies, Vol. 32, No. 1 (2012) 197–210.

Vickers, L., 'Religious Discrimination in the Workplace: An Emerging Hierarchy', Ecclesiastical Law Journal, Vol. 12, No. 3 (2010) 280–303.

Watkin, T.G., 'Vestiges of Establishment: The Ecclesiastical and Canon Law of the Church in Wales', *Ecclesiastical Law Journal*, Vol. 2, No. 7 (1990) 110–15.

Websites

Ascribed author

Bagehot, 'There is a Difference between Lacking Faith and Having No Religion', *The Economist* (10 Mar 2011), http://www.economist.com/blogs/bagehot/2011/03/british_2011_census

Cook, C., 'New Grammars and More Selection by Faith Proposed, *BBC News* (8 Sept 2016), http://www.bbc.co.uk/news/uk-politics-37312625

Cornock, D., 'Church in Wales Exempt from Same-Sex Marriage Law', *BBC News* (11 Dec 2012), http://www.bbc.co.uk/news/uk-wales-politics-20682574

Cranmer, F., 'Scottish Independence and the Establishment Principle', *Law and Religion UK* (19 May 2014), http://www.lawandreligionuk.com/2014/05/19/scottish-independence-and-the-establishment-principle

Duffy, N., 'Scotland: Faith Groups Can Opt Out of New Guidance Teaching Gay Relationships, *Pink News* (13 Dec 2014), http://www.pinknews.co.uk/2014/12/13/scotland-faith-schools-can-opt-out-of-new-guidance-on-teaching-gay-relationships

Dunbar, P., 'Why Should Childless Women Like Us Do Longer Hours to Cover for Working Mothers?', *The Daily Mail* (28 Jul 2013), http://www.dailymail.co.uk/femail/article-2380473/Why-SHOULD-childless-women-like-longer-hours-cover-working-mothers.html

Eaton, G., 'Clegg Calls for the Disestablishment of the Church of England – and He's Right', *The New Statesman* (24 Apr 2014), http://www.newstatesman.com/politics/2014/04/clegg-calls-disestablishment-church-england-and -hes-right

Fairbairn, C., Parliamentary Briefing Paper, Marriage (Wales) Bill [HL] Standard Note SN/HA/05347 (3 Mar 2010), http://researchbriefings.files.parliament.uk/documents/RP13-8/RP13-8.pdf

Flynn, J., 'Welsh Medics who Received Gallantry Medals in WW1 to be Honoured in Ceremony', *Wales Online* (15 Apr 2015), http://www.walesonline.co.uk/news/local-news/welsh-medics-who-received-gallantry-9048653

Mason, R., 'Nick Clegg Urges "Equal Rights" for Royal Girls as MPs Prepare to Debate Rules of Succession', *The Telegraph* (22 Jan 2013), http://www.telegraph.co.uk/news/uknews/theroyalfamily/9816620/Nick-Clegg-urges-equal-rights-for-royal-girls-as-MPs-prepare-to-debate-rules-of-succession.html

Meer, N. and T. Modood, 'A Jeffersonian Wall or an Anglican Establishment: The US and UK's Contrasting Approaches to Incorporating Muslims', *LSE US Centre*, http://blogs.lse.ac.uk/usappblog/2016/04/25/a-jeffersonian-wall-or-an-anglican-establishment-the-us-and-uks-contrasting-approaches-to-incorporating-muslims/#Author

Moore, M., 'Philosophy Tutor in Court for Leaving Anti-Religious Cartoons in John Lennon Airport', *The Telegraph* (3 Mar 2010), http://www.telegraph.co.uk/news/religion/7353643/Philosophy-tutor-in-court-for-leaving-anti-religious-cartoons-in-John-Lennon-airport.html

Pollock, I., 'Boy's Scurvy Death Prompts Home-Schooling Register Call', *BBC News* (8 July 2016), http://www.bbc.co.uk/news/uk-wales-36746094

Prince, R., 'David Cameron Declares Britain is Still a Christian Country', *The Telegraph* (5 Apr 2015), http://www.telegraph.co.uk/news/general-election-2015/11516804/David-Cameron-declares-Britain-is-still-a-Christian-country.html

Scott, K., 'Boys Avoid Jail for "Violating" Tomb and Beheading Corpse', *The Guardian* (24 Apr 2004), http://www.theguardian.com/uk/2004/apr/24/ukcrime.scotland

Vale, P., 'David Cameron Uses Easter Message to Praise Britain as a "Christian Country"', *Huffington Post UK* (5 Apr 2015), http://www.huffingtonpost.co.uk /2015/04/05/cameron-uses-easter-message-to-praise-church-as-living-active-force-doing-great-works_n_7007134.html

Vickers, L., 'Religious Discrimination Against Teachers in Faith Schools', *Public Spirit* (22 Oct 2013), http://www.publicspirit.org.uk/religious-discrimination-against-teachers-in-faith-schools/#_edn1

Wilkinson, M., 'Election 2015 Latest Poles and Odds: Labour Take Two Point Lead but Punters Prefer Tories', *The Telegraph* (8 Apr 2015), http://www.telegraph.

co.uk/news/general-election-2015/11519632/Election-2015-latest-polls-and-odds-Labour-take-two-point-lead-but-punters-prefer-Tories.html

Wynne Jones, J., 'Bishops Fear Position of Church under Threat', *The Telegraph* (17 Feb 2008), http://www.telegraph.co.uk/news/uknews/1578893/Bishops-fear-position-of-Church-under-threat.html

No ascribed author

BBC News 'Trojan Horse Reaction to Council and Government Reports', (18 Jul 2014), http://www.bbc.co.uk/news/uk-england-birmingham-28374058

BBC News, 'Atheist Guilty Over Cartoons Left at Liverpool Airport', (4 Mar 2010), http://news.bbc.co.uk/1/hi/england/merseyside/8549613.stm

British Humanist Association, 'Campaigns', https://humanism.org.uk/campaigns

British Humanist Association, 'Campaigns, Human Rights and Equality', https://humanism.org.uk/campaigns/human-rights-and-equality

British Humanist Association, 'Campaigns, Religion and Belief: Some Surveys and Statistics', https://humanism.org.uk/campaigns/religion-and-belief-some-surveys-and-statistics

British Humanist Association, 'Campaigns, Secularism', https://humanism.org.uk/campaigns/secularism

British Humanist Association, 'Campaigns, Schools and Education', https://humanism.org.uk/campaigns/schools-and-education

British Humanist Association, 'Marriage Law', https://humanism.org.uk/campaigns/human-rights-and-equality/marriage-laws

British Humanist Association, 'Public Ethical Issues', https://humanism.org.uk/campaigns/public-ethical-issues

British Humanist Association, 'Public Service Delivery', https://humanism.org.uk/campaigns/secularism/public-service-reform

Channel 4, 'Richard III: The Reburial', http://www.channel4.com/programmes/richard-iii-the-reburial

Christian Wicca, 'Christian Wicca: The Kingdom is Within You and All Around You', http://christianwicca.org

The Church of England, 'Crown Nominations Commissions', https://www.churchofengland.org/clergy-office-holders/asa/senappt/dbnom/cnc.aspx

The Church of England, 'A Detailed History', https://www.churchofengland.org/about-us/history/detailed-history.aspx

The Church of England, Research and Statics Department, Archbishops' Council, 'Statistics of Mission 2013', 6, https://www.churchofengland.org/media/2112070/2013statisticsformission.pdf

Church of the Flying Spaghetti Monster, http://www.venganza.org/about

The Church of Jesus Christ and the Latter Day Saints, United Kingdom and Ireland, 'Locations', http://lds.org.uk/locations

The Church of Scotland, 'Church Constitution', http://www.churchofscotland.org.uk/about_us/church_law/church_constitution

The Church of Scotland, 'The Church of Scotland and Education: A Guide to Good Practice for Church of Scotland Representatives on Local Authority Education Committees', http://www.churchofscotland.org.uk/speak_out/education/articles/the_church_of_scotland_and_education

The Church of Scotland, 'Frequently Asked Questions, Marriage', http://www.churchofscotland.org.uk/__data/assets/pdf_file/0019/2449/guide_marriage.pdf

The Church of Scotland, 'General Assembly', http://www.churchofscotland.org.uk/about_us/general_assembly

The Church of Scotland, 'How We Are Organised', http://www.churchofscotland.org.uk/about_us/how_we_are_organised

The Church of Scotland, 'Life Events', http://www.churchofscotland.org.uk/connect/life_events

Comhairle nan Eilean Siar, '2011 Census Barra and Vatersay Key Statistics', available via http://www.cne-siar.gov.uk/index.asp?tabindex=1

Comhairle nan Eilean Siar, '2011 Census Lewis Key Statistics', available via http://www.cne.siar.gov.uk index.asp?tabindex=1

Education Scotland, 'Religious and Moral Education', https://education.gov.scot/parentzone/learning-in-scotland/curriculum-areas/Religious%20and%20moral%20education

Sir Edward Cole, *The Reports of Sir Edward Coke in English, compleat in thirteen parts, with references to all the antient and modern books of the law. Exactly translated and compared with the first and last edition in French, and printed page for page with the same. To which are now added the pleadings to the cases*, Part IV, Adams and Lambert Case, 112, https://play.google.com/books/reader?id=O9YsAAAAYAAJ&printsec=frontcover&output=reader&hl=en_GB

Facebook, The Church of the Flying Spaghetti Monster Wales, https://www.facebook.com/pages/The-church-of-the-Flying-Spaghetti-Monster-Wales/1486947134916477

The Guardian, 'Prison Suicide Rate at Highest since 2007 Figures Show', (22 Jan 2015), http://www.theguardian.com/society/2015/jan/22/prison-suicide-rate-82-deaths

Home Education UK, 'Why Home Educate?', http://www.home-ed.co.uk/whyhomeed.html

Humanist Society Scotland, 'Assisted Dying Policy and Campaigns', https://www.humanism.scot/what-we-do/policy-campaigns/assisted-dying

Humanist Society Scotland, 'Female and Reproductive Rights', https://www.humanism.scot/what-we-do/policy-campaigns/female-and-reproductive-rights/

Humanist Society Scotland, 'Humanists and Education', https://www.humanism.scot/what-we-do/education

Humanist Society Scotland, 'LGBTI Campaigns and Policy', https://www.humanism.scot/what-we-do/policy-campaigns/lgbti-equality

National Secular Society, 'As Cameron Says UK Still a Christian country, 62% Tell YouGov They Are Not Religious' (8 Apr 2015), http://www.secularism.org.uk/news/2015/04/as-cameron-says-uk-still-a-christian-country-62-percent-tell-yougov-they-are-not-religious

National Secular Society, 'Challenging Religious Privilege', http://www.secularism.org.uk

National Secular Society, 'Chancel Repair Liability', https://www.secularism.org.uk/chancel-repair-liability.html

National Secular Society, 'Clerical Child Abuse', http://www.secularism.org.uk/child-abuse-and-the-catholic-chu1.html

National Secular Society, 'Collective Worship', http://www.secularism.org.uk/collective-worship.html

National Secular Society, 'Freedom of Expression', http://www.secularism.org.uk/freedom-of-expression.html

National Secular Society, 'Healthcare', http://www.secularism.org.uk/health.html

National Secular Society, 'Human Rights and Equality', http://www.secularism.org.uk/law-equality-and-human-rights.html

National Secular Society, 'Non-Stun Slaughter', https://www.secularism.org.uk/chancel-repair-liability.html

National Secular Society, 'Religion and Schools', http://www.secularism.org.uk/religion-in-schools.html

National Secular Society, 'Religion and State', http://www.secularism.org.uk/religion-and-state.html

National Secular Society 'Religious Influence in Parliament', http://www.secularism.org.uk/religious-influence-in-parliamen.html

National Secular Society, 'Sharia Law', http://www.secularism.org.uk/sharia-law.html

Office for National Statistics, '2011 Census: Key Statistics for Wales, March 2011', http://www.ons.gov.uk/ons/rel/census/2011-census/key-statistics-for-unitary-authorities-in-wales/stb-2011-census-key-statistics-for-wales.html

Office for National Statistics, 'Population Estimates for UK, England and Wales, Scotland and Northern Ireland, mid 2001–mid 2010 Revised' (17 Dec 2013), http://www.ons.gov.uk/ons/rel/pop-estimate/population-estimates-for-uk--england-and-wales--scotland-and-northern-ireland/mid-2001-to-mid-2010-revised/index.html

Office for National Statistics, 'Religion in England and Wales 2011: Key Points' (11 Dec 2012), 1–2, http://www.ons.gov.uk/ons/dcp171776_290510.pdf

OSCR Scottish Charity Regulator, 'About OSCR', https://www.oscr.org.uk/about/about-oscr

OSCR Scottish Charity Regulator, 'Meeting the Charity Test, Guidance: the Advancement of Religion', https://www.oscr.org.uk/charities/guidance/meeting-the-charity-test-guidance/c-the-advancement-of-religion

OSCR Scottish Charity Regulator, 'Thinking About Becoming a Charity', http://www.oscr.org.uk/public/thinking-about-becoming-a-charity

The Pagan Federation, Mid-West and Wales, http://www.paganfed.org/index.php/pagan-federation-districts/midwest-wales-pf

Royal Commission on the Reform of the House of Lords, *A House for the Future*, Cm 4534 (The Stationery Office) 2000, https://www.gov.uk/government/uploads/system/uploads/attachment_data/file/266061/prelims.pdf

The Scotsman, 'Corpse Ghouls Walk Free', (23 Apr 2004), http://www.scotsman.com/news/corpse-ghouls-walk-free-1-1009541

Scottish Government, 'Conduct of Relationships, Sexual Health and Parenthood Education in Schools' (11 Dec 2014), http://www.gov.scot/Publications/2014/12/8526/downloads

Scottish Government, 'Schools, Frequently Asked Questions', http://www.gov.scot/Topics/Education/Schools/FAQs

Scottish Government, 'Summary: Religious Group Demographics', http://www.gov.scot/Topics/People/Equality/Equalities/DataGrid/Religion/RelPopMig

The Secretary of State for Justice and the Lord Chancellor, *The Governance of Britain*, Cm 7170 (The Stationery Office: London) July 2007, https://www.gov.uk/government/uploads/system/uploads/attachment_data/file/228834/7170.pdf

STV News, 'Piper Alpha Memorial Service Takes Place', (8 July 2008), http://news.stv.tv/scotland/30409-piper-alpha-memorial-services-take-place

The Telegraph, 'Concern Over 1000 Boys in "Illegal" Schools Over Narrow Curriculum', (1 Apr 2016), http://www.telegraph.co.uk/education/2016/04/01/concern-for-1000-boys-in-illegal-schools-over-narrow-curriculum

UK Government, 'Faith Schools', https://www.gov.uk/types-of-school/faith-schools

UK Government, 'Home Education', https://www.gov.uk/home-education

UK Government, 'Marriage (Same Sex Couples) Act – A Factsheet', https://www.gov.uk/government/publications/equal-marriage-documents-explaining-our-policy

UK Government, 'Regulating Independent Schools' (Jan 2016), http://www.gov.uk/.../file/492994/Regulating_independent_schools.pdf

UK Government, Schools Admissions, 'Admission Criteria', https://www.gov.uk/schools-admissions/admissions-criteria

UK Government, 'Schools Admissions and Transport to School', https://www.gov.uk/types-of-school/faith-schools

UK Government, 'Statutory Guidance: Schools Admissions Code Department for Education' (19 Dec 2014, updated 17 Sept 2015), https://www.gov.uk/government/publications/school-admissions-code--2

UK Government, 'The Registrar General's Guidance for the Approval of Venues for Civil Marriages and Civil Partnerships', 5th edn (revised May 2014), https://www.gov.uk/government/publications/guidance-on-registering-a-venue-for-civil-marriage-and-civil-partnership

UK Parliament, 'Black Rod', http://www.parliament.uk/about/mps-and-lords/principal/black-rod

Vie Publique: Au coeur du débat public 'Les exceptions au droit de cultes issu de la loi de 1905' (24 May 2015), http://www.vie-publique.fr/politiques-publiques/etat-cultes-laicite/droit-local-cultes

Wales Online, 'Candlelit Vigil for April Jones in Machynlleth', (3 Oct 2012), http://www.walesonline.co.uk/news/local-news/candlelit-vigil-april-jones-machynlleth-2019746

Wales Online, 'Meet the Spaghetti Worshipper Battling the DVLA to Wear a Colander on His Head on His Driving License', (7 Apr 2015), http://www.walesonline.co.uk/news/wales-news/meet-pastafarian-member-church-flying-8997070

The Woolf Institute, http://www.woolf.cam.ac.uk

The Woolf Institute, Report of the Commission on Religion and Belief in British Public Life: Living with Difference – Community, Diversity and the Common Good (7 Dec 2015), http://www.woolf.cam.ac.uk/uploads/Living%20with%20Difference.pdf

Miscellaneous

General Assembly 2000 Act 5, Sacraments Consolidating Act.

Chapter 3

Books

Brunsman, D., *The Evil Necessity: British Naval Impressment in the Eighteenth Century Atlantic World* (University of Virginia Press: Virginia) 2013.

Domingo, R., *God and the Secular Legal System* (Cambridge University Press: Cambridge) 2016.

Ennis, D., *Enter the Press-Gang: Naval Impressment in Eighteenth Century British Literature* (Associated University Presses: London) 2002.

Gottlieb, A. and J. Deloache, *A World of Babies: Imagined Childcare Guides for Eight Societies* (Cambridge University Press: Cambridge) 2016.

Hartley, C. (ed.), *Secularism: New Historical Perspectives* (Cambridge Scholars Publishing: Newcastle) 2014.

Kramer, A., *Conscientious Objectors of the First World War: A Determined Resistance* (Pen & Sword: Barnsley) 2002.

Mitchell, C. and J. Reid-Walsh, *Girl Culture: An Encyclopaedia* (Greenwood Press: London) 2007.

Moskos, C. and J. Chambers, *The New Conscientious Objection: From Sacred to Secular Resistance* (Oxford University Press: Oxford) 1993.

Phelps, N., *The Great Compassion: Buddhism and Animal Rights* (Lantern Books: New York) 2004.

Roth, R., *That's Why We Don't Eat Animals* (North Atlantic Books: Berkley) 2009

Russell-Jones, G., *Conchie: What My Father Didn't Do in the War* (Lion Hudson: Oxford) 2016.

Stern, L., *How to Keep Kosher: A Comprehensive Guide to Understanding Jewish Dietary Laws* (Harper Collins: London) 2009.

Articles, book chapters and conference papers

Carey, H., 'Secularism v Christianity in Australian History', in C. Hartley (ed.), *Secularism: New Historical Perspectives* (Cambridge Scholars Publishing: Newcastle) 2014.

Cumper, P. and T. Lewis, 'Last Rites and Human Rights: Funeral Pyres and Religious Freedom in the United Kingdom', *Ecclesiastical Law Journal*, Vol. 12, No. 2 (2010) 131–51.

García Oliva, J. and H. Hall, 'Religious Decision-Making and the Capacity of Children in the United Kingdom', *Laicidad y Libertades: Escritos Jurídicos*, Vol. 1 (2013) 137–70.

Mac Sithigh, D., 'Flags, Priests and Morris Dancers: A Case for Medium Law', *SLS Paperbank* (2016).

McIvor, M., 'Carnal Exhibitions: Material Religion and the ECHR', *Ecclesiastical Law Journal*, Vol. 17, No. 1 (2015) 3–14.

Ouald Chaib, S., 'Procedural Fairness as a Vehicle for Inclusion in the Freedom of Religion Jurisprudence of the Strasbourg Court', *Human Rights Law Review*, Vol. 16, No. 3 (2016) 483–510.

Papworth, N., 'A Right to be Naked in A Public Place', *Criminal Law and Justice Weekly*, 177 JPN (2013) 843.

Peroni, L., 'On Religious and Cultural Equality in European Human Rights Convention Law', *Netherlands Quarterly of Human Rights*, Vol. 32, No. 3 (2014) 231–4.

Santino, J., 'Performative Commemoratives: Spontaneous Shrines and the Public Memorialization of Death', in J. Santino (ed.), *Spontaneous Shrines and the Public Memorialization of Death* (Palgrave Macmillan: Basingstoke) 2006, 5–16.

Su, A., 'Judging Religious Sincerity', *Oxford Journal of Law and Religion*, Vol. 5, No. 1 (2016) 28–48.

Websites

Attributed author

Australian Associated Press, '£5 Animal Fat Bank Note: British Vegetarians Being "Stupid" says Inventor', *The Guardian* (2 Dec 2016), https://www.theguardian.com/business/2016/dec/02/5-animal-fat-bank-note-british-vegetarians-being-stupid-says-inventor

BBC News, 'Animal Fat in New Five Pound Note Offensive, says Sikh Activist', (30 Nov 2016), http://www.bbc.co.uk/news/uk-38160291

Brooks, M., 'Conscientious Objectors in Their Own Words', *Imperial War Museums*, http://www.iwm.org.uk/history/conscientious-objectors-in-their-own-words

Brown, A., 'Paganism is Alive and Well – but You Won't Find It at a Goddess Temple', *The Spectator* (14 Feb 2015), https://www.spectator.co.uk/2015/02/paganism-is-alive-and-well-but-you-wont-find-it-at-a-goddess-temple

Copping, J., 'Morris Men Must Allow in Morris Women, but not to Dance', *The Telegraph* (24 Apr 2011), http://www.telegraph.co.uk/news/newstopics/howaboutthat/8469817/Morris-men-must-allow-in-morris-women-but-not-to-dance.html

Jones, S. 'Church of England and Church in Wales Protest at Gay Marriage Ban', *The Guardian* (13 Dec 2012), https://www.theguardian.com/society/2012/dec/13/anglican-church-protests-gay-marriage-ban

Sanghani, R., 'Thousands Call for Ear-Piercing to be Banned for Children in the UK', *The Telegraph* (11 Jun 2015), http://www.telegraph.co.uk/women/life/thousands-call-for-ear-piercing-to-be-banned-for-babies-in-the-uk

Wilcock, D. 'No Consultation: The Church of England attacks Government over Gay Marriage Plans', *The Independent* (14 Dec 2012), http://www.independent.co.uk/news/uk/home-news/no-consultation-church-of-england-attacks-government-over-gay-marriage-plans-8414180.html

No attributed author

The Badger Trust, 'Stop the Cull', http://badger.org.uk/campaigns/stop-the-cull.aspx

The Badger Trust, 'What We Do', http://badger.org.uk/about/what-we-do.aspx

BBC News, 'Animal Fat in New Five Pound Note Offensive, says Sikh Activist', (30 Nov 2016), http://www.bbc.co.uk/news/uk-38160291

BBC News, 'Gloucestershire Cheese-Rolling Off due to Safety Fears', (12 Mar 2010), http://news.bbc.co.uk/1/hi/england/gloucestershire/8563692.stm

British Humanist Association, 'Education for Teachers', https://humanism.org.uk/education/teachers

British Humanist Association, 'Human Rights and Equality Broadcasting', https://humanism.org.uk/campaigns/human-rights-and-equality/broadcasting

Cheese Rolling in Gloucestershire, http://www.cheese-rolling.co.uk/index1.htm

The Co-operative Groups, 'Values and Principles', http://www.co-operative.coop/corporate/aboutus/The-Co-operative-Group-Values-and-Principles/

The Daily Mail, 'Spitting, Threats and Arson? Gloucestershire Cheese-Rolling Festival Cancelled for the Second Year Running after Organisers Receive Abuse over £20 Entry Fee', (25 Mar 2011), http://www.dailymail.co.uk/news/article-1369824/Thoroughly-cheesed-Gloucestershire-cheese-rolling-festival-cancelled-second-year-running-organisers-receive-abuse-20-entry-fee.html

Humanist Society Scotland, 'Humanists Join Tributes at National Remembrance Day ceremony' (Nov 2016), https://www.humanism.scot/what-we-do/news/humanists-join-tributes-at-national-remembrance-day-ceremony

National Secular Society, 'About the National Secular Society', http://www.secularism.org.uk/about.html

National Secular Society, 'Homepage', http://www.secularism.org.uk

National Secular Society, 'News', http://www.secularism.org.uk/news.html

National Secular Society, 'Top Campaigns', http://www.secularism.org.uk/campaigns.html

National Secular Society, 'What is Secularism?', http://www.secularism.org.uk/what-is-secularism.html

Oxford English Dictionary (2016), http://www.oed.com/view/Entry/221868?rskey=3l3EwX&result=1#eid

Simple Magick, 'Pagans Want to be Included Too' (24 Apr 2007), http://www.simplemagick.com/2007/04/pagans-want-to-be-included-too.html
Stonewall, 'Our Mission', http://www.stonewall.org.uk/about-us/our-mission
Stonewall, 'Our Priorities', http://www.stonewall.org.uk/about-us/stonewalls-key-priorities
Stonewall, Education, 'Different Families: Same Love', http://www.stonewall.org.uk/get-involved/education/different-families-same-love
The Telegraph, 'Sikh Soldier First Guardsman to Parade Outside of Buckingham Palace Wearing a Turban', (11 Dec 2012), http://www.telegraph.co.uk/news/religion/9737480/Sikh-soldier-first-guardsman-to-parade-outside-Buckingham-palace-wearing-turban.html
Vegan Outreach, 'Environmental Destruction', http://www.veganoutreach.org/whyvegan/environment.html
Woodcraft Folk, 'Woodcraft Aims, Principles and Programme', https://woodcraft.org.uk/aims-and-principles
Woodcraft Folk, 'History', http://woodcraft.org.uk/history

Miscellaneous

Crown Prosecution Service, 'Nudity in Public-Guidance on handling cases of Naturism', cps.gov.uk/legal/I_to_o/nudity_in_public

Chapter 4

Books

Allan, T.R.S., *Law, Liberty and Justice: The Legal Foundations of UK Constitutionalism* (Clarendon Press: Oxford) 1993.
Anglican Consultative Council, *Principles of Canon Law Common to the Anglican Communion* (Anglican Communion Office: London) 2008.
Aquinas, T. (translation Fathers of the English Dominican Province), *The Summa Theologica of St Thomas Aquinas*, 2nd and revised edn, 1920.
Baker, J.H., *An Introduction to English Legal History* (Butterworths: London) 3rd edn, 1990.
Baskin, J. and K. Seeskin (eds), *The Cambridge Guide to Jewish History, Religion and Culture* (Cambridge University Press: Cambridge) 2010.
Beckford J. and S. Gilliat-Ray, *Religion in Prison: Equal Rights in a Multi-Faith Society* (Cambridge University Press: Cambridge) 1998.
Bingham, T., *The Rule of Law* (Penguin: London) 2011.
Boyce, M., *Zoroastrians: Their Religious Beliefs and Practices* (Routledge and Kegan Paul: London) 1987.
Camus, A., *L'Étranger* (Gallimar: Paris) 1972.
Cao, T.Y. (ed.), *Conceptual Foundations of Quantum Field Theory* (Cambridge University Press: Cambridge) 1999.
Childs, J., *God's Traitors: Terror and Faith in Elizabethan England* (Oxford University Press: Oxford) 2014.
Dean, M., *Japanese Legal System* (Cavendish Publishing: London) 2002.
Dicey A.V. and J.W.F. Allison (eds), *The Law of the Constitution* (Oxford University Press: Oxford) 2013.

Doe, N., *The Law of the Church in Wales* (University of Wales Press: Cardiff) 2002.
Dworkin, R., *A Matter of Principle* (Oxford University Press: Oxford) 1985.
Eisenberg, R., *The JPS Guide to Jewish Traditions* (The Jewish Publication Society: Philadelphia) 2004.
Elliott, M. and R. Thomas, *Public Law* (Oxford University Press: Oxford) 2nd edn, 2014.
Esposito, J., *The Future of Islam* (Oxford University Press: Oxford) 2010.
Ferguson, P. and C. McDiarmid, *Scots Criminal Law: A Critical Analysis* (Edinburgh University Press: Edinburgh) 2014.
Ferrari, A. and S. Pastorelli (eds), *The Burqa Affair Across Europe : Between Public and Private Space* (Ashgate: Farnham) 2013.
Flores. I. & K. Himma (eds), *Law Liberty and the Rule of Law* (Springer: Heidelberg, London, New York) 2013.
Green, N., *Bombay Islam: The Religious Economy of the West Indian Ocean 1840–1915* (Cambridge University Press: Cambridge) 2011.
Hawkings, S., *Goddess Worship, Witchcraft and Neo-Paganism* (Zondervan/Harper Collins: Michigan) 1998.
Hirsi Ali, A., *Heretic: Why Islam Needs a Reformation Now* (Harper: London) 2015.
Lewis, P., *Young, British and Muslim* (Continuum: London) 2011.
Lowe, N. and G. Douglas, *Bromley's Family Law* (Oxford University Press: Oxford) 10th edn, 2007.
Marranci, G., *The Anthropology of Islam* (Berg: Oxford) 2008.
Menski, W., *Hindu Law: Beyond Tradition and Modernity* (Oxford University Press: New Delhi) 2012.
Michell, H., *Sparta* (Cambridge University Press: Cambridge) 1964.
Munsey Turner, J., *John Wesley: The Evangelical Revival and the Rise of Methodism in England* (Epworth: Peterborough) 2002.
Nathan, M.A., *Buddhism and the Law: An Introduction* (Cambridge University Press: Cambridge) 2014.
Rack, H.D., H *Reasonable Enthusiast: John Wesley and the Rise of Methodism* (Epworth Press: London) 3rd edn, 2002.
Ripstein, A. (ed.), *Ronald Dworkin* (Cambridge University Press: Cambridge) 2007.
Rosen, J., *Understanding Judaism* (Dunedin Academic Press: Edinburg) 2003.
Sardar Z. and Z. Abbas Malik, *Introducing Islam* (Icon Books: Royston) 2004.
Scott, D., *Heavenly Confinement: The Role and Perception of Christian Prison Chaplains in North East England's Prisons* (LAP Lambert: Saarbrucken) 2011.
Spiro, M., *Buddhism and Society* (George All & Unwin: London) 1971.
Taekema, S., *The Concept of Ideals in Legal Theory* (Kluwer Law International: The Hague) 2003.
Tamanaha, B., *On the Rule of Law: History, Politics, Theory* (Cambridge University Press: Cambridge) 2004.
Yaran, C., *Understanding Islam* (Dunedin Press: Edinburgh) 2007.

Articles, book chapters and conference papers

Aluffi Beck-Peccoz, R., 'Burqa and Islam', in A. Ferrari and S. Pastorelli (eds), *The Burqa Affair Across Europe: Between Public and Private Space* (Ashgate: Farnham) 2013.
Atlas, S., 'Dina D'Malchuta Delimited', *Hebrew Union College Annual*, Vol. 46 (1975) 269– 88.
Beddard, R., 'Retrospective Crime', *New Law Journal*, Vol. 145 (1995) 663.

Bennett, M.J., 'Hart and Raz on the Non-Instrumental Moral Value of the Rule of Law: A Reconsideration', *Law and Philosophy*, Vol. 30, No. 5 (2011) 603–35.

Brown L.M. and F. Rohrlich, 'Chapter 17 Comments', in T.Y. Cao (ed.), *Conceptual Foundations of Quantum Field Theory* (Cambridge University Press: Cambridge) 1999.

Craig, P.P., 'Formal and Substantive Conceptions of the Rule of Law: An Analytical Framework', *Public Law*, Vol. 21 (1997) 467–87.

Dworkin, R. 'Political Judges and the Rule of Law', British Academy, *Proceedings of the British Academy*, Vol. 23, No. 3 (1980).

Dyzenhaus, D., 'The Rule of Law as the Rule of Liberal Principle', in A. Ripstein (ed.), *Ronald Dworkin* (Cambridge University Press: Cambridge) 2007, 56–79.

Etherton, T., 'Religion, the Rule of Law and Discrimination', *Ecclesiastical Law Journal*, Vol. 16, No. 3 (2014) 265–82.

García Oliva, J. and H. Hall, 'An Inevitable Challenge to Religious Liberty and Establishment', *Oxford Journal of Law and Religion*, Vol. 3, No. 1 (2014) 25–56.

Gethin, R., 'Keeping the Buddha's Rules: The View from the Sūtra Pitaka', in R. French and M. Nathan (eds), *Buddhism and the Law* (Cambridge University Press: Cambridge) 2015.

Hamara, C.T., 'The Concept of the Rule of Law', in I. Flores and K. Himma (eds), *Law, Liberty and the Rule of Law* (Springer: Heidelberg, London, New York) 2013.

Juss, S., 'The Secular Tradition in Sikhism', *Rutgers Journal of Law and Religion*, Vol. 11 (Spring 2010) Pt 2, 271.

Kieffer-Pulz, P., 'What the Vinayas Can Tell Us About Law', in R. French and M. Nathan (eds), *Buddhism and the Law* (Cambridge University Press: Cambridge) 2015, 46–62.

Laws, J., 'Law and Democracy', *Public Law* (1995) 72.

Laws, J., 'The Constitution, Morals and Rights', *Public Law* (1995) 622.

Miller, J., 'Bus Ad Ban Was Lawful', *New Law Journal*, Vol. 164, No. 7618 (2014).

Miller, M., 'Ministerial Foreword', in *Equal Marriage: The Government's Response* (Dec 2012).

Motis Dolander, M., 'Estructura interna y ordenamiento juridico de las aljames judias del valle del Ebro', *Segunda Semana de Estudios Medievales* (1993) 111–52.

Plunkett, D., 'Legal Positivism and the Moral Aim Thesis', *Oxford Journal of Legal Studies*, Vol. 33, No. 3 (2013) 563–605.

Raz, J., 'The Rule of Law and its Virtue', *Law Quarterly Review*, Vol. 93 (1977) 195–211.

Staiculescu, A. and M. Bala, 'The Rule of Law: Challenges and Opportunities', *Contemporary Readings in Social Justice*, Vol. 5, No. 2 (2013) 837.

Voyce, M., 'Ideas of Transgression and Buddhist Monks', *Law Critique*, Vol. 21, No. 2 (2010) 183–98.

Waldron, J., 'Why Law? Efficacy, Freedom and Infidelity, *Law and Philosophy*, Vol. 13 (1994) 259–84.

Websites

Attributed author

Al-Oadah, S., 'Obeying the Law in Non-Muslim Countries', *Islam Today*, http://en.islamtoday.net/node/604

Allen, P., 'Zoroastrian Faith Joins Queen's Coronation Celebrations', *The Telegraph* (4 Jul 2014), http://www.telegraph.co.uk/news/uknews/10097326/Zoroastrian-faith-joins-Queens-Coronation-celebrations.html

Bahnot, A. (General Secretary, Hindu Council UK), 'The Advancement of Dharma: A Discussion Paper for Faith Leaders', Hindu Council UK (20 Nov 2011), http://www.hinducounciluk.org/images/stories/report/the_advancement_of_dharma.pdf

Bingham, J., 'Sharia Law Guidelines Abandoned as Law Society Apologises', *The Telegraph* (24 Nov 2014), http://www.telegraph.co.uk/news/religion/11250643/Sharia-law-guidelines-abandoned-as-Law-Society-apologises.html

Fairbairn, C., '"Common Law Marriage" and Cohabitation', House of Commons Library, Briefing Paper 03372 (9 Mar 2017), http://www.parliament.uk/business/publications/research/briefing-papers/SN03372/common-law-marriage-and-cohabitation

Howse, C., 'The Trouble with Swearing an Oath on a Holy Book', *The Telegraph* (7 Mar 2015), http://www.telegraph.co.uk/comment/11455853/The-trouble-with-swearing-an-oath-on-a-holy-book.html

Jeory, T., 'UK Entering Uncharted Territory of Islamophobia after Brexit Vote', *The Independent* (27 Jun 2016), http://www.independent.co.uk/news/uk/home-news/brexit-muslim-racism-hate-crime-islamophobia-eu-referendum-leave-latest-a7106326.html

Lutz, M., 'Muslim World: Poll shows Majority Want Islam in Politics; Feelings Mixed on Hamas, Hezbollah', *Los Angeles Times* (5 Dec 2010), http://latimesblogs.latimes.com/babylonbeyond/2010/12/hamas-hezbollah-islam-sharia-public-opinion-muslim-countries.html/

Moore, M., 'If You Are Against Gay Marriage Don't Get Gay Married', *Pink News* (25 Oct 2016), http://www.pinknews.co.uk/2016/10/25/michael-moore-if-you-are-against-gay-marriage-dont-get-gay-married

Phillips, P., 'The Statutory Presence of the Church of England in Prisons should give it a Voice on Issues of Imprisonment, but it Remains Largely Silent', London School of Economics and Political Science, http://blogs.lse.ac.uk/religionpublicsphere/2016/09/the-statutory-presence-of-the-church-of-england-in-prisons-should-give-it-a-voice-on-issues-of-imprisonment-but-it-remains-largely-silent

Pigott R., 'Motion of End Bible Oaths in Court Defeated', *BBC News* (19 Oct 2013), http://www.bbc.co.uk/news/uk-24588854

Sacks, J., 'Living in a "Malkhut Shel Chessed", a "Kingdom of Kindness"', The Office of Rabbi Sacks (28 Oct 2014), http://www.rabbisacks.org/living-malkhut-shel-chessed-kingdom-kindness

Saul, H., 'Judge Stops Robbery Trial when Muslim Witness Swears on Bible instead of Koran', *The Independent* (28 Feb 2015) http://www.independent.co.uk/news/uk/crime/judge-stops-robbery-trial-when-muslim-witness-swears-on-bible-instead-of-koran-10075745.html

Sherwood, H., 'The Church of England backs same sex marriage', *The Guardian* (29 Jan 2016), https://www.theguardian.com/world/2016/jan/29/church-of-england-members-back-same-sex-marriage-poll

Singh, I., 'Religion and Society: A Sikh Perspective', Network of Sikh Organisations (20 Oct 2013), http://nsouk.co.uk/religion-and-society/#more-105

Talwar, D., 'Wedding Trouble as UK Muslim Marriages not Recognised', *BBC News* (3 Feb 2010), http://news.bbc.co.uk/1/hi/uk/8493660.stm

No attributed author

Amnesty International, Press Release: 'Great Britain Has a "Moral Responsibility" to Refugees from Syria say Faith Leaders'(28 Jan 2015), https://www.amnesty.org.uk/press-releases/great-britain-has-moral-responsibility-refugees-syria-say-faith-leaders

BBC News, 'Teenagers Deny Violating Corpse', (25 Mar 2004), http://news.bbc.co.uk/1/hi/scotland/3568075.stm

British Humanist Association, 'Humanist Thinking', https://humanism.org.uk/humanism/humanism-today/humanists-thinking.

The Church of England, 'Being An Anglican', https://www.churchofengland.org/our-faith/being-an-anglican.aspx

The Church of England, 'Common Worship Daily Prayer', https://www.churchof england.org/prayer-worship/worship/texts/daily2.aspx

The Church of England, 'Detailed History', https://www.churchofengland.org/about-us/history/detailed-history.aspx

The Church of England, 'Immigration and Asylum', https://www.churchofengland.org/our-views/home-and-community-affairs/asylum-and-immigration.aspx

The Church of England, 'Justice Issues and Prisons', https://www.churchofengland.org/our-views/home-and-community-affairs/home-affairs-policy/justice-issues-prisons/capital-punishment.aspx

The Church of England, 'Marriage after Divorce', http://www.yourchurchwedding.org/youre-welcome/marriage-after-divorce.aspx

The Church of England, Marriage (Same Sex Couples) Commons Second Reading Briefing, 'The Unique Position of the Established Church'

The Church of England, 'Measures', https://www.churchofengland.org/about-us/structure/churchlawlegis/legislation/measures.aspx

The Church of England, 'Social Care', https://www.churchofengland.org/our-views/medical-ethics-health-social-care-policy/socialcare.aspx

The Church of England, 'Thinking of a Church Wedding', https://www.churchofengland.org/weddings-baptisms-funerals/weddings.aspx

The Church of Scotland, General Assembly, 'Standing Orders', http://www.church ofscotland.org.uk/__data/assets/pdf_file/0012/705/standing_orders.pdf.

Daily Record, 'Former Grave Robber Loses Job after Colleagues Discover Past', (31 Jul 2009), http://www.dailyrecord.co.uk/news/scottish-news/former-grave-robber-loses-job-1032478

The Church in Wales, 'Marriage – Frequently Asked Questions', http://www.churchinwales.org.uk/life/marriage/faq

De La Salle, 'The Rule of the Brothers of the Christian Schools', Rome (2008), http://www.lasalle.org/wp-content/uploads/pdf/institucionales/fsc_rule.pdf

Duncan Lewis Solicitors, 'Aina Khan and Baroness Warsi Kickstart Muslim Marriage Project' (14 Jan 2014), http://www.duncanlewis.co.uk/news/Aina_Khan_and_Baroness_Warsi_kickstart_Muslim_Marriage_Project_%2814_January_2014%29.html#sthash.u3HEQ64F.dpbs

The Guardian, 'Signs of the Times of Racism in England that was All Too Familiar', (22 Oct 2015), http://www.theguardian.com/world/2015/oct/22/sign-of-the-times-of-racism-in-england-that-was-all-too-familiar

The Methodist Church, 'Vision and Values', http://www.methodist.org.uk/who-we-are/vision-values

The Movement for Reform Judaism, 'Our Core Values', http://www.reformjudaism.org.uk/about

The Muslim Council of Britain, 'Speech by Dr Shuja Shafi on British and Islamic Values' (29 Jan 2015), http://www.mcb.org.uk/shuja-shafi-speech-british-values-290115

Muslim Parliament of Great Britain, 'About the Muslim Parliament', http://www.muslimparliament.org.uk/about.htm

Muslim Parliament of Great Britain, 'Getting Married – Some Guidelines: Validation of Marriage', http://www.muslimparliament.org.uk/marriage_guidelines.htm
Order of St Benedict, 'Rule of St Benedict', http://www.osb.org/rb/text/toc.html
The Scotsman, 'Corpse Ghouls Walk Free', (23 Apr 2004), http://www.scotsman.com/news/corpse-ghouls-walk-free-1-1009541
Zarathustra, http://www.zarathushtra.com/z/article/overview.htm

Miscellaneous

Book of Common Prayer, Articles of Religion.
The Church of England, 'A Response to the Government Equalities Office Consultation: Equal Civil Marriage', Annex, Marriage Law: the Position of the Church of England.
European Court of Human Rights, Press Unit, 'Factsheet, Death Penalty Abolition' (Feb 2015), http://www.echr.coe.int/Documents/FS_Death_penalty_ENG.pdf
Faculty Office of the Archbishop of Canterbury, 'A Guide to the Law for Clergy' (1999)
Soka Gakkai International UK, http://www.sgi-uk.org
The Vatican, Code of Canon Law 1983.
The Vatican, Sacred Congregation for the Doctrine of the Faith, Declaration *Inter Signiores* on the Question of Admission of Women to the Ministerial Priesthood, http://www.vatican.va/roman_curia/congregations/cfaith/documents/rc_con_cfaith_doc_19761015_inter-insigniores_en.html

Chapter 5

Books

Arvind, S., *Modern Hindu Thought* (Oxford University Press: Oxford) 2005.
Bainham, A. and S. Gilmore, *Children: The Modern Law* (Jordans: Bristol) 2013.
Bamforth, N. and P. Leyland (eds), *Public Law in a Multi-Layered Constitution* (Hart Publishing: Oxford) 2003.
Bonwick, C., *The American Revolution* (University of Virginia Press: Charlottesville) 1991.
Brazier, R., *Ministers of the Crown* (Clarendon Press: Oxford) 1997.
Davidson, R. and G. Davis, *The Sexual State: Sexuality and Scottish Governance 1980–1950* (Edinburgh University Press: Edinburgh) 2012.
Eldin, D., *Judges and Unjust Laws, Common Law, Constitutionalism and the Foundations of Judicial Review* (University of Michigan Press: Ann Arbour) 2008.
Ellens, J., *Heaven, Hell and Afterlife: Eternity in Judaism, Christianity and Islam* (Praeger: Oxford) 2013.
Ferguson, P. and C. McDiarmid, *Scots Criminal Law: A Critical Analysis* (Edinburgh University Press: Edinburgh) 2014.
Goldsworthy, J., *Parliamentary Sovereignty: Contemporary Debates* (Cambridge University Press: Cambridge) 2010.
Gordon, M., *Parliamentary Sovereignty in the UK Constitution: Process, Politics and Democracy* (Hart: Oxford) 2015.
Hanson, T.B., *Saffron Wave: Democracy and Hindu Nationalism in Modern India* (Princeton University Press: Princeton) 1999.
Hart, H. *The Concept of Law* (Oxford University Press: Oxford)1994.
Hibbert, C., *The French Revolution* (Penguin: London) 2001.
Jennings, I., *Parliament* (Cambridge University Press: Cambridge) 1939.

Kiernan, K., H. Land and J. Lewis, *Lone Motherhood in Twentieth Century Britain: From Footnote to Front Page* (Clarendon Press: Oxford) 1998.

Lewis, P., *Young, British and Muslim* (Continuum: London) 2011.

Mackenzie, G., *The Laws and Customs of Scotland: In Matters Criminal* (Thomas Brown: Edinburgh) MDCLXXVIII (1678).

Meek, J., *Queer Voices in Post-War Scotland: Homosexuality, Religion and Society* (Palgrave/MacMillian: Basingstoke) 2015.

Menocal, M., *The Ornament of the World: How Muslims, Jews and Christians Created a Culture of Tolerance in Medieval Spain* (Little Brown: New York) 2002.

Mucciaroni, G., *Same Sex Different Politics: Successes and Failure in the Struggles over Gay Rights* (University of Chicago Press: Chicago & London) 2008.

Raina, P. (ed.), *A.V. Dicey: General Characteristics of English Constitutionalism – Six Unpublished Lectures* (Peter Laing: Oxford and New York) 2009.

Rawlings, R., P. Leyland and A. Young (eds), *Sovereignty and the Law: Domestic, European and International Perspectives* (Oxford University Press: Oxford) 2013.

Rosen, J., *Understanding Judaism* (Dunedin Academic Press: Edinburgh) 2003.

Saunders, C. & K. Le Roy, *The Rule of Law* (The Federation Press: Annandale) 2004.

Schmidt-Leukel, P., *Understanding Buddhism* (Dunedin Press: Edinburgh) 2006.

The Church of England, *Review of Clergy Terms of Service: Report on the First Phase of the Work* (Church House Publishing: London) 2004.

Yaran, C., *Understanding Islam* (Dunedin Academic Press: Edinburgh) 2007.

Articles, book chapters and secondary sources

Ahmed, F. and A. Perry, 'The Quasi-Entrenchment of Constitutional Statutes', *Cambridge Law Journal*, Vol. 73, No. 3 (2014) 514–35.

Akasoy, A., 'Convivencia and its Discontents: Interfaith Life in Al-Andalus', *International Journal of Middle East Studies*, Vol 43, No. 3 (2010) 489–99.

Allan, T., 'Parliamentary Sovereignty: Law, Politics, and Revolution', *Law Quarterly Review*, Vol. 113, No. 3 (1997) 443–52.

Arkush, A., 'Theocracy, Liberalism and Modern Judaism', *The Review of Politics*, Vol. 71, No. 4 (2009) 637–58.

Conan Doyle, A., 'The Empty House', in *Sherlock Holmes: The Complete Illustrated Short Stories* (Chancellor Press: London) 1989.

Craig, P., 'Sovereignty of the United Kingdom Parliament after Factortame', *Yearbook of European Law*, Vol. 11, No. 1 (1991) 221–55.

Dicey, A.V., *An Introduction to the Study of the Law of the Constitution* (ed. E.C.S. Wade, Macmillan: London) 10th edn, 1959.

Foster, J., 'Christianity and Democracy', *The Expository Times*, Vol. 63, No. 11 (1952) 350–2.

Fradkin, H., 'Judaism and Political Life', *Journal of Democracy*, Vol. 15, No. 3 (July 2004) 122–36.

García Oliva, J. and H. Hall, 'Same-Sex Marriage: An Inevitable Challenge to Religious Liberty and Establishment?', *Oxford Journal of Law and Religion*, Vol. 3, No. 1 (2014) 25–56.

Herring, J., 'The Human Rights Act and the Welfare Principle in Family Law – Conflicting or Complimentary?', *Child and Family Law Quarterly Review*, Vol. 11 (1999) 223–35.

Hobbes, T., *Leviathan* (Harvard Classics) 1909–14, Ch. XIII 'Of the Natural Condition of Mankind as Concerning Their Felicity and Misery', http://www.bartleby.com/34/5/13.html

Joseph, P., 'Parliament, the Courts and the Collaborative Enterprise', *King's College Law Journal*, Vol. 15 (2004) 321.

Jowell, J., 'Parliamentary Sovereignty under the New Constitutional Hypothesis', *Public Law*, Vol. 3 (2006) 562–80.

Knight, C. & T. Cross, 'Public Law in the Supreme Court 2011–12', *Judicial Review*, Vol. 17, No. 4 (2012) 330–55.

Lakin, S., 'Debunking the Idea of Parliamentary Sovereignty: The Controlling Factor of Legality in the British Constitution', *Oxford Journal of Legal Studies*, Vol. 28, No. 4 (2008) 709–34.

Laws, J., 'Law and Democracy', *Public Law* (1995) 72.

Letcher, A., 'The Scouring of the Shire: Fairies, Trolls and Pixies in Eco-Protest Culture', *Folklore*, Vol. 112 (2001) 147–61.

Lord Plant of Highfield, 'Foreward', in P. Raina (ed.), *A.V. Dicey: General Characteristics of English Constitutionalism – Six Unpublished Lectures* (Peter Lang: Oxford/New York) 2009, 9.

Moaddel, M., 'The Study of Islamic Culture and Politics: An Overview and Assessment', *Annual Review of Sociology*, Vol. 28 (2002) 359–86.

Rawlings, R., 'Introduction: Sovereignty in Question', in R. Rawlings, P. Leyland and A. Young (eds), *Sovereignty and the Law: Domestic, European and International Perspectives* (Oxford University Press: Oxford) 2013.

Tomkins, A., 'Talking in Fictions: Jennings on Parliament', *The Modern Law Review*, Vol. 67, No. 5 (Sept 2004) 772–86.

Tomkins, A., 'What is Parliament For?', in N. Bamforth and P. Leyland (eds), *Public Law in a Multi-Layered Constitution* (Hart: Oxford) 2003, Ch. 3.

Tucker, A., 'Uncertainty in the Rule of Recognition and the Doctrine of Parliamentary Sovereignty', *Oxford Journal of Legal Studies*, Vol. 31, No. 1 (2011) 61–88.

Wade, H.W.R., 'Sovereignty: Revolution or Revolution', *Law Quarterly Review*, Vol. 112 (1996) 568–75.

Wade, H.W.R., 'The Basis of Legal Sovereignty', *Cambridge Law Journal*, Vol. 13, No. 2 (1955) 172–97.

Young, A., 'Parliamentary Sovereignty – Redefined', in R. Rawlings, P. Leyland and A. Young (eds), *Sovereignty and the Law: Domestic, European and International Perspectives* (Oxford University Press: Oxford) 2013.

Websites

Attributed author

Allen, P., 'Zoroastrian Faith Joins Queen's Coronation Celebrations', *The Telegraph* (4 Jun 2013), http://www.telegraph.co.uk/news/uknews/10097326/Zoroastrian-faith-joins-Queens-Coronation-celebrations.html

García Oliva, J. 'Expert Comment: The Supreme Court's Decision – Article 50 and Parliament', The University of Manchester (24 Jan 2017), http://www.manchester.ac.uk/discover/news/article-50-parliament

García Oliva, J., 'Catalonia in Spain: The Significance of the 25th September 2015 Elections', UK Constitutional Law Association (25 Jul 2015), https://ukconstitutionallaw.org/2015/07/24/javier-garcia-oliva-catalonia-in-spain-the-significance-of-the-25th-september-2015-elections

García Oliva, J., 'Catalonia in Spain? The Future Ahead', *UK Constitutional Law Association* (10 Nov 2014), https://ukconstitutionallaw.org/2014/11/10/javier-garcia-oliva-catalonia-in-spain-the-future-ahead

Klug F. and H. Wildbore, letter published in *The Times* on the Human Rights Act, the relationship between domestic courts and the European Court of Human Rights and parliamentary sovereignty (24 Oct 2011), available via London School of Economics: Human Rights, http://www.lse.ac.uk/humanRights/documents/2011/KlugTimes24Oct.pdf, and http://www.lse.ac.uk/humanRights/whosWho/helenWildbore.aspx

Sales, B., 'The Haredim Look to Trump as a Pro-Israel, Traditionalist Tough Guy, Emphasis on "Guy"', *The Times of Israel* (7/11/2016), http://www.timesofisrael.com/haredim-look-to-trump-as-a-pro-israel-traditionalist-tough-guy-emphasis-on-guy

Slack, J. and S. Doughty, 'Britain Must Obey Strasbourg Judges or Quit the EU, Warns New Chief of the European Court of Human Rights', *The Daily Mail* (5 Jun 2013), http://www.dailymail.co.uk/news/article-2336021/Britain-obey-Strasbourg-judges-quit-EU-warns-new-chief-European-Court-Human-Rights.html#ixzz3eMMneYaD

No attributed author

Baptists Together, 'Politics and Christian Faith', http://www.baptist.org.uk/Groups/220649/Politics_and_Christian.aspx

BBC News, 'Metric Martyrs Loose Court Battle', (18 Feb 2002), http://news.bbc.co.uk/1/hi/england/1826503.stm

The Catholic Church in England and Wales, 'The General Election 2015 – Bishops' Letter to All Catholics in England and Wales' (24 Feb 2015), http://www.catholicnews.org.uk/Home/Featured/Features-2015/General-Election-2015/Election-Letter

The Church of England, 'Church of England Measures', https://www.churchofengland.org/about-us/structure/churchlawlegis/legislation/measures.aspx

The Church of England, House of Bishops, 'Pastoral Letter', https://www.churchofengland.org/media/2170230/whoismyneighbour-pages.pdf

The Church of England, 'The Clergy Discipline Measure', https://www.churchofengland.org/about-us/structure/churchlawlegis/clergydiscipline.aspx

Confederation of British Industry, 'Looking Ahead to 2015' (19 Dec 2014), http://www.cbi.org.uk/news/looking-ahead-to-2015

The Independent, 'In Full: The Letter from 1,000 Lawyers to David Cameron over EU Referendum', (10 Jul 2016), http://www.independent.co.uk/news/uk/politics/in-full-the-letter-from-1000-lawyers-to-david-cameron-over-eu-referendum-brexit-legality-a7130226.html

Komeito, 'On Politics and Religion', https://www.komei.or.jp/en/about/view.html

The Methodist Church, 'Elections', http://www.methodist.org.uk/mission/public-issues/politics-and-elections/elections

The Movement for Reform Judaism, 'A Jewish Guide to Voting' (2 Apr 2015), http://www.reformjudaism.org.uk/rabbi-dr-jonathan-romain-of-maidenhead-synagogue

Muslim Women's Network UK, 'Campaigns', http://www.mwnuk.co.uk/campaigns.php

Nuffield Foundation, Practical Physics, 'Light: Wave or Particles?', http://practicalphysics.org/light-%e2%80%93-waves-or-particles.html

Plymouth Brethren Christian Church, 'Plymouth Brethren and Politics', http://www.plymouthbrethrenchristianchurch.org/beliefs/doctrine

UK Parliament, 'Parliamentary Sovereignty', http://www.parliament.uk/about/how/sovereignty

Watch Tower Ministries, http://www.towerwatch.com/Witnesses/Beliefs/their_beliefs.htm

Miscellaneous

European Scrutiny Committee, Tenth Report, 'The EU Bill and Parliamentary Sovereignty', December 2010, http://www.publications.parliament.uk/pa/cm201011/cmselect/cmeuleg/633/63302.htm

Hansard, *HC Deb*, 22 May 2003, vol. 405, cc1174–85, http://hansard.millbanksystems.com/commons/2003/may/22/clergy-discipline-measure

Shakespeare, W. *The Tempest*, Act I, Scene II, 'Ariel's Song'

Chapter 6

Books

Babitt, E.C., *The Complete Jataka Tales* (Jazzybee Verlag Jurgen Beck: Atenmunster) 2012.

Bane, T., *The Encyclopaedia of Fairies in the World of Folklore and Mythology* (Jefferson: North Carolina and London) 2013.

Baron de Montesquieu, C., *The Spirit of Laws* (c1748) (translated by A. Cohler, B. Miller and H. Stone (eds), Cambridge University Press: New York) 1989.

Bogdanor, V., *The New British Constitution* (Hart: Oxford) 2009.

Bondy, W., *The Separation of Governmental Powers: in History, in Theory and in the Constitution* (The Law Book Exchange: New Jersey) 2004.

Bradley, A. & K. Ewing, *Constitutional and Administrative Law* (Pearson: London) 2014.

Carmichael, P. and B. Dickson (eds), *The House of Lords: Its Parliamentary and Judicial Roles* (Hart: Oxford) 1999.

Carolan, E., *A New Separation of Powers: A Theory for the Modern State* (Oxford University Press: Oxford) 2009.

Daly, R., *Apocalyptic Thought in Early Christianity* (Baker: Grand Rapids) 2009.

De Smith, S. *Constitutional and Administrative Law* (Penguin Books: Harmondsworth) 3rd edn, 1977.

Dharmapala, A., *The Maha Bodhi, Volume 105* (Maha Bodhi Society of India: Gaya) 1997.

Dicey, A.V., *Introduction to the Study of the Law of the Constitution* (ed. R. Michener, Liberty Fund: Indianapolis) 1982.

Farmer, D., *The Oxford Dictionary of Saints* (Oxford University Press: Oxford), 5th edn, 2003.

Feldman, D. *English Public Law* (Oxford University Press: Oxford) 2009.

Hall, T., *Anne Hutchinson: Puritan Prophet* (Pearson: Cambridge) 2010.

Hodgson, I., *Archbishop Oscar Romero: A Shepherd's Diary* (St Anthony Messenger Press: Cincinnati) 1993.

Jayapalan, N., *Modern Governments* (Atlantic: New Delhi) 1999.

Joppke, C., *The Secular State under Siege: Religion and Politics in Europe and America* (Polity Press: Cambridge) 2015.

Lindzey, A., *Animal Theology* (SCM Press: London) 1994.

Marshall, G., *Constitutional Theory* (Clarendon: Oxford) 1971.

Masterman, R., *The Separation of Powers in the Contemporary Constitution: Judicial Competence and Independence in the United Kingdom* (Cambridge University Press: Cambridge) 2011.

Mather, J., R. Anderson and J. Wood, *Octopus: The Ocean's Most Intelligent Invertebrate, A Natural History* (Timber Press: London) 2010.
Metaxas, E. *Bonhoeffer: Pastor, Martyr, Prophet, Spy* (Thomas Nelson: Nashville) 2011.
Palmer, M. and S. Burgess (eds), *The Blackstone Companion to Religion and Social Justice* (Blackstone: Oxford) 2012.
Pereiro, J., *Cardinal Manning: An Intellectual Biography* (Clarendon: Oxford) 1998.
Sardar Z. and Z. Malik, *Introducing Islam* (Totem Books: Royston) 2004.

Articles, book chapters and conference papers

Benwell, R. and O. Gay, 'The Separation of Powers', Library of the House of Commons, Standard Note SN/PC/006053
Brazier, R., 'The Second Chamber: Paradoxes and Plans', in P. Carmichael and B. Dickson (eds), *The House of Lords: Its Parliamentary and Judicial Roles* (Hart: Oxford) 1999, 53–66.
Dwivedi, O., 'Hinduism: Historical Setting', in M. Palmer and S. Burgess (eds), *The Blackstone Companion to Religion and Social Justice* (Blackstone: Oxford) 2012.
Ginsberg, T. & M Versteeg, 'Why Do Countries Adopt Constitutional Review?', *Journal of Law, Economics and Organizations*, Vol. 30, No. 3 (2014) 587–622.
Harlow, A., F. Cranmer and N. Doe, 'Bishops in the House of Lords: A Critical Analysis', *Public Law* (2008) 490–509.
Jivraj, S. & D. Herman, 'It is Difficult for a White Judge to Understand: Orientalism, Racialisation and Christianity in English Child Welfare Cases', *Child and Family Law Quarterly Review*, Vol. 21, No. 3 (2009) 283–308.
Krotosynski, R., 'The Separation of Legislative and Executive Powers', in T. Ginsburg and R. Dixon (eds), *Comparative Constitutional Law* (Edward Elgar: Cheltenham) 2011.
McColgan, A., 'Litigating the Public Sector Equality Duty: The Story So Far', *Oxford Journal of Legal Studies*, Vol. 35, No. 3 (2015) 453–85.
Miller, J. 'Court Protects Children from IS', *New Law Journal*, Vol. 165, No. 7670 (2015) 5.
Mistry, S., 'Naorojiin, Dadabhai', in D. Dabydeen, J. Gilmour and C. Jones (eds), *The Oxford Companion of Black British History* (Oxford University Press: Oxford) 2007.
Parry, K. and L. Maer, House of Commons Library Standard Note, SN/PC/05226, 'Ministers in the House of Lords' (15 Nov 2012).
Rush, M., 'The House of Lords: The Political Context', in P. Carmichael and B. Dickson (eds), *The House of Lords: Its Parliamentary and Judicial Roles* (Hart: Oxford) 1999.
Singh, A., 'Hinduism: Contemporary Expressions', in M. Palmer and S. Burgess (eds), *The Blackstone Companion to Religion and Social Justice* (Blackstone: Oxford) 2012.
Zuckerman, A., 'Super Injunctions – Curiosity-Suppressant Orders Undermine the Rule of Law', *Civil Justice Quarterly*, Vol. 29, No. 2 (2010) 131–8.

Websites

Attributed author

Abramowitz, J., 'Seven Universal Laws (of Noahides)', *Jew in the City* (20 Nov 2013), http://jewinthecity.com/2013/11/seven-universal-laws-of-noahides
Associated Press, 'Elf Lobby Blocks Iceland Road Project', *The Guardian* (22 Dec 2013), https://www.theguardian.com/world/2013/dec/22/elf-lobby-iceland-road-project

Ayra, D., 'Are Hindu Nationalists a Danger to Other Indians?', *BBC News* (12 Sept 2015), http://www.bbc.co.uk/news/magazine-33241100

Bingham, J., 'Church Condemns Government as Un-Christian over Stance on Drowning Migrants', *The Telegraph* (30 Oct 2014), http://www.telegraph.co.uk/news/uknews/immigration/11198140/Church-condemns-Government-as-un-Christian-over-stance-on-drowning-migrants.html

Casciani, D., 'Q & A Super-Injunctions', *BBC News* (20 May 2011), http://www.bbc.co.uk/news/uk-13473070

Coulter, P., 'Fairy Tales: Finding Fairy Bushes Across Northern Ireland', *BBC News* (13 Feb 2015), http://www.bbc.co.uk/news/uk-northern-ireland-31459851

Feldman, D. 'The European Court of Human Rights and the UK – Why Should Strasbourg Decide on Our Human Rights?', *UK Constitutional Law Association* (7 Dec 12), http://ukconstitutionallaw.org/2012/12/07/david-feldman-the-european-court-of-human-rights-and-the-uk-why-should-strasbourg-decide-on-our-human-rights

Hope, C., 'David Cameron: "I Want to Export Gay Marriage Around the World"', *The Telegraph* (24 Jul 2013), http://www.telegraph.co.uk/news/politics/10200636/I-want-to-export-gay-marriage-around-the-world-says-David-Cameron.html

Mortimer, C., 'Brexiteers Urge Supreme Court Judge to Stand Down from Article 50 Hearing over Wife's Pro-Remain Tweets', *The Independent* (19 Nov 2016), http://www.independent.co.uk/news/uk/politics/brexit-latest-supreme-court-article-50-hearing-judge-lord-neuberger-wife-tweet-impartiality-a7427511.html

Pavia, W. and C. Windle, 'Fairies Stop Developers Bulldozers in their Tracks', *The Times* (21 Nov 2005), https://www.thetimes.co.uk/article/fairies-stop-developers-bulldozers-in-their-tracks-dhk3qfz3rr7

Radford, B., 'Elves (Yes, Elves) Spark Road-Building Protest in Iceland', *Live Science* (14Jan2014),http://www.livescience.com/42547-elves-spark-environmental-protest-iceland.html

Riley-Smith, B., Liz Truss Breaks Silence over Article 50 Row to Defend Judiciary', *The Telegraph* (5 Nov 2016), http://www.telegraph.co.uk/news/2016/11/05/tory-mps-and-ex--ministers-call-on-government-to-defend-judiciar

Talwar, D. and B. Mostyn, 'No Sikhs in New Parliament', *BBC News* (12 May 2015), http://www.bbc.co.uk/news/uk-politics-32696615

Thakur, R., 'Parliamentary Democracy Isn't Perfect but It Is the Best Form of Government We Have', *The Japan Times* (24 Apr 2001), http://www.japantimes.co.jp/opinion/2001/04/26/commentary/world-commentary/parliamentary-democracy-isnt-perfect-but-its-the-best-form-of-government-we-have/#.WQYin4VOJuk

Thorp, L., 'Pagans Gather in Moss Bank Park for Anti-Fracking Ritual', *The Bolton News* (30 Sept 2013), http://www.theboltonnews.co.uk/news/10706465._/

Walsh, J., 'John Walsh on Monday: Irish Road Side-Tracked by the Fairies' Right of Way', *The Independent* 19/11/1999, http://www.independent.co.uk/news/john-walsh-on-monday-irish-road-side-tracked-by-the-fairies-right-of-way-1120744.html

No attributed author

Age UK, http://www.ageuk.org.uk/no-one

Age UK, 'Campaign to Tackle Loneliness', http://www.ageuk.org.uk/no-one/campaign-for-age-uk

Anglican Society for the Welfare of Animals, 'Campaigns: Threat to Hunting Bill', http://www.aswa.org.uk/page/campaigns/threat_to_hunting_bill

Animal Interfaith Alliance, 'Interfaith Celebration for Animals and AGM 2015' (13 Jul 2015), https://animal-interfaith-alliance.com/?s=AGM+2015

BBC News, 'Lord Carey Attacks PM over Christian "Support"', (30 Mar 2013), http://www.bbc.co.uk/news/uk-21979034

BBC News, 'Privacy Injunctions Unsustainable Says Cameron', (23 May 2011), http://www.bbc.co.uk/news/uk-13498504

BBC News 'UK Martyrs of the Modern Era', (9 Jul 1998), http://news.bbc.co.uk/1/hi/uk/129587.stm

Caritas Anchor House, 'Celebrating the Life and Legacy of Cardinal Manning' (11 Jun 2014), http://caritasanchorhouse.org.uk/blog/2014/06/11/celebrating-the-life-and-legacy-of-cardinal-manning

The Church of England, 'Bishops in the House of Lords: The Lords Spiritual', https://www.churchofengland.org/our-views/the-church-in-parliament/bishops-in-the-house-of-lords.aspx

The Church of England, 'Assisted Dying Bill 2015', https://www.churchofengland.org/our-views/medical-ethics-health-social-care-policy/assisted-suicide/assisted-dying-bill-2015.aspx

Churches Working Together, Joint Public Issues Team, 'Truth and Lies About Poverty' (1 Mar 2013), http://www.jointpublicissues.org.uk/truthandliesaboutpoverty

Courts and Tribunals Judiciary, 'About the Judiciary, Independence', https://www.judiciary.gov.uk/about-the-judiciary/the-judiciary-the-government-and-the-constitution/jud-acc-ind/independence

Courts and Tribunals Judiciary, 'About the Judiciary, Judges and Parliament', https://www.judiciary.gov.uk/about-the-judiciary/the-judiciary-the-government-and-the-constitution/jud-acc-ind/judges-and-parliament

Courts and Tribunals Judiciary, 'You and the Judiciary, Judicial Review', https://www.judiciary.gov.uk/you-and-the-judiciary/judicial-review

Dignity in Dying, 'Dignity in Dying Sir Terry Pratchett Dies' (12 Mar 2015), https://www.dignityindying.org.uk/news/dignity-dying-patron-sir-terry-pratchett-dies

Equality and Human Rights Commission Scotland, 'Public Sector Equality Duty FAQs', https://www.equalityhumanrights.com/en/public-sector-equality-duty-scotland/public-sector-equality-duty-faqs

HM Government, 'Safeguarding Children from Abuse Linked to a Belief in Spirit Possession', Non-Statutory Guidance, http://oxfordshirescb.proceduresonline.com/pdf/sg_ch_a_belief_spirit.pdf

House of Lords Appointments Commission, http://lordsappointments.independent.gov.uk

The Independent Crossbenchers, 'A List of Cross Bench Special Interests', http://62.32.116.90/interests.html

The Independent Crossbenchers, 'Who Are the Crossbenchers?', http://62.32.116.90/who.html

Museums Victoria, 'Coconut-Carrying Octopus', *YouTube*, https://www.youtube.com/watch?v=1DoWdHOtlrk

Mysterious Britain & Ireland, 'Fairies of St Fillans' (2005), http://www.mysteriousbritain.co.uk/scotland/perthshire/folklore/fairies-of-st-fillans-2005.html

Parliament Live TV, http://www.parliamentlive.tv/Commons

Scottish Government, 'Building, Planning and Design Policy', http://www.gov.scot/Topics/Built-Environment/planning

The Sunday Express, 'Any Wonder Remainers Won? Article 50 Judge Founded EU Integration Group', (5 Nov 2016), http://www.express.co.uk/news/uk/728460/Article-50-three-judges-blocked-Brexit

The Celtic Connection, 'The Wiccan Rede', http://wicca.com/celtic/wicca/rede.htm

UK Parliament, House of Lords, 'Checking and Challenging Government', http://www.parliament.uk/business/lords/work-of-the-house-of-lords/checking-and-challenging-government

UK Parliament, Commons Select Committee, Backbench Business Committee, 'How the Committee Works', http://www.parliament.uk/business/committees/committees-a-z/commons-select/backbench-business-committee/how-the-backbench-business-committee-works

UK Parliament, House of Lords, 'Who's in the House of Lords, Members and Their Roles, Diverse Experience', http://www.parliament.uk/business/lords/whos-in-the-house-of-lords/members-and-their-roles/diverse-experience

Miscellaneous

Alexander, C.F., 'Hymns for Little Children' (1848), http://www.cyberhymnal.org/htm/a/l/allthing.htm

The Chapters of the Fathers ('Pirkei Avot'). Cimpric, A., 'Children Accused of Witchcraft: An Anthropological Study of Contemporary Practices in Africa', UNICEF, Dakar (Apr 2010), https://www.unicef.org/wcaro/wcaro_children-accused-of-witchcraft-in-Africa.pdf

Daily Hansard (17 Jul 2014), 'India' and 'Fuel Poverty', http://www.publications.parliament.uk/pa/ld201415/ldhansrd/text/140717-0001.htm

Daily Hansard (18 Jul 2014), 'Assisted Dying Bill', https://www.publications.parliament.uk/pa/ld201415/ldhansrd/text/140718-0001.htm

Daily Hansard (13 Nov 2013), 'Children and Families Bill', http://www.publications.parliament.uk/pa/ld201314/ldhansrd/text/131118-gc0001.htm

Daily Hansard (3 Jun 2013), 'Marriage (Same Sex Couples) Bill, Second Reading', https://www.publications.parliament.uk/pa/ld201314/ldhansrd/text/130603-0001.htm

Exorcism of Children (Prohibition) Bill (15 Feb 2001), http://www.publications.parliament.uk/pa/cm200001/cmbills/033/2001033.htm

The Holy Bible (New Revised Standard Version). Metropolitan Police, Project Violet: Metropolitan Police Service Response to Abuse Linked to Faith and Belief, https://beta.met.police.uk/advice-and-information/child-abuse/faith-based-abuse

Sahih Bukhari.

Sri Guru Granth Sahib.

Stobart, E. 'Child Abuse Linked to Accusations of "Possession" and "Witchcraft"', Department of Education and Skills, Research Report RR750 2006, http://dera.ioe.ac.uk/6416/1/RR750.pdf

Chapter 7

Books

Ackroyd, P., *The Life of St Thomas More* (Vintage: London) 1998.

Al Aayed, S.H., (translation A. Alosh) *The Rights of Non-Muslims in the Islamic World* (Dar Eshbelia: Riyadh) 2002.

Allen, P., *The Concept of Woman, 2: The Early Humanist Reformation, 1250–1500* (Grand Rapids: Eerdmans) 2006.

Bainham A. and S. Gilmore (with specialist contributions from N. Harris and K. Holdsworth), *Children: The Modern Law* (Family Law: Bristol) 2013.
Baker, J.H., *An Introduction to English legal History* (Oxford University Press: Oxford) 4th edn, 2005.
Berend, N., *Christianization and the Rise of Christian Monarchy: Scandinavia, Central Europe and Rus' c.900–1200* (Cambridge University Press: Cambridge) 2007.
Bomgardner, D., *Roman Amphitheatre* (Routledge: Abingdon) 2000.
Broyde, M. *Marriage, Divorce and the Abandoned Wife in Jewish Law: A Conceptual Understanding of Agunah Problems in America* (Ktav: New Jersey) 2001.
Bruns, R., *Martin Luther King Jr.: A Biography* (Greenwood: London/Connecticut) 2006.
Domingo, R., *God and the Secular Legal System* (Cambridge University Press: Cambridge) 2016.
Drixler, F., *Mabiki: Infanticide and Population Growth in Eastern Japan 1660–1950* (University of California Press: Berkley) 2013.
Feldman, D., *Civil Liberties and Human Rights in England and Wales* (Oxford University Press: Oxford) 2000.
Føllesdal, A., B. Peters and G. Ulfstein (eds), *Constituting Europe: The European Court of Human Rights in a National, European and Global Context* (Cambridge University Press: Cambridge) 2013.
Gandhi, M.K., *Hindu Dharma* (Orient Paperbacks: New Delhi) 2005.
Hatton, J., *Betsy: The Dramatic Biography of Prison Reformer Elizabeth Fry* (Monarch: Oxford) 2005.
Heal, B. and O. Grell, *The Impact of the European Reformation: Princes, Clergy and People* (Ashgate: London) 2008.
Hostettler, J., *A History of Criminal Justice in England and Wales* (Waterside Press: Sheffield) 2009.
Ishay, M., *The Human Rights Reader* (Routledge: Abingdon) 2007, Introduction 'The History of Human Rights from Ancient Times to the Globalisation Era', xxi–xxviii.
Jackson, B. (ed.), *Jewish Law in Legal History and the Modern World* (Brill: Leiden) 1980.
Jaleel, C.T., *On Entering Deen Completely* (Google Books) July 2015.
Keown, D., C. Prebish and W. Husted (eds), *Buddhism and Human Rights* (Curzon Press: Padstow) 1998.
Lester A.P. and D. Pannick, *Human Rights: Law and Practice* (Butterworths: Kent) 2000.
Levitt, L., *Jews and Feminism: The Ambivalent Search for Home* (Routledge: New York and London) 1997.
Linzey, A., *Animal Theology* (University of Illinois Press: Illinois) 1995.
Lowe N. and G. Douglas, *Bromley's Family Law* (Oxford University Press: Oxford) 10th edn, 2007.
Mansukhani, G.S., *Introduction to Sikhism* (Hemkunt Press: New Delhi) 14th edn, 2007.
Marlow J. (ed.), *Votes for Women: The Virago Book of Suffragettes* (Virago: London) 2001.
Moeckli, D., S. Shah, S. Sivakumaran and D. Harris, *International Human Rights Law* (Oxford University Press: Oxford) 2013.
Nehustan, Y., *Intolerant Religion in a Tolerant Liberal Democracy* (Hart: Oxford) 2015.
Parekh, B., *Gandhi: A Brief Insight* (Sterling: New York) 2010.
Pomeroy, S., *Goddesses, Whores, Wives and Slaves: Women in Classical Antiquity* (Pimlico: London) 1994.
Robertson, A. and G. Merrills, *Human Rights in the World* (Manchester University Press: Manchester) 1996.
Rubin, E., *The Soul and Society: The New Morality and the Modern State* (Oxford University Press: Oxford) 2015.

Sharma, A., *Hindu Narratives on Human Rights* (Greenwood: Santa Barbara) 2010.

Tomkins, S., *William Wilberforce: A Biography* (Lion: Oxford) 2007.

Witte, J. and J. Van de Vyver (eds), *Religious Human Rights in a Global Perspective: Religious Perspective* (Martinus Nijhoff: Leiden) 2000.

Wollstonecroft, M., *A Vindication of the Rights of Men, A Vindication of the Rights of Woman, An Historical and Moral View of the French Revolution* (Oxford University Press: Oxford) 1999, 'A Vindication of the Rights of Woman'.

Articles, book chapters and conference papers

An-an'im, A., 'Islamic Foundations of Religious Human Rights', in J. Witte and J. Van de Vyver (eds), *Religious Human Rights in a Global Perspective: Religious Perspective* (Martinus Nijhoff: Leiden) 2000, 341.

Arzt, D., 'The Treatment of Religious Dissidents under Classical and Contemporary Religious Law', in J. Witte and J. Van de Vyver (eds), *Religious Human Rights in a Global Perspective: Religious Perspective* (Martinus Nijhoff: Leiden) 2000, 387.

Bates, E., 'History', in D. Moeckli, S. Shah, S. Sivakumaran and D. Harris, *International Human Rights Law* (Oxford University Press: Oxford) 2013.

Bessant, C., 'Protecting Victims of Domestic Violence – Have We Got the Balance Right?', *Journal of Criminal Law*, Vol. 79, No. 2 (2015) 102–21.

Bindman, G., 'Battle of the Giants', *New Law Journal*, Vol. 165, No. 7641 (2015) 8.

Collins, B. and N. Newbegin, 'HRA 1998: The End', *New Law Journal*, Vol. 165, No. 7662 (2015) 11.

Daube, D., 'Jewish Law in the Hellenistic World', in B. Jackson (ed.), *Jewish Law in Legal History and the Modern World* (Brill: Leiden) 1980, 45.

Epstein, R., 'A Buddhist Perspective of Animal Rights', based on a presentation given at San Francisco State University Conference 'Animal Rights and our Relationship to the Biosphere' (29 Jan 1990).

Ihara, C., 'Why There Are No Rights in Buddhism – A Reply to Damien Keown', in D. Keown, C. Prebish and W. Husted (eds), *Buddhism and Human Rights* (Curzon Press: Padstow) 1998, 43.

Johnson, P., 'Marriage, Heteronormativity and the European Court of Human Rights: A Reappraisal', *International Journal of Law Policy the Family*, Vol. 29, No. 1 (2015) 56–77.

Keown, D., 'Are There Rights in Buddhism?', *Journal of Buddhist Ethics*, Vol. 2 (1995) 3–27.

Letsas, G. 'The ECHR as a Living Instrument: Its Meaning and Legitimacy', in A. Føllesdal, B. Peters and G. Ulfstein (eds), *Constituting Europe: The European Court of Human Rights in a National, European and Global Context* (Cambridge University Press: Cambridge) 2013, 106, 124–5 'Introduction'.

Macklem, P., 'Human Rights in International Law: Three Generations or One?', *London Review of International Law*, Vol 3, No. 1 (2015) 61–92.

Middleton, J 'Spare the Rod', *History Today*, Vol. 62, No. 11 (2012).

Morris, B., 'Succession to the Crown Bill: Possible Untoward Effects', *Ecclesiastical Law Journal*, Vol. 15, No. 2 (2013) 186–91.

Parpworth, N., 'The Succession to the Crown Act 2013: Modernising the Monarchy', *The Modern Law Review*, Vol. 76, No. 6 (2013) 1070–93.

Phillips, J., 'The Structure of Electoral Politics in Unreformed England', *Journal of British Studies*, Vol. 19, No. 1 (1979) 76–100.

Rogerson, P., 'News: Human Rights Warning from Leading Jurist', *Law Society Gazette*, Vol. 3, No. 1 (22 Jun 2015).

Villa Vicencio, C., 'Christianity and Human Rights', *Journal of Law and Religion*, Vol. 14, No. 2 (1999–2000) 579–600.

Willey, P. 'Trials in Absentia and Cuts to Criminal Legal Aid: A Deadly Combination?', *Journal of Criminal Law*, Vol. 78, No. 6 (2014) 486–510.

Wiseberg L.S. & H.M. Scoble, 'Women's Rights and International Human Rights: A Bibliographical Note', *Human Rights Quarterly*, Vol. 3, No. 2 (1981) 127–35.

Websites

Attributed author

Balaji, M., 'Let's Not Forget These Hindu Voices in the World of Social Uplift', *Huffington Post* (20 Jun 2014), http://www.huffingtonpost.com/murali-balaji/lets-not-forget-these-hin_b_5514768.html

Barrett, D. and C. Duffin, 'Pagan Wins "Family Life" Human Rights Case', *The Telegraph* (18 Dec 2011), http://www.telegraph.co.uk/news/uknews/immigration/8963019/Pagan-wins-family-life-human-rights-case.html

Bland, A., 'Freedom of Speech: Is It My Right to Offend You?', *The Independent* (2 Feb 2014), http://www.independent.co.uk/news/uk/politics/freedom-of-speech-is-it-my-right-to-offend-you-9101650.html

Cox, D., 'Made in Dagenham: A Squandered Opportunity', *The Guardian* (30 Sept 2010), http://www.theguardian.com/film/filmblog/2010/sep/13/made-in-dagenham-first-look

Jeffries, S., 'The Beano – A Happy 75th Anniversary', *The Guardian* (20 Jul 2013), http://www.theguardian.com/lifeandstyle/2013/jul/20/beano-75-year-anniversary

Josephs, A., 'Shabbos Chazon: Why John Lennon's Imagine is Messianic', *Jew in the City* (24 Jul 2015), http://jewinthecity.com/2015/07/shabbos-chazon-why-lennons-imagine-is-messianic

Lady Hale, 'What's the Point of Human Rights?', Warwick Law Lecture (28 Nov 2013), para. 1, http://supremecourt.uk/docs/speech-131128.pdf

Lambrecht, S., 'HRA Watch: Reform, Repeal, Replace? Criticism of the European Court of Human Rights – a UK Phenomenon?', *UK Constitutional Law Association* (27 Jul 2015), http://ukconstitutionallaw.org/2015/07/27/hra-watch-reform-repeal-replace-sarah-lambrecht-criticism-of-the-european-court-of-human-rights-a-uk-phenomenon/

Levy, A., 'ZAKA Mission to Haiti "Proudly Desecrating the Shabat"', *Ynet news.com* (17 Jan 2010), http://www.ynetnews.com/articles/0,7340,L-3835327,00.html

Littlejohn, R., 'Democracy? No, Britain's Now a Judicial Dictatorship and It's Time for Revolution', *The Daily Mail* (13 Aug 2014), http://www.dailymail.co.uk/debate/article-2723472/Democracy-No-Britain-s-judicial-dictatorship-s-time-revolution-writes-RICHARD-LITTLEJOHN.html

Mackler, A., 'Edut Nashim K'Edut Anashim: The Testimony of Women is as the Testimony of Men' (Nov 2004), https://www.rabbinicalassembly.org/sites/default/files/public/halakhah/teshuvot/20052010/mackler_women_witnesses.pdf

Mehr, F., 'Human Rights in Zoroastrianism', *Association for the Revival of Zoroastrianism*, https://www.causes.com/causes/566882-association-for-revival-of-zoroastrianism/updates/504963-human-rights-in-zoroastrianism

Orr, D., 'For Human Rights to Flourish, Religious Rights Have to Come Second', *The Guardian* (27 Dec 2013), http://www.theguardian.com/commentisfree/2013/dec/27/human-rights-religious-rights-come-second

Pocklington, D., 'Succession to the Crown Bill Passed', *Law and Religion UK* (26 Apr 2013), http://www.lawandreligionuk.com/2013/04/26/succession-to-the-crown-bill-passed

Rubery, J., 'Equal Pay and Europe', in *Winning Equal Pay: The Value of Women's Work*, part of the Union Makes Us Strong website, a collaboration between London Metropolitan University and the Trades Unions Congress, http://www.unionhistory.info/equalpay/roaddisplay.php?irn=785

Toynbee, P., 'Narnia Represents Everything that is Most Hateful about Religion', *The Guardian* (5 Dec 2005), http://www.theguardian.com/books/2005/dec/05/cslewis.booksforchildrenandteenagers

Toynee, P., 'We must be Free to Criticise Without being Called Racist', *The Guardian* (18 Sept 2004), http://www.theguardian.com/world/2004/aug/18/religion.politic

No attributed author

BBC News, 'Giant Lobster Ate Like a Whale', (12 Mar 2015), http://www.bbc.co.uk/news/science-environment-31837024

BBC News, 'Kylie Minogue Wedding Waits for Australian Marriage Equality', (6 Oct 2016), http://www.bbc.co.uk/news/world-australia-37548760

BBC News, 'Royal Pardon for Codebreaker Alan Turing', BBC News (24 Dec 2013), http://www.bbc.co.uk/news/technology-25495315

BBC News, 'Spanish Slugs: Public Urged to Report Sightings',(19 Oct 2013), http://www.bbc.co.uk/news/science-environment-24593015

BBC News, 'What Future for India's Caste System?', BBC News (22 Jun 2013), http://www.bbc.co.uk/news/business-22724831

BBC News, '300 WWI Soldiers Receive Pardons', (16 Aug 2006), http://news.bbc.co.uk/1/hi/uk/4796579.stm

British Humanist Association, 'Conscientious Objection', https://humanism.org.uk/campaigns/human-rights-and-equality/conscientious-objection

British Humanist Association, 'Humanism', https://humanism.org.uk/humanism

British Humanist Association, 'Humanists and Civil Rights Groups Rally to Defend Human Rights Act ', 10/12/2016, https://humanism.org.uk/2016/12/10/humanists-and-civil-rights-groups-rally-to-defend-human-rights-act

British Library, 'English Translation of Magna Carta', https://www.bl.uk/magna-carta/articles/magna-carta-english-translation

British Library, 'Sisterhood and After: Timeline of the Women's Liberation Movement', http://www.bl.uk/sisterhood/timeline

British Library, Learning Timelines: Sources from History, 'The Magna Carta 1215', http://www.bl.uk/learning/timeline/item95692.html

Children and Young People's Commissioner Scotland, '5 Concerns about Children's Rights in Scotland' (8 Apr 2015), http://www.cypcs.org.uk/news/in-the-news/5-concerns-for-childrens-rights-in-scotland

The Church of Scotland, 'How We Are Organised', http://www.churchofscotland.org.uk/about_us/how_we_are_organised

City Sikhs Volunteering Initiative, http://www.citysikhs.org.uk

The Complete Jewish Bible (with Rashi Commentary), Tehillim, Psalms, Chapter 139, http://www.chabad.org/library/bible_cdo/aid/16360/jewish/Chapter-139.htm#showrashi=true

The Conservative Party, 'Protecting Human Rights in the UK: The Conservatives' Proposals for Changing Britain's Human Rights Laws' (Oct 2014), https://www.conservatives.com/~/media/files/.../human_rights.pdf

Equality and Human Rights Commission, 'About Us', http://www.equalityhumanrights.com/about-us

Equality and Human Rights Commission, http://www.equalityhumanrights.com/about-us/devolved-authorities/commission-wales

Equality and Human Rights Commission, http://www.equalityhumanrights.com/about-us/devolved-authorities/commission-scotland

The Independent, 'To the Manor Born: the Female Aristocrats Battling to Inherit the Title', (14 Jun 2013)

Khalsa Aid, 'Recognise the Whole Human Race as One', http://www.khalsaaid.org

Muslim Aid, 'What We Do', https://www.muslimaid.org/what-we-do

National Readership Survey, 'Newsbrands, April 14–March 15', http://www.nrs.co.uk/latest-results/nrs-*print*-results/newspapers-nrsprintresults

Natural England, Department for Environment, Food & Rural Affairs and Environment Agency, 'Environmental Management Guidance – Harmful Weeds and Invasive, Non-Native Plants: Prevent Them Spreading' (23 Sept 2014, updated 16 Jun 2015), https://www.gov.uk/prevent-the-spread-of-harmful-invasive-and-non-native-plants

NHS Choices, About the NHS, 'Principles and Choices that Guide the NHS', http://www.nhs.uk/NHSEngland/thenhs/about/Pages/nhscoreprinciples.aspx

The Pagan Federation International, 'Code of Conduct', https://paganfed.org/index.php/federation/pagan-federation-code-of-ethics/code-of-conduct#8_-_Animal_cruelty__

The Pagan Federation International, 'Three Principles of Membership', http://www.paganfederation.org/about-the-pf/#Functions

The Scottish Government, 'The UN Convention on the Rights of the Child: A Guide for Children and Young People', Art. 14, http://www.gov.scot/Resource/0048/00486690.pdf

Sewa International USA, 'About Us', http://www.sewausa.org

Society for the Protection of Unborn Children, https://www.spuc.org.uk

UNCRC and the Scottish Government, 'Do The Right Thing: Progress Report 2012', http://www.gov.scot/Resource/0039/00392997.pdf

Together (Scottish Alliance for Children's Rights), 'State of Children's Rights in Scotland' (Nov 2014), 3, http://www.togetherscotland.org.uk/pdfs/SOCRRTogetherReport2014.pdf

United for Human Rights, 'About Us', http://www.humanrights.com/about-us/what-is-united-for-human-rights.html

United for Human Rights, 'Champions of Human Rights', http://www.humanrights.com/voices-for-human-rights/champions-human-rights.html

UK Government, 'Guidance on Overseas Visitors Hospital Charging Regulations', https://www.gov.uk/government/publications/guidance-on-overseas-visitors-hospital-charging-regulations

UK Parliament, 'Living Heritage', http://www.parliament.uk/about/living-heritage/transformingsociety/electionsvoting/womenvote/case-study-the-right-to-vote/the-right-to-vote/winson-green-forcefeeding/cat-and-mouse-act

UK Government, 'Equal Marriage: The Government's Response' (Dec 2012) Executive Summary para 1.7, https://www.gov.uk/government/consultations/equal-marriage-consultation

UK Government, Succession to the Crown Bill: Deputy Prime Minister's Opening Statement (at the second reading in the House of Commons) (22 Jan 2013), https://www.gov.uk/government/news/succession-to-the-crown-bill-deputy-prime-ministers-opening-statement

Zoroastrian Online, http://zoroastrianonline.com

Miscellaneous

Adi Granth.

New Revised Standard Version Bible, Popular Text Edition with Apocrypha (Oxford University Press: Oxford) 1995.

The Official Website of the British Monarch, Coronation Oath http://www.royal.gov.uk/ImagesandBroadcasts/Historic%20speeches%20and%20broadcasts/CoronationOath2June1953.aspx

United Nations, 'Universal Declaration of Human Rights, History of the Document', http://www.un.org/en/sections/universal-declaration/history-document

List of interviewees

Joaquín Acedo, specialist in sport physiotherapy and former physiotherapist with Everton Football Club

The Rev'd Dr Will Adam, Editor of *Ecclesiastical Law Journal* and Church of England priest

Baroness Haleh Afshar, House of Lords and Professor of Politics and Women's Studies, University of York

Joe Ahearne, director and writer

Baroness Ros Altmann, House of Lords and former minister of state, Department for Work and Pensions

Danny Batth, footballer, Wolverhampton Wanderers (Wolves) Football Club

Mona Bayoumi, Approved Counsel on the Attorney General's List of Counsel and Junior Counsel to the Welsh Assembly Government

Professor Dame Jocelyn Bell Burnell, Astrophysicist, University of Oxford

Baroness Elizabeth Berridge, House of Lords and Co-Chair of All-Party Parliamentary Group for Freedom of Religion and Belief in the UK Parliament.

Philip Bird, actor

The Rev'd Dr Jason Bray, Church in Wales priest

Baroness Elizabeth Butler-Sloss, House of Lords and Chairwoman of the Commission on Religion and Belief in British Public Life

Stephen Castle, journalist, *The New York Times*

Rev John Chalmers QHC, former Moderator of the Church of Scotland

Samantha Chandler, Secretary of the Anglican Society for the Welfare of Animals

Iman Irfan Chishti MBE, Iman of Manchester Central Mosque and Director of Facets Consulting Ltd

Naveed Choudhry, actor

Dr Martin Clarke, Lecturer in Music, Open University

Andrew Copson, Chief Executive, British Humanist Association

Frank Cranmer, Research Associate, Centre for Law and Religion, Cardiff University

Dr Adrian Crisp MD, FRCP, Fellow of Churchill College, University of Cambridge

Professor Grace Davie, Sociologist, Exeter University

Sam Dick, former Director of Campaigns, Policy and Research, Stonewall

Professor Norman Doe, Director, Centre for Law and Religion, Cardiff University

Anne Duddington, carer and nurse

Dominic Dyer, CEO, Badger Trust

Sir Gareth Edwards CBE, former international Welsh rugby player

Carole Emmerson, nurse

Professor David Feldman, Professor of Public Law, University of Cambridge

Dr Hilary Firestone, Clinical Teaching Fellow, University Dental Hospital Manchester

Lillie Flynn, actress

Mark Gifford, Learning and Development Manager, ASHA Foundation

Zerbanoo Gifford, Honorary Director, ASHA Foundation; writer and human rights campaigner

Ashley Gilbert, Nottingham Pagan Network

Lucy Gorman, former Chair of Changing Attitude

Dominic Grieve QC MP, former Attorney General

Aled Griffiths, Principal Lecturer in Law and Social Policy, Bangor University

Joanna Griffiths, former magistrate and social worker

Thomas Haines, former employee at the BBC

Lady Brenda Hale, Deputy President, Supreme Court of the United Kingdom

The Rt Rev'd Christine Hardman, House of Lords and Bishop of Newcastle

Lord Richard Harries of Pentregarth, House of Lords and former Bishop of Oxford

David Harte, former Senior Lecturer in Law, Newcastle University

Grace Hatley, provision of services and model

Dr Elizabeth Healey, Honorary Lecturer in Archaeology, University of Manchester

Professor John Healey, Professor of Semitic Studies, University of Manchester

Sir Mark Hedley DL, former judge of the High Court of England and Wales

The Rev'd Professor Martin Henig, Anthropologist, University of Oxford and member of Changing Attitude

Elder Clifford Herbertson, The Church of Jesus Christ of Latter-day Saints

Jenny Hodge, former student of Speech and Language Therapy, University of Manchester.

Don Horrocks, former Head of Public Affairs, Evangelical Alliance

Wendy Huggett, Home Office

Shaina Huleatt, Bruderhof and legal adviser to various UK charities

Dr Myriam Hunter-Henin, Reader, University College London

Professor Ronald Hutton, Historian, Bristol University

Constance Jackson, founder of JAX Global Consulting Ltd

Ruth Jenkins, Lecturer in Accounting and Taxation, and folk dancer

Fr Roddy Johnston, Roman Catholic priest

The Rt Rev'd James Jones, formerly with the House of Lords, former Bishop of Liverpool and Chairman of the Hillsborough Panel

Professor Steven Jones, Biologist, University College London

Gurd Kandola, Financial Services, Deloitte

Michael Kennedy QC, Deputy High Court Judge in Civil and Chancery

Faisal Khan, provision of services

Professor Imre Leader, Professor of Pure Mathematics, University of Cambridge

Dr Tobias Lock, Senior Lecturer, Edinburgh Law School, University of Edinburgh

Kimberley Long, community worker, facilitator and activist in Glasgow

Gary McFarlane, former solicitor and therapist specialising in Singleness and Couple Relational Issues

Professor Sheila McLean, former Professor of Law and Ethics in Medicine, School of Law, Glasgow University

Nico McNenzie-Juetten, former employee with the Scotland Commissioner for Children and Young People

Sarah Miles, actress

Daisuke Miura, ballet dancer and teacher

Jessica Morden MP

The Most Reverend Dr Barry Morgan, Archbishop of Wales

Dr Catharine Morgan, medical doctor

Chris Morris, solicitor and Assistant Coroner for Central and South East Kent

Chikwan Nam, nurse

Thomas Nichols, personal trainer

Jon Nott, General Secretary, Woodcraft Folk

Eamonn O'Brien, former student of Politics and Modern History, University of Manchester

Una Mary Parker, Author and Journalist

Fr Ian Paton, Rector of Old Saint Paul's, Episcopalian Church of Scotland

Fr William Pearsall, Roman Catholic chaplaincy, University of Manchester

Dr David Perfect, Research Manager, Equality and Human Rights Commission

David Pollock, British Humanist Association and former President of the European Humanist Federation

Keith Porteous Wood, Executive Director, National Secular Society in the United Kingdom

Lucy Powell MP

Dr Hema Radhakrishnan, Senior Lecturer in Optometry, the University of Manchester

Baroness Kathleen Richardson, House of Lords and Methodist minister

Rev David Robertson, former Moderator of the Free Church of Scotland

Professor Dame Nancy Rothwell, Physiologist and President of the University of Manchester

Rabbi Lord Jonathan Sacks, former Chief Rabbi

Roque Santa Cruz, footballer, Olimpia Asunción CF (Paraguay) and former Manchester City player

Ian Scott, Events Manager, British Humanist Association and former Acting Chief Executive, Humanist Society Scotland

Rabbi Reuven Silverman, Reform Synagogue Manchester

Lucy Skilbeck, Director of Actor Training, Royal Academy of Music and Dramatic Art

The Most Reverend Peter Smith, Archbishop of Southwark, Roman Catholic Church

Alison Steadman, actress

Fr Paul Stonham, Abbot, Belmont Abbey, Roman Catholic Church

Ioannis Stylianou, provision of services and engineer in the renewable energy sector

Professor Sir John Sulston, Chair of the Institute for Science, Ethics and Innovation, the University of Manchester

Jim Sutcliffe, farmer and butcher

Bharti Tailor, Executive Director, Hindu Forum of Europe

The Rt Rev'd Tim Thornton, House of Lords and Bishop of Truro

Patricia Travis, provision of services

Jeff Tyldesley, public servant, trainee counsellor and freelance writer

The Rt Rev'd Dominic Walker OGS, former Bishop of Monmouth

Shaun Wallace, barrister and television presenter

The Rev'd Professor Thomas Watkin, former Head of the School of Law, Bangor University, former First Legislative counsel to the Welsh Government and Church in Wales priest

Frank Williams, actor

The Most Reverend Professor Rowan Williams, House of Lords and former Archbishop of Canterbury.

Janette Wilson, former solicitor to the Church of Scotland

Professor Lord Robert Winston, House of Lords and Professor of Fertility Studies, Imperial College London

Professor Linda Woodhead, Sociologist, Lancaster University

Index

For Product Safety Concerns and Information please contact our EU representative GPSR@taylorandfrancis.com
Taylor & Francis Verlag GmbH, Kaufingerstraße 24, 80331 München, Germany

www.ingramcontent.com/pod-product-compliance
Ingram Content Group UK Ltd.
Pitfield, Milton Keynes, MK11 3LW, UK
UKHW022005180926
475701UK00003B/202
9780367313128